Ernst Troeltsch

ERNST TROELTSCH

His Life and Work

Hans-Georg Drescher

FORTRESS PRESS   MINNEAPOLIS

ERNST TROELTSCH
His Life and Work

First Fortress Press edition published 1993.

Translated by John Bowden from *Ernst Troeltsch: Leben und Werk*, published 1991 by Vandenhoeck & Ruprecht, Göttingen, with additional material and corrections supplied by the author. English translation © 1992 John Bowden. All rights reserved. Except for brief quotations in critical articles or reviews, no part of this book may be reproduced in any manner without prior written permission from the publisher. Write to: Permissions, Augsburg Fortress, 426 S. Fifth St., Box 1209, Minneapolis, MN 55440.

Library of Congress Cataloging-in-Publication data available
ISBN 0–8006–2674–5

Manufactured in Great Britain

97 96 95 94 93   1   2   3   4   5   6   7   8   9   10

AF 1–2674

Contents

Preface

My interest in Ernst Troeltsch goes back to the confrontation between liberal theology and dialectical theology, which I felt keenly in my student days. It was against this background that I wrote on Ernst Troeltsch's philosophy of religion. Since then, I have never ceased to be preoccupied with his writings and his person.

I was stimulated to more detailed work by the 1975 Troeltsch Congress in Lancaster, the contributions to which were published in *Ernst Troeltsch and the Future of Theology* (1976). With newly kindled interest and the boldness of someone who does not quite know what he has taken on, I decided to make a major study of Troeltsch's life and work. In so doing I attempted to find a better starting point for the interpretation of his work and the understanding of his person and life by tracing and collecting unknown and undiscovered source material. I was helped by the fact that since the 1970s intensified attention to Troeltsch's work has produced a substantial number of investigations on which the present account could be based. Special mention should be made of the works of Apfelbacher, Groll, Rendtorff, Rubanowice, the Troeltsch studies edited by Renz and Graf, and the Troeltsch bibliography by Graf and Ruddies.

Given the present state of research, it now seems possible to present an overall account of Troeltsch's life and work: to combine biography with a historical account of the development of his writings. That is what I shall attempt here. The emphasis will be not so much on a detailed discussion of the secondary literature as on use and development of the sources. I am aware that such varied work as that of Ernst Troeltsch will constantly prompt new interpretations; I hope that the present book will also offer stimuli in this direction.

A study like this depends on a good deal of support. I found welcome and ready help in many archives and libraries. Friends and colleagues have helped me with critical and constructive suggestions after reading the manuscript. I am very grateful to Eberhard Warns of Bielefeld, Rainer Küster of Bochum and Friedrich Rapp of Dortmund. In particular I would like to mention Horst Renz of Obergünzburg; I am indebted to him for the sources he has discovered, and he has supported me in many other ways.

Claudia Gola, Elke Jüngling and Barbara Srodecki helped in preparing the typescript. As publisher, Dr Arndt Ruprecht followed the growth of the book with lively interest and friendly support.

My own explanatory additions to texts quoted are in square brackets.

Translator's Note

Some terms relating to institutions and posts in the German universities and churches are almost impossible to translate satisfactorily into English. I have therefore left them in German and offer an explanation here in the form of a brief description.

After going to the Gymnasium (grammar school or high school), a student (in Troeltsch's time predominantly male, so I shall use the masculine pronoun) would study at one or more universities. He would then write a doctoral thesis on which he would be examined for his Promotion. To qualify as a teacher he would then have to engage in further research; this examination, again based on a thesis, was the Habilitation. The successful candidate then became a Privatdozent, a lecturer with somewhat precarious tenure. A call to a chair marked the really important step in his career: he was appointed first, probably, as an extraordinarius (associate) professor, then as an ordinarius (full) professor.

Since a university teacher (like a Protestant clergyman) was also a civil servant, he would come under the Kultusministerium of the Land (state) in which his post was situated. This Ministry would have a range of functions (differing slightly depending on the Land) reflected in names which varied from one state to another.

Each Land had its own church, the Landeskirche, under the government of the local ruler ('state church' would be a misleading description for these churches); before becoming a minister in the church a candidate had to serve a Vikariat (a period as assistant minister). The central administrative authority of the Landeskirche was the Oberkirchenrat. It had a consistory, Oberkonsistorium, a member of which was known as an Oberkonsistorialrat.

I have added one or two other explanatory comments in the notes, in square brackets and marked [Tr.].

Abbreviations

1. Troeltsch's writings

GS I-IV	*Gesammelte Schriften* I-IV
AC	*Die Absolutheit des Christentums und die Religionsgeschichte*, Tübingen ³1923, ET *The Absoluteness of Christianity and the History of Religions*, Atlanta 1971 and London 1972
BP	*Die Bedeutung des Protestantismus für die Entstehung der modernen Welt*, Munich and Berlin 1911, for ET see *PP*
CT	*Christian Thought. Its History and Application*, ed. F.von Hügel, London 1923
DG	*Deutscher Geist und Westeuropa*, Tübingen 1925, reprinted Aalen 1966
ETWTR	*Ernst Troeltsch. Writings on Theology and Religion*, edited by R.Morgan and M.Pye, London 1977
GJ	*Die Bedeutung der Geschichtlichkeit Jesu für den Glauben*, Tübingen 1911, ET 'The Significance of the Historical Existence of Jesus for Faith', in *ETWTR*, 182-207
GL	*Glaubenslehre*, Munich and Leipzig 1925
GM	'Geschichte und Metaphysik', *ZTK* 8, 1898, 1-69
HK	*Das Historische in Kants Religionsphilosophie*, Berlin 1904
HÜ	*Der Historismus und seine Überwindung*, Berlin 1924, for ET see *CT*
LT	*Die wissenschaftliche Lage und ihre Anforderungen an die Theologie*, Tübingen 1900
PE	*Psychologie und Erkenntnistheorie in der Religionswissenschaft*, Tübingen 1905
PN	'Protestantisches Christentum und Kirche in der Neuzeit', in *Die Kultur der Gegenwart*, ed. P.Hinneberg, Part I, IV.1, Berlin and Leipzig ²1909
PP	*Protestantism and Progress*, London and New York 1912
RH	*Religion in History*, Essays translated by James Luther Adams and Walter F.Bense, Edinburgh 1991
RP	'Religionsphilosophie', in W.Windelband (ed.), *Die*

	Philosophie im Beginn des zwanzigsten Jahrhunderts, Heidelberg 1907, 423-86
RR	*Richard Rothe*, Freiburg 1899
SB	*Spektator-Briefe*, Tübingen 1924, reprinted Aalen 1966
SK	*Die Trennung von Staat und Kirche, der staatliche Religionsunterricht und die theologischen Falkultäten*, Tübingen 1907, ET 'The Separation of Church and State and the Teaching of Religion', *RH*, 109-17
SR	'Die Selbständigkeit der Religion', *ZTK* 5, 1895, 361-436; 6, 1896, 71-110, 167-218
ST	*The Social Teaching of the Christian Churches* (2 vols.), London 1931 (ET of *GS* 1)
VO	*Vernunft und Offenbarung bei Johann Gerhard und Melanchthon*, Göttingen 1891

2. Periodicals, Lexicons, etc.

Apfelbacher/ Neuner	*Ernst Troeltsch. Briefe an Friedrich von Hügel 1901-1923*, edited with an introduction by Karl-Ernst Apfelbacher and Peter Neuner, Paderborn 1974
CW	*Die Christliche Welt*
DLZ	*Deutsche Literaturzeitung*
ETB	*Ernst Troeltsch Bibliographie*, edited with an introduction and commentary by F.W.Graf and H.Ruddies, Tübingen 1982
EvTh	*Evangelische Theologie*
GGA	*Göttingische gelehrte Anzeigen*
HZ	*Historische Zeitschrift*
HWP	*Historisches Wörterbuch der Philosophie*, ed. J.Ritter
NZST	*Neue Zeitschrift für Systematische Theologie und Religionsphilosophie*
PrJ	*Preussische Jahrbücher*
RE[3]	*Realenzyklopädie für protestantische Theologie und Kirche*, [3]*1896-1913*
RGG	*Die Religion in Geschichte und Gegenwart*
TLZ	*Theologische Literaturzeitung*
TJB	*Theologischer Jahresbericht*
TR	*Theologische Rundschau*
TRST	*Troeltsch-Studien*, ed. H.Renz and F.W.Graf (Vols 1, 3 and 4), Gütersloh 1982, 1984, 1987
SchmJ	*Schmollers Jahrbuch für Gesetzgebung, Verwaltung und Volkswirtschaft*
ZEE	*Zeitschrift für Evangelische Ethik*
ZKG	*Zeitschrift für Kirchengeschichte*

| ZTK | *Zeitschrift für Theologie und Kirche* |
| ZRGG | *Zeitschrift für Religions- und Geistesgeschichte* |

3. Other

ADB	*Allgemeine deutsche Biographie*
ET	English translation
SS	Summer semester
UB	Universitäts-Bibliothek
WS	Winter Semester

Introduction

Ernst Troeltsch (1865-1923) is one of those Protestant theologians who had an influence on the scholarly world in the time before the First World War which extended far beyond the bounds of theology. A variety of circumstances led to his name and his work almost being forgotten in the generation after him, and his significance was recognized only in the narrower circle of professionals interested in the history of religion and theology. Beyond doubt one reason for this is that with his interests and approaches, Troeltsch, as a prominent representative of so-called liberal theology, seemed out of date to the next generation of leading theologians. For them the First World War was the sign of a complete collapse of a theology orientated on cultural history and the signal for a radically new theological beginning. The lack of more wide-ranging and ongoing discussion of Troeltsch's work may have been a contributory factor to his early death. No real school formed around him.

The intensive attention that has been paid to Ernst Troeltsch in the last fifteen years is a remarkable development, and stands in contrast to the widespread oblivion of earlier decades. However, it must be added that Troeltsch has had an influence outside theology. This is because of the great variety in his work, which goes beyond theology in various directions, to philosophy, history and sociology.

There has been another remarkable development recently: Troeltsch has also become increasingly a focus of interest as a person, with his biography. This has come about as a result of the recognition that in his case life and work belong closely together. If one adopts Wilhelm Dilthey's distinction that while Kant's work can be understood without his life, that of Schleiermacher cannot be understood without his biography, Troeltsch belongs to the second category. His work is shaped by the exchange of ideas, lively scholarly communication, keen perception and the assimilation of the events of his time. In his autobiographical sketch ('My Books'), Troeltsch himself described how his work and his person belong together, and how each sheds light on the other. Above all he showed how, if one takes them in the order in which he tackled them, the progress of his literary production, his 'books', is in this connection itself a piece of enthralling biography. That is particularly significant when the purely biographical source material is not as abundant as one could have wished. However, here too there has been a change in recent years.

Two reasons can be given for this newly-awakened interest in Troeltsch. First, the interval of time now separating us from the period of 'liberal' theology has cleared the air. Liberal theology can appear as what it really was – and no longer suffers from the instant assessment provoked by the global repudiation of the next generation. Troeltsch's life was devoted to a form of theology which addressed the basic questions of its time and tackled them constructively. This included the discovery of the non-Christian religions, the questions put to the Christian tradition by historicism, and the recognition in principle of the historical method, to mention only the most important factors. Furthermore, the 'dialectical' theologians and their work are now themselves open to historical criticism. Secondly, Troeltsch's work is of interest because of the breadth of his questions and the themes that he tackles. It takes up the thought of the history-of-religions school, raises the question of the epistemological basis of theology and extends to a diagnosis of the time and an assessment of the modern world in terms of the philosophy of culture.

So the present biography combines two approaches, one in terms of biography and the genesis of ideas, and the other in terms of the systematic discussion of themes. The chronological structure is fundamental. Nor is it purely formal; sections which dwell systematically on an interpretation of Troeltsch's works have been built into the biographical narrative and the account of his literary activity.

In assessing Troeltsch's work as a whole, it should be noted that Troeltsch varied what he said depending on the context, and that he clearly became involved in changing dialogue situations and confrontations. Therefore a genetic approach is much more suited to a scientific biography than a fundamentally systematic reconstruction. Troeltsch was a deeply dialogical thinker who, as his friend Carl Neumann, the Heidelberg art historian, once put it, carried on 'dialogues... with books and people'. This dialogical approach also played a part in determining the 'distinctive form of his books'.[1]

An important insight goes with this: because in his academic work Troeltsch was disposed to think in terms of development and differentiation, of the acceptance of other standpoints and a discussion of them, condensing material was ruled out, since that would fail to do justice to its real content, to what could be learned from critical discussion. Troeltsch's thought is bassed on a wealth of phenomena, broad horizons and a variety of possible approaches, the productive acceptance and development in controversy of other possible positions. His thought and his methods of working are characterized less by logical argument and a linear progress of ideas than by working round the whole of a problem to develop it, indicating its structure and making references to possible solutions. Troeltsch here represents something of the modern experience of the world by attempting to maintain the tension between the desire for clarity of intellect and position and the perception of change and alternation, which always at the same time shows alteration and richness to be broken.

For a long time Troeltsch was assessed above all in terms of what he did not achieve – and the criteria for this assessment were excessively taken from his critics' own dogmatics. This has distorted perception of the independence and fruitfulness of his work. By contrast, those who follow the paths of his thought, overgrown though indeed they sometimes are, and undertake to go along with him, will be able to derive rich benefit from the wealth and abundance of his work.

Part One: The Beginning of Troeltsch's Life and Work
(1865-1894)

I

Youth in Augsburg

Ernst Troeltsch came from Augsburg, or more precisely from Haunstetten, a village south of the city which was later swallowed up into it. His parents moved into the city itself the year he was born. Augsburg is an ancient mercantile city with a south German flavour. In addition to a concern for acquiring possessions, the citizens manifestly also had a tendency to invest what they acquired in things that could simultaneously satisfy both an artistic and a civic sense. The splendid Renaissance façades of the houses recall the heyday of Augsburg, the time of the Fuggers and the Welsers. Down the centuries, wide-ranging trading connections created a spirit capable of thinking beyond its own circumstances; a spirit of some liberality, which had room for others.

That even affected the relationship between the confessions. In the city of the *Confessio Augustana* the prevalent atmosphere was on the whole one of a concern for reconciliation; the churches of the Protestants, who were usually in the minority, stood right alongside those of the Catholics. Granted, in the long history of the city there had also been phases of lively controversy and mutual criticism between the confessions. But all in all, polemic and disparagement were kept within bounds. In the course of time Augsburg had declined from the significant position that it had during its heyday in the sixteenth century. However, what largely remained and was valued was the awareness of being a free city of the Reich and pride in the fact.

Ernst Peter Wilhelm Troeltsch was born on 17 February 1865. If we link his life with the wider course of historical events, we may say that his childhood coincided with the foundation of the Reich, his youth with the growing economic and political significance of the united Reich, and the end of his life with its collapse and the beginning of the Weimar Republic. We shall see in due course how his life was bound up with the far-reaching changes which these developments brought about, how he reacted to his time and acted in it. But at this point it can already be said that Troeltsch's life was on the one hand the quiet life of a scholar devoted to intellectual work and on the other was eminently bound up with wider cultural and political developments. This was not just a result of his personal involvement in contemporary events; it was also a fundamental consequence of his work and its aims.

Ernst Troeltsch (above left) in a family group, c. 1874

Troeltsch's father, who came from a family of Augsburg merchants, had settled in Haunstetten in 1862 as a doctor, a general practitioner. His ancestors were Bavarians and had mainly been engaged in trade. Ernst's father's move into medicine seems to have been an exception. His mother, Eugenie née Köppel, came from a Nuremberg doctor's family.

Ernst was the first child born to the young couple, while they were still in Haunstetten; further children born in Augsburg were Wilhelmine (1867), Rudolf (1870), Eugenie (1871), Emilie (1875) and Elise (1879). Their father was completely devoted to the medical profession; in addition to his studies he had also kept up an interest in science. Troeltsch later recalled the scientific collections at home, the 'skeletons, anatomical compendia, electrical machines, books of plants, books about crystals, etc.'.[1]

Although Ernst's father had little time after his professional duties and many public offices, he seems to have taken an intense interest in his sons and daughters. The family chronicle gives a glimpse of the open atmosphere in the family: 'For us children the living room was both a place to work and a place to romp in; all the furniture was often turned upside down and transformed by children's imagination into railway trains, steamships or huts. Family parties took place there, at Christmas and on other occasions; it was here on Sunday evenings that Uncle Carl and Aunt Dora came to visit, and the families of doctor friends met in turn for the monthly gathering.'[2]

The religious spirit in Ernst's home matched this open atmosphere to the degree that it did not seek to constrain inner convictions but nevertheless deliberately maintained the Christian tradition. Ernst later described it like this: 'Our home was always a Christian home, without any dogmatic or pietistic colouring, but holding firm to Christian custom.'[3] The political attitude at home was basically monarchical, tending to favour a single German state. Troeltsch shared this attitude; in his student days he had a high regard for Bismarck and took a nationalistic viewpoint for granted.[4]

Ernst Troeltsch kept up and cultivated links with his family all his life, and his native city of Augsburg played a major role in his reminiscences.[5] He keenly followed the fortunes of members of the family, and tried to help when difficulties cropped up. He was particularly oppressed by the fact that his father lost his money through the bankruptcy of a nephew, had to start practising as a doctor again, and for a long time was the victim of depression. Troeltsch wrote about this to his student friend Wilhelm Bousset: 'Through his nephew's frauds my father has lost his whole very considerable fortune, and only a small part of it will be able to be saved from the bankruptcy proceedings which have now begun. For the moment everything is in the hands of the administrators. You can fill out the situation for yourself. My brother isn't earning anyting and was in the middle of his second examination when the proceedings began [his brother became a lawyer]. Now my sisters have to go out, and my father, who wanted to retire, has to earn a living again. In these circumstances I had a very gloomy Christmas. I won't tell you all the details in this letter, but it's obvious that there was a good deal of anxiety, consternation and pain. Thank God that I am provided for and now can at least help my family.'[6]

Ernst had a strong emotional tie to his family. Not only as a student and Privatdozent, but also when he was professor in Heidelberg, he visited his parents in Augsburg frequently. Close contact with his brothers and sisters is also evident in letters from the Berlin period.

In a letter which Ernst wrote in 1918 to Gertrud le Fort on the death of her mother, he reflects on his own relationship to his parents: 'Pictures of my early youth now pass before me almost every day... The constant movement of life gives us nothing to hold on to and in the end also brings all kinds of friction. Only when the movement is at an end is the whole picture restored again. And then how deep and painful is the loss, how melancholy the remembrance! How fresh everything becomes again, and in a thousand details life returns to love! I now live more with my dear departed ones than I did during their lifetimes. Their pictures greet me every evening as I go to sleep, and during the day a thousand little things conjure up memories of my parental home.'[7]

Ernst's parents followed the academic progress of their oldest son attentively and with pride. Thus on the centenary of Schiller's death, in 1905, Ernst's father noted on the announcement of the ceremonial lecture: 'Given by my son Ernst in the Goldener Saal of the city.'

After attending the local primary school, from autumn 1874 to summer 1883 Ernst studied at St Anna, a gymnasium specializing in the classics which his father had attended before him. The school tradition combined Christian tradition with a humanist atmosphere. Later, Ernst recalled schooldays with amazingly few lessons, which left a good deal of time for other studies. In expressing his recollections like this, he was probably indicating not so much the actual timetable of school life as the ease with which he coped with the work. Moreover, he seems to have had a pragmatic approach and was therefore in a position to adapt to the demands of school rules.[8]

For the whole of his schooldays Ernst brought home brilliant reports. When he remarked later that he would be 'forever grateful to some of the teachers at the school at that time for their stimulation and teaching', he was probably thinking above all of Professor Mezger, who taught him for two years, and Inspector Boeckh, his religious teacher. Whereas Boeckh was remembered for his 'wealth of knowledge and warm piety', Mezger's influence probably lay more in conveying the cultural world of classical antiquity.[9] Ernst's later dedication of his licentiate thesis on *Reason and Revelation in Johann Gerhard and Melanchthon* to Professor Mezger along with his own father is an indication of his esteem and affection.

In July 1883 Ernst passed his final school examination with 'very good' in all subjects except for mathematics, physics and physical education, in which he was given 'good'. The general report stressed his academic zeal; his teachers expected 'that at college, too, he will devote the full force of his intellectual gifts to his chosen study and will achieve the utmost success'.

At the Speech Day on 6 August 1883, Ernst gave the school-leavers' speech. It shows a remarkably mature and free mind. He said that the 'greatest treasure' which the leavers would take with them from the school was a knowledge of classical antiquity. Then there was the religious world. In a way anticipating his later synthetic thought, Ernst took the two together and understood them as mutually critical correctives: 'Only those who adopt the positive principles of religion as their guide through the world of ideas will be preserved from falling by the wayside, and again only those who know the classical world will be able to attain the highest there is, by the highest way: truth through research.'[10]

At this time Ernst was not yet certain what discipline he would choose. His father would have loved him to study medicine. The period of military service which Ernst underwent as a one-year volunteer in an artillery regiment in Augsburg postponed the decision. Military service gave him enough time to pursue his lively intellectual interests, and so during this period he also went to lectures at the Royal Lyceum in Augsburg. The Lyceum provided basic philosophical training for Catholic theological students and was run by Benedictines. The lectures Ernst attended in the winter semester of 1883/84 were on logic and metaphysics, experimental physics, anthropology and philology; the next semester he attended further lectures on the history of art, natural history, the history of philosophy and again experimental physics.[11]

II

Student Years (1884-1891)

1. Beginnings in Erlangen

At the end of his military service, Troeltsch began his university studies. As I have already indicated, he appears to have been somewhat uncertain about a choice of subject. Law did not seem uninteresting to him, but the professional career which would eventually follow was not very attractive. 'I was also fascinated by classical philology, in which our school had taken us to unusual depths; but experiences with the schoolmasters of the time had shown all too clearly that Hellenic ideals of life cannot be realized in practice today. As it was then, philosophy as such was unattractive; my interest in medicine was purely theoretical. So I studied theology. At that time theology alone seemed to offer an approach both to metaphysics and to unusually exciting historical problems... The practical consequences for my own career could then follow as they would. A naturally vigorous religious drive seemed to guarantee that everything would work out somehow or other.'[12]

So primarily academic interests led Troeltsch to theology, rather than the vocation of a pastor or practical work in the church. He was so confident of his own strong religious feelings that even the pastorate seemed possible – here his religious upbringing at home and in school will have been contributory factors.

Troeltsch enrolled in the theological faculty of Erlangen university in the winter semester of 1884/85. It will have been natural to choose the local university to begin with. But given his tendencies and his interest, was Erlangen the right place for him to study? Erlangen, the citadel of Lutheranism and known for its preservation of the Lutheran doctrinal tradition with strong ties to the church? In retrospect Troeltsch remarked on his teachers and his own ideas: 'We had a cool respect for these gentlemen and regarded them as antiques from the time of the German Federation, as relics of the fight between neo-pietism and the Enlightenment. Our interests were different: in part contemporary political and social problems, and in part the scientific world-view of the time.'[13]

Troeltsch went to lectures on the history of the early church by the church historian A.Hauck and on pedagogics and didactics by the practical theologian

K.A.von Zezschwitz, who seems to have gained a great reputation in the Bavarian Landeskirche. In the second semester he also went to lectures on exegesis by T.Zahn and on dogmatics by F.H.R.Frank.

What kind of theology did Troeltsch meet in Erlangen? To generalize, it may be said that the Erlangen faculty derived its particular orientation from a close combination of Bible, confession and Lutheran doctrinal tradition. In this respect the faculty was homogeneous. Erlangen theology as it had developed in the second half of the nineteenth century and determined the spirit of the faculty when Troeltsch studied there was characterized by a dogmatics which began with faith in the form of experience and certainty, the association of personal faith with a traditional confession, an orientation on the Bible on the basis of a salvation-historical theology, and a conscious acceptance of the basic views of Luther on the relationship between the church and the world and on professional life.[14]

It will very soon have become evident that Erlangen theology was not going to give a long-term answer to Troeltsch's questions about the relationship between Christianity and the modern world-view, and the concentration on the word of scripture and the Lutheran doctrinal tradition did not correspond to what he had in mind when he associated the spirit of antiquity with Christianity in his school-leavers' speech. The stress on links with the church and the acquisition of personal certainty through the biblical tradition which was accepted as a norm certainly offered a firm theology and faith, but was also manifestly narrow.

The lectures by the philosopher Gustav Class (1836-1908) will have been more important for Troeltsch in arriving at a theological and philosophical position.[15] What particularly attracted him about Class was the way he put metaphysics at the centre and his interest in the philosophy of religion and ethics. And it was Class who referred Troeltsch to Kant, Lotze and Schleiermacher.

The philosophical work of Gustav Class went back to the tradition of German idealism. It aimed at a modification of Kantian doctrine to 'provide the foundation for a standpoint which, while maintaining essentials, goes beyond Kant but does not coincide with Hegel's standpoint'.[16] In the philosophy of religion this approach brought Class close to Schleiermacher, as when he stresses the idea of the individual and takes up the idea of God as a limit concept.

Class defined history as a constant interaction between historical content and individuals.[17] Historical content works on individuals in the form of demands; the individual responds by passing judgment. In the end this reciprocal relationship has an ethical aim, to the degree that the judgment which comes to be formed in this process entails a sense of obligation. Where a person is in a position to perceive the obligation in a demand on him over and above his own judgment, in principle the spirit and the life of the spirit come to be set above mere nature.[18]

In contrast to a view of the idea of God as a postulate, Class stressed the reality of the idea of God. The supreme reality, interpreted as absolute spirit and absolute love, is revealed in particular actions through which it participates in life, in the development of the spiritual realm.[19] By their service 'of a holy "you should", providential personalities' – here especially the heroes of religion – elevate themselves above the world of ordinary human conflicts and are evidence that God plays a part in the struggle of the human spirit against mere nature.[20]

In his first great systematic work on 'the independence of religion' Troeltsch uses ideas from Class's philosophy of religion. He follows one line of Class's thinking when he stresses the notion that religion rests on the living self-movement of God and evokes a resonance in human beings which discloses the deity at increasing depth.[21]

2. Friendship with Bousset – attempt at self-discovery

In his first semester at Erlangen Troeltsch made the acquaintance of Wilhelm Bousset, who later joined with him in founding the history-of-religions school. Bousset (1865-1920) was to become a lifelong friend; his studies on the New Testament environment and his exegetical work are still important today. Bousset, who came from Lübeck, had begun his theological study in Erlangen a semester before Troeltsch. Both were members of the student association Uttenruthia. The Uttenruthians, close to Wingolf, were a student association with Christian ideals and aims. Troeltsch was accepted in November 1884 and was given the nickname 'Strolch' (hooligan). From then on the affairs of the association, the friendships and quarrels among its members, were an important theme in Troeltsch's student life and between the two friends.

In retrospect Troeltsch said that his days as a young student were untroubled, marked by serious work and searching, but also full with all kinds of pranks. Students loved making up stories and were always trying to go one better than the next person. For example, Bousset, whose nickname was 'Moor', claimed that his grandfather, still a Moor, had played the tympani in the chapel at the Court of Mecklenberg. Bousset himself is said to have been a real master at inventing such stories. Many years later, when Troeltsch was already a well-placed professor of theology, he had to protest against fantasies which still stuck to him from his student days.

The flights of fancy and a friendship which today would appear over-close should not disguise the fact that already during these years Troeltsch had broad spiritual and cultural interests. A clear, lively mind and a deep interest in theological and philosophical questions were part of his make-up.

Troeltsch's many letters to Wilhelm Bousset give some information about his thoughts on theology and the world at that time. Thus in a letter of 11 September 1889 he wrote: 'For a long time now I have been used to making progress in companionship with you, and as one has a real need for some public, while I have quietly been working on I have involuntarily kept thinking what you would say about it.'[22]

There was a lively correspondence in July and August 1885 when Troeltsch had to go on military manoeuvres in Ingolstadt and Lechfeld. He found the firing and exercises required of him exceptionally difficult; he developed a real hatred of the 'Brown Bess'. On the other hand, he found life in the artillery barracks tolerable. He had plenty of spare time, which – as during his military service in Augsburg – he used for his own studies and interests. The officers were very obliging, so that Troeltsch did not have the pride of a free student insulted. However, he soon found himself in the role of an outsider, although this was not without advantages for him. He was quite happy not to be invited to the evening entertainments, with visits to the inns and taverns.

Troeltsch sought to avoid a direct confrontation. This concern to find a kind of balance between a struggle for independence and some compromise would also be characteristic of him in the future.

In describing events and people around him Troeltsch had the gift of being a sharp observer. He did not enjoy the hail-fellow-well-met student world. He was not impressed by the outward dash and the whole atmosphere of camaraderie, with its drinking and gossip. His antipathy to student elitism with its lack of intellectual content led him often to see his comrades in a negative light. He was very interested in other people, their behaviour and their mentality; he was stirred by their views of the world and religion. Here was someone who was close to reality - one might even almost say obsessed with reality – who wanted to perceive and assimilate the whole of reality.

One sometimes gets the impression that Troeltsch is almost talking down to Bousset in his letters. True, we do not have the letters which Bousset wrote in reply, but it becomes clear that Troeltsch did not take in much about what and who interested his friend; many passages in his letters are more reflections on himself.

It is amazing how self-critically and at the same time confidently the young student talks of the tensions in his personality and thought: 'I have two sides and I serve two masters – call them thought and feeling, or realism and idealism, immanence and transcendence, mechanism and supranaturalism, knowledge and disposition, or whatever. My whole work consists in attempting to give each of these masters its due. But here, of course, it is easy to be inconsistent, since the true mean is never the philosopher's stone – at least I have never found it – and so I will often be understood wrongly. Indeed, even those who love me often have sympathy and understanding only for the one side, and antipathy and censure for the other. They make the side that speaks to them my main side, my nature, and are infuriated with the inconsistency when they see the other... I suffer the fate of all those who want to do justice to two masters: they do not do justice to either. But I cannot do other than serve the two masters I know. I can only guess at the point which unites them, i.e. the master standing over them, and as my knowledge here becomes clearer, so my action on all sides will become firm and consistent. So I ask you never to keep to one side alone...' (letter of 30 July 1885).

This kind of concern for a balance brings us to something else which is largely typical of Troeltsch's position. He will have nothing to do with thinking in alternatives; he sees this as simplification and an attempt to fix things. Many years later, he wrote in a review that it was easy to put his whole thought 'on the dilemma' of an either-or and in this way to manipulate it.[23] Rather, in his thought he was concerned to arrive at a balance, to relate the possibilities of thought and belief. This concern not to take a one-sided view did not always make Troeltsch's relationships with other people easy, leaving him open to the accusation that he was unable to make up his mind.

The quest for a unitary standpoint which transcends and embraces the basic polar possibilities of life runs through Troeltsch's early letters. He asks Bousset to bear with him over his nature and the character of his thought. He is somewhere between 'guidance by the Lord' and a way which opens up through development: 'I cannot do otherwise; I have to take this course. The Lord will lead me in the right way. But do not let yourself be led astray even if you know otherwise or better. Those are the ways along which the development goes. I can do nothing about mine and you can do nothing about yours. But precisely by encouraging ourselves along these ways we shall remain what we were' (letter of 30 July 1885).

In the letter that I have quoted, Troeltsch sees the point of unity in personal terms as a master of whom he has only an inkling and cannot describe in more detail. The divergent principles, which are described as thought and feeling, immanence and transcendence, mechanism and spontaneity, cannot be re-conciled in a system, and all the drive towards intellectual and personal consistency at this point is hardly appropriate for him. This too is an abiding feature of Troeltsch's theological and philosophical work. At the end of his life, in his autobiographical sketch, he would comment critically on the ideas of a system and think that if he described his own work as a system at all, it could only be an open, an 'unstable' system.[24]

Bousset evidently criticized Troeltsch's view, and also asked for more clarity and consistency in his practical attitude to other people. He indicated to his friend that Troeltsch regarded important existential questions in too cool and detached a way. To this charge Troeltsch replied: 'There remain my two sides, however much you may chide my inconsistency and depict the relationship between thought and feeling as a kind of fencing match in which feeling always gets beaten. Where everything is still gaping open, where the foundations, the basic ingredients of a philosophical world-view, are still fluctuating in a nebulous way and struggling for shape in unruly haste, consistency is imposs-ible. But I go further and claim that there is no really consistent view of the world. No one will ever succeed in combining the two elements of mechanics and consciousness into a construction which has no gaps. There will always remain a tremendous, unbridgeable gulf between the two ingredients, and the end of the research will continue to be that my understanding tells me this, while my disposition tells me that. Both are right, since they are there. And if the results on the two sides do not match, this will probably be because the middle factors are missing from my calculation. So I would prefer not to take account of the world' (12 August 1885). Troeltsch describes his renunciation of a solution to the questions of principles addressed in the form of a 'system' as 'cautious resignation'. But such resignation is at the same time also interpreted in positive terms, because the basic elements of reality which are felt to be opposites are not bent together by force.

Troeltsch was also concerned from a theological aspect with the question how to bend together two polar principles to form a unitary system. He asked whether a distinction between 'children of God' and 'children of the world' could be appropriate; here his judgments were very cautious and critical. He thought that one cannot simply establish who belongs to one group and who to the other, nor is one of the two poles to be done away with. For if the children of God disappear, a requirement of human dispositions remains unfulfilled; and if the children of the world are no longer there, the existence of humanity is threatened. He makes this comment on a piety which is worn on the sleeve: 'Moreover there is so much hypocrisy, self-righteousness, manifest error and superstition, conscious and subconscious, in the very ranks of the "children of God", that it is difficult to present them as the only inhabitants of the world who live up to the idea. So there is no alternative but to decide on decreeing some degree of equal rights, though this goes against both my logic and my feelings. What should the theorist do now? If he is young, he will say: "I will grow older, and only then will I attempt to make a connection; until then I shall content myself with the facts and neither persecute one direction nor monopolize the other." I too say that.

But what is the practical person to do here? If theoretically neither of the two sides is to be eliminated, one has a free choice of one's way of life. That one does not have. My education, my conscience, my thought, my disposition, tells me which side I have to join, and this is enough to show me my way quite definitely...' (letter of 12 August 1885).

In practice, at this time Troeltsch seems to have been content with a remarkable combination of the Kantian view of duty and a cautious belief in divine guidance. The assumption of divine guidance is bound up with the doing of human duties. What Troeltsch can accept for himself as a personal view of faith differs in its lack of clarity and also its formal language from what he can say so vividly and convincingly elsewhere, in a non-theological sense, about the world, human beings and the basic elements of reality. On the question of the origin of the standpoint of faith and its justification, he observes that these things are 'in part given directly in the feelings and in part offered us by the historical revelation of God' (letter of 19 May 1886).

Troeltsch goes on to resort to the notion that the solution of the whole question can be postponed. 'Christianity is practical life, not a system; it came into the world as a living force, and as such it has continued to have an effect on all the heroes of our faith. Its content is not the canon but the Christian community, just as the life work of Paul is not his letters, useful though they may be to quote from, but the tremendous expansion of Christianity' (letter of 19 May 1886).

Troeltsch thinks that his basic argument is capable of improvement at various points, but remarks, not without pride, that it is all 'based... on my own work and does not follow anyone else' (letter of 25 June 1886). Subjectively, he is certainly right in feeling this, though concepts and notions indicate a clear relationship to the late idealistic philosophy of the time, especially to Class and Lotze. It is above all the concepts of the life of the spirit, value and interest which connect him with this philosophy. However, it should be noted how Troeltsch can deal independently with individual concepts and approaches. He stubbornly feels that materialism and naturalism must be taken seriously as counter-movements to an idealistic position.

The two friends argued over the question of the role of philosophy in its relationship to theology or religion. Bousset accused Troeltsch of having too high a regard for philosophy generally. He said this not least in view of the fact that Troeltsch was studying theology and might possibly be working later as a pastor. Troeltsch retorted with some agitation: 'You are being stupid again about philosophy. I believe that you have no feeling for it, but that's all right. People who approach pastoral work purely on the basis of faith, untroubled by the welter of philosophical reflection and relying purely on their faith to deal with this source of knowledge, indeed distress us, and difficult and rare though this art is, it is pleasant really to see such a disposition set to work. At the same time, though, we must not do an injustice to the others who share with us in working on the great task of humanity, using God-given reason to explain their mode of being and value and in so doing giving the human race not so much an understanding of its goal as increasingly general and certain knowledge' (letter of 6 December 1885).

Bousset is not misled by the irony and continues to press for the independence of the religious element from philosophy, whereas Troeltsch recognizes one of the main problems for his thought precisely at this point, namely, the appropriate relationship between philosophy on the one hand and religion and theology on the other. For him, an essential task of contemporary theology is to achieve 'a reconciliation between these modern forms of thought and the Western dispositional content (not the metaphysical content) of positive Christianity' (letter of 23 December 1885). But it is not yet clear to him what the solution to this task might prove to be: 'However, so far I cannot see the way to a solution anywhere; I do not have it myself; I'm very sceptical and almost sad about things. It is possible that the church will be completely destroyed and that the aesthetic forms of subjective religion which are now emerging will give very different religions to the educated and the uneducated, and to the semi-educated no religion at all; in short, that religion and religious feeling coincide, and the external forms no longer have any significance. That would be a sorry state, but it would be more tolerable than the untruth of Catholicism or orthodoxy' (ibid.).

However, quite apart from such basic philosophical and theological questions which at this time took up a good deal of space in Troeltsch's letters to Bousset and which are impressive for the unerring way in which Troeltsch here presses for an answer and will not be content with over-hasty solutions in terms of faith, other things which interest the friends are also discussed. But they are often once again bent back into reflections on basic issues.

To the degree that philosophy can offer a basic view of life, Troeltsch regards it as paramount; the special task of theology only develops on this basis. The work of dogmatics consists in making a connection between a general view of the world and life on the one hand and the special view of religion or the Christian faith on the other. However, for Troeltsch neither philosophy nor dogmatics are science in the strict sense. Rather, they are attempts 'to grasp the world, ourselves and God in a unity which satisfies the intellect as much as the disposition. Of course we are never successful here, and one can call one's dogmatics complete only when one has closed one's eyes. It lives and grows with the subject, reflects his career and is to a supreme degree dependent on his individuality. So on the one hand I attach no importance to dogmatics, but on the other every importance. For practical religious life it is secondary, but for the educated mind it is indispensable' (letter of 19 May 1886). Troeltsch's view of dogmatics here comes close to that presented later in his licentiate work: dogmatics is an attempt to connect with the spirit of the time, particularly as expressed in philosophical work.

If we look at the questions of the possibility of asserting and bringing together spiritual approaches to reality in the face of the mechanization of thought in the modern world, as expressed in Troeltsch's letters, it is clear that Troeltsch's theological teachers in Erlangen were unable to give a satisfactory answer. Frank's systematic thought relies not least on deriving the content of the theological doctrinal tradition from the strange certainty of the experience of faith. That is quite a different world, a world of marked theological demarcation from the reality of modern life and views opposed to Christian faith.

3. *The move to Berlin*

Troeltsch decided to leave Erlangen in the winter semester of 1885/86. He wanted to go to Berlin; his friend Bousset preferred Leipzig for his studies.

The change from the Bavarian university of Erlangen to the capital of the

Reich was a great spur to Troeltsch. Now twenty, he enjoyed the atmosphere
of the capital: 'The great metropolis with its remarkable architecture and life
constantly attracts one's attention, but it just as energetically stimulates
intellectual effort and delight in being able to take things in. In my view Berlin
is not a beautiful city, but a city with beautiful buildings; indeed, it is an
arena for every conceivable activity with amazingly developed means of
communication. Among the sometimes ugly or at any rate very ordinary rows
of houses, from time to time enormous palaces rise up in every style; the
streets and squares are adorned with a wealth of sometimes valuable statues
and monuments, past which the inhabitants of the city usually rush indifferently
about their business. One attractive corner is the square occupied by the
museums, hallowed by the wonderfully graceful seriousness of art. Otherwise
even the most splendid squares are spoilt by some tawdry regal façade, a
stinking cheesemonger's barracks, a sober hiring cage, a fragile art shop or
the ruins of torn down or incomplete buildings. Berlin had the misfortune to
be built at the time when taste was at its worst, and now it has great difficulty
in keeping its change of dress in step with its growth. But the historical
associations which crop up everywhere are elevating and inspiring. The days
of the great archdukes, the age of the Fredericks with its heroic acts in war
and peace, the humiliation of Prussia and the wars of 1813 and 1815, the
saving dawn of the spring of 1866, the consummation in 1870, all this presents
itself to those enthusiastic for the Fatherland with almost overwhelming power
and touching liveliness. I have never felt the greatness of Prussia, its significance
for Germany, as much as here, and in particular it is the royal house of
Hohenzollern which with its iron consistency, its truly royal dignity and its
brilliant understanding of history arouses ever-increasing wonderment in me'
(letter of 6 November 1885 to Bousset).

Of the wealth of intellectual stimuli and cultural delights he said: 'Here
there is truly a kind of ethereal region of pure spiritual, ideal life, and I do not
think I shall ever be able to enjoy it enough.'[25] So Troeltsch did not stick
narrowly to theology, but also turned to other areas of study. His wide-ranging
interest bore fruit later. Here were laid the foundations of his capacity to
analyse the scientific situation of the time and the confrontation of theology
with the spirit of the age, and he was encouraged by the nature of his
involvement. Hermann Köberle, a pastor's son from Memmingen who had
been a friend of Troeltsch's since they were at school together, now a member
of the same association and living in the same house, gave an impressive account
of the stimulating intellectual atmosphere which this close companionship
produced.[26] This is how Troeltsch's personality, life and way of working
appeared to Köberle. 'In his theology he is somewhat left-wing, but I too am
also partly so. However, for the moment he has more in mind than entering
the pastorate – and in Bavaria at that... Of course he has done an enormous
amount of studying; I only hope that his body can take it.'[27]

Troeltsch's wide-ranging intellectual interest is evident from his choice of lectures. He heard Ernst Curtius on 'The History of Graphic Art among the Greeks and Romans', and also Emil du Bois-Reymond on 'Physical Anthropology'.[28] At the centre, though, was theology – increasingly in the form of dogmatics and ethics.

Of his teacher in this discipline, Julius Kaftan, he wrote to Bousset that 'so far he has been imposing but in no way illuminating' (letter of 6 November 1885).[29] Troeltsch continued his search for an acceptable theological position.

Bousset, who was very interested in social questions, and for whom among many others Adolf Stöcker[30] was a kind of leading figure, waited eagerly for news of the impression that Stöcker and the Inner Mission had made on Troeltsch. What he was told will not have pleased him very much. 'To achieve his ideals, in his political activity, which in itself is quite noteworthy, Stöcker is forced to attract the sheep-vote of the mass at any price and keep it in line by constantly feeding it with slogans and taunts. A gathering of the Christian Social Party is not a very elevated experience: much empty rhetoric, many slogans, a mass of advertising and humbug, hatred of the better-off, satisfaction of political passions, a piety which misunderstands itself; a leadership which will soon no longer be able to banish the spirits it has conjured up – all in all it is not a very pleasant picture' (letter of 6 November 1885). True, this attempt to make Christianity practical compelled Troeltsch's respect, but he nevertheless thought 'that history will not approve of Stöcker, but, as everywhere else, will take its revenge on any amalgamation of politics and Christianity by a bad confusion of concepts' (ibid., reprinted in Dinkler-von Schubert, 22 n.4). Nor could Troeltsch get much out of the Inner Mission. Here he detected an American style at work, but thought that one had to 'distinguish between following the Christian Social Party and following Christ' (letter of 6 November 1885). Stöcker's antisemitism seemed to him essentially to be 'a policy of professional jealousy decked out with grandiose Christian phrases' (ibid). Although Troeltsch was quite impressed by Stöcker as a person, he stuck to his more sceptical verdict: 'In the meantime I have not made friends with Stöcker, for all my respect and admiration. To combine orthodox Christianity, politics and the mission of love goes beyond the powers even of a very gifted man' (letter of 20 February 1886).

The young Troeltsch's stay in the capital of the Reich was not without political influence on him. He had already been an admirer of Bismarck. Now, in Berlin, where Prussian history encountered him at every turn, the nationalistic slant of his thinking intensified. 'Here I feel my political views in particular being vigorously stimulated, and if possible here I am more enthusiastic than before for our imperial monarchy with the Hohenzollern crown' (ibid.). However, we may doubt whether specific political questions interested Troeltsch particularly strongly at this time. He later remarked that what had happened to him was like what happened to many of the cultured middle-class Germans: only at a very late stage did he arrive at a poitical awareness of his own.

Troeltsch remained in Berlin for the summer semester of 1886. He felt it 'too beautiful to leave after just one semester...'(ibid.). And he said quite casually of Kaftan: he 'is really a fine chap, and I would very much like to hear more of him' (ibid.). But he was quite specially interested in Treitschke[31] and the Berlin museums: 'And then above all I am captivated by Treitschke, whom I really revere far above all others; it is worth going to Berlin for him alone... Then the museums are also very important for me; I've not yet studied even half of them, and I just have to continue these studies; there's tremendous enjoyment in store. I shall never have it so fine again' (letter to Bousset, 20 February 1886).

However, the next winter Troeltsch did want to leave Berlin. Probably he did not see sufficient possibilities for himself within theology. Moreover, he was moved by another factor: 'I long above all for association life and for a smaller world' (letter to Bousset, 25 June 1886).

A letter to Uttenruthia of 19 January 1886 is illuminating for Troeltsch's attitude to the Erlangen association, which was as committed as it was critical.[32] In the summer of 1885 he had sent an anonymous letter to Uttenruthia in which he asked them to think of a question for the association, an existential question which went beyond 'just soup and beef'. He took a critical view of the situation, noting a number of customs that had crept in. 'There is no positive, creative life to breathe in new verve and above all the truly ideal characteristic of communal work and the encouragement of association life.' He felt it important that the number of new admissions should be reduced and that the choice of members should be made more firmly on the basis of intellectual calibre. 'Then we shall be fewer and be able to get to know one another better; then we shall also always fit together better; then our ideal, really lively atmosphere will return, and we will be truly at one and be respected by outsiders.'[33] Troeltsch's reflections show an idealistic young man who is disturbed by the general intellectual level of association life but becomes critically involved in it through his suggestions for change. On the other side, in the semester report there is mention of a reformer who in his zeal to reform the association has forgotten to put the 'better hand' on himself. He has shown some members of the association that they would not belong in the 'ideal association' which he had in mind. Troeltsch felt misunderstood and wrongly saw himself exposed to public criticism. The somewhat lofty tone of his reply can hardly conceal how hurt he is. Basically, he feels, it all boils down to the accusation that he is an 'arrogant and loveless simpleton'. Annoyed, he continues: 'Quite apart from the fact that I never proposed "reforms" and never thought that they were necessary, but felt that there was a need for a change of atmosphere generally, these words contain almost the worst verdict that one can pass on moral character and make the person concerned somewhat ridiculous. This does not surprise me at all..., but it does not need to be printed and announced in a newspaper to all the Philistines, who of course if they do not already know will ask just who this inflated and loveless reformer is.'

Troeltsch was occasionally incautious and unbalanced in the way in which he formulated his ideas; where something seemed important to him he could – at least formally – say hurtful things. He was aware of this himself, and so – as he had also indicated to Bousset – he made excuses for his character and nature: 'I none the less also use this opportunity to repeat my often-expressed request for a rather gentler and more correct verdict to be passed on my actions; I hope that such unconsidered verdicts will not be prompted by some harshnesses which have appeared.'

Despite such clouds, Troeltsch valued being with his friends in the association very highly and actively sought their company. Here a degree of polarity in his character becomes clear. He had to work on his own in seclusion; he was not afraid of occasionally going his own way with critical detachment. At the same time he needed the stimulus of his friends: he could be very sociable and was regarded as a lively conversationalist, full of wit and personal charm.

4. To Ritschl in Göttingen (1886-1888)

Troeltsch thought hard about the choice of a new place to study. Only Greifswald, Tübingen or Göttingen attracted him. In favour of Göttingen were the person and work of Ritschl. After a visit there he wrote to Bousset: 'Ritschl is in the air everywhere there, and with every breath one person supports him and another opposes him. I grant you, this movement has also had a powerful effect on me and I plan to go there, perhaps next winter' (letter of 23 December 1885, unpublished).

Troeltsch asked Bousset to come to Göttingen, too, so that they could continue their studies together. Bousset was willing, and so the friends were reunited there for the winter semester of 1886/87. Albrecht Ritschl (1822–1889) was the special attraction which made Troeltsch decide for Göttingen.[34] What he personally felt and said – 'Ritschl is in the air everywhere there' – was the basic feeling among the majority of that theological generation.

What was so special about Ritschl's work that it had even proved possible to speak of a Ritschl school, which in its prominent representatives Adolf von Harnack, Wilhelm Herrmann and Julius Kaftan had continued to be an impressive force right down to the second decade of the next century, to the beginnings of dialectical theology?

In his account of Ritschl's theology, Rolf Schäfer has spoken of a 'system which has almost disappeared without trace'.[35] And the way in which a later generation of theologians distanced themselves critically from Ritschl's theology was exemplifed to Göttingen theological students by a remark made in his lectures in the 1950s by the systematic theologian Otto Weber, who was influenced by Barth. He commented that if one looked at Albert Ritschl's house on the Herzberger Landstrasse, at the same time gloomy and monumental, one had an immediate impression of his theology.

Albrecht Ritschl began with historical studies, in order to gain a reliable picture of the teaching of the apostles and the significance of Gentile Christianity for the rise of the Catholic Church. He then extended his historical work to Reformation history, above all working out how Reformation theology differed from the Catholic view and any form of mysticism. However, Ritschl's decisive significance lies in the realm of systematic theology. Here, though, one cannot rightly assess his significance without noting how he started from exegetical-historical questions, and questions relating to the history of theology, especially Reformation history. His dogmatic position is essentially governed by the way in which he stresses the character of religious experience as distinct from all other forms of knowledge and world-view. Religion – and for Ritschl religion is essentially Christianity – is in a position to communicate a total impression of feelings about the world which, by going beyond mere nature and causality, offers a kind of control of the world in a spiritual and religious sense. Thus religion appears on the one hand as an independent entity and on the other in proximity to the life of the spirit, as this was understood by idealist/late idealist philosophy (Kant and Lotze). This connection between religion and a philosophy which puts the emphasis on human beings as spiritual beings is achieved above all by defining Christian faith in terms of ethical categories.

Ritschl's distinction between ontological judgments and value judgments attempts to set apart the value judgment made in Christian faith from any possible theoretical knowledge and define it independently. In making such a distinction between the theoretical forms of knowledge of the world and evaluative judgment Ritschl's basic idea is that this is a way towards relating theoretical knowledge to the possibility of defining the totality in the process of reliigous evaluation, as a view of the world, human beings and life.

Problems arise in Ritschl's theology especially through his assertion of the proximity of religion to ethics, in so far as the idea of the kingdom of God taken over from the Gospels is interpreted above all in a moral perspective; as an idea from biblical Christianity it here represents a remarkable combination of religious aim and inducement to action.

We cannot understand Ritschl's influence on the theology of his time properly unless we see that more sharply than elesewhere he put biblical-Reformation Christianity at the centre of his historical-systematic investigations and in so doing emphasized the special nature of the religious interpretation of life and its proximity to a spiritual personal view of the world and life. This proximity is given philosophical support by the adoption of an idealistic philosophy, but its problems are accentuated by the assumption of a similarity in ethical orientation which Ritschl saw motivated and called for above all by the biblical notion of the kingdom of God.

A few remarks in Troeltsch's letters make it clear how much he esteemed Ritschl as a teacher. Thus in 1889 he wrote to Bousset: 'I have the feeling that I must write something to you on the death of Ritschl, of which of course you know as well as I. I confess that the event has really shaken me, and that I had hoped that we might expect more academic works from him and be given more personal encouragement. Do you remember how we heard his last lecture course on dogmatics and how in the final lecture he remarked quite amazingly that he thanked God for having brought them to a conclusion. If you know more about his last days, please tell me' (card of 23 March 1889, unpublished).

And in 1896 Troeltsch expressed gratitude for a picture of his teacher Ritschl which his publisher Siebeck had sent. He wrote: 'The picture shows him as rather younger than he was when I knew him but gives the most vivid impression of him. It is a splendid memento of my student days, when I had much to do with Ritschl...' (letter of 12 January 1896, Mohr/Siebeck archives, Tübingen, unpublished).

In his three semesters at Göttingen Troeltsch heard Ritschl lecture on Dogmatics I and II (WS 1886/87 and SS 1887) and on Theological Ethics (WS 1887/88). He also heard lectures by Hermann Reuter (1817-89), of whom he said later that he had been a model for methodology,[36] on the church history of the first eight centuries (WS 1886/87). He went to hear Bernhard Duhm (1847-1928) lecturing on the Psalms (SS 1887) and on the history of religion (WS 1887/88). In addition, in his last semester at Göttingen he heard lectures on practical theology by Karl Knoke (1841-1920).

Later, Troeltsch assessed the influence that Göttingen had had on him like this: 'It was Ritschl whose powerful personality attracted us to Göttingen, who really first won us over to theology. With the friends whom I shall go on to mention, we formed his last school. It is difficult nowadays to get an idea of the authority, dignity and power with which this significant but completely unromantic, indeed unpoetic man, attracted us by virtue of his intellectual acumen, the grand yet strict structure of his systematic theology, his purity and superior character. Today's generation of students is less inclined to such dedication and there is no longer his like. He drove us above all into study of the New Testament and the Reformation, in which we began to engage with fiery zeal. In the background, however, Paul de Lagarde and Bernhard Duhm worked in quite a different direction. They both drove us into the history of religion and led us to an increasingly more fundamental break with Ritschl's view of the Bible.'[37]

Troeltsch mentions Paul de Lagarde (1827-1891) here, but it should be noted that he probably did not hear Lagarde during his time as a student in Göttingen and so was not his pupil in the narrower sense. Rather, Lagarde influenced Troeltsch by way of the young doctoral students and would-be lecturers whom he met in Göttingen in 1890.[38]

One theologian who was particularly close to Ritschl in Göttingen was Hermann Schultz (1836-1903). Troeltsch went to his exposition of Genesis (WS 1886/87), his Christian apologetics (SS 1887) and his dogmatic seminar (SS 1887 and WS 1887/88). Schulz, later one of the examiners of Troeltsch's licentiate thesis, was not really a pupil of Ritschl's. He was only fourteen years younger than Ritschl and moved close to him at a relatively late stage. In his dogmatic work Schultz was nearer to Schleiermacher than Ritschl was. For him, as for Schleiermacher, theological activity was based on the reflection of faith on faith. He agreed with Ritschl in the christological foundation of

Wir Prorector und Senat der Königlich Preussischen Georg-Augusts-Universität

bezeugen hiermit, daß der Studirende

Ernst Troeltsch aus Augsburg

auf den Grund eines Zeugnisses der Reife v. d. G. zu Augsburg u. s.

Z. d. U. Berlin

am 22 ten Oct. 1886 als der Theol.

Beflissener unter die Zahl der hiesigen Studirenden aufgenommen ist, und sich bis jetzt

Studirens halber hieselbst aufgehalten hat.

Während seines Hierseins hat derselbe, den beigebrachten Zeugnissen zu Folge, u. V. b.

Winter 1886/7.

Dogmatik I Theil bei Prof. A. Ritschl.

Erklärung des Genesis bei Prof. A. Schultz.

Kirchengeschichte I Theil bei Abt Reuter.

Sommer 1887.

Dogmatik II Theil bei Prof. A. Ritschl.

Symbolik bei Prof. A. Schultz.

Kolenne bei Prof. Duhm.

Systematisches Seminar bei Prof. A. Schultz

Kirchen-historisches Seminar bei Prof. A. Wagenmann.

Winter 1887/8.

Ethik bei Prof. A. Ritschl.

Praktische Theologie bei Prof. Knoke.

Religionsgeschichte bei Prof. Duhm.

Systematisches Seminar bei Prof. A. Schultz.

Katechetisches   Seminar.

Homiletisches

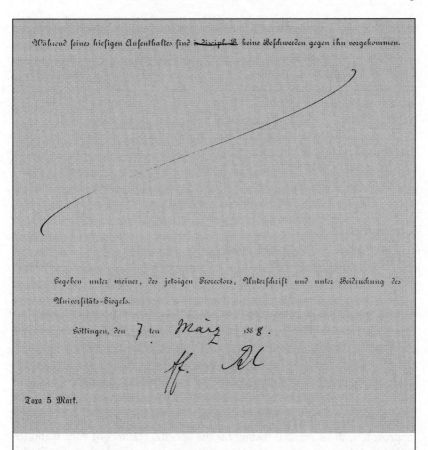

Report on courses attended at Göttingen

One reason why relatively few courses are listed is that a lecture course usually consisted of five lectures a week during the semester so that the fee for it would be relatively expensive. It is worth noting that Troeltsch went to Ritschl and Schultz each semester, and that in contrast to his broader studies in Erlangen and Berlin, in Göttingen he concentrated on theology.

dogmatics. For him, 'faith in Christ' was the mark of true and complete religious feeling. Faith resting on a 'value judgment' had to prove itself by releasing forces to shape the natural conditions of life.[39]

Along with Ritschl, Schultz, who had been called to Göttingen in 1876, determined the theological climate in Göttingen. After Ritschl's death in 1889 it was natural that he should devote special attention to works the author and subject-matter of which belonged in the sphere of Ritschlian thought.

However, that was still unthinkable in Troeltsch's first semester at Göttingen, and he first flexed his muscles in the prize essay set by the theological faculty in the winter semester of 1886/87.[40] The topic was *Hermanni Lotzii placita de conscientia recti quanti momenti sint in apologia religionis Christianae, demonstretur,*[41] which could roughly be translated, 'Describe how far Lotze's views on the conscience represent correct elements in an apologia for the Christian religion'.

The topic should be seen against the background of the situation in Göttingen. Hermann Lotze (1817-1881) had taught there for a long time and had influenced Ritschl's epistemology and theory of values.

Lotze's thought moved in two directions. On the one hand he rejected all naturalism and materialism, as these are grounded in the mere facticity of the real and thus tend towards an ideological absolutizing of the given. On the other hand, he is opposed to a neglect of the individual, to any underestimation of the individual in the context of an interpretation of the world and life. He saw Hegel's dialectical thought as an exemplary expression of a philosophical dissolution of the principle of individuality.

Troeltsch was influenced above all by Lotze's fundamentally idealistic approach, with its marked feeling for the specific features of nature and the individual figures of history. Moreover we can assume that Troeltsch's criticism of Hegel ('logicalization of the real') was also influenced by Lotze. Looking back on his life and work, Troeltsch commented that 'Lotze... was first of all the real determinative spirit' (*GS* IV, 5).

The topic of the prize essay attracted Troeltsch above all because it had a theological and a philosophical side, and moreover corresponded to his tendency to be stimulated by persons and an intellectual climate. The essay aimed to show first of all Lotze's own views on the conscience and then their significance for an apologia for Christianity. The presupposition of the topic was that Lotze's philosophy contains elements of such an apologia, making them worth closer investigation. However, Troeltsch thought that Lotze's philosophy was to be used for his own apologia for Christianity. That was a misunderstanding quite typical of him: he did not want to embark on a detailed investigation of the history of philosophy, but to use material from the history of philosophy so that it had an influence on contemporary theological work.

Troeltsch's prize essay is written with great verve and is extraordinarily mature for a student of twenty-two. It shows an amazing sense of structure and an independent approach to the diffuse theme. But Troeltsch's gift of rapid comprehension and combination, along with his attempt at an overall view, also brought the danger that he did not look carefully enough at details in their specific context. At the same time we can also see joins in the work. The use of theological formulae and the series of biblical quotations stands in strange contrast to Troeltsch's sovereignty in dealing with the philosophical material. One significant thing about its content is that this work adopts a critical attitude to the tendency of theological thought to dogmatize. Thus Troeltsch speaks of 'dogmatic mouse traps' (p.5), which living religion must rise above as a spiritual power. At the same time talk of the 'thousand hair-splittings of dogmatics' (30) does not fit very well with the formal dogmatic language which Troeltsch himself uses in other passages.[42]

How does he imagine an apologia for Christianity? For him this cannot be achieved by means of a rational proof or through ethics. Rather, an apologia has to regard Christianity as 'a coherent fact of disposition, albeit one which is based on positive historical conditions' (6). At first that looks like a 'modified Schleiermacher'; the difference lies in the stronger stress on the historical conditions. In general, Troeltsch does not see apologetics as an immanent theological task but relates it to thinking as a whole; for him, all thinking is an apologia, to the degree that any content of experience must be related to other experiences. But precisely for that reason 'the fact of religion experienced in faith as a whole needs an apologia, a link with the other facts' (8). Christianity, seen independently, faces the task of linking up with the other facts of thought and contents of experience. Here Troeltsch stresses that what is involved is not a rational argument but a beginning from faith. This understanding of the task of apologetics leaves plenty of room for academic work and the formation of a philosophical system, but in principle it is directed against any separation of philosophy and theology. This means that he dissociates himself from Ritschl, but also from the kind of Lutheran theology which he had come to know in Erlangen. Critically, in connection with the separation of philosophy and theology, he remarks that 'it is regarded by many as a redemption of the latter, but in truth is nothing but a way of plundering the philosophers without having to subject oneself to their inconvenient discipline of thought' (9). This view recurs later in his work on the history of Protestantism.[43] It is an implicit criticism of Ritschl to the degree that in its epistemological reflections it makes use of the philosophy of Kant and Lotze, whereas elsewhere Troeltsch stands at a critical distance from philosophy and in particular strictly repudiates all metaphysics in theology.

Troeltsch also makes critical remarks about a theology dominated by Hegel, which undertakes a 'dialectical march-past of formal concepts' (10) and in so doing attempts to demonstrate that Christianity is the supreme knowledge.

A theological return to faith as the primal datum of the consciousness is not to be understood as bracketing off the empirical facts. Troeltsch sees the difficulties bound up with his position in the ever-new task of linking faith to the empirical facts. At this time the solution seems to him to be the maxim which holds for Protestants, 'that he can communicate his faith to himself with personal certainty, and that includes above all a good scholarly conscience; for him the unity and stability lie only in an ever-changing bond with the person of Jesus Christ' (10).

So Troeltsch calls for free movement in the task of forming a dogmatics. His concern is a dogmatics within the horizons of the culture of the time and at the same time one which binds the conscience to the founder of this faith, to Jesus Christ. In comparison with later works, here the christological foundation is brought into the foreground. This is also matched by the motto set over the work: 'No one can lay any other foundation than that which is laid, which is Jesus Christ.' When later, in his *The Absoluteness of Christianity and the History of Religion* (1902), Troeltsch wanted to describe the special form of Christian faith and the idea of absoluteness, he resorted to this confessional formula.[44]

With a view to the topic of the prize essay, he concluded that Lotze's judgments of the conscience represented an independent body of thought. Troeltsch thought that the results were almost Christian. All that they lacked was something which for him was an unconditional element of Christian faith: 'We hear the dearest thoughts of our faith, but nothing of Christ, and without that we cannot think them, if we do not want to do harm to him and his church; moreover we hear nothing of the sin against the background of which we think that we experience the peace of the Christian conscience and the value of Christian hope even more; and finally we hear nothing at all of justification and reconciliation, without which the certainty of the love of God expressed by Lotze seems to us to be quite unthinkable' (16).

Many passages of the work, especially when Troeltsch is writing about the position of faith, do not really match what he is writing in his letters to Bousset at the same time. There he emerges as a resolute defender of philosophy and maintains his own philosophical standpoint. In the prize essay his estimation of the significance of philosophy in comparison with theology is different. To the degree that it shows a particular kind of proximity to Christianity, it is even to be regarded as a possible opponent. However, Troeltsch argues critically, the philosophy of the conscience as presented by Lotze is not really in a position to perceive the tormenting expressions of the conscience in all their acuteness and to find solutions to match. Only faith can achieve that.

At the end of the study one can find in Troeltsch a tendency to use traditional theological terminology more strongly; this was probably because he saw the pastorate as at least a possibility and was thinking of the practical tasks involved.[45] Certainly he can also speak later of the guilt-laden conscience, but not with the radicality and focus which can see the way out only in the forgiveness of sin through Jesus Christ.

Troeltsch's work was sent on to be examined by the dean of the faculty, the New Testament scholar A.Wiesinger, along with two other prize works (these were sermons). The dean's impression was: 'The work indicates an author who is well versed in philosophy, practised in thought, and has a competent mind. But it does not follow the course that I would have liked. The author has something about him of the one who speaks in tongues and edifies himself more than others; he is more concerned to describe his own attitude to Lotze's philosophy (he expands the topic) than to go into the topic demonstratively.'[46]

Hermann Schultz in his assessment remarked that he could not judge how far the work fulfilled the task set, since the topic was 'not available' to him.[47] He went on to criticize the assertiveness of many of Troeltsch's remarks, and indeed spoke of a 'tendency towards rhetorical verbosity' which appeared in the work. The description of Lotze's ideas on the whole seemed to him to be not unskilful, but it was too short and did not develop out of the whole of his philosophy. He saw the value of the discussion in the way in which it grappled with Lotze from a Christian standpoint, thus bringing out weak points in the system. The view of the church historian Reuter was very positive: 'I cannot remember ever having received from a student a work which bore witness to such philosophical training (not just knowledge), such a quick mind as this.' Granted, Reuter commented critically that the work often 'lacks the precision of methodical proof', but all in all it had a 'real verve' which promised much.

Probably at a loss what to decide, the faculty turned to the philosopher J.Baumann for advice.[48] Baumann thought that Troeltsch had misunderstood the topic and felt that he had to write an apologia for Christianity with the aid of Lotze.

In the end the work was awarded a half-prize by the faculty. The prizegiving took place in the aula of the university. The University Chronicle comments: 'On 8 June the University held a ceremonial prizegiving, at which the Pro-Rector Dr Ritschl delivered the address. The theological faculty granted E.Troeltsch from Augsburg... the half-prize.'[49]

5. Return to Erlangen and First Theological Examination (1888)

In the 'year of the three emperors', which was so significant for German history, Troeltsch changed universities. In the summer semester of 1888 he returned to Erlangen, to take his examination in Bavaria. Contemporary historical events do not appear directly in the letters preserved from this time; rather, the existential questions of Troeltsch's own position and his future calling stand in the foreground.

To Bousset, who had remained in Göttingen, he wrote how alien the city and the university had become to him in the meantime.[50] 'As you can see, I'm back in Erlangen. It's a remarkable thing when after a long and varied development one again treads the ground from which one first began and to which one has meanwhile become so very alien. Indeed, to begin with I felt very strange: strange people, customs and views; not a single friend in whom I could confide unreservedly. Almost automatically I keep comparing it with

those first days when I took in the first seeds of a broader education in so
much earnest conversation... I am very aware that the first period of searching
and blossoming is past and that now my powers and wishes belong to the goal
of a particular calling, that the horizon has become narrower, and yet alongside
this I cannot kill off the never-satisfied striving for some knowledge which
stretches out into the immeasurable blue, the indeterminate drive for life and
movement at any price. Moreover, with my views, as you know, here I am in
a rather alien world. Here people are dominated by Zahn, Frank, Köhler and
the philosophy of Rabus, and that is a world of which I understand nothing'
(letter of 6 May 1888).[51] In this semester Troeltsch went to lectures on canon
law by Kahl (1849-1932), a course on modern sects by Kolde (1850-1913),
and Caspari's seminar on homiletics (1847-1923).

How strongly the Göttingen influence continued is evident from his
correspondence with Bousset, which is now increasingly about technical
theological questions. Thus Troeltsch remarks that he is now having to revise
his original view that he can leave aside the problems thrown up by criticism
of the Gospels, a view which he could hold because he felt that the basic
material of the Gospels was essentially certain. He asks himself how the
emergence and preaching of Jesus can be distinguished from the style of other
religious founders and prophetic figures. It is quite clear how much he has
been disquieted by the history-of-religions approach.

The modification of central dogmatic statements which lie at the periphery
of accounts of church history claim Troeltsch's interest and at the same time
raise questions for him. 'In his mere abstractness, the Christ with whom
dogmatics has so far always claimed my attention, who as some kind of being
whose uniqueness is to be evaluated conceptually, has to have properties to
be concluded from certain general premises, has nothing to do with the
concrete figure in history with his wonderful, enigmatic wealth of forces and
living movement. I do not know why these questions, which were so customary
forty years ago, can now be discussed in so innocent a way' (letter to Bousset
of 6 May 1888). All the dogmatic talk about satisfaction and revelation cannot
prevent him from addressing intensely concrete questions to the Jesus
tradition.

There thus emerges a critical awareness of the New Testament Jesus
tradition; however, the history-of-religions criticism is still forced into the
background by Ritschl's view, which seeks to combine historical knowledge
of the person of Jesus and the content of his preaching with an estimation
which derives from an overpowering of the human heart and conscience, and
thus is orientated on faith. Like the first disciples, human beings today have
the choice between rejecting and following Jesus. If the decision is positive,
the result is a personal assurance of faith, which can provide support. 'I find
that the only way of coping with the matter is to allow oneself to be convinced
in one's conscience, as were the first disciples' (letter to Bousset of 12

September 1888, unpublished). This results in an approach to the divine side of the being of Jesus as absolute transcendence of the world.

However, the marked tension in the notion of transcendence then leads Troeltsch to a criticism of Ritschl. For him, Ritschl - like Schleiermacher – saw the idea of the call of Jesus too much in terms of the immanent development of Jesus' life, whereas a more markedly idealistic approach to the life of Jesus would be appropriate. Troeltsch himself wants the central access to the person and work of Jesus to be by the interpretative aspect which derives from an estimation according to faith. In contrast to his later criticism of Ritschl, here Troeltsch sees the historical approach and the introduction of a perspective of development as interference. Later, in the face of an idealistic estimation which is *a priori* taken as the starting point, he asks with what right one can interpret Jesus as absolutely beyond the world and so can remove him from having purely historical significance.

One does not approach a correspondence like that between Troeltsch and Bousset with the expectation of finding a systematic account: remarks are made which pick up conversations and what they have heard together. Moreover the ideas are still in flux. Nevertheless, the special significance of these letters lies in the way in which they address problems directly and spontaneously and offer solutions. And one thing above all is evident: Troeltsch is engaged in a learning process over against Ritschl's theological position, in which he increasingly works out a critical distancing from his teacher.

At the beginning of September 1888 Troeltsch went to Ansbach to take the theological examination for acceptance into the ministry. The written examinations and the work in practical theology were set for the first part of the week of 2-8 September.

The topic for ethics was: 'Show what the nature of the conscience is, how far it is dependent on the knowledge of the individual and how it can err. How does the conscience express itself, what weight is to be attached to its expressions and in what does Christian assurance consist?' The topic for the written examination on the history of dogma was: 'What is the distinctive feature of mediaeval scholasticism and how does it differ from mysticism? By whom was the scholastic method introduced into theology? Who are the most prominent representatives of scholasticism and which theologian is regarded as the last scholastic? What do you understand by realism and nominalism? Who was the first to attempt to establish nominalistic principles, and what scholastic theologian successfully renewed nominalism after a long gap? What significance did scholasticism have for the church and how is its method to be assessed?'[52] This account will concentrate on Troeltsch's written examinations in ethics, catechesis and preaching. Here one would most expect some information about his personal views; furthermore, we have no other works on practical theology from him, and in particular no sermons.

In the ethics examination paper, on the conscience, the account of principles and the analysis, including the history of philosophy and theology, is striking. Historical thinking and the problems which arise from it are taken into account. 'It has proved that moral concepts are neither innate nor identical everywhere. The conscience of the Muslim is different from that of the Christian and, say, that of the Buddhist, and over time it changes within the same groups of peoples and cultures.'

The definition of the Christian conscience begins from a phenomenological approach, according to which the Christian moral law can be regarded as the law to which the human conscience reacts most strongly. An apologia for Christianity can only consist in overcoming the human conscience.

Here Troeltsch's prize essay on Lotze evidently comes in useful, since he also refers to Lotze and says that Lotze's investigations are very much deeper than those of Ritschl.[53]

The report on this examination recognizes the academic ability of the candidate. However, it also states: 'It is to be hoped that with the rich gifts bestowed on him the author will also penetrate increasingly deeply into the depths of scripture.' The paper is then given a 'very good'.

In the qualifying examination for the ministry Troeltsch wrote a catechetical sketch on the fifth commandment which is constructed entirely on a question-and-answer basis. Uninhibitedly and suggestively the answer is already included in the question. Here we can detect a very clear bent towards a traditional education which seemed exaggerated even to the churchmen marking the examination, as is evident from the marginal notes.

The catechesis begins with the question: 'How may we then not talk with God if we may ask ever so humbly for what we need?' Answer: 'As though we had a right to it.' Further: 'Do you children have a right to ask your parents to grant your wishes?' Answer, 'No' (in the margin there us a clear 'Yes'). Troeltsch then continues: 'Now who stands very much higher above all of us human beings than parents? God. So what does a psalm say about the person whom God remembers? "What is man that you are mindful of him, and the son of man that you accept him" (Ps.8.5). So what does that mean for our understanding of ourselves and our prayers? We are not worthy of what we pray for'(again in the margin there is a 'worthy').

The assessment notes that while the catechetical material is well thought out, and the pattern of exposition follows Luther, the language is rather above children's heads. 'And the answers "no" or possibly "yes" should not be prompted by the question.' The mark for the catechesis is 'almost very good'.

Troeltsch's trial sermon for the first examination was on Galatians 6.14-16. The sermon is arranged according to the accepted pattern: introduction, two main points and a conclusion. In an ethical and psychological approach Troeltsch relates the human boasting mentioned by Paul in connection with the fulfilling of the law to human boasting and the respect that one can gain on the basis of riches or spiritual capacities. Troeltsch thinks – and this is a central idea in his sermon – that the Christian moral life makes such striving for praise a matter of indifference.

Troeltsch's remarks express a markedly conservative attitude which cannot just be understood as a demand on Troeltsch the candidate. Already from a psychological perspective Troeltsch relativizes the difference between poor and rich, educated and uneducated: the spiritual element is then heightened. Thus the poor are admonished: 'Bear in patience what cannot be otherwise, just as our Lord bore his suffering and his poverty in patience.' And they are recommended to 'Set aside envy and lead a quiet, modest life, without excesses in the inn and the market.' The rich who attempt to heap up riches in compulsive haste and whose family life is threatened are told that if they accept into their lives what is offered in the Christian faith and so become a new creation in the kingdom of brotherly love, the result will be peace in their hearts and renewed joys of family life, in the 'happiness of simplicity and moderation'. Humility is commended to the educated as an appropriate attitude, since their knowledge has not made them happy, but simply more acutely aware of the riddle of the world.

Where the sermon is concerned for the aestheticizing of life and at the same time a perception of the deep enigmas of life, Troeltsch certainly also has himself in view and is talking about his own personal situation. The letters from this time pick up these problems. That Troeltsch can include himself in such passages gives the sermon some depth: 'Your training has not made you happy, it has not lessened the hardships of life, but only opened your eyes to its enigmas, and it has also given you some splendid hours in fascinating conversation, in tasteful mood or fruitful research, and also some hours in superficial gossip, in forced and formal courtesy, in idle entertainment and mere curiosity. A few hours of enjoyment here or there with a beautiful picture or a good piece of music are no guarantee that the rest of your life, that the whole of the world, that you and I, will similarly come to a happy ending.'

In such passages it is clear that the impressiveness of the analysis bears no relation to the formal language in which the perspectives of faith are taken up. However, there are also passages in which a lively personal piety is expressed: 'And let the uneducated rejoice that they need no education here. They in particular will find it easier to grasp the salvation of the cross, because no wisdom makes their necks stiff nor do hundreds of blinding pictures deflect their eyes.' His wish is that intellectualism and education should not bar the way to simple piety, but that wish is one which he finds very difficult to realize.

In the face of the human transformation that comes about in faith, Troeltsch thinks that the differences between the educated and the uneducated, the rich and the poor, are done away with. But he hastens to say that this equality applies only in a religious respect. 'Otherwise our differences remain, and in our earthly position we are still what we were. The merchant remains a merchant and the farmer a farmer, and these differences will abide as long as this world stands.'

However, for the 'children of God' the word of the apostle Peter holds: 'Let each one serve the other with the gift that he has received...' Troeltsch then goes on: 'Let him who is rich undertake everything with his riches, but let him not make it an idle show. Let him use it to disclose new sources of gain which only a great fortune can open up.' And with some naivety about social conditions he then continues: 'Let him (the rich man) adorn his life with all beauty, but in such a way that others can delight in it, and above all let him serve his needy fellow Christians.' What is said about the principle of economic power fits in with this reflection. 'In order to be able to achieve great things, riches must be concentrated in one hand, but in addition the rich must also be sure that the profit of his work benefits the poor, through whose help he has achieved it.' At such points the didactic trait, the moral appeal of the sermon, in language which in many passages is more like that of an academic lecture, emerges clearly. The assessment was very positive: 'This sermon derives a proper theme from the text and divides it up appropriately. A wealth of references to public life and the life of the individual Christian, a series of promptings and inclinations of the human heart, are aptly depicted, and illuminated by the light of the gospel... The account is skilful and lively.' Troeltsch's sermon was given a 'very good'.

Having also got through the oral part of the examination, on 8 September 1888 Troeltsch passed the first theological examination with a mark of II+, i.e. 'almost excellent'. With relief he wrote to Bousset: 'It all went off very well; inevitably there are marked theological differences, and a couple of times I got ahead of the "modern masters"... But I was so well prepared that they didn't do anything more and left me completely in peace. Moreover the gentlemen were very kind and expressed their different viewpoints more in the form of benevolent admonition' (letter to Bousset, 12 September 1888, unpublished).

He wrote that his written work had caused a stir and that the members of the committee had advised him to pursue an academic career. After his time at a preacher's seminary, which was approaching, his plan was to look for a coaching job in Erlangen. His parents had promised him financial support for this.

Looking back on the time spent preparing for the examination, Troeltsch felt that this had been an 'audit of the conscience'. He reflected on the sense and meaning of academic work: 'The whole of academia teems like an anthill, except that it lacks the single leadership of the latter. People seek to understand things by inventing a single centre which dominates as far as possible; but the higher and more dominant this is, the more subjective is the product of such attempts at explanation. Science lives only by compromises between imagination and knowledge, constantly applied afresh and constantly attempted. We must not overestimate it or let our hearts be fired by it because we can know so little' (letter to Bousset, 12 September 1888, unpublished).

At the end of lengthy reflections of an academic kind this letter contains a poem which must be seen in the context of Troeltsch's situation, the conclusion of his study and the prospect of a still uncertain future. It is a kind of self-assurance with an audience. He explains that the verses had come to him while he was writing to Bousset: 'They tell you more than I can communicate explicitly, and perhaps also bear misunderstanding.'

What penetrated my young heart,
what was weighty and important to me,
now seems such nonsense,
so strange, so remarkable.

In the golden distance of knowledge
I kept taking risks,
and yet I know that at heart
everything is quite ordinary.

However, this foolish urge
has never disappeared from my head;

if I have now found rest,
I hardly know how.

Only defilement is criminal.
Great is great and simple simple,
and that sober discovery
does not injure the soul's faith.

On closer inspection one can recognize that the first two lines of each strophe depict a former position or an attitude which now seems problematical; the opposite movement in the next two lines then represents the newly acquired standpoint. Troeltsch describes ideas and ways which lie in the past as 'nonsense'. The speculative line of thought cannot make any particular claim in the face of the secularity of reality. Knowledge cannot reach further than is indicated by the remarkable nature and constitution of reality. However, speculative thought, an unlimited concern to know, cannot be banished from the mind. That Troeltsch has now found rest surprises him, but he sees no merit in this. He cannot find any rational basis for this rest or give it a rational foundation. The 'defilement' marks a limit beyond which thought becomes devoid of reality and therefore untrue, and loses itself in the boundlessness of aesthetic fantasy.

The subjective principle of wanting to know is countered by an objective principle of the perception of criteria in things themselves. For him, the 'sober discovery' of the character of reality may not injure the nature of faith.[54]

6. Assistant minister in Munich (1888/89)

With four other candidates, Ernst Troeltsch entered the preachers' seminary in Munich on 21 September 1888, attendance at which was restricted to the best candidates of any year. On 1 October he was presented to Dean Konrad Fikenscher; with a handshake, a 'yes' and a signature Troeltsch committed himself to service in the preachers' seminary and in the community.[55] So that the seminarians could be appointed auxiliary clergy as quickly as possible, ordination usually took place soon after entry into the preachers' seminary. That was also the case with Troeltsch, who was ordained in St Matthäus Church, Munich, on 2 December 1888.[56]

Theoretically, work at the preachers' seminary was not only biassed heavily towards practical activity but was largely practical church work. In addition to seminary sermons and academic sessions in which practical religious topics were discussed, there were catechetical classes, sometimes with the pupils of the Munich Deaconesses' Institution.

Troeltsch describes his activity as an auxiliary minister in the community like this: 'There I preached and engaged in casual activity, not only pastoral work but care of the poor and religious instruction in the schools and diaspora welfare in quite broad terms, and of course I gained a very deep and lasting impression from this teaching.'[57]

Troeltsch attempted to explain the shift in his work towards the practical sphere to himself and his friend Bousset in terms of the relationship to God: 'If God spontaneously comes to the searcher in his striving for knowledge as a thought thing, as the "concept of God" in an objective form, the serving minister must achieve the most immediate intimacy with him, in order to find courage and strength for his work. In the doubts, hesitations and questions which come upon him while he is preparing his sermon, he cannot pursue and expect their solution but must be able to receive grace upon grace from the one thing that is certain to him. The other things must be sorted out afterwards. Good for the person for whom this fountain of experience does not run dry! I am very well aware of the purely theoretical thirst by which it drives us towards an overall view and how this truth exists solely for itself, but I also feel that religious knowledge does not coincide with this, but consists in the power of prayer and faith. How the two are related is a difficult and sometimes anxious problem for me; yesterday this suddenly came upon me with painful force during my sermon' (letter of 15 December 1888, unpublished). Troeltsch felt preaching and hospital visiting 'always a heavy business' (ibid.). But despite all the problems of practical ministry and despite the relative heavy burden he seemed to enjoy the work: 'But don't think that I'm not content with my present position. On the contrary, I'm very satisfied and very happy, balanced and fulfilled, in a mood which is rare for me. I always enjoy my visits to the poor, scant though the help is that I can give. I love teaching my five lessons, and they are not as bad as I expected... I also enjoy the sermons, though not writing them. One is so void of thoughts, so feeble and lacking in the driving force of living faith which automatically forces the words to one's lips. I have problems over writing all my sermons and am always convinced of the weakness and powerlessness of my faith, and for all the trouble I take, I don't know whether the small congregation gets anything out of them' (ibid.).

Troeltsch's wide-ranging interests, which had been forced rather into the background during his studies in Göttingen and as a result of the pressure of the examination, now showed themselves again. He read Scherer's *History of Literature*, Grimm's *Goethe*, Wundt's *Ethics* and Ranke's *History of the World*.[58]

However, academic questions and discussion of them among the candidates had not completely disappeared behind the main focus on practical work. Not without pride, Troeltsch reported the exalted position of the 'Göttingen group': 'We encounter virtually no theological difficulties. It has soon emerged that we free theologians are inspired by a very active zeal and a lively conviction; so far we have only received kind words. Our president is particularly preoccupied with us Ritschlians and said once again: 'Surely you're bringing more good things to our church'; that is significant. Our immediate superior, Oberkonsistorialrat Buchrucker (since 1885 head of the Preachers' Seminary) said to me with great satisfaction: "I can see clearly that for you the kingdom

of God is more than mankind bound together in love of neighbour."
Unfortunately I could not interrupt him and say that it was also more than
that for Ritschl. Before our ordination the president gave a great lecture
acknowledging Ritschl, whom otherwise he tended to call a "swindler", but
our ordination address rose to direct polemic against Ritschl... Our younger
colleagues are usually very friendly and tolerant towards us over theology: at
any rate we are good propaganda for Göttingen. And indeed I can only be
glad that my course took me there. In purely practical terms, what I learned
there is standing me in good stead. We find many things easier than those who
have come from the Erlangen school' (letter to Bousset of 15 December 1888,
unpublished).

When during the course of his year at the preachers' seminary it became
evident that nothing would come of his hope for the post of a tutor in Erlangen,
in July 1889 Troeltsch applied to the Oberkonsistorium of the Bavarian
Landeskirche for a two-year vocation so that he could take the licentiate
examination in Göttingen. To back up his choice of Göttingen he used his
prize essay, which had already made him known to the lecturers; he also hoped
that he could expect support in particular from his teacher Karl Knoke.
Moreover there were fewer competitors in Göttingen, and it was easier to do
some teaching – and thus earn some money – as the Habilitation examination
was not tied to the Second Theological Examination. A further factor for
Troeltsch was that in Göttingen he did not have to do 'submit work and be
examined in Latin, a language to which he was unaccustomed'.[59]

After this two years' leave Troeltsch wanted to sit the qualifying examination
in Bavaria. He wrote to the church authorities that it was uncertain whether
he could achieve his aim and that in the long term theoretical work would suit
him better than practical work. In the latter case he would prefer to devote
himself to his native Landeskirche; it was the only one with which he was
familiar and he was closely bound up with it through 'loyal respect and all
kinds of links'.[60] The Bavarian Landeskirche accepted these arguments, and
so he was able to return 'to Michaelis' in Göttingen to take up his doctoral
work.

7. In Göttingen again: preparation for academic teaching

Troeltsch wrote his licentiate thesis on the topic 'Reason and Revelation in
Johann Gerhard and Melanchthon'. At the same time, the Göttingen faculty
accepted the work at the same time as a Habilitation thesis, giving him the
qualification to lecture.[61] The investigation was based on extensive knowledge
of the sources and showed considerable skill in discovering new connections.
All in all, therefore, the result was a novel picture of the dogmatics of early
Protestantism, above all in relation to the philosophical tradition and the
educational institutions of the time. Troeltsch made a comprehensive investigation of the way in which the tradition of faith and reason were connected at

Vernunft und Offenbarung

bei

Johann Gerhard und Melanchthon.

Untersuchung zur

Geschichte der altprotestantischen Theologie

von

Lic. theol. **Ernst Troeltsch,**
Privatdocent an der Universität Göttingen.

Göttingen,

Verlag von Vandenhoeck & Ruprecht.

1891.

Troeltsch as Privatdozent in Göttingen

that time. Whereas for him religion was something direct and original, dogmatics represented the attempt to mediate between the general awareness of a time and religious conceptions. He had already put forward the substance of this view in his prize essay. He investigated the form of this mediation at a point which is of great significance within the tradition of Protestantism, namely where the theology of Luther becomes 'Lutheranism'. There are already the makings of this transition in Melanchthon, who, in contrast to Luther himself, proceeds and thinks 'systematically'. Here Melanchthon uses Romans as a basis; Luther's scriptural principle has some influence and acquires validity in the formulation and structure of dogmatic statements.

The most marked systematization of the dogmatic material comes about in Johann Gerhard (1589-1637), one of the more significant representatives of Lutheran orthodoxy. Troeltsch sees that Johann Gerhard is taking up philosophical statements from the Aristotelian tradition; though he cites them as biblical ideas or dogmatic ideas originating in the Bible, in fact Aristotelianism forms the basis, or more accurately the anthropological and ideological presupposition, for a more specific terminological definition. This means that in the 'real explanation' of the terms heaven, earth, man, soul, understanding, hell, ideas are expressed from a teleological and formal system rooted in Aristotelianism and are interpreted in terms of an orientation on a goal, namely the event of redemption in Christ. Thus the possibility of combining reason and revelation is already given by the conceptuality used in exegesis. 'So it proved possible, without any principle whatsoever and in what was claimed to be a purely exegetical approach, to interpret the necessary foundation in natural philosophy in terms of the drama of redemption, to correct or ignore the former where necessary and yet fuse the two together so intimately that the one presupposes the other' (*VO*, 45). Whereas in nineteenth-century Lutheranism, e.g. in Tholuck, there was a tendency to attach great importance to the Protestant tradition of faith and to play down the wider connections with intellectual life generally, and especially philosophy, Troeltsch judged otherwise. He assessed the connections as follows: '... the significance of dogmatics does not lie in the furthering of general knowledge and science; rather, dogmatics tends to attach itself to an education which is already finished and philosophical elements which are already as widely recognized as possible, and simply seeks to assure for its own material, which can never be free of all brittleness, a secure place in or alongside them. In the process it usually alienates these from their original meaning by adapting them to its own ends' (*VO*, 2).[62] Troeltsch retreats from the idea of a self-sufficient dogmatics, isolated from the intellectual trends of a time, and finds endorsement for this in the Protestant tradition.

Whereas Troeltsch understands Luther as a one-sidedly religious figure who thinks radically in terms of a religious principle, he views Melanchthon as someone who does justice to the demands on a positive religious community and church in quite a different way. Melanchthon is aware of the need to keep a balance between autonomous reason and the idea of revelation and seeks to maintain and develop this balance in his thinking. The understanding of Luther emerging from Troeltsch sees Luther through psychological categories, and in particular takes up the idea of the genius. Troeltsch emphasizes the significance for the ongoing history of religion of people with one-sided religious concerns, but he finds their radicalism sinister. From a historical perspective he regards it as great good fortune that Luther's radicalism and genius was followed by the temperament and capacities of Melanchthon, who was concerned for balance and mediation.

Troeltsch incorporates into his reflections the structure of the system of education, the principles of the faculty of arts and the theological faculty, and thus dissociates himself from an isolated and dogmatically pre-formed definition of the relationship between reason and revelation. In his account he refers critically to the doctrinaire trait in Lutheranism which for him consists in the establishment of salvation through the word of the Bible and the institution of the church. As will emerge, this assessment has a role in his later works.

Troeltsch once said that the germs of intellectual work must be present in a person's youth.[63] This remark also applies to him. In this work almost all his later distinguishing features are already present: the sharp analytical understanding which takes up the historical tradition and works out its essential features, and the systematic capacity to derive basic questions from this for his own time. In terms of content, too, this writing by the twenty-six year old shows the approaches and outlines of his later work. For all the stress on the certainty of faith, Reformation theology which claims to derive from the divine word of revelation cannot dispense with questions about the mediation of this word. For this task of mediation in the period following Luther, elements were taken up which come from the Stoic natural-law doctrine. The adoption of Stoic natural-law thinking in Melanchthon's theology and its continued influence in the post-Reformation tradition demonstrate a remarkable perspective of continuity between Reformation theology and accepted tradition.[64] From here the world of the Reformation thinkers is brought close to the mediaeval tradition – closer, above all, than had previously been the case in the Ritschl school. So Troeltsch can speak of an old Protestantism which is distinct from the Neo-Protestantism of the subsequent period.

This subjects to criticism fundamental judgments of the Ritschl school on the significance of the Reformation tradition for contemporary theology. 'We no longer have that old basic pillar, nor any new one peculiar to us. What we have in common with them [the old theologians] stands on quite a different basis, to the degree that we have any basis at all' (*VO*, 213).

The impression which has its roots here, that theology is faced with a new task, will intensify increasingly with Troeltsch. He can no longer accept simple forms of self-assurance, which deem it possible to take up Luther's principle of the view of the Bible and the significance of the word of God. Luther and his world are further removed from theology than theologians have so far wanted to suppose. In view of the changed cultural and academic climate of the time, the question of mediation has been reframed. Theology must first of all understand that it cannot simply conserve its previous answers.

The assessors of the work submitted by Troeltsch were the systematic theologian and Old Testament scholar Hermann Schultz and Paul Tschackert, the successor to Hermann Reuter in the chair of church history. Schultz praised the work for its 'laudable thoroughness, openness and piety towards the material'. It took up numerous issues which for a long time had played no role in Protestant theology – like Jesuit scholasticism, the activity of the arts faculty, the methodology of theological instruction – and 'all in all investigates them independently'.[65] However, he thought the first part of the dissertation the better. Tschackert was particularly attracted by the methodology. The process of moving back from Johann Gerhard to Melanchthon met with his undivided approval; he also praised the author's careful study of the sources. Like Schultz, he had hesitations only over the second part. He speaks of the 'laborious breadth of the account'. Tschackert saw the real novelty of the work in the notion that the mediation of Luther's ideas brought about by Melanchthon was achieved not through the thought-forms of scholasticism but through those of humanistic science. At the end he made a remark about Troeltsch's style, which his fellow assessor found somewhat lax, and at all events not always in line with academic custom.[66] However, this was just a passing comment and did not mar the generally good impression. Both assessors recommended that the faculty should accept the work.

The oral examination took place at 4 p.m. on Saturday 31 January 1891 at the home of Dean Knoke. Knoke examined Troeltsch for half an hour on practical theology, and then Tschackert followed with church history and the history of dogma, the subject of the Habilitation.[67] The topics here were obvious ones: Melanchthon's *Loci* 'from the perspective of contemporary problems and the problems of the earlier history of dogma'.[68]

Hermann Schultz examined in dogmatics and ethics. The topics were the 'systematic theory of principles' and the 'concepts of religion set up on various sides', like the relationship between dogmatics and ethics. In the New Testament Wiesinger examined Troeltsch on II Corinthians, and in the Old Testament Haering examined him on Isaiah. Overall Troeltsch was awarded the *summa cum laude*.

The public disputation on the promotion theses then took place in the aula of the University on 14 February. Troeltsch's opponents were Alfred Rahlfs and Wilhelm Bousset, both of whom had already qualified. As in his dissertation, here too Troeltsch was allowed to use German instead of Latin. The seventeen theses which he presented had previously been communicated to the members of the faculty and the students.[69]

It was usual to formulate theses from as many disciplines of theology as possible, ranging from the Old Testament to practical theology. The theses which relate to matters of theological principle are particularly interesting. The detailed arguments for the theses and the development of the theses can only be ascertained from ths general course of the disputation, as no record was made. Of course the whole proceedings were also a ritual, the course of which, at least in outline, had been agreed between the young theologians.

The important first thesis mentions the conditions on which theology can be called a discipline of the history of religion. What is normative is neither its place in a general history of religion nor the assumption that the Christian religion is the expression of a special content but a comparison with the other great religions known to us. In his reference to the construction of a universal history of religion Troeltsch seems to be thinking of Hegel and Schleiermacher, and in the focus on the content of the Christian religion he seems to be thinking of Albrecht Ritschl. It is characteristic of Troeltsch's position that he wants to derive the character of theology from the history-of-religions work of comparison, with a view to the content. Ritschl's notions are expanded and corrected, assigning a real function for theology to the history of religions.[70]

Dogmatics is understood as being scientific in so far as it is concerned with questions of principle. Where the content of faith is developed, strictly speaking it can no longer be said to be a science (thesis 12). This basic distinction crops up later in Troeltsch's work in his definition of the relationship between dogmatics and the philosophy of religion. Thesis 15 is particularly illuminating in its assent to Ritschl and its critical movement beyond him. From it we are to conclude that even if one accepts the (Ritschlian) distinction between religion and metaphysics, the task for theology consists of a development of doctrine in the form of a metaphysics, albeit under the aspect of the philosophy of religion. There is impressive evidence of the way in which Troeltsch is moulded by history-of-religions thinking, as say when Thesis 13 states that in a systematization of the idea of faith – if this is to be commended at all – eschatology must stand at the centre of the relationships. Or when the religion of Judaism is spoken of as the 'nursery of Christianity' (Thesis 3).

When one remembers that systematically the Göttingen faculty had been shaped by Ritschl's theology, it is already impressive what independent thinking was allowed and encouraged here. This judgment applies even if we recognize that this public defence of theses was a particular kind of academic challenge offering the possibility of formulating one's own ideas in a pointed way.

The dialectical focus in the formulation, say, of Troeltsch's statement 'theology is as hard for the church to bear as to do without', almost at the end of his set of theses, anticipated something of his own career. All his life he thought that it was hard for the church to do without theology, and the church itself to some extent validated the other half of his thesis, in that his theology was difficult for the church of the time to take.

Troeltsch's theses breathe the spirit of history-of-religions thinking. He sees developments in connection with both the Old and the New Testament traditions, and stresses the task of comparison. Moreover one can also pick out his interest in matters of principle: what theology is, what its academic elements consist of, how ideas of faith can be systematized, how dogmatics and ethics can be separated. The theses as a whole have style, are all interesting, and show Troeltsch's capacity for terse and sharp formulation.

On 28 February Troeltsch then gave his trial lecture. The topic was 'The Doctrine of Justification in the Apology'. The other topics proposed by Troeltsch similarly came from the sphere of old Protestant orthodoxy ('The Position of Calixtus in Lutheran Scholarship' and 'The Development of Prolegomena in Old Protestant Dogmatics'). The day after the trial lecture the faculty unanimously gave Troeltsch permission to lecture in church history and the history of dogma, for two years.[71] Troeltsch reported the success of his Göttingen plans to the Landeskirche of Bavaria and announced – 'in humble gratitude' and 'as proof of diligent use of the leave granted'[72] – that he would send them his licentiate dissertation.

At exactly twenty-six Ernst Troeltsch was now a Privatdozent; he had achieved the first important step in his academic career. And now, in order also to complete the practical part of his training, in his first semester as Privatdozent he took the Second Theological Examination.

8. Qualifying examination in Bavaria (1891)

The examination in Ansbach began on 14 June 1891 and again lasted a week. Some of the examiners were already known to Troeltsch from the first examination, as was the course of the examination: presentation of a catechism topic, three days of written examinations, sermon and catechesis, and finally the oral examination. The discussion of the dogmatic concepts of faith, justification and sanctification[73] undertaken by Troeltsch was praised by the members of the examining committee for its academic content. However, they made the critical comment: 'It is only to be regretted that in developing the three concepts in question the author did not take as a basis the expiation of our sin and guilt through the suffering and death of the incarnate Son of God, as the church confession does quite definitely and clearly.'

Of course Troeltsch's catechesis and his sermon are particularly important in indicating his attitude to practical questions of faith and life. In the catechetical work he had to discuss a central problem of education, training in obedience.

In discussing this question Troeltsch begins from conflicting interests, the interest of the person to be educated in independence and freedom, and that of the educator in the observance of certain norms of community life. The important thing for him is that this tension should not be done away with on either side. For Troeltsch, the overall aim of education is moral maturity as one of the 'basic pillars of the life of the people'.

In the additional question of how boredom is to be avoided in instruction

Troeltsch came out with the following verdict: 'In my experience nine-tenths of all instruction that is given is extraordinarily boring. The simple reason for this fact is that the great majority of people, including both teacher and pupils, are boring...' As a means of combatting this desperate situation Troeltsch thinks that he can commend the 'lively and warm participation of the teacher in his subject' and also 'the use of frequent changes in the material and the way in which it is treated'.

Finally, to the amazement of his examiners, Troeltsch commented positively on the role of wit – something that he himself possessed. 'Nor is the significance of wit in instruction to be underestimated. A teacher who has wit, and is tactful in using it, can achieve an extraordinary amount through it; wit is uncommonly enlivening and refreshing...'[74]

The text for the sermon was Ephesians 2.4-9. Troeltsch stresses the idea of grace and relates it directly to the relationship between God and man. The christological elements in the text are largely left aside.[75]

In the exposition it becomes clear that Troeltsch is expounding the notion of grace which finds expression in the biblical statement 'He first loved us' in such a way as to make it possible to find an inwardly perceptible 'first' on the basis of the human disposition as created. What comes to human beings from outside, in the historical event and the word of forgiveness, is taken up into the depth of human knowledge about this 'first'. Troeltsch is concerned to stress that this is an event which can only be experienced, not dissected and given a rational foundation.

At the centre of all three sermons which Troeltsch presented either complete or in outline lies the question of the relationship between the natural and the reborn person, or the world and the kingdom of God.[76] Troeltsch is concerned that the natural life shall not be devalued in the light of a radical, overdrawn understanding of sin. The contradictoriness, the 'not being able to satisfy', which arises in the merely natural life must be recognized by people so that they can arrive at a particular depth of self-understanding. Only on this basis is it possible to understand the world in the light of God and to interpret life accordingly. It is important for Troeltsch that the transition from the natural person to the spiritual or the reborn person cannot be described; only the fact of the transformation in the human understanding of self and the world is visible.

All in all, the impression left by Troeltsch on the basis of his work is somewhat ambiguous. We see a young theologian with brilliant intellectual capacities. Troeltsch is in a position to make acute analyses, depict connections and state them briefly: he has rich comparative material from history at his disposal. His strong intellectual background, especially in the history of dogma and church history, is relatively out of balance with the degree of uncertainty evident in matters of practical theology. What he expresses here keeps mainly to traditional lines: religious sensibility is expressed in a language which seems more conservative. True, this impression is not so marked in the qualifying examination, but the basically conservative tone, which also extends to politics, a marked ethical focus and a morality of Christian provenance are also still present here. His sovereign way of dealing with the material is not really matched by his achievements in practical theology. His practical theology is like another world, somewhat narrow and occasionally ingenuous, dogmatic, and not very fruitful.

The churchmen, whose views on the whole show a clear and certain verdict, accepted the divergent views but noted the discrepancy. Nowhere is there any doubt of Troeltsch's academic achievement and capacity, but there is some doubt as to whether he has firm roots in the Christian doctrine of salvation, as for example in the examination on dogma and the sermon. So the final report on the qualifying examination was: 'Candidate Troeltsch has shown academic gifts and knowledge of such excellence in the written and oral examination that he was awarded a First Class. However, his views on the basic doctrines of Christianity give cause for serious doubt, and so if he wanted to return from his position as Dozent in Göttingen to the service of our Landeskirche, he would have to be required to give adequate guarantees that he was remembering to teach along the lines of the confessional writings of our church.'[77] As the candidate with the best marks in the examination, Troeltsch was given a travel grant, but his trip, which took him to Strasbourg and Switzerland, did not take place until 1893.[78]

III

Teaching Begins (1891-1894)

1. Privatdozent in Göttingen

In the summer semester of 1891, before the qualifying examination in Bavaria, Troeltsch began his teaching with a series of lectures on the theology of the old Protestant dogmatic theologians. Thus he chose an area which was familiar to him from his licentiate work. The faculty report at the end of the summer semester of 1891 noted that an audience of eight attended his first session. In the report, the dean remarked that Troeltsch also showed 'well-ordered knowledge in teaching which he can present with clarity and freshness'.[79]

The next semester Troeltsch was involved in two sets of teaching, a series of lectures on 'Introduction to the Augsburg Confession' and a class on 'Ritschl's *Instruction in the Christian Religion*'. In the lectures Troeltsch kept to the sphere that was familiar to him from the history of dogma, and the class took up something of the latest Göttingen theological tradition. At the same time this topic matched the last thesis of his Promotion, which had spoken of the need for a 'respectable textbook for religious teaching in schools'.[80]

For the next summer semester (1892) Troeltsch then announced a major set of lectures on the history of modern theology from the Reformation to the present, five per week, but he did not give them.

In addition to these official tasks in the university sphere, at this time the decisive thing for Troeltsch was what one could call the 'Göttingen atmosphere'. This was a particular intellectual mood and situation which had formed through a favourable constellation of persons and events. Troeltsch related very vividly how the influx of Privatdozenten and Habilitands had instilled a kind of terror in the faculty and how the older members of the faculty spoke reservedly and yet with appreciation of the 'little faculty'. It was at this time that the 'history-of-religions school' was born. It was not a 'school' in the usual sense, with teachers and pupils, but a loose association of young theologians who got on well with one another and who in a shared theological approach sought to go beyond the Ritschlianism of their elders by expounding the biblical texts as literature in the context of the religious tradition of their time and circumstances. They understood Christianity as one religion among others and applied historical thought or the historical method indiscriminately to the interpretation of religious tradition. Troeltsch very much enjoyed the intellectual restlessness and mobility of this group, the close friendly companionship with shared lunches, and many conversations and walks through the woods of Göttingen. We can understand how this led to closer links, both personal and academic, with one person or another, say Bousset or Wrede. Albert Eichhorn, who was somewhat older, and stood outside the circle of Göttingen friends, occupied a special position. He was a Privatdozent in Halle, and so was more of an outside influence on the group, but he provided a decisive stimulus to history-of-religions thinking.

Of Troeltsch, one can say that the atmosphere of this group very much suited his nature and his notion of academic work.[81] He was stimulated greatly by his history-of-religions friends Bousset, Wrede, Rahlfs, Hackmann and Weiss, but also boldly put forward his own ideas without laying any claim to originality. His theological friends, among them especially Alfred Rahlfs, were the ones who drew his attention to Paul de Lagarde,[82] who pointed the way forward for the history-of-religions school in the question of methodology. Troeltsch dedicated the second volume of his collected works to Lagarde, at the same time remarking that no false conclusions should be drawn from this.[83] Many aspects of Paul de Lagarde's broad field of activity did not affect Troeltsch much – his editorial work, studies of the sources, research into the Septuagint. What came over, rather, was a method of historical work and work in the history of religions. What attracted Troeltsch to Lagarde was the way in which Lagarde gave religious phenomena a place in history, and rejected any view of the religious with a speculative or dogmatic colouring.[84] Any possible isolation of the religious was to be transcended in favour of its association with the particular cultural, social and political spirit of the age. At this point Paul de Lagarde stimulated Troeltsch to further reflections on matters of principle.

In addition, ideas of Wellhausen's and Harnack's had a particular influence on the young Göttingen theologians, who could be described as the first-generation 'history-of-religions school'. That applies not so much to any detailed exegetical and historical work as to the spirit of the whole group and the method they used.[85] Along with Bousset and Troeltsch, William Wrede and Alfred Rahlfs (who has already been mentioned) belonged to the closer circle; in addition mention should also be made of Hermann Gunkel, though he left Göttingen as early as 1889.[86] The generally 'undogmatic' intellectual climate of this trend of research clearly emerges everywhere. It is concerned to grasp the religious in a free and living way and to be open to religion generally as an existential phenomenon of elemental significance.[87] However, to the degree that the 'undogmatic' element in the above sense came into the foreground,[88] questions of principle inevitably arose. These include, for example, the questions of the position of Christianity in the history of religions or the authoritative validity of New Testament texts.

The description 'systematician of the history-of-religions school' is apt for

Troeltsch in so far as he took up methodological and dogmatic questions within the group of historians of religion and in this respect played a particular role within the group.[89] But two closer definitions or qualifications need to be made: as I have already indicated, one can talk of a 'school' only in a very broad sense. That emerges, for example, from the mere fact that Troeltsch and Bousset did not agree in many individual questions of historical and exegetical work. The same can be said of the other theologians who were termed 'historians of religion'. The term 'history-of-religions school' needs therefore to be used very carefully. Moreover, the solidarity of these theologians resulted not least from some pressure from outside which led to an interest in differentiation and demarcation and which encouraged common features among them.[90]

2. *Extraordinarius professor in Bonn*

After a short period as a Privatdozent, in March 1892 Troeltsch was invited to become extraordinarius professor in Bonn.[91]

How did this rapid call come about? One cannot say that he had special success in teaching which made him known beyond the bounds of Göttingen, and so far only his licentiate work had been published. Granted, it had had a positive review which was quite long for a first work in the *Theologische Literaturzeitung*,[92] written by Julius Kaftan, Troeltsch's teacher in Berlin and his later adversary. Kaftan's judgment was: 'The author has thoroughly investigated from all sides the material which he presents, has ordered it happily with a sure hand, and knows how to present it in a way which holds the interest. His work is a thorough and careful discussion of an important period of the history of our dogmatics which not only deserves all praise as a first work, but would do credit to any scholar.'[93]

Another factor was probably decisive in Troeltsch's call, namely a report to the Prussian Ministry of Culture from Professor Bernhard Weiss.[94] Weiss went to Göttingen to find out more about the young theologians who qualified there. In accordance with his principle that no decision should be made on questions of appointment 'without some personal acquaintance with the person to be called',[95] Weiss observed the Göttingen lecturers closely for two days. Whether there was a specific appointment in view at first remained unclear to those 'visited'.

Weiss's report mentions Wrede first. Bernhard Weiss heard him in two different lectures. He was particularly attracted by the lecture on Jesus' view of parables, but was not so happy with one on a passage from I Peter. However, because Wrede taught only New Testament, according to Weiss he could not be considered for the extraordinarius chair in Bonn.[96] Weiss then went on: 'However, Licentiate Troeltsch, who has also already spent 1-2 years in practical church work in Munich, is in my view ripe for such a position, although he is only twenty-seven years old... I heard him give a very well attended public lecture on Schleiermacher's theology in which he discussed the great theologian's relationship to Kant in a way which was both lively and powerful and, taking up the threads of the history of his development, drew a very attractive picture of his relationship to his father, and of his life as a tutor. What I found even more valuable was that I was able to attend the seminar classes which he held with a large audience. In these he attempted to engage the rather stolid hearers in a conversation on Ritschl's *Instruction in the Christian Religion.* Here, too, he showed himself a complete master of material and method, was able to present this fluidly, and took a position quite independent of his teacher, whom he did not hesitate to criticize incisively.'

On the other hand, Weiss had gained a very unfavourable impression of Bousset, and the fact that this report by Weiss went to the Prussian Ministry of Culture will have affected Weiss's academic career. 'Licentiate Bousset satisfied me least of the three Privatdozenten, of each of whom I attempted to form a picture by personal conversations... his manner was quite assured and his presentations were not without skill. Nevertheless, his exegesis of a section from Romans 3 confirmed an experience that I have often had, that even very substantial achievements in a specialist sphere do not of themselves guarantee theological maturity. His exegesis was quite superficial, his solutions of the questions discussed were not very convincing and, even where he hit on the right point, were not sufficiently substantiated. Some were evidently quite wrong, and there were even very gross mistakes. Certainly Bousset still needs considerable practice in academic teaching.'[97]

It is amazing that Bousset and Wrede – both specializing in the New Testament – should ever have been drawn into the circle of possible candidates for an extraordinarius chair in systematic theology. First, one has to take into account that at that time there was still far less restriction to a particular sphere within a discipline, and secondly that such assessments could also serve generally as a basis for later possible calls.

The process of the call itself took a strange course. For the original proposal of the Bonn faculty was that the first nominee should be the gymnasium teacher Max Reischle (1858-1906) from Stuttgart, a member of the Ritschl school, and the second William Wrede from Göttingen, despite the fact that his specialist sphere was the New Testament. The faculty proposal ended with the observation: '... Like Reischle, Wrede too is renowned as a sound and pious person, a reliable and popular character, and a theologian with unusual academic gifts.'[98]

But in December 1891 the Berlin Ministry – evidently as a result of Weiss's report – issued an invitation to Gandtner, the Curator of the Royal University in Bonn: 'Pursuant to the report of 3 July of this year... concerning the appointment to the Lemme Ordinarius Chair for Systematic Theology, I humbly request Your Excellency to secure from the Protestant Theological Faculty there an opinion on Privatdozent Licentiate Troeltsch in Göttingen in connection with the question of the occupation of the chair.'[99]

The faculty replied that it welcomed this invitation, especially since 'as a result of it we have been led to expand substantially our former suggestions without abandoning these in any way. As we had the honour to inform Your Excellency in our earlier report, at that stage there was no occasion for us to take the above-mentioned Licentiate Troeltsch into account in any way, since he had not made himself known to the theological public at that time. However, that is no longer the case... It is also reported to us that Licentiate Troeltsch has also proved his abundant theological knowledge in his licentiate examination. Moreover, the reports that we have received of his teaching abilities are similarly very favourable. As for his personality, this seems to be remarkably developed given his youth, but attractive in its freshness and openness. Should... the Ministry have occasion provisionally to appoint merely an extraordinarius professor to the chair, we would confidently accept Licentiate Troeltsch as such.'[100]

The Bonn faculty's answer is a cameo of the problems of a faculty wanting to be able to assert its rights over appointments but not in fact being able to have its way – somewhere between firmness and readiness to compromise.

The Minister did in fact intend to appoint an extraordinarius professor in Bonn, and in February 1892 made enquiries of the Evangelische Oberkirchenrat as to how things stood with Troeltsch's confession and doctrine.[101]

The Oberkirchenrat replied that because of his great youth and the fact that Troeltsch had published only one work, there was not enough knowledge available to give a verdict. 'In these circumstances we believe that we should merely suggest to your Excellency to consider carefully the responsibility of the calling of so young a theologian, not yet inwardly proven and matured, particularly for systematic theology. However, at present we refrain from raising doubts about his calling on the basis of his confession and doctrine.'[102]

This left the way free for Troeltsch's call to Bonn. He was asked to organize his teaching so that it represented an extension of the work he had already offered in systematic theology.[103]

A few weeks after the beginning of the semester Troeltsch sent his first report to Bousset. He wrote of an only moderate attendance (eight) and thought that he was 'of all the Dozents here the weakest' (card of 5 June 1892, unpublished). But above all he still had a longing 'for dear Göttingen' (ibid.).

In October Troeltsch then found time for a longer letter to Bousset. In the meantime, he wrote, he had settled down well in Bonn; above all he had found what made a place attractive for him, the stimulating company of friends. 'Things are going very well with me here. I have already a very nice and pleasant set of friendships with colleagues from different faculties and hope to achieve quite a respectable social position. I am already very close friends with Grafe, who is a splendidly noble and aristocratic man and an uncommonly independent and skilled teacher, though more inclined to the pleasant enjoyment of witty and many-sided companionship than to productive academic work. I get on with him quite amazingly well and am very fond of him because of his character and his winning personality. I am also in very well with my colleague Meinhold and Privatdozent Meyer, who is very productive in Judaism and apocalyptic as a pupil of Spitta'[104] (letter of 1 October 1892, unpublished).

One particular occasion for the correspondence with Bousset was the latter's gift of his most recent book on *Jesus' Preaching in Contrast to Judaism* (1892). Troeltsch discusses it in detail. He points out that he himself has put forward many of the basic ideas in the book, 'as I often encountered ideas which were familiar to me from our conversations. I would also assume that you have recognized some as coming from the influence of friends' (letter from Bousset of 1 October 1892, unpublished). Troeltsch agreed with Bousset in 'regarding belief in God the Father and its consequences as the substance of the activity of Jesus which proved influential in history...'(ibid.). However, then comes his criticism: 'Nevertheless, I cannot conceal the fact that I personally feel predominantly antipathetic to it all... You have shifted the uniqueness (of Jesus) from the sphere of doctrine to the virtually personal level of a sense of life and normality [of the ethic of Jesus], into the true mean between asceticism and cultural bliss, and aimed at killing these two birds with one stone by detaching Jesus from Judaism. That is why the introduction painted Judaism as being so absolutely black, so as to be able to make something absolutely new from the undoubted relative newness and primal force of the piety of Jesus' (ibid.).

Troeltsch himself did not want either to explain the attitude of Jesus to morality in terms of Judaism or to detach him from it. He put Jesus in the sphere of prophetic piety, though Jesus deepened and consummated this. It is amazing to what extent Troeltsch criticizes Bousset, above all in a sphere of work remote from his own. It is a pity that letters from Bousset have not been preserved which could have indicated his reaction to such criticism.

Despite the conditions in Bonn, which Troeltsch found very 'pleasant', he still missed the close collaboration and academic stimulation of the Göttingen group. 'We got on particularly well together, and shared all the sorrows and joys of Habilitation' (card to Bousset, 16 June 1893, unpublished). In retrospect, he praised the Göttingen faculty highly for attaching importance to youth and restraining its suspicions in the face of such a great crowd of competitors for an academic post.

Troeltsch remarked that his own work and development 'is quietly progressing. In the meantime I have now thoroughly and definitively parted company with the Ritschlians' (ibid.). How far his next works would confirm this statement will emerge in due course.

In autumn 1893 Troeltsch took part in a Bonn vacation course which had been arranged a year earlier, on 'The Christian World-View and its Scientific Competitors'. This vacation course had been arranged to make it possible for pastors to continue their involvement in academic theology. Here Troeltsch had his first experience of the resistance to him in the so-called 'positive' camp in connection with the most recent theological research – especially that into the history of religions.[105]

The conflict first really broke out at a time when Troeltsch was already no longer a member of the Bonn faculty. However, it is a good illustration of the relationship at that time between critical theology and a more conservative trend which had support in church groups. On the third Bonn vacation course there was controversy over a lecture by Graf in which he had put forward hypotheses on the origin of the eucharist formulated by Harnack. Furthermore, in his Old Testament lecture Meinhold had made critical comments on the Old Testament creation stories and had spoken of the texts as 'sagas'. The so-called Bible-believing communities and the positive trend within theology reacted to these two lectures with vigorous criticism. Protest was organized in the form of an assembly of the 'Rhineland Westphalia friends of the Church Confession'. It was then continued in print, first regionally and then in the *Reichsbote* and the *Kreuzzeitung*. The 'positive' trend asked for the two professors to be investigated by the Ministry of Culture and the church governments. The 'Friends of the Church Confession' collected signatures and sent them to the ministry. In the course of this controversy plans were even mooted to establish a Protestant theological faculty with a 'positive' trend which would be loyal to the confession, in Herford. There was a call to appoint 'positive' lecturers as a counterbalance to the free-thinking professors in order to achieve a parity. Bosse, the Minister of Culture, thereupon considered the appointment of three Dozenten close to the 'positive camp' in Bonn; hence these posts were given the term 'penal professorships'.

With circumstances as they were, Troeltsch felt that these disputes were unimportant. For him, theology and church were under pressure from modern world-views. The position of theology and church in modern cultural life had to be rethought, and historical thinking had to be adopted in theology. These were crucial tasks which suggested a transformation of theology as a discipline and the church as a religious and institutional factor.

During his brief period in Bonn, Troeltsch devoted himself in particular to working out his lectures.[106] After three semesters there his audience had increased somewhat (to eighteen). However, Troeltsch was quite critical about his students: 'My audience is only there because it has to be, and the attendance is not very good' (letter to Bousset, 4 September 1893, unpublished).

In addition to the 'lecture business', Troeltsch began on some 'commissioned work', in the form of articles and a lengthy review of Lipsius' *Dogmatics* in the *Göttingische gelehrte Anzeige* (1894). Troeltsch was to be very occupied with reviews in subsequent years, especially in the *Theologische Jahresbericht*, in which he wrote on the philosophy of religion and fundamental theology.[107] He wrote these reports on theological works which had appeared in the course of the previous year between 1896 and 1899, i.e. on works published between 1895 and 1898.

Troeltsch had great skill in reviewing. He could write a survey of academic publications in a particular area very quickly, and found it easy to think himself into other positions and to formulate his critical objections briefly and pertinently. Nevertheless, he always found this work an extraordinary burden, and it did not leave him enough time for his own productive activity.[108]

3. The call to Heidelberg

In November 1893 Troeltsch had a major piece of news to report to his friend Bousset: he had been called to a chair in Heidelberg and was to go there in the summer semester of 1894. He described the situation in detail: 'Despite urgent requests Prussia has let me leave my faculty. It was all a hellishly diplomatic story in which I was trapped like a mouse, in that Althoff of Baden came to me and offered me a post on condition that I accepted without negotiating with Berlin...' (card to W.Bousset, 2 November 1893, unpublished).

In fact the Bonn faculty had been very concerned that Troeltsch should remain in Bonn; they sent a telegram to Bosse, the Minister of Culture in Berlin: 'Since no young talent for systematic theology and Troeltsch indispensable here given increasing demand, we earnestly ask you to appoint him to the second ordinarius professorship for systematic theology, still unoccupied.'[109]

A few hours early Gandtner, the University Curator, had informed the Ministry of the offer made to Troeltsch. He sent a telegram to Berlin: 'Troeltsch to Heidelberg as ordinarius on 4500 marks, decision by noon tomorrow.'[110] The Minister left the decision to Troeltsch. A few days later the Curator then added by letter that he had foreseen that the action would fail. 'I have to concede that Troeltsch was put in a hopeless position by the actions of the Baden government. The advisor concerned – I have forgotten his name – wanted an answer straightaway, but in the end gave him twenty-four hours to think it over and dropped anchor here that long. After the arrival of the answer by telegram Troeltsch accepted the offer, but the decision does not seem to have been easy for him.'[111]

So Troeltsch decided for Heidelberg, and at the end of November asked to be released from the service of the Prussian state. Minister Bosse was asked 'to excuse the haste of the decision on the basis of the urgent proceedings of the Ministry of the Grand Duchy of Baden and his (my) uncertainty about the possibility of his being retained'.[112] Otto Ritschl was called to Bonn as extraordinarius to be Troeltsch's successor.[113]

Troeltsch's call was approved by almost all the members of the Heidelberg faculty. In a majority vote (five out of six)[114] the faculty nominated to the Ministry in Karlsruhe Troeltsch in first place, Max Reischle of Giessen in second and in third place Privatdozent Johannes Werner of Marburg.

The resolution of the faculty indicates the reasons for the suggestion and the expectations set on Troeltsch: 'Professor Troeltsch, who is proposed in first place, is still a relatively young man whose academic career is not a long one... He has demonstrated his literary qualities... in a major academic study on *Reason and Revelation in Johann Gerhard and Melanchthon*. His work is characterized by learning, clear judgment, openness of standpoint, and a fine understanding of the religious phenomena and personalities of the past and the systematic needs of the present. Just as this led to the author being appointed to Bonn with laudable speed, so too it justifies the expectation that in the future, too, he will achieve splendid results in the sphere of systematic theology.'[115]

Troeltsch's call to Bonn marks the beginning of a new period of his life and work. His time of training and the beginning of his career was over. Externally he had achieved a firm position, but we have yet to consider his theological orientation, his professional work and his personal life.

Part Two: Professor of Theology in Heidelberg

I

The First Years (1894-1900)

1. The city and its university

Heidelberg is the place where Troeltsch lived and worked as a theologian for more than twenty years. Small in terms of population and without any great economic significance, the city owed its reputation above all to the university, its history and its beautiful setting. Heidelberg was a magnet for academic young people from Germany and abroad, but tradition and landscape certainly played a major role here.[1] Heidelberg was regarded as emphatically a 'summer university'.[2] The influx of students for any summer semester was considerable. However, the numbers and types of students coming to any one particular faculty were quite varied. The 'normal Baden student' gave the theological faculty its look.

The city to which the young professor of theology came was an attractive one; a city with a rich tradition, which had its place in the history of German intellectual life, associated above all with the names of the Romantics, but also with Hegel and Hölderlin, Goethe and Jean Paul.

Troeltsch here found the manageable circumstances that he had wanted earlier. Everything was very close together: houses and people, the university and the churches. However, there was hardly any possiblity for the more serious enjoyment of the arts. Anyone who wanted to see a good play or opera had to go to Mannheim, Darmstadt or Frankfurt. Still, the conditions were almost tailor-made for the first concentrated work of a young scholar. For a man like Troeltsch, the only other thing necessary was scholarly friendships to match, to give his whole life some style. And as will emerge, they were certainly to be had.

The charm of Heidelberg as a city lies on the one hand in its architecture and on the other in its setting. The past is alive; history becomes present in a series of architectural monuments, the ruins of the castle and the mediaeval part of the city on the castle hill. Then there is the old bridge over the Neckar which Troeltsch crossed so often when he lived with Max Weber on the other side of the river, and which sets the seal on the view of Heidelberg as a city. The setting of the city is dominated by the Neckar valley and the towering heights which frame it and hang over it. A mild climate with an early spring and a warm summer makes life here easier and more attractive than elsewhere. The old city of Heidelberg is dominated by South German and Italian baroque: the Corn Market, the Jesuit Church and the market place are evidence of this. And Troeltsch's articles on 'Two Paintings by Thoma in St Peter's Church, Heidelberg' are evidence of his eye for significant works of art.[3]

In 1891 the city had 28,000 inhabitants, and by the year 1900 the number had risen to 40,000 through an influx of population and the expansion of the city to take in outlying communities. The university, a very old foundation (1368), underwent a manifest boom in the nineteenth century when it was refounded as the Ruperto-Carola university (1803). Organizational changes went with this: the university became a state institution and the professors became civil servants. The local ruler was the Rector of the university. Every year at Easter a Pro-Rector, the real Rector as we would understand it, was elected from among the ordinarius professors by a secret vote.

In 1880 the University of Heidelberg had forty ordinarius professors, and by the year 1900 five new chairs had been added. Among the Heidelberg faculties, law had by far the largest number of students; up to the year 1880 half of all Heidelberg students were enrolled in it. The philosophical faculty also provided general education for the other faculties. Here student numbers rose only with the development of the secondary school system.

The philosophical faculty had an important historian of philosophy in its ranks in the person of Kuno Fischer, who from 1872 taught in Heidelberg as a disciple of Eduard Zeller. Fischer was famed for his rhetorical power and gifts, which he used to communicate the more recent history of philosophy to his students. However, he was said to have been very aware of his reputation and his importance. There are many stories which tell us a good deal not only about him but also about what conditions were like at the time. One day when Fischer could not think because he was distracted by the noise of a city plasterer outside his house, he went outside and called up to him: 'Shut up, or I shall accept' (viz., the call to another chair which he had just received).[4] The story was soon all over town.

The professors were well-known figures in the city, not just celebrities like Helmholtz or Kuno Fischer, but also Ernst Troeltsch or Max Weber. No wonder that in Berlin later Troeltsch felt that he had left behind the typical situation of a small German university city.

It is clear that the university developed continuously.[5] There were no great numbers in the theological faculty. Only 67 students were enrolled in it in the year 1905. By contrast, the philosophical faculty had 457 students. Another noteworthy feature was that in Heidelberg the number of student associations and clubs was very large, so that academic life and also city life was strongly influenced by them.

2. Conditions within the faculty, teaching and private life

When Troeltsch, not yet thirty, became ordinarius professor of theology, outwardly his academic career had proved a brilliant success.

Moreover, Troeltsch was aware of how well things had gone; he knew that so early an appointment was by no means usual. However, he was sceptical about the significance of this for his academic work. He wrote to Bousset: 'I had exorbitant luck. You must be reasonably content and not grumble at fate. Your bold achievements will still win you your place, though there will be some obstacles in the way. They are always there, especially in theology.'[6] Troeltsch said that he had enough work, but that it was unclear and dubious to him what one could achieve in theology.

What were the external conditions for his work? In particular, what kind of a faculty was it which accepted Troeltsch into its ranks and to which he was to belong for a good two decades? The reputation that the faculty was able to achieve in the nineteenth century was based above all on two names: Karl Daub (1765-1836) and Richard Rothe (1799-1867).

Karl Daub was a speculative thinker of impressive power who had shifted positions and finally attached himself to German idealism. Richard Rothe continued the tradition of speculative thought, albeit under a different star. The spirit of his theology and influence was still alive in the faculty and in the region in Troeltsch's time. Not only did Troeltsch deliver the memorial oration on him in 1899, but Rothe's theological aims also had an influence on Troeltsch's work.

In Rothe's speculative system, the universal history of redemption was seen as analogous to the individual history of redemption. He took up the idea of development, seeing both the individual and history morally purified and elevated in a purely religious experience.[7] According to Rothe, this process is connected with the activity of the Redeemer because the new life emerging from him is 'quite essentially both moral and religious'.[8] Rothe sees the religious and moral development of the individual and humanity held together and governed in salvation-historical terms by a christological thinking which embraces both.[9]

Rothe was moulded by the revival movement. He attached special importance to personal belief in God's move towards human beings in salvation. In the memorial address on the centenary of Rothe's birth, Troeltsch described this side of Rothe's theological work[10] along with his capacity to make a critical analysis of the cultural and historical situation in which Christianity is entangled, and emphasized Rothe's criticism of the church.[11]

In the subsequent period philological-historical work became increasingly significant in the faculty.[12]

The exegetical disciplines came into the foreground with Ferdinand Hitzig (1807-1875), Adalbert Merx (1818-1909) and Heinrich Holtzmann (1832-1910). The historical element in theology was represented by W.Gass (1813-

1889), who was distinguished for work on the history of dogmatics and ethics. The work of Adolf Hausrath (1837-1907), who for some time was a colleague of Troeltsch's, generally had a marked historical and biographical slant. His book *Richard Rothe and his Friends* (2 vols., 1902-1906) was also a piece of faculty history.

In 'positive' church circles there was a desire to supplement the faculty, which stressed the historical and philological element in theology and was largely liberal in church politics, by a more conservative theology. So Ludwig Lemme (1847-1927)[13] was appointed to Heidelberg, subsequently becoming Troeltsch's immediate colleague as a systematic theologian.

Troeltsch was appointed to Heidelberg on 1 April 1894;[14] however, because of a lengthy trip in Greece which he went on in March and April with two Bonn colleagues,[15] he could only take up his appointment on 24 April.[16] First of all he had to take the oath of office, which required him to be loyal to the Grand Duke and the constitution and to further the well-being of ruler and fatherland to the best of his abilities.[17]

Troeltsch made an arrangement with his colleague Lemme to maintain the previous programme of lectures. He left it to the faculty to decide when he should lecture, but said that he did not care at all for the period between seven and eight in the morning. The faculty sympathized, so Troeltsch gave his first series of Heidelberg lectures, 'Dogmatics I', for five days a week from 8 to 9 a.m. He had an audience of fifteen. They were keen to hear the new Ordinarius Professor of Systematic Theology, who was only twenty-nine years old, and of whom they knew virtually nothing except that he had come from Bonn. The figure they saw and the lectures they heard somewhat surprised them. 'When the door of the lecture room flew open, a man of youthful appearance with a stocky body mounted the podium; his fair hair and full, somewhat short-sighted face, suggested a young man storming into the daylight full of the joys of life and very sure of himself. There was no anxiety and caution, no treading gently. Coming from a strong temperament backed up by a vigorous inner commitment, the teaching flowed in a way which carried all before it, so that one needed to listen attentively in order to follow the rapidly moving train of thought.'[18] In addition to the lectures Troeltsch also supervised classes in systematic theology, on Mondays from 9 to 10. His capacity to react spontaneously to opinions aired in dialogue and his interest in other people and views were particularly important here.

The call to Heidelberg, which had clashed with his travel plans and which meant leaving Bonn when he had only just established himself there, initially introduced some unrest into Troeltsch's life. In the peace and quiet of the vacation, which at last once again brought contentment and rest, he wrote to his friend Bousset: 'During the summer I really wasn't my own master. Still full of all the varied impressions from my great trip, I was immediately caught up in the maelstrom of new conditions, completely new people and things, all the while recollecting the splendid situation which I had left, the visits and

invitations, the work on lectures and my review of Lipsius.[19] All this proved
utterly confusing. Naturally I did not feel at all pleased. Furthermore, I lived
in the last house in Heidelberg, way out on the Rhine plain,[20] so that I kept
having to make endless journeys and enjoyed very little of the real natural
beauty of Heidelberg. In addition I had a great many visits from my father,
who had fallen ill during the winter and sought a cure in the baths all though
the summer. It was good to see him, but the visits were distracting and anxious.
His state still causes me much concern and I'm very sorry for him. At any rate,
I had neither peace nor time to collect myself.'[21]

Troeltsch hoped that in Heidelberg, too, he would be able to create the
same sort of conditions for living and working as those which he had found
so pleasant in Bonn. External security and rest, and a feeling that the situation
was reasonably within his grasp, were very important factors for him. So he
wrote to Bousset: 'And above all nothing can deprive me of the awareness of
having a secure official position, which is an infinite blessing to me.'[22] He
could still remember vividly the risk associated with the status of Privatdozent,
and it is clear from the letters to Bousset how relieved he was about the
unexpectedly rapid progress of his academic career.

Troeltsch gives a vivid description of the impact made on him by his
colleagues and the faculty which shows the slightly malicious wit which is
occasionally a characteristic of his descriptions of people and circumstances:
'The make-up of the faculty is very curious and not very enjoyable. Merx [Old
Testament scholar and orientalist, who had been in Heidelberg since 1875],
who in some way is of the circumcision, is the real torment to me: his vanity
and know-all air are so ludicrous that I am hardly in a position to assess his
good sides. One can keep him off one's back to some degree only by pointed
insults. Hausrath [Professor of Church History, who had been in Heidelberg
since 1867] is utterly distasteful, having fallen out with God and the world;
he is a witty but temperamental and unfair conversationalist who utterly
despises all theology and all theologians, and sounds off to almost anyone.
Then there is the lovely Lemme, who is incredibly brash and uncollegial, but
outwardly very restrained: he only storms up and down outside in the region.
He has a great fixation on the Reformation and sees himself as God's saviour
in Baden. Fortunately he is not a particularly brilliant teacher, and understands
only solemn bluster. Anyway, I have my ground next to him and also have the
advantage of being regarded by him as a somewhat inferior creature, against
whom he does not need to make much effort. These three are quite enough
to make the faculty unattractive. Fortunately, the rest are much better.
However, Holsten [1825-1897, a New Testament scholar] is very old and
quite one-sidedly stuck in his theories. But he must be an excellent teacher,
since all the people hang on his words and swear by his views on the New
Testament, though I often come into conflict with him. Certainly he is a very
lovable and excellent person. Bassermann [1849-1909, a practical theologian
and a university preacher] is known to you. I find him by far the most congenial

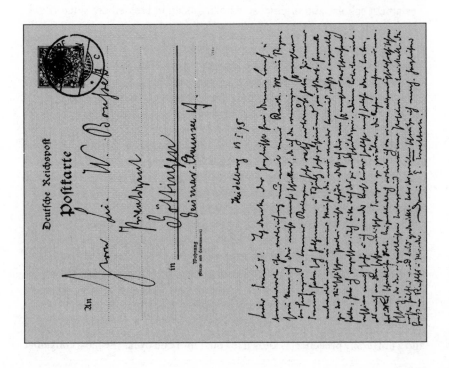

Card from Ernst Troeltsch to Wilhelm Bousset, 13 January 1895. The photograph shows Wilhelm Bousset as a Privatdozent in Göttingen (1892/3). The card reads as follows: 'Dear Friend, very many thanks for your letter; for the moment I'm just replying with a card. I can't send you my review now; I had very few copies of it and I used them up very quickly on colleagues here and in Bonn. To my delight Holtzmann and Schultz were very positive about it. Harnack replied in a way which showed me once again that he does not belong to the Ritschlian party. I had forgotten that I had promised you a copy; please forgive me. I'm very interested in your work and I would rather be doing that sort of thing myself than tormenting myself on systematic questions. Sometimes these problems are really oppressive. At the moment I'm working on an essay on the philosophy of religion which develops the real basis of my position. The first half will be printed soon; I'm still sweating over the second. Warmest greetings to Rahlfs and Wrede, Yours, E. Troeltsch.'

(The review mentioned was of R. A. Lipsius, *Lehrbuch der evangelisch-protestantischen Dogmatik*, which appeared in the *Göttingische gelehrte Anzeigen*; the essay Troeltsch was working on was 'The Independence of Religion'.)

person, and he is a strength and stay for me in the dark valley. At the same time he has the advantage of having a very attractive family with whom I spend Sunday evenings. Finally there is our Privatdozent Grützmacher [1866-1914, from 1896 Extraordinarius Professor of Church History in Heidelberg], whom Harnack directed here in order to advance his school to this post as well. However, I cannot learn much from him. His tremendous eloquence drives every thought from my mind and really provokes me only to irony. That's the way it is, and I have no idea of his real concerns. However, I fear that they don't amount to much, and that Harnack is not unhappy to have put him at some distance. This Berlin cobbler's apprentice is accompanied by the backwoodsman Kneucker, who on his very small pastor's stipend has to feed seven children and from Hitzig's heritage his very much smaller audience. It is clear that this is quite an odd faculty. But I feel all right here. There's no point in looking back, so I make what I can of the present, and hope that in due course I, too, may carve out a place for myself here in which at least I have my particular and secure sphere of influence.'[23]

Nine months later, with three Heidelberg semesters behind him, Troeltsch sent the following report to Bousset: 'So I'm increasingly getting settled into my academic work and am mostly having contact with colleagues from other faculties. There is nothing doing in my own. Holsten lives in quite a different, old, world and does not read anything new. He does not recognize any concrete historical work which goes beyond the New Testament; he does everything with logic and the NT, bursts out in blind enthusiasm on every occasion and delivers interminable speeches in which he constantly describes the Jewish, pagan and Christian consciousness. The others are not worth mentioning. It's a pity that this is such a dead and lifeless faculty. However, Bassermann is quite a different kettle of fish, though his practical theology does not give me any academic stimulation.'[24]

In the winter semester of 1894/95, Troeltsch lectured on Dogmatics II and also gave a public lecture one hour a week on Schleiermacher's life and teaching, which attracted an audience of thirty-three. In the summer semester of 1895 there then followed a 'History of Protestant Theology in the Nineteenth Century' (with an audience of fifteen), a series of lectures on ethics (with an audience of eight) and his classes on systematic theology.[25]

So it was not easy for Troeltsch to feel at home with his colleagues in the Heidelberg faculty.

It was essential for him to keep up with the academic work of others; this is not surprising, since he was particularly interested in the academic achievements of the former members of the 'little Göttingen faculty', especially Bousset, Wrede and Rahlfs. When Bousset sent him his *Antichrist* (1895), Troeltsch wrote: 'I detect in the work what, if I may say so, is a feature common to the young Göttingen school, an unrestricted history-of-religions method which investigates in purely historical and philological terms the varied material of the religious movements which supported and surrounded Christianity. I came upon this in Gunkel's book, and now I also find it in yours. Wrede works in a similar way... That is a real achievement.'[26]

To begin with, closer contact with Heinrich Bassermann and his family proved most enjoyable for Troeltsch. However, his relationship with Basser-man was more personal than based on any common interests.

A longer-lasting shift in mood began when one of Bassermann's daughter broke off her engagement to Troeltsch. Evidently Troeltsch had quite different views about such a liaison from those of his fiancée. He thought that marriage was above all a useful way of guarding against loneliness. He had already written from Bonn to his friend Bousset that having lost his Göttingen friends, now 'marriage seems the only refuge. But to whom? And then, on the other hand, it would be disruptive.'[27] That was the point – he did not want the whole business to disrupt his work. Troeltsch wrote to Bousset that he could not do justice to the quite enthusiastic inclinations of his fiancée, having been 'thoroughly accustomed to masculine company and piled high with work'.[28] He had not known how to behave as a 'bridegroom' and thought more of his own future household than of the 'reasonable and peaceful aim' of this alliance.[29]

It is quite in keeping with this very 'rational' and remarkably functional attitude of Troeltsch's that he should end by saying: 'Moreover it is a piece of good fortune that my position in Heidelberg has not been shaken in other respects as a result of the event. With few exceptions, relations with the families of friends have remained unchanged, and my various friends have been very kind to me.'[30]

The somewhat dull atmosphere in the Heidelberg theological faculty changed for Troeltsch in 1897, when Adolf Deissmann (1866-1937) was appointed to Heidelberg. Troeltsch got on with him like a house on fire.[31] He agreed with Deissmann in his inclination towards both the history of religions and historical method.[32] Moreover, Deissmann had a social and political concern, and in this respect, too, was an interesting conversation partner. But Troeltsch was not very happy about the situation in the faculty generally, although he tended more towards agreement and compromise than towards confrontation.

In the meantime, relations with Ludwig Lemme, Troeltsch's immediate colleague in the faculty, had become increasingly difficult. Lemme represented the 'positive' trend both inside, in the work of the faculty and in university life, and outside, in the church and public life. Lemme saw himself as a kind of bulwark against the 'liberal flood' in the faculty and kept attempting crudely to advocate the rights of a theology orientated on the Bible, confession and community. Lemme felt supported and sustained by the strong influence which church institutions and associations and conservative church circles sought to exercise on the faculty. One point of dispute which kept emerging was whether or not the faculty should be enlarged by the appointment of 'positive' professors.[33]

Lemme never wearied of presenting himself to the Ministry and the Court as the spokesman of a theologically interested public which saw in Heidelberg a faculty which was too strongly dominated generally by historical and philological methods and purely academic aims and paid far too little heed to church ties and the orientation which went with them.

If we keep in mind this pressure from outside and the situation within the faculty, it is evident that questions relating to appointments were almost bound to lead to vigorous controversies. That can be illustrated most clearly from the circumstances surrounding Bousset's call. Troeltsch made three attempts to secure Bousset's appointment to the New Testament chair in Heidelberg. In 1897 there was a debate over who was to succeed Karl Holsten, who had died that year. Troeltsch described the situation to Bousset like this: 'I will do all I can to get you here and have the support of Bassermann in this. I cannot say how things are with the others. It's all uncertain.'[34]

In parallel, however, Troeltsch wrote on 30 January 1897 to Adolf Jülicher (1857-1938), the Marburg New Testament scholar: 'After discussions with Hausrath it is clear that his chief wish is to get you here. You can imagine that nothing would be more congenial to me.'[35] But on 17 February 1897, Troeltsch then had to tell Jülicher that although Bassermann and he had backed Jülicher's nomination, they had not won the day. Shortly beforehand he had described progress to Bousset like this. 'Fortunately, Bassermann and I have prevailed and you are to be nominated in first place... True, we have proposed Schmiedel as equal first with you, but we have mentioned him second and indicated clearly that we would prefer you to be appointed. Deissmann, whose biblical studies have very much impressed me, is nominated in third place.'[36]

Even Troeltsch saw Bousset's political involvement as an obstacle in the way of his appointment. There was no doubt for Troeltsch that here Bousset had to some extent to backtrack.[37] He accepted this fully, and did not think it excessive that were Bousset to be appointed he should be asked for an assurance that he would not be invoved in political activity. He wrote: 'I would ask you to write me a letter which can be shown to the dean (only Dean Bassermann, to whom you can speak openly enough), which will give us something to go on in this matter.'[38] Troeltsch did not want Bousset's political attitude in any way to be a burden – either inside the faculty or out.

When the whole Jülicher affair was then made public, Troeltsch wrote to Bousset: 'So the government has asked about our attitude to a call. On academic grounds, initially I was very much in favour of this appointment and had already even won everyone else over (apart from Lemme); but suddenly Hausrath changed his mind once again and for his sake we backed off Jülicher's nomination. So when the Ministry itself proposed Jülicher to us, we readily agreed. So Jülicher was offered the post and declined it. And we are still faced with the question.'[39]

It has to be said that Troeltsch concealed from Bousset that he originally favoured Jülicher for the post, and only conceded this later. Evidently

Troeltsch, faced with the choice between Jülicher and Bousset, set more store by Jülicher, who had already achieved academic recognition, and allowed the prospect of renewed collaboration with Bousset to fade into the background.

In the majority resolution of the faculty that was finally agreed on, which put Bousset and Schmiedel equal first and Deissmann third, it was stressed that these were men of a 'critical direction'. The appointment of one of the candidates who were named in a separate opinion given by Lemme – with Steude[40] in first place – would have led to a 'change in the historical character of the Heidelberg faculty, above all in the difficult position of theology in relation to the other faculties'.[41]

So Adolf Deissmann was appointed. As I have already said, Troeltsch found him the kind of theological conversation-partner whom he had so far missed in Heidelberg.

The fronts were not only sharply drawn in such decisive things as appointments; there were also deep-seated differences of opinon in other questions, for example in 1899 over the issue of the admission of women to lectures. Merx, Hausrath, Deissmann and Troeltsch were in favour in principle, and Bassermann had no objections. But Lemme regarded theological study by women as senseless since they could not in any case become pastors or preachers. But above all he voted against the motion because he did not believe that women would have had a good enough education: 'How anyone with a state school education can understand my lectures is beyond me. I was asked to collaborate in the production of a school lexicon aimed at the level of the average pupil, but my articles, which were written as simply as possible, were sent back because they were too difficult for that level. And are we now to give our institutions the impression that they stand at the level of secondary schools?' Troeltsch thought that the last part of this argument was somewhat venomous. Lemme should 'omit arguments connected with self-esteem, as these contribute nothing to the subject and serve only to irritate other people...' In the end the faculty passed a majority resolution 'to admit women to lectures and to leave this admission to the judgment of individual lecturers, who must also decide on the adequacy of the qualifications which are presented'.[42]

One particularly spectacular occasion for controversy in the faculty was provided by the celebrations which were planned for the centenary of Richard Rothe's birth in 1899. The preparations began almost two years before the anniversary. Troeltsch, who was dean at this time, suggested that the Grand Duke should be invited: 'He will be interested because of his known respect for Rothe, and in any case he must be instructed.' He proposed that Hausrath should give the ceremonial address, as Hausrath had known Rothe personally. He mentioned himself in second place. Hausrath, who despite all the scurrility attributed to him[43] voted very objectively, argued: 'Of course my colleague Troeltsch will give the lecture, since as the representative of the discipline and the dean he alone has the right to. I would not be competent to comment on Rothe's systematic theology and ethics.'[44]

So this question was settled, but then something happened which brought the whole matter to the verge of a scandal – though it was also not also without its comic features. Troeltsch described what happened in a letter to Adolf von Harnack: 'Allow me to make a request in connection with a new war which our Lemme is in process of waging against our faculty. He has formed a committee from a few of our right-wing people to celebrate the centenary of Richard Rothe's birth and has put himself at their head. His intention is to invite all the theological faculties, but he has not communicated this to the faculty; he has just co-opted Bassermann on to the committee. Unfortunately Bassermann agreed to be co-opted, also without reporting the fact to the faculty... The whole affair was of course an attempt to force the faculty to the wall and to make an impression in Karlsruhe (and elsewhere). I want to report this to you simply in case a similar enquiry has come or should come to your faculty. We, i.e. the faculty, will in due course take official note of the event and allow the celebration by the committee to go ahead independently.'[45] Almost a year later, when the time for the celebrations was imminent, things were still unclear. Troeltsch again reported to Harnack: 'Now the faculty is officially represented on the committee... He (Lemme) has assured us that note will also be taken of the liberals. But I do not know how this will work out. All I know is that he has already told a variety of lies and I have threatened him with a boycott of his celebrations by the faculty.'[46] It did not come to that, and the celebrations took place in a 'worthy' fashion: Dean Troeltsch gave the ceremonial oration and the theological students sang a chorale to begin and end the celebration.

In 1897/8 Troeltsch struck up an academic friendship with Max Weber outside the faculty, which was to prove of long-lasting importance. Weber had come from Freiburg in 1897 to take up a chair of national economy in Heidelberg.

Weber, who was about the same age as Troeltsch, had a basic leaning towards political life, was open to philosophical and theological questions, and through the 'Association for Social Policy' and the 'Evangelical Social Congress' had developed a strong interest in social and political themes. Through the 'Evangelical Social Congress' he entered into closer relations with Friedrich Naumann and supported his Christian-Social views, though not uncritically. However, this did not lead to any break in their friendship. In Freiburg he had made closer contact with Heinrich Rickert, challenged his epistemological reflections on the relationship between science and history or cultural studies, and largely shared Rickert's views. Presumably Weber played an important role as stimulus and go-between when in the subsequent period Troelstch both became open to Rickert's neo-Kantianism and found his way into social and political questions and issues of practical social policy.

Marianne Weber has given a careful and critical account of the growing friendship between the two men – critical above all of Troeltsch's part in it. On the one hand she praised the breadth and freedom of his spirit, and his thought which was lively and refreshing, and also vivid. On the other hand, however, she referred to his quite conservative political attitude. She wrote of Troeltsch: '... his strongly bourgeois instincts were alien to social and democratic ideals. He did not believe in so much that the Webers were striving for, either in the intellectual and political development of the working classes or in the intellectual and cultural development of the female sex. And the temperaments of the two men were different: it was enough for Troeltsch that he had to fight for intellectual freedom and tolerance within theology – otherwise he was not a fighter, but concerned for conciliation and balance, and accommodating to human weaknesses.'[47]

The friendship with Max Weber became increasingly close over the course of the next year, above all after Weber had got over the serious illness which for a time condemned him to absence from Heidelberg. The two travelled together to the United States and later they shared a house on the far side of the Neckar.

Further friendly ties also developed with the art historian Carl Neumann (1860-1934) and the philosopher Paul Hensel (1860-1930), but these were not so important academically and intellectually. Carl Neumann, who had done his Habilitation in Heidelberg in 1894 in art history and then had taught there first as a Privatdozent, was particularly close to Troeltsch because of the latter's own interest in art and the history of art. Moreover, as a pupil of Jakob Burckhardt, Neumann was interested in how historical eras are formed; at a later stage he caused a stir beyond the bounds of his more narrow discipline with his thesis that the Renaissance was the maturing of the Middle Ages. Troeltsch repeatedly made mention of Neumann's book on Rembrandt,[48] in which Neumann interpreted Rembrandt's artistic achievement in terms of the 'Nordic' tradition and not Italian baroque. Neumann writes in his memoirs: 'It did not prove easy for the person changed by Rembrandt to become aware of the scope of his new insights in a constant struggle with Burckhardt, especially as respect for Burckhardt had given an almost tragic tension to this long, hard struggle. At this time I encountered Ernst Troeltsch, who came from quite a different background, and we had a long friendship and exchange of ideas. Sometimes we differed in our views, but it was always fruitful.'[49] Later, when Neumann went to Göttingen, Troeltsch commended him to the care and also to some degree to the protection of Wilhelm Bousset. He wrote to Bousset: 'With these lines I would like to commend warmly to you my friend Karl Neumann, who is coming to you as extraordinarius. He is an admirable person and his scholarship is stimulating and bold to the highest degree... However, he is somewhat long-winded, a bit Heitmüllerish, and to that degree you need to be patient with him. But that too brings its rewards.'[50]

There were also closer contacts with the philosopher Paul Hensel, who in 1898 came from Strasbourg to Heidelberg, where he first worked as extraordinarius alongside Kuno Fischer. In contrast to Fischer's predilection for the history of philosophy, he marked out his own special areas in ethics and the philosophy of religion, and also in the somewhat remote themes of philosophy and the history of ideas. He was a follower of Friedrich Naumann and in this respect could find a positive response and readiness for conversation with Weber and later also with Troeltsch. Hensel left Heidelberg four years later to take up an ordinarius chair of philosophy in Erlangen.

What picture does this give us of Troeltsch's life?

The intensive withdrawn work of the scholar who is beginning to develop his position, who has to work out the main lectures in his discipline, was supplemented by and also contrasted with life in a circle of friends. Troeltsch was ready to listen to all sides and to accept ideas of a non-theological kind.

He combined this broad horizon with a great capacity for intellectual concentration, and with this went a concern to make what he had perceived fruitful for his own academic work. Troeltsch would not allow himself to be forced into the preconceived image of a professor of theology. He made space for himself – and used it – for his own work and social converse with other scholars.

On the one hand he did not allow himself to be governed by superficial concern about the opinions of those around him, but on the other hand he was clearly concerned about his academic position, his reputation and his status. And sometimes there is a suspicion that he only played the lively Bavarian with the directness and boldness that goes with that in order to create freedom for himself and avoid contacts with boring people.

Troeltsch made one of his long journeys in 1899. It took him to Siebenbürgen and then on to the Bosphorus. He undertook the journey on behalf of Heidelberg University. He was part of a delegation – which also included Harnack – which went to Hermannstadt for the unveiling of a monument to Bishop Teutsch of the Siebenbürgen Saxons and which was meant to demonstrate the solidarity of the German universities with them. In his New Year's letter to Bousset, which over the years had become a custom, he wrote: 'The stay in Siebenbürgen was always interesting, instructive and enjoyable. Indeed, I believe that the bold, militant feelings of the Saxons there sparked off something in me, or that there at least I had a strong idea of the purpose of human struggles and anxieties. Moreover one also felt that one's own activity and existence had some purpose on encountering the great delight that these people had in the involvement of the universities.'[51]

There was also a literary account of the journey to Siebenbürgen in the form of a report in *Christliche Welt*.[52] Here too Troeltsch's gift for acute observation proved itself. He was able to set the contemporary Saxon Lutheran church of Siebenbürgen in a historical context and made positive mention of the 'untheological' nature of this church. Troeltsch had an eye for real connections, and saw not only the characteristics of the institutional church but also cultural links, local features and economic problems. His description of the formal ceremony showed how at the same time he could evaluate the whole event aesthetically, with a wealth of background humour: 'Like old, weatherbeaten admirals the pastors marched into the church with their cocked hats, the people from the country and the town behind them. At the end the Te Deum rang through the church like a mighty psalm of thanksgiving, for a moment overcoming past, present and future in the presence of the eternal God.'[53]

A critical perspective was part of Troeltsch's real view. He wondered how long this relatively united group of people would survive, and how they could assert themselves against the flood of modern life.

The journey on to Constantinople brought him new impressions. Even in retrospect one can see from his euphoric tone how impressive this detour had been for him. 'It was quite wonderful, the most glorious and the strangest thing that I had ever seen. For the first time I was in the realm of an alien religion and alien customs. One got a very vivid impression of this, and in any case Islam is not so bad a religion. The Turks there are the most respectable people. However, Europeans could not live with such a religion. Of course I have a good deal to tell, but I must keep that for whenever we may meet again. Here I can only note the effect, namely that this journey of two months did an enormous amount for me and spring-cleaned my head and heart in a way that I would never have expected.'[54]

Troeltsch, who kept succumbing to doubts about his capacities and powers, also regarded the journey as a way of recharging his batteries for work. He was a man with a good eye, who could assimilate new impressions in an open and lively way and who saw his travels as a great extension of the possibilities of life.[55]

That was already evident from his first major trip to Switzerland, which he had been promised by the Biarowski Foundation as a reward for his good examination. From Bonn he continued his travels with the trip to Greece that I have already mentioned, and they culminated in the visits to Siebenbürgen and to America, which I shall mention in due course.

II

Defining His Academic Position

1. The role of Christianity in the ideological controversies of the time

Troeltsch's first major scholarly publication after his licentiate work was concerned with the ideological criticism of Christianity which was emerging at that time.[56]

At first sight one might think that Troeltsch was engaged in apologetics, like so many others. But that is not an adequate definition, because a special understanding of the apologetic task lay behind his work. His was an 'open' apologetic which was not *a priori* moulded by a demarcation of interests from other world-views or philosophical positions, but set the self-assurance rooted in the Christian experience of salvation over against other forms of the modern experience of reality. Troeltsch did not want to demote the inner force of religious experience nor to play down the significance of the personal conviction of faith; rather, for him religious experience also involves a world-view which must be investigated in a concern to see the possibility of reconciling it with other modes of thought. There is a need to investigate whether the content of the Christian experience of faith can communicate to modern men and women an acceptable, illuminating way of interpreting the world. It is acceptable and illuminating if it can stand up to scientific insights, or more precisely if it can be reconciled with them.

Theology has to cope with a challenge to the Christian view of the world in the form of a variety of counter-tendencies: with the natural sciences and the acceptance of a regular causality which prevails in them; with the translation of scientific thought into the technological moulding of life; with a sensualism and materialism which appeals to the scientific way of thinking. Theology must take note of neo-humanism which, while accepting ancient tradition, sketches out a new ideal of humanity, which is the expression of a purely immanent intellectual stance with aesthetic components. Finally, the positivist criticism of church and Christianity has to be taken up, in that this criticism attempts to outline a picture of reality opposed to the religious interpretation on a natural and intellectual basis.

For Troeltsch, that at the same time raises the question whether philosophical or ideological tendencies can be recognized which interpret the facts disclosed by the sciences in a different way and which can be reconciled with a religious interpretation. The trends which he finds important here are an idealistic philosophy with an epistemological orientation, a philosophical religious theism and a historical science based on the theory of development.

Troeltsch sees an idealistic way of thinking above all as being in a position to coexist with the Christian experience of faith and the theology based on it. It recognizes 'the priority of mind to nature and creates a theory...that itself incorporates the fact of nature with its mechanical rigidity, apparently so dead and deadly, into the warm and mobile life of the Spirit'.[57] The acceptance of the value of the life of the spirit, the stress on the personal, are for Troeltsch the elements which unite idealism and Christian theology.

I think that we can accept the starting point that theology must be open to the scientific and philosophical trends of the time and must not just be polemic against the spirit of the time (in the sense of a positivism of revelation). The problem arises where faith in the value of the personality, understood in an 'idealist' sense, is harmonized with what is intended in or bound up with the Christian understanding, because the distinction once presupposed between natural and spiritual life can no longer be regarded as apt or requisite. The foundation for the value of the human being as a person which comes from the Christian experience of faith is not attributed to a higher value to be derived from the human being but must be communicated as truth in the face of situations of alienation which have to be perceived existentially. The categorial means for establishing the common basis – the distinction between nature and spirit – comes only from the idealistic tradition. The biblical concept of spirit is not involved here.

In part of his argument Troeltsch remained rooted in certain nineteenth-century traditions and thus left weak points where the subsequent generation of dialectical theologians could attack. For a long time this concealed what e.g. Gogarten, Bultmann and ultimately also Barth had in common, in relating theology and modern consciousness, especially as the new generation of theologians was not agreed in defining what the modern consciousness could be.

Troeltsch remained remarkably vague in the remarks about the understanding of revelation which he made within this framework. First of all revelation is brought close to a manifestation of the intellectual and moral determination of human beings and their personhood, and secondly revelation is spoken of in the sense of a communication 'from above'.[58]

In the question of the absoluteness of Christianity, which he developed further and in a more sophisticated way in later years, Troeltsch primarily presented the standpoint which was dominant in Ritschl and his school: what is decisive for asserting the absoluteness of Christianity is a self-assertion which is addressed to human beings as a 'claim' to truth and finds its expression in their firm assurance of faith. Troeltsch adopts this basis, but modifies it and gives it new accents. First, he sees more clearly and more keenly than is the case in the Ritschl school the development towards modernity in the history of ideas and in world-view, along with the critical question which lies in it or is to be found in it of the possibility of asserting the Christian faith. Secondly, he forces the theological controversy with opposing ideological trends because the reference to self-assurance in faith by itself is not enough for him. And finally, history-of-religions, comparative thought takes on a different significance for him from that which it has with the Ritschlians and in confessional Lutheranism.

The result is that in the question of the absoluteness of Christianity he has to make some qualifications. First of all he thinks it impossible to offer any proof that Christianity is the unsurpassable consummation of religon. That could only happen 'if one has already defined in advance the general nature of religion apart from its final Christian form'.[59]

Secondly, Troeltsch refrains from attempting to derive the supernatural origin of Christianity from an emphasis on inner experience, because he thinks that this would be to restore the old anthropomorphic supernaturalism.[60]

In the standpoint adopted by Troeltsch we can easily see the position from which he is marking himself off. It is less clear what positive support he can find for the form of absoluteness which he assumes. Troeltsch sets himself apart on the one hand from a 'constructive' philosophy of religion which thinks in conceptual terms, and on the other from a dogmatic supernaturalism. Accordingly, he dispenses with any positive proof for the absoluteness of Christianity and writes polemically against drawing false conclusions from the inner experience of faith. Nevertheless, a personal absoluteness with a confessional orientation has to be maintained. This is to be given a purely intellectual foundation, not through proof but through 'demonstration' that the truth-claim associated with Christianity is essentially justified. This demonstration, which seeks to work out how Christianity is in principle unique, will be enough for faith to arrive at the form of absoluteness appropriate to it. Later, Troeltsch will advance further considerations on this point, and his judgment will be more critical.

He also applies ideological criticism to Christian ethics. In this question he assumes a particularly close link between human religious development and the emergence of moral norms. Just as human beings gradually progress from their existence as natural beings to a relationship to God on the basis of a religious deepening of their being, so too the moral development of humankind moves from working out its special spiritual character in relation to nature to perceiving a personal relationship in inter-human encounter.

Here Troeltsch attaches importance on the one hand to the structural similarity of the process and on the other to the dawning recognition of the relativity of moral good which takes place in the course of personal development, so that the course of human development can ultimately issue in the relationship to God. Not only radically religious people like prophets or apostles will be able to identify with the last and supreme expression of this way. According to Troeltsch, the maxims of humane ethics also apply to the person with an average human disposition, and then a religious permeation and intensification is built up on them step by step.

Both the proximity of Troeltsch to Ritschl and the critical distance between them can be seen in this description. In his definition of Christianity as the absolutely moral religion,Ritschl brought ethics generally and Christian faith close together. The resultant connection can be described rather like this: whereas ethical action presupposes human independence, the concept of religion, understood in the Christian sense, signals human dependence. For Ritschl, the connection between the two views comes about in the fact that the person freed for tasks in the world through reconciliation with God can work towards the final goal of creation,[61] which is to be seen in the kingdom of God.

For Troeltsch, ethics generally is concerned with the relationship of human beings to other human beings and to nature. The ends are related to the origin and formation of cultural life. An ethic which derives from the Christian spirit is different. The relationship with God introduces an unconditional element into human life and thus a distinction from all conditions of 'natural ethics'. 'The bliss and security of the disposition which knows itself to be safe in God, the humbly joyful union with the divine being and the elevation of all men and women to this kingdom of the love of God are here the final moral good.'

At this point Troeltsch criticizes Ritschl. He believes that in the interest of bringing the content of natural and Christian ethics closer together, Ritschl has toned down the character of Christian ethics, i.e. its 'transcendence', but also the specific character of humane ethics.[62]

Troeltsch himself adopts a development model in which the connection and the difference between general and Christian ethics can be thought of in terms of historical development. Troeltsch believes that his position is an improvement on that of Ritschl in that it adopts a historical element with a general orientation which takes into account the history of the development of the individual. However, we have to ask whether the definition of the relationship by the development model against the background of a kind of two-tier ethics does not also lead to a toning down of the radical demand.

For Troeltsch, in all theological questions we must take account of the idea of development, the significance of which has already become evident within theology in the history-of-religions perspective. The idea of development has become the dominant concept in the scientific and philosophical discussion of the time. Therefore in questions of dogmatics and ethics theology is challenged to take a more consistent and radical attitude to this way of thinking than previously.

However, according to Troeltsch, anyone who wants to take up the idea of development in theology must construct the Christian world-view on the basis of a philosophy of history.[63]

Here the decisive question becomes whether the idea of development makes it impossible to believe in a self-disclosure of God in history. The way in which Troeltsch raises the question is significant for his view. He does not begin from the truth of the Christian principle of faith, and go on from there to examine the possibility of the truth or correctness of modern conceptuality or ideas, but takes the opposite course, moving from the assumption of the correctness of the concept of development to the Christian faith and its possible implications for the truth. The real reason for this is the change in the spiritual and ideological climate in modernity which I have already mentioned.

For Troeltsch, the application of the idea of development to history does not meant the acceptance of the scientific axiom 'nature does not make any leaps' (*natura non facit saltus*). For him there is an activity in history which 'produces value', which brings forth new things, so that one can speak of relative leaps in development. And in that case, Troeltsch thinks, there is no reason why there should not be a self-communication of God in history.

For Troeltsch, this consideration is a kind of apologetic interim idea, which when thought through consistently points in a religious direction. That emerges in the course of further argumentation. According to Troeltsch, the ideal belief in values cannot ultimately be really saturated by philosophy or a world view: 'If the drive towards an abiding truth is so deep and powerful, and if all ideal faith gains a secure basis only in such a truth, and all philosophical attempts to construct it from the development fall far short of their goal, there is no compelling reason for rejecting the claim of religion that it contains within itself the last and abiding truth of human existence and now reveals that truth from innermost communion with God.'[64] This notion both stresses the possibility of attaching the religious view to a particular kind of interpretation of history and at the same time maintains the 'excessive' element in religion.

But in that case the question is whether what is assumed as proximity on the basis of this interpretation of history is in fact the case, and above all whether it is enough to provide religious conviction with a foundation. For even the references to philosophers like Lotze and Eucken, who believe in an ideal positing of values as a continuum in the face of the variability of values in the course of historical development, at most makes a 'void' conceivable. In Troeltsch's approach, which consists in seeking to find a basis by attaching Christian faith to an understanding of history that 'allows' revelation in history, there is a tendency to succumb to the danger of levelling out the difference between ideal values and religion.

By his argument Troeltsch thinks that he has opened up the way to an 'internal perspective' on the matter, the perspective of faith. From a spiritual perspective, the Christian claim to truth is not isolated; there are possibilities of making attachments and connections. We shall have to see later whether the solution envisaged by Troeltsch here can withstand ideological and philosophical criticism, and above all whether it can be theologically successful.

2. *The independence of religion*

For Troeltsch, his next major work on 'The Independence of Religion' was an organic extension of the first. The more apologetic interest of his first work had put the basic question of religion into the background, so now it had to be retrieved. The new article appeared in 1895/6 in three issues of the *Zeitschrift für Theologie und Kirche*.[65]

Troeltsch's article on 'The Independence of Religion' is a model example of his early attempt at finding a position. He was really attempting too much here. Not without justification, Julius Kaftan criticized him for having failed to assimilate his wide reading completely, and for having illegitimately forced together different positions (cf. the section 'The dispute with Kaftan'). Nevertheless the article sheds light on Troeltsch's knowledge at the time and the solutions he was considering, and it gives us some insight into the problems that were preoccupying him and the way in which he worked.

The leading questions. If religion is a unitary phenomenon that goes with a cultural life and there develops according to its own laws, i.e. independently, the truth-content of religion cannot be communicated through ideological pretensions or an isolated claim to a supernatural truth. Rather, the truth-content has to be derived from the historical development.

That leads to two major complexes of questions. In an investigation into the psychology of religion Troeltsch examines the origin and significance of religion within the human consciousness. For him, only through an analysis of consciousness can 'what can be made out generally about the question of truth in religion' be demonstrated.[66]

The second complex of questions is directed to the regularity and forms of the development of the history of religion; here the question of criteria takes on special significance for the assessment of phenomena.

Given this presentation of the tasks, the question arises how investigations into the psychology of religion and the history of religion are connected. First of all Troeltsch indicates that psychological procedures have developed from individual psychology to social psychology and history. One presupposition of a methodology which adopts the historical perspective is that any possible connection with faith in the sense of a personal religious conviction to be thought of in isolation must for the moment be suspended. For consistency, that means that the starting point cannot be a religious truth posited as a norm, nor can a final religious goal be posited *a priori*. Rather, the goal can only emerge in the course of the development.

If asked about the meaning or possibility of a suspension of personal truthful religious involvement, Troeltsch would probably reply that it is the nature of the historical approach to dispense with or leave open any isolated claim to truth or impact of truth. The reason for this is evident. A Christian theologian who begins from the special character and uniqueness of the Christian experience of salvation does not do justice to the historical view of the phenomenon of religion. Such a theologian cannot take into account the history of religion generally and the consequences of the development towards modernity in particular. Here Troeltsch was criticizing the theology of experience. But this leads consistently to a criticism of the Ritschl school. While that school regarded religion as a totality, as something special, religion thought of independently was only a link, a transition, a way of arriving at the 'independence of Christianity'. The isolation of Christianity which comes about this way is achieved in systematic theology by an approach in terms of a history of revelation, which thinks that it can find security in the form of a 'value judgment' of absolute truth.[67]

The psychological analysis of religion. Systematically, the psychological approach to religion has to stand in first place. First of all it has to be established that religion is a special form of consciousness, which has specific consequences for the will: 'The whole always remains the same: the conception of superhuman powers or realities which are to be worshipped, of such a kind as to be accompanied by strong feelings which lead to some sort of deliberate actions of a cultic and mostly also of a moral kind; the whole dominating a large number of people in tradition and morality and consequently establishing themselves in all kinds of external forms' (*ZTK* 5, 381).

From this basic insight, Troeltsch attempts first of all to define religious experience more closely. He stresses that the whole soul is always active in the emergence of religious experiences. These experiences cannot be grasped by any reference to formal functions of logical and associative connections. Religion is not the satisfaction of an intellectual need, but stills the longing of the human heart, and so is related to questions of meaning.

Thus an important expression of religious experience is associative remembrance. Here we can see the connection between experience and imagination. Imagination creates the possibility of receiving and expressing, through the senses, impressions which are communicated through images, as ideal values for the disposition. So Troeltsch thinks that the notions of a world of ideas which communicate meaning can be distinguished from notions of the world of the sense. The ideas of the beautiful, the good and the divine arise out of the independent, underivable goals of the spiritual life. The emergence of these 'ideas' follows, through reciprocal interaction with the word of the senses, with compelling power and necessity.

The idealist position presented here by Troeltsch issues in a criticism of Kant. The defect of Kant's doctrine of freedom is that it thinks of the world of inner experience in analogy to the assumption of the reality of phenomena – in other words, the principle of causality is also applied to it. For Kant, the difference consists merely in the fact that inner experience is not governed by ideas of space and substance. Hence, Troeltsch thinks, in Kant the question of the reality which transcends the subject and underlies the ideas is ultimately left unexplained. The full extent of the idea of the reciprocal action between human beings and reality is not accepted.

Troeltsch thinks that the distinction between modes of experience is important. In the sphere of the senses, perception comes to the foreground and feeling retreats. The other sphere is the experience of spiritual reality, which itself corresponds to the innermost being of men and women. The value reference to be assumed here indicates some growth in the framework of the moral education of the human race as in that of the individual personality. In this form of philosophy of the mind, Troeltsch is close to Hermann Lotze.[68] At the same time, his reflections on philosophy are influenced, even down to individual phrases, by the views of Wilhelm Wundt (1832-1920).[69]

What Troeltsch finds illuminating in Wundt is above all the way in which thought is bound up with the psychological comprehension of reality (feeling, imagination, will) while at the same time an openness to the transcendent is preserved. The distinction made by Troeltsch between two spheres of perception, his peculiar understanding of the soul – functional, yet underivable and independent – the reference to the history of the development of the spirit, the stress on value judgments which relate to an idea as a sense of value – all these considerations represent an independent combination of approaches which are to be found particularly in Lotze, Class and Wundt.

In deriving religion from psychological factors Troeltsch has to tackle the explanation of religion as an illusion, especially as put forward by Feuerbach. The explanation of religion as an illusion rightly recognizes the practical intent of religious conceptions. However, a naive natural interpretation of religion in terms of fear and the assumption of help which is then produced seems untenable to Troeltsch. The progress of history cannot be made plausible in this way. In religion we have something which arose in an arbitrary way; it is, as Troeltsch says, a 'primal datum of the consciousness'.

The derivation of religion from a human need may gently be made, but the argument must then go beyond this narrow limit. For Troeltsch it is decisive that there is always also an objective element in religious need, because otherwise the connection between the need and the power of the unconditional which encounters human beings is not explained appropriately. It is typical of a thinker like Troeltsch that he does not formulate his argument with Feuerbach simply as a repudiation.

In analogy to the process of knowledge through the senses which comes into being through the reciprocal reaction between the human capacity for knowledge and the organization of the outside world, Troeltsch defines religion as an experience of the reciprocal relationship between the I and the not-I. So he assumes that the meaning of trans-subjective reality is grounded in the relationship with God and can only really be deciphered in this.[70]

So in what way, we may ask, is there talk of God here? Is God as it were apersonally the sense experience accepted by the soul in an act of experience? Or the interpretation of the totality of the impact of reality in the direction of a basic experience? This second notion seems more likely when we read: 'Thus religion rested on experience and built itself up in a sum of individual experiences, in that, grounded on the one hand in the living self-movement of the Godhead who bears us up and on the other in the reaction of the human soul, with the progress of the whole of spiritual life it experienced ever-deeper disclosures of the Godhead and did not establish these disclosures as the possessions of tradition without the involvement of human folly, weakness and sin. It would rest on revelation in the sense of an inner experience, like experiences of the good and the beautiful, and in this way would lend support to the usual belief in revelation...' (*ZTK* 5, 414). Troeltsch does not make it clear how religion can be understood on the one hand as an inner human experience, as the total impact of an encounter with reality in the form of an experience in which the meaning of the world dawns on people, while on the other hand there is talk of the foundation of religion on the deity itself or of a self-movement of the Godhead who bears us up. Here a tension remains between the description of a psychological process and normative statements about the nature of religion or the divine and the quality of the experience to be had with it.

Troeltsch thinks that his approach brings him near to countless theologians from Schleiermacher through the two Dorners, Biedermann and Weisse to Pfleiderer. However, in his view he differs from them by not beginning from a particular philosophical system but from a basic general idealistic approach and understanding religion as living religious feeling. Troeltsch also sees his views as being very close to those of Dilthey, especially the latter's 'introduction to the humane sciences'. However, Troeltsch then qualifies the link with Dilthey by arguing that Dilthey demonstrates consciousness as being what produces the world of the senses and the ideal world, whereas for Troeltsch consciousness comes about through the effect of both the world of the senses and the ideal world. Troeltsch criticizes Dilthey's acceptance of Kant's epistemological criticism and questions both Kant and Dilthey over what with Lotze he calls 'reciprocal relationship'. However, he only hints at this criticism. He accepts the counter-view that the transcendental philosophical approach of which he had accused Dilthey has the advantage of being unilinear and consistent, whereas in his own view psychological and epistemological considerations intertwine in a remarkable way.

Troeltsch reckons that his notion of the origin of religion has brought him only so far as an indeterminate experience. He has not been able to demonstrate a particular attitude of faith within the framework of the psychology of religion. But it is precisely that which he regards as typical. The religious sense that is experienced directly is poor in ideas, conceptually empty. Only afterwards are 'media' added, like the reality which surrounds us, a traditional concept of God or the personality of Jesus as the central medium of the Christian religion.

The experience of God is bound to an experience in which the bond between the soul and God is decisive and ideas only emerge afterwards and represent a support for what is purely experiential. In contrast to the living quality of the experience of God the dogmatics which follows appears a 'fossilization of religion', or 'the herbarium of its dried-up conceptions' (*ZTK* 5, 418). Troeltsch sees it as a kind of straitjacket of which the great religious spirits had known nothing. 'But living religion works through powerful and compelling images of the imagination which elevate and cast down, touch and charm, and in which the danger of a rank and tasteless luxuriance is never avoided. The purest and most powerful means of stimulation is, however, the moral conscience and its experience. Where the moral has differentiated itself so as to become independent knowledge of what should be, it enters into the closest connection with religion and becomes its most important medium' (ibid.).

Troeltsch attempts to explain the connection by incorporating the ethical perspective as it were into the process of experience. But he himself does not seem to see the difficulty which arises when one begins to think in terms of content, i.e. investigates the content of traditional religion and moral demands and seeks possible connections here. Troeltsch wants to avoid this by formalizing the difficulty; he assumes that the religious sense and moral life exercise a mutual attraction and find each other through their shared bias towards the unconditional.

Troeltsch thinks that 'moral purposes... change from the goods of social life within the world to the good of the innermost communion of the purified heart with the primal source of the good' (*ZTK* 5, 418f.). But a problem can be seen at precisely this point. How can the phrase 'primal source of the good' suddenly take the place of the designation 'God' – for here what is meant is not a closer interpretation of God, taking in the Christian tradition, but an independent or, as one can also say, a philosophical idea. The combination of ethics and religion evidently comes about when the concept of religion and its supreme expression, the concept of God, *a priori* stand in a clear connection with ethics.

An analogy to this difficulty is to be seen in the definition of the cult as an essential expression of religion. For Troeltsch, the real nature of religion is 'that human beings live by faith in the reality of a power which goes beyond nature and the senses. Precisely for that reason this faith directly contains the most powerful impact of feeling, which is what is really important and dominant for the practical life of religion' (*ZTK* 5, 422). The cult belongs in this sphere as a kind of ordered continuation of the impact of religious feeling with the assumption that it has an effect back on the Godhead. Cult belongs inseparably to religion, just as a philosophical religion is to be criticized above all because it lacks any living and ordered relationship to God.

Ernst Troeltsch

The understanding of religion which lies in the background here is clearly stamped by late idealistic thought. There the combination of ethics and religion in particular is seen as being constitutive, and spiritualization beyond the constraints of natural religion and the limitations of nationalism is understood as the way of true religion.

With this theme we reach the second basic question under which the categorial and evaluative perspectives of an analysis of religion are discussed.

The development of the history of religion and the question of revelation. Whereas the task for the psychology of religion consisted in marking out by analysis the framework for religious experience which underlies all possible manifestations of religion within history, the history-of-religions question is about the connection between the ground of religion which can be made out by psychology and its concrete form which emerges in history.

Troeltsch has a philosophical presupposition in answering this question. He speaks of a teleological grasp of reality. This assumption is based on a philosophy of the spirit and assumes a process of development in natural and spiritual life. Troeltsch thinks that only in this way can he understand the effective connection between natural and human life with a view to a spiritual potency which stands behind them. For Troeltsch this is not primarily an adoption of Hegel's philosophy or of Enlightenment ideas of development (Lessing), but an attempt to formulate his basic view of the 'progress' of the Spirit, which is significant for him in the progress of the sciences. However, it is clear that here he is also indebted to Hegel. 'The venture must be made to believe in the reason of reality, which with ever new and higher forms reveals itself to human beings and drags them on by the force of facts. It must be endured as a matter of course that the assessment of these powers emerging in this way is dependent on a personal attitude to them and that this judgment must be fought for with the solemnity of conviction' (*ZTK* 6, 77).

Troeltsch does not offer in advance any criteria for assessing the course of the development of religions: 'The criterion grows in and with history itself, in that the higher phenomenon carries within itself the certainty of its greater power and depth' (*ZTK* 6, 78). Thus finding the criteria has a basis in the objective course of history as a higher development. The basic personal assumption lies in the fact that one has a belief in law and development in reality generally, and indeed believes in a meaning which only unfolds itself in the course of development. The 'conviction of the progress and law of history' (*ZTK* 6, 79) is a presupposition of this thought.

We can see that Troeltsch attempted to make theological use of the insight into scientific development which is quite essential for him, instead of employing it to reject Christianity and Christian theology in principle. He accepted historical development as the expression of a spiritual and scientific process, just as he accepted the possibility of the comparison of religions which had become manifest in work on the history of religions, a possibility which put in question the 'absoluteness of Christianity'. His intellectual courage and his lack of concern are to be marvelled at, because on the one hand his personal faith and his trust in the revelation which becomes effective in the history of Christianity seem unbroken, and on the other hand he takes up the systematic and categorial aids of different teachers – like Lotze, Class and Wundt – in the firm trust that the clashes which seem irreconcilable will prove to be truly compatible when scholars have overcome dogmatic constraints. It is clear that Troeltsch mistrusted systems and sought open dialogue.

From a present-day perspective, how far religion is given a criterion by the assumption of feelings of superiority to the 'preliminary stages', by the idea of the inner 'power and capacity for enthusiasm' and the 'capacity for adaptation'[71] in religion, seems questionable. No decision on the question of truth of the kind that is necessary in the formation of criteria can be associated with a reference to the capacity for enthusiasm and power which are contained in the matter.

Presumably Troeltsch, too, was already moved by this doubt, so he added a further consideration. Translated into religious terms, the assumption of a principle of development within the course of history is an idea of the history of revelation. The history of religion appears as a continuing chain of divine revelations to the human race, so that the teleological movement of religion rests on the divine self-movement.[72] By the stress on the objective content of religion, on the basis of a movement of the divine itself, once again the criticism that religion is an illusion is averted. Here Troeltsch takes into account that a modified Christian understanding of revelation is the basis here. Thus the question of the criterion for assessing the development in the history of religion is 'decided in advance' in terms of Christianity. As Troeltsch sees it, this is a result of analysis by the history of religion.

In stressing the objective content of the history of religion on the basis of divine self-communication, Troeltsch knows that he is close to Hegel, and at the same time this leads to a criticism of Schleiermacher. For Troeltsch, Schleiermacher, with his stress on the feeling of dependence and thus the subjective side of religion, did not pay sufficient attention to the historical development.

As for Hegel, Troeltsch criticizes the fact that he thinks of the idea of the self-movement of God as a construct in the light of a concept of absoluteness, and in this way intellectualizes the history of religion. But according to Troeltsch the history of religion cannot be understood from the logical perspectives of progress.[73] It is connected with experiences, impulses, or – from a logical perspective – with 'leaps' which appear suddenly.

As I have already said, Troeltsch's criticism of Kant's epistemology is governed by Lotze's philosophy. Troeltsch saw Kant's solution as an unnecessary retreat to a minimum of knowledge, clad in the subjective presuppositions of manifestations in space and time and the categories. He himself argues that knowledge of the trans-subjective world is quite possible. Here Troeltsch, following Lotze, is governed by a basic metaphysical assumption about the connection between nature and the world of the spirit – by the assumption that a spiritual principle is at work in the world of nature itself, so that the world of nature and the spirit are linked together and there can be advances in knowledge.[74]

Belief in what Troeltsch calls the God-humanity of the history of religion is to be supported by belief in objective laws of the world of the spirit, such as the regularity of the collaboration of individuals and a central essence. Here Troeltsch regards a theistic philosophy of religion along the lines of the spirit of the time and guided by the historical influence of Christianity as having a prior advantage in connection with truth in the form of their possible link with religion.

In his critical discussion of philosophy Troeltsch does not spare the neo-Kantianism of the time. From it he accepts only the general presupposition of a critical analysis of consciousness, but not what one can call its subjectivity. Here the presupposition of all religion, namely that it has to do with a power standing over against human beings, is not sufficiently expressed.

Neo-Kantianism cannot do justice to what Troeltsch describes as an 'interweaving of divine and human effects' (*ZTK* 6, 83). A theology which takes up Neo-Kantianism will stop at the epistemological reflection of the subject and brush aside the question of the trans-subjective world as irrelevant.

This tendency becomes even clearer when Troeltsch understands the idea of the God-humanity of the history of religion as the goal of his reflections. He had argued that the criterion for the progressive self-manifestation of the divine Spirit in the development of the history of religion had to be found *a posteriori*. In connection with this task of thinking through the history of religion there was no discussion of the assumption that the course of the history of religion is grounded in God himself. But that is to omit the vital element from the discussion of criteria and to understand it as a religious presupposition which cannot be derived further. Troeltsch asserts that the course of history has to be followed a posteriori, but at the same time indicates the conditions on which it is possible to talk of an idea of development at all. Here 'development' is seen from the basic aspect of the connection between religion as an independent sphere of life and the whole of spiritual life. All that emerges in the later course of development must already be contained in embryonic beginnings. In the course of history it then proves that through various stages the whole tends towards the form of a goal. Troeltsch has a dialectical understanding of the connection between religion and the life of the spirit generally. Religion is related to the whole life of the spirit, but is not exhausted by it; it has an effect on this whole life and is influenced by it, but its nucleus remains independent.

One criterion which has not yet been mentioned plays an important role for Troeltsch in his assessment of the development of the history of religion. Those religions which can be connected in a living way with mature cultures are regarded as being on a high level of development. The idea of cultural level corresponds to that of 'religious level' and is an element which inspires the finding of a criterion.

In association with the cultural level Christian criteria are accepted as part of the history of religion generally, so that the history of religion appears under a twofold aspect: the possibility of a connection with culture and higher cultural development and the links between historical phenomena and basic ideas of Christian religious feeling. So Troeltsch's conclusion is: 'Even with the strictest scientific objectivity there can be no doubt about it. It is clear that Christianity is the deepest, most powerful and richest development of the religious idea' (*ZTK* 6, 200).

So what was mentioned as a premise in principle also applies to Christianity: its concept of God is the one which is most strongly spiritualized and moralized. All other religions have features of natural religion. They have not thought through with sufficient consistency the elevation of God above the world, because the idea of revelation does not have the same significance in them that it does in Christianity.

Now that does not mean that the difference from other religions which Troeltsch accepts as a matter of principle can be interpreted in such a way that only Christianity is a real religion. But it does mean that Chrisitianity is 'relatively the highest of religions so far' – and in this way the question of absoluteness is solved (*ZTK* 6, 206f.).

The application of the principle of development to Christianity represents a modification, in that to provide content there must be a discussion of central notions of Christianity. What is said to be the 'highest' in Christianity must be defined more closely in terms of itself and in respect of other religions. This view characterizes Troeltsch's history-of-religions and theological understanding, sheds light on the questions which he regards as central, and points towards a solution.[75]

Troeltsch wants to take the task of argumentation further – further, at any rate, than in the Ritschl school. Here there is a difference in the background to his considerations. On the one hand it is said that no more can be demonstrated scientifically than that Christianity is the 'highest level of development within religions and their history known so far' (*ZTK* 6, 206). From this is distinguished a 'claim' which is of the essence of Christianity itself. It is the claim to be the final revelation of salvation, and anyone who assents to this claim experientially has 'absolute religion' for themselves – but that is not tantamount to an academic proof. All that is to be demonstrated is that the claim to absoluteness is of the essence of Christianity. 'Christianity is by nature necessarily absolute religion, and in its faith in God and revelation has the power of absolute religion. Faith in this absoluteness is the nature of Christian belief, the dedication of the whole soul to an eternal truth which renews and perfects human beings' (*ZTK* 6, 212).

It seems to me questionable for Troeltsch in this way to distinguish between an approach in terms of the history of religion and the result which emerges in the light of developments in the history of religion on the one hand, and the personal experience of faith on the other. What kind of approach says of

Christianity that it must necessarily speak of a 'claim'? Is it influenced by personal faith or is it based on considerations from the study of religion? Furthermore, in what way is in fact a distinction made between a general perspective on the study of religion and the emergence of value considerations? And finally, if a distinction has to be made between faith or theology on the one hand and the study of religion on the other, what significance does the scientific approach to religion have for theology? What relationship is to be thought of here?

Troeltsch's understanding of the tasks for the study of religion and theology can be described as follows: the history-of-religions approach suggests that in Christianity we have the 'absolute' religion, in the sense that here we have the highest validity of the religious idea. Christian faith is therefore not in an isolated situation of decision which is represented as the opposition of claim and decision, but has a broad, 'objective' foundation in the form of a comparative treatment and evaluation.

For a theologian thinking 'post-dialectically', a basic difficulty in Troeltsch's ideas lies in the fact that he makes relatively innocent and thus ultimately too uncritical use of the psychology of religion, the sociology of religion and insights from the history and philosophy of religion. The differences in methodology which can be perceived are not maintained radically enough. The assumption that he is dealing with one and the same phenomenon, namely 'religion', sets back the differences in approach and aim – in contrast to materialism and positivism.

Its broad scholarly foundation is a characteristic of Troeltsch's work on the independence of religion. The philosophical and theological tradition is to be taken up in the context of contemporary questions and utilized for his own ends.[76] Here Troeltsch is concerned more with the viability of his position in principle than with its final and irrevocable form.

Troeltsch already indicates the two sets of accents in his work in his theme: on the one hand the emphasis lies on the independence of religion, the impossibility of finding any derivation for it and its special character even in the context of religious criticism. Here the right of religion to its special nature which cannot be replaced by any other capacity of the spirit is to be brought out – a right which has its foundation in its indispensable contribution towards explaining the world and humankind. And secondly, the emphasis lies on the independence of religion. Here it is made clear over against confessional theologies of all shades, and also against the Ritschlians, that the starting point is not to be taken as Christianity, assumed to be independent and grounded in faith, but religion – because Christianity is one religion among others and with these must clarify its 'claim' in the spiritual and cultural situation of the time.

In the light of this twofold aim something can also be said about Troeltsch's future opponents. They were to come, first, from the camp of the positivists and materialists, but also from the philosophers of religion in so far as these did not accept either the independence of religion or Troeltsch's ongoing concern with Christianity. And finally they were to be found among the 'positive' theologians and Ritschlians who could not share Troeltsch's basic philosophical position because it did not seem to them to do justice to the significance and value of the Christian faith.

3. *Collaboration with* Christliche Welt

In the last third of the nineteenth century German Protestantism in its institutional form was an impressive entity. The unity of the Reich under the leadership of a consciously Protestant ruling house meant a close association between Protestantism and the state which was expressed in public life. This external role, and the outward respect that went with it, did not correspond to the internal situation of Protestantism.

Theology and the church were exposed in a variety of ways to ideological attacks and were very disunited. Political questions like the attitude of the church to Social Democracy and the social question generally became disputed issues. Protestantism was split into trends which differed in their opposed assessments of cultural and social development at a time of industrialization. There was the conservative trend which was represented more by 'positive' theology, and the liberal trend which was open to the spirit of the time, to new developments in science and culture, and a more mediating trend. Wide stretches of the population were alienated from the church, especially the workers and the educated. Whereas open rejection largely prevailed among the workers, among the educated the tendency was more towards scepticism and lack of interest, and in both groups for the most part this mainly related to institutional links with the church.

One of the most important tasks of theology and the church at this time was to make themselves comprehensible to these groups in the population. Both the work of the 'Evangelical Social Congress'[77] and the programme and aims of *Christliche Welt* belong in the framework of these problems and aims. Whereas the Evangelical-Social Congress – at least ideally – addressed the workers, the audience of *Christliche Welt* was essentially the educated.

Closely bound up with the personality and capabilities of its co-founder and editor Martin Rade (1857-1940),[78] *Christliche Welt* was neither just a church newspaper nor a theological journal. It sought to take up general cultural questions of the time as well as theological and church questions. The non-theological readers of the paper criticized the increasing shift towards technical theological questions and the academic level that went with it.[79]

Of particular significance in the history of the paper are the extended commentaries on and discussions of theological and church-political events, like the dispute over the Apostles' Creed, the Jatho and Traub cases, and the foundation of the 'Evangelical Social Congress'. The discussion in the theological controversies within *Christliche Welt* was open and frequently very vigorous. The breadth and openness in questions of church politics and theology is unmistakable and reflects the liberal spirit of the journal.[80]

After the dispute over the Apostles' Creed,[81] the idea came up of a review of the discussion and support for those who were indebted to Harnack as pupils. This gave rise to the Eisenach meetings, which are an important chapter in the history of liberal Protestantism. The first meeting was held in Eisenach on 4 October 1892;[82] Troeltsch also took part. At this meeting a statement on the use of the Apostles' Creed was to be worked out. The discussion which was sparked off over this question made it clear that the theologians who flocked round *Christliche Welt* had both a right wing and a left wing. Rade was even afraid that the group might fall apart.[83]

The clash between Ritschlianism and history-of-religions thought which can be recognized in Troeltsch's theological development has as it were a parallel in the fights over direction within the circle around *Christliche Welt*.[84] The verdicts on the person and work of Ernst Troeltsch in this circle are interesting. Thus Ferdinand Kattenbusch (1851-1935), who belonged on the 'right wing', among the Ritschlians, wrote to Martin Rade: 'I'm quite open even about Troeltsch; I can take the rustic fellow. But I don't want even to seem to be acting with him, since my theological views are diametrically opposed to his.'[85] The formation of fronts emerged clearly. Even if personal sympathies also played their part, people like Kattenbusch, Kaftan or Bornemann had quite a different theological orientation from Troeltsch, particularly over history-of-religions thinking.[86]

Within the circle around *Christliche Welt*, Ernst Troeltsch increasingly became the spokesman of the younger theologians, the theological left, who sought to dissociate themselves from the Ritschlianism of the older ones, with their more marked leaning towards the church, dogma and confession.[87]

Already in his Bonn period Troeltsch was invited to give a paper at an Eisenach conference, but declined.[88] He gave his first lecture in 1895, on the 'Concept of Revelation'. He did not approach the theme in an immanently Christian or dogmatic way but in terms of the history of religions, by investigating statements about revelation in the individual religions and only then going into the special features of Christianity on this basis.[89]

The meeting in 1896 was to result in an outburst which Walter Köhler described in his book on Troeltsch. It has often been quoted, and is regarded as a kind of key scene for Troeltsch's understanding of theology and his times: 'The "Friends of *Christliche Welt*" were gathered in Eisenach in 1896; Julius Kaftan from Berlin had given a very learned and somewhat scholastic lecture on the significance of the Logos doctrine; the discussion began, and with youthful élan a young man sprang on to the platform and began his contribution with the words, 'Gentlemen, it's all tottering'. It was Ernst Troeltsch. Then he let loose, and in broad, firm strokes painted a picture of the situation intended to confirm his verdict. This to the dismay of all: as their spokesman, Ferdinand Kattenbusch spoke of a "shabby theology". Thereupon Troeltsch left the gathering, slamming the door behind him. But we young ones listened.'[90]

The scene might almost have come from a play: the young against the old, the youthful hero beginning unconventionally and provocatively, being censured, and making an effective exit. It is remarkable that Rade made no mention of this scene in the next issue of the journal. He certainly says that critical and radical remarks were occasionally to be heard, but his assessment is completely positive.[91]

On the other hand, it is in fact true that 'it's all tottering' is an evocative expression of Troeltsch's idea of the crisis, the changes in the spiritual and religious structure of the times, and what he had already said in his licentiate work about the failure of the old pillars in comparison with old Protestantism.

Troeltsch's thought was evidently less critical on practical social questions and questions of social policy. This impression is given, for example, by his review of Sudermann's play *Heimat*, which may be mentioned as an example at this point. In form and direction the review is of course shaped by the journal in which it was published, *Christliche Welt*.[92]

Troeltsch does not take any offence at the action, which seems very artificial. Because the daughter of Lieutenant Colonel Schwartze does not want to marry Pastor Heffterdingk, she is thrown out by her father. She becomes the mistress of councillor Keller, by whom she has an illegitimate child, has a great career as a singer, and then returns to her home town. There she again comes into conflict with her father. Troeltsch is interested less in the aesthetic than in the ethical questions. He sees two fundamental views of life presented in Sudermann's play, represented by the main characters, Magda and her father. According to Troeltsch these are in no way depictions of types, but of individuals.[93]

The review of this play by Troeltsch displays a quite conservative attitude. Thus he warns against arguing from the views of the father to a defect in the social order. 'Negative conclusions cannot in any way be drawn from his character about the existing order, though he may well be a justified warning to many.'[94] What is really crucial for Troeltsch is the moral and spiritual conflict which arises from the confrontation of two different views of life. The aesthetic ideal of life embodied by the artist Magda is confronted by the moral ideal. Troeltsch sums up his verdict: certainly a playwright is in a position to depict an aesthetic morality of individualism in vivid colours, but '... the need for state order and moral discipline, particularly in the sphere of sexual and family life, is so deeply grounded in the nature of things and human beings that even the most gripping play can only make one doubt it during the moments of one's first confusing impression'.[95] In the end Troeltsch regrets that the playwright has expressed important ethical ideas in the form of a play the content of which is unfortunately based on the influence of the social problem of fashion. One need not advocate a class-conscious aesthetic as does, e.g., Franz Mehring,[96] to recognize that the moral problems of Sudermann's play do not rest on 'social problems of fashion'.

Other contributions by Troeltsch to *Christliche Welt* were doubtless more important theologically, as for example his article 'On the Theological Situation',[97] which bears witness to his interest in principle in the theological situation and which in particular picks up the controversies within the Ritschl school. However, the review of the Sudermann play sheds more light on his personal attitude in ethics and social politics, which is why I have gone into it more closely.

4. The dispute with Kaftan

The critical questions. Julius Kaftan, Professor of Dogmatics in Berlin, reacted critically to Troeltsch's article on 'The Independence of Religion'. The opposing position is already indicated by the title of his contribution: he calls it 'The Independence of Christianity' (1896).[98]

At the beginning of his riposte Kaftan makes a basic theoretical distinction, between the positive sciences on the one hand and philosophy on the other. The sciences investigate what is, and philosophy what should be. The consequence of the epistemological distinction made here is that the religious sciences are not competent to deal with questions of what is the case, of the ideal, but only to investigate the material of historical facts. Christian theology is in principle different from the religious sciences, and belongs to the sphere of the philosophical and the ideal, but here too it has a special nature, i.e. is independent. The foundation of this independence is the character of the Christian religion as revelation, which justifies its claim to absoluteness. At this point Kaftan is at one with the other representatives of the Ritschl school – despite all the differences in detail that can be found. The claim to absoluteness can be affirmed by human beings only in a judgment of faith.[99] A judgment of faith is an act of knowing on the basis of inner certainty. The form of personal involvement is the only appropriate one in the sphere of the ideal.

Kaftan also holds that in questions of religion and morality the historical tradition is of decisive significance. History offers as an authority that which human beings can acknowledge in faith, namely revelation. The community, past and present, is the vehicle of this revelation. But in that case what about the scientific character of theology? Somewhat surprisingly, Kaftan now argues than one can start from the positive religious sciences which say something about the nature of religion and move on from there to theology without allowing oneself to be bothered by a possible claim from the philosophy of religion. One as it were accepts from religious science the general characteristics of religion; the question of the ideal and thus the possibility and the meaning of faith remain untouched by this. But it is simply impossible to accept from a universal philosophy of religion the scientific foundation for

Christian theology. 'However, one thing remains strictly excluded, namely that theology should in any way be grounded in the philosophy of religion. To this extent it must remain in opposition to the philosophy of religion. Revelation, i.e. Jesus Christ, Holy Scripture, is and remains the sole foundation. This is demanded by the faith that we confess and the community which theology has to serve. This also accords with the considerations of reason.'[100] For Kaftan, the philosophies of religion represent a historically changeable element with which theology can form a new union on each occasion. 'These [systems of a philosophy of religion] come and go, and in the great stream of spiritual life are, like the stream itself, subject to change and alteration. By contrast, Christianity abides.'[101]

The exclusion of Christianity from the general historical development constitutes a fundamental difference between Kaftan and Troeltsch, whose precise problem is his insight into the changeableness of Christianity and the consequences for faith and theology which arise from that. For Kaftan, Troeltsch's propagation of the philosophy of religion as the scientific foundation of theology is no real advance on Ritschl. So Kaftan's criticism is above all that Troeltsch has not distinguished clearly enough between a scientific observation directed towards facts and questions about establishing ideals.[102]

Here Kaftan has seen a certain imbalance in Troeltsch's account, which above all is produced by the relic of Ritschlianism that still remains, and which cannot at all points be reconciled with the history-of-religions position.[103] Kaftan seeks to illustrate his critical assessment of Troeltsch's position in more detail at certain points. For example, he very wittily describes Troeltsch's criticism of Kant as a 'modest log', taken to the pyre on which the sinner, who advocates sceptical subjectivism à la Kant, is being burned.[104] Troeltsch has failed to recognize that it is necessary to distinguish between a relationship of consciousness and the real relationship of being. 'Anyone who asserts the independence of Christianity confesses the absolute truth of the Christian faith. For such a person there is no last and highest knowledge alongside this faith. So he will in some way have to demonstrate that our knowledge of the world does not show us any way to the truth here.'[105] When Troeltsch states in his comments on epistemology that in this way he now seems to have come close to Hegel and Schelling,[106] Kaftan challengingly argues: 'To which one can only say, not only "seems to have" but "has", "has" – dear colleague! Only on this presupposition does the thing gain meaning and context.'[107] At a point like this the occasionally very emotional and high-flown style of Kaftan's criticism becomes clear.[108]

The next point criticized by Kaftan is connected with the psychology of religion. Kaftan sees its possibilities transcended in the direction of a judgment of faith or a metaphysical judgment when Troeltsch states as the result of his reflections that religion in the objective sense rests on an independent inner experience of 'divine power'. 'Either empirical analysis and at the right point the transition to the standpoint in the ideal, i.e. to personal conviction, to faith

– or the teaching of religion in the sense of metaphysics; there is no middle way.'[109] Anyone who like Troeltsch puts themselves betwen the two tasks has not advanced far enough in academic self-reflection for Kaftan. Certainly, in fact, here too Kaftan has recognized a weak point in Troeltsch's argument.

A further critical comment is directed against Troeltsch's view of the history of religion. The idea of the 'God-manhood' (*Gottmenschheit*) of the history of religion (here Kaftan gets the term wrong; Troeltsch writes 'God-humanity', *Gottmenschlichkeit*) could only express a conviction of faith and does not belong in the sphere of scientific accounts unless one has metaphysical presuppositions. Finally, Troeltsch has also failed to think through fully the relationship beween person and principle (of Christianity). The important question is whether we have to do with a principle or with the person of the redeemer. In principle, Kaftan thinks that Troeltsch does not want to deny the latter, but probably entertains the view that in the personal impact of faith the Christian religion stands out above the line of historical development as absolute. This leads Kaftan to express the hope that for Troeltsch the idea of Christianity as the absolute religion may prove to be the decisive one.

Troeltsch's retort. Troeltsch answered Kaftan's criticism with his article 'History and Metaphysics'.[110]

He maintains the ritualized forms of an academic response to criticism and at the same time uses them ironically. His retort to Kaftan's critical questions is on the one hand objective and detached, and on the other ironical in its brevity and exaggeration. Kaftan is presented as a kind of theological expert who has the right solutions for Troeltsch's fatal errors. Troeltsch pertinently counters: 'In this portrayal I cannot in any way find a correct description of my true intentions in my articles. Kaftan did not go more closely into this purpose, but has simply assessed me and corrected me by his rules' (ibid., 2).

Troeltsch's procedure is not to go one by one through the points of criticism made by Kaftan and to seek to refute them. Rather, he raises the question of the appropriate method. He sees the difference between himself and Kaftan in the latter's recognition of a special Christian method, whereas he himself follows the usual methods of the secular sciences in his approach.[111] Thus Troeltsch has modified Kaftan's criticism to the degree that he is no longer investigating the relationship between the scientific approach and the evaluative conviction of faith but the difference between a supranatural and a historical-critical perspective.

Troeltsch's objection emphasizes the significance of history-of-religions thought and insists on the validity of the method of historical investigation for all religious phenomena, including Christian phenomena. Anyone who detaches Christianity from its context in the hstory of religion is guided by supernaturalist premises. 'Only someone who touches on the history of religion merely as an apologetic hunter, simply lurking in the wilderness of proofs that the non-Christian religions are of less value, and who does not go through this exalted miraculous world as a quiet and reverent traveller, can bring his supernaturalism home from such forays intact' (ibid., 9). For Troeltsch, the question of the possibility or impossibility of adopting a supernatural approach and thinking supernaturally is the decisive point in the controversy. 'But starting from a similar position to Kaftan I have felt the pressure of historical-critical method much more strongly. Once admitted, it no longer allows us to draw any boundaries and, having been developed in connection with the events of nature, when applied to the supernatural it necessarily dissolves this into the natural, i.e. that which is analogous to everything else' (ibid., 5).

For Troeltsch, the presupposition for the perception of analogies is a 'provisional leaving aside of the question of truth' (ibid., 10). That leads him to dispense in principle with a 'theology of claim' in favour of an (open) philosophy of religion as the scientific foundation for theology, a philosophy of the kind that he intended in the article on the 'independence of religion'. This aim is formulated more clearly on the basis of a heightened awareness of method. All in all it can be said that the second article, which takes up Kaftan's polemic, expresses Troeltsch's ideas more precisely.

Troeltsch takes up Kaftan's criticism of his distinction between principle and person and gives an explanation of it. He describes Christianity as a 'principle' in the sense that here a religion is seen in terms of its whole development and thus of its changes. So he is interested not just in the 'embryonic form' of Christianity but also in the course of its development in the context of an ever-changing cultural situation. However, how the definition of Christianity is related to the significance of the person of Jesus as founder still seems to be an open question. There remains a critical question about his interpretation of the supernatural in view of the difference between the naive religion of Jesus and later 'dogmatic' theology. Now the new element is connected with Jesus' 'claim'.

In the end Troeltsch's remarks are rightly focussed on a special quality of Christianity, so we must ask how they are related to the idea of comparison in the history of religions and a foundation in that history. What is the relationship between comparability and incomparability? Throughout it is clear that Troeltsch assesses the scientific situation and its significance for theology in quite a different way from his opponent. For him the question put to Christianity and to theology is how they can survive in the present crisis. On cultural and ideological presuppositions, demands are made on Christianity which cannot be met by an exclusive supernaturalism. For theology, the scientific situation is characterized not least by historicism. Historicism has opened up a deeper understanding of historical events and historical documents than was available previously. At the same time there is the danger of an ideological relativism which subsumes everything into the process of becoming and so makes it difficult to take up a personal position. But it is no longer possible to go back behind historicism. It cannot be shaken off again, nor is it possible to restore supernaturalism. 'The dangers of the situation can only be overcome by a metaphysics of history which can emphasize the simple, abiding, true element in historical development as its nucleus and offer it to faith on the basis of faith in the rationality of human history.'[112]

Each of the two opponents, Kaftan and Troetlsch, has seen weak points in the other's position and has marked out clearly the task which faces him. The remarkable thing about the confrontation between them is that within the spectrum of the Ritschl school Kaftan is the one who through his understanding of theology to some degree comes closest to Troeltsch. In contrast to Ritschl himself, Kaftan is concerned to take up the history of religion; moreover, in a more fundamental way than Ritschl and Ritschl's other pupils he has an eye to the relationship between epistemology and theology. Finally, in contrast to Ritschl Kaftan does not dispute the significance of mysticism for the understanding of Christian faith. However, he differs characteristically in his aims from Troeltsch, for whom the orientation and task of the history of religion and also the mystical element in faith and religion stand in another context.

In his 'refutation',[113] Kaftan responded to Troeltsch's account and criticism, and then the controversy came to an end, at least externally. Kaftan pointed out that his questions had been about method. Now Troeltsch was insinuating that his real motive was the idea of supranaturalism and its defence. But that was no answer to the charge that Troetlsch's method was contradictory.[114]

Kaftan had seen rightly that Troeltsch had still to define precisely what he meant by the 'absoluteness of Christianity'. The question of the relationship between revelation and history proves to be a central theological point of difference between Kaftan and Troeltsch. For Kaftan, the conclusion here is that Christianity has no possibility of existing nor any reason for continuing to exist without a supernatural faith in revelation. Troeltsch cannot, Kaftan concludes, want to maintain the absoluteness of Christianity while at the same time rejecting supernaturalism.

That Julius Kaftan had little inclination and ability to work towards a real understanding of Troeltsch's position, and how clearly he repudiated Troeltsch academically and misunderstood him personally, is clear from the correspondence between the brothers Julius and Theodor Kaftan.[115] When Theodor Kaftan had to give lectures on Troeltsch at a theological conference, he wrote to Troeltsch and asked what books he should use as a basis for his judgment. Theodor Kaftan told to his brother that Troeltsch had replied in an amiable way and spoken of his theology 'as a kind of hibernation of Christianity for better times'.[116]

To which Julius Kaftan replied: 'Do you want to speak on Ernst Troeltsch? I hope you will have what you say published. Perhaps I shall then learn to understand what is really new and great about this man.'[117] Julius Kaftan then pointed out that Troeltsch had started out from the Ritschlian school. He continued: 'He is no longer aware of this connection, of course not; that won't change anything; I am only suprised that he now thinks that we others could have learned it from him. This is in the background for him, and in the foreground is the Enlightenment. The unprecedented turning inside out of everything so far, which Troeltsch is called on to proclaim, is for me the X that I do not understand. In the lecture I have mentioned ["The Absoluteness of Christianity and the History of Religions"] there are attempts at formulation which are based on a simple confusion. Karl Holl, who in general basically also thinks that the man is no more than the programme which he keeps re-inventing, referred me to "The Historical in Kant's Philosophy of Religion", and said that that was a solid work.'[118] However, Julius Kaftan took no pleasure even in this historical work and wrote: 'Is that what the "historical" method is supposed to be, whereas according to Troeltsch all the rest of us have a dogmatic (i.e. dogmatistic) method? Besides, Niebergall has repeatedly told me that there is also a Troeltsch who flees from the world, who sometimes even gains the upper hand in him. Perhaps this is the one who wrote to you about the hibernation of Christianity.'[119]

The controversy with Kaftan involves all the central questions relating to the philosophy of religion and theology which occupied Troeltsch at that time and were to do so in the immediate future. What is left open is above all the question of the 'absoluteness of Christianity' and the precise definition of the historical method in relation to theology. If we add that a foundation for theology in the philosophy of religion appears more as a desideratum than as something that is really described, then we have identified the decisive problems which would continue to occupy Troeltsch and awaited a solution.

5. Historical or dogmatic method?

Friedrich Niebergall's critical remarks and Troeltsch's answer. In the controversy with Kaftan, Troeltsch was concerned with the fundamental question of the tenability of supernaturalism in the form of a doctrine of the supernatural revelation of salvation, attaching to the person of Jesus, in view of a historical approach which took up the broad development of the history of religion and from there attempted to reflect on the question of personal commitment to faith.

Troeltsch defended this historical approach in countering objections from Kaftan's disciple Niebergall. In an article 'On the Absolute in Christianity'[120] Niebergall had criticized a pantheistic view of religion in Troeltsch. For Troeltsch, he argued, religion proved to be involved in a development in the history of revelation in which Christianity at best represented the conclusion of the development. According to Niebergall the presupposition for this assumption was a relativism which was itself postulated with historical thought, a relativism which could not find any absolute within history. His opposing position ran: 'We believe that the focal point for our generation lies in the past. We believe that we have attained the highest point there, and will reach no higher. And this point is Christ... Therefore we assert that only so much in other religions rests on revelation as corresponds with the Christian religion.'[121] Niebergall accused Troeltsch of having a twofold concept of the absoluteness of Christianity: first absoluteness was the highest form of religion so far, and secondly he spoke of absoluteness 'in the sense of a direct derivation from God'.[122] The relationship between the two concepts was totally unclear. Niebergall doubted whether Troeltsch in fact made an unprejudiced study of the whole breadth of the history of religion, as it were with a cool gaze, in order then to find the ideal of religion. 'But what happens is that before one extracts it [the ideal of religion], one has put it in.'[123] Niebergall comments that Troeltsch's procedure certainly shows a great sensitivity to the characteristics of other religions; nevertheless the central objection remains that '... the absolute character of Christianity can only be established by an investigation of the subjective factors of the heart and the conscience, which have nothing to do with considerations in the philosophy of religion'.[124]

Troeltsch similarly sees the decisive difference between him and Niebergall in the sphere of method. He describes this difference as that between dogmatical and historical method. His article 'On Historical and Dogmatic Method in Theology'[125] attempts to develop his own procedure in more detail.[126]

Troeltsch describes the historical method that he represents as follows. Three aspects are basic to it: historical criticism, the noting of analogies and the recognition of the reciprocal relationship between historical phenomena.

In principle, historical material has to be accepted critically. It follows from this that all judgments can be made only in terms of probability, because one has to be open to new discoveries, new source material and the new perspectives that these bring. The critical approach changes one's relationship to the traditional material in so far as it dissects it, makes hypotheses about its correctness and thus remains at a critical distance from it. Therefore from the point of view of method the whole content and all the modes of tradition, including religious tradition, have to be treated in the same way.

The second piece of historical criticism which makes criticism possible at all is the perception of analogies. Individual methodological concepts thus run into one another and indeed condition one another.[127]

The historical method begins from the assumption that an element of the tradition has analogies. The perception of these comes about through reflection in the field of one's own experiences, and that reflection is transferred to history. So the interpreter is in a position to associate his own judgment with that which comes over from history. If the historical perspective is sharp enough, analogies can also be perceived in the broader historical tradition. Here Troeltsch speaks of the 'omnipotence of analogy' (*RH*, 14). In his view the history of theology shows that people have ventured less and less to present pieces of the Christian tradition as being without analogy. The moral character of Jesus and the resurrection are still such remnants.

The third characteristic of the historical method is that of correlation.

Correlation means that no historical phenomenon stands in isolation, but rather has precedents and concomitant phenomena associated with it. Correlation relates to the way in which one historical phenomenon is interwoven with others.[128]

For Troeltsch, as he now says, these are 'principles' of historical thinking and working. For him, the art of the historian lies in being sensitive to what the tradition says, so that the character of the material can be perceived. At the same time it must be remembered that the changes in historical life are part of its character. 'The historian's ultimate problems arise from the attempt to understand the nature and basis of the whole historical context and to arrive at value judgments regarding its various forms' (*RH*, 15).

The theological relevance of the methodological dispute. Troeltsch's 'three aspects' of the historical method are recognized today in academic theology and his account has become almost a classic. However, some scholars would no longer follow Troeltsch's identification of historical method with the idea of a history-of-religions theology. To recognize that Christianity as a historical phenomenon is bound up with the history of religion and culture generally does not mean that individual passages in which experience is reflected can only be understood in terms of the general idea of religion. Understanding arises from an encounter with a living expression then, as it takes form in the text, and the quest for meaning in life today. Troeltsch doubtless allows the 'historical method' to end up in his own overall theological view in too much of a straight line and in only one dimension. In my view a hermeneutical theory could have helped to clarify the questions discussed by Troeltsch here. Troeltsch himself probably thought that he could dispense with such a theory – although it was available to him along the Schleiermacher-Dilthey line – by taking the individual tradition in the overall course of history and bringing this into a metaphysical connection in the light of the concept of the spirit.

What speaks decisively for the historical method is that it is in a position to bring the past alive and to communicate new insights. According to Troeltsch, anyone who adopts it, admits it at one point, cannot draw back: 'Give the historical method an inch and it will take a mile. From a strictly orthodox standpoint, therefore, it seems to bear a certain similarity to the devil' (*RH*, 16).

Troeltsch's description of methods as dogmatic on the one hand and historical on the other clearly contains a value judgment. In terms of value the designation 'historical' as applied to method is to be equated with 'modern', while 'dogmatic' can also stand for 'antiquated' or 'unscientific-ecclesiastical' method.[129]

That the general prejudice of educated Protestantism against the dogmas of the church, which had been widespread since the Enlightenment, is taken over by the systematic theologian Troeltsch in so pronounced a way, is certainly also to be explained in terms of the cultural and political situation of the time.

The Kulturkampf and Vatican I had intensified the criticism of dogma in connection with the repudiation of Ultramontanism, and educated Protestants felt that they were faced with the choice of either accepting piety as a private view or separating understanding and faith. Troeltsch is the most prominent theologian of the time to seek a way of holding together faith and critical thought as it were from within. He conjectured that all the characteristics of historical method – criticism, analogy and correlation – would have a destructive effect on the dogmatic method: what would be destroyed would be false certainty in the face of history, the idea of uniqueness in the sense of a complex of salvation history, and the idea that Christianity was a closed system. It is clear how the assessment of the method as 'dogmatic' is derived from the contrast with 'historical'.

Troeltsch's view is that two different metaphysical principles underlie the historical and the dogmatic methods. In one case there is the assumption of the overall context of the universe and the spiritual activity of human beings in history; the question of principles for evaluation has to be derived from that. In the other case, that of the dogmatic method, a metaphysical principle arises in the form of miracle and an authority with a supernatural foundation. Troeltsch simplifies by putting the question of method in a pointed way: either the unqualified recognition of the historical process, associated with general basic assumptions about history and value, or a metaphysical principle in a narrower theological sense which requires for its object miracle, a special epistemological method.

Troeltsch expresses his own position in assuming that there is a real breakthrough of the bond between religion and the rooting of the spirit in nature at only one point in history, namely in the religion of the prophets of Israel and in the person of Jesus. The religious power given here which brings inner conviction is the decisive characteristic in any talk of a new starting point for historical development.

Here, of course, we have to ask whether the idea of a development in the history of religion is being maintained consistently if such qualitative levels are assumed. Troeltsch would object that the significance of the comparison made in advance is that it avoids the impact of miracle, special causality, and salvation-historical thought with the assumption of two levels of reality.

In so far as the narrowness and intolerance of the breaking through of history in outward miracle, communicated as a finished doctrine, is shown up by the objection in terms of the history of religion, and the previously closed character of the salvation-historical mode of thought is broken up by a critical process of reflection and evaluation, one could describe this idea of the entanglement of Christianity in the history of religion generally as ideological criticism. In that case we have to ask how the critical thinking intended by Troeltsch could be taken up and preserved without being developed into a history-of-religions theology which assumed the constant comparability, nearness and parallelism of religious phenomena – which would in turn become an ideology.

However, Troeltsch was one of the few who assessed correctly and systematically the significance of the historical method for theology and the consequences which follow from it. As has constantly emerged in the more than eighty years since Troeltsch's article, the dispute over the legitimation and limitations of the historical method confirms Troeltsch's talk of the 'dynamite of historical method' for theology generally.

Today as then the basic question is whether or not the biblical texts can claim special rights in their interpretation on the basis of a prior evaluation grounded in the Christian faith. Karl Barth's discussion with Adolf von Harnack brought out the problem clearly in the context of the rise of dialectical theology.[130] And not least, this is also the methodological background to the debate over existentialist interpretation. A standpoint of post-critical exegesis of scripture which has emerged in recent years has felt able to speak of the need for historical method to be supplemented by a reference to the special claim of the tradition.

It is to the credit of Troeltsch that he was the first to perceive the methodological connections, the theological aspects and consequences of historical-critical work, to work out the principles of the new method and to see an ongoing problem in the relationship between exegesis and dogmatics.

III

In the Prime of Life and Activity (1900-1915)

1. Broadening his academic interests and establishing a goal

Whereas Troeltsch's first years at Heidelberg could be regarded more as a time of orientation in an academic and personal sense, the following period demonstrates more strongly and markedly his influence outside Heidelberg.[131]

The dispute with Kaftan, characteristic of the initial years, was the repulsing of an attack. Now Troeltsch himself took the initiative, not in direct attacks on other persons and positions, but in deliberate argument with them. This was true both of his acceptance of the theme proposed by Harnack on 'the essence of Christianity' and of his entry into discussion with Wilhelm Herrmann on ethical questions. Moreover in this period Troeltsch wrote two major historical works, *Protestant Christianity and the Church in Modern Times* (1906) and *The Social Teachings of the Christian Churches and Groups* (1911).

When Troeltsch wrote in a letter to Wilhelm Bousset, 'I'm always being hounded',[132] he was certainly saying something important about what he felt about life. The goals that he set himself, the pressure to which he exposed himself in order to discipline himself and make progress, were enormous. Even if one takes into account his proverbial vitality for coping with this burden of work, the impression remains of an effort which physically and psychologically went to the limit.

Troeltsch's way of working and his aims on the one hand give the impression of being planned and on the other seem discontinous. It makes good sense for a young theologian to attempt to get an overall view by intensive reviewing, and to take stock in a major systematic work of the basis he has chosen for his work and his aims. Is it not a good and well-considered plan then to engage in controversies and publish larger works? But on the other hand Troeltsch makes quite a different impression. He reacts very quickly to the demands of the present and allows himself to be influenced by persons and events. Plans are postponed and new commitments are taken on. Here Troeltsch often prefers the programmatic approach which analyses problems and indicates solutions but only just hints at, or completely omits, their systematic execution. However, both the planned and the contingent belong together on a higher level, and are an expression of his personality and his view of life. They have their foundation in specific capacities and limitations of Troeltsch's person, and are at the same time the expression of a basic philosophical and theological position which is as indebted to what is seen and required by reason as to the irrationalisms of life. The polarity which emerges in his work, his overall situation and his activity made it possible to increase productivity, but also led to difficulties. Troeltsch mentioned these problems quite openly: 'But I have to confess that I have not succeeded in bringing the separate streams together and that I follow impressions and feelings more than the need for the development of a strict conceptuality. I have a marked tendency towards an anti-rationalistic affirmation of life, but there are great difficulties in combining this with the rationalistic features of my thought and any thought.'[133]

2. A change in private circumstances

In the summer of 1900 Troeltsch had some news to pass on to Wilhelm Bousset: he had become engaged. The letter came from Toitenwinkel, a village near Rostock. Troeltsch wrote: 'I have been here for six weeks on the estate of retired Captain Fick with my fiancée, to whom I became engaged in the last days of the semester. I had made her acquaintance in Heidelberg during the winter. I had been missing bitterly that almost daily company which only marriage provides, and all the time could find no inner repose. Now I think that in a quite splendid girl, particularly noted for her affectionate nature and firmness of character, I have really found a consort who understands me and from whom I may expect my and her happiness.'[134] In April of the next year, Troeltsch could report to Friedrich von Hügel (1852-1925)[135] that he was in process of making a home of his own. According to Troeltsch, his fiancée, later his bride, came from quite a different background from his. 'She is the daughter of an officer and landowner in Mecklenburg and is completely from the conservative world. Her family has cast off or lost a former Swedish title, I don't know all the details. At any rate, this has given me some contact with completely different social circles.'[136]

The marriage took place on 31 May 1901. As an 'ideal' combination one could have wished for Wilhelm Bousset as best man. At any rate he was invited.[137]

The letter to Bousset announcing his engagement and its description of the situation suggest that Troeltsch, now thirty-six, had yet to get rid of his remarkably 'rational' ideas about marriage. He had no close companion, could not find any inner repose; now his inner state had improved. This basic attitude is matched by his later account to Bousset, just a short time after the wedding: 'However, this time of getting to know each other and living together is not very conducive to work and study. To begin with, one's former life-style is completely disrupted and it takes women time to understand that husbands have work to do and that the (?) focal point of their being lies in their work.

But all that will come about gradually, and then things will get more and more pleasant.'[138]

We may leave open the question how far Troeltsch found what he evidently looked for in a marriage, namely pleasant companionship which at the same time helped his work on. Marta Troeltsch seems to have been a somewhat frail woman, prone to becoming overwrought. Troeltsch speaks of a nervous heart disease or a nervous illness, and there is often mention of biliousness. In other respects, too, she does not seem to have been the easiest person to get on with. Because only a few accounts of Troeltsch's family life are available, it is worth including some evidence here which perhaps sheds some light on it. When Troeltsch's publisher Siebeck announced a visit to Heidelberg and said that he would also like to visit the Troeltschs, Troeltsch had to confess: 'She [his wife] has strictly forbidden me to have any guests when she is not present, because she does not fully trust the competence of her maid, so when I heard of your intention to come I did not dare to go against this prohibition and have given my colleague Schöll the honour of accommodating you.'[139]

The state of Marta Troeltsch's health seems to have improved only after the birth of their only child, Ernst Eberhard, in 1913. The long period without a child also seems to have been a burden for Troeltsch, not least also because of his wife.[140] When he reports the birth of his son to von Hügel, his joy is quiet rather than exuberant, and he also attaches importance to the beneficial effect on his wife's nerves.

It is impossible to say precisely to what degree Troeltsch's wife took part in her husband's scholarly work and perhaps even shared in conversations. Only later does she seem to have been intensively concerned with Troeltsch's work. Carl Neumann reports a meeting with Marta Troeltsch which suggests this.[141]

In Gertrud von le Fort's novel *Garland of Angels*, in which she fictionalized her recollections of Heidelberg, the wife of the 'guardian and professor' also plays a role.[142] The woman is called 'Silk'. This can mean two things: exclusive, brilliant, but also 'superficial', because it 'shimmers', makes an external effect. From the context the latter meaning seems to me to the one here: superficiality, because 'Silk' joins in everything and thinks that she can talk about anything. It is characteristic that the professor goes along with his wife with great good will, and indeed even gives way to her.[143]

A sentence which Troeltsch wrote down in his 1891 examination sermon and which makes it clear that scepticism was an element in his make-up may be an apt comment on his relationship with his wife and also with other people. 'Human love can never make two people one, can never give completely and receive completely. There are still always two people, each of whom have to support themselves.'[144]

3. Collaboration with the Evangelical Social Congress

The Evangelical Social Congress was an association for analysing social problems at a scholarly level, founded in 1890 in connection with the increased emphasis on the social question by theologians (A.Stöcker and L.Weber) and national economists (e.g. A.Wagner) in the Kaiser's Reich. How it differed from Social Democracy in principle was evident. Given the atmosphere in politics and the church, the decrees on social questions promulgated by the Kaiser in February of that year encouraged the foundation of the Congress and the beginning of its work. The more the Kaiser dissociated himself from the social and political aims expressed in the decrees ('Anyone who is a Christian is also "social", so to be Christian Social is nonsense'), the more markedly the Congress came into the firing line of the Evangelische Oberkirchenrat and official politics. Stöcker resigned in 1896 and founded a parallel conference with a more conservative stance (the Church Social Conference).

In the view of Marianne Weber, during the first years of their acquaintance in Heidelberg Troeltsch was not very open to social questions. On the whole, his political views seemed more conservative.[145] It fits this assessment that Troeltsch found his way into the Evangelical Social Congress only at a relatively late stage.[146] He took part in a congress in 1904 and gave a paper there. By then the Congress already had a history of fourteen years behind it; in both its origin and its history it was a significant reflection of contemporary Protestantism and its grappling with social questions.

The Evangelical Social Congress may be said to be a specifically Protestant institution in that it was more an organ with an academic orientation which sought to influence through teaching; its social policy tended more towards the provision of information and the exchange of opinions, and in social ethics its main stress was on an appeal to the conscience. The members met annually and aimed to arrive at an understanding on questions of social politics and social ethics through lectures and discussions. It can certainly be said that by its own intention the Congress was focussed on practical matters in social life, but both the lectures and the contributions by members of the Congress to the discussion largely remained at a theoretical level. Moreover the talk had a marked theological and ecclesiastical colouring, which got in the way of the wider influence that was hoped for. Such talk in the Congress's own circle hardly matched the social reality with its conflicts and the domestic political difficulties which arose as a result. Moreover, its members were largely above being corrected by those who were chiefly affected both socially and politically, i.e. the workers.[147]

Consequently only a very limited effect was to be expected from the proposals and resolutions of the body, since there was little possibility of its influencing those with political power. However, reservations about the external effectiveness of the Congress should not be emphasized so much that they obscure the historical contribution made in the purpose expressed in its foundation and activity, namely a concern with social problems in a form anchored in an actual organization.

In his *Social Teachings* Troeltsch described the Congress as a model of the type of 'mysticism'.[148] Here, for him, the basic ingredient of this type, the free exchange of ideas, a shared disposition, had become reality, without any fixed organization but also without the narrowness of a sect. The advantage and the weakness of the Congress were directly connected. Troeltsch could agree with the basic attitude expressed in the work of the Congress, but had doubts about its effectiveness for social and political life.

Whereas when the Congress was founded it had been assumed that it could provide a forum for discussing social questions in the spirit of the gospel, transcending all interests of party politics, it soon emerged that the integrating formula, 'Christian social commitment', was not enough. Rather, theological and political controversies arose which had their foundation in individuals and the programmes which they represented. First, mention should be made of Adolf Stöcker, his influence and his following. Politically, Stöcker was still under the sway of ideas about the nation state, and his social politics was dominated by the idea of aid that could be given in a patriarchal guise. His aim to win the working class for the church was combined with a sharp repudiation of Social Democracy.

A group round Friedrich Naumann (1860-1919) increasingly criticized Stöcker's ideas and following. This group stressed the need for social aid without direct church-political motives. The summons to social action arising from the gospel was to be understood as free Christian concern. Naumann thought that forms of personal initiative by the socially weak were essential, and moreover wanted to keep away from party-political narrowness. He later gave up the idea which he had first put forward, that social action could be derived directly from the gospel, and increasingly called for comprehensive measures in social policy by the state.

Two events in the history of the Congress before the year 1904 are of particular significance. First is Harnack's 1894 lecture on the social question in the history of the church, which sparked off a theological controversy. A biblicist and politically conservative trend made a noisy protest against Harnack's basic theory that the way in which the social task of the church was expressed had changed over the course of time, whereas the basic forms of its aim and social action had remained the same. The other event was connected with the first lecture by a woman. Elisabeth Gnauck-Kühne spoke at the 1895 Congress in Erfurt on the social position of women. The arguments with which the appearance of a woman were both rejected and defended are interesting. For even those in favour largely imply a form of critical dissociation, since the real sphere of women's work was seen as being the home. Martin von Nathusius, a professor of theology in Greifswald, was in favour of the Congress taking up the question of women's rights, but he was against a woman appearing at the Congress to give a paper. The appearance of Frau Gnauck led him to resign from the Congress.[149]

The subject of Troeltsch's lecture at the 1904 congress in Breslau was 'Christian Ethics and Contemporary Society'. For publication, Troeltsch chose the title 'Political Ethics and Christianity'.[150]

Troeltsch based his thoughts on the question what spiritual and political forces within the modern view of the state might be expected to produce a political ethic. He distinguished four forces or groups. First liberalism, whose view of the state is determined by limiting the state to questions of external order and the formation of economic power. Along with this the state is given a certain protective power both externally and in spiritual and religious terms. Here, according to Troeltsch, the devaluation of the idea of the state is obvious.

His second grouping was nationalism. This understands the nation as an orientating and normative power for politics and society. This perspective gives rise to a moral solemnity which expresses itself above all in the idea of the subordination of the individual to the principle of community. For all his approval of nationalistic feelings and nationalistic attitudes, Troeltsch could not see this principle as an appropriate basis for the development of a political ethic. One thing which already told against this, as far as he was concerned. was 'all the ghastly nationalistic bunkum that has gripped the peoples of Europe with a mixture of romantic ideas about the national spirit and the democratic awakening of the masses, pitting one against the other in senseless arrogance'.[151]

There remained only two other groups and the basic political views which went with them: democracy on the one hand and conservatism on the other.

Democracy, taken as a political principle, is based on the idea of human rights and stresses the moral right of the individual. The democratic constitution aims at the most equitable human participation possible in the material and spiritual goods within the commonwealth. According to Troeltsch, the presupposition for democratic thinking is a teleological view of reality which aims at a victory of rationality and ethics.

By contrast conservatism, understood as a political principle and the basis for a view of the state, rests on the assumption of human inequality. The different spiritual and social endowments or presuppositions are understood as natural necessities and not as a destiny to be overcome.[152] The slogan of conservatism is that authority, not majority, is the decisive factor. Social responsibility shows itself in a concern for the socially weak on the part of rulers and those with possessions.

It is not easy to discover Troeltsch's position in this account of political views and forces, because the principle for his analysis is a sympathetic approach to the self-understanding of a group or basic notion. On the one hand he wants to work out the historical manifestations of a particular view of the state from within, and on the other hand he attempts to trace connecting links among the various views, and between them and Christianity. The demonstration of historical threads and possible connecting links and the rejection of a position which stands above all this, along with the partial affirmation of a view, makes Troeltsch's remarks as stimulating as they are difficult.[153]

Christianity is not represented among the principles mentioned, since for Troeltsch no political ethic can be derived directly from the Christian idea. Christianity belongs in the personal sphere or – in ethical terms – in the sphere of private morality. So the effect of Christianity on political ethics can only be an indirect one. Therefore it is important to investigate individual views of the state to see whether and how Christianity can exercise any influence on their ethical conceptions.

Troeltsch's basic notion is that since religious ethics are by nature 'international rather than national',[154] their influence on the political disposition is shown within the framework of democracy and conservatism. Democracy can take up Christian ideas of freedom and personality; conservatism ideas of authority, obedience and order.[155]

Troeltsch distinguishes between the central religious idea of Christianity in the form of love of God and neighbour and concomitant religious ideas in the form of the conception of personality and the notion of order. The central idea has validity only in the sphere of personal life, the private sphere. The concomitant ideas are to be seen in the wake or the orbit of the central idea and have a tendency to influence communal human life in state and society. The difficulty is that the basic possibility for the concomitant ideas lies in the central idea, so that they are thus directly connected with it.

Troeltsch's interest in this distinction, which can probably be regarded as a modification of the Lutheran two-kingdoms doctrine, has the following basis. On the one hand it can stress the unpolitical character of the central Christian idea; on the other it can confirm a twofold tendency in Christianity both towards revolution as the principle of change and towards conservatism as the principle of maintaining and preserving.

Troeltsch now adds a theological basis to his argument. Only in the sphere of love of God and love of neighbour is God identical as a reality in the world and as a principle of grace; with their emergence from the sphere of inwardness 'its [Christianity's] ideas necessarily move into a polarity'.[156]

But how, historically and in terms of effect, is there an indirect influence of Christian ethics on corresponding political views? The possible connections can be realized in history through the conservative view that some things are superior and some inferior, which holds regardless of religious confirmation. It is possible to combine Christianity with a democratic view on the basis of the relationship between human beings and God which does away with all inequalities and offers freedom. The historical realization of this possibility is above all associated with the natural law of the natural equality of human beings.

The idea of natural law and the reactionary consolidation of the idea of order are to be regarded as 'additional ingredients'. Additional ingredients can be recognized as such with the help of historical thought. At the same time it transpires that Christian ethics cannot be the norm which produces all other moral ideas. Here Troeltsch gives an answer to the question whether a Christian political ethic is conceivable. It is inconceivable for him because there is no such thing as a Christian political ethic, but only a contribution of Christianity to political ethics.

The central religious idea of Christianity cannot become effective as a principle of political ethics, but only the 'concomitant ideas' in the form of the

Christian view of personality and the religious idea of order. In further developing his ideas Troeltsch presents a gradated ethic, depending on whether the religious norm or the higher moral ideal of the inner life is elevated above the humane ethic.

We can thus see that Troeltsch's own position on the whole tends more strongly towards an aristocratic, conservative way of thinking, for all its references to the principle of social responsibility and to links with democracy, which in principle are equally possible. The Christian idea, he says in a characteristic phrase, will 'resist all blandishments of natural law and egalitarianism, and will always recognize personhood only in terms of moral substance. It will never assent to the identification of these ideals (in the interests of the class struggle) with the spirit of the proletariat or with opposition to the ruling classes. It will always demand that modesty and patience, humility and respect, obedience and readiness for service remain moral ideals...'[157]

The impression of a more marked personal leaning towards conservatism is not decisively corrected by the fact that this too is criticized. Troeltsch's critical attitude is shown in the fact that for him the prevailing order is not to be defended at any price. Here is his fundamental objection to all radicalisms, to all the exaggerated expressions of a principle, whether from the political right or the political left. At all events, we can see that the democratic principle of equality is subjected to sharper criticism.[158]

To round off the overall picture and as an indication of Troeltsch's political position, another fact is significant. When Troeltsch again took part in a congress in 1907, the Freiburg national economist von Schilze-Gaevernitz was giving a lecture on 'Culture and Economy. The Neo-German Economic Policy in the Service of Neo-German Culture'. For the speaker, the nation was the highest of all cultural values; as such it was closest to religion. For him, nationalistic and social policies could not be opposites; the nationalistic and the social had to continue to be related.

In a long contribution to the debate Troeltsch criticized the idea of a 'Neo-German' culture. For him, cultural work had to transcend nationalistic frameworks; in the case of Germany it had to include Europe, and over and above that it had to link Europe and the New World together. For Troeltsch it was not at all historically significant or possible to see in German Idealism (as the lecturer did) the presuppositions for a German cultural development in isolation. Rather, alongside this strand of tradition, another type was to be noted, the Western European. Troeltsch could not say whether it was possible, in view of the general cultural and political situation, to bring the two streams of ideas together so that they supplemented and corrected each other. 'I do not venture, like the lecturer, to think one or two centuries ahead; it seems to me that there are many cracks in the old Europe and that the future may possibly be serious and gloomy.'[159]

Troeltsch's involvement in the Evangelical Social Congress seems ambiguous, and shows his greatness and his limitations. His basic critical attitude prevents him from seeking simple and rapid solutions in the political and social sphere, and his gift for analysis leads him to constantly new cultural criticism which is extremely explosive, but also very fertile. His references to powers of structure, constructive form, are often too abstract, and too readily result in a jump from analytical considerations and the acceptance of historical knowledge to a proposed solution which consists only of vague hints.

How Troeltsch aptly assessed the possibilities of his working with the Congress became blindingly clear when in 1911 Harnack asked him to be a candidate for the office of President in succession to himself.[160] Troeltsch suggested that his own capabilities did not lie in the organizational or bureaucratic sphere but more in the field of debate.

Characteristically, he suggested a 'double praesidium' to Harnack. He himself could appear above all as a spokesman, whereas the other president could take on the organizational tasks. Harnack was not persuaded by the idea of a double presidency. So Otto Baumgarten (1858-1934) succeeded Harnack in the office of President of the Congress.

4. The trip to America (1904)

For Troeltsch, journeys abroad were a useful and attractive way of avoiding to some degree the pressure from outside and inside, from church politics and his plans for work.

So we can imagine how he enjoyed the trip to America to the World Congress in St Louis in 1904, not least because of the pleasant company. For Max Weber, Frau Marianne Weber and Paul Hensel were also in the party. There had been problems before the Congress over the reimbursement of travelling costs, which had led to a decimation in the number of German speakers. Troeltsch wrote to Harnack that twenty-four German scholars had cried off, including such significant figures as Windelband, Jellinek and Husserl.[161] They had reported to Münsterberg that the travelling expenses offered to them were too low. Characteristically, out of a mixture of a sense of justice and national pride, Weber and Troeltsch complained above all about the 'unfair treatment' of the foreign scholars.[162] By contrast, Paul Hensel wrote happily to the painter and art-dealer Irene Braun (1861-1923): 'I too have been invited to raise my little voice at the universal academic show that will take place in St Louis, with a lecture on the methods and aims of ethics. For this three-quarters of an hour I shall receive 500 dollars and free lodging in St Louis, and that gives me the opportunity to make a very fine and interesting trip... at relatively low cost.'[163]

The destination was St Louis, to participate in the Congress of Arts and Science which was being held in connection with the World Exposition there. The relatively large number of guest speakers invited from Germany, despite the problems I have mentioned, is striking. One reason for this was perhaps that the former Freiburg psychologist Hugo Münsterberg was one of the vice-presidents of the organizing committee and had been responsible for the humanities.[164] The trip took place in the high summer of 1904. Marianne Weber reported: 'The couple [she and her husband] embarked towards the end of August: Ernst Troeltsch with his precious humour was also one of the party.'[165] All three escaped seasickness, but Troeltsch could be seen to have a remarkable tendency towards asceticism over food, which was not otherwise characteristic of him.

Troeltsch, full of amazement at the remarkable things that he saw, and at the same time detached and critical, with a sharp eye for detail, gave his wife a vivid description of his first impressions of New York. 'What a view and what a hubbub of people and vehicles! The skyscrapers rise up like a mass of unruly towers, tremendous twenty-storey office blocks, a kind of citadel and fortress of capitalism, all gathered round the bank and stock exchange like an exaggerated mediaeval citadel, in which money, the bank, capital, rule over countless thousands of subjects.'[166]

There is a critical tone in Troeltsch's amazement at what had become so stupendous. And he also voices the intellectual aversion to noise which is also attested in literature since Schopenhauer: 'The eternal thunder and noise of the electric train, partly on viaducts above the streets, partly on the ground. Ears here are often completely deafened by the eternal thundering and roaring.'[167]

His verdict on the city contained a mixture of aesthetic and social perspectives: 'On the whole the city is extremely inelegant, rough, upstart, with miserable street lighting, bad street cleaning, and houses next to each other with no sense of style or planning. There is a stink of horse dung everywhere. In the elegant asphalted parts there are extremely splendid houses, like Tiergartenstrasse in Berlin, toilets and plumbing very noble. But that's the same the world over. Everything is brand new.'[168]

Above all he was delighted with the Webers' company. 'It is a rich gain to see this land of businesses with him. Of course he too keeps studying what he sees and strives to take it in. But as he thinks aloud, I have the benefit.'[169]

Troeltsch kept noticing with great amazement the power and self-awareness of the young American people and at the same time asked critical questions about its individualistic view of morality. Here he saw 'a great ethical, political and social problem'.[170] The question for him was whether the future cultural development of mankind would emerge more strongly from this moral understanding or from the European understanding, which put more emphasis on the historical and social element. Here Troeltsch was tackling a theme which would occupy him later, during the First World War. Something else emerged for him to study here which was also of interest to Weber[171] – perhaps more strongly and more persistently than to Troeltsch – namely, the question of the 'connection between this morality and the religious foundations of American life'.[172]

At the Congress itself, which now also offered material for his reflections,

Troeltsch was very impressed by the welcome and friendliness of the American hosts. Externally the Congress was a mammoth undertaking, but it was very well organized.[173] All the needs of the foreign speakers were looked after. There were different opportunities for further trips through the country to gain information and see the sights.

How strongly the nationalistic element played a role at the Congress and indeed came to the fore is evident, among other things, from the fact that all the national anthems of the states represented at the Congress were played at the opening, and the American national anthem at the end. The opening took place on the afternoon of 19 September in the Festival Hall and the main programme began the next morning. Troeltsch's lecture was one of the short papers; its topic 'Main Problems of the Philosophy of Religion: Psychology and Theory of Knowledge in the Science of Religion.'[174] In this lecture, Troeltsch presented one of the main ideas of his philosophy of religion for the first time, namely the epistemological foundation of religion in the sense of a religious *a priori*.

The Congress ended with a solemn closing ceremony. Then special trains left for Washington, where there was a reception given by the President. After that the trip continued to Harvard, where Professor Hugo Münsterberg received the guests. Most scholars then returned to New York, to be guests of Columbia University, where the Association of Old German Students gave a great dinner.

Troeltsch's stay in the United States was not wholly without problems for him. Something seems to have happened, the details of which we cannot now discover, but which led Troeltsch to write a long letter of apology to Hugo Münsterberg. He speaks of an 'unfortunate expression' which for him was an expression of personal clumsiness and arose from his delight in the comical.[175] For him the comical element emerged in 'a thousand happy pictures of the European scholars lost in America'. However, Troeltsch adds an explanation and shows that this was not all: 'The comical element is not just on the side of the organization, but also on the side of our colleagues.'[176] Although the letter as a whole has markedly apologetic features, Troeltsch's final verdict was: 'I regard this journey as one of the most valuable achievements of my life.'[177] The other problem involved his family. The death of his mother-in-law led Troeltsch to break off the journey prematurely and return to Germany.

5. Work with students and in the faculty; Troeltsch's influence as a university teacher

As a professor of theology, for more than twenty years Troeltsch lectured for four or five hours a week each semester. There was also the systematics seminar which took up two hours a week. Since the winter semester of 1909/ 10 Troeltsch had begun to teach in the philosophy faculty, where he also

As professor of theology, 1906

Leaving the Aula after a ceremonial occasion with Friedrich Endemann (1857–1936); from 1904 Endemann was Professor of Roman and German Civil Law in Heidelberg.

lectured four hours a week on philosophy of religion, ethics and the history of modern philosophy, and gave an introduction to philosophy.[178]

The class on systematics which Troeltsch additionally had to give in the seminar on practical theology – alternating with Lemme – seems to have brought him little joy over the years. On several occasions he asked the Ministry in Karlsruhe to relieve him of this obligation – which led his colleague Lemme to put the same request to the Minister.[179] Both the class in the academic theological seminar and that in the practical theological seminar had to be given without payment. All in all, however, the salaries of professors at that time were not bad. In 1899 Troeltsch's professorial salary amounted to 5760 marks without the living allowance of between 600 and 700 marks, and by 1911 had risen to 7700 marks. In addition there were the lecture fees, which could be very considerable, depending on the size of the audience. The bursary ledger for the summer semester of 1911, in which Troeltsch lectured for four hours a week on ethics to an audience of 111 in the philosophical and theological faculties and had an audience of 28 in his lectures on symbolics, which were also four hours a week, indicates a payment of 2680 marks.

So study was a very expensive business. We can therefore understand the anxious question of a father to the 'director of theological candidates in Heidelberg' who was inquiring about the likely cost of his son's study. Dean Deissmann replied on 10 November 1905: 'Dear Sir, The school costs about which you are asking are probably the lecture fees. In our faculty these amount to between 4 and 5 marks per hour per semester, so that a student who goes to 20 lectures a week has to pay between 80 and 100 marks a semester. Enrolment costs 20 marks, matriculation 10. Lodgings cost between 25 and 30 marks a month. There are cheaper and more expensive rooms.'[180]

In view of the very high costs of study it is not surprising that many theological students tried to get a grant. This imposed a considerable burden on the professors, who had to approve a large number of grant applications and above all had to provide the certificates of diligence which had to accompany them. In grant applications it was necessary to indicate the lectures or seminars attended and to provide a certificate of diligence and good morals.[181]

In view of all these commitments, it is understandable that the organization of faculty business was done with the least possible expenditure of energy. Faculty sessions took place only on extraordinary occasions, for example when appointments were being made. As a rule two sessions were planned in such circumstances, one for discussion and provisional nomination of candidates and another after a period used for getting information. General information was usually to be communicated in writing by the circulation of minutes or other documents, like dissertations. The current dean made a list of pending questions and put forward proposals about how to proceed. Then the members of the faculty each contributed their views.

Troeltsch, who was against any long-drawn-out way of settling administrative matters, very much liked the pattern of circulating faculty documents – the disadvantage of the minimal amount of contact among colleagues and the possibility of misunderstandings were taken into account. He acted as dean of the theological faculty (a post which he held three times) with a degree of detachment and generosity in administrative matters. Thus he often openly confessed that he had 'lost a document'. He was concerned that business should go through as smoothly as possible; it was not to take a long time and to keep people away from real work. The proposals and comments made by Troeltsch were brief and precise; he was not afraid of being quite firm with faculty members to get faculty business through quickly. When Troeltsch terminated the discussion of a Promotion dissertation, his colleague Merx reacted angrily: 'In licentiate theses it is important to give members of the faculty time to read. It is quite unseemly to rush through things like this, and I for one will never tolerate it.' To which Troeltsch retorted: 'On a personal note, I have to comment on the discourteous remark by my colleague Herr Merx that... I simply spoke of his holding back the work in order to explain its absence and to give reasons for the new submission. There was no occasion for such pedantic outbursts, and with due respect to my older colleague I repudiate his tone.'[182]

So small differences were not uncommon. They also happened over the budget. Savings had to be made even then. Thus on 11 January 1905, in the faculty book Troeltsch asked his colleagues 'to be sparing with the expensive electric light or to keep an eye on the wasteful habits of the servants'.[183]

The faculty book reveals a rare case of complete unanimity between Troeltsch and Lemme when the colours for new gowns were to be chosen. Lemme was for the traditional violet. Troeltsch wrote on 12 February 1903: 'I agree with my colleague Herr Lemme. Black is dreadful.'[184]

When new arrangements for the licentiate examination and Habilitation were discussed in the faculty (1899), the difference of opinion on the conditions that the candidates should fulfil was illuminating. In discussing the regulations for Habilitation Deissmann agreed with Bassermann that greater importance should be attached to prior practical service. He wanted to prevent 'a personality with a quite sterile religion from escaping from the pastorate into a teaching career'. Troeltsch did not like the narrow way in which such a requirement would be fixed in statutes. In any case, his main interest was in academic qualifications; he was afraid that the rule proposed by Deissmann might be abused. In the prevailing 'church circumstances it might prove that a very competent scholar who is not at all sterile cannot get on in the church...' The passage about practical service was then omitted from the new Habilitation regulations.[185]

The question of church influence, above all on calls and on teaching matters, was a permanent problem. The various critical comments on theology in Troeltsch's letters are less the result of a surfeit of theology than above all references to external conditions; in other words they relate more to the situation of the theological faculty than to substantive matters. As he confessed in a letter to Rudolf Otto, doubts about faith, the theological disease, were certainly very well known to him, but they had 'never really seriously thrown' him.[186] That was also in part because he worked out a position which he understood as 'religious-theistic belief'; while it had its roots in Christianity, it rested on a free and sovereign use of tradition.

Troeltsch felt that with this understanding of faith it was quite legitimate for him to give lectures on doctrine. However, of course this was not enough for his critics from the 'positive' camp. So above all else the conflict with Ludwig Lemme as his 'positive' counterpart in the faculty, but also with the positive church groups in the region, was almost pre-programmed.[187]

Externally, despite all the differences over theological views and his outward detachment, Troeltsch maintained collegial loyalty and allowed relatively little of this ongoing conflict to emerge in public. He spoke about it only to close colleagues or friends. However, the *laissez-faire* principle had its limitations. For in the faculty people lived closely together and had to deal with one another over administrative questions and appointments. And finally, in teaching, i.e. in front of the students, it was impossible to avoid the clash over views. When Troeltsch rejected dogmatic exclusivist thinking with its narrowness and theological arrogance, one can well imagine that he had Ludwig Lemme in mind as a concrete example of this way of thinking.[188]

How justified on the whole Troeltsch's sensitivity to the 'believers' claims' to exercise influence on the theological faculties and the teaching activity of the professors of theology was is shown, for example, in a remark by Friedrich von Bodelschwingh: 'A flood of unbelieving and impious criticism flows inexorably from the theological chairs of our German colleges over our poor theological youth and shakes the foundations of our faith, namely Holy Scripture. The tears of many fathers and mothers cry out against such cruel pastors of souls in Protestant professorships.'[189]

Over the years there were changes in the composition of the faculty which Troeltsch regarded as going in a positive direction. Thus in 1908, when Adolf Deissmann had left for Berlin, Johannes Weiss (1863-1914) was appointed to the New Testament chair. Once again it proved impossible to secure the appointment of Wilhelm Bousset.[190]

Troeltsch, who always also thought in categories of academic recognition, both for himself and for the faculty to which he belonged, commented on the call of Johannes Weiss: 'With this our faculty is gradually reaching the heights; at all events it has become a respectable faculty.'[191]

The appointment of Hans von Schubert (1869-1931) to the chair of church history in 1906, in succession to Adolf Hausrath, also added to the reputation of the faculty on which Troeltsch put so much emphasis. He and Troeltsch became close friends, both professionally and personally. Von Schubert had made his reputation in studies on Reformation history and the Middle Ages, and in works on the history of law.[192] Although in Troeltsch's view the situation in the faculty, and above all the academic reputation of the Heidelberg faculty, had notably improved, he was not very happy about the academic and church-political situation as expressed in the pressure from 'positive circles': he was in principle against this.

On the whole, work with the students remained untouched by such burdens and such pressure. But how are we to assess Troeltsch's activity as a university teacher? What response did he get? What characterized his work?

Albert Dietrich thought that Troeltsch's effect on the students came above all from his unprejudiced thinking and his wide-ranging interests.[193] According to Dietrich, Troeltsch's seminar classes had been particularly impressive. Here he had no plan, was not guided by any direct didactic purpose, but gave a direct insight into his thought. 'But the whole thing was not improvised, though there were plenty of surprises, which often led to amazement, annoyance or hilarity on both sides.'[194]

Troeltsch evidently made considerable demands on the members of the seminar with his distinctive and lively spirit. He did not always follow a clear line in his teaching; rather, the seminar tended to be shaped by sudden ideas, the demonstration of connections in history and in subject-matter, and the tendency to turn solutions into new problems again.[195]

Troeltsch was evidently more a teacher for the intellectually demanding students, who were not merely out for knowledge that they could acquire but wanted to explore questions and have their horizons opened up.[196] The attraction of the approach that he practised lay in the way in which he communicated his personal way of thinking and being. But as he was a complex person, shaped by a broad spectrum of interests, who moreover had a tendency to see the provisional nature of tensions and solutions as characteristics of intellectual life or work, in the eyes of some students he had no clear position.

Rather more conventional people also found difficulties in the fact that Troeltsch's appearance, indeed his whole manner, were quite 'untheological'. Moreover, his remarks could occasionally prove somewhat devastating to 'those of another disposition'.[197]

Anyone who wanted to understand Troeltsch as an academic teacher and follow his thoughts had to be able to go along with his procedure or follow it afterwards 'by intuition and rational criticism of it'.[198] Intuition here evidently means direct access to something, seeing the essentials by taking in history and life, while criticism of this process investigates its possibility and tenability. Rational criticism thus leads to an interruption of immediacy. This character-istic of Troeltsch's approach has been attributed, probably rightly, to 'an intimate and lively interaction between immediacy and reflection' which was to be found in his person.[199]

One further point. The concept of individuality which meant so much to Troeltsch both theologically and philosophically also shaped his own view of life and his relationship to others. Troeltsch believed that teaching or upbringing should not make any violent intervention in the nature of a person

as determined by disposition and inclination. He attached more importance
to the organic unfolding of the characteristics and potentialities inherent in
the individual, which it was important to respect and cautiously to encourage.[200]
Anyone who accepted the personal characteristics of others so freely had
limitations as an academic teacher when it came to exercising influence and
above all forming a theological school. Those in search of an explanation why
Troeltsch did not form a school and had relatively few personal disciples –
theologians who understood themselves as his disciples could differ as widely
in their views as Georg Wünsch on the one hand and Friedrich Gogarten on
the other[201] – will have to take this understanding of individuality and
theological position into account, among other factors. Furthermore,
Troeltsch's way of thinking, which kept history and the world in view and
largely avoided concentration on a 'doctrine', made a striking breadth and
variety possible here.[202]

Troeltsch's style of thinking and lecturing, the combination of historical
orientation and subject-centred thought, suited the framework of philosophical
lectures better and were, at least outwardly, more appreciated by the students.
But perhaps they were better prepared here by the work of Kuno Fischer and
Wilhelm Windelband.

Significant characteristics of Troeltsch's personality and life-style appear
in his work with students and his association with colleagues in the faculty, so
we need to go into them more deeply at this point.

Troeltsch's personality was shot through with clear inherent contradictions.
These tensions were also his strength. Precisely because he was so many-
sided, assessments of him by others, whether friends, colleagues or critics,
varied. Whereas some people thought that he had a tendency to passivity and
resignation, others thought of him as active, as having a natural force, like a
rustic Bavarian. Some referred to his compelling way of thinking and acting,
whereas others described him as an acute critic, abrupt and dismissive to the
point of being devastating. But these contrasts seem to have been deeply
rooted in his nature. His 'powerful nature', his vitality, was at the same time
shot through with melancholy and scepticism. And his criticism, his detached
assessment of the situation or of other people, is only one side of his thought:
the other is a concern for understanding, for balance, for mediation. Perhaps
he himself regarded mediating thought as a corrective to the critical elements
in his position and his person.

Troeltsch was famous for his jokes. At the same time he had a streak of
melancholy which becomes evident above all in his letters. He was a very
creative person, always with many plans in his head, a man who always gave
himself an enormous burden of work. Along with this went dissatisfaction
with his own achievements and capacity for work.

He repeatedly remarked that he could not work and publish with sufficient
speed and concentration, and he was plagued by considerable nervousness
and unrest. It also becomes clear how highly he esteemed himself as a scholarly

mind. There is a fluctuation between self-doubt and the conviction of being able to make an important contribution to scholarship. The same is true of his attitude towards questions about Christianity and religion. Religious inwardness, a confessional tone, a personal piety, stand alongside his scholarly approach and critical spirit. The warm tone of personal piety often does not go well with his critical scholarly comments.

These tensions and contrasts are also expressed in photographs. Troeltsch was on the one hand someone who could be photographed in Heidelberg in bathing costume, and on the other the professor who was not antipathetic to being represented in cap and gown, who presided over solemn ceremonies in the university and greeted the Grand Duke. On the one hand he was simple and unconcerned, occasionally coarse; on the other hand he was extremely complicated, sensitive, and concerned for his reputation.

Troeltsch had a clear tendency towards what Harnack called 'solitariness', towards the quiet life of a scholar, withdrawal into his own work, withdrawal even from friends.[203] His need for contact and conversation was in tension with this.

Troeltsch had a good eye. This became evident at a very early stage from his enjoyment at looking at works of art. How else could it be that a young theologian in Munich to train as a minister not only went to the art exhibition there but also wrote about it?[204] This was certainly not out of a desire for publicity, since an article signed with a T. in a church paper would hardly attract much outside recognition. Troeltsch judged and took in art – sculpture and painting – relatively directly and naively. How fascinated he was by it is clear from his many visits to museums in Berlin; he gave vivid and lively reports of them and was so attracted by them that he could write that the museums in Berlin, taken with the academic possibilities, could deter him from changing his place of study.

Was Troeltsch also someone who could transpose this desire to contemplate into an open contemplation of nature? Can one imagine him going for long walks by the Neckar? He was certainly not like Niebergall, who went on famous expeditions with his students to the mill at Ziegelhausen – a happy crowd, to some degree anticipating a youth movement; Gertrud von le Fort and Friedrich Gogarten related these seminar expeditions as important impressions from their student days in Heidelberg, a special form of communal experience and exchange of ideas with an academic teacher who had a fondness for students.

These traits of contentment were largely lacking in Troeltsch. Bathing in the Neckar and holidaying in the mountains were something of a training programme for him; to meet people in his bathing costume became a particular kind of intellectual communication, as Rothacker later described it.[205] Nor is the extraordinary occasion when Troeltsch the theologian met one of his close colleagues while bathing and disappeared into the water in a headstand likely to be completely without significance. Above all, though, Troeltsch was always trying to keep fit, to sustain his power to work or to regain it.

Troeltsch also saw companionship partly in utilitarian terms. He was looking for a counterbalance to his lonely work at the desk, his penetrating reflections and also the feeling that as a theologian he could not hope for a direct response. So the circle of friends had to be drawn more widely. Looking through Troeltsch's life from his schooldays on, one can see first of all that he cannot have been too keen on making contact with people. School reports even mention his intellectual arrogance.[206] In the student association there were complaints that he was playing the reformer, regardless of whether he had in fact done so or indeed wanted to do so. And in Göttingen within the 'little faculty' he was regarded as the eminent systematic brain, which matched his own understanding of himself. One can always recognize links with a community and at the same time a desire to be different, a critical detachment.

One form of spontaneous behaviour is to be found in Troeltsch's verbal wit, the capacity to react immediately to a situation, a remark in a conversation, a person. Troeltsch had a ready wit and was well able to express it: points sat lightly on him. He was a charming entertainer and conversation-partner. But there was something more. His capacity for an immediate, even intuitive grasp of people and situations was relativized or put in question by the rational components of the assessment.

Troeltsch cultivated contacts with individual liberal clergy, and sometimes also with former pupils: there is often mention of, say, Dean Schmidthenner. But evidently there was virtually no correspondence with close pupils like Wünsch or even Gogarten.[207] Troeltsch was not particularly interested in the transition of his students from the academic world to the practical world of the pastorate, and only rarely kept in touch with them. It is almost impossible to imagine Troeltsch in close contact with church life, say as a regular churchgoer like old Zahn in Erlangen, who appeared in churh Sunday by Sunday on his daughter's arm, not without giving the impression of doing his duty. A particular kind of reading served as a means of edification and spiritual refreshment for Troeltsch; he mentions the Bible and Goethe, both of which go together.[208]

Troeltsch does not seem to have had any special feeling for music. There is virtually nothing to point in this direction in either his work or his letters. He was obviously not fond of music in the home, which was still commonplace in his time, nor did he himself play any musical instrument.[209] He is said to have gone to the opera in Berlin only occasionally, probably more as a social than a musical event.[210]

Travelling was particularly important for Troeltsch because he was very open to sense-impressions in the form of images. So new landscapes and peoples must have had a special attraction for him. In addition there was his intellectual curiosity in conditions abroad and other cultural streams. In this way he attempted to attain freshness and vigour of body and mind, which was very important to him.

Troeltsch certainly saw himself as a pious man, but his piety and his religion were always also under threat; they were put in question by rationality and a tendency to criticism. To the degree that he felt the ideological pressure on modern people, with a feeling of relativism on the one hand and dogmatic consolidation on the other, Troeltsch increasingly had the impression that human beings needed religion as a source of power, as a last support.

6. Pro-Rector of the university[211] (1906-7)

One of the external high points of Troeltsch's university life was his Pro-Rectorate in 1906/07. The instance of Lemme, who was passed over when it was his turn to be elected,[212] shows that the election was not a matter of course. However, there was no danger of this in the case of Troeltsch. He found increasing recognition in the university and in his discipline, but this was not synonymous with recognition in the sphere of theology and the church.[213]

It was customary for both the outgoing and the newly-elected Pro-Rectors to be escorted by the students in a torchlight procession, after which it was the duty of the newly-elected officer to give a speech to the assembled students.

In his torchlight speech, Troeltsch described the academic freedom expressed in self-administration and freedom to teach and learn as 'one of the highest and noblest forms of freedom, if at the same time, as it should, it represents self-discipline and a sense of responsibility'.[214] In this perspective the university was a school in which the students grew up to be 'civil officers' of the people and were best able to fit into the monarchical structure of the state.[215]

Troeltsch's speech at the opening of the Czerny Institute in Heidelberg may be seen as one example of the duties of a Pro-Rector. The Czerny Institute was a cancer institute, a significant new establishment in the university which at the same time was a relatively independent foundation and represented a great scientific achievement for the period. The Grand Duke attended the solemn opening; his presence was not only an indication of the importance of the institution but also a sign of the close connection between university and ruling house. Troeltsch, who was probably well aware of the scientific status of the event and therefore of what the foundation of the institute meant for Heidelberg, nevertheless did not want to approach it from this perspective. He emphasized that when one remembered the 'object of this gathering' the ceremony could not really be a 'festival' but was an act of concern and help for suffering men and women motivated by humanity.[216]

The content of the speech which Troeltsch gave as Pro-Rector of the university on 22 November 1906, the centenary of the refounding of the university as the Ruperto-Carola University, was more important, and more indicative of his position in the academic world and in church politics. His topic was 'The Separation of State and Church: State Religious Education and the Theological Faculties'.[217] In the speech he referred to the current significance of the question of the rights of the theological faculties in the overall structure of the university and then developed the theme historically and as a matter of principle.

Roughly speaking, the formation of fronts on the matter in question looked like this: there was criticism from the 'positive' trend within theology of the openness of purely academic work and thought, and for this reason a closer bond was sought between the theological faculties and the church and its confession. This demand corresponded with the views of the anti-church trend, not in its basis but in its effect. For them, theology was an alien body within the university because it was bound to norms. To these ideas, under the influence of history-of-religions thought was also added the demand for an expansion of the theological faculty into a faculty for the history of religion generally.[218]

In his speech Troeltsch identified three different forms of relationship between state and church: '1. the system of absolute establishment, where one church assures uniformity and is most intimately inseparably united with the whole of political life; 2. the system of disestablishment, where any number of different free churches are related to the state, essentially on the basis of the laws governing associations in general; and 3. the system of mixed establishment, where a small number of state churches are treated on a basis of parity'. He saw these three forms as three different understandings of truth and revelation. The views expressed here were later developed further in the *Social Teachings*, above all in the form of the types church, sect and mysticism.[219]

How was the role of the theological faculties within the university to be defined? Troeltsch thought it a serious error to suppose that one could dispense with theology.[220] The tradition of faith and culture generally had to continue to be seen engaged both in free critical discussion and in a possible relationship and alliance. According to Troeltsch, the contact between science and the religious tradition was of fundamental significance for any honest pious person.

But what form or what type of relationship did Troeltsch himself endorse? In his view, the system of Landeskirchen on equal terms should adopt individual features of the two other forms. The objective factor of the idea of the unitary church should be limited by the principle of personal conviction as represented by the free church. The idea of free will corresponding to the free church had to be supplemented by legal and social stabilizing factors.[221] So Troeltsch – and here lies the motive for all the ramifications of his line of thought – had in mind a gradated argument which was to make religious instruction and theological faculties seem meaningful even under changed historical conditions, in other words in the case of a separation between church and state.[222]

7. University representative in the Baden First Chamber (1909-1914)

It was in keeping with his deeper involvement in political questions that Troeltsch stood for election as representative of the University of Heidelberg in the First Chamber of the Assembly of the Grand Duchy of Baden. Here he succeeded Windelband from 1909 to 1914. This was certainly far from what Max Weber expected of him, namely general political or party-political activity, but it was at least a step in this direction.[223]

Troeltsch was capable of finding his feet quickly on particular political questions and could advocate his viewpoint convincingly. As chairman of a variety of commissions he was good at combining detailed analysis with an overall aim and had a special talent for describing the matter under discussion with vivid examples.

Troeltsch gained a hearing above all as an expert on questions relating to the politics of higher education. Appointments in the theological faculty were a particulary tricky topic of many debates. Troeltsch attempted to clarify the particular interests of the theological faculty to the members of the Chamber.[224]

He energetically countered accusations from the conservative side that the theological faculty preferred theologians from the liberal wing in appointments. He referred to the difficult position of theological faculties within the university. He argued that when there were disputes over particular trends in the faculty, they were connected with the cause that they represented. Therefore nothing was more important in the theological faculties than a degree of homogeneity.[225] Here Troeltsch was talking about things which had made life in theology hard for him. He wanted peace and quiet for his work and often saw himself exposed to petty squabbles among rival trends.

To the accusation that the theological faculty wanted to gain members who were as radical as possible, Troeltsch retorted: 'The opposite is the case: the faculty wants members who are as academically eminent as possible and as unradical as possible, mediating in a peaceful and sensible way.'[226] That was Troeltsch's ideal picture of a faculty colleague and at the same time his idea of the composition of a theological faculty. He spoke out equally resolutely when there were mutterings in circles committed to the church and also at court that the Heidelberg theological faculty influenced students in the direction of a theological or ecclesiastical radicalism. He commented: 'We take special pains to do justice to the various trends among the students...'[227]

Questions about teacher training and school instruction were controversial topics in the Chamber. In Troeltsch's view the deconfessionalizing of teacher training was to be striven for largely on ideological grounds. He was against a doctrinaire standpoint – there should be no change in conditions on the basis of a principle of simultaneity. He observed that one could not approach basic problems of state and religious instruction, school and church, in terms of an individual issue. 'No one should attempt, pressing forward with such small steps, to unfold the great question in this guise [the principle of simultaneity].

The question must be discussed for what is: a purely unpolitical, practical question.'[228]

In connection with a draft law on elementary education Troeltsch had to assess the submissions received from teachers' unions, associations, and city and country communities. He thought that the draft, about the relationship between private and state schools, was very important. When he was accused of presenting the relationship between state and church in his report essentially as a compromise, he replied: 'But that is my well-considered view of the matter, derived from a knowledge of history. Except that the word "compromise" is to be understood differently. It is not to be understood to indicate that the state reluctantly and without inner conviction merely has to make concessions to the churches because of its power. That is not the case. The state and society generally need the inner spiritual and moral power which emanate from the churches of all confessions, and also from the various lesser religious communities, among which I would include the Jews.'[229]

For Troeltsch it was of the essence of the church that in its work in school it went far beyond the aim of character-building. This resulted on the one hand in the idea of an educational task specific to the church and on the other in a concession to the state to limit the influence of the churches as organizations – which always also ended up in the development of power. This dual perspective produced the need for compromise.[230] Because of the overwhelming power of the church as an institution, Troeltsch thought it legitimate to put obstacles in the way of a law which allowed the church to set up private schools alongside public schools.

The question of the relationship between state, church and theological faculties came up once again in connection with the anti-Modernist oath. Troeltsch pointed out the difference in principle between the church's understanding of itself and that of the theological faculties. Catholic faculties were 'a concession of the church to the state'.[231] They would not lose anything if they were detached from the universities. The Protestant faculties were quite different. The strength of Protestantism did not lie 'in the regimented political coherence of the church organism... but in the free mobility and adaptation of religion to cultural life generally... Its theological faculties are now the essential organ for this accommodation with the whole intellectual culture.'[232] The other faculties within the university were necessary for the existence of theology in so far as they brought it cultural life.

Troeltsch thought the principle of a parity of the liberal and positive trends in the theological faculties quite inappropriate: this went against the spirit of an academic institution. 'It must be possible for the Protestants to leave academic work completely free and to trust that any intellectualist one-sidednesses of the school will be corrected by clergy through the practical experience of their profession. Here it must be possible for them to trust that they can also find the truth and understand it for themselves in different forms.'[233]

Troeltsch also commented on practical issues in university life: on research, the system of lecture fees and the salaries of teachers. In supporting the wishes of the lecturers – grants and a greater share in teaching – he had in mind not only his own experiences but also those of his circle of friends and colleagues: one need think only of Wilhelm Bousset or Rudolf Otto.

For Troeltsch, to transfer democratic constitutional ideals to the university meant making the university a great electoral institution with the representation of the individual interest-groups in academic self-administration. That seemed to him to be quite unnecessary: 'Now if democracy represents the right, the duty and responsibility of the individual in the formation of an overall will, it is surely an understandable and justified demand in politics. But we have no analogy to that in our scholarly bodies. Not only is scholarship very aristocratic by nature but, above all, the self-administration which could be brought into being by elections does not exist. Faculties and senates are not bodies which represent interests, and urgent warnings should be issued against turning them into such.'[234]

The later comment that his habit of analysing and describing situations made it difficult for Troeltsch to arrive at a decision does not apply to his work in the Baden Chamber. Here he could get an impression of practical politics in action: he knew what he wanted and had decided views about any matter under discussion. But he also tended to proceed cautiously, weighing up carefully and with deliberation the pros and cons of a decision.

Here are some striking features of Troeltsch's political ideas in the period before the First World War. He was evidently much less sensitive to politically conservative thought than to a theological or church-political conservatism. He was perhaps also less disturbed by what might be called a more conservative political attitude because at first it affected him less – less, at any rate than attitudes to theology and church politics. Generally speaking, in the first decade of his political activity Troeltsch did not show much interest in political questions; his academic work forced everything else into the background.[235] At the same time the idea of avoiding unnecessary offence by firm political involvement or activity also came into the picture. Different factors combined to shape Troeltsch's political interests as they gradually became stronger. The phase of establishing himself as a scholar was over. He was also stimulated politically by his friends in Heidelberg and by his involvement in the 'Evangelical Social Congress'. And finally, it has to be said that the period leading up to the First World War brought increasing political tension. Troeltsch's growing sense of political connotations was increasingly guided and encouraged by his own work on history and the analysis of culture.

There is no doubt that Troeltsch's attitude was basically nationalistic. However, here the nuances are important. Any exaggeration was alien to him. Nationalistic slogans and an outward-looking nationalistic consciousness were far from his thought. Even the designation 'national-social'[236] is not an apt description of Troeltsch's political attitude. That would not do justice to his basically liberal traits, and would fail to recognize what made him sensitive to any ideological fixation. We might get closest by speaking of a 'mixed form' which sought to combine national, liberal and social elements and at the same time contained a basically conservative trait. For despite all its social components, Troeltsch's political thought is not bent on change, and one cannot say that he has a fundamental concern to shake up society. Given this orientation, in terms of party politics Troeltsch fits best in the national liberal trend, though here we need to take into account his critical detachment from party programmes or official statements.[237]

However, Troeltsch proved increasingly open to a 'cautious reform', a change on the basis of existing conditions, with a deliberate adoption of the tradition. His critical verdict on a policy of merely keeping to the existing conditions in society is documented in a letter to Bousset from 1912. Given the situation, Troeltsch thinks that 'the ruling powers presuppose that we all affirm their position and do nothing towards a transition to new conditions in the hope that in this way they may be able to hinder it. Thus they are merely bridling radicalism and putting a brake on the centre.'[238] All in all, we can see in Troeltsch a process of development which leads from a gradually awakening political awareness, through a long shift in his moderate conservative position, in the direction of reform (albeit cautious).

8. Friendship with Max Weber

The friendly relations between Troeltsch and Max Weber became increasingly close over the years, to the point that in 1910 they both came to live in the same house. In his obituary of Max Weber, Troeltsch remarked, 'Of myself I will only say that for years I experienced the infinitely stimulating power of this man in daily converse.'[239] Here in particular he will have been referring to the time when they lived together in the house on Ziegelhäuser Landstrasse.[240]

However, they also had other opportunities for being together, for carrying on cultured companionship with an intellectual tone, for example in the Eranos circle to which both Troeltsch and Weber belonged, and which was characteristic of the cultural atmosphere of Heidelberg at that time. This circle had been formed by Adolf Deissmann in 1904 together with his old Marburg friend Albrecht Dieterich (1866-1908). It was made up of professors from a wide variety of disciplines, and non-theologians were in the majority. They met once a month on a Sunday afternoon in the house of one of the members, who was then the host in every sense of the word. Before they sat down to a meal, the host presented a scholarly paper to his colleagues and this was followed by discussion, which was usually very lively. The requirement was for the speaker to give a paper with some bearing on religion.

Deissmann acknowledged: 'I have never experienced scholarly exchanges which were at so high a level and so open, in friendly and cultured company.'[241]

Even if we remember the many bonds of friendship which developed for

The house in Ziegelhäuser Landstrasse, no. 17. Max Weber and his wife lived on the first floor; the Troeltsch family in the apartment above.

Max Weber 1917/18

Leif Geiges

Troeltsch in the course of time, including those that were still to come in Heidelberg, for example with Adolf Deissmann and Hans von Schubert, his friendship with Max Weber was of quite special importance. This friendship was not so much a warm-hearted personal relationship but rested on mutual attraction and also accepted the other's idiosyncrasies. Here above all, power of thought, intellectual stimulation by the other and his stature as a scholar were the things that were prized.

The friendship was based on a certain natural affinity, on kindred minds and capacities. This is evident, for example, from the letters written by the student Troeltsch or the student Max Weber. If we compare the two, common features emerge: first a sharp analytical mind, a capacity for a critical judgment on persons and situations, and secondly a delight in describing people and things with a particular sense of their comic and eccentric side.[242]

What attracted Troeltsch to Weber, quite apart from the subject-matter of his work and his academic interests, was above all a freedom of mind, an openness to new questions and a degree of independence from academic habits and a bourgeois life-style.[243] However, the latter can only be observed now and then. Both Weber and Troeltsch had 'aristocratic' traits in assessing their own work and the scholarly activity of the time.

In both men, as well as a disposition threatened by striking changes of mood, a basic scepticism is unmistakable. Both perceived the way in which individuals and wider groups become entangled in the course of time, both politically and culturally. Weber saw this basic feeling more strongly as a tragic entanglement, as something immutable which was to be accepted by fate, whereas Troeltsch, who was affected by it even in his work, thought that he could create hope for the future by his roots in the religious. His own feeling was that he could at least raise himself above entanglement in the political and cultural situation of the time provoked by this scepticism to a freedom which derived from a hope in the future with religious basis. He saw very clearly that this was a threatened future, and a hope with its ifs and buts. However, such a hope was there. The same cannot be said of Weber. Where from a cultural perspective Troeltsch posited a synthesis and thought it possible, for Weber there remained only a radical renunciation of the possibility of arriving at a scientific and rational solution to the question of meaning and value. In his studies of historicism and his obituary of Max Weber, Troeltsch described Weber's 'stoic greatness and harshness' with an expression of partial admiration and stronger scepticism and ideological detachment. Above all he thought false and fatal Weber's direct contrast between sociological and historical research into the real world on the one side and an evaluative decision on the basis of the 'irreconcilable polytheism of values' on the other.[244] Here we can recognize a last alienation of Troeltsch from Max Weber's temperament, in the face of the harshness of Weber's effort of will and his ideas of power. Troeltsch thought that despite all the relativisms which Weber perceived and advocated elsewhere, he knew only two basic dogmas: on the one hand the bond with the nation and on the other the 'categorical imperative of human dignity and justice'.[245]

It has been suggested that Troeltsch was particularly dependent on Weber's work above all in his book *The Social Teachings of the Christian Churches*.[246] This verdict is prompted by too great a stress on the capitalism thesis and its adoption by Troeltsch. Troeltsch's overall contribution here cannot be explained in terms of dependence on Max Weber. Such a judgment does not take sufficient notice or account of the wealth of Troeltsch's historical insights. Moreover, above all in the case of the capitalism thesis, i.e. the notion that Protestantism has a particular ascetic nature, the adoption of Weber's thoughts had long been prepared for by Troeltsch's own ideas.[247]

Both Troeltsch and Weber created a life's work which was broad and yet 'obsessed with detail', because what they recognized and understood had to be tested against concrete reality. Another factor which distinguished the two was the political view. Whereas Weber sought to avoid any thought of compromise, and regarded it more as a weakness than a strength, Troeltsch found compromise, the weighing up of both sides and the adoption of what was new and compelling, a quite acceptable possibility not only in the theological and philosophical sphere but also in the realm of politics. Carl Neumann, who was a sensitive and sharp observer, noted that Weber was a dominating figure, a kind of master-thinker as a scholar, who tried rigorously to bring others into line with his thought, midway between esteem and detachment: 'At the same time Max Weber laid down the network for his conquistadorial forays, through which the imperialist thrust of his gifts was to raise scientific knowledge to the level of an overall science.'[248]

The remark made by Friedrich Karl Schumann, that in principle each man enriched and encouraged the other, seems to me to be an apt one.[249] That is the case even if we assume that Weber's part may be defined more specifically and perhaps was also greater.[250]

The friendship was broken off at the beginning of the First World War as the result of an unfortunate event. Weber and Troeltsch had both registered for hospital service. Whereas Weber as a reserve officer had a leading role, Troeltsch was responsible for just one military hospital. In an atmosphere of heightened nationalistic feelings and with the fear of enemy spies, people in Heidelberg wanted to ban a professor from Alsace from visiting French prisoners of war in the military hospital. Troeltsch allowed his Alsatian colleague to visit the hospital under him only under military escort. Here he wanted to take account both the wishes of the population and the interests of the visitor (though the latter refused on these conditions). Weber just could not understand Troeltsch's tendency to this compromise. He was furious, spoke of chauvinism, and called Troeltsch's behaviour dishonourable. He demanded unlimited visiting rights, and broke off relations with Troeltsch completely. Marianne Weber commented: 'As often in such cases, cause and effect were unrelated. He apologized for his fierceness but also expected the other to see his mistake. When that did not happen, the break remained.'[251]

In the circumstances, Troeltsch's call to Berlin and departure from the house that they had shared was an external solution to a situation which had become difficult. Only years later did the two men meet again, through the mediation of their wives. However, they could not regain the earlier intensity of their relationship – and certainly not just because they were separated by physical distance.[252]

9. The call to Berlin

Troeltsch had twice had the prospect of a call to Berlin, first (in 1908) to the theological faculty and then (1908/09) to the philosophical faculty. In both cases the call had come to nothing because of resistance or reservations in the faculty concerned. Basically, he was too philosophical for the theologians and too theological for the philosophers.[253]

In the summer of 1914 Troeltsch received a call to a chair of philosophy in the university of Berlin. He must have felt a belated satisfaction that what had not been attainable years before was now to be fulfilled. This time he was going to occupy a chair which had been handed over to the philosophical faculty by the theological faculty. Troeltsch's double interest in philosophy and theology was again a stumbling block for some members of the faculty. This time the faculty asked rather more specifically whether Troeltsch might not seek a post in the theological faculty, thus undesirably blurring the boundaries between the two faculties. The Ministry dismissed this suspicion by indicating that it had no intention of giving such a teaching post. That took the wind out of the critics' sails. Troeltsch was thereupon put on the list in first place with a substantial majority. The Minister indicated assent, so now the initative lay with Troeltsch.

Various thoughts came to him in this situation. First, as has already been mentioned, there was a degree of satisfaction, not least because the theological faculty in Berlin had never approached him with a call. However, a further important factor was the idea of working at a more central position in German university and cultural life. He also took into account the prospect of liberation from the external pressure caused by the interference of church circles in faculty life and teaching which would become possible by the change in faculty. So we have to take into account the complexity of the questions which arose with the move to Berlin if we are to assess Troeltsch's decision correctly.

Having been informed of a generous financial offer from the Ministry in Karlsruhe should he remain in Heidelberg, Troeltsch wrote to the Pro-Rector of the university: 'In truth, the situation is that Berlin was so accommodating over everything, especially in structuring the teaching post, that after the usual prior negotiations... there was no longer any real possibility of going back on it. Nor can I deny that, for all my hesitations, the representation of my ideas at the centre of German life through a professorship which is realy tailored to me has proved a decisive attraction both personally and in terms of my discipline. It finally drew me from the small-state idyll of Heidelberg to the battlefield of Berlin.'[254]

The reaction among friends and colleagues was divided. Wilhelm Bousset does not seem not have been very pleased at Troeltsch's decision to move to the philosophy faculty. Troeltsch evaded his critical questions by referring in his answer to the political dimension of his call. He wrote: 'The situation was that pressure from the Reich Chancellor first set the Minister in motion (this in confidence), and the call to the philosophical faculty was the only one over which he saw himself in a position to make concessions to the liberals. Seeberg's system is very powerful and militates against me more powerfully than anyone else. Deissmann has turned Seeberg completely against me. Am I then to please all these people and not accept the chair?'[255] In this letter from Troeltsch to Bousset it becomes clear that the main factor in his decision to go to Berlin and the philosophy faculty was not a weariness with theology; he increasingly had in view the situation of the theological faculties and collaboration with his colleagues. He asked: 'Am I to refuse a chair which is tailor-made for me and which completely rescues me from my theological colleagues? They really have few merits. In the present situation in the church and politics I have little faith in theology and feel that the contrast between my theology and all present-day theology is so great that very little is to be hoped for here. I shall only arrive at complete truthfulness with myself when I am rid of these concerns.'[256]

In later interpretation of Troeltsch the move to Berlin has frequently been interpreted as a flight from theology, as resignation. For Troeltsch, however, the change to the philosophical faculty was not resignation nor a flight from theology. He remained committed to theology as he understood it, a theology with a foundation in the philosophy of religion and a marked historical orientation. We are to think less in terms of a violent break or renunciation on his part than of a transition to something new, in both his specific work and its external setting. For Troeltsch, theology and philosophy were far too close to each other in principle for him really to be able or want to accept a break. If the feeling of liberation emerges here, it is above all because of the removal of the external pressure of church politics.

It is impossible to say precisely why Troeltsch did not want to come to Berlin until the summer semester of 1915. Perhaps he just wanted to have longer for his move, and perhaps he also wanted to help to sort out the question of his successor. In fact this was decided quite quickly. Georg Wobbermin (1869-1936), Ordinarius Professor of Systematic Theology in Breslau, was nominated in first place in the faculty proposals for the appointment to Troeltsch's chair. The reason for the proposal was that he had been trained predominantly in philosophy and systematic theology, without 'leaving historical research completely aside'.[257]

The decision was made quickly. An order went out from Karlsruhe dated 30 December 1914 that His Royal Highness, the Grand Duke, had decided to release the Ordinarius Professor of Systematic Theology Ernst Troeltsch from state service 'in accordance with his humble request' with effect from 1 April 1915 and to nominate Professor Georg Wobbermin as Ordinarius in his stead.[258] For Troeltsch, 1915 marked the beginning a new period in his life, and just under eight years would remain to him for his activity in Berlin.

When Troeltsch left Heidelberg in the early summer of 1915, the city fathers gave him a farewell ceremony. There was even a public invitation to this in the newspaper. Regardless of rank and status, his fellow-citizens were once again gathered round him to say farewell.[259] The ceremony took place at 8.30 in the evening of 20 March in the tournament hall by the Klingenteich.

Part Three: Main Works from the Heidelberg Period
(1900-1914)

Introductory Remarks: Troeltsch as a
Theological Author

I remarked right at the beginning that Carl Neumann said of Troeltsch that he carried on 'dialogues... with books and people'.[1] This form of academic approach and work which was characteristic of him only really took shape in the main works of his Heidelberg period. His 'detachment' from the Ritschl school and argument with one of its leading figures, Julius Kaftan, lay behind him. What now followed was in a special way in accord with Troeltsch's nature and intellectual aims: a dialogical procedure, the assimilation of tradition and current scholarly statements in the interests of taking them further so that they issued in work of his own. This way of thinking finds classical expression in his critical discussions with Adolf von Harnack and Wilhelmm Herrmann.

Troeltsch's method of presentation is not simple, nor is his style exactly brilliant. He himself regretted this; others, like Wilhelm Herrmann, occasionally complained about it. But the often long accumulation of clauses and the illumination of a subject from a wide variety of angles bring readers under their spell because they sense that this form results from an unconditional dedication to the subject-matter, that the author is concerned to express reality as vividly and as comprehensively as possible.

First of all Troeltsch has an overall view, an overall picture of what he is aiming to describe which is gained by intuition, for example in the assessment of a historical phenomenon or a systematic conception. Closer definition, with the adoption of appropriate conceptuality, follows and is quite open to correction.

A further characteristic is connected with this. For most of the time Troeltsch, who often arrived at his topics and formulated them in relation to other positions, shows little interest in continuing literary dialogue following the usual academic customs. That means that he has no interest in the unconditional assertion of a position, nor even in specific arguments in support of it and the choice of concepts. He could admire a capacity for conceptual distinctions in others with a kind of detached, slightly aesthetic satisfaction, but set little store by them himself. He was concerned to deal with specific subject-matter in an approach for which conceptuality had only an auxiliary function; the decisive thing was to arrive at an existential position which had been achieved through theological and philosophical reflection or had simply been made or had become conscious.

This notion and aim also explains his sometimes rather violent treatment of material. In an apt image which takes up a well-known saying from the biblical tradition, C.H.Becker has said that the phrase 'I will not let you go unless you bless me' applies to Troeltsch and his struggle with the material.[2] This struggle with the material involves the concretizing of the intuition and overall view which stamp him from the start.

In principle, Troeltsch expects that the scholarly discussion following first publication will serve to bring further precision and differentiation to his work. *A priori* he is open to detailed criticism. In his counter-criticism, in particular he tackles methodological objections which prevent the 'modern world' with its legitimate demands for critical scientific reflection and the understanding of life shaped by this from being left out of account. In the light of this academic approach we can understand how in a variety of accounts Troeltsch as it were circles round the decisive question of the significance of the modern world for theology and the church.

Two features, one more on the periphery but nevertheless significant, and one at the centre, go with this kind of thought and description. The first is the way in which Troeltsch thinks it normal to change his mind and unusual to persist in the same view. For him, literary academic work is a forward-looking process in which new insights and recognitions are only to be expected. Thus he makes the following comment on a collection of his articles: 'I have indicated clearly where I have allowed earlier views to stand.'[3] And the central feature is his understanding of himself as a theologian, which is indicated in a remark in a letter to Friedrich von Hügel. He says of himself: 'I am more a theologian for people in general, for those who have been stimulated and are searching, than for a special church community.'[4] Troeltsch deliberately wanted to have an influence on a broad public beyond all the narrower limits of academic theology and its audience. He saw his educated contemporary as the ideal reader. His real interest was to provide access to a religious and theological perspective. It goes without saying that this is not true of all his writings equally, nor was that his intention. But it is obvious that he always had this overarching aspect in view in his academic works, even those which are theological in the narrower sense.

I

A Historical Description and Analysis of the Time

In his autobiographical retrospect, Troeltsch remarks that his 'concern for knowledge... was from earliest youth directed towards the historical world'.[5] It is in keeping with this basic drive towards historical knowledge that some of his works take up historical themes; however, they do so not as if in a 'museum', engaging in history as concerned with what lies in the past, but ultimately out of an interest in the present day.

1. Methodology and aims

It must have been the success of Troeltsch's first work on the history of Protestant dogma which brought him an enquiry from the publishing house Mohr/Siebeck in Tübingen as to whether he would be prepared to write a history of theology. At first Troeltsch said yes, but he found himself confronted with increasing problems, which had their foundation in both method and content. For him the prime need was for a major account of principles, a kind of continuation of Harnack's history of dogma, one which 'grapples with the specific character and essence of modern theology in the context of cultural history and contrasts this with all old theology from the rise of the dogma of early Christianity'.[6]

Troeltsch did not in principle abandon his plan of writing a history of Protestant dogma beyond the time of the Reformers and Orthodoxy, but it took shape in a modified form. When Troeltsch was asked by Paul Hinneberg to collaborate in the great composite work *Culture of the Present*, he accepted, and wrote the article 'Protestant Christianity and Church in the Modern Period'.[7]

In this project, Troeltsch felt freer in his description. He was not tied to the form and aims of a textbook series, but in practice had the possibility of writing a monograph. The incorporation of the history of theology into the general development of cultural history which characterizes this is a consequence of Troeltsch's historical thought, his feeling for method and his basic view of theology. 'For me everything issues in the idea of a history of the

European mind, i.e. of the religions and of scientific reflection. That is really my main scholarly idea, the one from which I take my bearings and seek a basis for answering individual questions.'[8]

At this point it is worth comparing Troeltsch's methodological approach with that of others. With this view Troeltsch differed from Ferdinand Christian Baur and his school, for whom the assumption of dialectical development from a principle had precedence over the understanding of individual features which proved resistant to the principle. 'It is not the dialectic of its [Christianity's] principle but the clash with and adhesion to a modern culture growing up independently alongside it which condition its modern development.'[9] But Troeltsch also cannot accept Harnack's ideas of a history of dogma which is to be thought of as being in principle independent, in which the essential features of the historical development of dogma are described out of a marked interest in the context of the history of concepts and ideas.

The methodological principles which Troeltsch himself follows can be inferred from an outline of his work on 'Protestant Christianity and Church in the Modern Period' (1906). It begins with a description of the relationship of Protestantism to the Middle Ages on the one hand and the modern world on the other. Then follows a description of the reform movements of the sixteenth century, in which the Reformation is incorporated into the general reformist tendencies of the time. Troeltsch describes the theology of the eighteenth and nineteenth centuries within the framework of remarks on modern culture generally. In other words, he investigates Neo-Protestantism to see what changes from old Protestantism take place as a result of its involvement in the modern world and what connecting links can be established. In the first perspective he stresses the Enlightenment and German Idealism, and in the second the religious impulses which emerge from the Baptist movement and the principles of humanistic thought.

The idea of a 'history of the European mind' presented by Troeltsch is governed by philosophical considerations which begin from the priority of the spirit or spiritual life over nature. The proximity to the aims and approach of Wilhelm Dilthey is unmistakable. Both are guided by an interest in intellectual history which derives the description of spiritual and religious phenomena from universal cultural involvements and connections and pursues their development. The multifariousness of historical reality is to be understood by deriving it from fundamental ideas, central questions and conceptual forms which extend beyond particular periods and yet are each seen in its special form. Here Troeltsch differs from Dilthey in that the analysis of a specific situation plays a major role, even down to social and political conditions.[10]

Troeltsch's intention to incorporate the history of Protestant theology and the church in an overarching cultural context and to understand its effect on modern conditions leads him to a twofold approach: that of the historian, who with a view to the present becomes an analyst of the time, and that of the systematic thinker, who seeks the connection between cultural tradition and present tasks and thus is forced to select and to criticize.

The scholarly world was quite unanimous in seeing Troeltsch's work on the history of Protestant theology and the church as an impressive achievement. This verdict is in no way diminished by the sometimes vigorous controversy over Troeltsch's account. Quite the contrary. Criticism was directed mainly at his assessment of the relationship between the Reformation and the Middle Ages and his account of the relationship between Protestantism and the modern world.

Thus while, for example, Wilhelm Herrmann recognized Troeltsch's work as a towering achievement in the history of theology, he vigorously criticized his view of dogmatics and the historical analysis which had led him to distinguish between old and new Protestantism. The influence of Troeltsch's historical work has shown that he was tackling major issues here. At the same time Herrmann saw correctly that in Troeltsch historical analysis and systematic insight belong together and condition or justify each other. The question whether Luther is to be put more in the Middle Ages or more at the beginning of the modern period cannot be separated from considerations of theology, the history of ideas and method. The same goes for the question of the significance of Protestantism for the genesis of the modern world. Here Troeltsch's understanding and assessment of the Enlightenment plays an important role.

2. The historical location of the Reformation

Troeltsch's location of the Reformation period within cultural history in the context of the Middle Ages is new for Protestant historiography. Troeltsch bases his thesis theologically on an interpretation of Luther and historically by references to the understanding of the world and the idea of culture.

Troeltsch sees a new solution to old – especially mediaeval – problems in Luther's stress on faith in the question of the appropriation of salvation by human beings. Mediaeval theology left questions open; Luther found new answers. The special character of the answer, its originality and historical significance, seems to be diminished by the combination of question and answer in this account and evaluation of Reformation theology. The general hermeneutical principle of relating question and answer must be open to the real novelty in an answer. Luther's pointed emphasis on the aspect of faith in the appropriation of salvation must as a possibility or in principle be able to lead in a different direction from the earlier view. Here Troeltsch's understanding tends to stress the combination more strongly than the possible difference, the connection more strongly than the novelty.[11]

For Troeltsch, the proximity of Reformation theology to mediaeval theology, indeed the continuity between them, emerges even more clearly in questions of ethics than in his understanding of faith. Protestant ethics maintains the basic idea, aim and outline of the view developed in mediaeval Catholic theology. The ethical concept is not governed by the separation of worldly and spiritual life but by the formation of the world in a Christian spirit, so that in the ethics of Lutheranism, as in those of Calvinism, there is a closed cultural idea, corresponding to Catholicism, which is to be assumed as a basis and an aim.

For Troeltsch, none of the fundamental ideas of Reformation theology are in the last resort original creations. They take up prior questions and continue views which are a matter of principle. As such basic notions Troeltsch mentions the idea of grace, the idea of faith, the shaping of the world by a basic universal idea of culture, the view of the state and finally the idea of the churches and authority.[12]

It is noteworthy and significant for Troeltsch's view that he mentions the concept of grace as the first 'basic idea' of Protestantism and only then that of faith. So he does not follow the priority he finds in the Protestant tradition. Troeltsch points out that the concept of grace in Reformation theology has a mediaeval origin, and in the history of its influence has a connection with the theology of Augustine. The concept of grace in Augustine is about the communication of the spirit and the guarantee of salvation. In Reformation theology there is merely a stress on the character of trust, which is bound up with the acceptance of grace on the human side. In this respect one can speak of a certain transformation of the mediaeval concept of grace. Nevertheless the significance of concept of grace as such for the understanding of the church is preserved.

Troeltsch then uses a similar argument in the case of the idea of faith. Here, too, essentially he can see only the connection, the continuity, with the Middle Ages, because the Protestant version merely takes up a problem which stems from mediaeval thought. Protestantism reponds to a question which is not really solved in Catholicism, namely how the appropriation of salvation can be seen as a task for the Christian's life of faith on the presupposition of infant baptism. Protestant theology answers the question by accepting Paul's understanding of faith, and at the same time goes beyond Paul. The sacramental event is internalized: it takes a turn towards the intellectual and the dispositional. To this degree one can say that it loses its supernatural character.

It is not always easy to follow Troeltsch's trains of thought. He uses a system of argument and description on various levels which stresses each different aspect. For example, he can think in terms of the self-development of the religious idea, but at the same time criticize Baur's view of history which is based on it. How proximity and criticism are combined here and partly transcend themselves is shown, for example, in Troeltsch's formulation that 'the Christian idea' was not exhausted with Catholicism,[13] but further historical manifestations of the idea had to follow as a process from the power of the idea. Or he points out that the concept of faith in Catholicism could not have the same significance as in Protestantism, for two reasons. Because of the missionizing of the Gentile world, in Catholicism it could not amount to internalization and the personal appropriation of salvation; rather, the idea of repentance and the proving of human beings had to stand in the foreground. Secondly, the concept of faith was already 'occupied', because it meant the act of subjection to the doctrinal statements of the church. Only in the course of the Middle Ages did the change in the spiritual situation generally and the religious possibilites which emerged with it produce a move to forms of personal piety. An aspect of cultural history clarifies the problem of the appropriation of an alien religious feeling by the Germanic people. From this wider perspective it can be said that before Luther there had already been attempts at internalization and a stress on the personal appropriation of salvation.

Troeltsch broadens the question historically and picks out psychological aspects of faith, so that he can say: 'Luther's concept of faith is simply the highpoint of this process of appropriation. He simplifies and internalizes it so that it is quite a transparent and simple event, trust in the gracious will of God who forgives sins. So he was also the first one to find a single name for this process.'[14]

The criterion for Troeltsch's assessment that no theological discontinuity can be perceived in Protestant ethics but rather that they are a solution to mediaeval problems is the 'identity of the Christian cultural idea'. At this point it becomes clear how the question of the relationship between the Middle Ages and the Reformation is connected with that of the relationship between the Reformation and the modern world. For whereas the Reformation, along with the Middle Ages, represented a universal Christian cultural idea, it was the Enlightenment which really liberated the secular element.

If we think of Luther's doctrine of the two kingdoms and its effect on the practice or the experience of faith, Troeltsch's association of the Middle Ages with the Reformation seems interesting but somewhat arbitrary. Here Troeltsch introduces the 'cultural idea' as a unifying perspective, in relation to which the distinctions made by Luther lose their significance. Troeltsch also approximates Luther's thought to mediaeval thought in connection with freedom and secularity, because he understands and evaluates freeing essentially as coming of age in the Enlightenment sense. However, the anticipation of Enlightenment ideas makes the historical intermediate tones of a relative freeing disappear in the comparison with mediaeval forms of thought and life.

When Troeltsch touches on the question of asceticism in connection with ethics it is quite evident that in the second edition his researches for the *Social Teachings* lie in the background and have led him to change what he originally said. Troeltsch's verdict is on the whole more cautious, and is aimed at avoiding misunderstandings. The new, Protestant, view is meant to appear as a modification of the Catholic form of asceticism, and is therefore described as 'inner-worldly asceticism'. However, this modification does not alter the basic notion that 'Protestantism, too, is familiar with asceticism and as a spiritual culture has its centre there'.[15]

The Protestant form of the state church is a continuation of the idea of a religious culture. Here, too, Troeltsch significantly speaks of the demands of the idea. The universal church needs universal culture. The idea of the 'church which alone brings salvation' and a 'supernatural concept of truth' are normative here. Both these two elements are 'developed as a matter of course by Protestantism'.[16]

Granted, the unitary church is turned into the Landeskirche, but that similarly lives by the ideal of a universal church culture, though this may be limited and capable of realization only in a limited area. Troeltsch does not conceal the fact that in Luther there are ideas which contradict this, but they are attributed to an early ideal of community and community piety. 'There remains the idea of the unitary church, the power of the true church of the pure word and sacrament which alone brings salvation, the absolute truth-concept of a clear supernatural revelation and the duty of the state to support the free activity of the word with all the means at its disposal and at least externally to keep down or do away with all stubborn resistance to the truth.'[17]

What is decisive for Troeltsch in this argument is that the idea of the church and the concept of truth have led to the same cultural and political consequences in both Catholicism and Protestantism. In other words, the role of the state over against the church is the same in both the mediaeval Catholic view and the Protestant view. At all events, the interests of the church have priority over those of the state.[18]

Troeltsch certainly sees that the hierarchical character of the relationship between church and state fades into the background in Protestantism. But the construction of the relationship suggests that on theological premises 'the free development of a unity of life in a state church is expected'.[19]

For Troeltsch, there is also a continuity between mediaeval and Protestant theology in the acceptance of Aristotelian philosophy. Since this is specifically not the case in Luther, he finds it the explanation of both Luther's particular character and the difference between Luther's theology and the subsequent period. His explanation is that Luther's definition of the relationship between faith and reason follows from the depths of his religious genius, just as the 'natural opposition of the religious genius to any philosophy' is significant.[20] This one-sidedness and self-sufficiency of the religious idea and the religious understanding were not maintained by the subsequent period. The tendency towards Aristotelian philosophy and a corresponding basis and ordering of theology and the activity of philosophical and theological schools was the logical conclusion.

Of course, not all the individual formulations and ideas put forward by Troeltsch always do justice to Luther's theology, for example, when Troeltsch speaks of the 'possession of the Word' which Luther sees as the foundation of the 'church which alone brings salvation'. In my view, neither the phrase 'possession of the Word' nor the formula the 'church which alone brings salvation' rightly fits Luther's intention. In Luther the emphasis on word and preaching is dynamic and not static; its orientation is more personal than institutional. However, what Troeltsch is trying to express in these formulations is clear enough. He wants to show that in the Reformation dogmatizing, one-sidedness and exclusiveness remained, even if the specific reasons for them had changed, so that in terms of practical consistency the relationship between church and world or church and culture went in the same direction as it did in the Middle Ages, namely in that of the compulsive character of a church culture.

Naturally Troeltsch sees that not everything that is said about the essence and significance of Protestantism as a historical phenomenon and its historical effects can be true. To supplement and counter the idea of ongoing continuity, Troeltsch speaks of the 'transcendence and abolition' of the mediaeval idea in Protestantism. This indicates that the new element introduced by Protestantism had an indirect role in laying the foundations for modern culture and the modern world-view. However, this 'new' element is not abrupt, nor is it to be seen or understood in isolation; rather, it was prepared for by the crisis of mediaeval theology and the mediaeval church. Troeltsch's formulae seek to convey a 'sublation' (*Aufhebung*) in the Hegelian sense.[21]

But what is the decisively new element which could thus lead to a sublation of the mediaeval idea in Protestantism? According to Troeltsch it is the destruction of the Catholic understanding of the sacraments.[22]

In the Catholic view, the sacraments are materializations of the divine and have an absolute character where salvation is concerned. According to Troeltsch, in Luther 'subjective' religion takes the place of 'objective' religion, and that means the requirement of a personal appropriation of salvation through faith. However, Troeltsch does not let this idea escape criticism either, so that despite all the changes continuity can again be recognized. For while in Luther miracle in the sacramental sense is replaced by the 'miracle' of the idea, it does remain a miracle, so that with the shift from the sphere of the senses to that of the spiritual we have only the beginnings of the modern understanding. This change 'corresponds to the modern tendency towards the notional and the immanent linking of all events in the soul, to the immanence of God in the very life of the spirit'.[23]

Heinrich Boehmer makes a critical comment on this assessment of Luther's idea of the sacraments in relation to that of the Middle Ages, to the effect that Troeltsch did not start from Luther's positive basic ideas but put a negative consequence at the centre of his account. If Troeltsch wanted to explain how the Catholic concept of the sacrament came to disintegrate in Protestantism, he should have gone back to the principle of justification, which was central for Luther. But here above all, his formal understanding which came from outside failed to note this.[24]

Troeltsch thinks that the breaking through of mediaeval sacramentalism lies in a view of religion as a religion of faith and the spirit, with a stress on the human disposition. He can use 'character of faith' and 'character of knowledge' of religion almost interchangeably. Certainly he fails to do justice to Luther's theological approach here. The main reason why Troeltsch's ideas are so difficult here is that his historical account sets out to be a generalization with a focus on cultural history and at the same time presents a wealth of individual perspectives to make this clear and provide a basis for it.

Some of the further remarks on Luther which were added later can be explained from the criticism of Troeltsch's account which had been made in the meantime. Thus for example Ferdinand Kattenbusch wrote in a review: 'At any rate Luther's name is mentioned here and there. But Luther above all would largely have rejected Troeltsch's interpretation and his ideas. Above all he would marvel, and I can only marvel with him, that Troeltsch does not accept that there is a break with the "Middle Ages" if Luther has only filled its 'form with new content'.[25] Kattenbusch goes on to complain that Troeltsch makes abstract psychological associations, that he brings his intuition into play, and that his results do not match up to the sources or to research into the sources.[26] Troeltsch then substantially expanded this part of his work by pointing beyond the 'central idea' of Protestantism which he cited, to individual manifestations.

Troeltsch sees a further form of the transcending and abolition of mediaeval thought, characteristic of Protestantism, in religious individualism. 'Just as faith stands over against the sacrament and the priestly power of redemption, so religious individualism stands over against church dogma and the teaching authority of the priest.'[27] But even here his verdict on Luther's theology is positive only to a limited degree. For Luther's opposition to religious dogma was only conditional, and could not go so far as to dissolve it. The dogma itself remains; all that changes is the way in which it is adopted, the basis for the authority. The individualism intended is thus not radically new, because the basic presupposition remains in the form of the supernatural basis of authority in the context of revelation.

Finally, in ethics a transcending and abolition of the mediaeval view can be seen in the way in which the religious idea has its practical consequences in the sphere of personal ethics, so that in general one can speak of a 'dispositional ethics' in Protestantism. However, this ethics is not yet constructed on the notion of radical autonomy. It still contains a supernaturalism which derives actual demands from the revealed law. In concrete terms, this is demonstrated by the emphasis on the idea of calling in Protestantism. For Troeltsch, the basis of this does not lie in the intrinsic value of the vocation in itself, but is derived from a divine foundation or appointment, so that here, too, limits are set to autonomy. Indeed, for Troeltsch the Catholic idea of a 'graduated ethics' which takes up and transcends the human ethic comes closer to the unity of life than the Protestant idea of the human vocation to be seen in the perspective of God and grounded in God, which is to include the character of suffering over the world and its conditions.

According to Troeltsch, all the 'new' ideas of Protestantism cited in this connection have a common root, namely Luther's idea of God. Luther's change in the concept of God can be explained in terms of his doctrine of the primal state and his view of the law. The concept of God is interpreted no longer on the basis of the categories of substance, but of those of personality. The relationship with God is about the divine concern which is affirmed and grasped by human beings in faith. In so far as the personal components take on a central significance, for Troeltsch there is a real and complete theism. In Troeltsch's view, one can also talk of a theism of immanence, namely the immanence of the natural spirit in the divine, which in Lutheranism is thought of more in terms of universal love, and in Calvinism more as an expression of groundless grace. However, in both forms of Reformation theology this personalistic theism is disguised by the retention of the dogma of the Trinity and the development of the idea of original sin, the substance of which is the separation of the empirical human being from God.[28]

3. Troeltsch's understanding of Luther

By way of anticipation it has to be said that in his interpretation of Luther Troeltsch has a tendency to psychologize the person of Luther and also judges Luther's work from this perspective. In his account Troeltsch incorporates biographical and psychological perspectives in such a way that the structure of Luther's personality becomes an essential starting point for the interpretation of his theology. Luther is described as a religious genius in whom the 'unspoilt naivety of the child of the people'[29] and a primal religious force are combined. Courage and a desire to dominate, inwardness and the idea of authority, form a contradictory unity in Luther. With this interpretation Troeltsch creates for himself a starting point for locating mediaeval and modern elements in the Reformation. His estimation of Luther as a 'great personality' is probably also connected with the early influence of Carlyle and Treitschke, and derives from an understanding of history which attaches to the great stimulators, the prominent personalities, an essential significance for the course of history. There are also connections here with the understanding produced in the history-of-religions approach.[30]

In Troeltsch's view the real impetus to the Reformation comes from outside. With his criticism of the sacrament of penance Luther rejects the principles of sacramental thought and the Catholic concept of grace. For him, the church is the fellowship of believers, and the hearers of the Word need no authority which goes beyond that. As I have already indicated, Troeltsch finds here a basic tendency towards a religion of disposition. A main problem of his understanding of Luther is how to see the relationship between Luther's almost automatic adoption of the supernaturalism of the mediaeval church and what Troeltsch calls his orientation on an autonomous religion of disposition. Troeltsch attempts to tackle the fundamental difficulty here by incorporating the orientation on a religion of disposition into the history of Luther's development.

He refers to Staupitz, Occamist theology and mysticism. Luther's nailing up of the theses and his position in the subsequent theological arguments over a new view of the sacrament of penance then show a tendency towards a religion of disposition. But even if one puts the course of Luther's development in this kind of setting, the difficulty remains how supernaturalism and an autonomous religion of disposition can go together: how – in other words – the individual force of religious feeling and the retention of the supernatural standpoint of the church moving along fixed tracks can be in any way compatible.[31]

No historical account will dispute that there are contradictions in Luther's personality. However, the question remains what theological significance to attach to them, and above all whether a strong emphasis at this point does not undervalue questions of substance and the assessment of historical constellations and possibilities.

Troeltsch's picture of Luther's personality seems remarkably fragmented. On the one hand he concedes special conditions to the religious genius, and on the other he emphasizes the problems of the religious radicalism which thus emerge. He takes an utterly positive view of the fact that in Luther there is a combination of religious power and a resolute awareness of criteria and limitations. But precisely these limitations which are perceived or accepted by Luther are now problematical for Troeltsch and can no longer be accepted, because in principle they presuppose an ecclesiastical supernaturalism.

One can grasp Troeltsch's understanding of Luther more firmly by looking closely at the exegesis of specific texts, like those of the main Reformation writings.[32] Here it emerges that Troeltsch's criticism of Luther emerges most clearly in his interpetation of the work on freedom.[33] Troeltsch stresses that an exaggerated religious principle of Luther's led to a focus on the contrast between a religious and a purely secular view. 'An ethical approach to the world and secular action is arrived at here only by way of corporeality, in which Christians with their fleshly desires and needs for social converse still continue to live.'[34]

Troeltsch interprets this passage in terms of the psychology of faith, in connection with both Luther himself and the Christian. He does not take enough account of the contemporary historical background and the theological tradition. Thus, for example, he does not ask from where Luther received the stimuli to formulate the idea of freedom, and where there are links between the mystical tradition of the Middle Ages and Pauline conceptuality.

Troeltsch cannot see clearly how the work on freedom and that addressed to the nobility can go together as the expression of a uniform overall theological and political view. Characteristically he derives the contradiction that he feels from a contradiction in Luther himself: a contradiction in his 'own being and will'.[35]

Troeltsch thinks that the idea that faith is derived only from the promise of the divine Word in preaching and feels completely free from secular conditions is incompatible with the idea that the gospel should renew life in secular conditions. Troeltsch's explanation is that this is the permanent contradiction in Luther's being and outlook. Luther then attempted to bring together the conflicting tendencies in his theology, which he could no longer understand in terms of the Catholic intention of the rise from nature to supernature, by adopting the idea of natural law.[36]

Troeltsch, himself critical of systems and strict systematization, emphasizes the lack of system in Luther. For him, Luther did not really have a theology but only the elements of one, which he formulated in relation to specific situations and as theological answers to the needs of a particular situation.[37] In the end he feels that a discrepancy remains: the tension between the subjective principle of faith and the objective orientation on biblical tradition and central dogmas like the dogma of Christ and the doctrines of the Trinity and the eucharist.

Perhaps it could be said that the conflict in Troeltsch's own life as a theologian, as in his theology, is reflected in his interpretation of Luther. It is the conflict between the element which is pure faith, the 'inward' element, and an objectification in the form of doctrine, an ordered form of community life and a movement towards the world. A further problem is how an emphasis on the personal principle of faith can protect itself from radicalizations which result in a devaluation of the world and lead the person with a religious orientation into cultural isolation.

Troeltsch discovered in the theology of Luther approaches from his initial period towards a more 'ideal' view of Christianity and a breaking through of dogmatic assertions. However, for him these were not enough to form a direct link to the modern world. Nor was what one might call the Protestant shaping of life or world-view in the context of post-Reformation thought enough either. Rather, there had to be a greater degree of subjectivity and freedom which cannot be found here, at any rate along the official line of Protestantism and its influence. In order to find this it was necessary to turn to peripheral phenomena, the 'left' wing of the Reformation, Spiritualism and the Anabaptists. If we add to the spirit of inwardness and freedom which has its roots here what can be said about the effect of humanism on the principles of scriptural research and the adoption of the idea of truth, then in Troeltsch's overall conception we have what in terms of its Protestant origins could be understood as a movement towards the modern world.

4. The contribution of Protestantism to the rise of the modern world

In his article on 'Luther and the Modern World' (1908), Troeltsch primarily wanted to demonstrate what links Protestantism with the modern world. So he chose a different method of description from the one he used in 'Protestant Christianity and Church in the Modern Period'.[38] He was prompted, not least by the different presentation of the theme, to work out the novel historical element in Protestantism. Only in a second and less emphasized step did he then note what separates the two, so that his assessment of Reformation theology does not point so much backwards towards mediaeval Catholicism as forwards towards modernity.

Here Troeltsch describes Protestantism as a religion of faith, which brings out a concentration on the conviction of faith in the individual in place of the communication of the substance of salvation. Troeltsch qualifies his description by observing that the close, biblical faith of the Reformation has ideological presuppositions about the validity of belief in God and the world of the Bible which are no longer permissible on the basis of the intellectual changes in the modern period. Individualism is restricted by the view that there should be a single form of the communication of truth which is the same for all. An individualism which corresponded to modern thought would have had to be freer and more mobile; it would have had to assume a variation in religious ideas and the possibilities of access to religious experience.

Ethically, the dispositional ethics of Protestantism, which in principle are to be seen in a positive light, have their limitations in the fact that they are governed by ideas which no longer correspond to modern thought, in terms of immanence – they include above all the ideas of heaven and hell and the theory of retribution. On modern presuppositions, what old Protestantism propagated ethically as an inclination towards the world is no longer enough. Science has detached itself from its links with the church. Therefore ethics must be rethought – something which is more possible for Protestantism than for Catholicism. In other words, attention must be paid to the emancipation of science and political life from the claims of religion, so that the Protestant position, too, must undergo a change for a new interpretation of the religious significance of 'openness to the world' to become possible. For that to happen, dogmatic presuppositions must be abandoned, above all in the form of the doctrine of original sin. In this way Troeltsch makes it clear that in an approach from a history of culture and religion understood in evolutionary terms he expects an appropriate theological understanding (in this case of Protestantism) only in a theological consideration and understanding of the changes.

A discussion of Troeltsch's arguments would have to take particular account of his understanding of sin in relation to the idea of freedom. Here Troeltsch takes up a key modern question. We must ask on what presuppositions the concept of sin can be understood as a limitation of human freedom, as it is by Troeltsch. Here Troeltsch understands sin as an ontological-anthropological concept. He does not find decisive the conception of the relationship with God which it contains. However, if in the biblical understanding the relationship with God is primary, then 'sin' is the negative side of the salvation offered in the relationship with God. It is simply the renunciation of the life that stems from God's salvation. In that case, however, there is no *a priori* limitation to autonomy in the sense of a modern idea of freedom either: rather, the relationship with God is an acceptance of the idea of autonomy in a qualitative sense.[39]

Troeltsch's reflections show that he has perceived the problem of secularization. He sees something of the effect of the history of the religious tradition in the development of modern thought. However, above all the Reformation, with its 'left' wing, represents a shift in the tradition towards free elements which stress subjectivity and disposition. If, as Troeltsch thinks, the religious form of autonomy is bound up with cultural ideas of autonomy generally, the independence of cultural life need not be disputed, and the modern person's feeling of value need not be destroyed.

Troeltsch assumes a line of cultural development which does not simply coincide with the actual course of history. To put it simply, his is a forward-looking line of development focussed on the formation of the modern idea of autonomy. The link between Protestantism and the modern world is developing, and for Troeltsch exists to the degree that the principle of autonomy and the idea of immanence can relate to an individualism which has a religious foundation. This relationship is possible and meaningful to the degree that religious individualism basically seeks a freedom from the world which includes or holds open the religious ties of human beings as persons.

We can certainly agree with Troeltsch that there are structural parallels and convergences between Protestant tradition and modern thought. However, the meaning of individualism in Reformation thought and then – on the basis of philosophical and theological development – of individualism in modernity would have to be defined more closely. More precisely, the relationship between individualism and autonomy would have to be clarified in a history and analysis of the concepts, since individualism does not of itself mean autonomy, but takes on a new value with the concept of autonomy, as that concept found special expression in the course of Enlightenment thought and German idealism.[40] The more Troeltsch takes up the idea of autonomy as an interpretative formula in relation to the modern world, the more disturbed he is that the Reformation idea of individualism seems to take back and limit what can be described from the perspective of modern intellectual history as 'autonomous'.

It is evident in both the general thesis and in the details that Troeltsch's assessment of the Middle Ages and the Reformation cannot be separated from his understanding of modernity. This is the new element which distinguishes itself both from the Middle Ages and the Reformation period, in both theology and philosophy and in cultural terms generally. Nevertheless, even the 'new' element in modernity always remains only relatively new. For reason and the spiritual life are always directed towards history. They cannot produce anything absolutely new which is binding on all in the same way. Even what is characteristic of the modern world binds this time to the prior epochs of culture, though not as clearly as in the relationship between the Reformation period and the Middle Ages.[41]

The fundamental significance of this question for Troeltsch's thought is evident from the fact that the concern with Luther and his theology and an interest in the history of the influence of Protestantism persists in his work and emerges in different themes and with different accents. In the 1906 lecture to the Stuttgart Historians' Conference on 'The Significance of Protestantism for the Rise of the Modern World' Troeltsch once again makes the connection betwen Reformation theology and modernity, now in a rightly different way. He evaluates the Reformation as the religious liberation of the individual. It is to be seen along with the Renaissance as the artistic liberation, and with the Enlightenment as the scientific liberation, of people from the tutelage of the church, politics and the spirit. With its view, Protestantism corresponds to the modern world in many respects.[42]

Here, too, Troeltsch sees the idea of autonomy as the fundamental principle for the rise of the modern world.[43] He takes up the distinction between autonomy and heteronomy in order to describe the relationship between modern culture and mediaeval culture. The question is, first, whether one can do justice to great eras like the Middle Ages and modernity in this way, in that they are complex and always also more than the simple conceptual view or distinction. Secondly, it has to be pointed out that since Kant, the idea of heteronomy has negative connotations and that justice cannot be done to mediaeval culture either immanently or from the aspect of cultural development on that basis. The general criterion for an assessment of a cultural development here is modern culture, which indicates a hermeneutical problem in that the criterion is taken from the complex which is being subjected to comparison. It will hardly prove possible to interpret culture in an overarching sense other than through such a process, which then brings a corresponding pre-understanding with it. However, this must be used critically and questions must be asked of it.

It should probably be conceded to Troeltsch that the nature of modern culture may be defined in terms of the idea of autonomy, understood as a principle of personal conviction, on a rational critical basis. But we are now far removed from the positive feature which, according to Troeltsch, persists despite all ideas of crisis and the ambivalence of culture because the problems of this culture of conviction have emerged more clearly in the meantime. It has largely proved to be a matter of asking too much, and the way in which human beings are hurled into instability and a void as a permanent threat to themselves and their culture has been brought into view in a different kind of radicalism. However, with the possibility of self-determination, which is surely to be rated highly, is there not a human capacity to perceive finitude, to accept handicaps in the form of a universal and individual fate? Not to mention the fact that large areas of the political life of our time cannot be subsumed under the specific character of the modern world cited by Troeltsch, because, far from being any autonomy, they prove to be irrationalisms, a failure in the face of the human interest in self-realization in work and society. The principle of autonomy and the idea of freedom present central aims of political action, the realization of which is as controversial as it is difficult, aims which result in negative forms as new dependences and losses. Troeltsch saw the beginnings of these threats; they are also contained theoretically in the notion of 'ambivalence' as a characteristic of modern culture. Nevertheless, the basic insight into the possibility of a move from freedom and self-determination to bondage and alienation is transcended or restrained by at least a latent belief in history and a guarded optimism about the possibility of cultural development and the creative human power which determines culture, an optimism which asserts itself at the end.

For Troeltsch, it is crucially significant for the rise of the modern world that the rational system of sciences has taken the place of theology as a single science. Here there is a connection with ideas of Wilhelm Dilthey.[44] However, the perception of actual conditions must be added to this perspective from the history of ideas. A tightly organized state structure, a capitalist economic organization and disposition emerge in connection with technological changes. All this leads to political clashes externally and social political struggles internally. Here Troeltsch leaves open the question of which factor is ultimately decisive, the ideal principle of autonomy or actual conditions. It is hard for him to decide whether the actual conditions 'determine that spirit or are on the other hand determined by it'.[45]

It is illuminating to see what normative figures Troeltsch mentions in connection with modern culture. He mentions Goethe above all; then come the great mystics – like Eckhart and Böhme – and Kant and Schleiermacher are mentioned as pioneer thinkers. The combination of names, which seems remarkable at first sight, results from the fact that Troeltsch is concerned both to offer an orientation for modern men and women and also to mention symbolic figures. He recognized that these figures have had, and still have, specific effects which go beyond the original content of their work or its primary intention. Troeltsch applies this insight to the question of secularization.

In general, Troeltsch could have shared the objections Hans Blumenberg has made to absolutizing theological thought,[46] which suspects and impairs purely human self-assertion. But the consequences which arise from that for a historical approach are not the same for Troeltsch as they are for Blumenberg. Troeltsch's understanding of mediaeval culture and modernity is governed by the notion that a further cultural development took place under the influence of religious life which is also positive, and so it would be impossible to talk of a 'culture guilt' as a possible burden on or suspicion of modern man and his cultural self-understanding. Blumenberg sees theology as an obstacle, a compulsion, a constriction. Modernity came into being against religion; for Blumenberg, intellectual curiosity could only prevail in the face of pressure from religion. Blumenberg reacts over-sensitively to the element of order and compulsion which is innate in any religion or cultural creation. It would not have occurred to Troeltsch to suppose that it was appropriate to derive the question of the legitimation of modernity from the assumption of a primarily religious use of the idea or the emergence of a 'problem of dispossession'. For Troeltsch, the modern world is indeed also *against* religion, but equally it grew up *with* it. What it owes to religion is a positive, constructive element which furthers culture.

Troeltsch sees the adoption of Reformation thought in the present sensibility of the world as coming through culture. What that means becomes clear, say, when we note the difference here from the procedure of Gogarten, who thinks primarily in terms of theological connections orientated on personal phenomena like freedom, responsibility and coming of age. In his adoption of biblical Reformation thought, Gogarten, like Troeltsch, is governed by a presupposition which is critical of culture, but the extent and evaluation of the cultural criticism are different. For Gogarten, true freedom and coming of age can be thought of only as a freeing of the relationship with the world for responsibility before God, and that means responsibility for human beings and the world. For Gogarten, 'purely worldly' is a qualitative statement which can only really embrace believers in so far as their 'being surrounded by the world' is translated and overcome in faith.[47]

Whereas modern historical thought – here Troeltsch is a representative for Gogarten – seeks to extract the 'essential' from history in a process of abstraction and understands it as a closed totality, Gogarten has a personal concept of historical totality. This 'totality' in principle precedes human action and activity, choice and commitment; it is a totality derived from God's being and action. Troeltsch is not concerned, like Gogarten, to interpret history on theological presuppositions and with a theological aim. Rather, he is concerned with universal considerations of the philosophy of history, and in contrast to Gogarten focusses on the actual historical development. Gogarten has entered into the heritage of his teacher Troeltsch to the degree that he takes up a question which Troeltsch also put, but answered in a different way. The fundamental difference lies in the fact that Gogarten has a different concept of autonomy from Troeltsch. In Gogarten the concept is not rooted in the Enlightenment, but is governed by the idea of creation and by christology.

Troeltsch is concerned to see the rise of the idea of autonomy, with the reference of all questions of authority to critical reason, as an event the substance and system of which can not only be ascertained historically but also evaluated positively. He can make a positive connection between the shift to the modern period expressed here and the Protestant Christian tradition only by seeing some beginnings of such autonomous thought in Luther himself and then – in the course of his deeper interest in the Baptist movement and Spiritualism – increasingly in the peripheral movements of the Reformation period.[48]

One can say only that Protestantism has a 'share' in the formation of the modern sciences, and this also applies to the other spheres of modern cultural development. For Troeltsch, modern science began among figures who were not tied to the church, among men like Descartes, Machiavelli and Hobbes. Certainly it was possible for Protestantism to ally itself with the spirit of modern thought, but it contributed only conditionally or partially to this development. There were severe struggles before this process of association began. Thus Protestantism did not introduce the principle of autonomy into science, but was itself confronted with this principle. However, as a result of the individual components of its theology and view of piety it was in a position to take a positive attitude towards the principle of autonomy. Protestantism itself developed historical criticism. This was first tested in the critical examination of Catholic church historiography, and then had an influence on modern times through the adoption of elements from humanism.

Troeltsch's summary verdict is that Protestantism 'could play a conspicuous part in the production of the modern world',[49] but was not its creator. However, Protestantism was in a better position than Catholicism to give culture room for independent development, indeed to adopt it, as individual modern theologians indicate.

Anyone who claims that Troeltsch had a secret predilection for the Catholic church and Catholic piety – and elements of such an interpretation can be found not only among some contemporaries but also today in Apfelbacher – must be told that for Troeltsch the approach to the modern world, which from a theological and religious perspective is absolutely necessary, can be made far more easily and consistently from Protestantism than from Catholicism.

In this connection reference should be made to Gertrud von le Fort, who reports of Troeltsch: 'In his lectures on symbolism one was sometimes tempted to think that he was putting forward his own ideas and not those of others. I still remember how after his lecture on the Roman church the students asked him, "Professor, are you trying to persuade us to become Catholics?", to which he laughingly retorted, "There could be worse things than that." For him, the worst thing was the idea of the quenching of the soul of the committed Christian, indeed of the religious soul generally.'[50] In my view, Troeltsch was certainly concerned to assert the value of a basic religious conviction in the face of the threat from modern ideological trends, and here he had something in common with modern tendencies in Catholicism. But there can be no connecting Troeltsch in some way with Catholicism because of a proximity to 'Modernism' which he himself accepted and his estimation of the Catholic church and Catholic theology, as Apfelbacher is attempting to do at present. I at any rate feel that this is tendentious. Apfelbacher writes: 'Troeltsch also felt affinities to Catholic modernists in his external fortunes in the church: "We both," he writes to von Hügel, belong to "minorities which are sorely threatened by 'officials' and which therefore naturally draw near to each other under the pressure of a common fate" ' (*Briefe*, 75).[51] However, Apfelbacher cannot or will not see that here already Troeltsch has to assume a greater proximity than was in fact the case because of his conversation partner. As a professor who represented a liberal theological position, Troeltsch was in nowhere near the same situation – in theology or church politics – as a Catholic theologian representing 'Modernism'. When Troeltsch points out that his background is Protestant, just as that of von Hügel is Catholic, the reference to these different backgrounds indicates what divides them, and that does not disappear by assuming some religious element that they ultimately have in common over against the materialism and positivism in the modern world.

For Troeltsch, it is of decisive importance to create a support, a basis for immanental thought and the principle of autonomy which is connected with freedom and therefore does not require subjection to an 'alien' principle. For Troeltsch, this element of personal conviction and the freedom it provides is offered in the Protestant tradition. Thus Protestantism is the form of religion that corresponds to the modern world. This does not exclude but includes Troeltsch's positive assessment of Catholicism as a historical pheonomenon, particularly in its mediaeval (consistent) form, and his leaning towards Catholicism above all where he sees a mystical enlivening of religion in it. It is one thing to acknowledge the achievements of the 'church' as the power of tradition in theology and cultural history, and quite a different matter to investigate specific individual associations and evaluations made in faith. No more can be expected from Troeltsch than an affirmation of Catholicism in the sense indicated. Above all, any more would not fit in above all with the individualistic features of his religious feelings, associated as they are with the principle of freedom and responsibility, or with his criticism of sacramentalism and a view of the church determined by the priestly office. Significantly, Troeltsch's friendship with Friedrich von Hügel came up against its limits at these very points. In his letters to von Hügel, Troeltsch repeatedly takes up the question of his own relationship to the Protestant tradition as over against Catholicism.[52]

5. The cultural situation of the time

For Troeltsch, the cultural situation was characterized by wealth and decay, by heightened possibilities for life and threats to life, by a reversal of all that had been achieved and had been possible. All in all the modern world was a time of latent and sometimes open crisis. The roots of this crisis reached back to the time of the Enlightenment; their effects shaped the face of the present.[53]

This basic insight into the character of the modern world as crisis emerges in Troeltsch at a very early stage.[54]

Three different levels of thought, each with their different thematic orientations and aims, can be distinguished in Troeltsch's historical analyses. There is the theological level in the narrow sense, the level of the history of ideas, and the level of culture generally, including political and social perspectives.[55]

The theological dimension is part of an analysis of the time in that questions must be asked about forms of the life of faith and the relationship between faith and the world which have an objective foundation and call for personal responsibility. Given the ideological and scientific changes in modern times it is important to learn how to rethink the faith. Like all other sciences, like all views of the world and life which have a theoretical foundation, theology must accept the conditions of a particular time. The points of reference for knowledge and the solution to the problems created for theology by the new situation are shaped in advance by tradition.[56]

According to Troeltsch, the compromise formula of the relationship of reason and revelation worked out in tradition is no longer acceptable in the present. It related to an understanding of science which regarded rational knowledge as 'natural' knowledge of God or a natural view of morality, so that 'supernatural' knowledge could attach itself to it. The twin terms 'natural and supernatural' solved the problems of both the connection and the distinction between general and special knowledge.

An empirical understanding of science and its division into individual sciences puts an end to the possibility of compromise on the scientific side. The break comes in theology and the history of ideas with Enlightenment thought, and since then the strict distinction between scientific work and religious conviction has been fundamental. Religion is increasingly limited to the personal sphere, personal conviction and personal life-style. In Troeltsch's view this process need not necessarily be a disadvantage, or detrimental to the cause of religion.

However, the presuppositions have changed not only on the side of science but also on the side of religion, of Christianity. Theology has made use of the patterns of thought and argument generally accepted in science and accordingly has taken a new form. From the principle of scientific thought there followed the reduction of the given, the positive, to a universal on the basis of which Christianity or religious conviction had to justify itself or into the context of which it had to fit without conflict. This provided the beginnings of the science of religion. The prejudice, deriving from scientific considerations generally, against the supernatural character of Christianity, which is supposed to be unique and therefore exclusive, was confirmed by the beginnings of historical-critical research. 'The meeting of the two considerations in particular made and makes the fall of supernaturalism all the more unavoidable.'[57]

Where theology was in a position to take up the heritage of the Enlightenment appropriately, it found the way to a scientific basis. Such a basis, in the form of a philosophy of religion, meets the demand to argue scientifically, and therefore critically, in matters of religion, and on the basis of this philosophy of religion then to build up theology in its dogmatic form as an expression of personal piety.[58]

Now it is striking how cautious Troeltsch is in specifically theological questions after his energetic general demands. He says that he does not regard his position as 'untenable'. At any rate, for him it does not have the untenability of a contrast between natural knowledge and supernatural revelation. That recalls what Troeltsch said to Kaftan about the 'hibernation of Christianity'. In both instances, what is meant is that in the face of the pressure from a scientific and technological age religion can be toned down by a specific epistemological foundation in theology.

The second dimension in this question relates to the approach in terms of cultural history. The crisis of theology belongs in the context of the general crisis which has been produced by the course of more recent intellectual and cultural history. The religious or theological crisis and the general crisis go together, and a reciprocal relationship is to be seen here. The presupposition for overcoming the crisis is insight into its character and basis, so that theology cannot dispense with an approach in terms of cultural history and thus a consideration of the wider, more general framework, which takes spirituality and culture into account.

In the course of his reflections Troeltsch remarks that in the history of theology there have always been times of crisis and times of conservation. This recognition of a 'permanency in change' is achieved by a detached view which passes judgment from a meta-level. Such an attitude is problematical because it can lead to relativization, in so far as the present, as an expression of history, is subject to universal regularities and it seems possible to gain not only insight but also consolation from a belief in history generally. The next generation of theologians then viewed the notion of crisis in a different way: they did not speak of the crisis in terms of cultural history but in terms of the radical crisis of human beings before God, from which only God can provide a way out with his Word which condemns and affirms.

In considering Troeltsch's reflections on the cultural crisis, we need to see that he is protected from the sweeping charge of 'culture Protestantism'.[59] That is because the issue is not one of a form of simple cultural attachment or relationship; rather, Troeltsch has a whole set of insights on the basis of which he draws attention to difficulties in defining relationships, and also allows partial, non-religious, answers aimed at relieving the crisis. The power of religion to sustain culture is not conceived of as being 'exclusive' in relation to other cultural forms and forces but as 'inclusive'. Certainly, the overarching aspect is focussed on culture, and religion as a part of culture, even as its foundation and centre. But religion at the same time evades a merely cultural perspective and classification, as it also remains an 'alien element' which shows culture to be limited and provisional, to the degree that religion rests on the experience of God's concern as a transcendent power.

The acceptance of the radical crisis situation of human beings before God comes as it were from the other end and makes the perspective of faith absolute. After the questioning of traditional political, social and spiritual values by the external crisis situation after 1918, the answer of a total 'No' (and 'Yes') was perhaps more acceptable as a religious answer than the cautious attempt that Troeltsch envisaged to take up the forces which sustain culture. However, we must not overlook the fact that Troeltsch found a way from this foundation of his views not only to a deep concern about contemporary events in the First World War and the post-war situation but also to a political commitment. If we want to see this not just as an expression of personal character and capacities but also as a mode of conduct in keeping with its objective and also theological basis, we must avoid the use of simple, derogatory formulas like culture Protestantism or the mere inwardness of bourgeois Protestant religion.

Finally, a general analysis of culture needs to be mentioned as the last dimension. This covers everything that Troeltsch said about the modern world and its striving for autonomy and rationality. His analysis in the lecture on 'The Scientific Situation and its Demands on Theology' is particularly brilliant. Here Troeltsch not only refers to the deep change in European society and culture since the Enlightenment but includes state life and politics, along with the changes in economic and social life, in his account.[60]

However, Troeltsch did not succeed in going beyond cultural analysis and the critical perspective contained in it to concrete proposals for reform in the light of political and social conditions. This is shown by his lecture on 'The Essence of the Modern Spirit' (1907). Here Troeltsch distinguishes in his analysis between 'hard' and 'soft' ingredients and applies this distinction to the difference betwen state and economic life on the one hand and spiritual forces and forms of life on the other. This distinction has first of all a heuristic significance, and is the expression of a view obtained through the adoption of the Marxist theory of substructure and superstructure. At the same time it sheds some light on his basic attitude to questions of reform. The 'hard' ingredients are clearly outlined, and permanently and inexorably determine the world situation. They are the 'basic pillars of our existence, the basic lines along which all our life and activity moves...'[61]

By contrast, the 'soft' ingredients are to be assigned to the spiritual sphere. They are connected with tradition, are variable and very mobile. But they are also somewhat diffuse. This closer definition certainly does not completely answer the question of the possibility of changing social conditions, but it does give a 'preliminary answer'.

If the possibility of changes is seen above all in the sphere of intellectual life, whereas work, economics and politics mainly run along fixed tracks, then the nature of the distinction limits the possibility and the breadth of reforms. Troeltsch thinks that this perspective is realistic.[62] One can share this view; but his basic distinction has the fatal consequence of not regarding ideas of reform and actual changes as all the more necessary; rather, it easily allows itself to be led into a feeling of helplessness. Troeltsch's basic distinction, like its theoretical and practical consequences, suggest to him a move towards the more mobile forces, which moreover have the advantage of representing 'the higher' as the spiritual element.

Troeltsch similarly indicates an ambivalence with his comment that on the presupposition of modern thought, culture is a culture of reflection. Over against the reflective form of understanding and its effect in positing and enabling freedom stands the power which addresses itself from here to human beings, in so far as it believes that it can understand human knowledge of the law as a mere product of the course of nature. Thus under the conditions of modern intellectual life a feeling of helplessness and scepticism can spread. This scepticism becomes perceptible both in the definition of morality and in the understanding of history. In both cases the question of what is binding and valid seems largely unresolved.

The impression of an unsettled and open situation, the perception of a confusing variety of offers of meaning, competing in form, brings religion on the scene and gives it a special opportunity, but it also shares in the fate of the modern world in the guise of a dissolution of the old binding forms. With these comments it becomes clear how closely for Troeltsch a diagnosis of the time and the discussion of particular issues in the sphere of theology and philosophy hang together.

II

Works on Theology and the Philosophy of Religion

1. A move towards south-west German neo-Kantianism (Windelband and Rickert)

The philosophical situation at the end of the nineteenth century was shaped by a lively methodolgical discussion on the rights and significance of the humanities over against the natural sciences, which were so successful. Wilhelm Dilthey had attempted to ground their independence in a contrast between the procedures of the natural sciences, which 'dissect' natural events into their causal sequence, and the approach of the humanities which aimed at 'understanding' historical processes. The context of the discussion was to be changed by neo-Kantian criticism.[63]

Epistemology and the notion of value. Dilthey based his methodological approach on the assumption of a basic incomparability between material processes and those in the mind and soul. Neo-Kantianism sought another solution by assuming a procedure specific to each in the face of the one reality. Wilhelm Windelband's 1894 address as Rector of Strasbourg on 'History and Science' is particularly significant here. Windelband differentiated between the experiential sciences, which strive to understand reality, and the sciences of law and event. The former focus on what always is, the latter on the unique and the special. The former proceed nomothetically, the latter 'idiographically'. Heinrich Rickert, a pupil of Windelband, further developed and systematized the ideas which his teacher had stated more as a principle.

Around the turn of the century, evidently in connection with the philosophical discussion I have just mentioned, Troeltsch began to reorientate the philosophical foundation of his views. He began increasingly to turn towards south-west German neo-Kantianism, especially to Heinrich Rickert (1863-1936) and his basic work on 'The Limits of the Formation of Scientific Concepts' (1896-1902), which went into many editions. Troeltsch speaks of a 'shift of philosophical standpoint from Dilthey and Lotze to Windelband and Rickert'.[64] He hopes that the new orientation of his philosophical ideas will help him answer questions which seemed insoluble on his previous approach. He is concerned above all with the validity of religious phenomena which can be grasped by historical investigation and described in psychological terms, and the critical question of their reality and truth-content. In retrospect he thought: 'There was no other course; in principle I had to go into the anti-psychologistic theory of validity.'[65] In other words, over and above the experience of the philosophy of life, which has to follow after the event, he sought a binding, substantial foundation of the kind that neo-Kantianism offered.

This philosophical orientation on neo-Kantianism now allowed psychology to have another place in his 'systematic thought', and – in connection with this – it also allowed the possibility of developing a philosophical theory in terms of the 'religious *a priori*'. If so far it had been the case that psychology alone could contribute what can be discovered about the question of truth, now this task fell to an 'epistemology of religion'.[66]

The emergence of this new offer of a solution and the thinking through of a usable foundation connected with it also had its personal side, as always in Troeltsch's biography. Granted, Troeltsch was an unusually perspective observer of the scientific trends of the time, the changes in the sphere of philosophy, but personal scholarly contact was always of great significance for him. So we may conjecture that his attention was specifically drawn to Heinrich Rickert by Max Weber and also Paul Hensel.[67]

When we consider the two great figures of the south-west German Kant school, Windelband and Rickert, it is at first sight amazing that Troeltsch turned primarily to Rickert and that the impact and influence of Windelband, who was the real founder of the school, faded into the background. There are probably two main reasons for this. The first is the influence of Weber and Hensel to which I have already referred. Secondly, as a pupil of Windelband, Rickert was more successful than in his master in achieving a systematization of the starting point common to both. It seems that Rickert was better able to achieve openness in the questions at issue than Windelband, who was more content with outlines and at the same time worked more specifically in the philosophy of history. However, there was a marked change in this estimation when Windelband was called to Heidelberg and also made personal contact with Troeltsch (1903). In the end, Troeltsch could find little pleasure in Rickert's procedure, which strongly emphasized the conceptual, above all in his studies of historicism.

First of all, however, Troeltsch felt 'attracted and challenged' by Rickert's logic.[68] Here in a remarkable way aesthetic categories were intermingled with the use that he wanted to make of Rickert's work: yet aesthetic satisfaction from the intellectual process, in this case systematic cohesion and purity, which was always important to him, could not be everything, since it was crucial for him to take things further, to develop.

In a way typical of Troeltsch, his reception of Rickert consisted in a combination of acceptance or assent and the awareness that here he was opening up an independent horizon of problems which might possibly again put him at a distance from the ideas and conceptuality that he affirmed. So it is worth examining in detail once again what attracted Troeltsch to Rickert, and what possible solutions he hoped for in the open questions I have mentioned.

Even before his main work on 'The Limits of the Formation of Scientific Conceptuality' (1886-1902), in his 1892 study of 'The Object of Knowledge', Rickert had described epistemology as a 'logical' task. All knowledge is thought, thought means judgment, and all judgment depends on the will, on assent or rejection, and thus ultimately on evaluation. However, 'values' do not rest on reality but are connected with demands to which human beings assent only in free decision, or which they can reject. A second article – which Troeltsch soon got to know – on 'Cultural Science and Natural Science' (1899)[69] then made a fundamental epistemological distinction between 'natural science' on the one hand and 'cultural science' on the other. Here Rickert was not thinking of two different spheres of reality, but orientating himself on the interest of the researcher. In contrast to the approach of the natural sciences, in cultural science this is governed by the question of value.[70] Accordingly, in each science a different relationship between the general and the particular emerges. In the natural sciences the particular is subsumed under the general with the intention of forming a conceptuality which amounts to a regular system. In the case of the cultural sciences the specific, the individual, is fundamental, and the general is regarded as following from it.[71]

Critical acceptance of Rickert. Troeltsch was very attracted by Rickert's work on 'Cultural Science and Natural Science'; he praised it as being clear and instructive, and found it full of fertile thoughts. However, he did not follow Rickert at a central point. He did not want to make any epistemological division. He thought that that Rickert the logician was causing problems which burdened his whole approach by dispensing with a metaphysical support for his views. In particular, he saw the unavoidable question of the real state of the spiritual and mental world as a problem which could not be solved in the way proposed by Rickert. So Troeltsch sums up: 'I for my part cannot share the purely immanent, anti-metaphysical starting point for this whole account...'[72]

Rickert's great book on the 'Limits of the Formation of Scientific Concepts' was a new challenge for Troeltsch. This study brought a wealth of ideas and concepts which had connections with Troeltsch's own work and occupied him further. This was true above all of the concepts of individuality, value, development, causality and type. In his major review article on 'Modern Philosophy of History',[73] Troeltsch shows great sympathy for Rickert's procedure of working out the character of the formation of historical concepts.

He can agree with the idea of the formation of historical judgment in the

form of the constitution of a particular individual value-whole, and this assent
makes itself felt above all in the caution with which he now considers the
sequence of historical phenomena, connecting and evaluating them on an
overarching principle of continuity and assessment. And Rickert's argument
that it is of central significance for the work of historians that in the wealth of
history they should distinguish and extract the essential from the inessential
clearly raises questions about the 'essence of Christianity'. Moreover, Rickert's
and Troeltsch's views meet in the view that considerable importance must be
attached to discussions of the principle of causality. Troeltsch's theological
concern was to preclude ideas of dogmatic exclusiveness through the rejection
of a 'causality of miracle'. For Troeltsch, Rickert's philosophical discussions
generally take on yet further relevance for the philosophy of religion and for
history. Rickert sees the difference between a scientific and a historical
definition of causality in the fact that the idea of causal connection in the
formation of concepts in history does not simply include that of natural
procedure and understanding. He is concerned for the assumption of an
individual 'historical' causal series to be held to be possible.[74]

In connection with historical causality, Rickert formulates an independent
concept of historical development.[75] This understands the historical process
teleologically, without associating it with the idea of progress. In this way one
epoch or event can be given special emphasis over against another and thus
be regarded as an immanently necessary means of attaining a goal.[76] The
teleological unity of the process of development from the aspect of uniqueness
has special significance for Rickert.[77]

However, Troeltsch also adds something to Rickert's view of the concept
of development, the significance of which for him is beyond question. This
issues in a consideration of the concept of the 'idea' and transcends Rickert's
notion of the historical individual by doing justice to real history in connection
with the development of embryonic ideas, 'embryonic purposes'.[78] All these
considerations are aimed at supplementing Rickert's purely formal ones, as is
shown for example by Troeltsch's positive reaction to the concept of a 'cultural
content' which is stressed by Class.[79]

Whether the concept of the 'type', which becomes significant for Troeltsch
in the framework of the *Social Teachings*,[80] can be used logically becomes a
problem for Rickert. Whereas Rickert regards the concept as ambivalent
because it refers on the one hand to the exemplary in evaluative terms and on
the other to the average, in general terms, Troeltsch intends a 'middle-concept'
which embraces the characteristic element of each particular historical
phenomenon as a set of instruments related to history.

Troeltsch sees the most important stimulus to his own thought in Rickert's
sketch of a historical logic and its development in the form of a history of
philosophy. He explains: 'My discussions of the "absoluteness of Christianity"
and the concept of the "essence of Christianity" have accordingly used

Rickert's philosophy of history and especially the connection which that teaches between empirical history and the philosophy of history as the most important means of solving problems which are felt to be difficult.'[81]

In principle, Troeltsch accepts two possible interpretations of experience in the approach to the development of a theory, the 'nomothetic' and the 'idiographic'. But he does not provide an adequate answer to the question of the relationship between them, given the unity of consciousness. He thinks that Rickert foists a metaphysical problem relating to the mode of being 'on to the contrast of modes of contemplation'.[82] His own notions arrive at a 'balance' in a way which is typical of him.[83] Evidently he wants to supplement and back up the concept which Rickert presents formally and one-sidedly in logical terms by making a distinction within the sphere of objects.

A central point of criticism is Rickert's combination of the philosophy of history and immanent awareness. Troeltsch sees an inconsistency here. If one's own possible of experience alone is valid, a real encounter with the life of others is ultimately made impossible. So it is not so much the notion of the individual in itself which is given sufficient attention in Rickert as the assumption of the working of an independent force transcending consciousness, which cannot be objectified but is to be postulated in the philosophy of history. On the presupposition of this additional insight 'history loses the ghostly character that it takes on from the standpoint of pure immanential experience, even in Rickert'.[84]

The significance of Rickert for the progress of Troeltsch's work in religion and the philosophy of history can be found above all in three respects: first, in the fundamental reference to Kant's thought, more accurately to a criticism made from a specific perspective; secondly, in a heightened awareness of epistemological methods and their application to history or the philosophy of history; and finally in ongoing attention to the conceptuality and categorical equipment for formulating a philosophy of history and religion. How Troeltsch takes up and assimilates Rickert's philosophy and yet remains independent will become even clearer in what follows.

2. The absoluteness of Christianity and the history of religion[85]

For Troeltsch, the problems which come under the heading of the 'absoluteness of Christianity' can be discussed appropriately only in the context of the history of theology. First, that means that a cultural-historical insight into the modern view of the world and life is necessary, the most important expression of which is the historical mode of thinking and the awareness of method which goes with it. Secondly, it means that two important breaks must be noted within the development of the history of theology, one in the early church and the other at the time of the Enlightenment.

The relativizing of the idea of absoluteness. Historical analysis leads Troeltsch to the insight that the unreflecting, simple confidence in one's own normative truth which prevailed as a matter of course in the initial period already gave way to an apologetic system in the early church. Here the first step was a branding of all that was not Christian as error and apostasy; the second, taken in the 'philosophy of the churches', was the working out of a special history of salvation transcending all that is human and earthly. The dogmatic safeguarding of access to the absolute truth is bound up with the church-philosophical version of apologetics. The theological argument which grew out of this way of thinking went on for centuries, ecpecially as the controversy with other religions and with philosophical criticism had lost its threatening character as a result of the state church of the Roman empire. When the claim of this first theological system had become questionable as a result of the rise of historical thought, another form of apologetics sought to replace the previous system. Here it should be noted that the application of a historical mode of thinking to theology led to a disputing of the dogmatic proof from miracle and the salvation-historical interpretation of the idea of the church. Theology and philosophy met the spiritual challenge with the 'construction of a universal history'. The concept of 'absoluteness' derives from this modern evolutionary (teleological) apologetic based on a philosophy of history. The apologetic system developed here rests on the incorporation of the religious ideal into a gradual development, the culminating point of which is seen as Christianity. According to this view the idea of religion coincides with Christianity, so that the concept has found its complete realization in it.

For Troeltsch, Lessing, Kant and Herder pioneered this approach in the philosophy of history: it comes to consummation in Schleiermacher and Hegel. He finds some merit in both forms of apologetic. The early church form attempted to express the special character of the religious, albeit in a questionable way. Modern, evolutionistic apologetic thinks in historical terms, but in a speculative way, and takes up the beginnings of comparative, history-of-religions, thought. The second form of apologetics is the real object of the critical dispute. The theological problem lies in the fact that if Christianity, mediated through the philosophy of history, is the absolute form of religion, then justice is not really done either to history-of-religions thought or to modern individual religious feeling, which as far as history and the form of truth that is communicated through history are concerned lives in the tension between provisionality and finality.

If as a result of the application of historical thinking to Christianity, Christianity is in principle recognized as a historical phenomenon, then it is a conditioned, relative expression of religion and not the realization of the 'essence' of religion generally. The philosophy of history constructed by the Enlightenment and German Idealism had apparently resolved the question of norms, which arises in the face of historical multiplicity. The universal concept of religion was identical with Christianity, and was the norm of religion. Now this question had to be put again to all religions because of the relativizing consequences of historical thought and its sweeping application to all religions.

Norm and history. The apologetic of German Idealism based on the philosophy of history allowed historical thought only conditionally, i.e. as immanent in the system. Now we have to take seriously the recognition that 'historical' and 'relative' mean the same thing.[86] According to Troeltsch, that does not lead to unbounded sceptical relativism; rather, the historical mode of thinking which destroys absolutes can provide the basis for a new constructive understanding.[87]

The destructive relativism which is a possible consequence of historical thought can be limited from two sides: on the one hand by the philosophy of history, and on the other by the individual value judgments of human beings. The two are directly connected. An approach in terms of the philosophy of history entails a concrete comparision of historical phenomena, and thus of religions. That results in the assumption of an aim and, bound up with that, a gradation of values. This variant of teleological thought favoured by Troeltsch differs from the teleological approach of the philosophy of history constructed in the wake of German Idealism by having a different understanding of revelation. For Troeltsch, the philosophy of history belongs to an approach in terms of the history of religions, rejects the universal concept of religion and accepts the evaluation of revelation as an element in historical development, in which 'universality', i.e. revelation generally, and 'particularity', namely the individual expression of revelation in history, are admissible epistemologically.

The destructiveness of relativism is similarly limited by the evaluative attitude of human beings as individuals. This evaluation can be linked to a history-of-religions value comparison. So normativeness is not tied to a universal criterion based on the philosophy of history, but takes place in the course of personal decision and is an expression of individual conviction. This conviction does not hang in the air, but can be understood as a quite consistent consequence of the attitude of the individual which takes both external and internal factors into account. According to this understanding, absoluteness is conceivable only at the end of history as the last real goal of the whole, whereas concrete history and thus all historical values-constructs have temporally limited, individual, and therefore relative form, but can at the same time be an expression of truth. Here, according to Troeltsch, three things should be noted: 1. the individual decision as to value finds support in the history-of-religions comparison, which shows Christianity as the relatively highest manifestation of religion. 2. The decision of the individual is supported by an empirical fact in the history of culture, namely the experience that Christianity is the religion of our cultural circle and that the acknowledgment of Christianity rests on a practical consensus of educated people. 3. The assumption of a historical transcendent goal here unites elements which according to Löwith's well-known theory belong together in the history of ideas: Christian eschatological thought and Hegelian thought in terms of universal history.

The idea of the 'creative synthesis'. Troeltsch evidently wants to avoid the alternative that either Christianity is a historical phenomenon, to be regarded and estimated as such, in which case it is purely relative – or it is the realization of the idea of religion or rests on a unique supernatural revelation, in which case it is absolute. Quite apart from the considerations already cited, the idea of a 'creative synthesis' plays a role in Troeltsch's attempt to overcome this alternative. In his view the absolute is given a time-conditioned but appropriate form by constant new creative combinations of cultural forces, especially religious. That means that speculation in terms of the philosophy of history and dogmatic supernaturalistic thinking is replaced by the dynamic absoluteness of historical concretion, which is in keeping with the situation and true in so far as it is not self-development, but is based on the exertion of the forces of many individuals.

The idea of this 'creative synthesis' is tied to two premises. First, to the presupposition from the history of revelation that truth must at any time create a specific expression which is appropriate to it, and secondly, to the idea that history and fate are not everything, but that an effort is needed, and thus an appeal to the individual capacity, to the formative power of the human beings at any period. The philosophy of history in German idealism is transcended and superseded by an existentialist enrichment in terms of the philosophy of culture.

The presupposition for such convictions as come from the philosophy of culture is ultimately a metaphysic of the Spirit.[88] According to Troeltsch, history everywhere shows the struggle of spiritual life as it strives against the merely natural. Apart from the ways in which individual phenomena are conditioned, the differences lie in the variations in the depth, power and clarity of the life that is revealed.[89] For Troeltsch, the comparability of historical formations presupposes a universal; not, however, one which is arrived at through abstraction but one which appears in the phenomena of life itself as the goal or ideal which is envisaged at any point. This goal is not realized anywhere, but remains an idea which envisaged as a final purpose of the whole. For Troeltsch, this notion from the philosophy of history is without doubt an analogy to the eschatology of Christianity.

Religious experience and history. But can such a form of relative 'absoluteness' satisfy true religious feeling? The religious person wants truth and certainty on the basis of a real encounter with God. Can it be enough if such a person is called on 'to follow the clearest, most simple and most compelling of the instructions of God which reach his ear and leave it to God how he is to develop them'?[90]

So the question remains how relativization through historical knowledge relates to the faith of the pious person who thinks in existential categories of absoluteness. Troeltsch attempts to counter the dualism inherent in this constellation by interpreting the essential content of the relationship between human beings and God as immediate, direct human experience. The attention of the religious person is directed to the encounter with God himself, for which the historical element is only a horizon and a means of stimulation. So absolute revelation can never be expected in the framework of history. Rather, 'absoluteness' rests in God himself, and in religious experience becomes existential event in a form accessible to human beings alone.

It is clear from the perspective of theological tradition that Troeltsch relates the concepts of God and history in such a way that an idea of revelation mediated christologically is not determinative. Rather, God himself is to be seen as the ground and goal of religious experience in a historical movement which is to be understood as the history of his being revealed.

The human being who lives in history has access to the God who shows himself in history through religious experience, though this differs in nature and depth. But this God does not bind himself uniquely and finally in a particular saving event. He is universally at work in the history of revelation. He is a power at work in history, but the revelation of finality and absoluteness is reserved for the end of history.

The question is whether a convincing theology is offered to the modern consciousness by this understanding of God and revelation. At any rate the sharpness, the radical nature of the 'dualism' between the experience of faith and historical consciousness is on the one hand toned down – and this is Troeltsch's intention – by being partly overcome in the religious experience, and on the other hand is completely dissolved in the finality of salvation to be expected.

Troeltsch asks many questions in his account about the origin of the Christian church and theology, including critical questions about the relationships beween Jesus and Paul and between the primitive community and the church of early Catholicism, questions about the relationship between faith and theology, faith and church dogma. By taking up critical considerations which are formulated in awareness of modernity, and at the same time accepting the positive presupposition of the possibility and necessity of religion even within modern critical thought, Troeltsch attempts to tackle historical questions systematically. By making the combination of theology and Greek philosophy in the early church a systematic question and redefining the apologetic thought which arises from this combination in terms of absoluteness, he thinks that he has found an intellectual approach to mediation. This procedure also enables him in principle to dispense with apologetic thought and makes it conceivable that Christianity can be detached from its previous ecclesiastical and historical form.

Naive absoluteness and scientific thought. Seen in terms of cultural history, the conception of the absolute is the characteristic of a naive attitude, while the scientific approach is from the start opposed to absolutizing naivety. In principle, theologians with an academic training face the question how their insights, gained at a critical distance from immediate piety, can also be communicated to those who do not have this professional training. Troeltsch's interest as a theologian is now directed towards finding room for this naive self-certainty and at the same time giving scientific thought its due place. How are the two to be related and interlinked permanently? However, this notion of Troeltsch's is not easy to explain. When he describes the self-assurance of faith as naivety and at the same time thinks in cultural-historical terms of a link with an original situation, the term 'naivety' already represents an evaluation and a distancing. How the naive element is then at the same time to be preserved and accepted despite this evaluation needs to be clarified. Troeltsch sees the mediation between naivety and reflection from the perspective of theology and cultural history as being divided into different epochs: psychologically, it is related to separate phases in the life of the individual. This offers an approach to the mediation but does not provide the mediation itself. That is achieved as follows: the aim of the scientific approach is the restoration of naivety, but at a higher level. According to Troeltsch, this higher level can be described either as thinking piety or as critical naivety.[91] In it emerges 'all satiated wisdom of thought... that does not destroy the naive element of reality but is seen in a higher context'.[92]

In the later generation of theologians, Rudolf Bultmann in particular concerned himself with this topic. Bultmann thought it inappropriate to use the term 'naive' for the original situation in the history of religion, i.e for the religion of Jesus. For him this introduced categories which got in the way of access to the proclamation of Jesus. In his preaching, Jesus calls to decision, but not in the terms of individual inwardness and experiential piety. In Bultmann, the notion of decision contains the problem of absoluteness; however, this is understood, not as the absoluteness of Christianity but as the 'absoluteness of faith'. According to Bultmann, it makes no sense to speak of the absoluteness of Christianity, but one can speak of the absoluteness of the decision of faith which has its place in the concrete history of existence and can only be perceived and taken up in it. Nor, as in Troeltsch, can the idea of development have any significance in this context. 'This view also parts company with the idea of development, according to which the moral judgment of man develops or the man himself develops and perfects himself. Here there is no relative standard, only the absolute. The decision is an absolute "Either-Or": the good which is here required is not a relative good, which on a higher level of development can be replaced by something better – it is the will of God.'[93]

So 'naivety' is ruled out because Bultmann will not allow any understanding of the man Jesus and his proclamation in terms of personality. For Bultmann, all references to personal enthusiasm, to heroism, readiness for sacrifice or religious energy are inappropriate, because anthropologically they are based on human beings in themselves and thus are judged psychologically and aesthetically. Instead, human beings must be seen over against God and his claim. This claim becomes event in the kerygma, and in faith takes shape as a response to the kerygma. In this dimension one can speak of absoluteness, for only in this way is the claim of the proclamation and of faith as a human response perceived appropriately, namely as entities which determine life.

Historicity of revelation and history of revelation. Troeltsch's idea is that as soon as theories are formed about the truth-claims of Christianity, naive self-assurance and thus 'naive absoluteness' disappear. In the theology of the church, theories of absoluteness replaced the immediacy of the relationship of faith lived out by Jesus. Whereas the statements of faith of the first period were the naive expression of what was necessary, their consolidation in dogma was a change from what was in fact felt to be necessary to what was 'conceptually necessary, unchangeable and abiding'.[94] In order to keep to the conceptuality which he puts in the centre as a result of his approach in terms of the history of theology and at the same time to do justice to the variety of historical approaches, Troeltsch varies the concept of absoluteness in a number of ways.

Thus he speaks of an 'artificial absoluteness' which can be located midway between religious immediacy and comparative thought. To the degree that, out of apologetic concern, this allows only the validity of its own view, it is a move towards a supernatural absoluteness. From this, Troeltsch distinguishes 'rational absoluteness', which allows relative truths to other religions. According to Troeltsch, the idea of artificial absoluteness is characteristic of the thought of a community which has no philosophical training, while the rational notion of absoluteness is the work of educated classes in the church. 'Church philosophy is the rational absoluteness of Christianity, just as the theory of incarnation, revelation and the church is its supernatural absoluteness.'[95]

The solution to the problems of absoluteness after the Enlightenment came about in 'evolutionary absoluteness' in which the modern notion of development takes up the idea of absoluteness in modified form. But Troeltsch wants to dissociate himself generally from this false development in dogmatic thought. In this approach, the supernatural grounding of the history of dogma, the theology of the incarnation, the theology of revelation and church history is obsolete. The notion of revelation in history has to be modified, so that it becomes the idea of the history of revelation. This historical differentiation must be supplemented with a systematic insight.

If the development of dogmatic thought is mainly seen as a kind of decline, then the basic question remains: what is the relationship of original naive faith to dogmatic thought? In understanding the history of theology up to the rise of the historical approach as a history with a tendency to dogmatize, Troeltsch expresses a deep mistrust of theology where it is not done through historical criticism.

The question how Troeltsch's distinction between what is conceptually necessary and what is in fact supreme and ultimate in Christianity is to be understood is of central importance. One difficulty for interpretation is that the thought here is on two different levels, first that of conceptual argument and then that of empirical history. However, that does not exclude the possibility that Troeltsch deliberately brought this difference of levels into play, so we have to go on to ask what historical phenomena he sees as being connected with one level of thought or the other, or where the idea of 'absoluteness' is justified.

Historically speaking, with the first form of evaluation Troeltsch has in mind the theology of exclusive supernaturalism and evolutionistic apologetics. According to Troeltsch, both forms seek to demonstrate that the special position of Christianity is in principle conceptually necessary. In the one case (supernaturalistic orthodoxy), this is done by contrasting and linking the terms 'heavenly' and 'earthly'. The contrast between heavenly and earthy is both maintained and transcended by an institution which brings supernatural salvation, in a contingent historical way and thus in a form which lays down salvation. In the other case (evolutionistic apologetics) the difference betwen idea and history is mediated speculatively: Christianity is the necessary expression of the idea.

Troeltsch rejects a solution of the question of the norm by the construction of concepts. Christianity is not necessarily an expression of religious absoluteness. Against this conception he sets the religious evaluation of Christianity as what is in fact the highest and the last.[96] Here 'in fact' is the counter to 'necessary', and it relates to history in two senses. First, to the fact of the significance of Christianity in the history of religion and culture, especially for our cultural circle. Secondly, to the individual's value decision, which is rooted in history and is always made only within historical facticity.

If in Troeltsch's view Christianity is thus shown to be supreme and final,[97] then the critical objection that a contrast between conceptual necessity and what is in fact recognizable as supreme involves thought at two different levels is again limited. For 'supreme and final', too, not only relates to what is actual and historical in the sense mentioned, but implies a value aspect. However, the normativeness which is possible here is not universal, but one which is possible for human beings on a particular occasion on the basis of their personal knowledge and decision.

By thinking in these terms Troeltsch has removed himself even more clearly from his theological beginnings, and above all has detached himself from a view close to that of Hegel, which connects the question of criteria closely to historical development itself. And he has freed himself even more markedly from the remnants of Ritschlian theology, which in this question ends up by identifying religion with Christianity, and in a 'theology of claims'.

To the degree that Troeltsch focuses on the question of the relationship between history and norm and in so doing refers to the value decision of the individual, influences of Rickert's philosophy are clearly recognizable. And Troeltsch also goes along with Rickert over the primacy of practical reason bound up with the value question, an emphasis on ethical obligation and the 'ought', to the degree that human collaboration in the formation of the 'creative synthesis' rests on a moral obligation. At the same time it becomes clear that here Troeltsch shares Rickert's own philosophical problem, namely the question of the link between the world of value and history. Moreover, it becomes clear that his own ideas of a solution on the basis of an orientation on cultural content and a metaphysics diverge from those of Rickert. It is also evident that to the degree that Troeltsch brings the individual's value decision into the foreground and the idea of a cultural circle gains ground (Christianity as the religion of our cultural circle), the significance of the history-of-religions comparison of Christianity and non-Christian religions fades into the background.[98]

Contemporary criticism and aspects of historical influence.[99] The most interesting and important contemporary criticism came from Wilhelm Herrmann.[100] Herrmann refers to the problems of the transition from religious to scientific language in Troeltsch and asks whether a clearer distinction should not have been made here. Certainly, for Herrmann the absoluteness of Christianity cannot be proved scientifically, but it can be arrived at through the history experienced by the individual. According to Herrmann, Troeltsch did not notice that two different epistemological principles are involved here.[101]

Herrmann sees Troeltsch's intention to protect religion scientifically from the suspicion of being an illusion as scientific understanding which is questionable where theology is concerned. He remarks somewhat caustically: 'Of course he has never let on to us the ontological foundation of which he often speaks. But simply because he talks about it, to many people to whom that shift [to a historical approach and reflection with a historical motivation] is fatal, he appears as a saviour in their deepest need.'[102] For Herrmann, the ontology claimed or propagated by Troeltsch has two aspects: on the one hand it is meant to be science, and on the other it is meant to help 'towards an acquaintance with absolute things...'[103] But in science only the relative significance of a thing can be known.

For Herrmann, the distinction which Troeltsch makes between naive and artificial absoluteness is a mere construction. It would have been unnecessary had Troeltsch recognized the significance of the notion of the personal certainty of salvation wihch emerges from religious experience and evaluated it accordingly. If the issue is really the confidence of faith, then it cannot be assumed that something greater or more appropriate, for example to be expressed in scientific language, should emerge. For Herrmann, Christian faith not only *has* the conviction of the absoluteness of Christianity but *is* this conviction. Both Jesus as a historical person and experience of the encounter with him play a decisive role in the formation of this conviction, so that in contrast to Troeltsch, from there the relationship to history is a permanent one, indissolubly bound up with the person of Jesus.

Other critical voices from the Ritschl school largely go along with Herrmann's criticism. The 'absoluteness of Christianity' can only be believed in and confessed; it cannot be arrived at rationally. Faith and confession are the forms which constitute access to the truth promised in Christianity and claimed by it. This personal and confessional element is the one expressed by Ritschl in his theory of the independent religious value-judgment. There we read that the evaluative judgment represents the only possible access to the content of Christianity. The claim to truth is matched by a personal faith which feels that the truth offered and communicated is a value for personal life. The believer experiences the influence of this truth in liberation for independence and moral action.

The criticism made by Ludwig Ihmels[104] is representative of the standpoint of Erlangen theology. Ihmels sees an unacceptable relativism in Troeltsch's position. Troeltsch is not in a position to avoid the intended certainty of scepticism. There is a contradiction in Troeltsch in that on the one hand the truth-claim of the Christian religion seems justified, whereas on the other it is put in doubt. Ihmels counters that the issue is the certainty of the Christian's experience of the person of Jesus.

Ihmels certainly thinks the history-of-religions approach important, but it becomes significant and really admissible for him only when a firm standpoint of faith has been achieved on the basis of inner experience. Furthermore, Ihmels doubts whether the notion of a history-of-religions comparison is a consequence of the influence of the historical approach on theology. He is not convinced that Troeltsch's concern is to build a way towards solving this problem specifically by accepting comparative history-of-religions thought.

The solution to the problem of the absoluteness of Christianity proposed by Rudolf Bultmann on the one hand presupposes Troeltsch's account, but on the other is to be put closer to that of Wilhelm Herrmann because of its theological conception. Bultmann is concerned that the 'offence' associated with Christian faith or the question of faith should be recognized in the dialogue with philosophy and with any educated contemporaries. This offence would be misunderstood were it regarded as an assertion of the absoluteness of Christianity. Rather, the issue is the claim of the Christian faith to absoluteness, which cannot be made 'on the basis of a comparison with other modes of faith, but only as a response to the address of the Word which has come to me'.[105]

For Ulrich Mann, the absoluteness of Christianity and tolerance belong together because the insight into unconditional tolerance which results from a knowledge of God's revelation transcending all reason is part of the truth of Christian religion. The claim to absoluteness must be seen in broad and dynamic terms and must lead to a refusal to absolutize a historical phenomenon. A 'synoptic' theology has to collaborate with all the disciplines which touch on religion and thus submit itself to rational control. Mann rejects the idea of a claim which transcends the sphere of faith because it attempts to avoid the critical objection from both outside and inside, i.e. from the sides of science and of the other religions.

For Mann, exclusiveness is part of practical religion; theologically it is marginal. By contrast, an important theological task is that of explaining the religious inclusiveness of Christianity. Very much along Troeltsch's lines he speaks of a suppression of the religious inclusiveness of Christianity by an exclusive kind of thought which arose in the course of the development of the early church.[106]

3. *The debate with Harnack's* Essence of Christianity

Harnack's book and its influence. In the winter semester 1899/1900 Adolf Harnack delivered his famous lectures on 'the essence of Christianity', in which he both as it were took a stand and gave a reckoning.

His retrospect on the beginnings of Christianity and the high points of its development was intended to help to clarify the question of what deserves to remain as the 'essential' element of Christianity and what – on the eve of a new century – could also define the future. Of course the decision to give a positive answer to this question depends on the individual; it depends on the living acceptance and assimilation of the powers of the gospel and its further influence in the history of the church and in history generally. The lectures, originally given without notes, soon appeared in print and had an extraordinary effect.[107]

Harnack's person and programme seem to have provoked many theological reactions from his contemporaries. The excited debate over his *Essence of Christianity* shows how most of the publications appearing at this time were written directly either for or against him.[108]

In keeping with this, particular notions in church politics or academic politics became clearly evident in the controversy. In the agitated discussion Troeltsch himself felt it important to direct attention back to substantive issues. He wanted a more fundamental discussion of the 'essence of Christianity' than was to be found in Harnack.

For Harnack, the question of the 'essence of Christianity' is a question of historical interest. Applied to the beginnings of Christianity, it runs: who was Jesus Christ, and what really was his message?[109]

But history should not just be interrogated in the interest of what happened; at the same time attention should also be paid to the present. Two basic distinctions are significant for Harnack's view of the 'essence of Christianity'. He distinguishes between religious teaching and religious life and, in the historical tradition, between 'kernel' and 'shell'. In the first distinction the accent lies on religious life. In the second, he holds that the assertion of a 'nucleus' makes it possible to assume that while Christianity does not correspond in all respects with its first form, in 'essence' it remains the same.

So the task of the account is to grasp the fundamentals, what is common to all historical phenomena; here the gospel offers the guiding line. According to Harnack, in this historical investigation the basic features of the gospel must also be subjected to examination, on the basis of what history has brought to light in its development. That leads to the question how the methodology of this examination can be defined more closely.

The process must take up reality as a question of origins and in turn regard the origin as a criterion for development. In other words, there must be something like the hermeneutical circle, with a stress on the question of the norm.

In his definition of the 'essence of Christianity', Harnack begins with the preaching of Jesus. In his preaching, Jesus, the founder of the Christian religion, merely had human beings generally in view, so that the situation of the hearer is basically irrelevant then as now. For Harnack, the gospel preached by Jesus consists of three groups of ideas: 1. the kingdom of God and its coming; 2. God the Father and the infinite value of the human soul; 3. the better righteousness and the command to love. In the first complex the preaching of Jesus includes a prophetic announcement of the kingdom, a rule which will become visible in the future, and an 'inward' kingdom of God which is already dawning with the message of Jesus. For Harnack, the idea of two kingdoms, the kingdom of God and the kingdom of the devil, rests on the thought of the time. The notion that the kingdom of God is an inward coming is an essential statement of the preaching of Jeuss. This view introduces a really new element. The significance of the distinction between 'shell' and 'kernel' becomes clear: the distinctive element as an expression of the person is the 'kernel', and differs from the traditional thought of the time.

The kingdom of God is characterized by three distinguishing marks. The preaching of Jesus points, first, to something other-worldly; secondly, to something purely religious; and finally, to the idea of liberation from the rule of sin. The main perspectives of the 'purely religious' are individuality and inwardness. Harnack describes the second group of ideas in the proclamation of Jesus with the remarkable formula: God the Father and the infinite value of the human soul. In this group the 'principles of the preaching of Jesus can be described progressively'.[110] The reference to the 'infinite value of the human soul' expresses a notion which is also used repeatedly by Troeltsch and had become a standard topic in the liberal theology of the time. Because human beings can say 'Father' to the creator of the world, they have a value which extends beyond the dimension of the finite.

In the third group of ideas, namely of the better righteousness and the commandment to love, for Harnack Jesus dissolves all ties between ethics and ritual. The moral demand is derived from the human disposition. Love is the real motive for moral action; as Jesus understands it, it is the beginning of a new life.[111]

For Harnack, the gospel is purely and exclusively 'religion'. Accordingly, it keeps free from any direct relationship to culture, to social conditions and to science. It is precisely in this that Harnack sees a decisive advantage. A tie to a particular phase of cultural development would have meant that the gospel was not free.

The harmony which the gospel has struck up has to be taken up afresh each time, both by individuals and by religious groups. A legal tie to the classical form of the beginning is neither necessary nor permissible. The essential elements of the gospel are timeless, and as such they can speak to human beings in their essence at all times.

The influence of this work is attested not only by the many editions and translations of it, but also by the many books and articles which took issue with it. One example is the book by Troeltsch's Heidelberg colleague Ludwig Lemme, entitled *The Essence of Christianity and the Religion of the Future.*[112] Lemme argued that the basic tendency of Harnack's work was towards a total destruction of Christianity. For Lemme, after this, there was nothing more that Harnack could deny.[113] His own position is made clear in the section 'The Eternal Validity of Jesus Christ'.[114] Lemme sees the basis for a definiton of the essence of Christianity in the 'eternal validity of the messianic personality of Christ'.[115] This eternal validity is his divine Sonship. There will be no further revelation of God after this. At the same time, 'the final judgment for the totality of humankind' is to be attached to his redeeming act.[116]

The thoughts of the Greifswald dogmatic scholar Hermann Cremer on *The Essence of Christianity* (Gütersloh 1901) go in a similar direction. Here the notion of reconciliation, understood in dogmatic terms, also stands at the centre of the account. Finally, simply because of the title, one might mention the contribution by the pastor Georg Lasson, who later edited Hegel: 'The Nonsense of Pseudo-Christianity. Remarks made Necessary by Adolf Harnack's Book on the Essence of Christianity' (*Das Unwesen des Pseudochristentums. Notgedrungene Bemerkungen zu Adolf Harnacks Buch über das Wesen des Christentums*, Grosse Lichterfelde = Berlin nd). Lasson calls on all friends of the church 'to rally again to the banner of Christ and choose the standard of confessing the eternal Son of God who came in the flesh'.[117]

Troeltsch's criticism and development of the ideas. Troeltsch entered the debate sparked off by Harnack's book with an article 'What Does the "Essence of Christianity" Mean?' which appeared in *Christliche Welt* (1903, later in II, 386-451, *ETWTR*, 124-80). The choice of journal shows that he saw the question as a basic problem going beyond academic theology, one which also concerned his educated contemporaries.

For Troeltsch, Harnack's *Essence of Christianity* is the 'symbolic book for the historicizing trend in theology'.[118] He is interested above all in a critical discussion and development of the meaning of 'historical' in Harnack and of what is normative for Harnack's conception of a definition of essence.

For Troeltsch, the expression 'essence of Christianity' is a term which belongs to modernity and is bound up with the idea of a history of development. In German Idealism and Romanticism the 'essence' of a historical phenom-enon is arrived at by a process of abstraction from the historical facts. The 'driving ideas' of a historical phenomenon are investigated by a survey and assessment of basic expressions. The overall view of a phenomenon in the history of ideas rests on an overall perspective along with an attempt at definition. Here the individual element, the wealth of individual historical manifestations, must not be passed over, but rediscovered in the attempt at a definition.[119] Thus anyone who speaks of the 'essence of Christianity' stands in a particular tradition of thought, and by adopting the concept takes up presuppositions in the history of ideas.

The process of defining the essence is therefore bound up with history generally and the methodological principles which apply there. The idea of a trans-historical identity of Christianity and religious truth must be abandoned. 'The essential in Christianity is not that about it which corresponds to a general truth with a basis of its own elsewhere.'[120]

For the new edition (on the fiftieth anniversary of the appearance of Harnack's book), Bultmann wrote an introduction which was critical but was positive about Harnack's basic questions. For Bultmann, Harnack's book is not just a document of the first order from the history of theology, but at the same time represents a contribution to the current theological discussions. Bultmann sees the weaknesses of the book above all in the absence of any insight into the significance of history-of-religions questions – here his criticism coincides with that of Troeltsch – and with the absence of an understanding of the eschatological dimension.[121]

However, Troeltsch and Bultmann do not have much in common. They differ over basic interests and theological intention. Bultmann is concerned with the character of the gospel as address: the gospel claims truth in an authoritative way, so that underlying it is the paradox of announcing finality, and thus the truth, in historical concretion. For Troeltsch, the notion of historical individuality is basic. What is essential historically is not the universal, but the specific which develops as an independent element in history and in so doing sets a development in process. In any particular situation this process of development also becomes a question about the essence of the historical phenomenon, in this case Christianity.

For Troeltsch a definition of essence cannot either depend on the biblical tradition or be made through the church and any authoritative claim which the church is to be allowed. A definition of essence is also independent of any non-Christian norm; it can only be made within Christianity, in other words through the history of Christianity.

When Harnack speaks of being governed by a 'purely historical interest', Troeltsch suggests that 'purely historical' is a whole world-view.[122] Anyone who investigates the 'essence of Christianity' must make use of the means of historical thought and the historical method and do so consistently. Here we can hear an implicit criticism of Harnack, just as the whole of Troeltsch's article is full of overtones and indirectly puts critical questions to Harnack, to the Ritschl school and to 'positive theology'.[123]

Troeltsch is concerned to point out the difficulties and problems connected with the question. If essence is defined by means of abstraction from history, the way is open for grasping the idea which underlies the whole course of history. That can be done, along the lines of the Hegelian school, with the aid of a speculative notion of history, through the idea of the God-man. But in keeping with the intentions of Ritschl and his school the idea could also be that of the kingdom of God, which unfolds in a dialectical development into history. Neither way is acceptable to Troeltsch; underlying both is a construction which begins from dogmatic premises. The Protestant way of thinking makes such a procedure impossible for Troeltsch.[124] But he thinks that a theory of development on an organic evolutionary basis, or a dogmatic notion of continuity of a Catholic kind, cannot be right either. The reason is that a radical distinction must be made. There are not only relative but also radical oppositions in the course of history. So there follows a criticism of individual statements of a theological or organizational kind, always on the basis of a particular conception. For Troeltsch, the idea of essence implies a degree of criticism in so far as value judgments must be made about the whole course of church history. The task of criticism is directed not only to the inessential but also to that which contradicts the essence. And the recognition of this task is possible only in Protestantism, because in it the notion of such criticism has taken shape and proved to have a fruitful historical influence.

But what criterion makes an evaluative distinction possible? For Troeltsch, this is the point at which objective and subjective assessments of the course of history must be brought together.

A first consideration of the kind attempted by Harnack will be directed towards the 'classical' form of Christianity, i.e. to earliest Christianity and especially to the preaching of Jesus, and seek to orientate itself through it, or better in the light of it.[125]

It is above all important for Troeltsch that the relationship between historical knowledge and personal value-decision is not determined by dogmatic pre-judgments. He is concerned that there should be a free, mobile relationship which in principle allows criticism. For him, the historical Christ and the impact of faith aroused by him cannot be seen as the basis of the personal confessional approach. Rather, the orientating power comes from the 'spirit of Christ released when the earthly manifestation is shattered in death. He takes everything away from the historical Christ, but he opens the spiritual eye and leads into all truth.'[126]

For Troeltsch, the significance of historical concern lies in relating what is perceived historically to the present in such a way that both the present and the future appear in a new light on the basis of the understanding that has been achieved. In the light of this understanding the question of the concept of essence as an ideal concept must be discussed. The term 'ideal' relates to a Christianity of the future, the image of which is to become effective in the formation of Christianity in the present. Thus the definition of essence is extended. It embraces past, present and future, and also relates to the task of formation. With this notion Troeltsch transcends Harnack's view and emphasizes his personal concern.

For Troeltsch, what is involved is an act of decision, made in the present in the face of the future, which is itself a piece of history. It cannot be detached from the particular historical conditions of a time, nor can its historical effect be left out of account. Troeltsch took up and developed this notion in the context of his account of Rickert.[127] There he speaks of the 'individual act of conviction' of the individual person, which is necessary for arriving at a synthesis of the psychological and epistemological subject. This act of the subject is in continuity with the historical developments of value, but remains bound to the decision of the human conscience.[128] Troeltsch's additional comment here that the action which becomes necessary at the end of all scientific concern with history is only a process which clarifies what 'takes place in the dark depths of the general consciousness' shifts the emphasis somewhat. Here the significance of intuition is stressed more strongly than before. Perhaps Bergson, who gained increasing importance for Troeltsch, is to be found in the background here.[129]

So the question is that of concretion as the combination of an orientation related to the past with a new definition in the present.[130] With the task of a new definition, the idea of an ethical goal and obligation enters into the considerations. Unlike Harnack, Troeltsch wants to see the requirement for objectivity in the definition of essence related to the question of the subjective, evaluative judgment. Here he believes that the achievement of the process of abstraction and the shaping of the essence cannot be asked of the average person. Rather, the 'spiritual leaders of a people' have to perform this task.[131] For the others there remain honest dedication and a 'belief in authority tempered by gentle individual adjustments'.[132]

Thus what is required in principle is modified and qualified by pragmatic considerations. Here we have to remember that a certain 'objective' consensus has developed on the basis of historical development.

So the special role of the subjective derives from the fact that the issue is not an intellectual problem but an attitude which relates to and defines the person himself.

There is hardly any other work in which Troeltsch speaks as personally and with such direct involvement as he does here. On the basis of the topic and discussion of Harnack's book he feels challenged to give an account which demonstrates his own conviction of faith without in any way breaking away from critical reflection.

The closing section of the article headed 'The Result' (*GS* II, 448-51, *ETWTR*, 177-81) was added later by Troeltsch. He probably wanted to give a more markedly scientific conclusion to remarks which were now appearing within the framework of his *Gesammelte Schriften* and at the same time take up further insights which had been gained. One particular element which is new is the idea of a clearer separation of the purely historical task from the normative task of the philosophy of history. This perspective leads him to distance himself further from Harnack. It seems that for Troeltsch, Harnack's book has in turn become a piece of history and must be supplemented and taken further by both insights into the philosophy of history and a changed awareness of method – in particular by adopting socio-historical thought. This critical insight marks a sharper view of the problem of continuity. 'The concept of the various possibilities for development inherent within the Christian idea will be more important for purely historical attainment of a general concept, than the demonstration of a simple continuum or even of a dialectical necessity in the sequence of ideas.'[133]

Troeltsch's comments on the separation of the historical and the normative tasks are guided by Rickert's views on the philosophy of history, in particular the idea of a 'value-free teleology'.[134] However, for Troeltsch this separation is only provisional. In the end both perspectives come together again in the unity of life and the question of the future.

When we consider Troeltsch's article, what is particularly striking is the combination of assent, extension of the horizon of the questions, and constructive development. For Troeltsch, the objections to a historicizing trend in theology expressed in the debate generally do not go far enough; they are not capable of dealing theologically with the whole complex of questions. Neither picking out details nor a dogmatic repudiation of the process is of further help.[135]

We need to ask ourselves whether it is still meaningful today to answer the question which arises out of historical thinking about the possibility of attaching Christian belief in the present to tradition and the associated question of continuity by means of a 'definition of essence'.[136]

Anyone who takes these questions seriously presupposes, both theologically and in faith, a critical distance from biblicism and in connection with this an awareness of the theological relevance of historical thought. Only those who have recognized this historical relativization will find the argument over the concept of essence theologically relevant.

At this point reflection on the history of theology is appropriate. The questions raised required an answer from the next generation of theologians, and that applied even if these were not inclined to follow Harnack and Troeltsch in discussing of the concept of essence. They refused to do this on principle. Their refusal was connected on the one hand with Barth's dogmatic approach through a theology of the Word of God but also with Bultmann's stress on the task of understanding in the context of existentialist interpretation. The refusal to accept a theological continuity here nevertheless contains an underlying continuity. It largely came about as a result of a shift in the problem. Through this shift the questions raised were at the same time both pushed to one side and implicitly answered. In a somewhat simplifed and exaggerated way one could say that for Barth, the 'essential' element is God's Word in or as Jesus Christ, and for Bultmann the 'essential' element is being addressed by the kerygma, which means that a historical event (Jesus of Nazareth) is the eschatological event. At all events, the questions discussed by Troeltsch in a great many ways were raised again. That is shown by Bultmann's questions about Barth's understanding of history and Barth's criticism of Bultmann's existentialist hermeneutics.

Friedrich Gogarten plays a special role. He stands in direct continuity with Troeltsch to the degree that he affirmed Troeltsch's approach in terms of the history of ideas and an analysis of culture; indeed he largely inherited it. At the same time, this brings him closer to the substance of Troeltsch's questions than Barth and Bultmann. But with him, too, it emerges that questions change if one thinks that one has found other answers. How near to and yet how far from Troeltsch's thought Gogarten is is shown impressively by his book *What is Christianity?* Gogarten largely adopts Troeltsch's position in the debate on the essence of Christianity, yet shifts the interest by introducing another concept of history.[137] His idea of history has a biblical basis: it rests on the interpretation of the New Testament doctrine of creation and eschatology. At the centre of his exegesis stand the questions of human freedom and the responsibility of human beings for the world as God's creation. Gogarten understands the capacity of modern men and women to think historically as the effect of Christian faith on the situation of human existence, or more precisely on its new development, and the responsibility to be accepted as a result.[138]

Finally, mention should be made of Paul Tillich, who took up questions arising in connection with the debate over essence above all in his work 'Biblical Religion and the Quest for Meaning'. For Tillich, biblical religion and ontology are to be seen in a correlative relationship of question and answer. This close connection between biblical tradition and ontology is a task posed anew to each era, and thus takes the place of what for Troeltsch is the 'definition of essence'.[139]

In Troeltsch the question of the essence of Christianity has basically a polemical and a constructive side. The polemical side is directed against a rigid traditionalism and an external faith in authority. The constructive trend seeks to think of the relationship between Christian faith and history in terms of a hierarchy of values from the perspective of revelation which at the same time has a horizontal link. Troeltsch sees the combination of the two aspects in the fact that the question of an 'essence of Christianity' attempts to address modern men and women, who have gone astray through a belief in authority and miracles, in such a way as to serve as a basis for an understanding. This is what makes possible a present orientation in the context of the tradition that has been taken over, which at the same time is able to define the future.

4. Troeltsch's critique of Herrmann's Ethics *and the outlines of his own scheme*

Wilhelm Herrmann, who was about twenty years older than Troeltsch, had already written two major works by the end of the century which had made him known beyond the Ritschl school and had made Marburg a magnet for liberally-inclined students.[140] By comparison, at this time Ernst Troeltsch was more an outsider in the circles of a theological avant-garde, a critical spirit who seemed to communicate new perspectives of thought but so far had not developed beyond the level of a local Heidelberg celebrity. The tone of a letter to Herrmann preserved from the early period (27 October 1898) reflects Troeltsch's respect and sympathy. Troeltsch is delighted to have made Herrmann's acquaintance at a meeting of the friends of *Christliche Welt* and sees Herrmann as an important dialogue partner. Then the correspondence breaks off; it was only resumed during the war, for political reasons.[141]

Though the personal conversation initially fell silent or faded into the background, the academic argument between the two theologians continued, and has a special significance both for the theological situation of the time and because of its later effect.

Herrmann's scheme. When Wilhelm Herrmann wrote an *Ethics* in 1900, Troeltsch reacted with a detailed review which in both extent and content amounts to quite a respectable article.[142] This article is an indication of how Troeltsch takes the opportunity of using the theological schemes of theologians close to him for developing his own thought.

At the time of its appearance, within Herrmann's overall development his *Ethics* represented the adoption of notions which had been formulated earlier.[143]

Troeltsch has to accept Herrmann's view that people of the present first have to have a way to ethics constructed for them, by means of a general clarification of the moral element. Only then, according to Herrmann, can the transition to Christian faith and its significance for ethics be made. Accordingly, Herrmann's ethics is divided into two parts: the first is concerned with natural life and the emergence of the ethical question in the natural conditions of life; the second with the character of the moral life of the Christian.

Ethics as an overcoming of the will to self-assertion and thus as a higher level of the view of life is set over against self-assertion as the natural form of life. So moral life cannot be derived from the sphere of natural life; it represents an overcoming of the natural on the basis of a new orientation. This happens through the direction of the human will towards an object which is to be regarded as the 'highest good'.

For Herrmann, it is clear that moral thought as expressed generally can only be comprehended formally. 'Formality' makes possible a relationship to the situation through which the individual can show the requisite moral conduct on the basis of insight and conscience. The concretion of action follows from the adoption of the general and the formal in the special situation of personal life.

According to Herrmann, for the phenomenon of the moral to be grasped requires a relationship of trust between persons. This changes the human relationship, which has a merely natural foundation. The moral law which the unconditional demand presents to us is an expression and presupposition of this relationship of trust. Whereas conflicts must arise in the acceptance of natural human interests and tendencies, interpersonal relationships can be given a 'trustworthy' form on a moral basis. With these reflections Herrmann has quite specifically come close to Kant's ethics.

So Herrmann wrote an *Ethics* which is to be located within the sphere of influence of Kantian philosophy. Nevertheless, the special character of his argument must be noted. This includes his reference to the phenomenon of trust, his stress on truthfulness, and a view of the relationship between individual and society governed by the principle of trust, along with a view of the reality of life and the world which is achieved through faith in creation. Herrmann understands the relationship of human beings to reality dialectically: on the one hand the reality surrounding human beings can in principle be accepted positively, on the basis of belief in creation, and on the other this reality cannot be simply be accepted, nor may it be regarded as ultimate. Rather, it is a means towards the realization of the ethical insight.

It is striking how in the analysis of the moral element Herrmann comes close to the language and thought of the Bible and the Reformers. He can interpret the moral insight as 'self-denial' because it forbids human beings to adapt to conditions. The sphere of freedom transcends the world which can be perceived empirically; it cannot be communicated rationally, but only through an 'experience'. Right down to his language, we can see how indebted Herrmann is to the intellectual tradition of German idealism on the one hand and biblical and Reformation thought on the other.[144]

According to Herrmann, radical perception of the moral demand leads human beings to recognize their guilt. The possibility of freedom and the imputing of guilt correspond, to the degree that obligations to action, freedom, and insight into the inadequacies of behaviour belong together. Where the perception of guilt becomes unavoidable, for Herrmann the insight of faith is already at work in human beings. But how is the relationship between morality and religion to be defined more closely? Here Herrmann does not make any necessary transition. Rather, he argues with Schleiermacher – against Kant – that religion is an independent expression of life which rests on human beings being 'grasped'. The combination of religion and ethics cannot therefore come about by the religious view as it were giving aid to the moral. Rather, there are points of contact between ethics generally and Christian faith. The human being governed by the humane ethos notes the same attitude in the Christian: the assertion of a reality from freedom and for freedom, which is taken as reality before all experience.

For the person orientated only on a humane ethic the contradiction between obligation to action and capacity for action, which he imputes to himself as personal guilt, is intolerable if he discovers 'true faith' in other people. In Herrmann, the dimension of guilt becomes the interface at which humane and Christian ethics meet. In concrete, this means that the person who takes account of his guilt finds himself drawn into a set of problems which are incapable of solution – and that means also from an ethical perspective.

The presupposition for action as a Christian is rebirth. As a power which changes human beings this brings about Christian-moral action. Rebirth, which rests on a personal human experience, resolves the tension between moral insight and moral realization, makes a change in life possible, and leads to new action.

The orientation on the Bible and the Reformation which at the same time takes up Kant's practical philosophy, along with a move towards Schleiermacher, becomes clear in Herrmann's definition of the relationship between religion and ethics: religion is about trust in a power on which we know ourselves to be dependent and which we regard as a power that awakens trust in us and summons us to particular actions. The moment we find trust, we are dependent and independent at the same time; we know that we are both bounden and supported. It is in this process that for Herrmann the origin of religion and morality lies. Both become possible in human beings because they are given an experience of trust.[145] For Herrmann, the religious expression of such dependence is faith – faith in the divine revelation. The revelation of God is communicated to human beings through the person of Jesus. In this connection Troeltsch speaks of the 'fact' of Jesus which makes possible the way to such an experience.[146]

Herrmann does not describe more closely how the encounter with Jesus comes about. It is enough that it is perceived through faith and effective in real life. Herrmann dispenses with any description because he rejects any psychologizing of faith. What has to be maintained is that 'in his religious experience the Christian thus achieves the solution of the moral problem posed to humanity'.[147]

Herrmann's ethics is conceived of as a dispositional ethics which combines the moral autonomy of human beings with the Christian experience of redemption. At the same time the individualism rooted in the dispositional principle is linked with the Christian principle of community. The two are related in such a way that the Christian as a witness perceives other witnesses alongside him who have the same bond with God and face the same demand to be responsible for the world.

The cohesion of the Christian community arises out of this fellowship in the service of witness. The task of the Christian in the world is therefore, to put it simply, to be a 'witness in the world' on the basis of his bond with the power of good mediated by Jesus Christ. The natural forms of life and community relations – family, culture, society and the nation-state – have a relative value for Herrmann, but they cannot be regarded as ends in themselves. For while Christ was indeed bound to the limited forms of natural life, at the same time he was inwardly free from them.

Troeltsch's assent and criticism. Ernst Troeltsch regarded Herrmann's *Ethics* as 'one of the most mature, well-thought-out and imaginative works of contemporary theology'.[148] At the same time this generally positive verdict was an occasion for him to reflect further on his own position. He criticized Herrmann for not having clarified sufficiently the way in which his account was conditioned by the historical situation and not having reflected on it systematically. It seems as if Troeltsch looked on this kind of thinking with some amazement and admiration, but not least also with sceptical detachment.

He recognized the simplicity and strength of this conception, but at the same time it brought out the critic in him. Typically, he finds a place for Herrmann's conception in the history of modern thought and theology and feels the need to counter it with his own ethical scheme. For Troeltsch, Herrmann's idea of the connection between morality in general and the Christian contribution to ethics in particular is not a theological or ecclesiastical notion stemming from history, but arises out of modern psychology. This prompts the question of the unity of the life of the soul and the analytical approach which goes with it.[149]

For Troeltsch, the course of the more recent history of theology since the Reformation went like this. Originally an understanding of Christian faith and religion which was not discussed further included a bent towards action; the result was that the methodological question of the relationship between dogmatics and ethics went unanswered. Rather, ethics retreated behind dogmatics and stood in its shadow. That changed with the Enlightenment and its concern to develop a universal theory of morality. Kant represents the end of a development in which the relationship between ethics and religion changed. Ethics was understood as the fundamental science, and religion was incorporated into it or subordinated to it. This definition of the relationship now in turn changed with the rise of the individual sciences in the form of psychology and history. That posed a new task for the understanding of religion, namely an analysis of religious feeling to be made from a historical and psychological perspective. That meant that the dogmatic element again became independent from the ethical element, as a result of a specific view of the concept of religon, namely the independence of the religious from morality and metaphysics. This understanding is to be found in Schleiermacher. However, it was crossed by Schleiermacher's inclusion of theological ethics in doctrine, as a result of which the idea of ethics as subordinate to dogmatics, which was believed already to have been overcome, once again emerged. So it was right for Richard Rothe in his ethics not to begin from Schleiermacher's theological ethics but from his general ethics and to be inspired by the idea of developing theology from an overall ethical view. According to Troeltsch, no account before that of Herrmann did justice to the possibilities presented positively by Rothe, which at the same time are a consequence of the modern development. Here already Troeltsch saw the remarkable merit and special achievement of Wilhelm Herrmann's *Ethics*.

In Troeltsch's view, the consequence to be drawn from the understanding of ethics grounded in Schleiermacher's ethics, taken up by Rothe and issuing in Herrmann's view, was that one should not start from Christianity in isolation, but from the universal, here ethics as a system of objective values from which an agreement on the special contribution of Christianity can then follow. Two aspects follow from this. First, the relationship of religion and ethics in the context of the historical development towards modernity must be seen as an intellectual challenge. Secondly, on the presupposition of a general definition of ethics as the doctrine of the ultimate goals and aims of human life, the Christian element can fit into this general context as a special contribution, whereas conversely there would be a dogmatic claim to validity which puts the special character of Christianity before or above the general. Christian faith then appears as the realization of what is generally possible and conceivable as ethics.[150]

In Troeltsch's view, Herrmann had correctly seen the fundamental difference in modern ethics. Modern ethics are based on the contrast between conditioned, natural and unconditioned purposes based on commandment and obedience and the resultant character of the moral as obligation which differs from occasion to occasion. However, he thinks that Herrmann's interpretation of this dualism is epistemologically inadequate. For him, the dualism between the relative and the absolute goal is in truth that between the psychological and ontological purposes. He makes this point primarily against Kant, and secondarily against Herrmann.

The central features of Herrmann's *Ethics* and Troeltsch's retort are shaped by the philosophical and theological tradition since Kant and Schleiermacher. According to Kant, the will as the capacity to have one's desires determined by concepts and purposes makes it possible for human beings to orientate their action on laws. A *purpose* is then said to be what objectively underlies the will, and if this is governed by pure reason, it must be capable of generalization. Whereas the hypothetical imperative which begins from individual notions and aims can always only apply conditionally, the categorical imperative calls for unconditional validity.

From these presuppositions Kant derives an ethic of goods and purposes. The world of the 'goods' is involved in historical movement and change, so an ethic orientated on it must similarly be variable. It could claim only time-conditioned, relative validity because it is dependent on empirical factors. Kant uses the concept of final purpose to explore the possibility of breaking through sequences of purposes which again merely become means, in so far as this 'needs no other (i.e. purpose) as the condition of its possibility'.[151] In the moral sphere, the unconditional affirmation of the autonomy of the moral will under the notion of duty, which goes beyond any subjective goal of a eudaimonistic kind, can be seen as such a final purpose. Herrmann, who agrees with Kant on the question of the merely formal definition of what is required of human beings through the moral will, repeatedly uses the terms 'purpose' and 'final purpose'. In so doing he follows Kant's conceptuality, but for him the concept of the 'final purpose' takes on another, theological, significance which goes beyond Kant. For Herrmann, the 'final purpose' is the filling of huamn life with meaning and thus the perception of the real purpose as human independence and freedom. So the real final purpose is taken up into the event of redemption and forgiveness.[152]

Troeltsch wants to preserve the form of moral obligation grounded in Kant through the autonomy and value of the person; however, he wants to extend it by a reference to material values and their cultural tradition. Only through this perception of the values and purposes mediated through the history of culture is it possible to define the concrete content of morality alongside the general validity of its formal side, which is to be defined *a priori*. In his explanation of the notion of 'purpose', Troeltsch refers critically back to Schleiermacher. For his part, Schleiermacher criticizes the merely imperative character of Kant's ethics and the derivation of general validity from the formal notion of duty. When it comes to the special tasks of the individual, the possibility of accomplishing them must be a matter for the individual himself. Schleiermacher sees man in his unity as a natural and rational being. Schleiermacher's ethics culminates in the notion of the 'supreme good', which embraces the totality of all human relations and purposes in such a way that they arise out of it organically. Troeltsch criticizes Schleiermacher for falling short in his theological ethics of the level of argument which he has achieved in his philosophical ethics. Whereas in the philosophical outline religion appears alongside the other objective cultural values as a distinctive form of expression with an organic relationship to it and incorporated into it, theological ethics has lost this basic notion because the concept of redemption gives rise to a principle of exclusiveness which no longer allows the perception of the wealth of ethical phenomena from history and the present gained in philosophical ethics.[153] Troeltsch criticizes Schleiermacher's way of making the Christian religion absolute, in which Christ is constructed as the 'model of perfect religious feeling which has a productive effect'.[154] Troeltsch observes that in the question of the relationship between religion generally and Christian religion, Herrmann takes his bearings from Schleiermacher, though in a modified form. The moral knowledge which is communicated through the experience of Christ and the liberation for truly moral action which results from it represent the fulfilment of the general ethic. Troeltsch develops his own scheme by the combination and interweaving of historical and systematic criticism which is distinctive of him; this scheme brings out the independence of the religious or the Christian without demoting the significance of objective cultural values.

Troeltsch's own scheme. The reservations presented above put the basic approach of Herrmann's ethics in doubt and oblige the critic in turn to describe how he conceives an ethic. But in accordance with Troeltsch's way of thinking and working, the positive development of his thoughts now comes about essentially in and through the proces of interpretation, by an indication of wrong decisions or aporias, by expanding and changing – to the point of bringing out basic features (and only basic features) of his own way.

For Troeltsch, two conclusions follow from the basic notion presented by Herrmann of a distinction between relative purposes and an absolute purpose through the affirmation of the 'higher life'. One relates to the working out of the notion of guilt. Troeltsch cannot agree with it, because here he sees statements of faith introduced in a violent way. Anyone who calls for moral knowledge as stubbornly as Herrmann cannot think that in principle this cannot be realized. Secondly, Troeltsch sees a metaphysical shift of thought in Herrmann. For Troeltsch, this consists in the fact that in their moral action human beings think of the good as the power of the real. In his view, at this point Herrmann reinterprets Kant by coming close to Fichte. For Fichte does not attempt, as Kant does, to balance claims to happiness and moral worth through the postulate of human immortality; rather, he tends towards a recognition of metaphysical presuppositions of moral action. Troeltsch now remarks in amazement that this metaphysical shift of thought in Herrmann in the direction of belief in an ultimate meaning of reality is not yet 'religion'. Had Herrmann already seen religion in this metaphysical shift, then according to Troeltsch it would have been possible for him really to perceive the distinctive character of religion and develop its effects on ethics appropriately. According to Troeltsch, it was not without reason that Kant and Fichte had seen the advantage of Christian ethics over general ethics as one of degree rather than of principle.

For Troeltsch, one 'painful' difficulty lies in the drawing of a picture of a Jesus with power to save purely from the historical tradition, without any supernatural guarantees. He doubts whether one can speak of a 'fact' if one approaches the Jesus tradition by means of historical criticism. He cannot imagine how anyone can arrive at the experience of trust claimed by Herrmann if the issue is one of realizing the moral in personal life.

As Troeltsch rightly observes, for Herrmann the christological derivation of the 'fact' of Jesus is the foundation of the link between general and Christian ethics. The direction in which Troeltsch himself is moving becomes clear in his critical rendering of Herrmann's intention: 'So here the root of everything is trust in Jesus, belief in God for the sake of Jesus, not belief in Jesus for the sake of God.'[155]

Apart from this theological criticism, as it were from the other end there is criticism of the effect of the moral life, on such a basis, on the modern world of culture. To the degree that Herrmann takes the natural forms of community as a basis for the development of moral character, but does not assign them any value of their own, he does not find any satisfactory and consistent solution for the relationship between Christianity and culture. And according to Troeltsch, what should form the centre of Herrmann's considerations, namely the adoption of Kant's ethics with a theological intent, is not carried through consistently. He sees only the apologetic tendency in this argument, for in his view neither the way in which Herrmann grounds certainty nor the relationship of final moral purpose and natural community match Kant's formalism.

So Troeltsch's agreement with Herrmann's general analysis of the moral in terms of Kant's formalism and autonomy has its limits. He sees a contradiction in the fact that on the basis of the assumption of purely subjective purposes, an objective, formal necessity for objective purposes is excluded. 'For this reason, the relationship between the *a priori* characteristic of the necessity for experience which constitutes the moral must be different and more complicated than that constructed by Kantian ethics, with its simple reference of *a priori* moral necessity to the morally indifferent material of experience.'[156]

Troeltsch thinks that – if the question is one of 'necessity' – in moral reality judgments can be made not only on the basis of the subject but also on the basis of objective values (state, society, science) or with reference to them.[157] So he wants to extend the principles of a merely subjective morality in favour of objective values and their involvement in a culture.

To the degree that Troeltsch requires more note to be taken of the concept of the purpose and the definition of the purpose, he shifts in the direction of an ethic of goods.[158] He thinks that subjective and social virtues could be differentiated by a distinction between individual and social purposes. Troeltsch is offended that Herrmann regards everything towards which Christian moral action can be directed as mere matter, so that the subjective process of decision and self-discovery stands in the foreground.

For Troeltsch, it is necessary to distinguish between subjective and objective ethics. Only in this way can the moral element be grasped completely, because it embraces cultural values and can be experienced through history. Troeltsch is clear that he therefore has to abandon the certainty of the Kantian formation of judgments and that with the recourse to experience and history he is accepting some variability in his approach. But he also sees that if experiential judgments are allowed, and in this way ethics is directed beyond notions of 'objective' morality to history, then ethics needs a philosophy of history which associates this historical orientation with value judgments. He sees the link with tradition as follows. Schleiermacher's attempt to derive objective goods abstractly from the character of reason must be modified by taking into account the historical formation of these goods; one could even say that Schleiermacher has to be supplemented with a basic intention of Hegelian philosophy. The result of this is a relationship to religion which is different in principle: for Troeltsch, religion is an objective good, and its association with ethics does not come about through the notion of autonomy.

In the specifically theological sphere, the interpretation of the New Testament tradition becomes the touchstone: it brings out differences between Troeltsch and Herrmann. Troeltsch stresses the eschatological character of the preaching of Jesus and thus pays greater attention to more recent research into the New Testament than Herrmann does. However, we have to ask what significance this knowledge has for ethics. Here it emerges that for Troeltsch, Jesus' talk about the coming of the kingdom of God has the time-conditioned form of the fundamental recognition of the purpose which embraces all final purposes. According to Troeltsch, Jesus' eschatological mode of thinking and speaking was an interpretation, a historical enabling of the idea of the universal significance of the divine purpose. He thinks Herrmann's attempt to understand redemption in an ethical sense unsuccessful. 'Redemption' is not to be understood in purely ethical terms but at the same time cosmically, and to this degree also with a future orientation. 'This future redemption is related to a present redemption only in the way that the present kingdom of God is related to the coming kingdom of God, i.e. as a mood of hope and confidence, as the exalted power of those who may see the goal before them...'[159]

From the beginning, or more precisely from the transformation of the preaching of Jesus into the cult of Christ and belief in Christ, the content of the moral demand has always been a combination of natural, philosophical and religious ethics, albeit in a modified way. Here what is really Christian was established in the bestowing of grace and in justification. This pattern was preserved in Reformation ethics, and in a modified form governs the course of the more recent history of theology and thought generally through Kant to Herrmann. 'This scheme was produced by the church and is closely connected with its inner being. The church of the mass of the people cannot envisage binding all its members to the ethics of the Sermon on the Mount. It may be possible for the whole cultic and hierarchical organization to be based on the founding of salvation by the God-man, but not on those heroic-radical moral commandments.'[160]

For Troeltsch, in the question of the relationship between faith and ethics, the concept of redemption cannot stand in first place; rather, it comes behind the notion of God and that of the 'objective religious goal'.[161] It follows from this that 'redemptive power may be conceded also to non-Christian belief in God in its own way, because faith itself in any shape or form brings forces from the world above and is at least a germ of redemption'.[162] Troeltsch sees the denial of religious forces outside Christianity as a brusque assertion, the expression of a crude apologetic aim. He puts the stress on the notion of an idea of God independent of the Christ event with the offer of a communion with God which presents itself to human beings as the supreme purpose. In connection with communion with God, the notion of redemption attached to Jesus is one historical form of communication and clarification.

However, Troeltsch can also formulate the basic notion of the connection between belief in God and christology like this: 'Faith, and that means faith in the basic Christian moral idea, is itself redemption; conversion and justification are none other than the origin of this faith. This faith, which in the first place is directed towards God and the goal which he has shown us, is *at the same time* [my italics] directed to Jesus as the one who has brought us and guaranteed us this faith and whose image re-establishes it more strongly in ups and downs, temptations and exhaustion than any self-tormenting attempts at revival. He is the redeemer precisely because he is the bringer, the model and the support of faith in God.'[163]

Thus Troeltsch remains somewhat ambivalent about the relationship between the idea of redemption as communion with God and redemption understood in christological terms. His interpretation of New Testament eschatology also needs to be questioned. How can the possibility asssumed by Troeltsch of immersing oneself in the original situation of the formation of religious ideas have a life-giving effect for the faith of people in the present if at the same time the time-conditioned character of eschatology is recognized? People after the Enlightenment, as Troeltsch understands things, will hardly be able to see the element of truth in the tradition in its historical origin if at the same time they are aware of the way in which the sayings in the tradition are historically conditioned. Here Troeltsch should have explained more closely the relationship between an understanding in terms of the history of ideas and the notion of an immersion in the original situation, thought of in basically mystical terms. At least it becomes clear what he is dissociating himself from, and in what positive direction his thoughts are taking him. It is essential to him that redemption should not be understood as 'finished' and in this way removed from history. Rather, for him the essence of redemption lies in the fact that it is 'the pledge of the real coming redemption, which will be not merely an ethical but also a metaphysical event'.[164] Now if in this way a reference is made to the real redemption at the end of history, then according to Troeltsch the artificiality of a theological or ecclesiastical apologetic can disappear and its place can be taken by the notion of development, which includes the emergence of the Christian powers of redemption in the development of the life of the Spirit. In that case 'ethics and doctrine can be formed for the present in a free synthesis of living Christian forces'.[165]

This account can be supplemented with references to Troeltsch's lectures on ethics.[166]

One striking character of his practical Christian ethics is that Troeltsch combines exegesis, historical aspects and analyses of the time with substantive questions which begin from the Bible and are pursued into the history of theology and the church.

What Troeltsch says about the notion of autonomy and its relationship to theonomy is particularly important. For him, autonomy and theonomy are not in conflict; rather, theonomy, rightly understood, is the foundation of autonomy. Theonomy means 'autonomy interwoven with God'.[167]

Two notions illuminate Troeltsch's own attitude to questions of Christian belief and ethics: his understanding of the God-man relationship and his view of the immanence-transcendence relationship. On the former, it becomes clear that for Troeltsch God and man are not separated from each other by an abyss, but that connections exist in the depths, in the origin. So we read: 'In the ultimate depths of the soul the self goes over into the divine. God and man are not essentially separate. We do not draw on our natural being, but on that point where this divine-human connection exists.'[168]

In the definition of the relationship between immanence and transcendence, transcendence is seen as a force, as a penetration of immanence which is to be regarded as qualitative. Transcendence is not related to an absolute beyond; it is not a matter of an 'arrival' from somewhere else in the human world, which then puts that world in question. Rather, for Troeltsch everything is divine and human at the same time.

In his investigation of Troeltsch's ethics, Benckert comes to the conclusion that Troeltsch's significance does not lie either in what he said about the nature and principle of morality generally or in his wrestling with the question of personal morality. Rather, Troeltsch's significance lies in what he developed in relation to the ethics of cultural values, incorporating the notion of historical changes.

The interpretation presented by Pannenberg is particularly fruitful. He works out how Troeltsch's criticism of Herrmann is implicitly also directed against Schleiermacher, to the degree that in Schleiermacher the relationship between redemption and ethics generally is governed in a similar way to that in Herrmann, by isolating the idea of redemption from the concept of the kingdom of God while at the same time combining it with a natural ethic. Here Pannenberg rightly distinguishes between what Troeltsch explicitly indicates as a connection with Schleiermacher and what in addition they really have in common in their thought. Here Pannenberg makes particular mention of the notions of the supreme good or the purpose, which belongs in a line of tradition with Schleiermacher. In a further exploration of the notion of purposes adopted by Troeltsch, Pannenberg wants to arrive at a more appropriate interpretation of the relationship between the kingdom of God and ethics, by utilizing positively Troeltsch's notions of the independence of the secular sphere and the plurality of purposes within the world.

However, Pannenberg gives a different theological definition of 'provisionality' and 'finality' from Troeltsch. For him, provisionality can in 'anticipation' be defined in terms of finality, because Jesus' preaching of the coming kingdom of God proclaims God as the power of the future. Problems arise where Pannenberg interprets passages from Troeltsch's text which contradict this (common) basic direction. That is the case where the kingdom of God in Troeltsch is a future entity, though it is not seen one-sidedly, but at the same time grasped in terms of the present, and is put in a metaphysical context or interpreted in terms of inwardness – and not just in terms of the future.

5. The approach and structure of Troeltsch's philosophy of religion

Introductory remarks. If one surveys Troeltsch's works on the philosophy of religion, the dominant impression is one of incompleteness. What he published were in the strict sense preparatory works and programmatic outlines. He intended to develop them systematically in the form of a major account, but never managed to realize his aim.

In view of the significance of the philosophy of religion for Troeltsch's theological work and for his philosophy of culture, this lack of a systematic development is particularly regrettable. Troeltsch also felt this himself. He repeatedly assured his publisher that the working out of a philosophy of religion was one of his most important aims.[169]

At the beginning of his preoccupation with the theme, which was relatively concentrated on the years 1904/5, comes a work on 'The Historical in Kant's Philosophy of Religion' (1904).[170] In it Troeltsch discusses the possibility of a reception of Kant in the philosophy of religion and theology which at the same time contains a critical historical discussion of the question of the relationship between Enlightenment thought and history. The book represents a remarkable combination of historical and systematic questions typical of Troeltsch. Here Troeltsch at the same time discusses in the guise of history the views of the theological Kantians. Moreover, in connection with his own position he examines the possibilities of a link in the philosophy of religion with Kant.

Some months later an article of Troeltsch's appeared in the Festschrift for Kuno Fischer under the title 'Philosophy of Religion' (1904). In accordance with the overall intention of the Festschrift, this article was concerned more to sketch out the present state of the philosophy of religion as a philosophical discipline than to move towards finding Troeltsch's own position.[171]

The work which probably had the greatest outside influence and made Troeltsch known to a wider public in the philosophy of religion is the lecture that he gave at the World Congress in St Louis, which appeared under the title 'Psychology and Epistemology in the Study of Religion' (1905). The

title[172] makes it clear that here there are connecting links with both Troeltsch's
work on the philosophy of history and his contribution to the Festschrift.

Four more of Troeltsch's articles must then be mentioned from the subsequent period.
First the one on 'Essence of Religion and the Study of Religion' (1906). It introduces
reflections on the history of religion and philosophy into the discussion of the philosophy
of history. The article 'On the Question of the Religious *A Priori*' (1909) belongs in
the controversy over the religious *a priori*. Finally, mention should be made of the two
articles 'Empiricism and Platonism in the Philosophy of Religion' (1912) and 'Logos
and Myth in Theology and the Philosophy of Religion' (1913). In the first, Troeltsch
discusses the significance of James for the psychology of religion and develops this by
applying a series of types (empiricism on the one side and Platonism on the other) to
the establishment of positions in the philosophy of religion. The second article attempts
to define more closely the element in his theory which Bousset thought irrational.

In conclusion, reference should be made to Troeltsch's numerous reviews in which
he made critical comments about others or countered criticism of his own ideas. The
lectures which he gave now and then on the philosophy of religion, some of which have
been preserved in note form (e.g. by Gertrud von le Fort), cannot be a real substitute
for a systematic account. They contain much material and discuss theories in history
and the present which are revlevant to the philosophy of religion, but there is no
working out of the substance of his own position.

There are vaguenesses and obscurities as to what Troeltsch understood by
'philosophy of religion', some of which go back to his generous use of
terminology. In principle he tended to distinguish between the scientific study
of religion and the philosophy of religion. Nevertheless, he rightly saw
connections and overlaps here. The scientific study of religion works empirically, excluding the religious question of truth. Certainly it leads up to this
question, but it does not answer it. The philosophy of religion in the narrower
sense – understood as an epistemology of religion – takes this very question
of the truth and the reality of the religious as a theme. Issues from the
philosophy of history and metaphysics are associated with it. The religious
philosophy of history and metaphysics sometimes appear in Troeltsch as part
of the philosophy of religion, but at other times also as a development and
consequence of it. For Troeltsch, an overlap between the two disciplines is in
the nature of things. Now if he occasionally comes to equate the scientific
study of religion with the philosophy of religion, it is because on the one hand
in both cases one can speak of a scientific intention which is distinct from
living religious feeling, and on the other hand he regards the scientific study
of religion and the philosophy of religion as a possibility or necessity of an
approach to religion which is in keeping with the time and the subject-
matter.[173]

The psychological analysis of religion. In his philosophy of religion Troeltsch
begins with the psychology of religion. It is fundamental, to the degree that it

opens up access to religious phenomena. Nevertheless, from the aspect of the philosophy of religion it is not enough, but needs expansion.

For Troeltsch, the way has to go through the psychology of religion because the way through the church's dogma is blocked, as is the assumption of a natural religious sense in terms of the 'enlightened' understanding.[174]

The way which still remains open leads through the psychological analysis of religion. This is focussed on something that is indisputable, namely the religious consciousness itself. Another reason lies in the nature of the question: the access to religion must come about through the reality of the religious life.

Troeltsch sees the work of the psychology of religion in his time being carried on by two groups of researchers. There are the anthropologists with their interest in the religion of the primitives, and the experimental psychologists with their focus on the observation of religious phenomena. The historians of religion are to be put between the anthropologists and the psychologists: they investigate the great religions from the perspective of both the essential and the changeable and therefore occupy a middle position, because they are interested in both the past and the present of religious life. Troeltsch rejects a dominance of anthropological-prehistoric work in the psychology of religion. He regards as an ideological prejudice the assumption that it is possible to gain a fundamental access to religion generally through the world of the primitives. He thinks that this preconception rests on a positivistic view of the world which is not concerned with a real analysis of religion, but with a pejorative assessment which has the aim of making religion ultimately superfluous. The main defect of this view is not to be foisted on psychology but on the world-view underlying it, which claims to be scientific but is basically rooted in ideology. Information is to be gained about the essence of religion not through supposedly primal religion but through living experience of the present. Historical material can and should be taken up, but without constraints and impairments caused by an ideological judgment.

Troeltsch accepts experimental psychology to the degree that it is really concerned to observe religious phenomena. But in his view the assumption that here it is possible to proceed by measurability and quantitative definition fails to do justice to the essence of the matter. Wilhelm Wundt (1832-1920), who comes to mind in this connection and who was apostrophized by Troeltsch as the 'leader of German psychology',[175] cannot do justice to the special character of the religious either through his experimental psychology or through his psychology of peoples. The assumption that religion (like ethics and aesthetics) is a 'complex phenomenon' leads Wundt astray into the error that one can approach the essence of religion by a resort to simpler phenomena.[176]

As Troeltsch cannot consider approaches in terms of either anthropological-genetic or experimental psychology, he considers another possibility. He finds this in William James's empirical psychology of religion. James (1846-1916), professor of philosophy in Harvard, opposed the traditional rational view of psychology, which he felt to be indebted to the old metaphysical tradition, according to which the soul is understood as a spiritual essence endowed with special possibilities or, better, a special capacity.[177]

In particular, James criticizes the notion that by virtue of their intellectual endowment human beings seek to distance themselves from their concrete environment and over against this stresses the compulsion to pragmatic action. He insists that the inner capacities of human beings are *a priori* directed towards the structure of the world in which they live. The capacity of the human soul is functionally tailored to specific environmental influences, especially demands which arise from a particular concrete situation.[178]

Troeltsch called James a master of psychology who showed a 'real understanding for the most intimate phenomena of religion and complete openness to all the problems caused by the colourless of metaphysical thought and the heat of a fanaticism for causality'.[179] Troeltsch thought that he could take up James's psychology of religion because it expressed religious experience as a document and a manifestation of the character of religious feeling. He was convinced by the empirical approach to be found in James, i.e. the repudiation of a physiological derivation of religion and the renunciation of a metaphysical construction.

Perhaps Troeltsch's acceptance of James's methodology prevented him from asking what the empirical factor in James in fact looked like. In his work James above all followed literary testimonies of people who had had particular religious experiences and at the same time had a corresponding capacity for verbal or literary expression. Troeltsch saw it as a positive factor that here religious phenomena were speaking for themselves. For him this meant that in principle the spontaneity and special character of religious experience was preserved.

James answers in biological terms the question of what knowledge and truth is contained in religion, to the effect that religion leads to a heightened capacity in human beings to adapt to their environment. For Troeltsch the pragmatism expressed here rests (implicitly) on a rational presupposition. It includes the assumption of a preceding relationship between individuals and their natural and human environment, arrived at through the senses, and at the same time postulates 'meaning' in respect of the world as a whole.

Despite this criticism, Troeltsch maintained his basic endorsement of the empirical psychology of religion, of which he saw James as a representative.[180] Starting from the perception of the independence of religious life, he thought it possible to work out characteristic features on the basis of a general definition of form. He sees inspiration, revelation, prayer and meditation as the basic categories to be used here. The one-sidednesses and inconsistencies in James which Troeltsch brings out demonstrate to him that work in the philosophy of religion must be carried on in the form of an epistemology of religion. It is not just inherent in the form of a scholarly discussion that Troeltsch should also formulate objections to this approach; that also corresponds to his way of receiving stimulation. Because he finds his way to his own view through assent and criticism, taking note of his critics has a hermeneutical function. Three points are particularly significant: 1. Troeltsch thinks that James puts too much stress on the element of feeling in the definition of religion. This leads him to neglect the role of thought. 2. He criticizes the fact that because of James's psychological approach, he has a false estimation of the significance of community life for religion.[181] 3. He questions whether James answers the question of the truth and reality of religion in an adequate and convincing way. Whereas James believes himself to be following a purely pragmatic and scientific procedure, his account contains rational factors – which are more or less hidden.

Epistemology of religion. For Troeltsch, the main task of the philosophy of religion in the narrower sense consists in developing an epistemology of religion. This is an analysis of concepts and formal structures and not merely a matter of empirical perception and assimilation. An epistemology of religion which works on the basis of conceptual thought and strives for general validity can resolve the dilemma in which the psychology of religion necessarily finds itself if it wants to respond to the question of the knowledge of religion in its own terms.[182] By referring to a general definition of the form of religious life, the psychology of religion already points towards universalization, because this approach already goes via the multiplicity of religious phenomena and the great variety in the expression of them.

Whereas Troeltsch's first attempts indicated a philosophical standpoint close to that of Hegel, it was Kant's philosophy which now became increasingly significant for his investigations in the philosophy of religion. So we can read that 'it can only be the old Kant, ever given new life, by whom we have to go'.[183]

For Troeltsch, Kant recognized the basic problem in the philosophy of religion of how to develop empirical work in psychology in the direction of an epistemology and saw correctly the problem which arises here of a distinction between and a combination of irrational and rational elements.

Kant showed the direction for the philosophy of religion by his repudiation of a religion of pure reason, his attention to the history of religion and his assumption of the proximity of the psychological and the intelligible. Therefore for Troeltsch the philosophy of religion must 'in principle go the way of Kant'.[184] The qualification and thus the criticism of Kant is addressed above all to the excessively close bond between religion and morality which can be found in Kant's writings. By contrast, for Troeltsch, emphasis needs to be put on the independence of religion: a view which found an eloquent advocate, say, in Schleiermacher.

In view of his orientation on Kant, Troeltsch must of course also tackle the reception of Kant in the Protestant theology of his time, primarily the Ritschl schoool. He rejects a theological interpretation of Kant which loses sight of one of the main aims of the formation of a theory of the philosophy of religion, namely the relationship between the religious and reality. That comes about in the so-called theology of value-judgment (i.e. in Ritschl and his school) which, because it distinguishes between theoretical reason and the reason which makes a practical evaluation, is not in a position to maintain 'the necessary existence of the object in which these values are rooted'.[185]

In his own formation of a theory of the philosophy of religion, Troeltsch is guided by two essential motives. First, there is the dilemma in the psychology of religion which we have already addressed. It is impossible to restrict it to the description of religious phenomena; the 'value question' must be discussed. Secondly, there is the philosophical and ideological objection in the form of materialism and positivism, which challenges the truth and significance of religion. The dilemma has to be removed; the challenge to the claim of religion to validity and truth must be countered. Both motives are closely connected, indeed overlap. To take up the value question is to make a critical investigation of the possibility and significance of the assertion of the form of truth which emerges in individual religious experience – or to claim to do so.

Troeltsch felt that while Kant had seen the basic problem for the philosophy of religion of a combination of psychology and epistemology and had also offered pointers towards its solution, these had to be taken further, since they were inadequate both in principle and in a modern setting. So to take up Kant's philosophy for the philosophy of religion meant to go beyond him. Troeltsch sums up his criticism of Kant and the concern for modification which results from this criticism in four points. 1. The demonstration of the rational over against the merely empirical rests on an epistemological circle which progresses from the psychological perception of the facts to knowledge (or to the logical) and then goes back again. Very much along the lines of the south-west German Kant school, he speaks of a value decision of the will, which validates the rational over against the merely empirical. The laws of consciousness which are to apply are extracted from experience by analysis, and this is a task which needs constantly to be understood afresh. Here both the achievement and the limits of a concern for logical thought become evident.

For life is more than the rational and logical element. Nevertheless, the logical cannot be dispensed with in the interest of demonstrating 'rationality' in religious phenomena. Since there is always mere appearance and even error in the religious sphere, the questioning necessitates a distinction between appearance and reality, even if it also emerges that in the end the rational approach cannot be total, but confronts an inexplicable remnant.

Thus there will be no complete logicalization or rationalization of reality – a point already made earlier against Hegel: this is forbidden both by the reality and the capability of reason. Nevertheless, there remains a struggle between reason and what comes from the senses and is mere folly. Applied to religion, that means that the demonstration of what is 'valid' from religious reality is always unfinished. It rests on a human decision to regard as true on the basis of inner necessity and consistency the event perceived in religious life which is to be derived from a single basic experience.[186]

2. The second objection relates to the same subject-matter, but approaches it from a different angle. For Troeltsch, it is necessary to assert epistemological regularity over against the merely psychological, but this can only be got from the actual facts of religious life. In this context it is necessary to perceive and allow the special character of the religious.

3. The question which is connected with this relates to a central notion in the philosophy of religion, namely the relationship between the empirical and the intelligible I. Here once again it becomes clear how the philosophical adoption of Kantian philosophy comes about from an interest in the philosophy of religion which thinks that it can satisfy both the empirical and the rational factors in religious feeling. 'Empirical' relates to the religious experience, and its anti-intellectual character; 'rational' means the possibility of grounding the religious sense in a rational element.

For Troeltsch there is a contradiction in first finding the intelligible I in the world of the law and secondly allowing it to go beyond that. He does not think it possible to assume parallelism and difference simultaneously. Rather, in his view, both the intelligible and the empirical I must be 'interleaved', so that the intelligible is grasped as the element which is effective in reality.

In Kantian terms, this is the question of causality from freedom. Troeltsch opposes a view of causality for which natural life is governed by the causal nexus, and understands the intelligible in the course of a transcendental determination based on the idea of freedom as an autonomous production of reason, but does not allow it to have an effect on empirical life. However, the notion of an 'interleaving' of the empirical and the intelligible I which Troeltsch has in mind would do away with the distinction between the two Is in the context of a specific understanding of causality in each instance: on the one hand from nature and on the other from freedom. In Kant, we find causality according to nature as the succession of phenomena in the world of the senses according to a rule, that of cause and effect. By contrast, causality from freedom is not subject to the natural sequence of cause and effect which takes place within the framework of time. Rather, freedom is to be spoken of as a transcendental idea. As a transcendental idea, however, it does not correspond to what is given through experience. This leads reason to create for itself the idea of a spontaneity which can begin to act of itself.[187] Given the postulatory character of the idea of freedom, it is hard to escape the coherence and consistency of Kant's thought. If one does that nevertheless, as Troeltsch intends with his idea of 'interleaving', then one has fundamentally moved further beyond Kant than he is ready to concede. In that case we have to investigate the basis and the intent of Troeltsch's criticism of Kant.

Kant's conception at this point contradicts Troeltsch's interest in the philosophy of religion, which while it does not want to turn religious self-expression in the form of its experience of transcendence into a proof, does want to keep it open as a possibility. One can also say that in Troeltsch the place of the postulatory idea of freedom is taken by the assumption of an experience of transcendence. This is based on the perception of the presence of the divine in religious experience.[188]

One consequence of this modification of Kantian thought is a change in the concepts of both time and causality. The phenomenality of time is to be changed into an intelligible temporality. That means that not everything that belongs to time is also to be thought of in terms of 'phenomenality', but it is to be assumed that there is an intervention in the course of time on the basis of autonomous forces.

The notion of causality is connected with the new version of the concept of time. Troeltsch's letters to Rudolf Otto show how deeply he was concerned with a version of the concept of causality which was acceptable to the philosophy of religion. Thus he writes (on 3 December 1904): 'For me the focal point lies in the logical character of the principle of causality. I believe that this is very varied and multi-layered and must leave room at many points for the incomprehensible.'[189]

The new version of the concept of causality relates above all to the fact that the starting point is a definition of the courses of history in terms of strict regularity, in the interest of the assumption of an 'ordered interaction between phenomenal and intelligible, psychological and rational awareness of reality...'[190]

The assumption of an interaction in this sense serves the notion that the presence of the divine claimed in religious experience need not necessarily be fundamentally impossible, i.e. impossible on rational grounds.

4. The last point of a critical modification of Kantian philosophy means that an abstract concept of religion can never take the place of concrete religion, no matter how it is arrived at. Nevertheless, in the cause of the philosophical discussion of religion a process of abstraction must take place, in the interest of working out its validity. However, given the presuppositions in the form of religious life, and the aim, namely to root it in a specific act of reason, this is of a special kind. Troeltsch thinks that he can link up with Kant here, in so far as in accordance with his reflections on the *a priori* basis of theoretical reason Kant assumes aprioristic laws of consciousness of a practical kind for the ethical, the aesthetic, and also (fundamentally) the religious sphere.

There are laws of consciousness 'which are already contained *a priori* in the elementary phenomena of these spheres and produce these very activities of reason when applied to concrete factuality'.[191] So Troeltsch's own view is that his development could be very much in keeping with Kant. However, this is questionable in the framework of an interpretation of Kant.[192]

Troeltsch finds in reason remarkable confirmation of the impression gained through the history and psychology of religion of a unitariness of the religious as a sphere of life displaying mutually consistent, specific basic forms through reason. Reason for its part sees itself compelled to assume an aprioristic law of consciousness for this life. This process of deriving concrete religion from an *a priori* of reason is based on the notion of inner necessity and consistency. The knowledge of truth rooted in individual religious experience and the epistemological insight that the content of this knowledge can make a claim to validity coincide.

We need to ask some further questions about fundamental ideas and aims. First, how, in Troeltsch's view, must we imagine the relationship of the religious *a priori* to the other aprioristic forms of consciousness and reason as a whole? For Troeltsch, the religious *a priori* belongs with the ethical and the religious *a priori* among the other 'practical' forms of consciousness. Here, in contrast to the 'theoretical' *a priori*, the validity of a sphere of experience is indicated by the possibility of deriving its actual expression from a capacity of reason. As the ethical *a priori* cannot and should not replace practical-moral action and the aesthetic *a priori* cannot and should not replace artistic activity, but rather presupposes it, the religious *a priori* is a link between practical religious feeling and a distinctive capacity for reason. It cannot be further derived or dissolved, but rather has its own right and its own significance, as the last universal that can be found. While this does not make it possible to prove religious feeling, it does make it seem rationally possible and meaningful.

Together with the other practical *a priori* forms, the religious *a priori* displays a fundamental difference from the 'theoretical' *a priori*, in that the latter is concerned with the 'experience of reason which understands in a scientific way'.[193] In the case of the practical *a priori* forms, the particular *a priori* is elevated above the actual processes of life because these processes themselves, following a distinctive course and compulsion, allow the inference of a rational capacity which proves to be the basis of the possibility for this expression of life and thus a meaningful rational tie to and validation of a particular sphere of life.

A further question arises. What is the significance, the function, of the religious *a priori*? We have seen that the religious *a priori*, derived from religious reality, proves to be a formal capacity of reason by virtue of which the economy of the consciousness can first be regarded as 'organic'. The regularity to be found in the consciousness has a parallel in the reality of religious life and vice versa. Here is a parallel which for Troeltsch ultimately has a metaphysical foundation.

These presuppositions lead to the assumption that religion can purify itself on the basis of its own *a priori*. Troeltsch states: 'The validity of the truth of religion can be based on this rationalism alone, and on this basis it is possible to regulate critically the wild growths of the life of the psyche.'[194] This activity of reason has a support as it were in the religious life itself. All in all, there is a reciprocal relationship between religious reality and the aprioristic capacity of reason and a relative certainty deriving from this that here is a fundamental feature of the development in the history of religion from which the criterion then derives. In this context Troeltsch speaks of an evidential feeling which can appeal to an objective support. So the solution of the question of the criterion has two poles, one the essence of reason and the other religious reality. 'From the essence of reason' arises the possibility of associating the religious *a priori* with the other practical *a priori* forms. On this presupposition, 'the harmonization of religion with ethics and only then with the logical and aesthetic life is a further criterion of its validity or its truth-content'.[195] The reference to religious reality is derived from the assumption that a tendency to development can be recognized in the history of religion.

In the end there emerges what Troeltsch describes as the 'essence of religion' and which for him finds its expression in an ethical religion of personality. But in terms of content, i.e. of what he wants to achieve for the philosophy of religion with the theory of the religious *a priori*, there can only be a criterion of validity which does not have a dogmatic foundation but shows an inner mobility, because it must be thought of in analogy to 'mobile' history.[196]

In his theory of the religious *a priori* Troeltsch begins from two indisputable elements of the empirical world: from his own religious self-awareness, which could not be refuted by any of the critical ideas in the whole history of philosophy since Plato, and from the historical entity 'religion', which despite its multiplicity must be regarded as a distinctive, unitary phenomenon. The concept of the religious *a priori* has 'apologetic' significance to the degree that it indicates that there cannot be the beginnings of a social, materialistic explanation of religion. Religion and theology do not have any functional significance in the framework of the social system but are pointers to a new reality which exists independently, alongside art and ethics. Now since this reality cannot be seen anywhere in its pure form, as the history and psychology of religion show, we need criteria for distinction and evaluation. The assumption of the religious *a priori* assures us that irrationality, abnormality, exaggeration, fantasy can be recognized as such. That religion is in origin experience, not the result of rational knowledge, but can then very well assert itself in the sphere of reason, again becomes comprehensible through the *a priori* of religion. Conceptually, this assumption causes difficulty. As a variation on an old theological formula we could say, *simul* empirical, *simul* rational – both at the same time. Troeltsch believes that the fruitfulness of his conceptuality and his intellectual approach lies precisely in this twofold direction.[197]

However, the understanding of a religious *a priori* in terms of the reality of religious life must not lead to a standstill in this procedure, nor must the thinking be in isolation. Rather, it has to be kept moving in a twofold direction. First it is necessary to perceive that there is a formal reduction here which may not take place at the level of real life. The religious *a priori* may indeed necessarily be derived from the world of religious experience through knowledge or recognition, but this experience itself remains the constant ground for this process, which brings about unity, demonstrates connections or regularities, and provides the basis for a claim to validity.

Secondly, this process leads to what Troeltsch calls the 'actualization of the religious *a priori*'. This process issues in the reflections on the philosophy of history which Troeltsch offers in the context of his philosophy of religion.

The philosophy of history in religion. For Troeltsch, the task of the philosophy of history in the context of the philosophy of religion follows necessarily from this theoretical discussion. The way leads from actual religious feeling (the psychology of religion and comparative religion) through the asking of fundamental questions (epistemology) to the reality of religious life. A further development in or conclusion of the theoretical discussion then lies in the metaphysics of religion.

The philosophy of history as a 'subsequent problem' means that the epistemological demonstration of a rational law of consciousness, a 'religious *a priori*', cannot be the last word in the philosophy of religion, because having a religion is always practical. Troeltsch says that it is necessary to move as it were from the state of rest to the actual state; he has already expressed this task in the context of epistemology in the formula the 'actualization of the religious *a priori*'.[198]

For Troeltsch, the actualization of the religious *a priori* comes about through an interaction between the necessary as the 'legitimate' essence of religion and actual religious activity, which can be demonstrated by the psychology of religion and has created special forms of expression for itself at different stages in the history of the development of religion. Reflection on the philosophy of history is now concerned with the last point, i.e. the development of the history of religion, and thus the awareness that the religion of the present is bound up in a historical form. For Troeltsch, a 'philosophy of the history of religion' is necessary which presupposes research and knowledge in the history of religion but is not exhausted by it. So to be consistent, this poses the problem to the philosophy of religion of the unity of the religious in the face of its historical multiplicity and, in connection with this, of the tendency to development in the history of religion. Now this means that levels of values must be discovered which provide support for an assessment of history. So the question is not a historical one, nor can it be solved by empirical means, but relates to the philosophy of history and presupposes a fundamental theory of religion.

For Troeltsch, the levels of values in the development of the history of religion found an impressive solution in Hegel, but this was no longer acceptable to him. With their use of the notion of development in a metaphysical perspective, Hegel and his theological and philosophical successors fail to do justice to historical reality. The question then is why Troeltsch did not take a step further and put in question all possibilities of speaking about development here.

In this context, Troeltsch's reflections on the problem of the development of the history of religion appear as follows. The notion of a 'series of levels' –

on the presupposition of a regularity to be assumed here – can only be modified or, better, accepted in moderation, by a renunciation of continuity and exclusivity. For Troeltsch, in the history of religion, there are degenerations, just as there is also an ongoing development of religious feeling. In his view the notion that religion has made itself superfluous or become superfluous in the course of the development of the history of culture must be rejected.

So Troeltsch sees himself compelled to make differentiations and distinctions in different directions, in order to avoid a dogmatization or to prevent an opening for ideological prejudices. What then remains?[199]

What Troeltsch thinks that he can maintain is the notion of a development of religious life, constantly becoming stronger, in the direction of ever greater depth and clarity, without any detailed regularity being either ascertained or demonstrated. In the history of religion he thinks it possible to speak of deeper and higher levels of development. However, here the criterion is not taken from outside; it can only come from the impulse towards development inherent in the religious. The basis for this assumption is not historical but is 'religious in terms of the present', and follows from present religious experience.

Now what do the 'levels of values' proposed on these presuppositions look like? Troeltsch first of all makes a fundamental distinction between natural religion and an ethical religion of personality. Whereas natural religion is focussed on myth and cult and thus on a kind of 'objective' set of principles and assumptions, the ethical religion of personality arrives at a symbolization. 'Symbolization' means that all that is normative is summed up and shown in the person of God, so that the direct acceptance of nature is transposed to a higher level. This happens through the use of the symbolizing power of imagination and thus through a kind of analogical procedure.

Another basic notion is that in the ethical religion of personality, which is above all what Christianity is, immanence and transcendence are indissolubly connected. That which transcends the world in religious experience is referred back to an ethic which takes shape in personal moral life.

The assumption of a basic series of levels in the development of the history of religion undergoes a further differentiation in Troeltsch. In connection with the history of religion generally Troeltsch speaks of 'religious centres of revelation'. The assumption of centres of revelation which derive from the foundation of the great historical religions introduces a principle of plurality which on the one hand denies relativism and on the other indicates that religious tolerance is necessary and meaningful; which on the one hand makes revelation possible as a religious reality and on the other challenges the absoluteness of Christianity. The consequence of the plurality to be assumed here is a notion of toleration which understands Christianity in 'liberal' terms, in other words as being open both to other religions and to culture.[200] In this free Christianity the personal view replaces an authoritative faith mediated by the church. An 'institutional' boundary and foundation is given up, and its place is taken by the free formation of religious life in individual terms, taking up Christian life from the forces of the past.

Troeltsch has no thought whatsoever of arbitrariness, nor does he in any way have in view our present-day increasingly multi-religious society. He begins from Christianity as the religion of our cultural circle. Here he also has in mind the antipathy of the educated classes and the workers to the church life of his time and therefore wants to encourage persistence with the given. Moreover he sees in the notion of Christianity as the religion of our cultural circle an argument which supplements or rounds off the comparative history of religion and the notion of levels of values. This idea also suggests itself because in the end all 'objective' references to levels of value issue in the personal action and decision of the individual and have their ultimate ground and meaning there.

In Troeltsch's view, all this will have a twofold effect: the renewal of Christianity on the basis of its own religious structure, and an 'incarnation' of the religious forces in culture, in human social life.

The metaphysics of religion. The question may perhaps arise from a present-day perspective why Troeltsch does not take his account of the philosophy of religion one stage further. On the one hand his 'metaphysics of religion' is to be derived from philosophical tradition, while on the other Troeltsch is the theologian who around the turn of the century attempted once again to cover the whole of reality and knowledge in a survey of theology and philosophy and to introduce the questions of epistemology down to the ultimate question, the question of metaphysics. Troeltsch derived the factuality, special character and distinctiveness of human life and rationality as what is reasonable and universal from an ultimate unity in the 'cosmic' reason. It constitutes the great mystery of life, which cannot be understood rationally, but in the last resort can only be experienced.[201]

The particular and the universal, the irrational and the rational, are combined in this cosmic reason in one last incomprehensible unity which Troeltsch describes with the metaphor of 'harmony'. The philosophy of religion reflects this ultimate unity, in which the mystery of reality has its ultimate ground, in the twofold structure of its psychological and epistemological orientation. This mystery is perceived as the working of the divine only through a free ungrounded action of the autonomy of thought and practice. It is a harmony of the creative primal power of the divine and the autonomous action of human beings as free action which has no further ground and derivation.

On the basis of this structure, religious activity is always at the same time both divine activity and human action. The nature of what human beings produce is at the same time divine. The divinity of what they bring forth is evident in the human. The autonomy of the human spirit which makes it possible to speak of freedom and the establishment of freedom here is not only the starting point for this divine activity, but also an emanation of this divine and similar to it in structure. Therefore the contradictoriness which rests on the assumption of religious truth as divine encounter on the one hand and as human action on the other is controlled structurally and at the same time incorporated through the potentiality towards freedom as the autonomy of personhood inherent in the human personality itself. Troeltsch's basic notion is that on the one hand religion is assumed to be alive in the psyche, resting on an experience and on concrete forms, and as such may not be curtailed; but on the other hand the addition of the rational element 'direct it towards its basic content and its organic relations to the totality of the rational life of intellectual, moral and artistic achievements'.[202] The word 'directs' indicates an open process which combines graphicness, liveliness and concretion on the one hand, and rationality and a firm basis on the other. Given the twofold structure and openness of this approach, it must necessarily leave some questions in the air. How is the basic content developed and by what is it measured? Troeltsch speaks on the one hand of a 'permeation' of religious experience by the rational and on the other of the possibility of deriving the concrete from the rational as a measurement by the ideal. 'By this ideal we measure the different things that human religious life produces, and in the power of this ideal we work on the ongoing formation of our present religious life.'[203]

From his perspective Troeltsch adopts a basic position which he understands as a corrective to misunderstandings and false interpretations. Religion is not to be replaced by science: science in the form of an aprioristic universal is to have the significance of clarifying and regulating religion, but it is not to put it in question critically and challenge it; it is not to seek to dissolve it.

Nor is religious activity merely to be accepted descriptively. 'The important thing about such a scientific treatment of religion is that it leaves religion its freshness and life, its mysticism and irrationality, by virtue of which alone it is what it is, but also provides a criticism and regulation, a self-deepening and ongoing development of the religious life by virtue of which it is and can be more than it in fact seems to be at any point as a gloomy mass phenomenon.'[204] Science is to criticize psychologically deranged religious life; to provide regulation on the basis of a connection with the *a priori*; to help to achieve self-deepening by extracting the rational nucleus from the subjective religious sense of truth; to bring about development as an approach to the constructive development of religion as an ethic that shapes life. That is the basic intent of the programme. Demarcations and corrective functions become clear. It is possible to recognize the combination in principle of empiricism and rationalism, of psychology and epistemology. But Troeltsch does not explain in detail how this mutual interpenetration is to come about. His reference to history offers a clue as to how the whole is to function. 'The science of religion leaves religion as religion and regulates it only on the basis of its own *a priori*, which each time emerges in the great historical centres of revelation with deeper clarity and with the invitation to a closer association with reason as a whole in the religious centre.'[205]

An indication is sought in history, as it is sought in an *a priori* of reason, where reason, thought of as the overall economy of consciousness, also has an *a priori* form of religion alongside other *a priori* forms. And finally the argument becomes metaphysical: the belief of religion that it rests on a divine revelation has support to the degree that it is connected with reason, to be thought of as the reason of the world or the whole. The religion which springs up from unconscious depths of life is to be seen from the beginning and in principle as being connected with the world reason. First Troeltsch thinks of the relation between religious and non-religious metaphysics in terms of the special character of the approach and the aim in each case, and secondly he sees a remarkable proximity of the two on the basis of idealistic approaches thought through consistently to the end. And finally, he can assume a reciprocal effect, as proposed, for example, by Wilhelm Wundt. Philosophical metaphysics is preceded by religious metaphysics in spiritual life and cannot ignore the influence of that metaphysics on it. For both are instances of thinking of the whole of world and life, of sketching out a unitary conception. And on the other hand, religious-metaphysical thought will be concerned with a well-grounded relationship to the 'generalizations of the empirical sciences', one which is concerned to achieve a balance.[206]

Where the intent for reform associated with the religious *a priori* lies is explained in three steps. 1. Religion involves the coming together of the divine and the human. 2. The idea of exclusiveness is to be corrected by a greater or lesser disclosure of the depth of the divine. 3. Any self-sufficiency of religious life must be changed into a combination of the religious with reason as a whole and includes the shaping of the world which results from the religious attitude.

In the end, the philosophy of religion moves from considerations leading to ultimate methodological questions to its pragmatic beginning in the form of a European civilization moulded by modern science and by historical criticism. If the end of a religion is in sight, then another should be sought; if it does not come, does not suggest itself, then life has to be lived in the power of the religious feeling so far. If people think that they are living at a culmination of life hitherto – here there is an allusion to Christianity – then this culmination must be confirmed by comparison with the history of religion, and people must act in the power of the faith offered here. That must happen for there to be 'increasing conviction of the correctness of the fortifying and purifying effect of this faith on life, on the deepening and clarification of reason as a whole which emerges from it'.[207] Here the whole is once again bent round in a remarkable way, in that religious activity, the formation of religion, is expected to purify reason as a whole. That assumes an open process of reciprocal action between reason as a whole and religion within history.[208]

6. Troeltsch's 'positive' views (the Glaubenslehre *and 'The Significance of the Historical Existence of Jesus')*

When in 1900 the publishing house Mohr/Siebeck in Tübingen was considering whether to found a new journal for systematic theology, Troeltsch was also asked for his opinion. He wrote: 'Systematic theology belongs in general journals... I do not believe that anyone will have the courage to devote a special journal to it at a time when dogmatic theology is falling apart.'[209] The fact that Troeltsch had always had the intention to publish a collection of his 'positive' views does not contradict these thoughts.[210]

The idea of the dissolution of dogmatic theology is to be seen against the background of Troeltsch's distinction between dogmatics and the doctrine of faith (*Glaubenslehre*). In the history of religion Troeltsch sees dogmatics as a distinctive feature of Christianity which emerged in connection with the formation of a community, an exclusivist view of history and a speculative development of ideas. The concept of 'the doctrine of faith' resulted from the Protestant criticism of the idea of the authoritative laying down of teaching by the church and the assumption of universal normative validity in matters of faith. According to Troeltsch, modern Protestantism fundamentally overcame the domination of dogma and dogmatics by the destruction of the supernaturalist way of thinking and an understanding of revelation extending to the whole of Christianity. The summary description of ideas of Christian faith and the life of faith resting on personal conviction is aimed at handing down insights of faith to others, with the goal of evoking a corresponding personal resonance in them.

Here Troeltsch feels that he is in line with Schleiermacher. He observes: 'So Schleiermacher, who introduced this new concept for the first time into theology proper as a result of the stimuli of modern philosophy and out of his own brilliance, abolished the name dogmatics and introduced the designation, the doctrine of faith.'[211]

The Glaubenslehre *lectures.* The authenticity of the text, which derives from lecture notes, is guaranteed to the degree that at the beginning of each section Troeltsch dictated a précis. He then went on to develop what he had dictated in an extempore lecture. So a distinction must be made between the authenticity of the dictated material and that of the explanations which follow. The subjective factor of selection may have influenced the recording of the extempore lecture. A perception of the difference between dictation and extempore lecturing is significant for interpretation. The highly compressed, conceptual and thetic procedure of dictation is developed in a vivid and lively way, and many passages from the extempore lectures are almost like sermons. They seek to evoke a personal echo in the audience, to win them over to agree with this view of faith, and at the same time they have the future practical work of the audience in view.[212]

On the one hand, in the outline and arrangement of themes, Troeltsch's *Glaubenslehre* has the traditional form of a 'dogmatics' (prolegomena, doctrine of God, christology, anthropology, ecclesiology and eschatology). On the other hand, he distinguishes in principle between historical-religious and metaphysical-religious statements. This division matches his definition of the Christian 'principle' as the religious rebirth of man and the gathering together of the reborn with others in a 'kingdom of the divinely filled Spirit'.[213] So at the centre there stands the relation of man to God, which, as experienced and lived out in the present, needs to be clarified and rooted in history. Thus in a first part, under the heading of the historical-religious, there is a discussion of Jesus Christ as the object of faith. The usual themes of dogmatics are then discussed from the perspective of present-religious experience.

In detail, Troeltsch's *Glaubenslehre* displays a complex structure of argumentation and mode of description which is dovetailed with itself. First, Troeltsch adopts a descriptive approach, as it were proceeding from the outside inwards, and attempts to approach the complex of questions under review by means of a history-of-religions comparison. Then the specifically Christian view is worked out. In the process of this, different historical manifestations are pursued and the controversy with the modern feeling about the world and life is taken up. Secondly, Troeltsch has an immanently theological approach aimed at working out the traditional main concepts of Christian faith, which develops these and relates them. In this procedure, which focusses on the essentials without too narrow an interpretation, Troeltsch attempts to draw the hearers into a thought-process which from a more external perspective is centred increasingly on his own view of faith and piety and seeks to bring together historical knowledge, criticism and a personal approach. When, for example, in an account of the concept of God along analogical lines he works out how God is supreme moral freedom and is in a will which thus acts in a personal way, he raises the critical question how this statement or view can be combined with the conception of God's infinity. Here Troeltsch is concerned to show that analogical thought which attempts to deal with the concept of God from the principle of human freedom does not avoid tensions, in which a polarity becomes evident. 'We take up that analogy which is most capable of divinization, in which the human being breaks open mere existence and there is surrender to values which are valid in themselves.'[214]

Troeltsch assumes that the central statements are inherently conclusive and can be combined, but also sees that polarity lies at the heart of the matter.

The intrinsically theological discussion of the main concepts of Christian faith is then usually followed by the personal perspective, which develops what has been said to the hearers as an expression of personal piety (directly, i.e. in the light of Troeltsch's own person, or as an existential possibility). While for Troeltsch the decision of faith in the background here is subjective, it is not arbitrary, since it rests on inner necessity and consistency. That becomes evident, for example, in the way in which the side of a personal address or emotion, which in the first place is to be assessed in psychological terms, is developed by this form of reaction, of effect, being defined more closely and given a foundation in an intellectual process.[215]

For Troeltsch, the development of a 'doctrine of faith' is a creative procedure which presupposes religious experience and takes up the present Christian life as a horizon against which the closer definition is to be made. As the Christian life in the present is led within the framework and under the conditions of a modern view of the world and of life, these have both a critical and a constructive significance for the process of exegesis.

In contrast to what the dialectical theologians – Karl Barth in particular – said about the foundation of dogmatics, Troeltsch dispenses with any claim that the Word of God is a source and authority. That gives his whole work nowadays a certain strangeness and at the same time a power of attraction, because the account represents an expansion of theological horizon.

Troeltsch allows the possibility of thinking theologically in a 'plural' sense. That is inherent both in his history-of-religions approach and also in the attention he pays to the modern feeling about the world and life. In a 'cautious' apologetic, Christian faith, the Christian world of ideas, is shown to be decisive, relevant in a religious sense. Here the criterion is taken from within, by a reference to personal experience. For Troeltsch, Christian faith provides power to cope with life, opens up perspectives of meaning and possibilities of understanding which relate to the world and to life.

It is quite clear that in the confessional statements Troeltsch brings into play his own conviction as an element of authority. But he thinks that to the degree that it takes up the wealth of historical manifestations and notes possibilities, his *Glaubenslehre* can only be 'an incitement to produce one's own personal insight into faith'.[216]

Perhaps one reason for the limited effect of this free theological approach, based on individual authority, is that Troeltsch does not really note and reflect on the problem of mediation. The question of the ordered transmission of what is perceived and believed personally largely remains open.

Many explanations have been given of why the *Glaubenslehre* is divided up as it is. As I have already indicated, this follows from the definition of the Christian principle, from the view of faith and history, and from the relationship between knowledge and faith. The last has the function of being able to judge and in some cases to criticize concrete historical instances.

In so far as the content of the *Glaubenslehre* does not characterize specifically historical situations, for Troeltsch it is not orientated on science or philosophical knowledge (nor does it presuppose this); its epistemological character is, rather, to be termed atheoretical.[217] We may recall Troeltsch's ideas from the philosophy of religion that the nucleus of religious experience is to be called 'mystical'.

Troeltsch is directly influenced by Schleiermacher when he distinguishes the task of theology from that of science and philosophy.[218] Here, too, Troeltsch agrees with Schleiermacher's view to the degree that for him theological statements about God do not express God himself but always only God as he appears in our religious experience, in other words our idea of God. For Troeltsch, the knowledge of faith is bound up with 'revelation', but in accordance with his thinking, this is revelation understood not as a unique and final revelation in history, but as progressive and ongoing. As such it has high points, but is not exclusive. And the acceptance of this revelation in the human experience of faith as in the 'doctrine of faith' must on each occasion find a specific expression: both generally, i.e. in keeping with the time, and individually, in keeping with the life of the individual. However, this nearness to Schleiermacher is also marked by a number of breaks, modifications and critical objections. The main agreement consists in the 'dogmatic agnosticism'[219] which in the religious sphere favours the confessional and practical in place of theoretical knowledge. Dogmatic agnosticism as an expression of a specific religious epistemology is the presupposition of the approach in which for Schleiermacher the 'doctrine of faith' issues in practical theology, in the sense that he sees it investigating and reflecting on possible ways of communicating religious thought and proclamation. This basic line, which on the one hand leaves religious epistemology independent and on the other understands it as a basis for mediation with other forms of knowledge, meets with Troeltsch's assent. However, with it he combines an invitation to the theology of his time to 'take up in complete freedom and with the broadest academic education' the reform of theology seen by Schleiermacher but not really carried through as he intended.[220]

The crux of Troeltsch's criticism of Schleiermacher is that because he came from Herrnhuter pietism and was close to the world of Romanticism in his early years he expressed his theological programme in a fantastic and unworldly way. In particular his ideal of the church seems to Troeltsch to be utopian and alien to the world.[221] In the mature Schleiermacher Troeltsch criticizes above all his assimilation to current circumstances, to life in the Prussian church. For Troeltsch, Schleiermacher's programme, particularly his definition of the 'essence of Christianity', is dependent on a dogmatics which puts the emphasis on the concept of redemption and which allows itself to be directed by church thinking, by an accentuation of the concept of the church.[222]

At the centre of Troeltsch's reflections, as I have already indicated, lies the notion of the religious rebirth of man which presupposes or indicates an experience of faith based on a transcending of all merely natural forms of life as an 'organ and means of establishing and gaining oneself'.[223] The elevation of human beings to religious experience and understanding is also derived from the encounter of God with man which takes place within the framework of the history of revelation: while Jesus is to be seen at the centre of the redemptive activity of God here, he is not given any exclusive significance.[224]

God's approach to man and the reaction which takes place in man in the form of knowledge and surrender are constitutive of the 'higher birth of man' which finds its expression in the kingdom of God, constituted by spirit and disposition, and in the involvement of human beings who are orientated on this kingdom. The soteriological aspect is addressed without any christological focus or narrowing; emphasis is put on the working of salvation; a change in human life is brought into view; and reference is made to the continuation or effect of this change in a special form of communal life.

Systematic articles in Die Religion in Geschichte und Gegenwart. Troeltsch's reflections in the *Glaubenslehre* are expanded and to some degree also explained and defined more closely by his systematic articles in the lexicon *Die Religion in Geschichte und Gegenwart*, above all by his major articles on faith, redemption, grace and predestination.[225]

Troeltsch, who was responsible for the systematic part of the lexicon, did not really enjoy doing the editorial work which fell to him; it does not seem to have been to his taste. Thus he writes to F.M.Schiele, the editor of the lexicon: 'I agree fully with your [editorial] proposals and have the feeling that I am not up to real editorial work alongside other very difficult and extremely complicated work. Besides, a dogmatics in the form of a lexicon is a monstrosity. Then I tend to get annoyed with the contributions and would much prefer to write them all myself. But given my present work-load, that is quite impossible, and my dogmatics cannot pile up under the usual catchwords. In short, I'm delighted to be relieved of anything.'[226] In agreeing to collaborate, Troeltsch was moved above all by the thought that he would also have to make his presence felt as a dogmatic theologian somewhere.[227]

His basic approach is repeated in the lexicon articles. One leading thought of the account which is given in Troeltsch's articles is that the traditional dogmatic views and positions should be rendered in a way which at the same time contains modifications and explanatory additions. It is not easy to determine where Troeltsch is merely reporting and where his own position begins or comes in. Troeltsch develops a special procedure which is based on first giving historical information and details about the subject-matter and then adding an interpretation of the particular subject or theme which begins from within as a corrective to the merely descriptive account; finally, he gives the reader material for thought and orientation.

The article on 'Faith and History' is particularly significant, both for its subject-matter and because of the precision it brings. According to Troeltsch, in defining the relationship between faith and history the need of believers has to be taken into account and it is necessary to go back to the starting point of their belief in history. The religious world of ideas is established in a 'primal picture' and then derives power and life in the present from this. Faith is nourished and kept alive by history. As Christian faith, it is not 'conceivable without deliberate reference to Christ... even if one sees his belief in God as asserting itself to a considerable degree through its own inner evidence and power. It came into being from a historical disclosure of the divine life, and for clarity and power needs constantly to be referred to this foundation, which is present to the imagination in a living way.'[228]

So the notion of redemption remains strictly related to the personal element; redemption is taken up into faith, which as a result is seen in strongly functional terms in which the definition of the content largely remains open.

The historical orientation of faith consists in the acceptance of a power which elevates us and draws us on. Faith is indeed by nature present experience which, while expressing itself directly, for its foundation and its continuation indirectly needs 'the historical statements in which it is given revelation, assurance and an illustration of its powers'.[229]

It is striking that Troeltsch does not choose the same perspectives or formulations when he is arguing in terms of the psychology of faith as when he thinks he can combine or balance the link between faith and history with the modern notion of autonomy. There the emphasis lies on the need of faith or believers for a superior power; here the communication of power from history is stressed as a help in the gaining of autonomy. For him there is a possibility of connecting the two perspectives closely: if on the presuppositions of modern thought the facts of history are changed, so that here a communication of power contributes to the development of personal independence, then reference can be made to the inner consistency of faith, which is focussed on experience in the present.[230]

For Troeltsch, the meaning and significance of the link between history and faith are to be seen as having different levels, depending on whether the focal point is the situation of psychological need or the autonomy of the person. For him, on the one hand this is grounded in the subject-matter itself, and on the other is connected with the formation of the individual view of faith and piety.[231] The advantage of the first differentiation (which at first seems unusual) for the practical understanding of faith is that Troeltsch accepts both a systematic basis for the difference between the individual understanding of faith and the view handed down by the church, in conflict – which was the norm for intellectuals at the turn of the century – but gives priority to the individual, living understanding.

Troeltsch sees very clearly that faith can be a power determining human life only if it is brought into the present from a purely historical perspective. But the immersing of oneself in history which is claimed for communication with the present, the reference to the communication of power which derives from history, are understood in markedly functional terms. Here the thought is more from the outside than from the inside, and the focus is more on the possibility of agreement or approximation, rather than there being a discussion of the question of truth-content. The positive basic notion of an opening up of the offer of faith which is to be communicated from history to the present, and the form of argument on different levels, above all in connection with the adoption of the notion of autonomy, are weakened by the fact that the question of a possible bond to be provided by the factor of personal experinece is not discussed. This critical observation applies even if one perceives and accepts Troeltsch's interest in a twofold demarcation, over against an aestheticizing religion of mood and a theology of saving facts.

The historical existence of Jesus and faith. Troeltsch's 1911 lecture on 'The Significance of the Historical Existence of Jesus for Faith'[232] takes up the central theological question of the relationship between faith and history in a particular direction and with particular emphases. The contemporary background should be noted: a radical approach making use of the means of historical-critical thought judged not only individual elements of the Christian tradition but also the person of Jesus of Nazareth from a critical perspective. In particular, Arthur Drews and Peter Jensen had achieved much publicity with their views.

In his book on 'The Christ Myth' (Part I, 1901; Part II, 1911), Arthur Drews (1865-1935) argued that Jesus was not a historical figure. For him the picture of Jesus drawn in the Synoptic Gospels is an expression of metaphysical ideas or religious experiences the real motive of which is the later historical legitimation of Jesus as a cult deity of the community. For Peter Jensen (1861-1936), both Jesus and Paul were mythical figures who derive from the Gilgamesh epic, a religious epic from the time of Assurbanipal (668-626 BCE) transmitted on twelve clay tablets. Jensen saw the outline of the life of Jesus prefigured in the speeches and charts of this era, so that Jesus could not be accepted as a historical figure.[233]

In his lecture, Troeltsch takes contemporary questions back to basic problems of method and content. For him the disputing of the historicity of Jesus is one of the consequences of the acceptance of historical thought into theology. What significance can a picture of Jesus exposed to historical criticism or worked out by it have for faith? That is the question at issue. From the perspective of the history of ideas the effect of historical criticism is to destroy the classic picture of Jesus. What can stand up to historical criticism is a reference to the fact of the existence of Jesus and a demonstration of basic features of his proclamation. But is that enough?[234]

The questions resulting from the theological situation make sense for Troeltsch only on two presuppositions: 1. The dogma of the divine-human redeemer in the early church, his mediating function in respect of the saving work of God, is finished. 2. Faith is directed towards God. Faith is God's work in human beings, so that in practice faith and redemption coincide, because in faith human beings take up God's will to forgive sins.

The historical development of critical questioning has a twofold effect, one destructive and the other constructive. What is destroyed is the christology of the early church; what remains – and can remain – is faith in God as a human experience of salvation which is not mediated historically.[235] A differentiated, systematizing survey of cultural history and the history of theology shows where, in Troeltsch's view, a new understanding is developing which transcends the old dogmatic version. Fundamentally here the mystics like Meister Eckhart and Sebastian Franck, with their polemic against a dogmatic version of the notion of redemption, had already got further than Erasmus, Locke and Leibniz, who maintained the necessity of the historical link because they gave the miracles of Jesus the function of authenticating doctrine. The tension between historical legitimation and the living experience of faith then led to ever-new attempts at a solution in subsequent centuries. Lessing and Kant critically opposed the notion of a historical legitimation of faith and evaluated biblical history as a means of inserting the Christian idea into history. David Friedrich Strauss then distinguished the 'Christian principle' from its historical starting point. The ideas of Schleiermacher, Ritschl and Herrmann represent 'mixed forms', which did not take over the distinction between Christian principle and the person of Jesus. Here a relative, inner necessity for the tie to the person of Jesus is assumed in respect of the Christian certainty of redemption. At the same time, ever-new redemption in the form of faith or the knowledge of faith is recognized alongside a redemption to be thought of as unique on the basis of a particular historical act. For Troeltsch this 'mixed form' points in the right direction, as it appropriately puts the emphasis on personal faith, human knowledge in faith. But the critical objection is that for that function it no longer needs the historical Jesus if because of historical insights he can no longer be used as a ground of legitimation.[236]

Dispensing with the historical foundation has a liberating effect and removes a burden, but its place can be taken by inner conviction of 'the grandeur of prophetic Christian faith in God'.[237] In theological terms, the acknowledgment of Jesus is not a presupposition but a consequence of belief in God.

But in that case how is the relationship of Christian faith in God to the person of Jesus to be conceived? 'Is this connexion something contingent, purely historical and factual, for pedagogy and symbolism not to be dispensed with, but nevertheless not required by the idea itself? Or is it something unchangeably and eternally inherent in the essence of the Christian idea?'[238]

In the first case one is independent of historical research, in the second not. But the assumption of a bond to the person of Jesus which lies in the essence of the Christian idea is consistent only on the basis of the dogma of the ancient church. In that case there remains only the idea that the link is historical and factual, and the significance of the person of Jesus for faith is to be understood in terms of pedagogical symbolism.

These questions and the alternative they contain are governed by a distinction between historical facticity and idea and focus on a possibility inherent in the essence of the Christian idea, of being able to experience salvation in a direct experience of God without any link to history. On the basis of more recent developments in cultural and theological history the second way seems natural. Its defect is that it has not proved to be effective enough, and it underestimates the role of community life and cult for religious faith.

If the original question was the possibility and significance of the relationship of present-day people to the person of Jesus, Troeltsch now modifies the questioning by asking with a systematic intent what is the role of community and cult for faith. He sees himself driven to this question both by the experience of more recent history and by the intrinsic essence of the matter. In this connection he speaks of observations of the church as a social body, sees a lack of community and cult as a disease of modern life, and advances insights from the history and psychology of religion.

For Troeltsch, from a historical perspective the history of the church developed like this. The original faith of the followers of Christ initially had no dogma and no teaching, but was the practice of the life of prayer and communion with Christ in the Lord's Supper.[239] The emergence of the Christ cult was necessary as a means of fulfilling the religious need for community. For Troeltsch, this historical development corresponds to a law of social psychology, namely that of the need for a cultic centre for religious fellowship.

Troeltsch's clear stress on cult and community comes as something of a surprise, given the systematic theological statements in this direction that we can find elsewhere in his work. In my view there are two aspects which help to explain this emphasis on cult and community. First, at this very time Troeltsch was preparing his *Social Teachings* for publication; in solving contemporary theological problems he was guided by central ideas in this work. Furthermore, Troeltsch delivered his lecture to hearers who were interested in practical questions of faith because they were either actually or about to be involved in the service of the church. For them he presented his ideas as a theological possibility of advancing from a position which is obligated to rigid dogma – above all in the form of the doctrine of original sin and the exclusiveness of the conception of salvation in Jesus Christ.

In scholarship at that time – as is still the case even now – there was a discussion of the development of liturgy in earliest Christianity. Troeltsch's view of the interpretation of the historical starting point in the earliest community was this: originally there was no dogma and no cult, but only prayer and 'living union with Christ in the Lord's Supper'.[240] The motive for the transformation of this conception and praxis was the need of Christians for cult and community; following a universal law of social psychology, this created a corresponding base and point of orientation in the cult of Christ.[241]

So in the beginnings of church history Troeltsch found confirmation of the law of social psychology that the meeting of individuals in religious activities can continue and be stabilized only if it has a specific cultic centre which offers a way of making belief vivid in the form of imagination and feeling. Troeltsch stressed that: 'The connexion of the Christian idea with Christ's central position in cult and doctrine is not a conceptual necessity inherent in the concept of salvation.'[242]

Troeltsch's account is open to criticism at different levels and in different directions. First, the question arises which was already put by Wilhelm Bousset, as to whether this 'law of social psychology can be confirmed',[243] and whether the cult of the founder is not a peculiarity of Christianity. Troeltsch explained: 'By the cult which we can construct I understand merely cultic representation in preaching and devotion, not a new worship, and merely believe that the motives are similar today to what they were then.'[244]

All in all, at many points it becomes clear how Troeltsch is arguing on two different levels, on the one hand on the universal level which starts from the notion of essence in connection with religion and Christianity, and on the other on the factual and historical level, which is orientated on actual situations and experiences.

In order largely to dismiss the claim of an exclusive necessity of salvation, Troeltsch resorts to the means of demonstrating the significance of the person of Jesus for faith by a law of social psychology which is historically questionable because of a lack of comparisons. This motive governs Troeltsch's thinking here. In it one can see a characteristic of his systematic theology: he is not afraid of the risk of thought and legitimation, does not deduce conceptually, but explores by raising questions, accepting ideas, and being open to a explanation after the event. He is concerned less with terminological exactitude and precise historical justification than with the possibility of providing a basis at all. In terms of content the question arises whether the perception of a universal law of social psychology which is put forward so decisively, along with its validity for the history of religion and thus as a category which embraces dogmatics and history to an equal degree, does not also emerge here with a kind of 'dogmatic' claim. Troeltsch's nervous sensitivity to dogmatic forms of thought should really have made him more observant at this point. But he was probably so fascinated by an undogmatic form of argument which could therefore even satisfy the intellectual demands of modern people trained in history that he did not notice the problem.

Wilhelm Bousset and Wilhelm Herrmann are particularly interesting as critics of Troeltsch's position. Wilhelm Bousset already dealt with the question discussed in Troeltsch's letter in his lecture at the World Congress for Liberal Christianity in Berlin in 1910. The title of his lecture was 'The Significance of the Person of Jesus for Faith'. There are characteristic differences between the positions of Bousset and Troeltsch – despite the proximity of their theological thought in comparison with the radical challenge to the historical existence of Jesus and the 'positive' trend in theology, and despite their common ground in history-of-religions thought and historical criticism. For Bousset, history points beyond itself; if one understands religion as an element connected to human reason, not introduced from outside by revelation in history, then one can dispense with the conception of a supernatural revelation. Religion is seen as a basic human possibility which has unfolded into history. According to Bousset, the ideas are not dependent on the authority of history but are rather the criterion by which historical phenomena must be measured. But as the ideas are intangible and schematic, if they are to take on practical religious life, they need to be clad in imagery, they need symbolization. For Bousset, Jesus belongs in the long series of religious personalities who have become symbols, albeit with the concession that a qualitative difference may be noted here.

The different views on the connection between faith and history which emerge in this way, focussed on the question of the significance of the historicity of Jesus for faith, find expression in the correspondence between the two friends.[245] It becomes evident that Bousset's history-of-religions approach is more radical than that of Troeltsch. For Bousset, the cultic significance of Jesus is not a lasting one, an indispensable part of the Christian community for all times, but is time-conditioned. Since the cultic worship of Jesus – being unique – cannot either be derived from a law of the psychology of religion or related to the circumstances of earliest Christianity, the aspect of change is to be seen in more radical terms. For this reason Bousset asks Troeltsch critically whether he is not 'idealizing the faith of earliest Christianity', in other words, whether he is paying enough attention to the historical situation. For Bousset, 'historical situation' means that the cultic worship of Jesus becomes understandable particularly through reflection on his setting in the history of religion. Here Bousset is evidently thinking of the influence of the Hellenistic mystery religions, which he then attempted to demonstrate in more detail in his work *Kyrios Christos*. The difficulties Troeltsch has with the reconstruction of historical developments is also evident. He attempts to understand the faith of earliest Christianity in terms of the intention to set apart a new religious community which creates a corresponding expression of itself in the cult. It should be noted that the new cult 'may probably have emerged from the Lord's Supper, the expectation of a return, and messianic doctrine. How? That I do not know. At all events, things were finished by the time of Paul; he was not the first to do them.'[246] The discussion between Troeltsch and Bousset is carried on at two levels: they are concerned, first to arrive at a historical verdict, and secondly, to find a foundation in the philosophy of religion. In questions of the precise historical foundation, Troeltsch is inclined to accept Bousset's judgment or to learn from him. His hesitations relate more strongly to Bousset's philosophical foundation. 'Our differences relate on the one hand to immanent rationalism and its relationship to history, which I see as being much more complicated than you think, and where I am not completely free of historical positivism, on the other hand to the idea of earliest Christian history and the origin of the Christ-cult.'[247] Contrary to Bousset, and dissociating himself from him, Troeltsch thinks that reason cannot be thought of before all history and above it, but only from it and together with it.

The criticism of Wilhelm Herrmann is also directed at this critical point in the discussion between Troeltsch and Bousset.[248] For Herrmann, the real defect in Troeltsch's position is that there is no intrinsic connection betwen religion and history. Troeltsch does not interpret religion in terms of an inner experience but in terms of a universal idea or principle. Herrmann thinks that Troeltsch wants the link with history for practical reasons, because otherwise the church cannot exist, and in this connection he notes that this has brought Troeltsch near to the modern, 'positive' trend in theology. However, he adds that Troeltsch has 'far too much taste to give himself the decoration "positive" '.[249] Herrmann's criticism focusses on the fact that what is a justified reference to the practical requirements of the church makes clear a notable defect in Troeltsch's arguments, because they do not follow from the subject-matter. For Herrmann, Troeltsch is caught in the dilemma of wanting to maintain a connection which he cannot justify in terms of subject-matter, but only in terms of a need, namely the need of religious community for a point of orientation and support.[250] In his criticism of Troeltsch Wilhelm Herrmann rightly recognized that the level of his discussion and arguments shifted when after his systematic reflections on the context of the history of dogma and the more recent history of theology and cultural history, and the basic alternatives which result from historical knowledge (knowledge of historical facts – thinking in terms of the idea), he referred to the laws of social psychology in connection with the formation of religious communities. It emerges that in rejecting an uncritical adoption of the dogma of the early church – in order to keep in contact with his critical conversation-partners among scientists and theologians – Troeltsch is clear and uncompromising, but in his readiness also to build bridges to modern positive theologians and the nurture of piety in the church, in the tradition of theology and the church, he is relatively open.

7. Statements on controversies within church politics ('Modernism' and the 'Jatho case')

Troeltsch was not particularly interested in specific issues in church politics. Here he differed from Julius Kaftan, and also from theologians who stood closer to him like Harnack and Rade. However, what increasingly interested him – in line with his growing openness to political life – were fundamental questions like the relationship between state and church or law and justice. It is in keeping with this general line that Troeltsch took up an explicit position on only two controversies in church politics, the papal condemnation of Modernism on the Roman Catholic side and the 'Jatho case' on the Protestant side. In Troeltsch's view, both cases were more than events of the day in church politics. They were questions of principle with considerable significance for the future development of theology and the church in relation to society and the modern consciousness.

The papal condemnation of Modernism. It is obvious and understandable that Troeltsch would sympathize with theologians who attempted to go new ways in Catholic theology and piety because they had recognized cultural and scientific changes in the modern world. In particular, he would be in agreement with the adoption of historical-critical exegesis and theological attention to modern religious experience. Therefore the papal condemnation of a 'modernist' theology would disturb him all the more and provoke his critical reaction.[251]

Troeltsch's remarks on Modernism and its condemnation by the church differ in a positive and at the same time in a characteristic way from the general dispute. That is true above all in respect of the anti-Roman tendencies in the Protestant camp.[252] Troeltsch does not react with crude polemic, say out of a feeling of Protestant superiority or a superiority that might be generally called modern, but differentiates critically and self-critically. He notes various aspects of the condemnation and also attempts to do justice to the encyclical and the intention evident in it. Thus, for example, he remarks that 'from the standpoint of Curialism and strict Catholic dogma there was in fact a real danger'.[253] Moreover, his view was that one could not in any way regard the encyclical as theologically insignificant; rather, as far as he was concerned, it had brought out the basic problem sharply and clearly.[254]

In both publications Troeltsch was primarily addressing the intellectuals: not a church or theological public, but rather a political public interested in culture generally. His argument is certainly coloured by the readership to be assumed here. He gives the intellectuals who regard themselves as enlightened and liberal an object lesson in how complex the problem is in this instance and how subtle and cautious one must be in passing judgment on it. In particular he wants to draw the attention of Protestant critics to the problems in their own house, their own church and church politics, so that they can (at least also) turn their critical tendency inwards.

Troeltsch's polemic is against a wrong estimation of church and religious life by the intellectuals. In part this rests on sheer ignorance, and in part it is also connected with an immunization against everything connected with church and religion. Here on the whole people fail to see that believers in the two great confessions find dogmatic statements or demands by the churches easier to take than exaggerated criticism and deprecation from outside. They put their hope on a reform of the church rather than expecting something from political liberalism in alliance with ideologized Enlightenment thought. And at any rate in principle, both Protestantism and Catholicism are affected by the religious crisis in the modern world.

So Troeltsch wants to counter the prejudices which are to be found among intellectuals generally, and at the same time to repudiate Protestant arrogance which thinks that something of this kind could not occur in its own camp. He wants to engage in the work of enlightenment in the broadest sense, so that there can be a better and deeper understanding of religious and church questions.[255]

For Troeltsch, Catholicism cannot be equated with the theology which emerges in the encyclical either as a historical phenomenon generally or in its present form. Historically, it is more and other; in the present, too, it has to be understood in wider terms than Protestant polemic wants. Indeed, Catholicism can be a compensation for the weaknesses of Protestantism as a religion of ideas with its stress on preaching. It can fill abiding religious human needs by taking up the cultic element and integrating the forces of popular religion. In this connection Troeltsch's description of Catholicism is a remarkable mixture of endorsement and criticism, a kind of thought from within which adopts a Catholic self-understanding, and a critical element coming from outside.[256]

As an entity which is living in this sense, Catholicism is concerned to preserve its identity without losing contact with the spiritual or cultural forces of the present. So Troeltsch's argument is nuanced and detailed, deliberately adopting a great variety of perspectives and judgments. According to Troeltsch there is a real 'change of scene and lighting'[257] depending on the perspective from which one views.

Troeltsch was critical of the reaction to events in Protestant circles. He saw a blatant contradiction between the vehement criticism of the encyclical in the Protestant camp and the failure to see the pressure exerted by church governments and church assemblies on liberal theology.[258]

Troeltsch's concern to evaluate Catholicism positively as a historical phenomenon is to be understood not least from this dialogue situation. For him, Catholicism has to be understood as a world system which does not rest on doctrines and dogmas, but 'has its focal point... in the living persons of the priesthood deriving from Christ and filled with his Spirit'.[259] On these premises Troeltsch then comes to a surprising conclusion: if that is the case, then in his view Catholicism could allow room for efforts like Modernist theology. Indeed one could even say that Modernism was in line with the best of the Catholic tradition. It was in keeping with this assessment that the work of the representatives of a 'Modernist' trend – both theologians and laity – was governed by questions of theological content, and moreover that the religious impulse which guided them was unmistakable. Troeltsch thought that the concentration of official criticism on the allegedly harmful influence of modern philosophy was mistaken.

Troeltsch mentions George Tyrrell (1861-1909) and Alfred Loisy (1857-1940), one an English Jesuit and moral theologian and the other professor of biblical exegesis in Paris, as typical representatives of Modernism. Both represent in a specific and at the same time exemplary way the 'Reform Catholicism' of the time.

In the case of Tyrrell attention should be drawn first to his personal piety, and secondly to his position in the philosophy or religion: he attempted to incorporate historical development into the definition of the essence of Catholicism. For him, inwardness and the symbolic exegesis of traditional doctrine are a critical corrective to belief in the letter and theological narrowness. However, all this does not point to a religious individualism: on the contrary, for Tyrrell, an understanding of the church as a community based on religious experience is central. For Troeltsch, Alfred Loisy, the other, is the historian among the modernists, a theologian who uses the history-of-religions method in a sovereign way, who allows the significance of dogmas to take a back place in favour of an ethical theism, because for him this ethical theism is substantially identical with Christianity.

For Troeltsch, the spirit of Modernist theology and piety emerges most convincingly with Friedrich von Hügel (1852-1925), because von Hügel is personally most attractive to Troeltsch.[260] In a letter to von Hügel (of 4 April 1908) Troeltsch expresses his assent to and personal sympathy for the theologians involved even more clearly than in his public statement. His remarks to von Hügel are almost pastoral. They communicate sympathy through a deep, inward reflection. For Troeltsch, things take on a different status *sub specie aeternitatis* from when they are judged and assessed in purely human terms. For him God governs the world and 'the great ethical and religious truths of humanity cannot perish'.[261]

Belief in a divine guidance is not conceived of in merely intellectual terms, but is focussed on a theology of history. For Troeltsch, it does not exclude a perception of the dark and incomprensible elements in history.[262]

Von Hügel and Troeltsch shared a common starting point in religion and theology. There was agreement between them on the significance of religious experience for faith and theology. Moreover, both agreed on a view of the relationship between religion and culture governed by an organic notion of their connection. Here they were largely agreed in their assessment of ideological problems. Both agreed on the central problems for the theology and church of their day. Broadly speaking, their agreement might be described like this: a piety strongly rooted in human experience is to be combined with a modern view of culture determined by individuality and human autonomy. However, there are different ways to this and also different individual determinations. On Troeltsch's side, special mention should be made of his difficulties with particular forms of church life and Catholicism in particular. He was mainly disturbed by the Catholic understanding of the priestly office, the hierarchical structure of the church and sacramentalism. What was predominant, and could shape his relationship with von Hügel in so positive a way, was a personal attitude which the two of them shared beyond all specific issues. It was shaped by a form of piety which was accepting and inclusive, i.e. not 'exclusive', and thus in principle was tailored to breadth and tolerance.

Troeltsch's links with Modernism, his concern for the fate of those who were accounted Modernist, does not emerge only in letters,[263] but also in his publications. Troeltsch can say of 8 September, the day of the promulgation of the encyclical, that on it 'in Dante's heaven all the saints will have wept for the earth despite their gaze on God's unchanging entourage'.[264]

The papal condemnation had considerable consequences for the Catholic clergy. It meant the indexing of literature, the obligation on clergy to oppose Modernism, a restriction on openness. Nevetheless, Troeltsch rejected any short-term partisanship in church politics and spoke, rather, of the need to arrive at a balanced judgment. For Troeltsch, if historical and contemporary thought are taken into account, there is no denying that, given the cultural conditions, the situation of religion and the church in the modern world is a difficult one. The soullessness of modern technological civilization is matched by the lack of religion in broad circles of the population. That is one side of the matter. The other is represented by the churches (Troeltsch deliberately uses the plural), which have a tendency to false thinking in terms of autonomy and to dogmatization. Here it is hard to say what solutions are available and what approaches can be adopted. For Troeltsch, the most important thing is that criticism of the church should come from within, so that to leave the church is a false step. This would fail to take account of the key issue, namely that a new religious life is dawning which is leaving hardening and externalization behind.

However, alongside this, another feature becomes evident in Troeltsch, namely a degree of resignation. He is sometimes inclined simply to let things run their course. But perhaps that is also an expression of trust in God, coupled with a remarkable retreat into personal religious feeling.[265]

A piece of concealed hope is also connected with the question how things will develop in the future. If culture is deprived of its foundation in the form of religion, then the trend towards the ideologizing and mythicizing of science can no longer be sustained. Troeltsch thinks that the time will come when the consequences of an attitude which is critical of religion and Christianity will become visible and there will be amazement at the 'modern hypertrophy of science... at the many things which "science" has not seen'.[266]

The Jatho case. The other controversy in church politics which Troeltsch also took up in his writings, and which was of particular concern to him, was the 'Jatho case'. Carl Jatho (1851-1913), a pastor in Cologne, was able to attract a wide range of people through preaching and parish work which was firmly orientated on individual experience and which contained aesthetic elements. However, he first became known through the 'Jatho case', which ended in a hearing before a tribunal (of the Church of the Old Prussian Union) and finally resulted in his being dismissed from office.

From as early as 1905, Jatho's activity, which for many years was not discussed publicly, had led to enquiries and protests from conservative circles in the church because of its particular stress on a 'personal religon' in which the confession and dogma no longer had any verbally binding significance.[267] However, the grounds for an intervention by official organs of the church, which also had an impact on a wider public, only emerged when in 1910 a law relating to heresy was enacted in Prussia.

To understand this law correctly, it is also necessary to perceive its positive intent. This was that there should explicitly be no disciplinary authority legitimated by the state, but that matters of doctrine should be settled within the church. A tribunal of theologians and church lawyers was appointed to supervise this task.

Over and above these positive aspects for church law and church politics, in its origins and implementation the law of heresy was deeply entangled in interests and party loyalties within the church. Above all, it had an anti-liberal focus and effect, even if in the end only real outsiders with a tendency towards freethinking were affected by this law. Be this as it may, in his person and work Jatho was an ideal figure of whom to make an example. It might even be said that Jatho's person and teaching were also a reason for the establishment of this law, so it was only consistent that it should first be applied to him.[268]

The 'Jatho case', his teaching, the complaints about his doctrine, the hearing, and finally his dismissal from office, sparked off a vigorous debate within those circles in theology and the church which were liberally inclined. Very different positions emerged in this debate. Sharp critics of Jatho's theological views, like Wilhelm Herrmann, were opposed by spokesmen like Artur Bonus and Gottfried Traub. Even these last were less concerned to support Jatho's doctrine than to regard individual doctrinal deviations as tolerable. Adolf von Harnack, to whom Jatho made a special appeal, was hesitant to adopt a position. So in this debate once again all the problems of the circle surrounding *Christliche Welt* emerged, namely that, in essence, theologically it was split into a left-wing and a right-wing group with a centre party in between, and was completely at odds over both theology and church politics. However, we must not overlook the fact that this openness was at the same time a principle, and was the programme of the journal or the group.[269]

Ernst Troeltsch, too, intervened in this debate, which was carried on vigorously over a long period, produced a variety of reactions, and on the whole was very controversial. He wrote an article for *Christliche Welt* entitled 'Freedom of Conscience'.[270]

Troeltsch did not go into the Jatho case in any detail, whether into Jatho's account of his theology in answer to the enquiries of the Oberkirchenrat, or into the protest in principle against the new law which emerged from lay circles and the criticism of this protest by Adolf von Harnack. Even more strikingly, Troeltsch did not discuss the tribunal and its verdict.[271]

Rather, Troeltsch was interested in what was symptomatic of theology and church politics in this procedure and was also somewhat of a matter of principle. On Jatho's person and teaching, he took a mediating line. In *Christliche Welt*, Martin Rade put it like this: a rejection of Jatho's theology on the one hand and a plea for him to be allowed to remain in office on the other. The latter was regarded as toleration of Jatho because of his special contributions to the Cologne community.[272]

What do we make of Troeltsch's argument for his position, which ends up in the propagation of 'freedom of conscience'? For Troeltsch, Jatho's type of religion is mystical, and he comes close to the old spiritualists like Sebastian Franck and Angelus Silesius. According to Troeltsch, a man of this type of piety will argue that one cannot speak appropriately of God at all, either in theological language or even, strictly speaking, in the language of piety. For people of this kind, an element of dissatisfaction or inability is part of their way of believing. All that is important to them is that basic religious statements like the Bible should be accepted by an act of symbolization or poeticization, and clarified by the community in such a way as to have a religious influence.

For Troeltsch, Jatho differs from the old mystics in that he is fundamentally governed by the optimism and immanent thought of modern man. However, he does not share the basic attitude expressed in this in a reflective way – and thus with the possibility of critical detachment – but on the basis of a personal faith which might be called childlike.

So Troeltsch draws a picture of the pious man Jatho who is not so much a theologian but rather has remained basically naive in matters of faith. And Troeltsch also stresses that Jatho had had a marked religious influence on his community. He contrasts the church with the pious outsider Jatho, who represents the type of the 'mystic' in a specific way – similarly on the basis of thinking in terms of types. Troeltsch speaks of the church as an organization, the emphasis on institutional ties and authoritarian relationships in quite a negative way. On the one hand, then, there is the pious individual and his links with mystical religion, of which the theologian must certainly take a critical view, and a fundamentally optimistic view of the world which moves towards the aesthetic. And on the other hand there is the institutional church with its immobility and its claim to authority.

The basic problem which arises for Troeltsch from this confrontation is primarily that of freedom of conscience, which he now does not want to solve simply in individualistic terms but also in terms of the church community.[273] The Jatho case poses questions for the self-understanding of the church in the face of changed feelings about life and modern man's view of the world. For Troeltsch, there must be some recognition of the church as an institution and as an element in society, but at the same time attention must be paid to the general situation in terms of both culture and the church and religion. There are difficulties, almost pre-programmed conflicts here. That applies not only to individuals, but, in Troeltsch's view, to around half of church people.

Troeltsch sees that the 'Jatho case' has consequences for relations between church and state which could spur on the opponents of the state church. But he is against a disestablishment of the church in line with a liberal political programme. In such a solution the link with the church as a historical entity is largely lost, and with it a potential for tradition which can order and hand on religious forces. The demand in principle for freedom of conscience in the church is to be addressed to the conditions and possibilities of the established church on the one hand and the need to accept the church as a vehicle of tradition and an element of order on the other.

One can best assess Troeltsch's attitude in the Jatho case by comparing it with the attitudes of other theologians at the time. First there is Julius Kaftan, who comments on the controversy in letters to his brother Theodore.[274] For Kaftan, in world-view Jatho is a monist akin to Haeckel. Like Haeckel, Jatho is concerned with the unity of the world on the basis of a thoroughgoing acceptance of the law of causality.[275]

Moreover Kaftan thinks that the loyal members of the community in Cologne who argue so vehemently for Jatho cannot distinguish between the symbolic expressions which he uses and the subject-matter which has to be given appropriate expression.[276]

The pastor and the individual community cannot insist on their rights to such a degree that the whole body of the church and its claims must fade into the background before them. Therefore, according to Kaftan, there are definite limits to the attitude of the individual pastor, which is shaped by the bonds of conscience. They lie in the orientation of both the pastor and the community on the confession and thus on a definite content of faith. It is evident that for Kaftan the question of the individual's freedom of conscience does not by any means play the kind of role that it does for Troeltsch. Kaftan approaches the resolution of questions of order in the church in a different way from Troeltsch. He sees the whole 'Jatho case' as an outbreak of individual arbitrariness in matters of faith. And the case is so serious for him because here the fundamental problem of the relationship between state and church arises. He describes his concern like this. 'I do not know what will become of Protestantism if state and church fall apart and we cannot hold them together.'[277]

Alongside Kaftan, mention should also be made of Adolf von Harnack, who was a kind of figurehead for theological liberalism and who was deliberately drawn into the affair by Jatho.[278] The correspondence makes it clear how Harnack sought to stand by Jatho without showing solidarity with him. The theologian trained in the interpretation of historical texts shows a concern to understand what moves Jatho and what his concern is. Jatho interests him as the expression of a subjective experience and Harnack puts it in a wider historical context. He assures the Cologne pastor: 'You are certainly right: the two natures doctrine is quite untenable; but in the form of an antiquated speculation on the historical truth about Jesus Christ it comes nearer than your "unauthorized quester for God".'[279]

For Harnack, the right of the subjective element in religion and in questions of faith cannot be asserted without qualification. For him pastors should certainly be able to express their opinion freely and openly, but they must also reckon with the fact that not every Landeskirche will be able to tolerate them. Here Harnack points in a way which resembles Lutheran theology to the possibility of accepting suffering.

Martin Rade expressed Harnack's ideas on Jatho, which could be regarded as central, in the formula: 'God does not = nature, does not = development. And Jesus is in the middle as indispensable.'[280] According to Rade, Jatho's subjectivism had to be corrected and supplemented by Harnack's view of religion. He therefore remarked pointedly: 'So I say Jatho alone – without Harnack – will not do.'[281]

Troeltsch sees the problem in a different light when he removes the possible conflict from the personal level and raises it to a more general level. He regards Jatho and his theology as a type which at the same time must be seen against the background of more recent developments in intellectual and cultural history. In that case the question ultimately focuses on the fundamental conflict between individual experiential piety based on inwardness, and objective ties to the Christian tradition and the church. Jatho is an model example of this basic theological conflict, and finding a solution is an essential task for present-day theology generally. Now for Troeltsch that does not exclude specific indicators for this individual case.

His basic intent in seeking a solution is mediation – but not without characteristic additions and further definitions which are important. The religious right of the individual, both the pastor and the individual Christian, and the right of the church as an individual community and an institution, must be brought together in a relationship which can be advocated and accepted. The expression and concrete figure of the religious personality of both pastor and individual Christian must be subjected to critical investigation on the basis of a meaningful and necessary link with the community. The community, even in its institutional form, must look out for the possibilities of tolerating individual religious manifestations on the basis of a conscientious bond and renounce the use of external means of pressure.

The specific suggestion which Troeltsch puts forward at the end must be distinguished from the fundamental problems and the generally open offer of a solution (as it were in the grand style). Troeltsch specifies his desired goal by proposing a free election of pastors by relatively independent communities.

The communities may decide on their own pastors, depending on their own needs. The pastors are to make a basic confession that they stand in the Christian tradition, and that should suffice. For Troeltsch, the other aspect will sort itself out almost automatically, since neither atheists nor radical critics of the church will want to become pastors.

It is typical of Troeltsch that he first sees the fundamental difficulties as lying in the changed situation in the modern world, and secondly argues for the possibilities of a balance in which orientation on tradition and concern for individual features play a role.

Troeltsch's view is not that this will remove difficulties both on the side of the church or the communities and within the personal life of pastors and community members. But he does think that in this way a radicalization and the fatal use of external pressure can be avoided.

As I remarked elsewhere, the concept of antinomy plays an important role in Troeltsch's thinking generally, and it also does so here. Troeltsch assumes an antimony between religious individualism and links with the community. For him, religion is always about the individual; it relates to the individual and seeks to take shape in the individual. On the other hand, 'the trees of individualism must not grow up to heaven',[282] as the religious community has inalienable rights.

The nature of the antinomy is that in principle it cannot be dissolved, because both forms of the expression of religious life are right. The consequence of this insight is that any simple and one-sided expression of these two forms must be questioned or limited. If the fundamental determination is shaped by such an antinomy, then any solution must be provisional and in need of reform.

In the case of the pastor – and that is the primary concern – it seems that a personal confession of his ties with the Christian world of ideas whould be accepted as generally sufficient. To some people today that will not seem very terrifying, but it must be seen in the context of the time, the ideological and religious controversies, and the situation in the Prussian church.

Even if one is of the opinion that Troeltsch's practical suggestions create difficulties because, drawing on liberal principles of thought, they leave great play for the individual freedom of conscience of the pastor, argue strongly in terms of the 'religious needs' of the community, and pay too little attention to the necessity and significance of forming a consensus, they neverthess remain acceptable. Here it is particularly necessary to understand that it would be more meaningful to have freedom of conscience *in* the church and not despite the church, and that in this connection attention must always be paid to the established church, the Volkskirche. For official church action this means that the church must be concerned for more liberality, so that there can be a balance between a meaningful link with the community and the orientation of individuals on their consciences.

8. The Social Teachings of the Christian Churches and Groups[283]

Ernst Troeltsch said that the *Social Teachings* was his favourite book.[284] He gave it a central place among his works. Moreover, the effort, the nervous and mental energy that it had taken, made the book particularly close to his heart. In retrospect he remarked: 'This time I dispensed with any programmatic preliminary work and instead of all the mere spitting I devoted myself with indescribable toil to piping.'[285]

Purpose and method. Difficulties arose because Troeltsch often felt that he was treading new ground in both method and subject-matter. Once the *Social Teachings* was finally out as the first volume of his collected works he felt freed from a great pressure. He had great hope for the book: not without pride he remarked that with the *Social Teachings* he had created a new discipline.[286]

However, in typical fashion, when the book was there in front of him, finished, he was already busy with new plans.[287]

At first sight Troeltsch's preoccupation with the theme seems to be completely new. However, this is only partly true, in that he was working towards sociological questions and using relevant historical material. On the other hand it is possible to recognize a connection with, a continuation of, the line that he had already taken. This line is the interest in a link between historical analysis and interpretation of the present, in which the question of the relationship between culture generally and religion has a central place. Moreover, by a cultural-historical approach which integrated the social and the political elements, he prepared the way for sociological, social-historical thought. This interest in history and contemporary analysis continues in the *Social Teachings*, where it creates new paths and makes a new impression.[288]

The immediate occasion for writing the *Social Teachings* was an invitation to review a book on 'The Collaboration of the Church in the Solution of the Social Question' by the Greifswald theologian von Nathusius.[289] In retrospect Troeltsch spoke of a 'wretched book' which showed him the whole sorry state of theologians' knowledge of social and social-ethical questions. Instead of giving a review, he set to and himself wrote a book of around a thousand pages.[290]

Troeltsch sees the advantage of the churches (in the plural!) as being that they can adopt a position on social questions and questions of social policy out of a conviction which has a metaphysical foundation. However, he argues that this conviction must be aware of its historical origin and the problems arising from that.

Troeltsch adopted the 'Marxist doctrine of substructure and superstructure' for his account, understanding this to be an impulse which was essentially methodological in the sense that it took real conditions into account for the development of the idea.[291]

Already in earlier works he had not adopted an approach purely in terms of the history of ideas, but had chosen a methodological approach which also took account of political and social factors.[292] This changed with the *Social Teachings*, in that now the rise of religious communities and the social theories represented by them were seen in the context of intellectual-cultural and also political, economic and social factors, on the assumption that in principle there was a reciprocal interaction here. For Troeltsch it could not simply be a question of the economic basis having an effect on religious conceptions or cultural conceptions generally; rather, the ideas also contributed to changing actual conditions.[293]

So Troeltsch wanted to take economic conditions into account, as factors which determine historical development. The independence of religion was not open to discussion or, better, to disposition. Thus in Kautsky's account in particular he noticed the absence of an appropriate consideration of the religious element: because of his 'popular Marxism', Kautsky overlooked the dialectics of the religious idea and therefore assessed the development wrongly.

A further point for Troeltsch was the relationship between sociological formations of a Christian kind and origin, and the social dimension, i.e. the state and society. He noted that the theological discussion of the time was not sufficiently clear on this question, in either conceptuality or method. In Christianity, as in all other manifestations of human life, he was concerned with the sociological working out of ideas. So the religious element did not have a special position, but an independence or character of its own.

In defining the 'social', Troeltsch draws lines on two sides, in one direction theological and in the other ideological. In both instances the view is 'dogmatic'. In the one instance (e.g. von Nathusius) the social is dissolved into the Christian and in the other (e.g. Kautsky) the Christian is dissolved into the social.

Troeltsch's authority on this question is Lorenz von Stein. He adopts Stein's 'dualistic' concept of society in the form of an opposition of state and society.[294] Von Stein's understanding of society is largely tailored to questions of economic life, and to state and society is added the family sphere as the presupposition of the two.[295]

For Troeltsch, the question of the unity of cultural life is of basic significance. 'If one recognizes that state and society, alongside countless other forces, are the main formative forces of culture, the ultimate question is how the church can combine with these forces to form a cultural unity.'[296] In this way the focus of the investigation takes up his theological reflections and his interest in the philosophy of history.

Where could Troeltsch start from here? Above all mention should be made of the theme and the orientation of Gerhard Ullhorn's work on 'Christian Charitable Activity' (*Die Christliche Liebestätigkeit*, Stuttgart [2]1895). Troeltsch respects the spirit of the book, which investigates the history of Christian charitable activity from a Christian social impulse and in so doing incorporates a vast amount of source material. Troeltsch cannot accept Uhlhorn as a forerunner or stimulus for his own work, for two reasons. First, because of Uhlhorn's remarkable basically apologetic and dogmatic attitude which excessively exalts Christianity, and has a tendency to deprecate all humane ethics and a social practice which results from them.[297] Secondly, because as a result of his view of the history of theology, Uhlhorn is not sufficiently critical of his sources.[298]

Troeltsch made a particular claim for his work, namely that it was a parallel to Harnack's *History of Dogma*.[299] This claim is understandable if we consider its methodology and form. In line with Harnack's *History of Dogma*, which is governed by the notion of a self-unfolding of the religious idea, Troeltsch sets out to write a history of the formation of sociological ideas, taking into account their actual effect on social life. Both works contain a historical survey from the early church to the time of the Reformation (Harnack) or the eighteenth century (Troeltsch). Troeltsch presupposes research into the history of dogma because he can only treat his first main point (the history of the formation of sociological ideas) on the basis of work on the history of dogma. So his outline is to be understood as a supplement to and development of Harnack's work. But it is new to the degree that actual conditions are noted (in the second main point). So as compared with Harnack it is concerned with both connection and proximity and development and difference. Troeltsch shows the limits of previous work in the history of dogma by raising a new set of questions and adopting a method appropriate to them.[300]

There is no disputing the fact that Troeltsch's work has to be taken further and its historiography corrected – how could it be otherwise? This process already began with Wernle's extensive review of the *Social Teachings*[301] and then continued on the basis of the specializations which had come about in the meantime, both in the field of theology and in that of sociology and history. Since then, above all the simple descriptions or main concepts adopted by Troeltsch, like early Catholicism, Lutheranism, Calvinism, confessionalism have been defined more precisely, qualified or broken down further. This has produced greater differentiation and greater exactitude in the assessment of historical developments.[302] However, we must not let our overall view, our verdict on the whole achievement, be distorted by the question of Troeltsch's knowledge of the sources or research into the sources.[303] Troeltsch was concerned to combine historical work with systematic aims, to have a better and deeper analysis of the time on the basis of historical knowledge and insight. He sketched out a picture of all the social teachings of the churches from the early church to the eighteenth century, drew attention to central questions and concepts, referred to junctures in the development, indicated lines of contact and showed the limits to both Christian apologetic and claims and the ideological criticism of Christianity.

The beginnings in the early church. Troeltsch begins from a fact which is significant for both history and systematic theology: the preaching of Jesus, like the formation of the earliest community, was not governed by any direct social interest. Rather, in both cases a 'purely religious' character has to be assumed. The consequence is that in its first form, Christianity has to be understood in the light less of the conditions of social history than of those of the history of religion. Here we are to see more than an interest in demarcation (e.g. from Kautsky). For Troeltsch, what appears in Christianity from a social perspective as a 'movement from below' is connected with the nature of new religious formations generally. With their power to form communities they derive from the living character of religious life, which in its unreflected and direct nature is to be encountered primarily in the lower strata of the population. However, the criterion for the authenticity and duration of the new religious forms of life is their capacity to attach themelves to reflective culture.[304]

For Troeltsch, the content of Jesus' preaching is to be understood from one basic notion, talk of the coming of the kingdom of God.[305] According to Troeltsch, this idea has not only a future but also a present significance. In his view, the demand to conform to the kingdom of God implies a 'dispositional ethic'. The preaching of Jesus displays a radicalism which makes unconditional demands on the basis of the total orientation of life on God. The question is how the radicalism which emerges in the gospel fits in with the idea of a cultural attachment, i.e. the capacity to make connections with a culture of reflection. The answer is that the twofold commandment to love provides a kind of framework within which the moral contents undergo an evaluation through the gift and demand of communion with God. In this way Christianity is in a position to take up ethical constructions of very different kinds, both religious and philosophical.

According to Troeltsch, on the basis of the twofold commandment to love, the gospel has the twofold sociological structure of an individualism and a universalism. The individualism is governed by the relationship to God, which bestows on the individual his worth as a human being. To the degree that the human being is aware of being bound to God, this notion establishes a relationship of communion and is ultimately resposible for universalism.

One difficulty is that Troeltsch does not always mark clearly the transition from the theological perspective to a sociological understanding. In other words, the thinking sometimes starts from inside and sometimes from outside; first from the self-understanding of faith or the believer and then from sociological considerations. To give an example: in Troeltsch's view the significance of Jesus' preaching for assuring people that God is graciously disposed towards them can initially be left out of account, since in sociological terms this is merely an intensification of the motive. However, the sociological-functional interpretation gives rise to an eminently theological problem, because it fails to consider whether and to what degree the preaching of Jesus (and the preaching about Jesus as the 'Christ') takes on significance as a ground for faith.

It is the same when Troeltsch makes the introduction of the idea of authority plausible on sociological presuppositions. He says that authority is necessary in the case of the God of Israel who makes himself known to people as the God of the will. That can only come about through a revelation, which is given authority as a sign of God to human beings. Here Troeltsch is arguing in terms of social psychology, but the theological focus on the question of how authority is to be recognized here, and what points of contact are valid for it, is not discussed further. Another point is connected with this: in Troeltsch's view, can the community which was founded by Jesus as a historical person and in which he was then worshipped cultically as the Christ be understood as a free community of the Spirit and of knowledge? This question admits an intellectualism into the account which fails to recognize the way in which the first community was aware of being bound up with Jesus' death and resurrection.

It is possible here only to follow the main aspects of the subsequent development (up to the time of the Reformation) and the assessment of it, the interpretative categories preferred by Troeltsch and the ideas for solutions which left their mark on history.

A new notion of community arises with Pauline Christianity. It is based on the worship of Christ in the cult and introduces new elements of religious commitment like baptism and the Lord's Supper. Here, too, the notion of the resurrection, which had played no role in the account so far, makes its mark. Troeltsch brings it into the circle of Pauline theology and Paul's view of community. There is an imbalance here, both historically and in terms of subject-matter, which is connected with Troeltsch's basic view of christ-ology.[306]

The notion in Pauline communities that people are divided into Christians, Jews and Gentiles, into those inside and those outside communion with God, necessarily also raises the sociological question of human equality. This question is particularly relevant for the modern understanding of human beings, because 'equality' is one of the basic demands of modernity. The question arises on several levels in connection with earliest Pauline Christ-ianity. In Troeltsch's view, equality consists primarily in two things, in the assertion that all human beings are equally distant from God because of sin and the perception that all have an equal relationship with God in the perspective of love.

Paul distinguishes religious equality from all possible forms of inequality in the life of the world. He stresses the connection between ideas of inequality and equality in such a way that human equality in the life of the world becomes the means of moral obligation for all on the basis of a fundamental religious impulse. This leads to the social application or working out of the ideas, but not to a change in social relationships themselves. The working out of the sociological idea emerges in changes in the social structure of the church.

The sociological type created in this way is that of Christian patriarchalism. It consists of an interpretation of human life and human conditions in faith, in the light of the principle of care and obligation. Earlier forms of this sociological type can be found in late Judaism; on the presupposition of the Christian idea of love it came to full fruition in the Middle Ages.[307] Here compromises were necessary with the world, because with its assumption of a simple world situation, the gospel could not be handed down and continue to have an effect in its radical form.[308]

However, this accommodation to the circumstances of the world is not to be interpreted as it is on Marxist presuppositions. It cannot be demonstrated that the construction of a spiritual-moral world depends on the previous structure or the character of a so-called basis.[309] The independence of the 'religious idea' is recognizable not least from the fact that there is no really intrinsic connection with the situation in the world. It is evident that the natural basis is shattered where it cannot be fitted into the context of ideas. That is evident, for example, from the notion of asceticism.

For Troeltsch, the formation of 'early Catholicism' is, after Paulinism, the second great historical form of the development of the gospel. A new understanding of ministry and the sacraments led to new definitions of the relationship with God and Christ. Troeltsch sees here an ongoing movement of the original religious forces present at the beginning. However, he suggests that the need for consolidation and association is quite understandable, given the historical situation.

The situation alters, the moment when the church not only becomes larger, but changes in structure and status, i.e. when it becomes a state church. The church's charitable activity is depersonalized. An organized system of charity takes up the ascetic idea, but at the same time understands works of love against the background of the salvation of the individual soul.

Whereas in the lower classes the religious myth continues to retain its significance, a combination of ancient philosophy and science with Christian theology is characteristic of the upper class. Platonism gives the Christian notion of redemption a theological foundation. Redemption is regarded as the consummation of the process of the origin of the world grounded in the Logos (starting from God and returning to God). Stoic philosophy is significant for ethics. Natural-law thought may be combined with Christian ideas here. Sociologically, the natural moral law of the Stoa, the property of all human beings and at the same time tending towards universality, because it makes a unitary structure and leadership possible (through the principle of reason), had the significance of deriving state and economy, family and property from this principle and structuring them by it. The combination was brought about intellectually the moment the natural moral law was held to be grounded in the divine will, the state of sin was understood as a relativization of the demands of the Decalogue, identical with the moral law, and Christ's demand qualified as the form of a new ethic which went beyond it. Troeltsch sees the Christian reception of natural-law thinking as being that absolute natural law belongs in the primal state and relative natural law belongs in the state of sin: the Lex Christi marks the special form. In Troeltsch's eyes, a Christian theory of natural law understood in this way is 'the real culture dogma of the church and as such it is at least as important as the dogma of the Trinity, or other main dogmas'.[310]

Sociological references and references to the history of culture do not of themselves make the course of tradition from the biblical period and the foundation of that tradition plausible. In particular Troeltsch asks what has become of the radical ideas of the gospel. Have they changed in this process of tradition? Or were they shunted on to another track? First of all, it is necessary to recognize that the Christian faith or the Christian notion of redemption could take over only those elements of ancient philosophy and knowledge which had a dualistic pattern. Secondly, Christian natural-law theory represents a toning down to the degree that natural life is seen as a basis grounded in the relative natural law. Furthermore, there was an institution in which the radical demands remained alive and were handed down, namely monasticism. Sociologically, this is a kind of return to the small and intimate conditions of the time of the beginning, to the personal proximity and ties originally to be found in the group of the disciples and the community of the disciples. So whereas the radical elements remained alive in the New Testament tradition, in the idea of the absolute natural law and monasticism, the church functioned as a mediating authority which achieved a practical compromise with the world and at the same time maintained its claim inwards, in the direction of the person.

The social teachings of mediaeval Catholicism. According to Troeltsch, the Christianity of antiquity could not find any really clear relationship to culture. There was no overall view and overall connection among the ideas of Christianity. Here lies the fundamental difference from mediaeval Catholicism, which developed the idea of a unitary Christian culture: the combination, or better the subordination, of all cultural forces to the religious idea, of which the church was to be seen as the representative.

How did this unitary Christian culture come to be formed historically? Troeltsch thinks that the difficulties of the process are underestimated in the usual accounts. It has to be recognized that the unitary Christian culture is not to be seen as an organic development or consequence of the Christian idea; rather, special historical forces were at work in conjunction with a particular historical constellation which first made possible this form of the relationship between church and culture.[311]

Troeltsch cites the sects as an example of the course of historical development. He sees here a dialectical development of the idea, but one in which movement and counter-movement are always present at the same time in the historical process. For there is 'no dialectic which would have been in a position to establish such a relationship [the interpenetration of spiritual and worldly being] programmatically from the Christian idea itself; here the possibilities and necessities which the actual course of affairs contributes to the develpoment of social life outside the church have their effect.'[312]

It remains to be asked whether the assumption of a dialectical development of the idea and attention to real conditions can be so related that interpretations of history emerge which do not contradict one another (and if so, how). In terms of both method and content Troeltsch wants to achieve a wealth of aspects which take up the fullness of historical life and get beyond one-sided approaches.[313] But is it not the case that the factor of 'spirit' plays a decisive role in what Troeltsch calls the real conditions, despite all the concrete points of contact, and that therefore it is the spirit of circumstances which is assumed and filtered out here, so that the link with the historical dialectic of the Christian idea can follow?

For the form of mediaeval Catholicism, reference must be made above all to the idea of the papacy, which is a decisive factor for the rise of church universalism.[314] Troeltsch, who is alienated from and critical of a dogmatic Christianity, stresses the significance of dogma where it has to be evaluated historically in connection with law and cult. He says that the idea of papal primacy lies in the basic sociological tendency of the idea of the church, indeed that one could even speak of its consummation in the papacy.[315] Troeltsch sees this consummation in the fact that the notion of the 'mystical Christ' was taken up again once it had been split up locally by the previous notion of the office of bishop. Here Troeltsch is judging from a sociological perspective. But the question is how the account which grew out of the sociological perspective is related to his criticism of the papacy expressed elsewhere. If Troeltsch is addressing a phenomenon from a sociological aspect, he can speak, for example, of 'needs' to be assumed. These are needs which then with intrinsic consistency lead to the formation of an idea. But what status does whatever is thus developed have in substantive theological criticism? Here countless questions remain open. The relationship between theological and sociological argument and the evaluation of phenomena which goes with it largely remains unexplained.

Thus for example on the basis of his 'sociological approach' Troeltsch accepts the 'power of the sacraments' as an intervention by the church in the life of the believer,[316] because this establishes the notion of a unitary Christian culture. The aim of trying to understand a theological argument, a church entity or a whole epoch primarily in its own terms accentuates the tendency to a withdrawal of theological criticism, at any rate in the relevant context.[317]

In Troeltsch's understanding, natural-law thought was eminently significant for the combination of secular and Christian ideas. The Stoic concept of natural law and the idea of natural justice based on it were on the one hand a rival by virtue of the way in which they corresponded independently to the sociological views of Christianity, and at the same time offered a potential solution to theological problems through reception and transformation. The conceptuality and idea of natural law were suitable for giving inner legitimation to the compromise with the world which was forced on the church by actual circumstances. For Troeltsch, the Christian relative natural law, together with the idea of theocracy, is the presupposition for the very formation of a unitary church culture. However, the ideas orientated in Stoic fashion on reason and incorporated into the church through natural-law thought could then become an explosive force which brought about the end of the unitary church culture in the seventeenth century.[318]

In Troeltsch's view, the idea of a mediaeval unitary culture is suitable for allowing a relative contrast between the world and the kingdom of God. The principle of unity is not endangered by this, but rather supported by the assumption of a series of levels. A system of co-ordination and distinction is introduced, which leads from the relative purposefulness of the inner-worldly ethic to the Christian form, which is again understood as having different levels.

For Troeltsch, Thomistic social philosophy is the definition of the relationship between church and culture expressed in a concept and embraced in a system. With his system Thomas depicts a combination of natural and supernatural forces, of morality and grace, in which Christianity makes a universal claim and the church appears as an absolute authority on the basis of its function of mediating salvation. That means that in this sense theology forms the theoretical interpenetration and foundation of the notion of the unitary culture.[319]

In Troeltsch's view, it is decisive that the Middle Ages defined the Christian ethic and Christianity generally as a 'supernatural' entity. This supernatural character is both a distinctive religious and a logical principle, which directs human beings as creatures of God towards the supernatural and leads to participation in God's being. Thus the task no longer consists – as in the early church – in mediating between absolute and relative natural law, but in mediating between nature and supernature.[320]

If the fundamental sociological scheme of the gospel was based on a radical religious individualism and universalism of love, and a cultic community in which the social differences were cushioned by patriarchalism was first formed through the notion of the Kyrios, it can now be said that both the idea of the organism and the notion of patriarchalism were taken over into mediaeval social doctrine. That happened in particular through the new version of the natural-law idea. The natural law was regarded as a natural level ready for an elevation and heightening brought about by the principle of grace. For Troeltsch, the notion of organism is an active, critical element of the system; he speaks of it as the 'revolutionary principle of Christian sociology'.[321] By contrast, patriarchalism represents the conservative element. Its function is to stabilize social conditions, for existing social differences are largely accepted.

Immanent difficulties and tensions can be indicated in each of the two elements, patriarchalism and the idea of the organism. In patriarchalism the difficulty lies in quietism, in the high esteem for a readiness for suffering and humility. In the principle of the organism, the significance of the individual is connected with its participation in the overall tasks and is determined by the idea of the organism as a whole. If the idea of religious authority is added to the notion of the organic, the organic principle of combination changes, and with it the position of the individual in the system. The organism is directed from above, and the individual is required to trust the authority given.

Even if mediaeval social philosophy did not develop any programme for shaping society, and its problematical points generally cannot be overlooked, Troeltsch nevertheless finds it an imposing entity. Both the early church and the Middle Ages are similar in their lack of a social programme, though the reasons for this differ. The early church believed in a disruption of the order of creation through human sin and attempted to do away with or at least tone down this disruption through the charitable actions of the individual and the community. The Middle Ages thought in terms of a balanced relationship between nature and grace, and in practice sought to direct conditions in the church by the Christian ideal. So the idea of church authority was normative. Thus whereas from the beginning it was hard for the early church to think of social reform, this was superfluous for the Middle Ages, because the actual situation could be accepted from a religious perspective as the preliminary form of a 'supernatural structure'. For Troeltsch there is no question that an 'undercurrent' of the ideals of the gospel was always maintained in the Christian tradition, the power of faith at work under the surface which was never given up. In this undercurrent, an alienation of faith from the world which could not be suppressed was carried down. This line of tradition also continued in the way in which the gospel continued to be handed down through the ideas of absolute natural law.[322]

For Troeltsch, the medieval sects belong in this context. He wants to counter the impression that the church was the only effective historical factor in the history of Christianity. That would be to deny, even in theory, those groups which in the course of history had in any case to experience so much harm and rejection. For Troeltsch, the special character of the sects, their 'radical' nature, lies in their denial of all mediating thought.

Troeltsch stresses that both the church-type and the sect-type could appeal to the establishment of Christianity in the form of the gospel and the early church. Because of its radical nature, the sect-type comes closer to Jesus; by contrast, the church-type goes back to Paul or Paulinism and his idea of redemption and understanding of mission.[323] Troeltsch certainly stresses that the term sect has nothing of the value judgment about it, but is merely meant to denote a sociological type. However, the reader cannot help noticing that for Troeltsch the price which the sects pay for their power and the vigour of their religious life seems too high.

In this connection – the church on the one hand and the sect on the other – we must note an important distinction made by Troeltsch in the reception of Christian tradition and the nature of its relationship to culture. This is the distinction between radicality and compromise. 'Radicality' is presented as a religious form of thought and understanding which is related to itself and at the same time excludes outsiders, and 'compromise' as a view which governs relations with the world and is thus supported by the notion of a mediation between Christian tradition and culture. There is no mistaking the fact that Troetlsch passes a relatively positive judgment on the attitude of compromise that emanates from the church. However, this positive evaluation turns into a negative one where the church appears as an 'institution'. Certainly Troeltsch sees and appreciates the significance of the radical nature of the sects for the formation of the churches' social teachings, but he passes a negative judgment on their ambivalent character – lived-out religious feeling on the one hand and legalistic narrowness on the other. Whereas Troeltsch as a historian and sociologist is interested in painting a picture of historical reality, Troeltsch the theologian has an ambiguous atittude. Certainly he can criticize both the radical character of the sects and the churches' attitude of compromise, but his fear of the radical character of the sects is greater than that of the compromise attitude of the church.

By his (modified) acceptance of this ideal-typical conceptuality, Troeltsch has a means of describing great, over-arching, epoch-making connections. He can survey and bring together historical material; he has critical perspectives at his disposal and at the same time a possibility of making surveys of historical development. In approach and intention this conceptuality stems from Max Weber and in academic terms it belongs in the context of the discussion of the theory and conceptuality of the humanities around the turn of the century.[324] Here the ideal types have above all a heuristic function. They aid the epistemological process of understanding reality historically. Here any simple co-ordination or assertion must be transcended by the assumption of an open horizon.[325]

Troeltsch's concept of sect corresponds to that of Weber. At the same time, Troeltsch points out that here the works of Scheel, and also of Simmel and Kawerau, have been significant. And finally he mentions his own article 'Religion and Church' from 1895.[326] The last reference in particular suggests that Troeltsch is claiming a degree of independence in the formation of concepts. This seems to me to be correct, simply because Troeltsch, without using the conceptuality, in substance addresses the 'typical' when he argues that radicalism has associations with the element of the sect, and compromise or mediation has associations with the church.

In Troeltsch, as in Weber, the sect is characterized by the voluntary character of the association of its members and the consistent adoption of religious conceptions in its way of life. All this stands in contrast to the church, which is already presented as an entity into which one is born and for which compromise with the situation in the world is significant.

However, the differences between Troeltsch and Weber in their adoption and use of conceptuality are quite unmistakable. Whereas Weber extends the ideal-typical approach to the history of religion as a whole, in accordance with his theme Troeltsch keeps to the Christian tradition. But above all, in contrast to Weber, Troeltsch speaks of 'types', meaning by this historical reality itself, over and above any conceptual or logical interest or set of instruments. And finally, to Weber's ideal types of sect and church, from the Middle Ages on Troeltsch adds the type of mysticism.[327]

Troeltsch's definition of this third type which he adds, mysticism, is somewhat unclear. In Weber the ideal types of church and sect are arrived at through the different motive of co-ordination to which each community relates and an assessment from the perspective of the religious qualifications which are expressed as a result. There is no possibility of this with mysticism. Mysticism is universal communion of the Spirit, and as such must transcend all fixed organizations. If one puts the emphasis on the universality of mysticism, then there is a relationship to the church. But if the free communion of the spirit comes to the fore, then in turn the difference from the church becomes evident. And mysticism comes close to the sect through the way in which an individual feature resting on personal experience comes into the foreground. However, mysticism differs from the sect by its lack of a close link with a religious grouping.

For Troeltsch, the view of individuality which finds expression in the mystical type has a parallel to or comes close to modern thought. The advantage of mysticism lies in the possibility of taking up elements of freedom and leaving room for the autonomous formation and bond of the conscience. The weakness of mysticism lies in its lack of organization.

The problem of co-ordinating or understanding individual historical phenomena by types emerges clearly in the way in which Troeltsch distinguishes church and sect here.[328] By this procedure, wide areas of church history are forced into the background because they are not covered by the types: for example, the development of the idea of the church in early Christianity and the Reformation: in early Christianity, because here the community principle has a significance which does not involve the institutional element; and in the Reformation because the standpoint of faith involved in belonging to the church is brought out. Certain difficulties also emerge with the sect-type. Troeltsch tailors this in a remarkable way to asceticism, because the sect 'refers its members directly to the supernatural aim of life' (cf. *GS* I, 362, *ST* I, 331). But this stress on the notion of asceticism applies to only one particular manifestation which Troeltsch emphasizes as applying to the type generally. In his interpretation Troeltsch stresses how close the sects are to the original form of Christian tradition: at the same time this procedure neutralizes the question of their heritage by subsuming them under the 'type'.

Troeltsch is convinced of the necessity of a reciprocal corrective function of the three types – churches, sects and mysticism. The radical character of the sects, which signalizes a lack of culture, is criticized in the light of the church-type and approached with a view to the necessary clarification of the relationship of the sect to the world. By contrast, the church must be asked critically in the light of the concept of the sect whether its compromise formula can be sustained on the basis of the biblical tradition and whether there is not a danger that with the idea of the institution it fails to do justice to personal decision and commitment.

Much as Troeltsch sees mysticism as the type which best corresponds to modern Christianity in its cultural development, this type, too, is not spared criticism. Mysticism was not really in a position to develop a sociological idea from itself; and it could not bind people together in a community and give this bond external, visible form.

From this perspective we can understand Troeltsch's efforts to emphasize Jesus as the centre of cultic worship, precisely because he observes that it is here that the difficulties of the mystical type lie. His own position is only approximately identical with the mystical type. For in the light of the two other types he also recognizes the defects of this type. The end-result is something like an 'ideal position', which analyses all three types critically and brings them together again at a meta-level. On the whole, there is a greater distance both from the church-type and that of the sect-type, and a greater inclination towards mysticism. What is decisive in connection with mysticism is the idea of personal freedom. Moreover there is a possibility of adopting such a metalevel in the freedom perceived and asserted by the mystical type.

Behind the notion of a mutual corrective function Troeltsch has a theological idea which pursues as its goal the communication of truth in accordance with faith and a relative affirmation of culture. This 'implicit theology' governs not only the construction but also the co-ordination of the types and the idea of their variability.

The Social Teachings of Protestantism: Luther and Lutheranism. The next major group, in both history and substance, is Protestantism.[329]

For Troeltsch, Protestantism faces the question whether it wants to remain a church or become a sect. The conclusion he draws is that it has remained a church and has thus continued, at least in principle, the idea of a unitary Christian culture. In the *Social Teachings* Troeltsch is concerned above all to show the framework common to mediaeval Catholicism and Protestantism in the form of the rule of a religious authority. He does not overlook deep-seated differences, but they remain within the framework of the church and have a full effect only when a change has taken place here, in the modern world. In view of the change in his questioning, which is now focussed on the sociological aspects, Troeltsch stresses the originality of Luther more strongly than before. Thus Luther is credited with the rediscovery of a religion of grace of the Augustinian-Pauline kind, and this is contrasted with the Catholic religion of the law.[330]

Troeltsch formulates five conclusions from the principle of a religion of grace or conviction in order to describe the new element in Luther's religious ideas. 1. There is a concentration on the knowledge of God and his means of grace rooted in personal faith and communicated through the apostolic picture of Christ. 2. A religious individualism is predominant, which finds its expression in a verbal view instead of objective mediation, and in so doing makes the ministry of the word the objective foundation of the communication of salvation. 3. Mention must be made of the principle of dispositional ethics, which has its foundation in personal human responsibility and its criterion in the conscience. 4. This ethics is to be termed world-affirming, in distinction from monastic asceticism on the one hand and sectarian understanding on the other. 5. Finally, a fundamentally different view of religious concepts like God, the world and humanity is to be noted as following from the whole approach.[331]

While Troeltsch finds influences from Luther which change the idea of the church, in the end the church remains 'the church'. The church of scripture and preachers takes the place of the church with a hierarchical structure and governed by sacramental thinking. Luther's distinction between the minister and the private person and the associated distinction between the morality of ministry and private morality has considerable significance for Troeltsch's critical interpretation of Luther. Here Troeltsch speaks of a twofold view of morality, which transfers this duality into the Decalogue and the law of Christ. According to Troeltsch, in resolving the contradiction between the demands on the Christian as a private person on the one hand and as the holder of an office on the other, Luther resorts to the idea of natural law: the principles and demands of natural law are applied to the conditions of the state of sin. Troeltsch sees an intrinsic contradiction here. What in Catholicism is made the principle of a move to a higher morality by the adoption of thinking in levels, remains a double morality and threatens to break apart the unity of the person.

This interpretation does not seem to me to apply to Luther himself. It differentiates human relationships in a specific context, and is about the different roles which the human person plays in different spheres. Luther does not strive for any separation but for a combination of different spheres in tension, a combination which includes the idea of conflict. Faith knows that the various orientations of the person are done away with in God himself in so far as God is creator of the world and its redeemer.[332]

The fundamental assessment of Luther's ethics ends up in the assumption that a 'prevenient holiness' is no longer related to the idea of the church, to priesthood and the sacraments, but to the prevenient word of the forgiveness of sins. Now the word – and this is decisive – is the 'supernatural producer' of the church.[333]

On the one hand Troeltsch can put relatively great emphasis on the new element in Protestantism, and on the other he can describe the nature of this new element as a refounding of the Christian unitary culture.[334] So for Troeltsch Protestantism is something which in principle is old and is simply based on changed presuppositions.[335]

Lutheranism arose from Luther's thought, and Reformation theology is a new entity of relative uniformity and one which can be defined historically (and is historically significant); for Troeltsch, as a social entity it largely represents a compulsive church culture. The theoretical distinction between secular and spiritual power can hardly gain any practical relevance, because the notion of the state church stands in the foreground.[336]

It emerges particularly clearly in the account of Lutheranism how Troeltsch draws lines down to the present and constantly has present circumstances in view. It can be seen that all in all he has become critical of the state and authority – from around the turn of the century.[337]

For him, the ideal of a Christian society is normative in the state ethic of Lutheranism. In the course of the development a home-made, even petty-bourgeois, feature emerges increasingly strongly, which stylizes the local ruler as the father of the Land and has an influence right down to the spheres of school and family.

The social ideal established by Luther and Lutheranism seems to have as a theological basis a conservative view of conditions in the world, professional life, the classes, because the prime issue is the freedom of the person and not any effect on the outward circumstances of life. The shaping of society is largely seen as a matter for the authorities, and it comes about in accordance with principles to be derived from reason, which are to be seen under the aspect of a religious and ethical modification in the face of conditions as they are. In principle, reference is made to the distinction between word and inwardness and to the allocation of secular things to reason. If there is no presupposition of a Christian authority, then in practice Lutheranism is of no more use as a principle for shaping society.

Calvinism and the capitalistic tendency of its business ethics. Two further historical forces which were influential are discussed alongside (mediaeval) Catholicism and Lutheranism – before the account ends with the eighteenth century:[338] Calvinism, and sect and mysticism within Protestantism. Lutheranism provides an appropriate background for Troeltsch's account of Calvinism, which he regards as the real main force in Protestantism.[339] By a comparison which ends up above all in a contrast, he achieves concentration and a vivid presentation. He is primarily concerned with essential characteristics, with an overall impression. The basic passivity of Lutheranism is contrasted with the activity and formative power of Calvinism. The power of church organization takes the place of a spiritualized idea of the church; the international significance and orientation of Calvinism is contrasted with the ecclesiastical narrowness in Lutheranism; the attention to economic factors in Calvinism stands in glaring contradiction to the wide-ranging exclusion of the world in Lutheranism.[340]

According to Troeltsch, the notion of asceticism is above all normative for the ethics of Calvinism, in the form of an 'inner-worldly' aceticism. While this is significant for Protestantism as a whole, it assumes a special form in Calvinism. In general, one can say that 'inner-worldly asceticism' means a religious and ethical permeation of the life of the world while at the same time preserving a distance between human beings and the world. Here, however, the differences between Calvinism and Lutheranism are significant: what is lacking in Lutheranism and marks out Calvinism is the planned way in which life is shaped, the understanding of a rationalization of life as an invitation to glorify God in the circumstances of the world. By comparison, the feeling of the world in Lutheranism is characterized more strongly by an acceptance of circumstances, by involvement in the course of the world.

All earthly gifts and possibilities of both a personal and a substantive kind are put in the context of the 'goal' of establishing the rule of Christ on earth. This conception appears in secularized form in the lands shaped by Calvinism, as an ideal of unselfish, unresting work, coupled with a sober aim for action generally and the sphere of business life in particular.

According to Troeltsch, Calvinism shares a basic sociological scheme with Catholicism and Lutheranism. All three presuppose or strive for a Christian culture and society. Thus Calvinism also has quite conservative features. It maintains human inequality and does not take any offence at the way in which people have such different positions in political and economic life. This inequality is explained theologically by God's will to rule, by his principle of election. The idea of human equality is therefore not rooted in Calvinism, but in Stoic natural law; it gains its influence on the modern world through the Baptist movements and the modern view of natural law.

A comparison of the democratic tendencies which are without doubt present in Calvinism and the democratic ideas of modernity leads Troeltsch to a qualified verdict. On the one hand the origin of the democratic idea is something else, and on the other, in Calvinism one can recognize a readiness to combine this idea with Christian notions. It is true of both Calvinism and the Baptist movement that 'they have prepared the way for modern democracy, and given it a spiritual backbone, rather than actually created it'.[341]

For Troeltsch, Calvinism had its strongest effect on modernity in secularized garb through its business ethic. It shaped the capitalist view of business and the business temperament and contributed to its origin. This is not to assume any causality, but a proximity, a religious and spiritual possibilty of contact. In this respect, Max Weber's investigation of capitalism and the history of its origins is fundamental.

Troeltsch refers back to Max Weber's theses on the connection between Protestant ethics and the spirit of capitalism. In Weber these are concentrated on the question of the rationality of work and business, after which he then focuses on the question of the modern world and rationality. Weber does not want to dispute the influence of economic factors on the rise of this rationality, but he himself takes a different course by investigating their spiritual origin. Within the forces which govern human beings, for Weber religious ties are of central importance. That leads him to ask whether and to what extent the capitalistic economic disposition was not encouraged and brought out by a particular religious attitude. Hence he assumes a connection between a capitalist business temperament and a specific form of asceticism which has its roots in Protestantism. The 'spirit of capitalism' is defined in Rickert's sense as conduct which attempts to grasp historical individuality and bind it together into a historical whole. The origin and meaning of this whole only emerges gradually through a consideration of individual features. The 'spirit' of capitalism is not the essence of a historical manifestation, but the disposition which is to be conjectured behind this phenomenon as its author. Weber is therefore not concerned to explain the capitalist economic system in terms of religious motives – Calvinistic ethics and a possibility of proving people before God which accords with this; rather, he is investigating the contribution of religious notions to the shaping of this spirit and, conversely, the effect of the capitalist spirit on the religious.

A closer definition of the relationship between Troeltsch and Weber in connection with the origin and understanding of the theses on capitalism would have to compare how belief in election, the interpretation of the sacraments, the 'demystification of the world', the role of professional work in connection with the principle of election, the estimation of good works in Calvinism and in Lutheranism and their effect on human conduct, along with Christian asceticism from the aspect of rational self-control, are understood by each of the scholars.

We should not allow ourselves to be deceived by what is striking or glaring, for example the adoption of a terminology (the church- and sect-types), into thinking that all in all the dialogical element predominated between Weber and Troeltsch and is to be counted a gain on both sides. At all events, Troeltsch was never petty about the originality of ideas, and was more concerned to make them fruitful. However, he was aroused out of the tranquillity of such thought and work by the controversy with Felix Rachfahl. Rachfahl's assumption that Weber and Troeltsch had produced a kind of collective work on the question of the confessional origin of the modern capitalist spirit insulted Troeltsch's scholarly honour.[342] He vigorously remarked that it was quite misleading for the two to be seen from Rachfahl's perspective as a joint academic firm in which each 'can be burdened with the real or supposed passivity of the other'.[343] And Weber pointed out that both he and Troeltsch had arrived at the same result by asking different questions.[344]

Sect-type and mysticism in Protestantism. In his account of sect and mysticism within Protestantism, Troeltsch benefits from his interest in people who are on the periphery, in theological exceptions and church outsiders. One even gets the impression that here he thinks that he has in some way to make good in the face of traditional theological historiography (leaving aside Gottfried Arnold and his history of heresies) an idea which accords with his marked sense of justice.

Despite his fundamental distinction between the two types, sect and mysticism, Troeltsch assumes that there are 'mixed forms' between them, so that he can assign a 'bundle of motives' to match a particular type.[345] That means two things. First, he is ready to understand the historical allocation to a type as falling short of a final definition, and secondly, the limits of his procedure become visible.

On the basis of the concentration on 'objective elements' (the church as an institution, truth understood in absolute dogmatic terms) which emerges increasingly strongly in official Protestantism, from a historical perspective it is understandable that the two other types and the motives prevailing in them should emerge: sect and mysticism are on the one hand complementary movements to the official form, but on the other hand they lead beyond themselves and display a form and doctrine of their own.

For Troeltsch, the character and significance of the sect-type on Protestant ground, apart from the other features which are specific to the type, lie in the decided links with the Bible. Here in particular mention should be made of the orientation on the Sermon on the Mount, where the ethical-radical element is dominant. The life of individual Christians, like that of particular groups, is thus increasingly put under the pressure of radical demands.[346]

The idea of the sanctification of life leads to a distancing both from the state and from existing church forms of community. The distinction between the suffering and the aggressive sects which is already anticipated by Troeltsch in his account of mediaeval sects is taken up again here.[347]

However, now the ideal of the suffering sects is neither possible nor asked for in the modern world, according to Troeltsch, in connection with either a historical analysis of the time or an assessment of its nature. The idea of suffering and the acceptance of suffering no longer has any power of attraction. What has a stronger influence is the radicalism and militancy of the sects in the form of a denial of and hostility to culture, coupled with an interest in transforming the situation in the contemporary world.

Troeltsch's account of the nature of sects extends from the Anabaptists in the time of Luther and their radicalization at the time of the English revolution through pietism to John Wesley and Methodism. What is constitutive and lasting for the sects is the principle of free will and a radical ethic; their relationship to the world and the church is variable.

The religious earnestness of the sects, the consistency of their reflection and action, deeply impressed Troeltsch. That does not prevent him at the same time from referring to the weaknesses and dangers that are in principle associated with the type. The form of suffering sects with their withdrawal, their encapsulation from the world, has no effect on history. The aggressive sects made their mark, but the price they paid was narrowness and a lack of culture.[348]

Whereas Catholicism was quite successful in receiving the sect motive by the founding of orders and associations – i.e. through simultaneous acceptance and separation – Protestantism found things much harder here. It had to put up with the sects as a particular form of community, and finally found room for their spirit in the form of pietistic thought and activity. Christian socialism, which for Troeltsch belongs in this connection, shows a leaning towards the sect-type, but because of its limited intention, existing circumstances act as a regulator.

The type to be mentioned alongside the sects on Protestant soil is also a tributary of the mainstream of church devlopment. This is mysticism or, as Troeltsch also calls it, spiritualism.

Here too it emerges that Troeltsch was not always sufficiently concerned to define terms accurately or to use the concepts which he had chosen consistently.

Often it is only the context which gives a clearer indication of the significance Troeltsch intended. So it is not clear in a specific instance whether mysticism and spiritualism are the same thing for Troeltsch, or whether he assumes differences. Sometimes he refers to 'mysticism and spiritualism' together; sometimes he talks of 'spiritualism' alone, so that one can assume that each term has a special meaning. Troeltsch was led, probably above all by criticism, to define and differentiate the mysticism type more closely in the manuscript notes for the second edition (on *GS* I, 878). He notes: 'Protestant mysticism and spiritualism a special form of the idea. Characteristic name spiritualism, which fits better. The personal-individual-auto-nomous and the cultless-notional are expressed better here.' Troeltsch's intention in the addition (two closely written pages) was on the one hand to define the type more accurately and on the other to look more closely at the historical phenomenon.

There is a line of historical continuity for mysticism, as there also is for the sect, on the basis of biblical motives, their ongoing influence in the time of the Reformation, and their continuation in more recent church history. In the sixteenth and seventeenth centuries spiritualism then found a way to its own religious and theological expression.

The difficulty of description arises from the fact that mysticism and the sect-type became associated in many ways or came close to each other, but nevertheless, as far as Troeltsch is concerned, have to be fundamentally distinguished. In principle, as a type, for Troeltsch mysticism is characterized above all by its pressure towards an immediacy and presence of religious experience. It has neither the cultural significance of the church nor the religious radicalism of the sect, but on the basis of its stress on religious inwardness and freedom it has been able to form a complex of tradition which has become very attractive to the modern educated world. According to Troeltsch, one can speak of mysticism as the 'secret religion' of the educated.[349]

For Troeltsch, the emergence of mysticism, the effectiveness of this type, presupposes that religion was already able to create an objective expression in cult and dogma, so that mysticism could develop over against these as a free and personal form of religion.[350]

The notion of a paradox, which Troeltsch takes up, refers to the indissoluble juxtaposition and opposition of immediacy and purpose. In my view the paradox of separation and unity would be more illuminating, a paradox which finds its philosophical expression in the encounter and interaction of becoming and being. The theological notion that mysticism pursues the goal of a unity with God is overlaid in Troeltsch with an approach in terms of the psychology of religion with references to the deliberate introduction of religious states of excitement, enthusiasm, hallucination and visions.[351] In Troeltsch's definition of mysticism, too little justice seems to have been done to the content of mysticism: inwardness and immediacy are not a sufficient description of mysticism, because it is concerned with a particular aim, that of the 'vision of God'.[352]

It is evident that Troeltsch has a double concept of mysticism: on the one hand a wide one, which is characterized by the immediacy and present character of religious experience, and on the other the narrower concept, which presupposes a criticism of the objectification of religious life and thus a reflectiveness and purposiveness in the process. In the narrower definition a specific interest is at work: part of the historical development is that in mysticism a criticism of the objectivity of the religious emerges in the form of doctrine and cult, and in connection with this an emphasis on the principle of subjectivity and a transition to modern structures of thought.

At all events, it is the case that a new form of religious life and thought emerged with mysticism, which is to be distinguished from official Protestantism but nevertheless had a marked influence on it. With this view of history, Troeltsch insists on a distinction between mysticism and the Baptist sects.[353]

Mysticism starts from the assumption of a divine spark in the soul; the Baptist movement attaches importance to the suddenness of the divine intervention in human life. Furthermore, on the basis of its enthusiasm, mysticism is freer and less regulated than the Baptist movement. Ethically, a radical orientation by the 'law of Christ' among the sects stands over against an idea of freedom with an antinomian orientation in spiritualism. This difference then emerges openly in the question of external order. Whereas community and the sacramental principle are determinative among the Baptists, spiritualism accentuates spiritual belonging and association.[354]

The theological characteristic of spiritualism is an individualism which differs from that of the sect as isolation through ethical strictness and opposition to the world. Particularly at the points where in spiritualism there is stress on the anti-dogmatic tendency and the aristocratic principle of belonging to a community mediated by the Spirit, in contrast to the mass organization of the church, Troeltsch is full of commitment and evidently in agreement with the tendency.[355]

He attaches special significance, where influence is concerned, to the proximity of the spiritualist tradition to rationalism. He sees here a link with the modern scientific principle. His reason is: 'Mysticism, which draws its nourishment from the immediate perception of the presence of God, is a process which is repeated everywhere and always in the same manner, and thus it comes into touch with the autonomy and universal validity of scientific thought. Each is assimilated to the other.'[356]

For Troeltsch, the acceptance of a mystical spiritualistic view by a modern consciousness lies in the renunciation of religious and theological exclusiveness in favour of a life in direct relationship to God which is possible everywhere, and is in principle the same.[357] However, its presuppositions are shaped by an objective link and effect which are to be assumed here. So Troeltsch also says of his own theology that it is 'certainly spiritualistic'.[358] He points out critically that both the question of the relationship of faith and history and that of the incorporation of the devout individual into the wider context represented by cult, rite and dogma present a problem or leave something to be desired. As a solution Troeltsch considers a synthesis in which the subjective and objective elements are combined and associated. The individualizing features of spiritualistic piety and incorporation into the pre-existing entity, the church, and thus also involvement in its cult and dogma, must be combined in such a way that one can conceive of a living permeation by the spirit of religious inwardness and openness of the greater whole and the fixed traditional forms.

Concluding reflections. For Troeltsch, all the insights which the investigation has brought to light belong with the changing situations and conditions of historical life. Nevertheless, he believes that attention must be paid to the question of an offer of orientation for the present which, while it cannot be called scientific in the strict sense, is not completely arbitrary either. Knowledge of an abiding ethical value has to be described. This description is based on 'selections from life in history which the living conviction and the active will fully apprehend in the certainty that here we perceive absolute Reason in the revelation that is addressed to us and formed in our present context'.[359]

Troeltsch sees such abiding ethical insights into value, as the content of Christian social ethics, in ideas of personality, in a specific form of socialism, in a basic moral view concerned with overcoming of social inequality, in the development of Christian charitable action and in the formulation of a central notion for future development.

He derives two lessons for the formation of Christian community life. First, cult and organization are indispensable for the transmission of and the possibility of describing Christian faith. Secondly, history shows the fundamental superiority of the church-type over the two other types; here the church-type at the same time represents a diminution of the Christian idea itself to the measure of the possible and what is required by the situation. Therefore the church needs change: an insight which would have to appropriate the advantages of the two other types and here has to learn from the character of Protestant Christianity and its history. Whereas Catholicism is the classical expression of the church-type because it is consistent, there are in Protestantism additional elements of subjectivity and inwardness, though as a result of this Protestantism needs state support and help. For the present situation, 'The days of the pure church-type in our culture are numbered. What the modern view of life takes for granted no longer coincides with what is taken for granted in the church.'[360]

So changes are unavoidable. They involve first the relationship between church and state, and then within the church the position of individual communities, and finally, from the perspective of the type, a mediation between the basic motives of the sect and mysticism and those of the church-type. Troeltsch is on the one hand convinced of the need for change, while on the other he sees a process at work here and rejects any use of external violence or pressure. The development presaged by the history of the Protestant church consists in a detachment from the ties to the state and a strengthening of the individual communities and their legal position.

It should be noted that one possible corrective function of the two other types over against the church-type is in the realm of theory. However, this is not without significance for the real stuation, for notions of reform. The interrelating of the motives from the individual types will ultimately bring into play the notion of a reconciliation which is of immediate significance for the situation of the church in the present and the future, in that it excludes radically confessional thought with its defensiveness against both other confessions and the modern world. What dogmatics was unable to achieve in the history of Christianity, namely to produce unity and thus reconciliation, must now, according to Troeltsch, be attempted in other ways. The church must be reformed from within; its equilibrium is not sufficient to achieve validity for itself in the present as well. But its framework can be made to serve other purposes. Troeltsch sees these other purposes as being a greater tolerance,

Ernst Troeltsch

the allowing of freedom of conscience, and thus a breadth and generosity brought about under the conditions of the established church, the Volkskirche. The concern must no longer be uniformity, but rather permission for a relative plurality of views and activities in an organism which takes over only remnants from the historical shape of the church and no longer concomitant forms in the shape of authoritative statements and a concern to impose itself.

It is remarkable that Troeltsch sees the notion of a unitary culture as something that both fascinates and repels the church. 'Unitary culture' in the Middle Ages, in contrast to modern times, meant not least the abolition of any splits in a greater whole which could support and be a norm for all individual manifestations. But at the same time 'unitary culture' is the compulsory culture of the church. According to Troeltsch, we must now put on a spiritual basis what at that time rested on a concern for external representation and power. The remains of the church can provide a buttress from the tradition, the 'historical substance of life', but must be open to change.[361] Whereas the insight into the problems in church politics and culture generally for the present and the future is oppressive, Troeltsch's notions of a solution do not always convey the impression of being sufficiently close to reality; they are not concrete and detailed enough to have any chance of being actually realized. For him, goals are sometimes also daydreams. At all events, it is clear where his 'liberal' heart beats: on the side of freedom of conscience and mobility in the church and thus a Volkskirche modified in the direction of greater openness and the free power of the spirit.

The same goes for Troeltsch's ideas in the sphere of Christian social philosophy and ethics. The two historical types which are relevant to social ethics, namely mediaeval Catholicism and ascetic Protestantism, are no longer acceptable. Their time is past: new solutions are not in sight. In clear parallel to Max Weber's talk of 'iron cages', which fatefully enclose modern people, Troeltsch speaks of the 'rock' of social reality against which all notions of reform, however well intended, will smash in vain.[362]

All in all, then, the result of Troeltsch's historical investigation, which constantly included the present situation, thought in terms of it and was directed towards it, was essentially negative. That is, unless one regards the insight into the problems of the present gained by historical knowledge as a positive result, which at least was also part of Troeltsch's intention. Awareness of the problem communicated in this way also includes an insight into the need for a new conception which has yet to be found, has not yet been thought of, and which relates the Christian heritage to the social-ethical needs of the present. Here Troeltsch can only make theoretical statements. These include above all the view that a recourse to the Bible cannot be enough, and that the history of Chrsitianity must also be included. Moreover, even a new conception, like all ideal constructions, will have to match up to reality.[363]

Right at the end, after both addressing the expectations of the future and bidding farewell to all ideas of absoluteness in respect of a Christian ethic which is always valid and timeless, the book contains a confession. This seeks to ignore all external factors and to point to the abiding ground of faith and hope, which is to be sought within human beings, the 'indwelling Kingdom of God'. However, this 'ground' does not make people passive, but provokes activity, and includes a relationship with God in the shaping of conditions in the world.[364]

The confessional conclusion has no connection with Troeltsch's academic reflections and thus draws attention to an aporia. For Troeltsch this aporia seems to be part of the content of his study. In the end people must be content with the recognition that there are limits to their scientific insights and that there is no alternative, at least where Christianity is concerned, to seizing the opportunity of belief in God and through it being given both forward impetus and rest and security.

It is also an open question how the acceptance of the future kingdom of God is related to its 'inwardness'. For Troeltsch the solution probably lies in the fact that the future kingdom of God as inalienable hope and ground of faith lies in the human heart itself, and thus cannot be threatened or attacked from outside. The certainty of the future becomes present in a faith which knows that the goal of history is at the same time both safe and hidden in God's being and activity. For Troeltsch, the tension both between the future and the presence of the kingdom of God and between the hiddenness of God and security in him is part of the matter itself. Thus tension is the expression, the form, of the only solution of the riddle of history possible for human beings.

Part Four: Philosopher of Culture in Berlin
(1915-1923)

I

Personal Situation and Contemporary History

1. The outbreak of the World War and Troeltsch's first political statements on the war

Troeltsch had already decided for Berlin when the First World War broke out, and the war made the idea of going to the capital of the Reich particularly significant and apposite for him. However, he spent the first months of the war in Heidelberg. It is hard to say whether he shared the (almost) universal enthusiasm for the war, even on the basis of speeches in 1914 which made him well-known to wide areas of the population. It is certain that the events which were heralded in July 1914 filled him with great anxiety. Thus he wrote to his old friend Bousset: 'However, the danger of war leads one to think of other things [than questions of a call and the theological situation]. God preserve us from a conflagration.'[1]

After the announcement of mobilization, Troeltsch gave a speech to the patriotic assembly convened by the city council of Heidelberg and the university. Troeltsch's address gives way to emotion and takes up propagandist slogans, like Slavonic wiles and French vindictiveness. In the face of these, rational political judgments take a back seat. The tone of appeal, the summoning up of a feeling of solidarity predominate, and there is also a political perspective in Troeltsch's remarks when he says: 'However, come what may, we are fighting for existence and life, and by not allowing Austria to be trampled underfoot we are fighting for ourselves, for freedom and human dignity.'[2]

We can also hear echoes of the anti-bourgeois, anti-intellectual perspective which understands the war as the outbreak of elemental forces, a perspective which could be found among some of the young students. Probably under the pressure of the commitment demanded of him by the situation, Troeltsch made statements which see merely verbal support for the cause of the Fatherland as inadequate: 'If only the person speaking at this hour could change every word into a bayonet, into a rifle, into a cannon! If only he could change it into a man who quietly and honourably, after the fashion of our people, joined up with the great hosts as though this were a matter of course! If only the human river could not rise high enough!'[3]

Walther Köhler thought that the strong point of this speech was that it did not simply stick to realities but deliberately raised its audience to a 'higher' plane.[4] This assessment certainly does justice to Troeltsch's intention, but the taking to a 'higher' plane relates to a transcending of all external forms of bravery in the direction of a brave disposition which is then capable of corresponding deeds. However, we can see that Troeltsch's speech contains a certain corrective to mere nationalistic solemnity, and especially all romanticism about the war, by referring to the seriousness of the situation and to the crises and emergencies which are to be expected.

Very much in keeping with the spirit of the time, Troeltsch refers to the German virtues of bravery, doing one's duty, simplicity and seriousness. At the end the speech takes up the religious perspective. There is no victory without faith. And faith, in Troeltsch's view, is at work at this time in many forms, from the philosophical-metaphysical to the Christian. The decisive factor is a shared orientation 'upwards', to the heights or to the ultimate, hidden ground of things. The speech concludes with a prayer which, Troeltsch believes, can say everything, whether in terms of religion or of bourgeois politics. 'It is the simple prayer of the Germans in time of need: "God save Germany, our Fatherland!" '[5] The public reaction was extraordinarily strong. While Troeltsch's rhetorical talent had always been recognized, now people realized and brought out his ability as a popular orator.

A little later, Troeltsch gave another major speech in Mannheim.[6] In it he defended militarism understood in the right way. In his view, as a result of its geographical situation and the political circumstances, Germany had to be a well-armed people, capable of defending itself. Rational political arguments followed from the analysis of the situation. However, Troeltsch overplayed his form of rational argumentation, and his attitude, presented as realism, is at the same time an ideal construction or turns into one. So his speech is a remarkable mixture of sober assessment and a theoretical edifice, which grows almost imperceptibly from the matter-of-fact assessment in which he speaks of the positive effect of military organization on civil life and above all on industry (railways, the mail, insurance).

Granted, it is evident that Troeltsch is averse to all crudely imperialistic ideas; nevertheless, nationalistic tones clearly ring through. And again a general religious aspect emerges. The political talk already has an undertone which invites a religious interpretation.

For Troeltsch, the notion that the religious depths of the soul and a sense of obligation must go together takes on central significance. Religion provides a deeper foundation, which goes beyond the bounds of ethics.

There is a more implicitly religious interpretation of the war in Troeltsch's ideas as a result of his recourse to the categories of experience, in the form of being thrown back on the ultimate questions of humanity and the nature of life.[7]

Troeltsch sees as one essential task, mainly to be achieved in a literary form, the appropriate presentation of the German standpoint in the cultural war which is developing. The cultural and ideological polemic against Germany which is emerging in enemy propaganda must be countered effectively. Here the political line advocated by Troeltsch presupposes an objective account along the lines of a history of ideas. The enlightenment gained from the power of political thought is to be exploited politically in order to give an account of the essence of the Geman spirit. Here his account is dominated by a combination of the principle of individuality and typification.

What Fichte said about the nature of the German spirit must be taken up and adapted to changed historical circumstances. Troeltsch does this by moving from the outside inwards in his train of thought and mentioning the following basic features of the German spirit: we are a monarchical, military, working people.[8]

The inner traits of the German essence, which can be seen as the source of order, meaning and depth of feeling, are to be found in a metaphysical-religious spirit: 'The Germans are metaphysicians and musers by nature, who strive to understand the world and things, human beings and destinies, from within, in terms of the spiritual inwardness of the universe.'[9]

For Troeltsch, all these individual characteristics are summed up in one last decisive expression, namely the German idea of freedom. It is a synthesis of individualism and the formation of community. The fundamental element is not a formal understanding, based on the idea of equality, but one in terms of content, which can conceive of both the great variety of personal expression and a 'totality' as a combination of the individual elements. Certainly this German idea of freedom can learn something from a 'Western' understanding. However, for Troeltsch, all meaningful and convincing changes in political life must come from the power of the Germans' own being. So all individual political questions, above those associated with reform, are connected with the 'expression of being' of the national spirit. And according to Troeltsch, this gives grounds for hope. The spirit which descends into the depths of a basic cosmic feeling of a metaphysical kind is at the same time capable of scaling the heights and thus finding objectivity and political toleration.[10]

Troeltsch's view that the political and ideological effect of the war on peace is that it can and must lead to a process in which the German essence purges itself is a consistent expression of these reflections. All constructive and critical notions are first of all directed towards his own nation, and anything beyond that, for example going in the direction of features common to Europe, appears only at the periphery.[11]

Troeltsch's notion of a historical tradition which applies to all European peoples is not easy to follow, since at the same time he stresses the various national characteristics. He evidently wants both to emphasize the common historical tradition of Europe and to maintain the special character of the German spirit, the German idea of freedom.[12]

Already in the Heidelberg period Troeltsch found the beginnings of a different attitude from the view which is evident in his very first remarks. In this connection reference might be made to his article on 'The War of the Nations and Christianity'.[13]

Here Troeltsch dissociates himself both from purely nationalistic questions and from a utopian view, directed towards the future, which skips over ethical questions. Both have their weaknesses in an understanding of the ethics of the state, either glorifying the state or seeing it in functional terms. Troeltsch thinks that a morality which starts from the idea of the state and relates to it is desirable: but he qualifies this to the degree that he assumes that it leads higher, to a more developed form which is to be found in Christianity. This higher Christian form is independent, and at the same time offers specific points of contact for state ethics. Here Troeltsch follows the line of the idea which he expressed in his 1904 article on 'Political Ethics and Christianity'.

The form of an aesthetic culture emerging alongside Christianity is politically inactive, and by comparison fades into the background. Troeltsch locates the tension between a religious interpretation of the national as an individualization of the divine reason and the Christian notion of the personal bond with God in the divine life itself. Here he is being consistent with his philosophy of religion, according to which a relationship of tension is assumed in the divine life which in human existence is spread over different levels and degrees of realization. Troeltsch does not give either an intellectual or a dogmatic answer to the question of the unity of the 'national' and the 'Christian' gospel which causes people great difficulties at a time of war between the nations; rather, his answer is metaphysical. This does not completely dispel doubts about the possibility of bringing these two gospels together, but for him these doubts have lost their urgency and acuteness because they are transcended and done away with in God himself.

2. Private life and university work

The move to Berlin followed at Easter 1915. There were considerable difficulties, and Troeltsch gave a vivid account of them to his sisters.[14] Certainly things were not simple. The effects of the war were evident everywhere. But at the same time there is clear evidence of the demands of a professor's household which were almost taken for granted and still seemed reasonable despite the events of the time. A cook, nursemaid and cleaning woman supported the housewife in a well-run household. It is also evident that this expenditure on staff caused problems, and there was no guarantee that the daily routine would run without a hitch.

The Troeltschs found somewhere to live in Charlottenberg, by the Reichs-kanzlerplatz. This was one of the better neighbourhoods of Berlin, though not comparable with Zehlendorf or Grunewald and a far cry from the fine old house in Heidelberg and its idyllic situation. Troeltsch himself seems to have

Reichskanzlerplatz (now Theodor-Heuss-Platz) in Berlin-Charlottenburg. The Troeltsch family lived in the house on the right-hand side of the picture.

been most content with the new circumstances. His pragmatic sense made
the move easier for him; in addition there was the attraction of novelty, both
in the university, and in politics and culture. Troeltsch's insatiable need to get
to grips with reality, to be able to take decisions with all the facts at his
fingertips, seemed to be satisfied in the fact that he was living in the city where
important decisions were taken, where one of the power centres of the
contemporary world was to be found.

If the situation and surroundings were not to be compared with Heidelberg,
Troeltsch did begin to create a substitute and believed that he could even see
some improvements. 'In the meantime a glorious spring has come. The
immediate surroundings are very attractive; baby goes into the wood every day
and plays in the sand. I go to visit gardens and fruit trees which are now in
splendid bloom, and on Sunday afternoon I go to the Havel, which is about
three-quarters of an hour away. That is really beautiful and one can feel
somewhat compensated for Heidelberg. One thing is better here: the air. It is
beyond question stronger and healthier. But of course I miss the house and
garden very much. Now that's behind me, and such a thing will not happen
again.'[15]

Troeltsch began his lectures in the summer semester. The newspapers
reported the first lecture. 'Yesterday the distinguished philosopher gave his
inaugural lecture. The packed Auditorium Maximum welcomed the new
Ordinarius and indicated the great delight which is felt about him here.'[16]
Troeltsch lectured on 'The Philosophy of Culture and Ethics'. By way of
acknowledgment and indeed admiration the newspaper report commented:
'He began to treat the extraordinarily extensive material with an attractive
verve...'[17]

Marta Troeltsch was also there. The move to something greater and more
significant than Heidelberg, the greater impact he could make on the outside
world, seem to have impressed Troeltsch and spurred him on.

The report on the first lecture shows that Troeltsch's remark 'I came to
Berlin to overcome the anarchy of values'[18] must not be taken in isolation.
Here Troeltsch is quoting Dilthey, and he indicates that he is not thinking of
following the course of either Dilthey (anarchy of values) or Weber (polytheism
of values) but wants to take up the value question in his own way, namely by
means of a religious/metaphysical value-decision aimed at a cultural synthesis.

The thought of being able to work at the centre of German intellectual life
and also to make more of a political impact made the change easier for
Troeltsch, and enabled him to put up with some injustice. For otherwise the
external situation left much to be desired. First generally, given the nature of
big city life, and then because of the war. Everything was impersonal, was dear
and scarce, and the renown of professors in Berlin did not match what
Troeltsch had been used to in Heidelberg.

The external interferences to life lost significance and importance in the
face of the war. Everything was overshadowed by the war, even the joys of life;

the war was permanently present, and dominated mind and senses. In a letter to his sisters Troeltsch speaks very personally and directly, giving eloquent expression to his fears and his longing for peace.[19] What still remains and he feels able to refer to is a bravery of heart or disposition. 'Bravery is everything, and today there are countless wounded hearts. They must all overcome, and we all have the better part of our life behind us.'[20]

His son Eberhard seems to have been a particular joy to him, and he kept a very close eye on his development. 'The boy is a real ray of sunshine and is doing splendidly. He is also very good, except for the inevitable spoiling.'[21]

Troeltsch's whole hope was fixed on an outcome of the war which would be tolerable for Germany. He seems to have been bolstering up his courage when he said: 'It is no use tormenting oneself; no one knows anything, not even the governments. They are quite unclear about things. One must be patient and trust that a people with so many good qualities cannot go under, despite all the fools and braggarts who speak in public.'[22]

However, we also find the inevitable references to his wife's state of health, occasionally with the indication that things are better again and that 'she takes care of her household duties admirably'.[23] There is certainly also a more or less veiled criticism here, which goes to makes this apologetic tone understandable. A request to his sisters in Augsburg shows how difficult the food situation had become in the meantime: 'If you could send us a basket of vegetables express, that would be very good.'[24] Despite the war, in some respects an outward show of normal life could be kept up. Thus Troeltsch repeatedly spent the summer holidays in Warnemünde, near his wife's family home in Mecklenburg. In Warnemünde he also met Getrud von le Fort. A photograph shows Troeltsch with his wife and son in wicker chairs, with Gertrud von le Fort sitting on the sand in front of them.

Troeltsch's links with the family and his concern about how members of the family are getting on are often evident, when he supports his brothers and sisters with advice and help, and repeatedly gives them some financial aid.

Troeltsch owed some of the social life which was beginning for him in Berlin to his time in Heidelberg. Thus mention is often made of the Kaisers,[25] and above all relations with Gertrud von le Fort became increasingly friendly. At the beginning of the war she had gone with her mother and a sister to Mecklenburg, where the family had the Boek estate by the Müritzsee. From there she travelled regularly to Berlin, either to study or for visits. Gertrud von le Fort kept up contact with Troeltsch both by letter and personally. In her sympathetic way she was very oppressed by the unimaginably bad food supply in the capital, where in the restaurants there was only 'turnip soup, turnip schnitzel and turnip pudding'.[26] These impressions were certainly one of her reasons for keeping in touch with the Troeltsch family. Troeltsch can report the happy arrival of a 'splendid parcel of smoked goose'[27] or can gratefully report to Boek the arrival of other nourishment. He attempted as far as possible to do something in return, for example by sending his most recent works. He knew that this help was not to be taken for granted, and he treasured above all the way in which such presents were offered him. 'Furthermore, I would now like to thank you from all of us, with all our hearts, for all your valuable help and the personal kindness which adds extra splendour to this help and so delights us.'[28]

In 1916, Troeltsch visited the von le Forts' estate for a few days and there showed his cheerful and charming side. One can also conjecture that he might perhaps also have sought deliberately to play down the outwardly dreadful situation. Gertrud von le Fort writes in her memoirs: 'A further delight for me was to be able to welcome Ernst Troeltsch in Boek as well. Those were hours of cheerful company in the midst of such oppressive days. Troeltsch had the gift of being infinitely droll, and at that time he told us one funny story after another.'[29]

The chapter 'Cheerfulness and Relaxation' also contains a letter to Getrud von le Fort, written by Frau Marie Kaiser and Troeltsch, which is full of charm and wit in its discreet allusion to Gertrud von le Fort's veneration for Troeltsch. It runs: 'Dearest Baroness, having leaped out of your automobile, the farewell greeting still in my eyes and my hand, I rushed home, and there I found – Troeltsch. I can't help laughing at you for your lack of feeling in not noticing anything about the Reichskanzlerplatz, when the spiritual sun has already been shining on it for twenty-four hours. So that you believe me, here is the signature of the key witness.' Troeltsch joins in and writes: 'It is indeed possible that I was still in Heidelberg in the spirit and consequently could not enliven the Reichskanzlerplatz and its gable-ends sufficiently. Anyway, I am sorry that I did not find it enlivened by you, which would certainly have done it good.'[30]

One form of social life which was rather like the Eranos circle in Heidelberg was the Gräca, a private circle for the cultivation of the Greek spirit – to give a rough description – into which Troeltsch was accepted. Troeltsch, who evidently became a member of the circle as early as the summer of 1915, described its aims and atmosphere to Friedrich Meinecke, whom he wanted to get as a further member: 'The sessions take place once a month (during the semester): at the moment we are reading Aeschylus, and his *Oresteia* will occupy us this winter. When the reading is finished we have a simple supper. We meet on Fridays, usually at the beginning of the month.'[31]

In composition and aims, the circle will have fallen well short of the Eranos group. But what Troeltsch particularly liked was the cheerful familiar tone, which made him soon feel at home. Moreover, he saw it as a positive feature that special effort and preparation was not required, since the main burden of interpretation fell on the philologists.[32]

Troeltsch's personal relationship with Friedrich Meinecke went beyond the evenings they spent together in the Gräca. They arranged to take walks together – which I shall describe in due course – had similar academic and political views, and evidently also got on well personally. Meinecke, who had come from Freiburg in 1914 to Berlin, where he had been reunited with his old friend, the historian Otto Hintze, writes: 'Once Otto Krauske, who was now... ordinarius in Königsberg... had been the third in our alliance, and indeed was really the leader. Now a stronger than he had come to Berlin who soon made a new triumvirate with us, not so personal but deeper in spirit – this was Ernst Troeltsch. He left his chair of theology in Heidelberg at Easter 1915 and became *the* philosopher of history in the Berlin philosophical faculty. Within Hintze's and my generation of scholars, he and his Heidelberg friend Max Weber were by far the most striking and universal, the ones who moved their contemporaries the most.'[33] In scholarship, Meinecke assumed a mutual influence, but all in all he described Troeltsch as being the more universal of the two of them and conceded that he had probably learned more from Troeltsch than vice versa. Like others, Meinecke also praised the intellectual effort which was evident in Troeltsch's struggle to achieve an overall cultural picture. However, he then continued critically: 'He often said that one must not stop at mere contemplation and that this had to be translated into creative and constructive cultural work – but his own gifts did not lie in the practical sphere but in shaking people up to venture on new ways.'[34]

In Berlin, Troeltsch seems to have remained true to his custom of having little contact with his colleagues and taking his intellectual bearings more widely. And this seems to have been the case with both his professional theological colleagues and the philosophers. One exception here was Adolf von Harnack, of whom Troeltsch had a very high opinion because of his scholarly achievements, and with whom he largely agreed on political questions. However, it is doubtful whether the personal contact was very close. The difference in age played a part here; in addition there was also some detached respect, quite apart from the fact that Harnack was more the type of the classical university professor, and saw himself and acted wholly as a scholar, whereas Troeltsch was always something more and something else. Troeltsch was more inclined than Harnack to leave the purely academic world and his scholarly status behind him.[35]

During the war, with its burdens both internal and external, drawn to and fro between budding hope and deep depression, Troeltsch seems more than usual to have found support and rest in his academic work. Thus after travelling or oppressive events in the outside world he constantly writes that he is glad to be able to get back to work, to the world of the spirit, which for him was a counterbalance to the barbarism of the war, to all the forces of destruction and degradation.

Here we should think not only of his work at his desk but also of his tasks in the university. If we are to be able to evaluate Troeltsch's position, his significance and his possibilities properly here, something must be said about the faculty and his colleagues.

The Berlin philosophical seminar was etablished in 1909 with the call of Benno Erdmanns to a chair in philosophy, and he is said to have organized it in an exemplary way.[36] Further directors of the seminar were Alois Riehl and Carl Stumpf.[37] If we reflect on the composition of the staff of the philosophy faculty it can soon be seen that with his capabilities and his interests Troeltsch must have been a remarkable addition. Furthermore, his generous approach to questions of organization and hierarchy will certainly have had a positive influence. In his memoirs Max Dessoir,[38] who like Erdmann and Stumpf was interested in psychological research and therefore a rival, reported difficulties within the faculty when it came to his nomination as ordinarius. He wrote: 'My relations with Ernst Troeltsch were free of such burdens. What a capacity for work, what a wealth of knowledge, what a stormy tempo he had! If one were talking with him, he would pace around with short, restless steps, wearing his crumpled trousers, a "many-sided" wanderer, always inclined to laugh loudly, ready to listen and of great intellectual charm.'[39]

The first lecture course offered by Troeltsch in the summer semester of 1915 on the philosophy of culture and ethics was of programmatic significance both for his university work and for his subsequent literary work. It took up a theme that was discussed in the studies of historicism and was addressed in the lectures intended for England. The theme recurs repeatedly in Troeltsch's lecture programme.

What form did it go on to take? The focal points of Troeltsch's lectures were the philosophy of culture and ethics, the philosophy of religion, and the philosophy of history; he also lectured on topics relating to the philosophy of history.[40] In his teaching Troeltsch clearly went back to lecture material which he had worked out in Heidelberg and discussed new themes to the degree that they fitted into his literary plans.

There were a striking number of women among the students at this time. This was mainly because of the war, but it was also a sign of increasing emancipation.[41] Troeltsch's direct use particularly of seminars for his literary work was noted critically by others. Thus Max Dessoir wrote: 'He was not very bothered about his students; the seminars served to prepare his own books.'[42] What attracted the students to Troeltsch's work was that his own unfinished preoccupation with philosophical questions was evident. Ludwig Marcuse described Troeltsch's unorthodox, spontaneous approach like this (perhaps with some exaggeration): 'He was a brilliant speaker, full of sympathies and antipathies even in the seminars from which his work on *Historicism and its Problems* emerged. He began the reading of a book enthusiastically, by the second chapter he threw it into a corner with a curse, and in the end we read an enthusiastic critique.'[43]

Troeltsch set little store by academic conventions, was flexible and ready for an exchange of ideas, while at the same time holding firm to convictions which he then showed clearly and defended outside as well. His Berlin pupils emphasized his free, generous procedure in academic examinations. Thus Gerhard Lehmann, who worked with Troeltsch on 'The Constants of Individuality', described his oral examination like this: 'I had visited him at home before, but had not been to his seminar – which he did not hold against me or require. He and Spranger examined me (*magna cum laude*). The difference was like that between day and night. Troeltsch asked me quite personally about what I had read; Spranger's questions gave me a headache. Only later did I enjoy him lecturing, where he spoke extempore and kept mopping at his sweat, pacing around like a lion. When I asked him at home which of his works I should read, he said that they were very scattered and difficult to find.'[44]

Troeltsch's conduct in connection with two appointments involving problems over both individuals and substantive issues are of interest in connection with university politics. These were the calls of Werner Sombart (1863-1941)[45] and Max Scheler (1874-1928).[46]

Despite all his detailed criticism, especially of Sombart, in the context of Sombart's studies of capitalism, Troeltsch's overall view was positive and extraordinarily candid where his own knowledge was concerned: 'The account is enlightening at important points. Much that I suspected and conjectured now has a shape and features, and there are reasons for it.'[47]

Troeltsch concedes that he does not find Sombart's character anything special. Then he continues: 'But I have a deep need for justice. And that tells me irrefutably that this is a major achievement. The whole outline, the definition of modern capitalism in relation to any other as distinctive and modern, the whole individualizing formation of concepts in the sphere of economic theory in contrast to the former identifications of anything economic as earning a living, etc., these are great, significant and rare insights.'[48] Troeltsch argued that Sombart should be put on the list of candidates. He was subsequently appointed to the chair of national economics at the University of Berlin in 1917.

Things were more difficult with Max Scheler, above all at a personal level. When the question arose of appointing Scheler to a chair in Berlin or Bonn, Troeltsch was asked by C.H.Becker for his view. He wrote: 'Scheler is one of the best philosophical talents and one of the most independent minds. That is beyond question. What is open to question is his personal and academic integrity and reliability... I personally have always regarded him with respect and caution. As for his chances in Berlin in particular, Erdmann, Riehl and Meinecke are resolute opponents. I assume that very few of the faculty would support him. I personally would support him with reservations, but it would be with reservations.'[49]

These personal reservations were connected with the bitter conflicts involving Scheler and going on around him, not only in Munich but also in Jena and Göttingen. However, Troeltsch did not feel in a position to refuse Scheler a chair on the basis of a fair assessment of his achievements in philosophy.[50]

Life in the philosophical faculty was quite different from what Troeltsch had grown accustomed to in Heidelberg and in theology. By tradition, the enormous faculty, comprising more than eighty members, met each Thursday evening. There were not enough chairs, and so people stood chatting in the corners; the proposals of the Promotion committee were usually accepted without a long discussion. And these proceedings made hardly any impression on the flow of talk from the small debating clubs standing in the corners. 'It was like a Polish parliament in the old days, or like a stock exchange. But people got to know one another through it.'⁵¹ When Meinecke, who was called to Berlin in 1914, wanted to sound out the historian Max Lenz over the situation in faculty politics, Lenz told him: 'The Göttingen clique dominates the faculty.'⁵² He was referring to colleagues who had come from Göttingen, like the philologist Wilamowitz, the Germanist Gustav Roethe and the Indologist Heinrich Lüders. Meinecke saw scholars with a considerable reputation and great capabilities in this 'clique', but felt repelled by their hybris and their pretentiousness. With Hintze and Troeltsch he watched the goings-on at a distance and stirred things up a bit, but on the whole felt that there were far more important things to do and watch in the war than faculty business.⁵³

Apart from his speeches on the war, Troeltsch made some major public speeches in the university and the city, for example on the Kaiser's birthday in 1916, when he spoke on 'The Criteria for Judging History' or the lecture he gave on 'Humanism and Nationalism in our Educational System'.⁵⁴.

Troeltsch's involvement in the 'Pedagogical Conference' which was held at the Ministry for Clergy Affairs and Education in May 1917 belongs in this connection.⁵⁵ He argued for seeing pedagogics as a theoretical science. It was not to be half science and half praxis, as it had been in the past. This programme was to be developed on the basis of the 'philosophy of history and culture or ethics developed from and based in philosophy...'⁵⁶ On this basis, pedagogics had to develop as a science for the whole of schooling. In practical matters like the establishment of academic chairs and scholarly organizations Troeltsch was uncertain, and thought there were different possible approaches. For him the development of the discipline depended above all on having the right people.

The many demands made on Troeltsch by the university, academic work and politics are obvious, and consequently he had to seek ways to counterbalance them and relax. In comparison to Heidelberg there were few possibilities. Social activities declined or were tailored directly to political ends, and there was no longer any question of swimming in the Neckar baths, as he used to. What he could still do was travel, and he did travel and enjoyed it. Here the sea and the mountains were his main destinations. Keeping in touch with Heidelberg also played a major part in his plans. Already in summer 1915 Troeltsch spent some days in Heidelberg on the way to a holiday in the mountains. He stayed with Carl Neumann and went to see Hans von Schubert. At the beginning of 1917 he had a longer stay in Heidelberg. His reaction makes it clear how strong the link with the city and his old friends there still was. Thus he wrote to Gertrud von le Fort: 'In the meantime I have spent two weeks in Heidelberg, and while I could not enjoy the spring there, I did enjoy peace and friendship, to return with new strength to work which gets incrasingly difficult.'[57]

In 1917 Troeltsch made a journey of a special kind with Friedrich Meinecke and some other professors to Tournai in northern France, on so-called army classes. In the end, however, these produced more entertainment and chat than serious academic work. The aim of this activity seems to have been to apply scholarship and minds to war purposes.[58]

3. Troeltsch's political attitude in the war

Troeltsch's political commitment to the intellectual and cultural legitimation of the German cause, which was already evident in the Heidelberg period, continued in Berlin and indeed intensified. With its atmosphere and its varied private and official contacts with diplomats, economic leaders and civil servants, the capital provided better possibilities than Heidelberg for gaining information and intensified his political interest.[59]

The 'Dahlem walk' was characteristic of a more private opportunity for meeting and conversation. Troeltsch would meet the historians Meinecke and Hintze and the economist Herkner every other Sunday afternooon in Dahlem for a walk to which others were usually invited: it became a kind of excursion with a political purpose, namely the exchange of views and information.[60] In addition Troeltsch belonged to the 'Deutsche Gesellschaft 1914'. This was a political club with evening lectures and discussions, at which members of Berlin's 'leading circles' gathered.[61] There was also the 'Mittwochabend', directed by Hans Delbrück; this, too, was a political club, meeting on Wednesday evenings, and bringing together university professors, deputies, industrialists and senior government officials.[62] Mention should also be made of a group of so-called moderates who met in the Agitationsbüro Hobohm – named after one of Delbrück's pupils.[63]

In his first statements, Troeltsch continued the line he had already taken in Heidelberg with his version of the 'culture war'. This is evident from a lecture given on this topic a few months after he arrived in Berlin.[64] To put it simply, Troeltsch's view was: apologetics abroad, above all aimed at neutral countries, and propaganda at home.[65]

In July 1915 Troeltsch was then among the signatories to a petition to the Reich Chancellor which opposed the annexationist demands made by some associations (the German Farmers Federation and the Industrial Federation) and intellectuals (in the so-called Seeberg Address).[66] The aims expressed in the statements of the Pan-Germans and the groups close to them covered a broad spectrum, extending from calls for a wider colonial empire, through annexations in the eastern part of Europe, to demands for territory or the granting of a sphere of influence in the West. The repudiation of such ambitions came about above all from an initiative of Harnack and Wolff.[67]

The Mittwochabend group already mentioned provided support and a background for discussion. It is not that there were no annexationist ideas in this group. Rather, those who signed the counter-declaration wanted exaggerated political claims to be rejected. They sought moderation, not least for tactical considerations, not a total anti-imperialistic renunciation. The central point of their argument was that the significance of nationalistic thought for Prussian-German history would be rejected if Germany now turned against the national statehood of other peoples. The formulation adopted in the text, that in a peace Germany's legitimate economic and political interests and German strategic needs would have to be satisfied, was open to interpretation in the direction of later 'moderate' claims. All in all, this was a political line with which Troeltsch could agree. In principle it coincided with his critical detachment from the ideas of the Prussian conservatives and confirmed his aversion to political and ideological radicalism, which at this time also extended to political demands. A letter written by Troeltsch while he was still in Heidelberg (in February 1915) to G.Traub (1869-1956) helps us to see some of the individual features of his line. In it Troeltsch argues that Germany had so far come out well as a military power, but then he continues: 'However, I hardly think it conceivable that we can really force our enemy to his knees.'[68] This assessment of Germany's military strength suggests to him an attitude of moderation over war aims. In his view, major annexations do not seem possible. What do seem conceivable, however, are 'alliances of central European states, at any rate a protectorate in Belgium, and improved frontiers where that is necessary. Also preservation of the fleet, the freedom of the seas and a colonial empire in Central Africa. That seems to me the most that can be expected. But that is not imperialism if one sees it more as the merely natural development of the power of the home state...'[69]

The conversation noted by Theodor Wolff, in which there was a discussion of the content of the counter-petition, largely corresponds to the Traub letter in portraying Troeltsch as the representative of a moderate line which merely makes certain demands westwards, concerning Belgium and France, on the basis of the German interest in security.

Troeltsch proves to be a mediating thinker, who advises moderation abroad and also over the situation in Germany. While he thinks political reforms in Germany necessary, ideologically they must take into account the special features of German history. What he is thinking about above all here is the German idea of freedom as an expression of the transcending of individual rights to freedom in favour of a principle of community. In the interest of rejecting all attempts to copy Western European political ideas in the form of freedom and equality, Troeltsch can even defend particular features of the authoritarian state and the division of society into classes, and allow them some justification.

Consistently – in connection with practical politics – this orientation on history means above all that political changes cannot come about without consideration of historical developments, and they need time. So for Troeltsch there is a degree of contemporaneity in the affirmation of democratic ideals and an ongoing persistence with the *status quo*. For him this attitude is legitimate and, above all, realistic.

According to Troeltsch, any political renewal must take into account the conditions and the possibilities emerging in the situation. This applies first to the war situation and then to the development of Germany into an industrial state. 'Relative' haste is needed as far as the war is concerned; the change to an industrial state means that in the long run Germany cannot rule out a development which takes the the mass of the people into account to a much greater degree in politics and constitution.

To this twofold aspect is added a basic perspective: politically and historically the powers rooted in the German nature and German history must be taken up and developed further. So while there must be change, it must not be abrupt change, a break with the past. This complex of notions, which has in view both the history of ideas and economic factors, the present situation and future possibilities, explains Troeltsch's critical reserve towards the Western European understanding of freedom and democracy.

In this connection it is remarkable how Troeltsch's criticism of Russia is different from that of the Western nations. If in the latter case a positive element can also be recognized in spite of all the criticism, an element which deserves notice and which must be analysed with a view towards possibilities of creating ties, his attitude towards Russia is almost exclusively negative. Troeltsch is polemical against any Russian idea of world rule and sees a possible Russification as a threat and danger.

These ideas of Troeltsch's find specific expression – and also support – in connection with power politics and political ideas in the notion of the formation of a central European block. Here Troeltsch takes the same line as Friedrich Naumann, who had been putting forward similar ideas since 1915.

Naumann's idea of Central Europe was based on a narrow political and economic collaboration, indeed a growing together, of Germany and Austria-Hungary. This was a process in which further states could be involved, like Rumania, Bulgaria, Italy and even, ideally and in the future, France. But Germany and Austria-Hungary would form the nucleus. In Naumann's notion their land in the middle of Europe would have to be thought of 'as a unity, as a land of brothers with many members, as a defensive alliance, as an economic sphere!'.[70]

A federal system was to protect Central Europe from the greater powers – here the thought was primarily of Russia, but also of England. Naumann's defensive notion was thus brought into the foreground, and here Troeltsch followed him. He rejected, or declared impossible, a manifest, real German imperialism because of the geographical situation and the size of the population. However, it must be said that Troeltsch was also led to see the idea of German imperialism in an increasingly critical light by the military situation.

Whereas in January 1915 he had termed 'anti-imperialistic' the view that after a peace treaty it was 'impossible that Germany's position in the world could be essentially changed',[71] a year later (in May 1916) his notions were far more cautious and qualified, and he regarded imperialism in a different way. In his earlier remarks, going beyond military and economic notions, Troeltsch had spoken of an imperialism of the idea or of culture, a notion which was at least open to misunderstanding, but which fitted the concept of the culture war and the German idea of freedom. He rejected this 'imperialism of the idea' in connection with a possible world-wide validity of German culture, and applied it to the tasks falling to each individual people in forming and changing themselves. During the course of 1916, he gave up the view of a limited imperialism thought to be compatible with this view of tasks, an imperialism in the form of economic and colonial claims and a safeguarding of frontiers in connection with the self-assertion of the German spirit.

The question of precisely when Troeltsch arrived at a different view in both foreign policy and domestic policy, and thus about both war aims and ideas for reform, a question which is significant for both his biography and his thought, is a complicated one. Right at the beginning of the war Troeltsch adopted a position beyond the extremes of radical nationalism or a pacifist ethical condemnation of the war. This central position, in which judgments were made especially from cultural and ideological perspectives, and detailed questions were pushed into the background, offered the starting point for a more moderate attitude which emerged during 1915 and then made itself felt increasingly from 1916 on.[72]

The changes can be seen in both the form and intent of his articles and speeches. Not only do his statements become more sober and factual, not only do they emphasize more firmly that the German idea of freedom merely has its own rights, but they are also shaped more markedly by the notion of defence and have a clear anti-imperialistic focus in connection with Germany's political and cultural claims, so that they push the idea of annexations, even in the present remaining instances, increasingly into the background. The changes in the tone and the content of the argument can be seen clearly in the article on 'The German Idea of Freedom' (1916). Here Troeltsch takes up the critical questions from the West about the German idea of freedom. He concedes that the criticism is partly right, and at the same time indicates the need to find the way to a distinctive form of creating ideas. A tendency towards self-criticism is evident from Troeltsch's concession that there are ideological political tensions; however, against this background he calls for a central authority, the monarchy, to be maintained.[73]

The line of political toleration which Troeltsch generally strives for is expressed in the way in which he concedes to the Western nations their political notions and their democratic idea of freedom. However, Troeltsch's distanced reference to the Western idea of freedom shows how critical of democracy his thought is at this time. In his view, democracy is not viable as a rational dogma. If anything were to threaten the German idea of freedom, it would be 'the adoption of a democracy which only requires free opportunities for business and fuels its idealism exclusively with universal equality, which in truth would be universal mediocrity and shallowness and about which the more subtle spirits are complaining even there'.[74]

For Troeltsch, the advantage of the understanding of autonomy in the German form of freedom is that the German conception does not have the material social interests and the ties of convention and public opinion characteristic of the American one. In his view, greater freedom can be found in Germany in the form of intellectual mobility and productivity. Of course in view of the political dimension of the question that is an evasion at the cultural and intellectual level. Moreover, this argument does not fit well with the phenomenon of a German spirit of subservience, which is criticized elsewhere.

Troeltsch's ideas are permeated by a political apologetic aim. This is also confirmed by his retrospective view of 'the ideas of 1914'. In contrast to the ideas from the time of the German revolt against Napoleon, these are not arrived at from rational principles, from ties to a moral world order, but derive from the depth of immediate experience. Troeltsch mentions four forms of experience which are rooted in the ideal, namely 1. the experience of the spirit or the spiritual; 2. the discovery of the people as a unitary entity; 3. the constitution of Germany as a cohesive trading state; and finally 4. the experience of the intellectual isolation of Germany and the fact of being thrown back on the German idea of freedom. A precise analysis shows that Troeltsch is on the one hand following the lines of his previous thought but on the other is introducing new emphases and that he is formulating some things more cautiously. Thus there is a critical comment that the effectiveness of the German idea of freedom has been hindered by a view and division of society in terms of classes. Something similar is said about state institutions: 'We still often lack the idealistic, spiritual view of a totality transcending the individual and the participation of the individual in bringing it forth. We still often move in the false alternatives of the mediaeval standpoint of domination and French equality, the trusting reverence of officials and liberal stateless-ness.'[75]

Politically, the question arises for the future as to whether the German idea of freedom, which envisages the incorporation of the individual into community life, can make plausible a system which indicates the rights and duties of members of society in a gradated way. What is the relationship between the sacrifice out of duty, rooted in the idea of freedom, and the coming of age of the individual in the form of the right to join in and criticize? Troeltsch sees the free decision of the individual in the face of the demands of community life as an expression of coming of age. On the other hand, the sacrifice of the individual to society out of a sense of duty does not exclude the possibility of criticism.

Perhaps it is because of the tense political and military situation that

Troeltsch argues in a one-sided way. He refers to abuses of democratic thought and procedures. To be fair, he would have to reflect that the idea of duty can be misused in the interest of the political struggle for power and the imposition of imperialistic goals. So here some questions remain open; there is some restraint or cautious statement out of apologetic wisdom or tactical considerations. More than elsewhere we have to remember the situation from which and for which Troeltsch formulated his thoughts. Two different levels of argument can be recognized: the level of insight in principle and the recognition of political and military factors.

Troeltsch's attitude to pacifism shows that there can also be instances where principles and an assessment of the situation coincide.[76] He rejects pacificism as an ideological or religious principle on the basis of both the ethics of the state and a rational insight into the natural conditions of human life. For him this does not exclude a personal disposition towards peace and a love of neighbour, but that has another basis. It results from a specifically Christian disposition, and belongs in the sphere of *private* morality. With this definition Troeltsch comes close to the double morality that he criticized in Luther. However, he see the problems inherent in this view and attempts to find ways of combining the two worlds in which human beings live. Still, on closer inspection these considerations seem governed more by the idea of a personally orientated progress from one sphere to another than by the aim of combining them in principle.[77]

The claim of the state on its citizens, national obligation, has an ethical significance. However, religious knowledge and orientation, the bond of the soul with God, stand on a higher level. This thinking at different levels limits not only the radical nationalistic obligation but also the Christian bond and orientation. It is always just a question of relative levels; in addition, in principle orientation on compromise as what is possible and meaningful in a limited situation continues to apply.

After 1916 Troeltsch occupied himself with the question of the future of Germany after the war. He included explicitly in his reflection considerations that were evident earlier only in embryonic form. In this period Troeltsch can only imagine the war being ended by a peace of reason and balance. This is certainly also an effect of the situation after the battle of Verdun, which in military terms was seen as a stalemate.[78]

In Troeltsch's view, the people who had proved themselves in the war and made great sacrifices could no longer be simply the object of legislation, as before, but would have to be understood as its subject.[79] But what does recognition as a subject of legislation mean? Troeltsch emphasizes a general tendency. It is a form of anticipation of the ideas of electoral reform.[80] Whether Troeltsch's reflections went beyond this must remain open; presumably Troeltsch himself also saw them as open.

The political argument presented by Troeltsch in this connection is also interesting. He gives three reasons for the need for a change. 1. Political wisdom requires this step. The leaders on the left, who have laid the foundations for the work of popular solidarity, must not be left in the lurch. 2. The substance of the demand can be justified, in so far as it is a consequence of political justice. 3. There are still sufficiently conservative counter-balances in the federal state system.[81]

It is striking that even where Troeltsch claims to be arguing about an issue on its merits, he does not really think in terms of state and constitutional policy but brings in political wisdom; in other words, wartime and what is permissible or just in war play an important role in his argument. In connection with the issue itself he also adds that there must be transitions and intermediaries between the master culture on the one hand and the democratic mass culture on the other, so that the doctrinaire figures on the right and left are given no material, no possibility of joining in with the aim of forming a following. Moreover the idea of electoral reform can be made appealing to the conservatives by arguing that without the mass of the workers and their partial political saturation, the German Reich cannot have great-power status. With this latter notion Troeltsch is politically in line with Friedrich Naumann, for whom peace in domestic politics is the presupposition for any German claim in the foreign sphere. Troeltsch soothes possible critics of his view by adding: 'No abstract enthusiasm for democracy is needed to draw such conclusions.'[82]

If we consider the year 1916, it is striking that Troeltsch said nothing on the question of the all-out U-boat war, and did not utter such clear words of warning as did, for example, Max Weber.[83] This may be a coincidence, but there may also be good reasons for it. Perhaps Troeltsch saw the heightening of the U-Boat war as the inevitable military reaction to the English blockade. At any rate, that is what his argument looks like after the entry of America into the war.[84] That Troeltsch even now does not want to think in merely pragmatic and political terms is evident from his attempt to look behind the political arguments put forward, and from his investigation of the actual differences between the Western democratic understandings of freedom and the German understanding. On the one hand Troeltsch maintains his line, arguing politically in terms of the history of culture and ideas. But here too he has new emphases. He sees the presupposition for a possible peace in a work of enlightenment because in this way he wants to prepare people's minds by an act of political reason. Therefore he feels that the situation does not call for moral and dogmatic judgments but for a sober, detached historical perception which allows a plurality of understanding in place of an ideologically fixed judgment.

In his view it is necessary to distinguish between three different views of freedom. First, one in which the emphasis is on the individual's right to freedom. Secondly, one in which freedom appears as the expression of a modern formation of ideas; and thirdly, the participation of the individual in the formation of the political will, which comes about on a democratic basis. In the first form, the advantages of the Western nations are indisputable. The second version addresses the modern understanding of autonomy which the Western peoples have similarly made a beginning of forming. 'Only,' according to Troeltsch, 'in the meantime we have caught up with and more than caught up with this advance.'[85] In the discussion of the third point it is striking that Troeltsch's argument is not primarily about the political substance, but refers to a discrepancy between propagandist self-portraits and the real understanding. It is obvious that this in turn is used for propaganda, namely by Troeltsch himself. Thus it remains to ask what he actually intends. According to him, democratization is not an abstract process stemming from an idea, but a development on the basis of the changed life of the state and the economy. Here it is evident that the modern major state cannot really guarantee democracy, understood as an ideal conception.[86]

The argument is carried on on two different levels, that of historical facts and that of ideas, and its main aim is to force Western political claims on Germany. On the other hand, this form of argument represents a piece of mediation, a bridge towards the Western European understanding of democracy which does not involve losing face. This assessment is matched by the political conclusion which Troeltsch draws: neither of the two systems, democracy or the monarchical state system, is automatically more inclined to peace than the other.[87] In concrete, this means that a form of renunciation must be accepted on both sides, in the sense of an ideological non-intervention in the sphere of the other.

In the next year the question of peace became particularly acute for Germany. In July 1917, through the peace initiative of the Reichstag, there was a discussion about ending the war, which seems primarily to have been occasioned by the military situation, but was also connected with the goals and perspectives of domestic policy. The formula resounding from Russia, 'Peace without annexations and contributions', commanded a majority among the parties of the centre and the left wing and their power was sufficient to overthrow Chancellor Bethmann-Hollweg, who was proving a drag. Troeltsch had a realistic estimation of the general situation. He sympathized with those who supported a compromise peace and defended their ideas against the polemic from the conservative side. Thus he wrote in July 1916: 'The essential thing is that the U-boat war does not bring a decision by the autumn, so that the duration of the war becomes incalculable. Here some things are dawning on people and some illusions are foundering... The situation is getting serious, and the question is whether the present Reich government will last or whether new men are appointed. Today no one still knows whether the Chancellor will stay. I'm not particularly interested in him. His lack of resolution towards the Pan-Germans and Conservatives has made me very sceptical about him.'[88]

Troeltsch displays a remarkable temperament which in part was characteristic of an individual of the time, though it takes special forms in him. A quest for truth, a sober rational procedure in the form of analysis and criticism both of the military situation and events in politics abroad and at home, contrasts with a way of thinking which seems illusory, which sticks to individual phenomena, composes them into a mosaic that at least makes the future seem tolerable, sees positive developments, above all negotiations, on the way and has Germany emerging relatively unscathed from the threat at home and abroad.

How much pressure thre was on Troeltsch's feelings during the war, and how difficult he found it to bear the internal and external burdens is often evident from his letters. Friedrich Meinecke is also a key witness: 'I recall how he [Troeltsch] was once on the verge of collapsing in sheer despair during a Grunewald walk in 1917, and I thought that he saw me as the stronger one. But that only seemed to be the case, because I held on longer than Troeltsch to the faith that the modest war aims which we both advocated were also attainable.'[89]

Troeltsch constantly seems to have had illusions about the progress and above all the end of the war, partly also encouraged by the way in which the situation developed. Thus at the end of 1917 he writes to Hans von Schubert that he can breathe again politically because the real danger has now passed. For, 'The Bolsheviks and our influence on the Russian situation... have saved us. So we will also be able to cope with the rest, at least in a tolerable way.[90]

In December 1917 a People's Alliance for Freedom and the Fatherland was founded. Troeltsch discovered here a place for becoming active in practical politics. The foundation must be seen in connection with the initiative by the Fatherland Party to express its ideas and aims through a high membership and well-focused propaganda. As a counter, the People's Alliance for Freedom and Fatherland attempted to argue for moderation in every respect. The People's Alliance included representatives of trade unions and other interested bodies, parliamentarians and professors. Troeltsch, who was one of its founders, explained its aims in a letter to Martin Rade: 'It [the founding] emerges from the similarity between the wishes of Grabowsky, Meinecke and me to create an organization for agitation with a moral-political platform (above all aimed abroad) and those of the Christian trade unions, who think it necessary to revive and console the people, "since otherwise they will not be able to pull through". In this last respect the background is very serious. The workers' leaders fear a revolution – demonstrations over food shortages or disillusionment and indifference. The other organizations agreed, so they put domestic politics, the right to vote and parliamentarization in the foreground. The Catholics have joined in enthusiastically; the Protestants remain outside because of "sentimentality" and "too narrow demands"... In these circumstances the alliance is a difficult instrument, especially over the question of a moralized compromise policy. It was enormously difficult to get it together and I learned all the problems of detailed political work...'[91] In his opening speech at the foundation of the People's Alliance Troeltsch began from the notion that in principle the state of society in general required the involvement of each individual in the formation of a political will.[92] So in his view the aim was not a rule of the masses, because other organs of government formed a corrective to that. The democratic principle could only appear in a modified form, taking account of the historical forces which had grown up. Reforms, which were in any case unavoidable in the long term, would have an encouraging moral effect because of the military situation. Anticipating possible criticism, he said of these reform tendencies: 'These too I do not see in general theories of equality and right, about which one can dispute endlessly, but in the indispensable satisfaction of the sense of political honour which each indiivdual citizen has.'[93] For Troeltsch, in this connection the discussion of war aims was moving increasingly into the economic sphere. England would have to take note of the position of Germany as a power in world trade. His reflections move in the direction of a peace treaty, or more precisely a peace treaty orientated on a world economy, which in his view would not be possible unless both sides wanted it. Troeltsch fully agrees with the principle of a 'demobilization of spirits'.[94]

From the perspective of real politics, progress in the direction of peace could be bound up with this. From a moral aspect the acceptance of this notion was inescapable for the ongoing existence of Europe.[95] For Troeltsch the slogan of the People's Alliance was 'Freedom *and* Fatherland, not one against the other, but one through the other and one for the other'.[96]

Two further events are worth mentioning. In May 1918 an article appeared in *The Times* under the headline 'Truth for the Enemy'.[97] It was about a proposal made in the British Academy by the Anglican theologian William Sanday to invite German scholars, after the war had been won, to co-operate over a re-education of Germany. However, the precondition of this on the German side was to be a political confession, condemning the German war crimes.[98] In this connection mention was made of three scholars, Ernst Troeltsch, Adolf von Harnack and Friedrich Loofs. The very next day Troeltsch was sharply attacked in *The Times*, and his remarks on the war were cited and condemned.[99] This criticism was followed a little later by a much sharper one. In it Troeltsch was said to have expressed thoughts of war against England as early as 1907, and above all to have spoken out in this connection for considerable annexations.[100] Troeltsch was supposed to have had a conversation with the Oxford physiologist C.S.Sherrington (1857-1952). In a newspaper article Troeltsch rejected this information as nonsense and called the whole thing 'a fictitious conversation'.[101]

This condemnation of Troeltsch on the English side shows on the one hand how German professors of theology had an international reputation and on the other how little relevance Troeltsch's moderate position had abroad.

However, the charges levelled against him by 'enemies' abroad did not in any way prevent him from being caught in the millstones of German criticism with his attitude of a cautious toning down of radicalisms. That is shown by the other instance of a polemical work specifically directed against Troeltsch. This was Hans Volkelt's critique of his political attitude.[102]

Volkelt's account not only criticizes Troeltsch's political attitude but also engages in crude polemic which even gets personal.[103] Troeltsch's repudiation is generally to the point, but does contain some barbed remarks: 'Just as the sacred unity of the Middle Ages could explain heresies only as the work of the devil, so evidently Herr Volkelt can explain thought deviating from the commonplaces of today's patriotic German literati only in terms of the intellectual seductions of Western democracy and the weaknesses of an unpolitical intelligence and will-power.'[104] Troeltsch regarded hs own ideas as both 'real-political and moral'.[105]

How severely the defeat of Germany and the outbreak of the revolution affected Troeltsch is evident in a very personal and direct way from his letters, even when we take into account Troeltsch's tendency to come to a perhaps exaggerated conclusion because of his mood. Here a letter to Gertrud von le Fort is particularly significant, combining as it does personal involvement with matter-of-fact analysis. Troeltsch describes the toing and froing of officers and men, gives a detached and critical account of the Kaiser's resignation and reports that Max von Baden has handed over affairs to the 'capable' Ebert. He remarks critically in respect of the most recent past: 'They have not recognized the people and have thrown all warnings to the winds. In truth the officer corps waged the war, the Reich government was a dummy and the Kaiser a helpless weakling... Ludendorff's game was in the end that of a desperate bankrupt, who had previously been a bold player. People did not want peace as long as it was possible – though always with heavy losses. Now we have to capitulate.'[106]

Troeltsch ends the letter with personal remarks which go over into a general religious interpretation of history. 'I can no longer have any compassion. Despite everything it is a kind of relief that the tremendous tension of the last four years is at last easing. Only the murdering is at an end, the illusion is dispersed, the old system has collapsed under its sin. The enemy will not have much to give thanks for either. As man is now, he can no longer bear an excess of tension, and we were near to the end. All is now uncertain and in the air, but the end is certain, and what one has rescued in one's own soul from the tremendous collapse. God be gracious to us all! Now one really has faith if one can withstand all this inwardly.'[107]

The future had to show what political consequences the insights contained in the analysis would have.

II

Collaboration in the Building of the Weimar Republic

1. Troeltsch's activity as a political journalist

For Troeltsch, a realistic assessment of the situation brought about by the military collapse and the revolution called for an adaptation of nationalistic thinking to external circumstances. He felt that what was to become of the world as a whole could safely be left to God. In particular, as far as Germany was concerned, his view was that now that God had either willed or allowed the German defeat, it was important to draw conclusions, personally or for the situation, from the event. Here his religious belief in history coincided with his political insight. It was important to do what was necessary at the moment and to avoid prognoses which went beyond reality. While belief that history was guided by God did not bring Troeltsch any concrete hope for the future, all in all it did keep such a hope open. Troeltsch suggests that the world situation can change surprisingly, so that 'a revival even of the political concept of "Germany" as after Jena and Tilsit' is possible.[108]

From November 1918 to September 1922 Troeltsch had his own political column. In the bi-weekly 'Spectator Letters' he described and commented on the political events of the time.[109] The offer of the column came from Ferdinand Avenarius, editor of *Kunstwart*. Troeltsch says of his intention: 'I took advantage of Avenarius' offer to have a speaking tube which I could use regularly, as I do not have real access to the patriotic and liberal press. I do not fit in anywhere and have also fallen out with the big papers...'[110] It proved that all did not go as he would have liked even with *Kunstwart*. Avenarius tried to soften the tone and content of the letters in order to make them more to public taste.[111]

For Troeltsch, the German situation in November 1918 was marked not only by the military collapse but also by the collapse of the political system. So he felt that there should be neither legends about a stab in the back nor a lack of readiness for reform. New thoughts and aims enter his analysis, which takes back and modifies assessments made during the war with an apologetic aim. His was a balancing act which did not want to see the collapse combined with a total loss of orientation by a renunciation of the values of the past, but sought possibilities of taking up the tradition. Here we first find a negative selection. 'At the moment, the clarity that we have to achieve can only consist in our becoming clear about what is finished and at an end in all circumstances and in all future possibilities. That is militarism, the building up of the state and society on the Prussian military constitution which has existed hitherto, and the spirit that goes with it.'[112]

For Troeltsch, the cease-fire with the conditions laid down by the negotiating commission was a 'veiled capitulation'.[113] It made the desperate military situation of Germany obvious to him. In his view one could speak of a 'revolution' only to a very limited degree. In reality there was no general overthrow but only a change in circumstances limited to the military and emanating from them.[114] Troeltsch's criticism as a 'spectator' becomes sharp when he speaks of the reaction of the average citizen to the events of the November days. 'Sunday, 10 November, was a wonderful autumn day. In Grunewald, masses of citizens went for walks as usual. No elegant dress, just citizens, some of them probably deliberately dressed simply. All rather subdued, like people whose fate will be decided somewhere far in the future, but peaceful and content that things have turned out so well. Trams and the underground ran as usual, the pledge that all immediate needs in life were in order. On all faces there was written: we'll keep getting our wages.'[115] Here we find a feature which characterizes all Troeltsch's reporting and commentary. He combines a view of conditions, a description and analysis of the general political situation, with journalistic 'close-ups', cameos of what he sees or experiences directly. It is like changing to another approach and way of writing, but such vivid detail is also significant both for both contemporary history and his biography. One thinks, for example, of the point at which the changed circumstances in society are demonstrated by the reaction of a batman to an army captain: he refuses to be called 'batman' and wants to be called 'assistant and reader'. Or when Gertrud von Le Fort's brother makes an appearance – he is not named but can be recognized from the Troeltsch letters – and there is mention of his private war in Mecklenburg in connection with the Kapp Putsch.[116]

Troeltsch's report of Hans Delbrück's seventieth birthday party sheds light on conditions and Troeltsch's own mental and psychological state. He relates how his wife did not want him to go without a revolver, as some of the journey is through the woods. His description of the party ends in an account of the speeches. In this situation, a reference to Goethe, so familiar to Troeltsch and apt in both form and content, cannot console him.[117]

However, at the centre of Troeltsch's accounts stands national politics, both domestic policy and foreign policy. He discusses and comments on the Prussian National Assembly (20 March 1919), the National Assembly in Weimar (6 February – 21 August 1919) and the signing of the Versailles Treaty (20 June 1919) as the outstanding events of 1919. For him, the most important thing was the establishment or restoration of order, to be interpreted in three directions: 1. the 'regulation' of the revolutionary forces; 2. the preservation of the unity of the Reich; and 3. the return to law and order.

In his letters Troeltsch argues for a notion of order; he points out its significance for politics abroad and at home, because it will help not only Germany but the world as a whole.[118] He agrees with the criticism voiced on many sides of the resignation of the government and parliament: they do not have real style, something approaching spiritual greatness. At the same time he argues for compromise. The circumstances hardly allow anything else. The policy of the victorious powers, the desperate economic situation, the failure of intelligence – for him, these are the real signs that there is no other prospect, that there can be no forward progress like this and that every foot of (democratic) ground in Germany will have to be fought for.[119]

Troeltsch vigorously criticizes the peace conditions laid down by the victorious powers. For him the peace in prospect is 'a peace of vengeance, of deceit, of force and of perpetuated arson...'[120] Specifically: 'England is annihilating trade, France and Poland are tearing the territory of the German state to pieces and both together are destroying German finances and the productivity of German work...'[121] Troeltsch combines criticism directed outwards in the direction of the Entente powers with criticism directed inwards. He sees a threat emerging in the old division into political left and right wings; he recognizes that social democracy has become the political power of the centre and is thus sustaining and supporting the state. He finds a lack of the right spirit: among the victorious powers, a disposition towards peace and the broad political view that is necessary; in his own people, right through all parties and groups, of the capacity for a rational insight into the situation and the readiness or the will for fundamental moral and spiritual renewal.

Troeltsch agrees with the great majority of the people, and also with the political parties who are ready to collaborate in the building up of the Republic, that the demand for an acknowledgment of guilt in the Versailles Treaty is nonsensical, indeed dangerous. Troeltsch speaks of a dogma of guilt, the establishment and effect of which reminds him of the old witch-hunting. Here, on the basis of the form of injustice, immoderation and short-sightedness which he finds in the peace conditions generally and the dogma of guilt in particular, Troeltsch comes dangerously near to 'right-wing' political interpretations. He speaks of the 'revolutionary self-disarming' of Germany through the deception of Wilson's Fourteen Points and of a hatred of Germany which is going through the world with no moderation and no understanding.[122]

His criticism of the domestic situation represents a critical corrective to this right-wing tendency determined by the situation in foreign policy. On the whole Troeltsch's position on domestic policy clearly differs from both right and left: he distances himself from the independent Social Democrats and the Spartacists on the one hand and the German nationalists and all those of their ilk on the other. According to Troeltsch, neither thought of world revolution nor renewal of the nationalistic view can help in the present situation. But he also sharply condemns the clericalism which emerges with the Centre Party.[123]

This position, which avoids the extremes of right and left, is aimed in the direction of a basic agreement with the politics of the government, but with a critical reserve towards the ideological remnants to be found among the Social Democrats. For him, these can be found above all in their view of economics and their policy for education and the churches.[124]

There are times when Troeltsch sees the danger coming more from the left, and then again times when he sees the enemy on the right. The former was the case above all in the first year after the revolution, as a result of the system of councils and the political orientation on Russia; later, especially after the Kapp Putsch and the murders of Erzberger and Rathenau, his critical comments are directed more against the political right.

In his December 1919 article on 'The Wave from the Right', Troeltsch discussed the conservative tendencies in the bourgeois camp and in this connection pointed to the civil service, the country population, academic education and the Protestant church. The inveterate monarchists, those who think without qualification in nationalistic terms, are charged with having falsified historical truth about the outcome of the war with their legend of the stab in the back. Troeltsch regards as illusionary and dangerous their ideas for the restoration of the monarchy and a new war against the former enemy powers. 'It's dashing and splendid to think like that. But they cannot detach themselves from the old and learn to think new thoughts.'[125] Troeltsch describes the powers behind the Kapp Putsch as a 'military caste': 'It will neither think nor see, will not take psychological and political account either without or within.'[126]

Troeltsch finds confirmation of the notion that the course of history shows particular regularities. A comparison with other revolutions, for example the French and the English, but also with the 1848 revolution in Germany, shows him certain laws of movement within the course of revolutionary events. After the first stormy phase of breaking loose, shaking off old ties, there is usually a phase of weariness, indeed of disappointment. In the concrete instance, developments in Germany, that means that the second phase has begun in the form of weariness and satiation, which allows a rise of the conservative forces. For Troeltsch, an acceptance of this rule has two effects: it generalizes and allows detachment. Both effects are to provide help in understanding and are also a form of self-protection.

Troeltsch did not choose the pseudonym 'Spectator' unadvisedly. It was meant to indicate that he was observing and commenting on the events of the time. However, it should be noted how this observation from a distance also turns into an extremely subjective form of involvement and assessment.

Troeltsch's distance from the political right wing is not to be seen as an indication that he has finished with nationalistic thought and a conservative view. Rather, he wants to allow their validity in a higher sense. How markedly nationalistic Troeltsch's thought continues to be can be detected on every page, and one can largely see in this mode of thinking the real motive force behind his accounts. Only it must be a changed national feeling, one which has learned from history, which is free from chauvinistic traits and a tendency to power politics. The new nationalist thinking must have a spiritual and cultural, moral foundation.

Here Troeltsch's article 'Aristocracy' (1919) sheds light on the more specific purpose of his thoughts. On the one hand, he regards the aristocratic spirit and disposition as finished, not just since 9 November 1918, but long before. Any truly aristocratic thought prevented any narrow-minded politics of interest and class. Here it is evident how Troeltsch's criticism of the state of the ruling classes has become increasingly more radical. He speaks of the ideology of the reserve officer, of his setting store by privileges, of his pursuing purely class interests. But what demands are to be put to an authentic aristocracy? 'An aristocracy of status and privilege must be replaced by an aristocracy of achievement and personal worth.'[127]

If this change, this reorientation, is really accepted, it means that society is on the move, because rise and fall will correspond. All the disadvantages which may be associated with this principle must be mitigated by 'upbringing'.[128] Troeltsch thinks that the Christian ethic is in a position to become effective as a principle for combining aristocratic and democratic elements. Catholicism with its choice of talents and acceptance of leadership has advantages for him here. By contrast, because of its fundamental attitude and history, Protestantism is more bound up with conservative conditions of power and therefore has difficulties in accepting change. For all his affirmation of the democratic way in principle, Troeltsch still implicitly criticizes democracy. However, one must distinguish three things in his writing. First, democracy taken as a type, an idea; then its realization in historical form and differentiation, above all in Western Europe and America; and finally the political form which the democratic idea is to take in Germany. Democracy as an idea rests positively on the granting of individual rights of freedom and, associated with that, on a heightening of popular readiness for responsibility and increased intellectual and political productivity. Negatively, it has a tendency to level out spirit and origin, both for the individual and for society. It leads all too easily to battles between economic and political interests and on the whole bears within it the danger of anarchy.[129]

The democratic idea appears in a particular historical form in each instance. Whereas in Western Europe the battle against feudalism and aristocracy was the essential political motivation, this political background was lacking in North America; moreover, the relationship with Puritanism created special possibilities for spiritual penetration and political construction. Thus because of the history of its origin, American democracy is freer; it could not develop without the need to form a contrast and be a counter-movement. It has, rather, to be able to find a way to what Troeltsch calls 'conservative democracy', with positive connotations. By that he understands a basically positive attitude to history, so that the culture of the spirit is not put in question by a negative revolutionary disposition. We must consider here whether Troeltsch's assessment of American democracy, its history and present form, is not shaped by current political perspectives. As victorious powers, the Western European states seemed demanding and threatening in another way from America, materially, intellectually and politically.

Finally, the third form of the idea of democracy, which for Troeltsch represents the current political possibility in Germany. Here he thinks he can see certain historical points of contact for the republican and democratic spirit in the political history of Germany. However, all in all, he cannot see the character of the German people, combined with German history, as providing a good breeding ground for democracy. Still, this is just one perspective. What really counts is the real political position, the loss of the war, the collapse of the old system. According to Troeltsch, for anyone whose thought is realistic and critical here there is no political way which by-passes democracy.[130] However, the all-important thing is what democracy will look like in Germany, what possibilities it is accorded, what form it will take.

Troeltsch's aim is a social democracy which is at the same time marked by conservative traits. Democracy as a form of the state, based on the will of the people and the constitution, cannot mean a sudden reversal of the old situation of power, so that a proletarian class rule takes the place of the old form of rule. Rather, social conditions must be reshaped. But the basis for this must not be dogmatic, nor the expression of a political doctrine; rather, a cautious, gradual transformation of social conditions must be envisaged. Above all, this includes a change of ownership in agriculture and industry, and also a much fairer tax system. For Troeltsch, this democratic transformation cannot come about without the 'spirit'. Unless it has a tie to culture as a whole, the democratic idea has no roots.

The social democracy which is affirmed and intended politically thus has 'conservative' features, to the degree that there is a link with 'culture as a whole': it is the powers of tradition which need to be accepted and changed.[131]

Troeltsch's capacity for critical analysis is limited, and shot through with a significant weakness. On the one hand he is in a position to see and discover political connections, perceive tendencies and recognize dangers, for example that coming from the right in the form of nationalist or later Fascist thought. On the other hand, in his account Troeltsch is often too ready to draw consequences from his view of the situation in the grand style, and does not avoid forced constructions and speculative assumptions.[132]

That is probably the grain of truth in Meinecke's criticism of Troeltsch: 'One will soon perceive that he strove more to grasp things than to have an influence on them with a political will. In conversation I often noticed that when he was developing his view of the situation in the style of a great fresco and had brought together scattered elements in established causal complexes, on being asked what was to be done with it all he just shrugged his shoulders. He certainly did not lack a practical concern on a large scale – his whole philosophy of history bears witness to that – but he did when it came to having a direct influence on the course of things. He left that to those who were called to do this, though he did provide some help in his analysis of things, which no practical statesman could provide because he could not see it other than *sub specie aeterni*.'[133]

However, one must not be unfair to Troeltsch here. The period after the First World War, after the defeat, the revolution and the subsequent changes, was difficult to analyse even for those with political training, and the possibilities of a constructive development were hard to define. The lack of a capacity for political constructiveness in Troeltsch is probably also particularly striking because he was more capable than others of making an acute analysis of political conditions. So people thought they could assume that he would also define the next political step to be taken. Thus for example he was wrong in his assumptions of the final distribution of power on a world scale. He was wrong in his assessment of the role of England and Europe generally. What was more important, however, was that he perceived the threat of political dangers at home, above all the rise of Fascism and antisemitism, that he warned of the danger of a new world war, and that his social criticism of an unfair distribution of possessions and a polarization based on that were accurate. From a present-day perspective, Troeltsch's capacity to think in ideological-critical terms is a very positive factor – particular in relation to nationalist and Fascist thought.

References to the 'masses' appear particularly frequently in Troeltsch's political vocabulary. The masses are said to be hard to reassure, to react nervously according to their own laws, and to be largely irrational. These comments stem from a mixture of elitist detachment and an attempt to understand. Troeltsch also moves in the direction of elitist thinking when on the one hand he praises the Social Democrats for doing great service in the cause of national unity, preserving law and order and creating a consitution, while on the other he fails to find intellectual stature, a broad political view and above all diplomatic skill based on upbringing and capability in Ebert, Scheidemann and their colleagues.[134]

But these bourgeois-intellectual prejudices are also corrected. Troeltsch learned from history, from the political developments which had taken place in the meantime. He increasingly recognized the significance of the working class and argued for a coalition of the workers and the middle classes as the presupposition for a constructive political development in Germany.[135]

Troeltsch's sharp criticism of the middle class, the civil service and especially the academics is striking. For him the middle class had largely failed, had not recognized the demands of the historical moment, and had largely evaded its responsibilities. His criticism of Protestantism, especially in its church form, also goes in the same direction. Out of a mixture of a basically conservative attitude and a churchmanship wrongly understood, the Protestant forces tend towards a negative assessment of the new circumstances, the form of state, politics and politicians. However, this criticism of tendentiousness is also directed against Catholicism – above all in the form of clericalism, though Protestantism is criticized more clearly.

Here Troeltsch shows clear sympathy for the middle class in another respect, for its intellectual and cultural claims, for the sense of responsibility and duty which can still be found among it – all things the basic features of which are to be preserved on the presupposition of an acceptance of the changed political conditions. Here is the world from which he comes and to which he knows that he belongs – intellectually, culturally and politically – albeit not without criticism and a tendency towards reform.

Troeltsch calls for an endorsement in principle of the new situation and readiness to collaborate in building up the Republic. His thoughts are governed by the demands of the situation, which in his view allows no other choice. 'The fact remains that the Republic is the only possible course and... is necessary to consolidate conditions at home.'[136]

Troeltsch called himself a 'rational democrat',[137] seeking to distinguish himself from democrats by conviction and passion, and to indicate the significance of rational insight into the facts of the political situation. The political course chosen by Troeltsch and his like-minded colleagues – like Friedrich Meinecke, Max Weber and Friedrich Naumann, though there were differences between them – subsequently earned respect and recognition, above all by comparison with the course advocated in wide areas of society and the church. At the same time we have to note that this detached assessment and self-assessment bore within it something of the political tragedy of the Weimar Republic generally and Troeltsch in particular. It has rightly been pointed out that the youth could not really be attracted and drawn in by such a rational attitude, combined with a critical detachment from the state, the parties and the constitution – as the National Socialists were later able to draw them in with their irrational aims, their offers of emotional identification and their mythical call for sacrifice.[138] And Troeltsch's personal tragedy lies in the fact that with his differentiated criticism on all sides, in a sense he was politically homeless – and at the same time his critical potential could be exploited by all parties.

So the question whether Troeltsch increasingly found a positive relationship to the Republic has to be answered with a qualified 'Yes'. If one spreads the biographical net wider and takes in the previous development, then one cannot describe Troeltsch's political course simply as a transformation from a monarchist with a basically nationalist attitude to a republican. Rather, this was a transformation with elements of continuity, a process which began in the pre-war period in the form of a criticism of political conditions and continued after the war. But guidelines from the philosophy of history and ethics remain; they can be read above all out of Troeltsch's ideas about mediation and an ethic of compromise.

How important a consideration of the contemporary situation was for the accentuation and development of Troeltsch's ideas is evident from the fact that he saw a Bolshevik take-over of Germany as the initial danger. In the face of the activities of German-nationalist and revanchist forces, Troeltsch could some years later adopt the slogan of the Reich government, 'the enemy is on the right wing': dissociation from a right-wing tendency was now the demand of the hour. For Troeltsch, the Kapp Putsch and the murder of Rathenau were visible signs of a negative development which he wanted to oppose with all his might.[139]

The label 'professorial philosophy' is not the right one to describe Troeltsch's political journalism. Certainly he tends to toy with political forces and possibilities, and his accounts are not free from speculation and bold prognoses. His is a form of thought in the spirit of historicism, which attempts to understand the formation of political ideas in terms of historical development, take them up in a comparative way and relate them, combine them. But it is not a merely 'ideal' trait which governs this journalism; the 'ideal thought' is guided by an orientation on reality and keeps getting back to the facts, to the political, economic and social situation. Thus the politics of the day becomes the object of his interest and his account. Troeltsch was not a passionate, a full-blooded politician, as he had seen Max Weber to be.[140] He was a political journalist as the result of a combination of inner necessity and interest, originally very intellectual and theoretical, who later also became practical and went into detail. It is to his credit that he acted and sought to be influential to the best of his ability.

There are many passages in Troeltsch's articles where the beginnings of resignation are to be noted. The contemporary situation is judged in a detached and critical way in an attitude of nostalgic retrospect on the past and the spiritual and cultural tradition. However, this attitude is not to be seen as inactivity, nor as 'mere' resignation. Rather, for Troeltsch such an attitude is a visible expression of a real assessment of the situation; it is the presupposition for appropriate political activity in the present. Resignation is to be understood in positive terms because it represents a renunciation of mere wishes, of a maximum taken as an ideal.[141] With such reflections Troeltsch's political journalism takes up his work in the philosophy of history and culture or goes over into this.[142]

2. Troeltsch's involvement in practical politics

In addition to his political journalism, after the war Troeltsch was also involved in party politics in the German Democratic Party, the DDP. This was founded on 16 November 1918, just a week after the overthrow, by a group of intellectuals and leading businessmen, and was based on the recognition in principle of the republican form of state. The preservation of the unity of the Reich, the maintaining or restoration of law and order, and equal rights for all citizens, are further points of its first programmatic declaration.[143]

Troeltsch's political journalism after the war was largely within this intellectual framework and represents a free acceptance and exposition of these principles and aims. Two things should be noted about his link with the party and his orientation on the principles of the Democratic Party. Politically speaking, Troeltsch came from the national liberal tradition, but with reservations, with a certain break from it. He had suspicions about an excessively strong nationalistic trend, and was critical and detached about the bourgeois liberalism of the time with its economic views and its theory of the state. To the extent that the principles of the Democratic Party came near to this line, he had been prepared to assent in the light of his own political development. The second thing was that the idea which became evident in the official party line of a rejection of extremes, a repudiation of radicalism on the right or the left wing, the social tendency in the sense of an effort to change the distribution of property and possessions, and the concern for reconciliation between the workers and the middle class, was in line with his own thinking. If any party fitted him, then it was the German Democratic Party. The founders and first spokesmen of the party like Theodor Wolff, Eberhard Gothein and Max Weber came close to his own convictions, as they did to him personally.

However, a year later, the party programme in 1919 made rather more moderate statements than it had at the beginning. Whereas originally in November 1918 there was talk of sacrifices by those with possessions, of giving away property and limiting estates, now the emphasis was on the idea of the private economy,[144] economic self-interest and self-responsibility. However, these general economic principles were qualified by references to the good of the people and social justice. The formation of an economic monopoly and speculation in land, social injustice in the distribution of possessions and the level of salaries were criticized. At the same time, however, the principle of achievement was advocated in setting pay levels, and the significance of private initiatives was brought to the fore. Concrete social policy appeared first and urgently in references to a changed tax legislation.[145]

It is hard to say when Troeltsch joined the party. At the very beginning there is no mention of his name, but it is beyond question that he tended towards the group mentioned above and had a positive attitude to the founding of the party. In addition to the principles already mentioned, what is said about the relationship between state and church, about school, upbringing and education, and about science and culture, are of interest for Troeltsch and his own work. Here it is evident that Troeltsch's own ideas about schools and the relationship between state and church could find points of contact or parallels in the party programme. The favouring of a simultaneous single school and religious instruction, the priority of which was to familiarize pupils with the history and nature of religion, was very much in line with his own aims. The same is true of the relationship between state and church, where the party programme envisages a fundamental separation. Troeltsch has reservations only where the idea of separation is seen in ideological terms, and there is no attention to historical development, the situation of the established church, and the possibility of a free constructive collaboration.[146]

How much Troeltsch's own political line basically coincided with that of the Democratic Party is evident from the DDP election campaign in January 1919 for the constituent National Assembly. The main aim was the repudiation of left-wing radicalism, and there was a certain tendency to dissociation from the right wing as well: all in all this was a strengthening of the middle-class centre. At the election itself the DDP won seventy-five seats, and entered into the Weimar coalition with the Social Democrats and the Centre Party. Before the National Assembly met, the Prussian State Assembly was elected. Here the main electoral slogan of the DDP was an undivided Prussia. At the election to the Prussian State Assembly the DDP was able to win 65 of the 405 mandates. Troeltsch became a member of the Prussian parliament and when, as he writes, 'the formation of the government depended on the under-secretariats of state', he had himself nominated for this office.[147] In March 1919 he was appointed to the post of parliamentary under-secretary of state in the Prussian Ministry of Culture.[148] Although his relations with the Social Democrat minister Konrad Haenisch were not free of tension, he held the office until 1921.

Troeltsch's basic condition for accepting this honorary post at the Ministry was that he should be able to keep on his lecturing at the university. 'Only the seminar will be dropped, because it involves an enormous amount of work.'[149] He attempted to dispel doubts which he saw arising in the faculty about his double position, as a professor on the one hand and a member of the Ministry of Culture on the other. 'At any rate I can hope in this way to be useful to schools, to science and to the universities, and above all to protect proven institutions. I can also assume that the new post will not last very long. It goes without saying that I am not to be regarded as a representative of the Ministry of Culture and therefore will essentially remain a professor and member of the faculty.'[150] Troeltsch's main responsibility as an under-secretary of state was church policy, including questions of school policy. According to Troeltsch, that alone justified his double position as professor and member of the Ministry.[151]

If we are to understand and evaluate Troeltsch's views on church politics, we need to note the conditions generally. German Protestantism after the defeat and the overthrow had suffered a double shock: on the one hand, more internally, in religious politics; on the other, more externally, in terms of legal organization. The two were not unconnected. Protestantism, which had been marked by a special closeness to the state and a special awareness of it, had lost an essential landmark and support. Here it clearly differed from Catholicism, which had a state counterpart in the Kaiser's Protestant Reich in the Centre Party. By contrast, for German Protestantism the year 1918 marked a break in continuity. The ending of church government by local rulers, and the legal and financial disorientation which followed, combined with freethinking propaganda and propaganda against the church to cause great disquiet. The resultant situation was an invitation to find a remedy as soon a possible, and that meant above all giving the Protestant church a new legal form.

In the discussion about the legal situation of the Prussian church since the nineteenth century, alongside the question of the Union and the separation of church and state, the question of church order, the church constitution, had had a central position. The main problem here was what relevance should be accorded to the democratic principle, especially with a Reformed stamp: the synodical principle on the one hand and the consistorial principle, approximating to the structure of the state authorities, on the other. Friedrich Julius Stahl (1802-1861, professor of constitutional and church law) had spoken here of dualism, of a separation of the consistorial and presbyterial-synodical elements, though without excluding reciprocal correction and supplementation. In the following period there were those, above all the canon lawyer Emil Herrmann (1812-1885), who strove for the union of these two basic elements of the church constitution.[152] It proved that these aspects always also involved political questions. For, to put it simply, the consistorial element was associated with a principle of administration and law similar to the state and subordinate to it, and the synodical element was associated with a more democratic element, rooted in the notion of the community and in the church principle of mission. A trend, as in Herrmann's view, towards the notion of a unitary organism which combined both the consistorial and the synodical elements, because both are needed to form this organism, relativized the government of the churches by local rulers and the consistorial principle.[153] The discussion of legal and constitutional questions in the reconstruction of the Protestant church after the First World War must be seen against this background.

Article 137 of the Weimar Constitution of 31 July 1919 contained the stipulation: 'No state church exists'. This principle was then interpreted in the direction of church autonomy in matters of law as follows: 'Each religious community shall order and administer its affairs independently within the limits of the law which has universal validity. It will bestow its offices without the involvement of the state or the civil community.' However, the principle of the separation of state and church operative in this stipulation is relativized by the church being given the status of a 'corporation in public law', with an additional privilege extending beyond that of other organizations or institutions: the right to levy taxes.[154]

A distinction must be made in Troeltsch's ideas and activity in church politics and questions of church constitution. He had no doubt about the significance of religion generally, both for culture and for personal life. But his criticism of conservative Lutheranism, of the Prussian conservatives and their use of religious tradition to maintain hierarchical order and nationalistic thought, continued. His basic question in church politics was: how can the positive religious function of the church be maintained in changed circumstances, and how can these be cautiously reformed for the future? He thus denies the ideological view of the separation of state and church politically, but does not dispute that both state and church have laws of their own. In cultural policy, Troeltsch fears that if the church is not seen as a cohesive force, it will lose its function as a mediator in the religious sphere; a 'void' will remain which can be filled by every possible kind of radicalism.

In this situation it is quite understandable that in his report on cultural policy to the Second Extraordinary Party Conference of the DDP in 1919, Troeltsch should have opposed all attempts to understand or constitute the Democratic Party as an ideological party. The reasons he gave for this were pragmatic,[155] but certainly also went deeper. Troeltsch was concerned that the party should be differentiated from the Social Democrats and the Centre Party, both of which were ideological parties. But the critical focus was also against liberalism as the ideological basis of the DDP.

For Troeltsch the DDP had also to be orientated on the middle-class centre, the progressive intelligentsia, and find its special field of activity here.[156] In his survey he combines fundamental insights with concrete aims. Here his points on the relationship between state and church and on religious instruction, connected with his practical work at the Ministry, are of special interest. On the separation of state and church, Troeltsch suggests that the singular is not in place here and that one should talk of 'churches'. He stresses the positive side of a church free from the state and state intervention, but then goes on to the negative side, namely the strengthening of church autonomy associated with it. 'It [church life] is no longer kept in check by the state and adapted to general interests. So it will go its own way and impose its demands in a social and democratic fashion. With things among our people as they are, a German democracy will have a very marked clerical colouring.'[157] He believes that the most important church-political task of the present 'is to carry through the difficult business of separation from the old Protestant state- and Land-churches, because these churches must create their own representation and thus become involved in conflicts of interest'.[158]

On the question of schools, very much along the Party line, he argues for the single school. He regards it as a necessity on political and ethical grounds. But he opposes all tendencies towards levelling out, which he sees rooted above all in Social Democracy. Troeltsch sees problems emerging over religious instruction: he argues pragmatically and theoretically at the same time. On the one hand the people wants religious instruction, and on the other (and this is the crucial thought) religious instruction must be an organic element of instruction generally, since 'religion cannot be a mere appendage to instruction'[159] in school, which is seen as an institution for upbringing and the schooling of dispositions. As a 'spiritual power which is the basis of everything', religion cannot dominate or be dominated, but must embrace and penetrate everything, all disciplines and the school's task of upbringing.

In concrete, this entails taking account of the rights of parents, and confessional schools where these are desired and can be defended on pedagogical as well as organizational grounds. Troeltsch ends his comments with an expression of hope: 'Faith in ourselves and in the Spirit – in the present situation that is the most essential and necessary cultural programme. God has not abandoned anyone who has not abandoned himself.'[160]

A paper written by Troeltsch at the beginning of 1919 – some months before the party conference – shows even more clearly the degree to which his reflections are governed both by history and by questions of principle, and how with his many ifs and buts he finds it difficult to indicate a clear aim. Nevertheless his work is marked by a wealth of thought, including political thought, and by a consideration of the realities in schools and society generally, which extends right down to details. At the end, in the discussion of aims, a complicated theory emerges composed of different elements. First, dogmatic instruction belongs in church, not in school. Secondly, schools cannot dispense with religious education, on grounds of education and upbringing. Thirdly, religious instruction in schools should be essentially historical and phenomenological. Troeltsch ends his comments by remarking: 'I shall not discuss here how this is to be achieved in detail, or how it will turn out in practice.'[161] Presumably Troeltsch's personal notions move in the direction of small likeminded groups which give the individual 'spiritual warmth and companionship' and which come somewhere between religious individuality and the institutional church or the practices of the established church.[162] His proposals relating to the law and constitution of the Evangelical Landeskirche of Prussia also in principle take the form of historical diagnosis. It is important to note what has been the custom hitherto (supreme episcopate, state religion) and at the same time prepare the way for something new. 'It [Protestantism] must give itself a new form, both externally and internally; it must become more Chrisitan and independent. The orthodox or semi-orthodox zeal for "positive" teaching can no longer function as something like a surrogate for real religion. Whether and how it can preserve its unity here is a question which cannot be answered today.'[163]

Troeltsch's comments on the Dresden Kirchentag show how critical he was of the way of reforming itself which the Protestant church had adopted.[164] In his view, the statements made by the Kirchentag were conservative throughout: all hope of avoiding religious narrowness and political confrontation and achieving a 'massing and revival of religious forces' in the direction of a 'living and forward-moving Protestantism' rested on the Protestant church people.[165] Troeltsch seems to have shared the interest of the liberal wing in church politics and theology in taking note of the synodical element in the church constitution: this was basically in line with his own ideas. The strengthening of the synodical principle found expression in two electoral laws, relating to the local community and to the synod. These laws addressed the community principle and in principle opened up a 'democratic way'. Troeltsch noted: 'This electoral law for local communities has a very liberal basis. It provides for both general suffrage for both men and women and for proportional representation, and in this respect is not at all offensive.'[166] It is clear that Troeltsch felt that the Protestant church should take its own initiative over the constitution: this was in line with his basic conviction, and there was also historical evidence for it.[167]

Troeltsch did not like being put under pressure in his ministerial work. He wanted to safeguard his personal standpoint, but perhaps was not always skilful and tactful in doing so. That doubt is appropriate here is evident from the following controversy. In an impending official condemnation of a head teacher called Borg, who had a nationalistic attitude, Troeltsch was evidently disturbed by the lack of evidence and the tone adopted, the 'incredibly pastoral, moral dressing down'.[168] Various personal and political views were concealed behind questions of form and organization. Troeltsch, it became known, had evidently been able to achieve only a distant relationship with Minister Haenisch; he often did not agree with the minister's style and the way in which he worked. Troeltsch's attitude was characterized throughout by a marked sense of justice.[169] All in all, the unattractive side of work in the Ministry is evident from this case: the hassle, the feuding, the direct or hidden snubs or hostilities. At the end of his report Troeltsch states: 'Here I am simply fighting as an honest man for truth and justice.'[170] The affair then clearly went much wider, and after discussion in the 'headmasters' conference' was referred to a formal disciplinary tribunal. Troeltsch indicated that he was prepared to resign his honorary position as under-secretary of state, but first wanted to hear the views of the Minister as to how, as he put it, he could depart 'in peace'.[171]

Another incident similarly coincided with Troeltsch's characteristics. In a meeting Troeltsch had exclaimed, 'Conditions in the Ministry are like a pigsty!' As this remark reached the Minister by some obscure channel, Troeltsch felt compelled to explain. First he tried to play things down by saying that the expression was common in Bavaria and pointing out that the conversation was a private one. As for the substance of the remark, he explained: 'The remark was not directed against you. I would have expressed myself differently about you and your administration, as indeed I always have done, even in a private conversation.'[172] Here Troeltsch wanted to indicate that he was criticizing conditions in the Ministry generally. He explained that he saw work in the Ministry endangered by outside pressure, from the parties.[173]

Troeltsch did not resign, but came to an agreement with the Minister. His activity as parliamentary under-secretary of state in the Prussian Ministry for Science, Art and Popular Education ended in 1921, with the expiry of his parliamentary mandate.[174] Troeltsch, richer by some political and also human experience, was happy to be able to go back to concentrating on his scholarly work.

It is virtually impossible to give a satisfactory answer to the question how significant and efficient Troeltsch's work in practical politics was.[175] He certainly also saw it as doing his duty. Or better, and more accurately, it was symbolic action which he required of himself, which was to show his basically positive attitude to the Republic and to prompt others to do the same.

III

New Thematic Focal Points

1. Works on the history of culture

Even in the war years, although he was interested in and committed to politics, Troeltsch did not completely neglect his academic work. Above all in his own judgment ('I live and work only for the war') it retreated into the background; nevertheless what he wrote and produced at this time remains impressive.

As early as 1913 Troeltsch had announced that his articles on the rise of the modern spirit would appear soon.[176] But his plans soon took another direction. Now he wanted not only to investigate the development towards modernity from a purely historical aspect but also to combine his work with practical aims of a cultural philosophical kind. He wanted to demonstrate what historical heritage was culturally relevant for providing points of contact with and a foundation for the modern spirit. This concern was always present for him, but he devoted two works specifically to it, 'The Faith and Ethics of the Hebrew Prophets' and 'The Early Church'.[177] Here Troeltsch was concerned with the religious part of the tradition, not secular thought stemming from the Graeco-Roman spirit.

Troeltsch sees Hebrew prophecy as a historical phenomenon of towering significance. That is true immanently within the history of religion, but also as a religious presupposition for the handing down of an irreplaceable spiritual attitude. In the history of religion prophecy is significant for its new understanding of the relationship between human beings and God, an understanding which is based on the spirit of personal faith and trust. The history of the prophetic influence is characterized by the production of a new view of history which extends beyond short-term historical goals and turns towards the universal. It is the knowledge of an all-embracing goal of history which is detached and independent, open to other, universally spiritual determinations. Troeltsch's reflections are focussed on the assumption of a regularity which rests on the perception of the ongoing influence of spiritual contents or motives over and above their original historical context.

Troeltsch sees the relationship between the cultural past and present tasks as one of co-ordinations and modified links, not as a process of oppositions and exclusions. For him, the 'original' has changed in the course of history.

Anyone who wants to think in religious terms must at the same time think in historical terms, not in the sense of an abstract historicity, but in awareness of concretion, of the development of the original in its historical effect into a tradition, a process in which the concretion is part of the substance itself as a particular historical expression. Because the essence manifests itself only in such concretions, everything presses towards new emphases in the present.[178]

He has a further thought about Hebrew prophecy. The type of ethics which emerges here has particular power and strength, but at the same time it is restrictive and hostile to culture because of its radical concentration on the notion of love of God and the brethren. It acquired special significance for development by being taken up into the proclamation of Jesus, albeit with the difference of a qualitative change into yet greater inwardness, yet stronger humanity, and also a more clearly marked other-worldly character.

The clash between this ethics, which was hostile or at least indifferent to culture, and a theology based on compromise with culture, runs through the whole history of Christianity. The transformation of a conception with an originally nationalist orientation into a general, universal form of ethics is based on an affinity of choice between the activism and individualism of Hebrew prophecy and the Greek way of thinking, which goes over into the universally human. Troeltsch emphasizes that the synthesis which became possible as a result is a specific feature of Western intellectual history. He sees this event of secularization as a historical process; but the question of a possible return to the old original content does not arise for him. He is not prepared to sacrifice the historian's knowledge of the irrevocable character of past eras to the systematic concern of the theologian or philosopher. Troeltsch sees the historical process of a detachment of religious content so that it becomes independent, but he does not question the legitimacy of the new. Troeltsch could have shared Blumenberg's critical questions here, as the assumption of a 'cultural guilt' and thus an 'illegitimacy' of modernity would presuppose a primacy of systematics and a jurisdiction of theology over the philosophy of history, which was quite remote from his undogmatic thought.[179]

Troeltsch calls his article on 'The Early Church' from 1916/17 a study in the philosophy of culture. The article demonstrates the relationship between Christianity and culture by means of historical examples. At numerous points he takes up the insights gained in the *Social Teachings*, for example in the case of ethics and asceticism or natural-law thought, and develops them from another perspective. A letter to Wilhelm Bousset indicates his intention: 'But above all many thanks for your remarks on my article. It is a piece from a book that I plan on the philosophy of culture. Hence the stress only on the things which are of lasting importance for us in the West. But I shall note your comments, most of which seem to me to be justified, in the final version. I am not a professional; I read the sources but do not research into them. I have got out of them what I need for my purposes...'[180]

Troeltsch makes a methodological distinction between the self-understanding of contemporaries or those involved and a verdict coming from outside. That leads to a distinction between church and Christianity corresponding to that in Enlightenment thought. Here Troeltsch follows his old notion of the independence of religion, from the perspective of the philosophy of culture. He sees the relationship between the Christian church and ancient culture dialectically, and a distinctive logic of the religious is expressed on the side of the church or religion.[181]

Troeltsch distinguishes the element of the religious from any form of the rational in the form of repeatability or abstraction. The early church is a dynamic interplay of forces. Its cultural significance lies in the fact that it is a link between the ancient and the modern world. With it a new historical entity emerges which, going through oppositions, in a complicated process of development becomes what it appears to be later, in retrospect. The contrasts emerging in it are not solved in logical and dogmatic fashion, but in a historical process through the actual course of history. Troeltsch does not see any syncretism here, of the kind that there was supposed to be in history-of-religions research, but a 'tremendous synthesis going far beyond the earlier simplicity and closed nature of existence and therefore incapable of organic systematization'.[182] Troeltsch can use Nicolas of Cusa's scholastic figure of thought, the *complexio oppositorum*, by way of clarification.

A relative opposition was maintained as the two traditional entities of antiquity and Christianity grew together; they were not dissolved into each other, but there was an abiding dialectical interplay. Awareness of these historical roots makes an essential contribution to present-day knowledge, and from a structural perspective is the occasion for a new version of the relationship of Christianity and culture.[183]

Troeltsch's theological thought also developed further along this cultural-philosophical perspective. The religious, different from all the rationality of the world as it is, is stressed more strongly than before as a phenomenon *sui generis*, and as a result, any simple possibility of a mediation between culture and religion or the Christian tradition is denied more firmly than ever. At the same time Troeltsch develops the stimulus towards moral action more clearly in terms of the security of human beings in God. What Bultmann understands as a dialectical relationship of indicative to imperative on the basis of his interpretation of Paul, as knowledge of the grace promised to human beings along with the demand to live in accordance with this grace, is regarded by Troeltsch as the dialectic of the religious idea. Some of the objections raised against him thus appear in a new light. Troeltsch's criticism of a modern Protestantism which delights in culture, which does not think dialectically enough, and knows nothing of a 'breaking of natural self-reliance' through the transcendent does not fit into the picture of the usual criticism of his work.[184]

Troeltsch wants to combine recognition of historical influence with cultural philosophy; he wants to demonstrate the incorporation of the religious into culture and its formation in concrete historical processes without abandoning the special character of the religious dimension. For Troeltsch, two things are true. Religion is an element of culture; religion is more than culture, can be the basis of it, transcends it, is the 'other' over against culture. Transcendence and immanence, contingency and development, event and formation, religion and secularization are to be equally valid; Troeltsch wants to be a man of the Enlightenment and religious at the same time – that is his intellectual ideal.

The synthesis of antiquity and the Christian culture or view of life which is to be found in the early church has historical and substantive significance which extends down to the present. However, the nature of this connection cannot be repeated, but must be rediscovered in the conditions of present culture.

This brings up a further thematic focus in the form of discussions on the philosophy of history. Here the question of the possibility of a cultural synthesis in the present is the goal of Troeltsch's historical and systematic reflections.

2. *Historicism and its problems*

Troeltsch's occupation of the chair of philosophy in Berlin became the most important external stimulus for an intensive preoccupation with the philosophy of history. What had so far been part of his work on the philosophy of religion and theology, now became a main theme. The events of the time had encouraged this development. They had made the question of the meaning of history and the possibilities of a reconstruction of culture not only a general existential issue but also a personal issue for a thinker like Troeltsch. Academically the thematization of the philosophy of history was a presupposition for the history of the rise of modern culture that he planned, since in his view mere history was not enough: first of all the theme of history had to be discussed in principle.

Structure and aim. Troeltsch arranged his work on 'Historicism and Its Problems' in two part-volumes, one of which was to be more focussed on conceptuality and logic, the other more on history itself. The second volume never appeared, so the work remained a fragment.[185]

The history of the origin of the book – or more precisely, of the first part-volume – is connected with one of Troeltsch's characteristics, his style of thinking and working. He had already published almost the whole text beforehand, and then published it a a book, with additions and modifications. A letter to his publisher shows how much this was planned, and what Troeltsch promised himself from this procedure. He writes: 'At one stage I scattered the individual parts around... as I had also done earlier, and it proved very worth while... In this way I can accept countless invitations, slowly arouse interest, profit from criticism and reworking, and have the basis for an improved final redaction, as I can put all later thoughts and further literature in the copies.'[186]

One feature of the systematic structure is that the reflections on the significance of the philosophy of history which are put at the beginning are explained and backed up by a history of recent schemes and solutions of the problem; then at the end, history as it were satisfied, questions can be asked about its relevance for the present situation. In the final section Troeltsch moves from a discussion of logical problems to a material philosophy of history, with the two thematic focal points 'cultural synthesis' and 'universal history'. The goal of all his efforts in the philosophy of history which appears in this framework, namely the building up of culture in the present, is discussed in the reflections on issues of principle, but not in any concrete shape and form.[187]

Despite some critical questions which one can have about the structure of the book, its overlappings and repetitions, and its fragmentary character, the work on historicism has a charm of its own. Troeltsch includes the reader in the process of his reflections and shows his mastery in the methodological combination of analyses of the time, a critical discussion of literature on the philosophy of history, and an account of the substantive problems developed from it, to which are attached suggestions for a solution. At the same time the book is a contemporary document of the first rank, since it reflects the spiritual, religious and political situation of the war and the immediate post-war period. Troeltsch does not want either to lapse into an attitude of cultural resignation, which at this time often resulted from a disillusioned nationalistic feeling, or to succumb to utopian thinking born of religion, philosophy and politics. He is concerned to make a sober assessment of the situation which can convey a touch of scepticism rather than fix on false hopes. For him, soberness and a realistic estimation of the situation must be combined with the courage to reconstruct culture.

Troeltsch begins with a description of the situation, relates the problem of the philosophy of history to it, and develops the two main tasks of a formal logic of history and a material philosophy of history. The fundamental question of the possibility of assessing history and then of developing a cultural ideal for the present results from this analysis and the survey of the material categories. The long chapter on the concept of historical development and universal history is a historical reassurance from the perspective of contemporary possibilities of reception. The problem of the relationship between the individual and the universal, historical reality and the general course of development, is central here. Just as the discussion of the problem of criteria ends meaningfully with the question of the relationship between history and the definition of values, so the investigation of universal history and the concept of development ends equally meaningfully with the problems of epistemology (history and epistemology), because these go beyond purely logical questions. The closing chapter on the construction of the European history of culture makes the account issue in the topical questions of the time, clarifies the two main themes of the material philosophy of history, namely cultural synthesis and universal history, and thus creates a transition to the development in the second volume, which was intended but never carried out.

Logically clarified vividness – the formal logic of history. The logic of history is fundamental reflection on the logical categories which are appropriate to the investigation and understanding of historical events and differs from a logic applied to natural events. Only the most recent past opened up for Troeltsch the perspective on a concern with the logic of history. What was particularly necessary was the overcoming of a methodological monism resting on scientific thought and the scientific recognition of the independence of historical research and knowledge which went with that. Unlike scientific work, historical work is not concerned with well-defined elements and general, abstract regularity, but with individual units which are relatively self-contained and have formed in the course of a development as a context of life.[188] This process, and logical attention to it, are fundamental for Troeltsch: the category of individual totality corresponds to it. From this it is possible to read off the fact that the decisive element is not logical dissection but a return to the shaped form of historical life. In their practical work historians instinctively turn to these individual entities, and become logically aware of them only in a subsequent course of reflection.

What can be regarded as individuality, and like it be defined more closely, depends on the particular interest of the researcher or observer: individualities can be individuals or families, a tribe or a state, and even an epoch. The boundaries are fluid, and therefore the conceptualization of them depends on the observer. Anyone who wants to perceive such historical individualities must investigate their 'qualitative unity and peculiarity'.[189]

This question is taken up in connection with the concept of originality and uniqueness. Thus it is noted that history has to do with life-processes which cannot be derived or traced back further.[190]

However, in their procedure historians must make a choice or selection of what is essential from the historical entities, their multiplicity and variety. Here Troeltsch speaks of a 'combination of knowledge of the matter and intuition';[191] for him orientation on the object and the openness of the historian must coincide. However, the process of abstraction leading to a concept must never be pushed so far that historical vividness is lost. According to Troeltsch, it is important for there to be a real balance between the reality of experience and conceptual order, the sovereign handling of which makes a historian great.[192]

The threat of a loss of important elements, through the process of selection, to historical life on the one hand and historical knowledge on the other is kept in bounds by the notion of representation. In its relational character this is focussed on the need to represent the wealth of individual features in the historical account by something other, significant or exemplary. In its adoption of the characteristic or representative element this concept resembles that of the type. The difference consists in the fact that through the power of historical imagination it is possible to go beyond the individual phenomenon, so that an approximation to the unique and symbolic follows.

Troeltsch conceives of the categories of the logic of history generally in connection with the lively interaction between historical object and understanding subject. That is true of the other categories, like the unity of value or meaning, the contingent or the unconscious. There must always be mediation between a vivid perception of the object and conceptual ordering. What is called for is a 'logically clarified vividness'.[193]

Troeltsch's notion of a system of categories in the logic of history lies between an empathetic understanding as Dilthey sees it and the logical subjectivism of Rickert, understood as a form of producing the object. Troeltsch seeks a synthesis and sees it in the extension of traditional logic in the form of an 'irrationalist logic' which is in a position to perceive the new and creative element of the historical process or events of life generally.[194]

He explains the necessity of a specific logic of history in the face of the independence of historical life by means of the concept of development. The assumption that the course of historical phenomena is significant is still far from producing any schematic or dogmatic understanding of causality. In history, one phenomenon cannot be conclusively derived from another; nor can any general principle of continuity be detected within historical entities like Christianity, feudalism or the Renaissance. Rather, understood historically, 'development' means that continuity and discontinuity overlap, so that the course is not a smooth one, but goes in leaps or with counter-movements. However, all in all that does not put in question the principle of becoming and the fundamental connection in an individual totality. The important thing is, rather, to assume creative originality at the two end-points, i.e. both in the historical process itself and on the side of the historian. And from this perspective, counter-movements or so-called aberrations can even be productive for the development of historical life. So for Troeltsch the concept of historical development has an objective basis in the facts, but to this must be added the historical sense of the observer, who recognizes the historical principle of becoming.

Troeltsch demarcates his reflections in two directions: first, against any idea of progress grounded in the philosophy of history; and secondly, against an acceptance of the idea of evolution. For Troeltsch, the idea of progress represents a secularization of Christian eschatology: the universal goal and the religious foundations are made immanent, i.e. transferred to the historical development. However, the question here is whether Troeltsch's reference to the idea of universality is already sufficient to allow talk in a comprehensive sense of the secularization of Christian content. The Löwith-Blumenberg controversy has shown what detailed differentiations become necessary here.

The demarcation in the other direction relates to the notion of evolution.

For Troeltsch, this is inappropriate for covering the special features of historical life and knowledge, because the development of meaning in a historical process is of a creative, qualitative kind. But as such it cannot really be perceived by thought in terms of evolution.[195]

According to Troeltsch, the logic of history is to be conceived of as a distinctive version of logic, because the independence both of historical life and of historical perception must be taken into account.[196] This leads to a co-ordination, or better an ordered interplay, of forces and possibilities. Troeltsch described with some emphasis the liberation inherent in this conception from a pressure on history in the form of determinism and splintering, as follows: 'We live again in the whole, the mobile, the creative, and understand the responsibility of the moment and personal decision.'[197]

The concept of historicism. For Troeltsch, the question of the logic of history must be seen in the context of more recent intellectual history. There are two towering phenomena which have shaped modern thought in a specific way: naturalism, which understands the world as only being determined by laws, and historicism, which draws everything into a historical perspective. Troeltsch understands both naturalism and historicism as the two last great creations of the scientific spirit of modernity. For him they ultimately come from one root, namely the Cartesian philosophy of consciousness.[198]

In keeping with the time, Troeltsch uses a neutral concept of historicism, prior to all evaluative tendencies.[199] As Troeltsch explains, the evaluative understanding of the concept of historicism is ambivalent in its philosophical and ideological development and effect. The negative effect of historicism is a shock which people have because eternal truths become questionable. If everything is caught up in an infinite flow of becoming, then there can only be relative knowledge and communication of truth. The positive effect lies in the way in which thought is brought to life and extended by the wealth of historical perception.[200]

In my view, critical questioning of Troeltsch's understanding of historicism should move in two directions. First, it must remembered that the sensitive acceptance of even what is most remote and distant in history and the possibility inherent in it for enriching life always has limits. The past always remains something alien, even to a finely developed historical sense, something lying in the past and resting in itself. On the other hand, the assumption that as a radical historical way of thinking historicism leads to a dissolution of all that is fixed and normative, because everything is seen as caught up in a flux of coming-to-be and passing away, also contains an unhistorical element. On the one hand the notion of development is radicalized, and on the other, from the metahistorical level an infinite process of development is assumed.[201]

Another thing to which Troeltsch fails to do justice is the question of the obligation which understands a past expression of life as an offer and a question from the perspective of the communication of truth. This addresses an existential level of encounter with historical life which is fundamentally different from the epistemological-metahistorical level. These critical reflections again lead to Troeltsch himself, because his whole intention is to 'overcome' historicism by giving in to it consistently, by arriving at a selection of the essentials and deliberately coming to a decision which has an 'objective' basis. This, then, is existential overcoming through character and will, made in a decision and not through knowledge.

A look at Friedrich Meinecke[202] shows how one can judge historicism differently on similar presuppositions to those of Troeltsch. Certainly on the one hand one can see here an extension of Troeltsch's position to the degree that Meinecke investigates the formation of historicism in terms of the history of ideas and shows its origin in representative figures (Herder, Möser, Goethe). The difference is that Meinecke has an essentially positive understanding of historicism, which is connected with his focus on the factor of individuality and thus on the character of historical life. In Meinecke the notions of development and individuality are bound together in such a way that general derivation and individual versions become visible. In my view Troeltsch sees the problematical sides of historicism more clearly because while he makes the category of individuality the dominant one in the formal logic of history and in connection with the character of historical life, he does not attribute to it a role which is constitutive of real historical events and its effect on intellectual history, as Meinecke does. Rather, from the beginning, i.e. from his theological beginnings, he combined both a positive and a negative view of historicism.[203] For Troeltsch, the double structure of historicism always includes both the danger of ideological relativism and the possibility of an enrichment of life.

Ritschl and Hegel as open and hidden conversation partners. Both the critical and the positive tendencies of Troeltsch's philosophy of history are best understood if one sees Rickert and Hegel as his main conversation partners. The dialogues with them appear both directly and indirectly, and they have both open and hidden traits.

Rickert's significance lies in his general methodological considerations, his references to the historical formation of concepts, and his philosophical reflections on the assumption or objectivity of values.[204] Unlike Rickert, Troeltsch wants to keep close to empirical historical research, to identify the difference between this and the conceptuality of the philosophy of history, and at the same time to understand their reciprocal ordering as a task. Troeltsch utilizes the conceptual distinctions made by Rickert and nevertheless seeks above all to make progress in the question of the relationship between history and the philosophy of history. He wants to supplement the definitions made by Rickert which, while they similarly have the concept of individuality at the centre, formalize it and logicize it, in the direction of a 'much more real version of the concept of development, more steeped in reality and more full of life', to use it to 'get further on the basis of the Rickert-Windelband theory'.[205]

In the course of these reflections Troeltsch takes offence at the violent procedures of Rickert, the logician and conceptual thinker, who does not truly realize the peculiarities of the historical object and the invitation to the person thinking historically to perceive history vividly and empathize with it.[206] In

Troeltsch's view, Rickert's recognition of the special quality of historical objects does not go deep enough, because it puts the subject of the knower too markedly in the foreground. 'But the logical subjectivity of the historian cannot be too alien and external to its object, but must be intrinsically interwoven with it; they must mutually condition and supplement each other...'[207] With the epistemological logic of Rickert, schooled in formal conceptuality, Troeltsch contrasts Dilthey's insight into the philosophy of life.

For Troeltsch, the historical subjectivity of the person who 'was' must replace logical subjectivity.[208] That means that the task of historical logic must be shifted to a logic of the historical understanding of meaning which recognizes the reciprocality of relationship and thus a fundamental equality of historical subject and historical object. Only in this way can the proximity to historical science be maintained and justice really be done to the historical object in its individuality.

The other point of criticism which Troeltsch makes relates to the question of value. Troeltsch sees that in Rickert there is a gaping chasm between the historically fortuitous, individual moulding of values on the one hand and the general rational value system on the other. As a result the assumption of an overall meaning of history in the face of the multitude of historical manifestations becomes a basic problem, which Rickert can solve only through a forced emphasis on the general system of value and its significance for ethics.[209]

With his rejection of a theory of values of a Neo-Kantian kind, understood in purely formal *a priori* terms, Troeltsch has come closer – if not explicitly, then in tendency – to the phenomenological school. He is concerned with the forms of association and principles of formation relating to the actual content of life, so that possibilities of evaluation have to be understood in terms of expressions of the content of life. Although Troeltsch here has only indicated the main accents for the focus of his reflections, his criticism of Rickert must also be seen against this background in the philosophy of history.[210] Even where Rickert is not mentioned, and there is no direct argument with him, he is continually present as it were as a conversation-partner, and is in the background of Troeltsch's reflections. In the critical argument with Rickert, Troeltsch sets the direction for his own scheme, but this then takes a different view both of the formation of historical concepts and of the relationship between history and value.

The second dialogue partner, whose significance in terms of content goes far beyond that of Rickert, is Hegel. Troeltsch's interpretation of Hegel forms the hidden centre of his philosophy of history. For Troeltsch, Hegel's great intellectual achievement is his dialectic, 'which is none other than the theory of the identity of opposites, while these opposites at the same time have complete reality, the logic of movement...'[211] Hegel's logic of movement can encompass the individual and the process in which it stands. It is an appropriate way of understanding the essence of history, which always represents both individual expression and principle of becoming at the same time. However, while Troeltsch fully accepts the idea of a logic of movement in connection with historical individuality and development, it is also clear that he maintains a critical distance from Hegel and Hegel's philosophy of identity, according to which 'the all-spirit is identical with the moved expression of itself and therefore through analysis can go back to itself from any point of its individual realization'.[212] One problem for Troeltsch in the philosophy of history is the assumption of the necessary sequence of historical events and a heightening of the historical realizations of value in the direction of a final aim which is connected with it.

Troeltsch wants to take up Hegel's thought in the direction of a logic of movement, without the view of dialectic and its premises in the philosophy of identity which constricts such logic and ties it down. For Troeltsch, Hegel is certainly already going in the right direction when he repudiates an *a priori* version of the dialectical principle and speaks of the 'courage to think'. But what he misses in Hegel is any awareness of the task of actively shaping the future. What stands completely in the shadow of the past and a present which is coming to a conclusion need not, as in Hegel, be taken up creatively and related to the present by an active process of formation. However, precisely here Troeltsch sees an unconditional demand on a philosophy of history which seeks to do justice to present tasks. The way in which Troeltsch combines admiration and criticism of Hegel is particularly evident from his acceptance of Hegel's dialectical view of the state. In the last resort Troeltsch's notion of a cultural synthesis goes back to Hegel's history of influence, albeit with distinctive modifications and expansions.[213]

According to Troeltsch, what is ultimately lacking in Hegel is any actual estimation of the individual and the concrete, undisturbed by speculation on the philosophy of identity or its claims. And above all, what is lacking is the assumption of a goal of historical development which is not already given by the beginning, but is shaped by creative power. Troeltsch's own position in the philosophy of history develops out of assent and criticism, admiration and critical distance from Hegel. According to Troeltsch, one needs to be able to speak of crossroads of historical development, of a tendency to connect the individual and the general, which has its basis, before or beyond all human powers of reflection, in the historical events themselves. Human beings are summoned to look out for such high points in the development and the tendency of the development which can be read off from them. This puts the task of the philosophy of history in another dimension. It is taken up into the very movement of life and at the same time, independently of all the dynamic of historical life, is given a concrete teleology, immanent in creation, which is bound up with the human capacity for decision and formative power.[214]

The notion of development and the knowledge of criteria for judgment. Historical development represents a central philosophical problem for the modern historian. Who develops, what develops, and how can one appropriately recognize developments? Of course the discussion has a history: Lessing, Kant, Hegel, Marx, to mention just a few important names. Troeltsch seeks his own differentiated answer as a historian, philosopher of history and theologian.

If history always always rests on development, the question of a criterion for assessment inexorably arises. For Troeltsch, the criteria required for the assessment of historical things may not be abstract and timeless, but must be individual and historical. That means that they must continually be formed anew. Troeltsch wants to avoid two false courses: on the one hand the assumption of a rationality in the formation of criteria which goes beyond time and on the other a merely intuitive form of address through historical objects. For him reason is not abstract but 'momentaneous'.[215]

Instead of a universal formal absoluteness as a dogmatically consolidated, conclusive supposition, Troeltsch strives for a self-certainty which is steeped in experience, which sets out on the process of selection from tradition critically, i.e. with rational justification, while at the same time being sure of having chosen what is apt and valid for the historical moment. That means that there is an appropriation of history for the purpose of providing an orientation for action and not simply to justify reason as a modern theodicy, as in Hegel.

The resultant self-certainty can be interpreted in religious terms or given a religious basis to the degree that it empathizes with an overall movement of history which has a divine intention and inspiration. Troeltsch also says with slight detachment that theology describes this process as 'revelation', but then accepts this notion in the garb of a philosophy of history. For him there is a kind of interplay between the divine movement of history and the human understanding which perceives it.

Thus Troeltsch strives to form a criterion which mediates between historical relativistic and rationalistic dogmatic appropriation. For him, historical criticism is only immanently possible in respect of strange times and events in the past, i.e. it must be relativized. But what does it mean to measure a historical phenomenon by itself? For Troeltsch, in keeping with Ranke's comment that each age has an immediate relationship to God, it means that the specific characteristic and value of a historical phenomenon or a time must be perceived. Thus any criterion which does not have a basis in the historical process is to be rejected. Whether the polemical repudiation or the positive acceptance of a historical goal follows then remains a matter of practical use and interest.

These reflections by Troeltsch on the formation of criteria provoke critical questions in return. Historical phenomena are in principle complex, and their contradictoriness calls for a prior criterion by which the aim, the 'distinctive idea', of a historical phenomenon, is to be measured. The application of criteria is concealed in the process of filtering out this 'distinctive idea' that is to be brought to consciousness and investigated for its origin and aim – and is so from within, i.e. from the phenomena, and from outside, from the historian. So Troeltsch's work needs to be supplemented by hermeneutics and ideological criticism. At different points in his account, in essence he has the hermeneutical problem in view, but he does not give it a theoretical basis or explain it. Reference should be made above all to Karl Mannheim for the connection between historicism and ideological criticism.[216]

Here Troeltsch distinguishes between a first-degree and second-degree assessment. In the former, researchers or observers empathize with history and primarily measure its phenomena by its own ideas or forces. The second-degree assessment deliberately introduces its own criteria into the assessment. Both forms of assessment are to be distinguished analytically, but in essence belong together. The researcher perceives lines of contact and oppositions. The criterion which develops in the course of the comparison is focussed on a distinction between the beneficial and the detrimental, the receptive and the repellent. In this work of comparison the view that the researcher has of historical development becomes significant. The important thing is to recognize or make connections by discovering hidden lines of continuity. Leaps and counter-movements are perceived in the historical process of development.[217] According to Troeltsch, in the end faith associated with a philosophy of history is necessary, which extracts meaning and depth of life from the historical processes. The will for being, for sense, which transcends the level of merely empirical perception must always also be there. Troeltsch is deeply impressed with the significance of modern historical insights and feels the revolutionary explosiveness of questions which relativize everything, but he seeks to ground in the same reason the existential recognition of meaning and human responsibility which he feels so strongly.

Consequently, here he takes up Kierkegaard's doctrine of the 'leap' and applies it to the philosophy of history, so that the 'leap' is the decision for the cultural heritage in the face of future tasks. For him, the 'leap' as a decision is not blind faith, but a balanced decision for a new cultural synthesis as the solution indicated by history to contemporary cultural problems.

For Troeltsch, the concept of development has a twofold significance: on the one hand, it is a category of the formal logic of history, a reference to a distinctive historical causality, and on the other a main concept in the philosophy of history through which and with which the possibility of the universal coherence and the goal of history is considered.[218]

In Troeltsch's view, neither Hegel's nor Marx's dialectic, neither the organology of the German historical school nor the positivistic view of development, nor that held by the philosophy of life, are really enough. All of them have one-sidednesses, for example the German historical school, which, spurred on by an intuitive view of organic connections in development, cannot grasp and ground the idea of a universal development.

By contrast, while Marxist dialectic has a universal trait, it has purchased it through a construction of the course of history in the interests of a revolutionary goal. One-sidedness, and thus widespread dissatisfaction in the light of the task posed, can also be found in positivism. Here too little room is given to the notion of development because of the accentuation of a causal thought concerned with fixing and calculating, understood along the lines of the natural sciences. The notion of development also has philosophical one-sidednesses in historical realism, in the context of its particular philosophical components, and cannot be philosophically adequate either for a notion of development or for a construction of one in terms of universal history. What is always left as an unsolved problem is how the special character and dynamic of historical life can be combined with an overarching element which represents the connection and the goal of history. And it is Troeltsch's intention that this link should take place in such a way that both aspects, the historical movement and the notion of unity and goal, are given their due right and significance.[219]

It is Walther Köhler's view that Troeltsch's declared intent is not to offer a history of historiography here but to destroy false absolutes.[220] However, by way of supplement it must be said that Troeltsch can often recognize partial truths in the schemes of the philosophy of history which he describes, so that he sees possibilities of accepting them.[221]

The metaphysical levels of knowledge as the offer of a solution. Troeltsch's quest for what gives history an ultimate ground, a ground which transcends and holds together all individualizations and relative generalizations, reaches its goal in metaphysics. Metaphysics is the offer of a solution at a last, highest level, so that partial answers to questions in the philosophy of history are to be thought of as included in it. Thus Troeltsch is following in modified form a notion known from the philosophy of history. All thought is both confirmed in understanding and deepened and transcended in the polarity of multiplicity and unity, of movement and rest. In details he looks to support from Leibniz (1646-1716) and Malebranche (1638-1715).

Troeltsch bases his philosophy of history on the central category of individuality and at the same time negates it as a 'merely finite' form. The dialectical 'sublation' is aimed at the essential 'identity of the finite spirits with the infinite spirit', so that individual distinction and essential belonging can be predicated equally.[222]

Troeltsch only sketched out and indicated the beginnings of the foundation for this speculative conception. He applies his categories from the philosophy of history of selection, representation, essence or the essential. In his view, it is necessary to part company with Descartes' concept of substance and thinking in terms of substance, even if this is seen from the perspective of the establishment of norms, and to go over to Leibniz's concept of monads. He sees the advantage of monadology in the fact that it takes up the principle of individuality and is able to conceive of a link between the finite spirits and the infinite Spirit through the relationship of the primal monad to the individual monads. This notion of belonging to an essence allows on the one hand the assumption of a participation of the finite spirits in the total content of reality and on the other the perception of an external world and thus of life alien to the soul. Here, however, Troeltsch has abandoned Leibniz's inherently consistent thought of the 'windowlessness' of the monads, in the interest of the perception of real courses of history which take place or are made possible through the metaphysical bond with the infinite Spirit.

As with all metaphysical schemes, here too there is a tension of conceptual logic which cannot be completely resolved. Who are the monads or the spirits? Who or what is the primal monad? If, for example, the infinite Spirit is identified with God, this has far-reaching consequences for theology or the philosophy of religion.

Troeltsch finds in metaphysics an answer to the question how the principles of vividness and abstraction are to be justified or how their limitations are to be understood at the level of conceptual thought. Here he finds a solution in the struggle within the philosophy of history between the philosophers of life on the one hand and the 'thinkers of form' on the other: for him, the answer to the question is not logical, but can only be resolved epistemologically, by an epistemology with metaphysical components that take it further. In his theory of monads Leibniz could 'see and conceive of the connections of life streaming through finite spirits as continuous movements within God, grounded in the ontological and teleological unity of the divine life...'[223] The notion of individuality, understood monadologically, becomes very significant for Troeltsch because he can simultaneously both maintain and transcend the individual form of historical life. The historical mobility of finite life finds its way to power, rest and unity through participation in the infinite Spirit. The infinite Spirit is itself to be thought of historically to the degree that it does not represent a fixed entity, but an infinite entity moved within itself. The other philosophical point of reference for Troeltsch is Malebranche, whose thought went in a similar direction and who can therefore be taken up into the speculative approach. The link between Leibniz and Malebranche passes through the idea of the participation of the finite spirit in the infinite, as a result of which all knowledge is grounded in God and is to be thought of as communicated through him as a living entity.[224]

It would certainly be perverse to say that the value of Troeltsch's philosophy of history is vitiated or put in question by this metaphysical conclusion. Rather, the metaphysics is meant to be a bond which brings about unity, a conclusion which crowns the whole. So we must note the level at which Troeltsch puts his metaphysical thought. It is hard to judge speculative conceptions. One either recognizes them or one does not, can identify with them or finds them aberrant. Like works of art, they must be taken as a whole. What is certainly problematical philosophically is the way in which Troeltsch uses conceptions from the philosophy of history as a potential solution for difficulties which arise in his understanding of history and here evades the constraints of the philosophical or systematic context by functional use and reinterpretation to suit himself.

We must rid ourselves of the notion that this metaphysical conception is to be guided immediately by religious experience. It remains in the realm of thought, of reason, albeit in a way which is extended by speculation. We should further note that while metaphysics and a religious view coincide in assuming an ultimate reality which transcends the reality of given conditions, they differ over the way in which this ultimate reality comes into being and is expressed. Whereas metaphysics is to reach its goal through reflection, through reason and logic, the religious understanding of the unconditioned rests on the intuitive perception of it in human experience. The goal to be achieved here also differs. On the one hand it is a divine foundation of the world or the absolute Spirit, and on the other a concept of God understood in personal terms.

However, Troeltsch seems to have relativized this distinction in his last works, since there are transitions and assimilations. We could see as one indication of such transitions the assumption of the coincidence of the philosophical doctrine of God and speculative theology. Troeltsch is thinking in terms of both the philosophy of history and religion at the same time when he sees the ultimate mystery of history in predestination and grace, or when he wants to abolish the distinction between religious experience and intellectual recognition in the concept of the notion of revelation.

The reaction of Otto Hintze is one example of the systematic difficulties Troeltsch expected with his metaphysical solution to the history of philosophy and the humanities generally. Hintze remarked on Troeltsch's metaphysical notions: 'I cannot follow Troeltsch along this way. In my view the creative principle of life which rules in nature and history must be distinguished from the idea of God that we bear in our human spirit.'[225]

Hintze thinks that one cannot call this creative principle of life divine, because nature and spirit, good and evil, are not distinct in it. Because a corresponding distinction only comes about in the human spirit, it could not belong to an extra-human reality. In this connection Friedrich Meinecke speaks of Troeltsch having made a metaphysical confession. However, according to Meinecke, 'he shrank from treading the ground of metaphysics more firmly, but contented himself with general intimations and hints'.[226] Of the subsequent generation of theologians, only Friedrich Gogarten undertook to subject Troeltsch's understanding of historicism, including his intent to offer a metaphysical solution, to criticism without radically opposing it from the start. However, it is clear that Gogarten's remarks issue in a criticism of the supra-historical element. In connection with Troeltsch's thoughts on the philosophy of history, Gogarten speaks of 'a secret inner necessity... which compels them to strive beyond the merely historical'.[227]

The culture of the present: the need for a cultural synthesis. The criterion of history is the presupposition for investigating the relevance of past history for the present and its cultural tasks. This is to make a qualification from the beginning. For Troeltsch, the question of the relevance of the content cannot produce a global criterion – the example of Hegel shows him how one can engage in excessive speculation here[228] – rather, the thought has to be of the present concrete unity of meaning, one's own cultural circle. Here Troeltsch picks up a notion which had already taken shape in his work on absoluteness and which followed consistently from the presupposition of the recognition of historical individuality.

From the perspective of the philosophy of history, the notion of the cultural circle lies midway between individuality and universality, and is an individual entity with a universal tendency. Of course this notion also gave rise to critical questions. Carlo Antoni's interpretation is original – because his questions come from the direct context of Troeltsch's thought. In a kind of philosophical modification of Max Weber's capitalism thesis he put forward the view that something of the Protestant ethic of vocation underlies Troeltsch's idea of the cultural circle and the idea of the acceptance of a destiny given by history which is connected with it.[229] Here he rightly recognized that the notion of the significance of one's own cultural circle not only marks out the framework of action, but as an affirmation of a pre-existing structure of meaning indicates a belief in history. However, for Troeltsch, too, the concentration on what is already given and real is also based on a pragmatic attitude. For him, the insight of faith and pragmatic thought can be reconciled.

One might add that Troeltsch's belief in history is not unilinear and unbroken. Thus Karl Löwith argues that while Troeltsch himself ultimately maintains to the end a belief in history, despite all the critical dismantling of absolutes, he does not see how threatened – assailed, in Lutheran terms – this belief is.[230] It is constantly assailed in a quite modern way, by scepticism and resignation. However, one must add that, for Troeltsch, in conditions of acute cultural crisis scepticism and resignation are not only justified but also have a necessary and stimulating function of challenge.

The comment that 'times of blossoming, harmony and an equilibrium of values, a matching of physical and spiritual power' are rare[231] is evidently based not only on an experience of history which is generally objective, but also on his own personal experience. Unbroken amazement at human power over history is qualified by the recognition that the history known to us covers only a short span of time and represents an incomplete phenomenon in the general process of life. In connection with the life of the individual, for Troeltsch the analogous insight becomes pressing: 'And is it different in individual life? Only a few moments of silver lining and the heights in an otherwise trivial and laborious life?'[232]

I have already mentioned that the concept of cultural synthesis follows from Troeltsch's notion that the significance of history for the present lies in the acceptance of elements from the tradition. The concept of cultural synthesis, which has a central position for Troeltsch, on the one hand takes up his early theological and philosophical notions of the cultural circle and creative synthesis, and on the other corresponds to the basic mood of the time in the philosophy of culture. Troeltsch's adoption and use of the concept are not without problems. These are connected with the breadth and impreciseness of his concept of synthesis, which extends from simple co-ordination with a corrective function to fusion. Furthermore, the concept has both an objective and a subjective side. On the one hand it relates to the activity of historical forces, so that the synthesis 'takes place' as a fate which befalls at a particular time. On the other hand, the cultural synthesis is bound up with the human will to form.[233] Troeltsch thinks that one can give an appropriate answer to questions which arise about concrete content and thus to the question of truth by attaching the philosophy of history to ethics and thus binding it to a value system. The criterion for the unity which is thus achieved is 'inner synthesis', which means a living combination of the elements of tradition with a new aim and conveyance of power which results from this. In Troeltsch the term is not just to be understood philosophically. It takes on special significance by having a programme and aim attached to it. The intention of historiography, grounded in the philosophy of culture, is aimed at forms of renewal which have both an intellectual and a political orientation and are meant to show the way between pessimism with an ideological foundation and optimism. Troeltsch is concerned to concentrate on the possible and to do what is meaningful in the moment by selecting, taking up and combining traditional cultural forces in a productive way. To the idealist and political enthusiast this may seem resignation, but in reality it is moderation.

Troeltsch repudiates the spirit of the time to the degree that he does not reverence either a religious or a political radicalism, and also turns his back on thoroughgoing scepticism. He wants to take up the best forces of the past, wants to offer encouragement, in a critical and well-considered way, to attempt it with the culture that has been inherited. A 'synthesis' of cultural forces is to be found in a kind of process of purification with a constructive tendency, from reason, but not just from reason; freely, but not in an arbitrary way.[234]

Troeltsch recognizes even more sharply than before that the cultural situation is determined by the notion of crisis. But he combines serious attention to the notion of crisis with a constructive move. Times of crisis also have their good side; they represent a spiritual and cultural challenge and opportunity, to the degree that they bring out values of preservation more clearly, and all in all lead to a purification of forces. This brings Troeltsch near to social Darwinism.

In his concept of synthesis framed in terms of the philosophy of culture, Troeltsch stresses the side of human activity in the shape of a cultural will for form. For him, the counterbalance and enlargement of this is the concept of revelation extended into the philosophy of culture. Revelation is the self-movement of the divine Spirit, which is to be thought of as drawn into the human spirit, so that all power of formation, all capacity for cultural expression, has its real ground in this event.[235]

Specifically, this means that for Troeltsch the solution of problems of world history, say in the light of a fundamental idea of humanity,[236] does not come into focus. He is concerned with the reconstruction of his own cultural circle, which is now defined as the 'European-American cultural circle'. If we think of his work on absoluteness, it becomes clear how he sharpens the notion of the cultural circle, but at the same time extends it by deliberately taking in the elements of geography and climate and paying attention to perspectives of historical influence (like influences on the American continent).[237]

Troeltsch speaks of a 'present cultural synthesis' in order to indicate the practical tasks of his own time. To understand the present in terms of a philosophy of history means, in this respect, combining the assumption of an 'is' direction with a 'should' direction. So this is no teleological conception of a course of history which is defined objectively and would be recognizable from a principle or an idea. Rather, the notion of development and ethics must be connected. Here the philosophy of history in its material expression goes over into a practical aim, i.e. the ethical dimension.

That does not rule out the idea of a universal history as a fundamental question. But it is represented in its speculative, constructive form, because all reflection on a universal history is to serve a cultural aim in relation to the demands of the present. Thus the concept of individuality moves beyond all definitions of formal logic into content, into the material side of the philosophy of history. 'Individuality' means on the one hand the actual separation of historical life and on the other the embodiment of an idea lying in this separation, which leads to 'the concretion of a should-be on each occasion'.[238]

In terms of the philosophy of history this emphasis on the principle of individuality rests on the reconciliation between 1. a definition through the formal principle of validity in terms of transcendental philosophy; 2. a simultaneous preservation of the notion of objectivity though a historical understanding of meaning; and 3. an existential way of thinking which picks up the level of the concrete decision of the individual.[239]

One form of concretion is the idea of building up European cultural history. This is not Europeanism on the philosophical presupposition of a relatively unitary context of meaning. 'European way of thinking' is a philosophical answer to the intellectual and political situation of the post-war period with its often narrow-minded nationalistic thought. Here we can at the same time determine the intention of arriving at a demarcation from cultural alienation by an 'Eastern' form of thought, whether this is understood in terms of religion and culture, or politically in connection with the most recent changes in Russia.[240]

In order to be able to go more specifically into the evaluation and analysis, Troeltsch uses structural terms with which forces and movements in the present may be grasped. Thus the problem of the time presents itself to Troeltsch as the question of the 'stratification of structure'. How does this come about? What is to be said about the elements and structural connections in this respect? The issue is that of the basic forces which are to be derived from history, to structure it in respect of the present. Troeltsch thinks that such basic forces or basic authorities include Hebrew prophecy, classical Greece, ancient imperialism and the Western Middle Ages. These forces determine the spiritual field of force and the structure of the modern world and are to be relieved of all that is superfluous and invalid in the interest of their present effectiveness. Of course Troeltsch sees that such a task is hard to define, and that the solution is hard to arrive at. It is clear to him that any possible answer is always in danger and that a distinctive weight rests on it, so that sometimes the result is only fragmentary. So he thinks that the best and most effective thing would be the emergence of an artistic symbol which could bring about unity and have a significance which both represented and spurred on cultural forces, as once happened with the Divine Comedy or Faust. 'Only it is a happy chance when an era is given such symbols, and usually they come only at the end. One has also to go on without them...'[241]

The linguistic expression really leaves open what we are to understand by 'cultural synthesis'. The demand for a cultural synthesis for the present also seems to contain Troeltsch's answer to the historical changes between the Middle Ages and modern times. The idea of a unitary church culture with its compulsive character is introduced and transformed into a cultural synthesis. This results in a merely relative uniformity; it allows free play of forces and has a binding factor in the form of individual responsibility. Cultural synthesis is synthesis *of* and *through* culture. It is a co-ordination and combination of traditional elements of culture into a new totality in the present, but also a unification of life and living forces generally by means of culture, so that the elements of tradition take on a particular significance. Troeltsch evidently had both in mind. The imprecisions of the concept and the consequent need to interpret it were probably deliberate. In Troeltsch we find approaches to a differentiation in three directions. First, cultural synthesis is bound up with the destinies which history has in store for a people and a time. Secondly, there follows the decisive basis of obligation through the tie with the individual's conscience. And finally, far more effective than a merely intellectual goal is the artistic symbol which transcends the powers of understanding and will. But as Troeltsch also speaks of a 'limit' in connection with the extrarodinary, uncontrollable power of artistic symbols, we can ask critically whether a cultural synthesis is possible at all. Is it not an abstract idea, the binding character of which on a community remains uncertain, and for the individual cannot take the place of the experience and affirmation of concrete truth?

3. Troeltsch's last works

One might almost think that Troeltsch had an intimation of the brevity of the span of time still left to him when in 1921 he wrote: 'If life and strength are left me, I would lastly like to return to the religious sphere and finish my philosophy of religion. That is my first love, and in the present cultural synthesis to be outlined by the philosophy of history, the religious remains at the centre.'[242] Troeltsch did not finish his studies of historicism, nor was he able to return to the philosophy of religion. So did his work remain a fragment? Yes and no. He did not develop what he had worked out into a system of any kind. But in method and position what might have been expected would doubtless have been along the lines of what he had already worked out and described. The present interpretation has attempted to show how on the one hand questions run through his life's work like scarlet threads, and on the other how progress in thought is evident in his works as variations of interpretations and the formation of concepts. In Troeltsch the transition from the historical work of analysis to the systematic side, to the 'system', is fluid. Historical analysis has systematic features, and systematics are won out of history. The working out of the content which he had planned would have corresponded to this way of thinking and working.

So what remains to be said of Troeltsch's last works? The lectures intended for England show and bring together his interest and aims, and in part take the issues further.[243] If we add the review article on 'The Revolution in Science'[244] and the essay 'The Crisis of Historicism',[245] then thematically we once again have essential parts of his work as a whole: theology, the philosophy of history, and ethics.

The revolution in science.[246] Troeltsch sees the cultural situation at the beginning of the 1920s as a time in which the symptoms of crisis have also intensified in human perception and awareness, and at the same time there is a tendency to move towards a new authoritarian culture. His study sets out to make a broad diagnosis of this phenomenon of the time, tracing out the background and the connections, and at the same time to offer indications of a solution.

What had already emerged in the pre-war period as a cultural phenomenon, namely the criticism of intellectualism and science, now emerges in intensified form, favoured by the events of the time. A stress on liveliness and originality is combined with intellectual aristocracy and elitist thinking. While contradictory in itself, this very thought tends towards the authoritarian, is ready to subject itself to dogmas, to recognize authorities.[247]

At this point questions about education and upbringing become significant for Troeltsch. This is a sphere which was a new one for him; at any rate it was not one which he had considered and described systematically. Three things moved him in this direction: first his appointment to the chair of philosophy in Berlin, then his experience in the war, and thirdly his activity in practical politics.[248]

For Troeltsch, the ideas of the pedagogue Hermann Nohl (1879-1960) about the contemporary crisis in education moved in the direction of his own reflections. Nohl had above all noted forms of rigidity and intellectual fragmentation. Whereas Troeltsch largely agreed with Nohl's analysis, he criticized Nohl's suggestions for overcoming the crisis.[249] Nohl saw current pedagogical efforts defined by a leading aim, namely achieving unity in a new form of education in order to arrive at a new form of German humanity. For Nohl, the combination of the centrifugal and intrinsically contradictory forces into a single formation of the cultural will, the idea of education, called for an ethical effort. This could go back to a longing for ties which was detectable in the spirit of the time, a search for a new form, a new law. For Troeltsch, what Nohl regarded as a means of overcoming the crisis in the sphere of education and intellectual life tended towards authoritarianism and a dogmatic restriction of thought.[250]

For Troeltsch, Nohl's question about a new law, a new unity, is symptomatic. He sees it as an effective expression of the struggle for a 'revolution in science'. This 'revolution' is a struggle against naturalistic and historicistic scepticism in favour of an overall view, a unity on the basis of originality and a free expression of life. An attempt was being made to counter the problem of relativism, which emerged as an ideological result of the new thinking, with a reference to authority and law.[251]

Troeltsch thought that he could describe and sum up the phenomena which were emerging under the term 'neo-Romantic'. For him this did not describe any content but rather a specific intellectual drive and direction. This was a movement of emancipation from intellectual rigidity, from the scientific domination of the spirit, in the direction of personal experience and existential involvement. However, it takes a closer definition of what is intended, what is meant positively, to indicate special forms and individual manifestations. And here, according to Troeltsch, the spectrum is very broad. Theologically, Troeltsch referred above all to Friedrich Gogarten as a representative of theology with a neo-Romantic orientation.[252] Troeltsch sees his analysis confirmed when the stress on the factor of 'experience' is overturned theologically and becomes a flight to dogma. The tendency towards a personal commitment of faith ends in a new religous bond and acceptance of authority. Troeltsch is not prepared to take this course.

What interests Troeltsch in his critical analysis over and above these religious and theological questions are the elitist forms of thought which emerge in the new intellectual movement that he is considering, the intellectual aristocracy falsely understood. He sees this spirit alive in the George circle – but this is only a blatant example of a widespread way of thinking which is lacking in goodness and understanding for others. That does not mean that for Troeltsch there may not be a special self-understanding among

Ernst Troeltsch

intellectuals, that he recognizes no intellectual aristocracy; however, as far as he is concerned this self-understanding must be combined with a sense of responsibility, must be inoculated against mere aestheticism and cultural encapsulation.

Apart from the George circle, Troeltsch finds similar forms of thought in Oswald Spengler, Graf Keyserling, Frobenius and Alfred Weber. From the religious side, Jatho, Traub, Bonus and Johannes Müller are to be mentioned in this connection, but also 'the followers of Kierkegaard like Heim and Gogarten who are now making contact'.[253] Troeltsch also sees a lack of concern for social factors, the problematical promise of new insights by-passing the old science or going beyond it, in Oswald Spengler's *Decline* and Graf Keyserling's *School of Wisdom*.[254]

The abiding significance of historicism. The basis of the situation which Troeltsch describes as the 'crisis of historicism' does not lie in political events and the changed political situation since the war, but in history and the philosophy of history. The effects of this in the form of specialization on the one hand and the relativizing of 'meaning' on the other have led to a dilemma which a philosophical dilettantism has been able to exploit. The consequence has been simplifications and ideological justifications. The World War and the political revolution have simply brought to light what had been the concerns of the science and the spirit of the time. Troeltsch's criticism is directed against those who exploit the crisis ideologically, and want to make ideological capital out of the situation. In his view, historicism is not to be abandoned, because it represents the only possibility of providing a relationship with past culture and past values. All criticism must start from this fundamental insight. Troeltsch is concerned to demonstrate the ideological and political consequences for historical thinking of a one-sided attribution of guilt. For him these consist in irrationalism and ideological violence, anti-historicism and authoritarian religious thought. The folkish interpretation of history and authoritarian religious thought are then the individual phenomena. In anti-historicism, rational argument has been replaced by a subjectivism which relies on concessions and thinks that it can commit others to this. Here the opposing position is marked by a radical rationalism. Another fatal idea for resolving the crisis is the folkish way, in the form of a limitation of universal history to the history of one's own people or race. Irrationalism and the totalitarian claim characterize the thought which expresses itself here. Troeltsch sees what amounts to a 'class ideology of a bourgeoisie whose existence is threatened'[255] in the folkish view of history and the corresponding politicizing which has chosen Jewry as its declared opponent.

For Troeltsch, the only possible way out of the crisis is a new combination of history and philosophy. The link back to historical forces must remain, but it must be brought to consciousness and put in order. There is no need for any violence through one-sidedness and self-justification. All references to history have to justify themselves through their creative power, through their rendering of new impulses. Troeltsch thinks that this way is not only viable but necessary because it gives or allows what is necessary to rational, scientific control.

IV

Preparations for the Trip to England and Troeltsch's Sudden Death

The lectures destined for England really produce hardly any new insights beyond the book on historicism, so their German title, 'The Overcoming of Historicism', is misleading.[256] Nevertheless, the lecture sequel is significant in terms of content. It makes some things more precise and develops thoughts on ethics, the absoluteness of Christianity and the relationship between politics and religion.

In connection with the first theme, Troeltsch stresses that in the solution of its main problems the philosophy of history must adopt an ethics of cultural values. Of course Troeltsch knows that this intention is burdened by a recognition of the variability of norms. In the quest for universal and objective norms, Troeltsch thinks that he can go back to an ethics of conscience to the degree that it is possible to demonstrate the obligatory moral character of action with reference to the phenomenon of the conscience. However, on the basis of his aim Troeltsch can only put forward this assumption because the demands expressed in an ethics of conscience have already been shaped by tradition – by means of a kind of consensus. The development towards fixed forms indicates that we have here demands which can be universalized on the basis of their formality. As we know from his discussion with Wilhelm Herrmann, Troeltsch incorporates the dimension of historical formations of value, the ethic of goods, into his reflections, so that beyond the purely formal character of the 'should' it is important also to take note of the substance of its demands. When applied to the argument, that means that history communicates an assessment of values as objectively given by a process of consolidation. By contrast, Troeltsch thinks that it is impossible to develop objective norms from the structure of the moral personality, so that a morality of personality or conscience cannot be thought to be sufficient. He responds to the problem of the relativism of moral values because of their historical derivation by indicating that any ethics is always a compromise. Every human being is on the one hand a natural being and on the other a spiritual being. The conflict to which this gives rise is in principle insoluble – in the present context it can be resolved only by a balance which always has to be achieved anew: compromise. The emphasis here on personal morality on the one hand and moral conduct determined by responsibility on the other has points of contact with Weber's distinction between dispositional ethics and an ethics of responsibility.

If the ethic of conscience is formal and supratemporal, the ethic of the good results from the historical development of cultural values. In taking up his main philosophical concept of individuality, Troeltsch indicates that this has a quite different status in the ethics of cultural values from the status that it has in personal morality.[257] On the question of the relationship between natural basis and moral superstructure, in the morality of conscience one is to assume an opposition, and in the ethic of goods an abiding bond on the basis of historical roots. From this Troeltsch concludes 'that the cultural ethic imposes itself more strongly and victoriously than the ethics of conscience'.[258] The solutions proposed by Troeltsch to the question of the relationship between the philosophy of history and ethics culminate in his notion of cultural synthesis, well known from his studies on historicism, but with a specific accent. According to Troeltsch, the combination of cultural values follows primarily from the sphere of the unconscious. However, in addition to this there is a need for a deliberate aim, though as an *a posteriori* construction it links up with the pre- or sub-personal levels of the formation of a synthesis which have already been addressed. What can at one stage be developed as the central value of a cultural circle is bound up with a human decision, is both living personal action and the acceptance of historical personalities at the same time. In a modification of the notion of justification and the Lutheran *pro me* principle, Troeltsch argues that here faith alone justifies and that truth must always be truth 'for us'.

With reference to the subjectivism which was developing at this time, the Romantic stress on experience, the quest for simplicity and concentration on life-style and questions of value, as a conclusion Troeltsch plans a combination of a moral of conscience, an ethic of cultural values and the 'situation'. Whereas earlier the churches appeared when questions of such a co-ordination arose, Troeltsch is now certain that the common spirit which is needed here can also originate and have an effect alongside and outside the churches.[259] The modern longing for more originality and more community always has to be accepted, but in connection with a stronger expression of a sense of responsibility and the perception and practice of an overarching love.[260]

Troeltsch's position on the question of the absoluteness of Christianity shows that his tendency towards the freely religious, the undogmatic and his leaning towards tolerance intensified.[261] In the question of absolutenesss, the notion of the supreme value of Christianity on the basis of a comparison of religions also fades into the background, and the notion of the cultural circle, with the idea of an involvement of human beings in a particular time and culture, comes more clearly to the fore. And whereas in the work on absoluteness the question of intolerance is considered within the framework of the history of the church and theology, on the basis of dogmatic positions, now the notion of tolerance becomes a specific theme and is developed. According to Troeltsch now, a comparative assessment of religions is fundamentally impossible. The investigations of historicism probably also contributed to this judgment, above all through the emphasis on the notion of historical individualism which is to be found there.

Christianity has two spheres of special significance in the comparison of religions. First, the idea of the truth 'for us' in the cultural circle, which is emphasized by Troeltsch, is an indication of the special task of the cultural synthesis, which takes note of the tradition of the West. And secondly, this offer and this challenge do not do away with the individual question of truth. In this connection Troeltsch speaks of a personal courage to believe.

It remains open how this personal position of faith is ultimately to be reconciled with the result of the approach in terms of cultural history. Troeltsch speaks of an 'ultimate unknown height' to which all religions strive. But none of the existing religions represents a unitive power in the sense of an objectively given human life of the spirit. God is indeed taken up into the earthly movement of life, or better, he moves into it, but according to Troeltsch the consummation is reserved for an ultimate unknown goal in the world beyond. Here Troeltsch gives original and apt expression to the feeling about life among many intellectuals at the end of the nineteenth and beginning of the twentieth century, the mixture of intellectual relativism, distance from dogmatic church life and a basic but conceptually blurred acknowledgment of Christianity on the basis of personal origins and cultural necessity. What remains a problem is that while the element of personal faith is prepared for in a way by the notion of the cultural circle,[262] the real approach is bound up with the experience of the individual, with an immediate inner certainty. In Troeltsch's argument the question of substance, of what should now be believed, fades into the background behind the quite justified reference to the existential form of the discovery of truth. Evidently it is enough for Troeltsch to bring divine life and human experience together in what can be called the course of development in the history of revelation, which then finds specific expression on each occasion in personal experience. For him this personal faith must be measured by the essence of love. Practical understanding of one another, the notion of tolerance, became increasingly important for Troeltsch. So talk of the 'multiplicity of religious truth' is his last word in this matter.[263]

The last point relates to the question of the relationship between politics and religion. Troeltsch indicates that here he mainly wants to adopt a theoretical approach. However, practical questions also crop up in his reflections. According to Troeltsch, the relationship between politics and religion becomes problematical where religion is understood as a spiritual and personal power (as it is especially in Christianity). So to put the question more generally, he is concerned with the relationship between spirit and power. In his view there are four possible solutions: 1. Naturalism, and thus a renunciation of religion understood in universal terms. 2. The purely religious view, which renounces power and only knows a morality of suffering and hope for the beyond. 3. The notion of a world empire based on a unitary principle of rule which in principle does away with the conflict between religious attitude and power, as was the case, for example, with the Roman empire. 4. And finally, the notion of a league of nations based on treaties and reciprocal respect.

Troeltsch finds difficulties in all four conceptions. His aim is to arrive at a practical compromise. In concrete, that means that politics should be human- ized, ethicized. The important thing is 'recognition of the value of persons at home and mutual respect for the necessities of life abroad'.[264] So here the notion of (political) tolerance comes through against the background or on the basis of an ethic of compromise. But that is not all, since for Troeltsch the realm of the spirit and of religion elevates itself above the level of political thought and action. 'This realm creates a spiritual unity and bond between people...'[265] So Troeltsch's thoughts ultimately culminate in a transcending of patriotism and politics, at any rate in theory. But he has no illusions about the changes needed in this direction in the self-understanding of the states and human beings bound by a national feeling. So first of all practical compromise, a concern for balance between naturalism as the level of the factual (including national ties) and idealism, as what really should be and is required, is the order of the day. The main advantage of this compromise thought is that it is realistic and gives some idea of its aim.[266]

It is hard to say what effect Troeltsch's lectures, which would doubtless have been seen by the people and institutions who invited him as creating a bond between peoples, would have made on their English audience – and also on a wider German public – had Troeltsch been able to give them. Their tendency was to take up and focus Troeltsch's thoughts on the philosophy of history and ethics, and at this level they were without doubt full of political ideas which, while they could not be understood to create any concrete bond betwen the peoples, did point to the possibilities of mutual acceptance and understanding. The later years of political reality in the Weimar Republic, especially the rising radicalism on the left and particularly on the right, hardly gave reflections at this level any chance of being heard.

The invitation to the lectures which Troeltsch was to give in the period between 14 and 19 March 1923 to the universities of London, Oxford and Edinburgh (and to the London Society for the Study of Religion) came as the result of an initiative by von Hügel. The journey was finally to realize a plan from years before, which could not be realized then for personal reasons.[267] And not least the invitation to Troeltsch also had political connotations: he was to be a sign of 'another' Germany, a Germany concerned for balance and compromise. There were enough reservations on the English side: they were above all political, but also religious. People either did not want to let a German professor speak, or they doubted his faith. But von Hügel and his friends would not be put off: the difficulties were set aside.

Preparations for the journey had to be made, and the host even thought of such external matters as the question of clothing. To an anxious enquiry in this area Troeltsch replied that he had a tail coat and a dinner-jacket with trousers and a waistcoat, in a very presentable state. 'The waistcoat is a bit worn, and I can have a new one made here. That is simpler than what you propose...'[268] Von Hügel had evidently planned to have a tail coat made for Troeltsch, for which Troeltsch was to send the measurements. Troeltsch was already looking forward to the journey. His last letter to von Hügel is dated 11 January 1923. Troeltsch writes: 'Now I'm again caught up in an enormous mountain of work. But there will be time to get a passport and prepare for the journey. I must also study the route: I think through Holland and Rotterdam.'[269]

But it was not to be. In January he fell sick. He developed a pulmonary embolism which also weakened his heart. Just as he seemed to have got over the illness, he had a relapse and died, on 1 February 1923.

To Ludwig Marcuse, who had visited him some days beforehand and had congratulated him on having come through the illness so well, Troeltsch replied: 'It does one no harm all at once to be taken very close to the abyss.' Marcuse adds: 'For a fleeting second there was a knowing smile on his lips. Then he spoke as vigorously as ever about travel plans, about his forthcoming lectures in England...'[270]

Marta Troeltsch replied to Baron von Hügel's letter of condolence with some moving words: 'Others can judge better than I what scholarship and the German nation has lost; no one knows better than I what has been lost with the human being Ernst Troeltsch.'[271] The official ceremonies show more than his immediate intellectual, and especially theological, influence had been able to do, that he had been 'one of the most venerable spirits of Germany and our time'.[272]

Adolf von Harnack gave the address at the funeral.[273] Harnack stressed Troeltsch's power of spiritual 'consumption', his readiness to learn from others, to assimilate what he had learned, and allow it to issue in his own work and thoughts. What seems to have moved him most, and where he probably also felt a direct spiritual bond with Troeltsch, was his perception of Troeltsch's repudiation of the 'violent actions of the rationalists and the distortions of the systematicians'.[274] But Harnack also did not suppress his critical view of Troeltsch: 'He was not an comfortable person, and he made it very difficult for many people to get to know him... He could wound by his arrogance and offend by his impetuosity: he did not make it easy for anyone to get inside him.'[275] However, even this judgment of Harnack's was made with deep understanding, indeed sympathy, since here was a man who – as Harnack put it – was free enough to give himself as he was.

The obituaries of Troeltsch indicate something of the wide influence of his person and work. Special mention should be made here of the article 'On the Death of Ernst Troeltsch' by Carl Neumann, who concludes by saying: 'He fought in changing scenes and with changing opponents; above all he fought with himself. We strive for totality and unity of personality. But life, which has so many forms and keeps changing so much, shakes us and pulls at us, and so contradictions are our lot.'[276]

What is striking in any assessment of Troeltsch's life undistorted by dogma is the tremendous breadth of his interests, his activities and his publications. None of the subsequent great theologians could show anything like this, and the same was true of very few before him. For the leading representatives of dialectical theology Troeltsch (together with Harnack) was the last great representative of an epoch of theology which had come to an end, which was shaped by the philosophy of idealism, by metaphysics, and by an inappropriate assimilation to modern culture. In so judging they failed to recognize that the problems which Troeltsch took up are characteristic of modern times generally – and therefore concern us even now. Moreover the 'post-dialectical' period sees this very multiplicity and openness as an impressive characteristic of his theology, which is to be evaluated positively. He saw the counterbalance to cultural plurality and a lack of orientation in a cultural synthesis supported by a religious centre. An ultimate trust in the course of history preserved him from a destructive pessimism. Troeltsch perceived clearly the gulf between the subjective inwardness of the religious conviction of faith, which is particularly characteristic of modern Protestants, and objective obligations in the form of church and doctrine. In his attempts at a solution, aimed at balance and mediation, an unexplained remnant remained which he dealt with personally by a simple, unconditional trust in God.

Paul Tillich was right in saying of Troeltsch's significance for theology that he was 'the negative presupposition for any coming structure',[277] in that we have to move beyond Troeltsch and his work, like everything in history. But we have to supplement Tillich's judgment. It has proved that Troeltsch was both the negative and the positive presupposition of future theological development, and, if one thinks on a long time-scale, he remains so. He was the negative presupposition, because it was necessary to move beyond him; the positive presupposition, because he recognized and thought through questions and considered solutions which must not be lost.

Sources and Bibliography

1. Primary literature (published and unpublished sources)

(a) Publications by Troeltsch

The pre-prints of the *RGG* articles (1907ff.) are not included here, and the 'Spektator-Briefe' (1918-1922), which were collected together later (1924), are not cited separately. For detailed references and a complete listing see F.W.Graf and H.Ruddies, *Ernst Troeltsch Bibliographie*, Tübingen 1982

1888

'Von der Münchener Kunstausstellung', *Korrespondenzblatt für die evangelisch-lutherischen Geistlichen in Bayern* 13, 393-5, 402-5, 405-8, 409-11

1891

Vernunft und Offenbarung bei Johann Gerhard und Melanchthon. Untersuchung zur Geschichte der altprotestantische Theologie, Göttingen

1893

'Die christliche Weltanschauung und die wissenschaftlichen Gegenströmungen', *ZTK* 3, 493-528 (continued in 1894)
'Sudermanns Heimat', *CW* 7, 568-78

1894

'Die christliche Weltanschauung und die wissenschaftlichen Gegenströmungen', *ZTK* 4, 167-231, later in *GS* II, 227-327
Review of R.A.Lipsius, *Lehrbuch der evangelisch-protestantischen Dogmatik*, Brunswick ³1893, in *GGA* 156, 841-54

1895

Die historischen Grundlagen der Theologie unseres Jahrhunderts, Karlsruhe
'Religion und Kirche', *PrJ* 81, 215-49, later in *GS* II, 146-82

'Die Selbständigkeit der Religion', *ZTK* 5, 361-436
'Atheistische Ethik', *PrJ* 92, 193-217, later in *GS* II, 525-51

1896

'Die Selbständigkeit der Religion', *ZTK* 6, 71-110, 167-218
'Religionsphilosophie und theologische Principienlehre', *TJB* 15, 376-425
'Zur Abwehr und Berichtigung gegen den Verfasser der "Religiösen Liquidation" ',
Deutsche Revue 21, 231-9
Reviews of R.Eucken,'Der Kampf um einen geistigen Lebensinhalt. Neue Grundleg-
ung einer Weltanschauung', *TLZ* 21, 405-9; J.Köstlin,'Der Glaube und seine
Bedeutung für Erkenntnis, Leben und Kirche', *GGA* 158, 673-85

1897

'Moderner Halbmaterialismus', *CW* 11, 98-103, 157-62
'Christentum und Religionsgeschichte', *PrJ* 87, 415-47, later in *GS* II, 328-63;
ET'Christianity and the History of Religion', in *RH*, 77-86
'Religionsphilosophie und theologische Principienlehre', *TJB* 16, 498-557
'Aufklärung', *RE³*, Vol.2, 225-41, later in *GS* IV, 338-74
Review of G.Class, *Untersuchungen zur Phänomenologie und Ontologie des menschlichen
Geistes, TLZ* 22, 51-7

1898

'Geschichte und Metaphysik', *ZTK* 8, 1-69
'Zur theologischen Lage', *CW* 12, 627-31, 650-7
'Religionsphilosophie und prinzipielle Theologie', *TJB* 17, 531-603
'Deismus', in *RE³*, Vol.4, 532-59, later in *GS* IV, 429-87
Reviews of C.A.Bernouilli, *Die wissenschaftliche und die kirchliche Methode in der Theologie,
GGA* 160, 425-35; M.Rade, *Die Religion im modernen Geistesleben, TLZ* 23, 570-3;
A.von Oettingen, *Lutherische Dogmatik*, Vol.1, *GGA* 160, 827-32; R.A.Lipsius,
Glauben und Wissen, GGA 160, 870-1; A.Sabatier, *Esquisse d'une philosophie de la
religion d'après la psychologie et l'histoire, DLZ* 19, 737-42

1899

Richard Rothe, Freiburg im Breisgau
'Religionsphilosophie und prinzipielle Theologie', *TJB* 15, 485-536
'Erinnerungen an Siebenbürgen', *CW* 13, 1233-8
Review of G.von Below, *Die neue historische Methode*, and H.Rickert, *Kulturwissenschaft
und Naturwissenschaft, TLZ* 24, 375-7

1900

'Die wissenschaftliche Lage und ihre Anforderungen an die Theologie', in *Sammlung
gemeinverständlicher Vorträge und Schriften aus dem Gebiet der Theologie und Religionsgeschichte* 20, Tübingen

'Ernst Haeckel als Philosoph', *CW* 14, 152-9, 171-9
'Ueber historische und dogmatische Methode der Theologie', in *Theologische Arbeiten aus dem rheinischen wissenschaftlichen Prediger-Verein*, Neue Folge, 4, 87-108, later in *GS* II, 729-53; ET 'Historical and Dogmatic Method in Theology', *RH*, 11-32
'Idealismus, deutscher', *RE*³ 8, 612-37, later in *GS* IV, 532-87

1901

'Voraussetzungslose Wissenschaft', *CW* 15, 1177-82, later in *GS* II, 183-92
Reviews of R.Seeberg, *Lehrbuch der Dogmengeschichte*, Part Two, *Die Dogmengeschichte des Mittelalters und der Neuzeit*, *GGA* 163, 15-30, later in *GS* IV, 739-52; J.Steinbeck, *Das Verhältniss von Theologie und Erkenntniss-Theorie*, *DLZ* 22, 710-12; A.D.Dorner, *Grundriss der Dogmengeschichte*, *GGA* 163, 265-75

1902

Die Absolutheit des Christentums und die Religionsgeschichte, Tübingen 1902; ET of ³1929, *The Absoluteness of Christianity and the History of Religions*, ed. J.L.Adams, Richmond, Va and London 1971
'Grundprobleme des Ethik', *ZTK* 12, 44-94, 125-78, later in *GS* II, 556-72; partial ETs 'The Formal Autonomous Ethic of Conviction and the Objective Teleological Ethic of Value', in *The Shaping of Modern Christian Thought*, ed. Warren F.Groff and Donald E.Miller, Cleveland and New York 1968; 'The Ethic of Jesus', *The Unitarian Universalist Christian* XXIX.2, Spring/Summer 1974, 38-45
'Der Ehrhardsche Reformkatholizismus', *CW* 16, 462-8
'Leibniz und die Anfänge des Pietismus', in *Der Protestantismus am Ende des XIX. Jahrhunderts in Wort und Bild*, Berlin, 353-76, later in *GS* IV, 488-531
'Theologie und Religionswissenschaft des 19.Jahrhunderts', in *Jahrbuch des Freien Deutschen Hochstifts 1902*, Frankfurt am Main, 91-120
Reviews of: A.von Oettingen, *Lutherische Dogmatik*, Vol.2, *GGA* 164, 317-23; R.Eucken, *Das Wesen der Religion philosophisch betrachtet*, *TLZ* 27, 386-7; O.Ritschl, *Die Causalbetrachtung in den Geisteswissenschaften*, *TLZ* 27, 387-9; G.Hoennicke, *Studien zur altprotestantischen Ethik*, *GGA* 164, 577-83

1903

'Moderne Geschichtsphilosophie', *TR* 6, 3-28, 57-72, 103-17, later in *GS* II, 673-728; ET 'Modern Philosophy of History', in *RH*, 273-320
'Zwei Thoma-Bilder in der Heidelberger Peterskirche', *CW* 17, 355-6
'Was heisst "Wesen des Christentums"?', *CW* 17, 443ff., later in *GS* II, 386-451; ET of ²1913, 'What Does "Essence of Christianity" Mean?', in *ETWTR*, 124-79
'Moralisten, englische', in *RE*³, Vol.13, 436-61, later in *GS* IV, 374-429
Reviews of F.Medicus, *Kants Philosophie der Geschichte*, and E.Lask, *Fichte's Idealismus und die Geschichte*, *TLZ* 28, 224-51; F.Loofs, *Symbolik oder christliche Konfessionskunde*, Vol.1, *DLZ* 24, 954-7; A.Bonus, 'Religion als Schöpfung', *TLZ* 28, 275-6; F.Kattenbusch, *Von Schleiermacher zu Ritschl*, *DLZ* 24, 1949-51; F.Overbeck, *Über die Christlichkeit unserer heutigen Theologie*, *DLZ* 24, 2472-5; G.Wobbermin, *Theologie und Metaphysik*, *GGA* 165, 849-56

1904

Politische Ethik und Christentum, Göttingen; ET 'Political Ethics and Christianity', in
   RH, 173-209
'Das Historische in Kants Religionsphilosophie', *Kantstudien* 9, 21-154
'Religionsphilosophie', in *Die Philosophie im Beginn des zwanzigsten Jahrhunderts*,
   Heidelberg 1904, 104-62
Reviews of: E.Cassirer, *Leibniz' System in seinen wissenschaftlichen Grundlagen*, *TLZ* 29,
   639-43; W.James, *The Varieties of Religious Experience*, *DLZ* 25, 3021-7; M.Reischle,
   'Theologie und Religionsgeschichte', *TLZ* 29, 613-17

1905

Psychologie und Erkenntnistheorie in der Religionswissenschaft, Tübingen
'Ethik und Kapitalismus, Grundzüge einer Sozialethik von G.Traub', *CW* 19, 320-6
Reviews of F.H.Lipsius, *Kritik der theologischen Erkenntnis*, *DLZ* 26, 206-10; A.von
   Oettingen, *Lutherische Dogmatik*, Vol.2, Part 2, *GGA* 167, 685-92; A.Dorner,
   Grundriss der Religionsphilosophie, *GGA* 167, 761-72

1906

'Die Mission in der modernen Welt', *CW* 20, 8ff.; later in *GS* II, 799-804
'Protestantisches Christentum und Kirche in der Neuzeit', in *Die Kultur der Gegenwart*,
   ed. P.Hinneberg, Part I.IV.1, Berlin and Leipzig, 253-458
'Wesen der Religion und der Religionswissenschaft', in *Die Kultur der Gegenwart*, ed.
   P.Hinneberg, Part I.IV.1, Berlin and Leipzig, 461-91, later in *GS* II, 452-99; ET
   of ²1909, 'Religion and the Science of Religion', in *ETWTR*, 82-123
'Die Bedeutung des Protestantismus für die Enstehung der modernen Welt', in *HZ*
   97, 1-66 (also published independently, Munich and Berlin 1911); ET *Protestantism
   and Progress*, London and New York 1912, reissued Boston 1958

1907

*Die Trennung von Staat und Kirche, der staatliche Religionsunterricht und die theologischen
   Fakultäten*, Tübingen 1907; ET 'The Separation of Church and State and the
   Teaching of Religion', in *RH*, 109-17
'Zur modernen Religionsphilosophie', *DLZ* 28, 837-41
'Das Wesen des modernen Geistes', *PrG* 128, 21-40, later in *GS* IV, 297-338; ET
   'The Essence of the Modern Spirit', in *RH*, 237-72
'Autonomie und Rationalismus in der modernen Welt', *Internationale Wochenschrift für
   Wissenschaft, Kunst und Technik* 1, 199-210
'Kant bleibt im Ansatz', *ZTK* 17, 231-3
'Missionsmotiv, Missionsaufgabe und neuzeitliches Humanitätschristentum', *Zeit-
   schrift für Missionskunde und Religionswissenschaft* 22, 129-39, 161-6
Review of K.Holl, *Die Rechtfertigungslehre im Licht der Geschichte des Protestantismus*,
   DLZ 17, 1101-3

1908

'Katholizismus und Reformismus', *Internationale Wochenschrift für Wissenschaft, Kunst und Technik* 2, 15-26
'David Friedrich Strauss', *Die Hilfe* 14, 57-9
'Luther und die moderne Welt', in *Das Christentum*, ed. P.Herre, Leipzig, 69-101, later in *GS* IV, 202-54; partial ET 'The Dispositional Ethic', in *RH*,168-72

1909

'Modernismus', *Die Neue Rundschau. XXter Jahrgang der Freien Bühne* 2, 456-81, later in *GS* II, 45-67
'Rückblick auf ein halbes Jahrhundert der theologischen Wissenschaft', in *Zeitschrift für wissenschaftliche Theologie* 51, 97-135, later in *GS* II, 193-26; ET of ²1913, 'Half a Century of Theology. A Review', in *ETWTR*, 53-81
'Calvinismus und Luthertum', *CW* 23, 669-70, 678-82, later in *GS* IV, 254-61
'Zur Frage des religiösen apriori', *Religion und Geisteskultur* 3, 263-73, later in *GS* II, 754-68; ET 'On the Question of the Religious A Priori', in *RH*, 33-45
'Berufung', *RGG*¹, Vol.1, 1070-1
'Concursus divinus', *RGG*¹, Vol.1, 1879
Reviews of H.Mulert, *Schleiermacher-Studien* I, *TLZ* 34, 277-80; H.Hermelink, *Die theologische Fakultät in Tübingen vor der Reformation*, *GGA* 171, 508-22

1910

'Die Kulturbedeutung des Calvinismus', *Internationale Wochenschrift für Wissenschaft, Kunst und Technik* 4, 449-68, 501-8, later in *GS* IV, 783-801
'Schleiermacher und die Kirche', in *Schleiermacher der Philosoph des Glaubens*, ed. F.M.Schiele und L.Zscharnack, Berlin-Schöneberg 1910, 9-35
'Aus der religiösen Bewegung der Gegenwart', *Die Neue Rundschau. XXter Jahrgang der Freien Bühne* 3, 1169-85, later in *GS* II, 22-44
'Dogma', *RGG*¹, Vol.2, 105-6
'Dogmatik', *RGG*¹, Vol.2, 106-9
'Erlösung: II Dogmatisch', *RGG*¹, Vol.2, 481-8
'Eschatologie: IV Dogmatisch', *RGG*¹, Vol.2, 622-32; ET 'Eschatology', in *RH*, 146-58
'Gericht Gottes', *RGG*¹, Vol.2, 1320-1
'Gesetz', *RGG*¹, Vol.2, 1373-87
'Glaube', *RGG*¹, Vol.2, 1437-57; ET 'Faith', 'Faith and History', in *RH*, 121-45
'Gnade Gottes: III. Dogmatisch', *RGG*¹, Vol.2, 1469-74
'Gnadenmittel', *RGG*¹, Vol.2, 1475-6
'Die Bedeutung des Begriffs der Kontingenz', *ZTK* 20, 421-30, later in *GS* II, 769-78

1911

'Die Zukunftsmöglichkeiten des Christentums', *Logos* 1, 165-85, later in *GS* II, 837-62; ET 'On the Possibility of a Liberal Christianity', in *RH*, 343-59

'Das stoisch-christliche Naturrecht und das moderne profane Naturrecht', *HZ* 106, 237-67, later in *GS* IV, 166-91; ET 'Stoic and Christian Natural Law and Modern Secular Natural Law', in *RH*, 321-42

Die Bedeutung der Geschichtlichkeit Jesu für den Glauben, Tübingen 1911; ET 'The Significance of the Historical Existence of Jesus for Faith', in *ETWTR*, 182-207

'Die Kirche im Leben der Gegenwart', in *Weltanschauung. Philosophie und Religion in Darstellungen von W.Dilthey u.a*, Berlin 1911, 438-54, later in *GS* II, 91-108

'Die Sozialphilosophie des Christentums', in *Jahrbuch des Freien Deutschen Hochstifts*, Frankfurt am Main, 31-67, later as 'Epochen und Typen der Sozialphilosophie des Christentums', in *GS* IV, 122-56

1912

Die Soziallehren der christlichen Kirchen und Gruppen, Tübingen 1912 (*GS* I); ET *The Social Teaching of the Christian Churches*, London and New York 1931, ²1949, reissued New York 1960

'Empiricism and Platonism in the Philosophy of Religion', *Harvard Theological Review* 5, 401-22, later in *GS* II, 364-85

'Kirche: III, Dogmatisch', *RGG*¹, Vol.3, 1147-55

Review of T.Kaftan, *Ernst Tröltsch. Eine kritische Zeitstudie*, Schleswig 1912, *TLZ* 37, 724-8

1913

Zur religiösen Lage, Religionsphilosophie und Ethik, Tübingen 1913 (*GS* II)

'Religion und Wirtschaft', in *Vorträge der Gehe-Stiftung zu Dresden* (5 vols.), Vol. 1, later in *GS* IV, 21-33

'The Dogmatics of the History of Religions School', *The American Journal of Theology* XVII, 1-21 (later in *GS* II, 500-24); revised ET in *RH*, 87-108

'Logos und Mythos in Theologie und Religionsphilosophie', *Logos* IV, 8-35, later in *GS* II, 805-36; ET '*Logos* and Mythos in Theology and Philosophy of Religion', in *RH*, 46-72

'Die wissenschaftliche Theologie im letzten Vierteljahrhundert', *Nord und Süd. Eine deutsche Monatsschrift* 37, 320-3

'Renaissance und Reformation', *HZ* 110, 519-56, later in *GS* IV, 261-96

'Religion', in *Das Jahr 1913. Ein Gesamtbild der Kulturentwicklung*, ed. D.Sarason, Berlin and Leipzig 1913, 533-49

'Die Religion im deutschen Staate', *Patria* 13, 122-49, later in *GS* II, 68-90

'Die Restaurationsepoche am Anfang des 19.Jahrhunderts', in *Vorträge über wissenschaftliche und kulturelle Probleme der Gegenwart von A.Harnack u.a.*, Riga, 47-71, later in *GS* IV, 587-614

'Naturrecht, christliches', *RGG*¹, Vol.4, 697-704, later in *GS* IV, 156-66; ET 'Christian Natural Law', in *RH*, 159-67

'Offenbarung: III, dogmatisch', *RGG*¹, Vol.4, 918-22

'Prinzip, religiöses', *RGG*¹, Vol.4, 1842-46; ET 'Religious Principle', in *Twentieth-Century Theology in the Making*, ed. J.Pelikan, New York and London 1970

'Protestantismus: II, Protestantismus im Verhältnis zur Kultur', *RGG*¹, Vol.4, 1912-20, later in *GS* IV, 191-202

'Free-Thought', *Encyclopaedia of Religion and Ethics*, ed. J.Hastings, Vol.VI, 120-3
'Historiography', *Encyclopaedia of Religion and Ethics*, Vol.VI, 716-23
'Neunzehntes Jahrhundert', *RE*³ 24, 244-60, later in *GS IV*, 614-49
Reviews of: H.Süskind, *Christentum und Geschichte bei Schleiermacher*, *TLZ* 38, 21-4;
F.Traub, *Theologie und Philosophie*, *TLZ* 38, 116-19; O.Lempp, *Das Problem der Theodicee in der Philosophie und Literatur des 18. Jahrhunderts bis auf Kant und Schiller*, and R.Wegener, *Das Problem der Theodicee in der Philosophie und Literatur des 18.Jahrhunderts mit besonderer Rücksicht auf Kant und Schiller*, *TLZ* 38, 213-315; P.Wernle, *Renaissance und Reformation*, *TLZ* 38, 239-42, later in *GS IV*, 759-62; O.Dreske, *Zwingli und das Naturrecht*, *TLZ* 38, 369-71, later in *GS IV*, 779-80; A.Jülicher, *Die Entmündigung einer preussischen theologichen Fakultät in zeitgeschichtlichem Zusammenhange* and E.Vischer, *Die Zukunft der evangelisch-theologischen Fakultäten*, *TLZ* 38, 401-3; H.Rickert, *Kulturwissenschaft und Naturwissenschaft*, *TLZ* 38, 440; P.Mezger, *Die Absolutheit des Christentums und die Religionsgeschichte*, *TLZ* 38, 502; W.Köhler, *Idee und Persönlichkeit in der Kirchengeschichte*, *HZ* 111, 137-41, later in *GS IV*, 721-4
'Theodizee: II.Systematisch', *RGG*¹, Vol.5, 1186-92

1914

Nach Erklärung der Mobilmachung. Rede gehalten bei der von Stadt und Universität einberufenen vaterländischen Versammlung am 2.August 1914, Heidelberg
Deutscher Glaube und Deutsche Sitte in unserem grossen Kriege, Berlin
Unser Volksheer. Rede gehalten am 3. November 1914 in der vaterländischen Versammlung im Nibelungensaale zu Mannheim, Heidelberg
'Der Krieg und die Internationalität der geistigen Kultur', *Internationale Monatsschrift für Wissenschaft, Kunst und Technik* 9, 51-8
'Friede auf Erden', *Die Hilfe* 20, 833-4
'Weiterentwicklung der christlichen Religion', *RGG*¹, Vol.5, 1881-6
'Idealism', *Encyclopaedia of Religion and Ethics*, Vol.VII, 89-95
'Kant', *Encyclopaedia of Religion and Ethics*, Vol.VII, 653-9
Reviews of J.Mausbach, *Die Ethik des heiligen Augustinus*, *HZ* 112, 341-8; O.Schilling, *Die Staats- und Sozial lehre des hl.Augustinus*, *HZ* 113, 562-7; E.Förster, *Die Enstehung der preussischen Landeskirche*, *HZ* 113, 371-8; H.Scholz, *Glaube und Unglaube in der Weltgeschichte*, *HZ*, 113, 83-7; N.Söderblom, *Natürliche Theologie und allgemeine Religionsgeschichte*, *TLZ* 39, 609-11

1915

Das Wesen der Deutschen. Rede gehalten am 6.Dezember 1914 in der vaterländischen Versammlung in der Karlsruher Stadthalle, Heidelberg
Augustin, die christliche Antike und das Mittelalter, Historische Bibliothek, Vol.36, Munich and Berlin
Der Kulturkrieg. Rede am 1.Juli 1915 gehalten an der Berliner Universität, Berlin
'Imperialismus', *Die neue Rundschau. XXVIter Jahrgang der Freien Bühne*, 1, 1-14
'Der Völkerkrieg und das Christentum', *CW* 29, 294-303
'Der Geist der deutschen Kultur', in *Deutschland und der Weltkrieg*, ed. O.Hintze et al., Leipzig and Berlin, 52-90

'Die Kirchen- und Religionspolitik im Verhältnis zur Sozialdemokratie', in *Die Arbeiterschaft im neuen Deutschland*, ed. F.Thimme and C.Legien, Leipzig 1915, 167-83
'Zum Gedächtnis Otto Lempps und Hermann Süskinds', *CW* 29, 653-7
Reviews of: H.Cohen, *Die religiösen Bewegungen der Gegenwart*, *TLZ* 40, 383-5; O.Schilling, *Naturrecht und Staat nach der Lehre der alten Kirche*, *TLZ* 40, 434-8

1916

Deutsche Zukunft, Sammlung von Schriften zur Zeitgeschichte, Vol.19, Berlin
Über Massstäbe zur Beurteilung historischer Dinge, Berlin 1916, later in *GS* III, 111-220
'Die deutsche Idee von der Freiheit', *Die neue Rundschau. XXVIIter Jahrgang der Freien Bühne*, 1, 145-69, later in *DG*, 80-107
'Privatmoral und Staatsmoral', *Die neue Rundschau. XXVIIter Jahrgang der Freien Bühne*, 1, 145-69, later in *DG*, 134-66
'Die Ideen von 1914', *Die neue Rundschau. XXVIIter Jahrgang der Freien Bühne*, 1, 605-24, later in *DG*, 31-58
'Das Ethos der hebräischen Propheten', *Logos* 6, 1-28, later in *GS* IV, 34-65; ET of Part One of *GS* version, 'Rival Methods for the Study of Religion', in *RH*, 46-72
'Politik des Mutes und Politik der Nüchternheit', *Das neue Deutschland, Wochenschrift für konservativer Fortschritt* 4, 374-7
'Konservativ und Liberal', *CW* 30, 647-51, 659-66, 678-83
'Eine Kulturphilosophie des bürgerlichen Liberalismus', *PrJ* 165, 353-77
'Zum Begriff und zur Methode der Soziologie', in *Weltwirtschaftliches Archiv*, Vol.8, 259-76, later in *GS* IV, 705-20
'Das neue Programm der "Christlichen Arbeiterbewegung" ', *Deutsche Politik. Wochenschrift für deutsche Welt- und Kulturpolitik* 1, 1931-43
Reviews of: W.Dilthey, *Gesammelte Schriften* (2 vols.), *TLZ* 41, 13-15; P.Wernle, *Jesus*, *TLZ* 41, 54-7; A.Görland, *Ethik als Kritik der Weltgeschichte*, *TLZ* 41, 131-3; W.Günther, *Die Grundlagen der Religionsphilosophie Troeltsch'*, *TLZ* 41, 448-50; H.Rickert, *Wilhelm Windelband*, *TLZ* 41, 469-71

1917

Humanismus und Nationalismus in unserem Bildungswesen, Berlin 1917, later in *DG*, 211-43
'Die ethische Neuorientierung als christlich-sozialen Programm', *CW* 31, 146-52
'Über einige Eigentümlichkeiten der angelsächsischen Zivilisation', *Die neue Rundschau. XXVIIIter Jahrgang der Freien Bühne*, 1, 230-50, later in *DG*, 108-33
'Die alte Kirche', *Logos* 6, 265-314, later in *GS* IV, 65-121
'Plenges Ideen von 1914', in *Annalen für soziale Politik und Gesetzgebung*, Vol.5, 308-43
'Der Ansturm der westlichen Demokratie', in *Die deutsche Freiheit. Fünf Vorträge von A.von Harnack u.a.*, Gotha, 79-113
'Von einem der bekanntsten Theologen Deutschlands. Briefe über religiöses Leben und Denken im gegenwärtigen Deutschland, I.', *Schweizerische Theologische Zeitschrift* 34, 259-64
'Luther und das soziale Problem', *März. Eine Wochenschrift* 11, 983-90

'Luther und der Protestantismus', *Die neue Rundschau. XXVIIIter Jahrgang der Freien Bühne*, 2, 1297-1325
'Ernste Gedanken zum Reformations-Jubiläum', in *Deutscher Wille. Des Kunstwarts 31.Jahr*, 87-91
Reviews of: A.Dorner, *Die Metaphysik des Christentums, TLZ* 42, 84-7; G.Heinzelmann, *Die erkenntnistheoretische Begründung der Religion, TLZ* 42, 148-9; W.Windelband, *Geschichtsphilosophie, TLZ* 42, 319-20; E.Cassirer, *Freiheit und Form, TLZ* 42, 368-71; G.Simmel, *Das Problem der historischen Zeit, TLZ* 42, 343-4; O.Scheel, *Martin Luther, HZ* 118, 304-8.

1918

Die Bedeutung der Geschichte für die Weltanschauung, Berlin 1918, later in *GS* III, 1-110
'Von einem der bekanntesten Theologen Deutschlands. Briefe über religiöses Leben und Denken im gegenwärtigen Deutschland II. und III.', *Schweizerische Theologische Zeitschrift* 35, 24-31, 57-66
'Das Wesen des Weltkrieges', in *Der Weltkrieg in seiner Einwirkung auf das deutsche Volk*, ed. M.Schwarte, Leipzig, 7-25
'Freiheit und Vaterland. Eröffnungsrede des "Volksbundes für Freiheit und Vaterland"', *Deutsche Politik* 3, 72-6
'Der Volksbund für Freiheit und Vaterland', *Deutsche Arbeit. Monatsschrift für die Bestrebungen der christlich-nationalen Arbeiterschaft* 3, 49-54
'Ostern', *Deutscher Wille, Des Kunstwarts 31.Jahr*, 2-7
'Anklagen auf Defaitismus', *Deutsche Politik* 3, 661-9
Reviews of: A.Wach, *Staatsmoral und Politik, TLZ* 43, 137-9; E.Schaeder, *Religion und Vernunft, TLZ* 43, 11-12; H.Cohen, 'Der Begriff der Religion im System der Philosophie', *TLZ* 43, 57-62; 'Zur Religionsphilosophie. Aus Anlass des Buches von Rudolf Otto über "Das Heilige" ', *Kantstudien* 23, 65-76

1919

Deutsche Bildung, Darmstadt, later in *DG*, 169-210
Die Dynamik der Geschichte nach der Geschichtsphilosophie des Positivismus, Berlin 1919, later in *GS* III, 371-464
'Für unsere Selbsterkenntnis', *Deutsche Wille. Des Kunstwarts 32.Jahr*, 25-6
'Spectator, Links und Rechts', *Deutsche Wille. Des Kunstwarts 32.Jahr*, 167-70
'Der Religionsunterricht und die Trennung von Staat und Kirchen', in *Revolution und Kirche*, ed. F.Thimme and E.Rolffs, Berlin, 301-25
'Von einem der bekanntesten Theologen Deutschlands. Briefe über religiöses Leben und Denken im gegenwärtigen Deutschland IV. und V.', *Schweizerische Theologische Zeitschrift* 36, 86-95, 140-8
'Über den Begriff einer historischen Dialektik (1. und 2.) Windelband – Rickert und Hegel', *HZ* 119, 373-426, later in *GS* III, 228-77
'Spectator, Produktivität', *Der Kunstwart und Kulturwart* 32, 252-6
'Die Kundgebungen des Dresdener Kirchentages', *Die Hilfe* 25, 565-7
'Spectator, Der neue Geist', *Der Kunstwart und Kulturwart* 33, 27-31
'Spectator, "Der Untergang des Abendlandes"', *Der Kunstwart und Kulturwart* 33, 83-7

'Aristokratie', *Der Kunstwart und Kulturwart* 33, 49-57
'Spectator, Zentralisation und Dezentralisation', *Der Kunstwart und Kulturwart* 33, 115-20
'Religiöser Subjektivismus', *Die Hilfe* 25, 697-701
'Über den Begriff einer historischen Dialektik. 3. Der Marxismus', *HZ* 120, 393-451, later in *GS* III, 314-71
Reviews of G.Simmel, *Grundfragen der Soziologie*, *TLZ* 44, 207-8; O.Spengler, *Der Untergang des Abendlandes I*, *HZ* 120, 281-91, later in *GS* IV, 677-84

1920

'Spectator, Vorherrschaft des Judentums?', *Der Kunstwart und Kulturwart* 33, 11-16
'Sozialismus', *Der Kunstwart und Kulturwart* 33, 97-107
'Die Krisis der Geschichtswissenschaft', *Die Hochschule. Blätter für akademisches Leben und studentische Arbeit* 3, 321-5, later in *GS* III, 1-7
'Die "kleine Göttinger Fakultät" von 1890', *CW* 34, 281-3
'Luthers Kirchenbegriff und die kirchliche Krisis von heute II. Erwiderung', *ZTK* 1, Neue Folge, 117-23
'Spectator, Kritik am System', *Der Kunstwart und Kulturwart* 33, 261-6
'Max Weber als Gelehrte', *Deutsche Allgemeine Zeitung*, 19 June 1920, evening edition, 1
'Max Weber', *Frankfurter Zeitung und Handelsblatt*, 20 June 1920, first morning edition, 1-2, later in *DG*, 247-52; ET 'Max Weber', in *RH*, 360-4
'Der Aufbau der europäischen Kulturgeschichte', *SchmJb* 44, 633-80, later in *GS* III, 694-772
'Der historische Entwicklungsbegriff in der modernen Geistes- und Lebensphilosophie I', *HZ* 122, 377-453, later in *GS* III, 464-530
Review of F.Overbeck, *Christentum und Kultur*, *HZ* 122, 279-87

1921

Der Berg der Läuterung. Rede zur Erinnerung an den 600jährigen Todestag Dantes, Berlin 1921
'Die geistige Revolution, Berliner Brief', *Der Kunstwart und Kulturwart* 34, 227-33
'Bethmann-Hollweg, Berliner Brief', *Der Kunstwart und Kulturwart* 34, 289-92, later in *DG*, 253-7
'Ein Apfel vom Baume Kierkegaards', *CW* 35, 186-90; ET 'An Apple from the Tree of Kierkegaard', in J.M.Robinson (ed.), *The Beginnings of Dialectical Theology*, Richmond, Va. 1968, 311-16
'Der moderne Atheismus', *Die Hilfe* 27, 136-9
'Adolf von Harnack und Ferdinand Christian von Baur', in *Festgabe A. von Harnack zum siebzigsten Geburtstag*, Tübingen, 282-91; ET 'Adolf von Harnack and Ferdinand Christian von Baur 1921', in W.Pauck, *Harnack and Troeltsch: Two Historical Theologians*, New York 1968, 97-115
'Zum Dante-Jubiläum', *Der Kunstwart und Kulturwart* 34, 321-7
'Zum Gedenktage an Dostojewskij', *Der Kunstwart und Kulturwart* 35, 76-8
'Der historische Entwicklungsbegriff in der modernen Geistes- und Lebensphilosophie, II', *HZ* 124, 377-47, later in *GS* III, 530-95 'Meine Bücher', in *Die deutsche*

Philosophie der Gegenwart in Selbstdarstellungen, Leipzig 1921, 2, 161-73; ET 'My Books', in *RH*, 365-78
Reviews of: H.Graf Keyserling, *Das Reisetagebuch eines Philosophen*, *HZ* 123, 90-6, later in *GS* IV, 691-6; E.Cassirer, *Das Erkenntnisproblem in der Philosophie und Wissenschaft der neueren Zeit* (3 vols.), *TLZ* 46, 160-1; O.Scheel, *Martin Luther. Vom Katholizismus zur Reformation*, Vol.2, *HZ* 124, 110-16, later under the title 'Zur religiösen Entwicklung Luthers', *GS* IV, 774-8; G.Simmel, *Lebensanschauung*, *TLZ* 46, 211-12; R.Köhler, *Der Begriff apriori in der modernen Religionsphilosophie* and R.Jelke, *Das religiöse Apriori und die Aufgaben der Religionsphilosophie*, *TLZ* 46, 270
'Die Revolution in der Wissenschaft', *SchmJb* 45, 1001-30, later in *GS* IV, 653-77

1922

Der Historismus und seine Probleme, Erstes Buch: Das logische Problem der Geschichtsphilosophie, Tübingen (*GS* III)
Die Sozialphilosophie des Christentums, Zurich 1922; ET 'The Social Philosophy of Christianity', in *RH*, 20-34
'Die deutsche Uneinigkeit, Berliner Brief', *Der Kunstwart und Kulturwart* 35, 285-91, later in *SB*, 248-53
'Die Krisis des Historismus', *Die neue Rundschau. XXXIIIter Jahrgang der Freien Bühne*, 1, 572-90
'Die Geisteswissenschaften und der Streit um Rickert', *SchmJb* 46, 35-64
'Eine Reise in Holland, Berliner Brief', *Der Kunstwart und Kulturwart* 35, 90-7
'Der historische Entwicklungsbegriff in der modernen Geistes- und Lebensphilosophie III', *HZ* 125, 377-437, later in *GS* III, 595-649
'Erwiderung', *SchmJb* 46,567-9
'Dem ermordeten Freunde', *Die neue Rundschau. XXXIIIter Jahrgang der Freien Bühne*, 787-92, later under the title 'Walther Rathenau, dem ermordeten Freunde', in *DG*, 258-64
'Die Logik des historischen Entwickelungsbegriffs', *Kantstudien* 27, 265-97, later in *GS* III, 656-93
'Naturrecht und Humanität in der Weltpolitik', *Weltwirtschafliches Archiv* 18, 485-501, later in *DG*, 3-27

1923

'Die Zufälligkeit der Geschichtswahrheiten', in *Der Leuchter. Jahrbuch der Schule der Weisheit* 4, 31-61
Review of E.Hirsch, *Die Reich-Gottesbegriffe des neueren europäischen Denkens*, *TLZ* 48, 23-4

Works or reprints published posthumously

Spektator-Briefe. Aufsätze über die deutsche Revolution und die Weltpolitik 1918-22, with an introduction by F.Meinecke, collected and edited by H.Baron, Tübingen 1924, reprinted Aalen 1966
Christian Thought: Its History and Application, ed. Baron F.von Hügel, London 1923 reissued Cleveland 1957; German text published as *Der Historismus und seine*

Überwindung. FünfVorträge von Ernst Troeltsch, with an introduction by F.von Hügel, Berlin 1924

Deutscher Geist und Westeuropa. Gesammelte kulturphilosophische Aufsätze und Reden, ed. H.Baron, Tübingen 1925, reprinted Aalen 1966; partial ET, 'The Ideas of Natural Law and Humanity in World Politics', in Otto Gierke, *Natural Law and the Theory of Society, 1500 to 1800*, Cambridge 1934, I, 199-22

Glaubenslehre. Nach Heidelberger Vorlesungen aus den Jahren 1911 und 1912, with a preface by M.Troeltsch, ed. G. von le Fort, Munich and Leipzig 1925

Gesammelte Schriften, IV, *Aufsätze zur Geistesgeschichte und Religionssoziologie*, ed. H.Baron, Tübingen 1925 (*GS* IV)

(B) Troeltsch's letters

No consecutive correspondence has been published apart from the letters to Friedrich von Hügel edited by K.E.Apfelbacher and P.Neuner (*Ernst Troeltsch. Briefe an Friedrich von Hügel 1901-1923*, Paderborn 1974) and to Wilhelm Bousset edited by Erika Dinkler-von Schubert (*Ernst Troeltsch. Briefe an Wilhelm Bousset, 1894-1914*, Heidelberger Jahrbücher 20, 1975, 19-52). In addition, mention should be made of the seven letters or cards from Troeltsch to Stefan Jacini included by G.Moretto in his 'Ernst Troeltsch e il Modernismo', *Archivio di Filosofia* 1982, 169-80. Quotations from letters in the Troeltsch literature have been indicated as far as possible.

This list is only a selection, the choice being determined by quantity and quality.

Letters from Troeltsch to:

Barth, K., 1 card (1912), Karl-Barth-Archiv, Basel
Becker, C., 13 letters (1910-1920), Geheimes Staatsarchiv, Berlin
Bernhart, J., 1 letter (1922), Bayerische Staatsbibliothek, Munich
Bousset, W., 104 letters or cards or letter-cards (1885-1920), UB Göttingen
Bousset, M., 1 letter (1922), UB Göttingen
Breysig, K., 1 letter (1920), Staatsbibliothek Preussischer Kulturbesitz
Delbrück, H., 10 letters or letter-cards (1895-1919); 5 letters (1907-1917), Deutsche Staatsbibliothek, Berlin
Fulda, L., 1 letter (1915), Freies Deutsches Hochstift, Frankfurt
Gogarten, F., 2 cards (1913-1914), in the possession of M.Bultmann
Häring, T.L., 1 card (1920), UB Tübingen
Harnack, A.von, 11 letters (1897-1920), Deutsche Staatsbibliothek, Berlin
Herrmann, W., 3 letters (1898-1918), UB Marburg
Jäger, P., 1 letter (1907), Landesbibliothek, Karlsruhe
Jülicher, A., 7 letters (1897-1913), UB Marburg
Kähler, M., 1 letter, UB Göttingen
Kerschensteiner, G., 1 letter (1917), Stadtbibliothek, Munich
Knittermeier, H., 1 letter, UB Bremen
Le Fort, G. von, 18 letters or cards (1917-1922), UB Heidelberg
Meinecke, F., 7 letters or cards (1917-1922), Geheimes Staatsarchiv, Berlin
Meyer, A.O., 1 postcard (1912), UB Göttingen
Misch, G., 3 letters (1913/1914), Nachlass W.Dilthey, UB Göttingen
Münsterberg, H., 2 letters (1903-1904), Boston Public Library

Natorp, P., 4 letters (1915-1919), UB Marburg
N.N., (1910) Sammlung Darmstädter (= 2d 1880), in the possession of Staatsbibliothek Preussischer Kulturbesitz
Nohl, E., 1 card (1922), UB Göttingen
Oncken, H., 5 letters (1915-1917), Niedersächsisches Staatsarchiv in Oldenburg
Otto, R., 4 letters (1904-1905), UB Marburg
Rehm, A., 1 card (1918), Stadtbibliothek, Munich
Rothacker, F., 2 letters (1921-1922), UB Bonn
Ruprecht, W., 6 letters (1902), Verlagsarchiv Vandenhoeck & Ruprecht, Göttingen
Schiele, F.M., 15 letters or cards (1906-1909), Verlagsarchiv Mohr/Siebeck, Tübingen
Schubert, H. von, 7 letters (1908-1920) in the possession of E.Dinkler-von Schubert
Siebeck, P., or to Verlag Mohr/Siebeck, Tübingen, 87 letters or letter cards (1891-1922), Verlagsarchiv Mohr/Siebeck, Tübingen
Tönnies, F., 1 card (1920), Schleswig-Holsteinische Landesbibliothek, Kiel
Troeltsch, Elise, 6 letters and 1 card (1915-1920), Bundesarchiv Koblenz
Troeltsch, Marta, 2 letters (1904), in the possession of H.Renz
Vaihinger, H., 6 letters (1903-1918), UB Bremen

(C) Lectures

1. Lectures on General Ethics, SS 1911 (§1 is missing). Typescript notes by Gertrud von le Fort (37pp.)
2. Lectures on Practical Christian Ethics, WS 1911/12 (§§1-3 are missing, 32pp.)
3. Lectures on the Philosophy of Religion (SS 1912). Typescript copy of the shorthand notes by Gertrud von le Fort
4. Typescript copy of no.4 of the lectures on the Philosophy of Religion
5a. Introduction to Philosophy, notes by Gertrud von le Fort. Typescript (130pp.)
5b. Id., corrected typescript copy by E.von la Chevallerie (60pp.)
5c. Id., the original of the lecture notes by G. von le Fort, 2 oilcloth volumes (pp.1-148, 149-294)
5d. Id., lecture notes by G.von le Fort, typescript copy by E.von La Chevallerie
This lecture material is in UB Heidelberg, Heid.Hs 3653 1-6
6. There is a copy of the outline of the lectures on Ethics (SS 1899) and Practical Christian Ethics in H.Benckert, *Ernst Troeltsch und das ethische Problem*, Göttingen 1932, 110-11

2. Secondary literature

Adams, J.L., Introduction to: Ernst Troeltsch, *The Absoluteness of Christianity and the History of Religions*, Richmond and London 1971, 7-20
Albertin, L., *Liberalismus und Demokratie am Anfang der Weimarer Republik*, Düsseldorf 1972
Antoni, C., *Vom Historismus zur Soziologie*, Stuttgart nd [1939]
Apfelbacher, K.-E., *Frömmigkeit und Wissenschaft. Ernst Troeltsch und sein theologisches Programm*, Munich 1978

Bainton, R.F., 'Ernst Troeltsch – Thirty Years Later', *Theology Today* 8, 1951, 70-96

Barth, K., 'Der christliche Glaube und die Geschichte', *Schweizerische Theologische Zeitschrift* 29, 1912, 1-18, 49-72

Baumgarten, E., *Max Weber, Werk und Person*, Tübingen 1964

Becker, G., *Neuzeitliche Subjektivität und Religiosität. Die religionsphilosophische Bedeutung von Heraufkunft und Wesen der Neuzeit im Denken von Ernst Troeltsch*, Regensburg 1982

- 'Die Funktion der Religionsphilosophie in Troeltschs Theorie des Christentums', *TRST* 3, 240-56

Benckert, H., 'Der Begriff der Entscheidung bei Ernst Troeltsch', *ZTK* 12, 1931, 422-42

- *Ernst Troeltsch und das ethische Problem*, Göttingen 1932

Birkner, H.-J., 'Über den Begriff des Neuprotestantismus', in H.J.Birkner and D.Rössler (eds.), *Beiträge zu einer Theorie des neuzeitlichen Christentums*, Berlin 1968, 1-15

- 'Glaubenslehre und Modernitätserfahrung. Ernst Troeltsch als Dogmatiker', *TRST* 4, 325-37

Blumenberg, H., *The Legitimacy of the Modern Age* (1966), Cambridge, Mass 1983

Bodenstein, W., *Neige des Historismus. Ernst Troeltschs Entwicklungsgang*, Gütersloh 1959

Böhme, K. (ed.), *Aufrufe und Reden deutscher Professoren im Ersten Weltkrieg*, Reklam, Universal-Bibliothek 9787, Stuttgart 1975

Bornhausen, K., 'Das religiöse Apriori bei Ernst Troeltsch und Rudolf Otto', *Zeitschrift für Philosophie und philosophische Kritik* 139, 1910, 193-206

- 'Ernst Troeltsch und das Problem der wissenschaftlichen Theologie', *ZTK* 4, 1923, 196-223

Bosse, H., *Marx-Weber-Troeltsch. Religionssoziologie und marxistische Ideologiekritik*, Munich and Mainz 1970

Brachmann, W., *Ernst Troeltschs historische Weltanschauung*, Halle 1940

Braun, J., *Historismus und Säkularisierung*, Munich dissertation 1978

Bräunlich, H., *Das Verhältnis von Religion und Theologie bei Ernst Troeltsch und Rudolf Otto*, Bonn dissertation 1978

Brieger, T., 'Randbemerkungen zu Troeltsch's Vortrag über "Die Bedeutung des Protestantismus für die Enstehung der modernen Welt" ', *ZKG* 27, 1906, 348-55

Bruch, R.von, *Wissenschaft, Politik und öffentliche Meinung. Gelehrtenpolitik im Wilhelminischen Deutschland 1890-1914*, Husum 1980

Brüning, W., 'Naturalismus – Historismus – Apriorismus. Das Werk Ernst Troeltschs', *Studia Philosophica* 15, Basel 1955, 35-52

Cantillo, G., *Ernst Troeltsch*, Naples 1979

Clayton, J.P. (ed.), *Ernst Troeltsch and the Future of Theology*, Cambridge 1976

- 'Paul Tillich – ein "verjüngter Troeltsch" oder noch "ein Apfel vom Baume Kierkegaards"?', *TRST* 4, 259-84

Coakley, S., 'Christologie "auf Treibsand"? Zur Aktualität von Troeltschs Christusdeutung', *TRST* 4, 338-51

– *Christ Without Absolutes. A Study of the Christology of Ernst Troeltsch*, Oxford 1988

Colpe, C., 'Der Wesensbegriff Ernst Troeltschs und seine heutige Anwendbarkeit auf Christentum, Religion und Religionswissenschaft', *TRST* 3, 231-9

Dahm, K.-W., 'Ernst Troeltsch', in *Unbefangenes Christentum*, ed. W.Schmidt, Munich 1968, 127-40

Dietrich, A., 'Ernst Troeltsch', in *Deutsches Biographisches Jahrbuch 5, Das Jahr 1923*, Berlin and Leipzig 1930, 349-68

- *Ernst Troeltsch. Eine Gedächtnisrede*, Einzelschriften zur Politik und Geschichte 2, Berlin 1923

Dilthey, W., *Weltanschauung und Analyse des Menschen seit Renaissance und Reformation*, Gesammelte Schriften II, Stuttgart and Göttingen [8]1969

Dinkler-von Schubert, E., 'Ernst Troeltsch. Briefe aus der Heidelberger Zeit an Wilhelm Bousset, 1894-1914', *Heidelberger Jahrbücher* XX, 1976, 19-52

- , 'Heidelberg in Leben und Werk von Gertrud von le Fort', *Heidelberger Jahrbücher* XVI, 1972, 4-22

Döring, H., *Der Weimarer Kreis. Studien zum politischen Bewusstsein verfassungstreuer Hochschullehrer in der Weimarer Republik*, Mannheimer Sozialwissenschaftliche Studien 10, Meisenheim 1975

Drehsen, V., 'Die "Normativität" neuzeitlicher Frömmigkeitsgeschichte. Zur aktuellen Bedeutung der klassischen Religionssoziologie Ernst Troeltschs', *TRST* 3, 257-80

Drescher, H.-G., *Glaube und Vernunft bei Ernst Troeltsch. Eine kritische Deutung seiner religionsphilosophischen Grundlegung*, Marburg dissertation 1957

- 'Das Problem der Geschichte bei Ernst Troeltsch', *ZTK* 57, 1960, 186-230

- Review of G.von Schlippe, *Die Absolutheit des Christentums bei Ernst Troeltsch auf dem Hintergrund der Denkfelder des 19.Jahrhunderts*, Neustadt a.d.Aisch 1966, *ZKG* 93, 1968, 278-80

- 'Ernst Troeltsch's Intellectual Development', in J.P.Clayton (ed..), *Ernst Troeltsch and the Future of Theology*, Cambridge 1976, 3-22

- 'Entwicklungsdenken und Glaubensentscheidung. Troeltschs Kierkegaardverständnis und die Kontroverse Troeltsch-Gogarten', *ZTK* 79, 1982, 80-106

- 'Ernst Troeltsch und Paul de Lagarde', *Mitteilungen der Ernst-Troeltsch-Gesellschaft* III, Augsburg 1984, 95-115

- 'Demokratie, Konservatismus und Christentum. Ernst Troeltschs theologisches Konzept zum Umgang mit politischer Ethik auf dem Evangelisch-sozialen Kongress 1904', *ZEE* 30, 1986, 84-94

Ebeling, G., 'Luther und der Anbruch der Neuzeit', *ZTK* 69, 1972, 185-213, later in *Wort und Glaube* III, Tübingen 1975, 29-59

Ecke, G., *Die theologische Schule Albrecht Ritschls*, Berlin 1897

Engelmann, H., *Spontaneität und Geschichte. Zum Historismusproblem bei Ernst Troeltsch*, Frankfurt am Main dissertation

Erbe, M., 'Das Problem des Historismus bei Ernst Troeltsch, Otto Hintze und Friedrich Meinecke', *TRST* 4, 73-91

Escribano Alberca, I., *Die Gewinnung theologischer Normen aus der Geschichte der Religion bei E.Troeltsch*, Munich 1961

Eucken, R., *Der Wahrheitsgehalt der Religion*, Leipzig 1901

- Review of Ernst Troeltsch, *Die Absolutheit des Christentums*, *GGA* 165, 1903, 77-106

Fellner, K., *Das überweltliche Gut und die innerweltlichen Güter. Eine Auseinandersetzung mit Ernst Troeltschs Theorie über das Verhältnis von Religion und Kultur*, Leipzig 1927

Fischer, H., 'Luther und seine Reformation in der Sicht Ernst Troeltschs', *NZST* 5, 63, 132-72
- *Christlicher Glaube und Geschichte. Voraussetzungen und Folgen der Theologie Friedrich Gogartens*, Gütersloh 1967
- 'Die Ambivalenz der Moderne. Zu Troeltschs Verhältnisbestimmung von Reformation und Neuzeit', *TRST* 3, 54-77
- 'Kulturprotestantische Brechungen. Beiläufige Anmerkungen zum Problem der Funktionalisierung von Religion', *Vierteljahrsschrift für neuzeitliches Christentum*, Tübingen 1987, 54-67
Freisberg, D., *Das Problem der historischen Objektivität in der Geschichtsphilosophie von Ernst Troeltsch*, Münster dissertation, 1940
Fülling, E., *Geschichte als Offenbarung. Studien zur Frage Historismus und Glaube von Herder bis Troeltsch*, Berlin 1956
Fürst, E., 'Christliches und profanes Ethos. Ernst Troeltsch und Rudolf Otto', *Tübinger Quartalschrift* 134, 1954, 333-51

Gabriel, H.-J., *Christlichkeit der Gesellschaft? Eine kritische Darstellung der Kulturphilosophie von Ernst Troeltsch*, Berlin 1975
Gerhard, W., *Ernst Troeltsch als Soziologe*, Cologne dissertation 1975
Gerrish, B.A., 'Protestantism and Progress. An Anglo-Saxon View of Troeltsch', *TRST* 3, 35-53
- 'Ernst Troeltsch and the Possibility of a Historical Theology', in J.P.Clayton (ed.), *Ernst Troeltsch and the Future of Theology*, Cambridge 1976, 100-35
Glockner, H., *Heidelberger Bilderbuch*, Bonn 1969
Gogarten, F., 'Die Krisis unserer Kultur', *CW* 34, 1920, 770-7, reprinted in Moltmann, *Anfänge der dialektischen Theologie* II, 101-21
- 'Die Not der Absolutheit', *CW* 36, 1922, 498-602, reprinted in Moltmann, *Anfänge* II, 122-7
- *Was ist Christentum?*, Göttingen 1956
- 'Wider die romantischen Theologie', *CW* 36, 1922, 498-502, 514-19, reprinted in Moltmann, *Anfänge* II, 140-53
- 'Historismus', *Zwischen den Zeiten* 2, 1924, 7-25, reprinted in Moltmann, *Anfänge* II, 171-90
- *Verhängnis und Hoffnung der Neuzeit*, Stuttgart 1958
Gothein, M.-L., *Eberhard Gothein, Ein Lebensbild, Seinen Briefen nacherzählt*, Stuttgart 1931
Graf, F.W., ' "Kierkegaards junge Herren". Troeltschs Kritik der "geistigen Revolution" im frühen zwanzigsten Jahrhundert', *TRST* 4, 172-92
- 'Religion und Individualität. Bemerkungen zu einem Grundproblem der Religionstheorie Ernst Troeltschs', *TRST* 3, 207-30
- 'Mystische Theorie der Subjektivität?' Review of Becker, G., *Neuzeitliche Subjektivität und Religiosität*, *Philosophisches Jahrbuch* 93, 1986, 217-20
- 'Ernst Troeltsch: Geschichtsphilosophie in praktischer Absicht' (with H.Ruddies), in *Grundprobleme der grossen Philosophen*, Philosophie der Neuzeit IV, Göttingen 1986, 128-64
- 'Max Weber und die protestantische Theologie seiner Zeit', *ZRGG* 39, 1987, 122-47
- 'Fachmenschenfreundschaft. Bemerkungen zu "Max Weber und Ernst Troeltsch"',

in *Max Weber und seine Zeitgenossen*, ed. W.J.Mommsen and W.Schwentker, Veröffentlichungen des Deutschen Historischen Instituts 21, Göttingen and Zurich 1988, 313-36

Groll, W., *Ernst Troeltsch und Karl Barth – Kontinuität im Widerspruch*, Munich 1976

Günther, W, *Die Grundlage der Religionsphilosophie Ernst Troeltsch'*, Leipzig 1914

Harnack, A. von, *What is Christianity?* (1900), London 1901 reissued New York 1957
- 'Das Urchristentum und die sozialen Fragen', *PrJ* 131, 1908, 443-59
- 'Rede am Sarge Ernst Troeltschs', *CW* 37, 1923, 101-5

Heiler, F., *Erscheinungsformen und Wesen der Religion*, Stuttgart 1961
- 'Die Frage der "Absolutheit" des Christentums im Lichte der Religionsgeschichte', *Una sancta* 30, 1975, 4-21

Herberger, K., 'Historismus und Kairos. Die Überwindung des Historismus bei Ernst Troeltsch und Paul Tillich', *Theologische Blätter* 14, 1935, 129-41, 161-75

Herrmann, W., *Ethik*, Tübingen and Leipzig 1901
- Review of E.Troeltsch, *Die Bedeutung der Geschichtlichkeit Jesu für den Glauben*, *TLZ* 37, 1912, 245-9
- *Schriften zur Grundlegung der Theologie*, ed. P.Fischer-Appelt, Theologische Bücherei 36, Vol.1, Munich 1966; Vol.2, Munich 1967

Hintze, O., 'Troeltsch und die Probleme des Historismus', *HZ* 135, 1927, 188-239, later in *Zur Theorie der Geschichte*, Gesammelte Abhandlungen II, Leipzig 1942, 20-70

Holl, K., *Der Modernismus* (1908), in *Gesammelte Aufsätze zur Kirchengeschichte* 3, Tübingen 1908, 437-59
- *Briefwechsel mit Adolf von Harnack*, ed. H.Karpp, Tübingen 1966
- *Gesammelte Aufsätze zur Kirchengeschichte*, 1, *Luther*, Tübingen 1932

Hübinger, G., 'Kulturkritik und Kulturpolitik des Eugen-Diederichs-Verlags im Wilhelminismus. Auswege aus der Krise der Moderne?', *TRST* 4, 92-114

Hügel, F.von, Introduction to Ernst Troeltsch, *Christian Thought. Its History and Application*, London 1923, xi-xxxi
- 'Ernst Troeltsch. To the Editor', *The Times Literary Supplement*, 29 March 1923, 216

James, W., *The Varieties of Religious Experience*, London 1902

Jelke, R., *Das religiöse Apriori und die Aufgaben der Religionsphilosophie*, Gütersloh 1917

Jellinek, G., *Ausgewählte Schriften und Reden*, Vol.1, reprint of Berlin 1911 edition, Aalen 1970 (this includes Camilla Jellinek, 'Georg Jellinek. Ein Lebensbild', 6-140)

Kaftan, J., Review of Ernst Troeltsch, *Vernunft und Offenbarung bei Johann Gerhard und Melanchthon*, Gütersloh 1891, *TLZ* 17, 1892, 208-12
- 'Die Selbständigkeit des Christentums', *ZTK* 1896, 373-94
- 'Erwiderung, 1.Methode, 2.Der Supranaturalismus', *ZTK* 8, 1898, 70-96

Kaftan, T., *Ernst Tröltsch. Eine kritische Zeitstudie*, Schleswig 1912

Kalweit, P., 'Das religiöse Apriori', *Studien und Kritiken* 81, 1908, 139-56

Kasch, W.F., *Die Sozialphilosophie von Ernst Troeltsch*, Beiträge zur historischen Theologie 34, Tübingen 1963

Kattenbusch, F., 'Im Sachen der Ritschlschen Theologie', *CW* 12, 1898, 59-62, 75-81

Klapwijk, J., *Tussen historisme en relativisme. Een studie over de dynamiek van het historisme en de wisgerige ontwikkelingsgang van Ernst Troeltsch*, Assen 1970

Klemm, H., 'Die Identifizierung des christlichen Glaubens in Ernst Troeltschs Vorlesung über Glaubenslehre', *NZST* 16, 1974, 187-98

Köhler, R., *Der Begriff a priori in der modernen Religionsphilosophie. Eine Untersuchung zur religionsphilosophischen Methode*, Leipzig 1920

Köhler, W., Review of *Die Bedeutung des Protestantismus* (Ernst Troeltsch), *HZ* 110, 1912, 437-8
- Review of *Die Soziallehren der christlichen Kirchen* (Ernst Troeltsch), *HZ* 114, 1915, 598-605
- *Ernst Troeltsch*, Tübingen 1941
- 'Ernst Troeltsch', *Zeitschrift für deutsche Kulturphilosophie* 9, 1943, 1-21

Kohls, E.-W., 'Das Bild der Reformation bei W.Dilthey, A.von Harnack and E. Troeltsch', *NZST* 11, 1969, 269-91

Kollmann, E.C., 'Eine Diagnose der Weimarer Republik. Ernst Troeltschs politische Anschauungen', *HZ* 182, 1956, 291-319

Korsch, D., 'Zeit der Krise und Neubau der Theologie. Karl Holl als Antipode Ernst Troeltschs', *TRST* 4, 211-29

Lannert, B., *Die Wiederentdeckung der neutestamentlichen Eschatologie durch Johannes Weiss*, Tübingen 1989

Leese, K., *Recht und Grenze der natürlichen Religion*, Zurich 1954

Le Fort, G., *Hälfte des Lebens. Erinnerungen*, Munich 1965

Lempp, O., 'Troeltschs theologischer Entwurf', *CW* 28, 1914, 362-70, 410-14, 434-41

Lessing, E., *Die Geschichtsphilosophie Ernst Troeltschs*, Hamburg 1965
- 'Die Bedeutung des religiösen Apriori für wissenschaftstheoretische Überlegungen innerhalb der Theologie', *EvTh* 30, 1970, 355-67

Liebert, A., 'Ernst Troeltsch, *Der Historismus und seine Überwindung*', Kantstudien 29, 1924, 359-64

Liebrich, H., *Die historische Wahrheit bei Ernst Troeltsch*, Giessen dissertation 1937

Little, H.G., 'Ernst Troeltsch and the Scope of Historicism', *Journal of Religion* 46, 1966, 343-64

Lübbe, H., *Säkularisierung. Geschichte eines ideenpolitischen Begriffs*, Munich 1965
- *Politische Philosophie in Deutschland*, Basel 1963

Lüdemann, G., 'Die religionsgeschichtliche Schule', in *Theologie in Göttingen*, ed. B.Moeller, Göttingen 1987, 325-61
- (with M.Schröder), *Die Religionsgeschichtliche Schule in Göttingen. Eine Dokumentation*, Göttingen 1987

Meier, K., 'Krisenbewältigung im freien Protestantismus. Kontinuitäts- und Umbruchsbewusstsein im kirchlichen Liberalismus nach 1918', *TRST* 4, 285-304

Mehnert, G., *Evangelische Kirche und Politik 1917-1919. Die politischen Strömungen im deutschen Protestantismus von der Julikrise 1917 bis zum Herbst 1919*, Düsseldorf 1959

Meinecke, F., 'Ernst Troeltsch' (Obituary), *HZ* 128, 1923, 185-7, reprinted in *Werke*, Vol.VI, 364-6
- 'Ernst Troeltsch und das Problem des Historismus', in *Werke*, Vol.IV, 367-78
- *Die Enstehung des Historismus*, *Werke*, Vol. III, Munich 1965

- *Ausgewählter Briefwechsel, Werke*, Vol.VI, Stuttgart 1962
- *Autobiographische Schriften, Werke*, Vol.VIII, Stuttgart 1969
Mertineit, J., *Das Wertproblem in der Philosophie der Gegenwart unter besonderer Berücksichtigung von Ernst Troeltsch*, Berlin 1934
Moretto, G., 'Ernst Troeltsch in Italien', *TRST* 3, 287-307
Müller, G., 'Die Selbstauflösung der Dogmatik bei Ernst Troeltsch', *Theologische Zeitschrift* 22, 1926, 334-46

Naumann, F., *Schriften zum Parteiwesen und zum Mitteleuropaproblem, Werke*, Vol.4, Cologne and Opladen 1964
- *Schriften zur Tagespolitik, Werke*, Vol.5, Cologne and Opladen 1964
Neumann, C., 'Zum Tode von Ernst Troeltsch', *Deutsche Vierteljahrsschrift für Literaturwissenschaft und Geistesgeschichte* 1, 1923, 161-71
Niebergall, F., 'Über die Absolutheit des Christentums', *Theologische Arbeiten aus dem rheinischen wissenschaftlichen Predigerverein*, NF 4, Tübingen and Leipzig 1900, 476-86
Nome, H., *Det Moderne Livsproblem Hos Troeltsch Og var Tid*, Oslo 1950
Novak, K., *Evangelische Kirche und Weimarer Republik*, Weimar and Göttingen 1981
- 'Die antihistoristische Revolution. Symptome und Folgen der Krise historischer Weltorientierung nach dem Ersten Weltkrieg in Deutschland', *TRST* 4, 133-71

Ogletree, T., *Christian Faith and History: A Critical Comparison of Ernst Troeltsch and Karl Barth*, New York 1965
Oncken, H., 'Das alte und das neue Mitteleuropa. Historisch-politische Betrachtungen über deutsche Bündnispolitik im Zeitalter des Weltkrieges', in *Perthes' Schriften zum Weltkrieg* 15, Gotha 1917

Pannenberg, W., 'Reformation und Neuzeit', *TRST* 3, 21-34
- 'Toward a Theology of the History of Religions', in *Basic Questions in Theology*, Vol.2, London and Philadelphia 1971, 65-118
- 'Christianity as the Legitimacy of the Modern Age', in *Basic Questions in Theology*, Vol.3, London and Philadelphia 1973, 178-91
- 'Die Begründung der Ethik bei Ernst Troeltsch', in *Ethik und Ekklesiologie*, Göttingen 1977, 70-96
Pauck, W., *Harnack and Troeltsch. Two Historical Theologians*, New York 1968
Pretzel, U., 'Ernst Troeltschs Berufung an die Berliner Universität', in *Studium Berolinense*, ed. H.Leussink et al., Berlin 1960, 50-714
Przywara, E., 'Ernst Troeltsch', in *Ringen der Gegenwart. Gesammelte Aufsätze*, Vol.1, Augsburg 1929, 180-90

Rapp, A., *Il Problema della Germania negli Scritti Politici di E.Troeltsch (1914-1922)*, Rome 1978
Rathje, J., *Die Welt des freien Protestantismus*, Stuttgart 1952
Reist, B.A., *Toward a Theology of Involvement. The Thought of Ernst Troeltsch*, London and New York 1966

Reitsema, G.W., 'Einheit und Zusammenhang im Denken von Ernst Troeltsch', *NZST* 17, 1975, 1-8

Rendtorff, T., *Theorie des Christentums*, Gütersloh 1972
- 'Säkularisierung als theologisches Problem', *NZST* 17, 1975, 108
- 'Die umstrittene Moderne in der Theologie. Ein transkultureller Vergleich zwischen der deutschen und der nordamerikanischen Theologie', *TRST* 4, 374-89
- 'Theologische Orientierung im Prozess der Aufklärung. Eine Erinnerung an Ernst Troeltsch', *Aufklärung, Interdisziplinäre Halbjahresschrift* 2, 1987, 19-33

Renz, H., 'Grundlagen der geistigen Entwicklung von Ernst Troeltsch', *TRST* 1, 13-32
- 'Eine unbekannte Preisarbeit über Lotze', *TRST* 1, 33-47
- 'Troeltschs Theologiestudium', *TRST* 1, 48-59
- and Graf, F.W. (eds.), *Untersuchungen zur Biographie und Werkgeschichte. Mit den unveröffentlichten Promotionsthesen der "Kleinen Göttinger Fakultät" 1888-1893*, Troeltsch-Studien, Vol.1, Gütersloh 1982
- *Protestantismus und Neuzeit*, Troeltsch-Studien, Vol.3, Gütersloh 1984
- *Umstrittene Moderne. Die Zukunft der Neuzeit im Urteil der Epoche Ernst Troeltschs*, Troeltsch-Studien Vol.4, Gütersloh 1987

Rickert, H., *Die Grenzen der naturwissenschaftlichen Begriffsbildung*, Freiburg 1896-1902, Tübingen ⁵1929
- 'Geschichtsphilosophie', in *Die Philosophie im Beginn des zwanzigsten Jahrhunderts, FS Kuno Fischer*, Heidelberg 1907, 321-422

Rintelen, F.J.von, 'Der Versuch einer Überwindung des Historismus bei Ernst Troeltsch', *Deutsche Vierteljahrsschrift für Literaturwissenschaft und Geistesgeschichte* 8, 1930, 324-72

Ritschl, A., *Justification and Reconciliation*, Vol.3, Edinburgh 1900
- *Unterricht in der christlichen Religion*, Bonn 1875
- *Drei akademische Reden*, Bonn 1887

Ritzert, G., *Die Religionsphilosophie Ernst Troeltschs*, Langensalza 1924

Röhricht, R., *Zwischen Historismus und Existenzdenken. Die Geschichtsphilosophie Ernst Troeltschs*, Tübingen dissertation 1954

Rollmann, H., 'Troeltsch, von Hügel and Modernism', *The Downside Review* 95, 1978, 35-60
- 'Die Beziehungen Ernst Troeltschs zu England und Schottland', *TRST* 3, 319-34

Rubanowice, R.J., *Crisis in Consciousness. The Thought of Ernst Troeltsch*, Tallahassee 1982

Ruddies, H., 'Soziale Demokratie und freier Protestantismus. Ernst Troeltsch in den Anfängen der Weimarer Republik', *TRST* 3, 145-74
- 'Karl Barth und Ernst Troeltsch. Aspekte eines unterbliebenen Dialogs', *TRST* 4, 230-58
- and F.W.Graf, 'Ernst Troeltsch: Geschichtsphilosophie in praktischer Absicht', in *Grundprobleme der grossen Philosophen*, Philosophie der Neuzeit IV, Göttingen 1986, 128-64

Rückert, H., 'Die geistesgeschichtliche Einordnung der Reformation', *ZTK* 52, 1955, 43-64, later in *Vorträge und Aufsätze zur historischen Theologie*, Tübingen 1972, 52-70

Ruh, H., *Säkularisierung als Interpretationskategorie. Zur Bedeutung des christlichen Erbes in der modernen Geistesgeschichte*, Freiburg 1980

Salomon, F., *Die deutschen Parteiprogramme*, Vol.2, *In deutschen Kaiserreich 1871 bis 1918*, Leipzig and Berlin [4]1932

Sato, S., 'Ernst Troeltsch und der Fall Jatho im Jahre 1911', *Mitteilungen der Ernst-Troeltsch-Gesellschaft* IV, 22-45

- 'Das Problem des Religionsunterrichtes am Anfang der Weimarer Republik, dargestellt am Beispiel von Ernst Troeltsch', *Mitteilungen der Ernst-Troeltsch-Gesellschaft* IV, 46-69

Schaaf, J.J., *Geschichte und Begriff. Eine kritische Studie zur Geschichtsmethodologie von Ernst Troeltsch und Max Weber*, Tübingen 1946

Schäfer, R., *Ritschl. Grundlinien eines fast verschollenen dogmatischen Systems*, Tübingen 1968

- 'Welchen Sinn hat es, nach einem Wesen des Christentums zu suchen?', *ZTK* 65, 1968, 329-47

Scheler, M., 'Ernst Troeltsch als Soziologe', *Kölner Vierteljahresheft für Soziologie und Sozialwissenschaften* 3, 1923/24, 7-21, reprinted in *Gesammelte Werke*, vol.3, 377-90

Schlippe, G.von, *Die Absolutheit des Christentums bei Ernst Troeltsch auf dem Hintergrund der Denkfelder des 19. Jahrhunderts*, Neustadt a.d.Aisch 1966

Schmidt, G., *Deutscher Historismus und der Übergang zur parlamentarischen Demokratie. Untersuchungen zu den politischen Gedanken von Meinecke, Troeltsch, Max Weber*, Historische Studien 389, Lübeck and Hamburg 1964

Schmidt, M., 'Züge eines theologischen Geschichtsbegriff bei Ernst Troeltsch', in Kantzenbach/Müller (eds.), *Reformatio und Confessio* (FS W.Maurer), Berlin 1965, 244-58

Scholz, H., *Religionsphilosophie*, Berlin 1921

Schrey, H.-H., 'Ernst Troeltsch und sein Werk', *TR* 12, 1940, 130-62

Schwarz, G.M., 'Deutschland und Westeuropa bei Ernst Troeltsch', *HZ* 191, 1960, 510-47

Schweitzer, A., *Geschichte der Leben-Jesu-Forschung*, Tübingen [4]1951

Sleigh, R.S., *The Sufficiency of Christianity: An Enquiry concerning the Nature and the Modern Possibilities of the Christian Religion. With Special Reference to the Religious Philosophy of Dr Ernst Troeltsch*, London 1923

Sösemann, B., 'Das "erneuerte Deutschland". Ernst Troeltschs politisches Engagement im Ersten Weltkrieg', *TRST* 3, 120-44

Spaleck, G., *Religionssoziologische Grundbegriffe bei Troeltsch*, Bleicherode/Harz 1937

Spiess, E., *Die Religionstheorie von Ernst Troeltsch*, Paderborn 1927

- , 'Zur Frage des religiösen apriori', *Religion und Geisteskultur* 3, 1909, 207-15

Spörri, H.M., *Ernst Troeltsch. Geschichtsphilosophie, Kulturphilosophie. Aktuelle Stellungnahme*, Zurich dissertation 1973

Spranger, E., 'Ernst Troeltsch als Religionsphilosoph', *Philosophische Wochenschrift und Literatur-Zeitung* 2, 1906, 42-57, 60-80, 97-110

- 'Ernst Troeltsch über Pädagogik als Universitätsfach', in J.Derbolav and F.Nicolin (eds.), *Erkenntnis und Verantwortung. Festschrift für Theodor Litt*, Düsseldorf 1960, 451-63

- 'Das Historismusproblem an der Universität Berlin seit 1900', in *Gesammelte Schriften*, Vol.5 (ed. H.Wenke), Tübingen 1969, 425-43

Stephan, W., *Aufstieg und Verfall des Linksliberalismus 1918-1933. Geschichte der Deutschen Demokratischen Partei*, Göttingen 1973

Stolz, E., *Die Interpretation der modernen Welt bei Ernst Troeltsch*, Hamburg dissertation 1979

Süsskind, H., *Christentum und Geschichte bei Schleiermacher. Die geschichtsphilosophischen Grundlagen der Schleiermacherschen Theologie*, I, *Die Absolutheit des Christentums und die Religionsphilosophie*, Tübingen 1911
- 'Zur Theologie Troeltschs', *TR* 17, 1914, 1-13, 53-62

Thadden, R. von, 'Protestantismus und Demokratie', *TRST* 3, 103-19

Thimme, F., 'Volksbund für Freiheit und Vaterland', *Deutsche Politik* 3, 1918, 92-4
- and Rolffs, E. (ed.), *Revolution und Kirche. Zur Neuordnung des Kirchenwesen im deutschen Volksstaat*, Berlin 1919

Tillich, P., 'Ernst Troeltsch. Versuch einer geistesgeschichtlichen Würdigung', *Kantstudien* 29, 1924, 351-8
- *Die religiöse Substanz der Kultur*, Gesammelte Werke IX, Stuttgart 1967

Timm, H., Review of Kasch, *Die Sozialphilosophie von Ernst Troeltsch*', Tübingen 1963, *ZEE* 9, 1965, 371-5

Tödt, H.E., 'Ernst Troeltsch', in H.J.Schulz (ed.), *Tendenzen der Theologie im 20.Jahrhundert*, Stuttgart 1966, 93-8
- 'Ernst Troeltschs Bedeutung für die evangelische Sozialethik', *ZEE* 10, 1966, 227-36

Tönnies, F., 'Tröltsch und die Philosophie der Geschichte', *SchmJb* 49.1, 1925, 147-91, later in *Soziologische Studien und Kritiken* II, Jena 1926, 381-429

Traub, F., 'Die religionsgeschichtliche Methode und die systematische Theologie. Eine Auseinandersetzung mit Tröltschs theologischem Reformprogramm', *ZTK* 11, 1901, 301-40

Treue, W., *Deutsche Parteiprogramme seit 1861*, Quellensammlung zur Kulturgeschichte 3, Göttingen 1962

Troeltsch, H.A., *Beiträge zur Geschichte der Familien Troeltsch*, privately printed, Passau 1973

Veauthier, F.W., 'Das Religiöse Apriori: Zur Ambivalenz von E.Troeltschs Analyse des Vernunftelementes in der Religion', *Kantstudien* 78, 1987, 42-63

Verhandlungen der Ersten Kammer der Ständeversammlung Badens. Protokollhefte 1909-1914, Karlsruhe 1910ff.

Verheule, A.F., *Wilhelm Bousset. Leben und Werk. Ein theologiegeschichtliche Versuch*, Amsterdam 1973

Volkelt, H., *Demobilisierung der Geister? Eine Auseinandersetzung vornehmlich mit Geheimrat Prof. Dr. Ernst Troeltsch*, Munich 1918

Wagner, F., *Was ist Religion? Studien zu ihrem Begriff und Thema in Geschichte und Gegenwart*, Gütersloh 1986

Wanger, G., *Geltung und normative Zwang*, Freiburg and Munich 1987

Weber, M., *Gesammelte Aufsätze zur Wissenschaftslehre*, Tübingen ⁴1973
- *Zur Politik im Weltkrieg, Gesamtausgabe I, Schriften und Reden 1914-1918*, Vol.15, Tübingen 1984
- *Zur Neuordnung Deutschlands, Schriften und Reden 1918-1920, Gesamtausgabe I*, Vol.16, Tübingen 1988

Weber, M., *Max Weber. Ein Lebensbild*, Tübingen 1926

Wendland, J., 'Zum Begriff "Entwicklung der Religion" ', *ZTK* 20, 1910, 226-31
- 'Philosophie und Christentum bei Ernst Troeltsch in Zusammenhange mit der Philosophie und Theologie des letzten Jahrhunderts', *ZTK* 24, 1914, 129-65
Wernle, P., 'Vorläufige Anmerkungen zu den *Soziallehren der christlichen Kirchen und Gruppen* von Ernst Troeltsch', *ZTK* 22, 1912, 329-68; 23, 1913, 18-80
Wichelhaus, M., *Kirchengeschichtsschreibung und Soziologie im 19.Jahrhundert und bei Ernst Troeltsch*, Heidelberger Forschungen 9, Heidelberg 1965
Wieneke, F., *Die Entwicklungen des philosophischen Gottesbegriffs bei Ernst Troeltsch*, Soldin 1929
Wiesenberg, W., *Das Verhältnis von Formal- und Materialethik erörtert an dem Streit zwischen Wilhelm Herrmann und Ernst Troeltsch*, Königsberg 1934
Wölber, H.-O., 'Dogma und Ethos: Christentum und Humanismus von Ritschl bis Troeltsch', in *Beiträge zur Förderung christlicher Theologie* 44, Gütersloh 1950
Wright, J.R.C., 'Ernst Troeltsch als parlamentarischer Unterstaatssekretär im preussischen Ministerium für Wissenschaft, Kunst und Volksbildung. Seine kirchenpolitische Auseinandersetzung mit dem Beamten', *TRST* 3, 175-206
Wünsch, G., 'Ernst Troeltsch', in W.Zorn (ed.), *Lebensbilder aus dem Bayerischen Schwaben* 9, Munich 1966, 386-425
- 'Ernst Troeltsch zum Gedächtnis', *CW* 37, 1923, 105-8
Wyman, W.E., Jr, 'Troeltschs Begriff der Glaubenslehre', *TRST* 4, 352-73
- *The Concept of Glaubenslehre. Ernst Troeltsch and the Theological Heritage of Schleiermacher*, Chico, Ca 1983

Zahn-Harnack, A. von, *Adolf von Harnack*, Berlin ²1951

Notes

Introduction

1. Cf. Carl Neumann, 'Zum Tode von Ernst Troeltsch', *Deutsche Vierteljahrsschrift für Literaturwissenschaft und Geistesgeschichte* I, 1923, 164.

Part One: The Beginning of Troeltsch's Life and Work (1865-1894)

1. 'My Books', *GS* IV, 3f., *RH*, 365.
2. Family chronicle, 'Lebensbericht des Hofrats', from H.Renz, *TRST* 1, 16. Carl Troeltsch ran a colonial goods business, in which the doctor was a sleeping partner (report by H.Renz).
3. Letter to F.von Hügel, 4 September 1913, in *Ernst Troeltsch. Briefe an Friedrich von Hügel 1901-1923*, ed K.E.Apfelbacher and P.Neuner, Paderborn 1974, 100 (henceforward Apfelbacher and Neuner).
4. In a speech which Troeltsch gave later as university representative in the Baden First Chamber he said: 'I need only recall my own youth. We were all sons from families with strong monarchical sensibilities and were enthusiasts for a united Germany' (*Verhandlungen der Ersten Kammer der Stände-Versammlung des Grossherzogtums Baden*, session of 15 July 1912, proceedings, 657). And in an article commemorating the death of his friend Wilhelm Bousset, he said of himself that 'as the son of an old family from an imperial city' he had 'grown up with a mild rationalism' and politically saw himself 'as an unqualified Bismarckian' ('Die "kleine Göttinger Fakultät" von 1890', *CW* 34, 1920, 281).
5. Thus Georg Wünsch, a pupil of Troeltsch and like him from Augsburg, writes: 'He received his first impressions from his surroundings, the landscape, people and language, and these also influenced his attitude and behaviour later...' (Georg Wünsch, 'Ernst Troeltsch', in W.Zorn, ed., *Lebensbilder aus dem Bayerischen Schwaben* 9, Munich 1966, 384-425: 385). For Troeltsch's origins and youth cf. above all H.Renz, 'Augsburger Jahre. Grundlagen der geistigen Entwicklung von Ernst Troeltsch', *TRST* 1, 13-32.
6. Letter to W.Bousset, 27 January 1897, UB Göttingen, unpublished. Family anxieties continued and above all affected his father who, while physically healthy, fell victim to a kind of depression (letter to W.Bousset, 5 August 1898, UB Göttingen, unpublished).
7. Letter to G.von le Fort, 2 December 1918, UB Heidelberg, unpublished.
8. Troeltsch evidently distinguished between his idea of school generally and his

personal experience during his Augsburg schooldays. In connection with a distinction between school learning and education he says this: 'School is simply a breaking-in agency and you soon have it behind you. I do not regard it as being very important... Moreover my experiences in Augsburg are not at all relevant here. The school did not trouble us much and left us plenty of spare time. I was very happy with it' (card to A.Rehm, 7 January 1918, unpublished, Bavyerische Staatsbibliothek, Munich).

9. According to the CVs which Troeltsch wrote both for his church examinations and his call to Bonn. The first piece of information comes from the CV for the Second Theological Evamination, the second from his Bonn CV. The CVs for the church examinations are in the Landeskirche archive in Nuremberg; that for Bonn in the personal records of the Central State Archive, Merseburg; the school reports are in the Bundesarchiv, Koblenz.

10. School-leavers' speech by Ernst Troeltsch, given at the Speech Day on 6 August 1883, made available to me privately by H.Renz.

11. Cf. H.Renz, 'Troeltschs Theologiestudium', *TRST* 1, 48-59.

12. 'My Books', *GS* IV, 4, *RH*, 366.

13. 'Die "kleine Göttinger Fakultät" von 1890', *CW* 34, 1920, 281. However, Troeltsch also passed a kinder judgment on his teachers at Erlangen and on his time as a student there. Thus he says that through the 'teaching of the admirable Erlangen theologians of the 1880s I gained a thorough knowledge of contemporary Lutheranism' (*GS* II, viii).

14. Cf. R.Seeberg, *An der Schwelle des zwanzigsten Jahrhunderts*, Leipzig ³1901, 94ff.; also F.W.Kantzenbach, *Die Erlanger Theologie*, Munich 1960, esp. 179ff.

15. These were lectures on the philosophical theories of law and state, on psychology, epistemology and metaphysics, and on philosophy of religion. Seen merely in terms of quantity this is an extraordinary work-load for a theological student, even taking into account the situation in Bavaria, where philosophy had an important role in theological study.

Thus later in one of his CVs (on the occasion of his call to Bonn in 1892) Troeltsch remarks that in addition to making the acquaintance of the Erlangen stars Frank and Zezschwitz, he had mainly studied philosophy. For Class cf. also H.Will, 'Ethik als allgemeine Theorie des geistigen Lebens. Troeltschs Erlanger Lehrer Gustav Class', *TRST* 1, 175-202. Class's lectures on the philosophy of religion have been edited posthumously by H.Renz in *Mitteilungen der Ernst-Troeltsch-Gesellschaft* III, 140-80. The student letters quoted by Renz (to his association friend J.Braun) show impressively how highly Troeltsch esteemed his teacher Class, though he also criticized him.

16. G.Class, *Die Realität der Gottesidee*, Munich 1904, 6.

17. G.Class, *Untersuchungen zur Phänomenologie und Ontologie des menschlichen Geistes*, Erlangen 1896, 103.

18. Cf. Class, *Realität* (n.16), 38.

19. For the idea of development in Class's philosophy see the Erlangen dissertation by Herrmann Bechmann, *Der Entwicklungsgedanke in der Philosophie Gustav Class'*, 1906. The work discusses the question of development in the history of religion and the absoluteness of Christianity from a normative aspect, and thus is also of interest in connection with Troeltsch.

20. Cf. Class, *Realität* (n.16), 71.

21. *ZTK* 5, 1895, 415. Troeltsch wrote a generally positive review of Class's book

Untersuchungen zur Phänomenologie und Ontologie des menschlichen Geistes (1896), cf. *TLZ*1896, 51-6, and *TJB* 1896, 534f. The summary in *Theologischer Jahresbericht* runs: 'The book contains a metaphysics of the spirit and history and thus the main presuppositions for an evaluation of history, including the history of religion. The main problem which arises for any such account of the relationship of the individual to the spiritual elements which transcend him is resolved with the postulate of the immortality of the spiritualized soul, not without leaving a good deal still obscure in this key question of an idealistic-teleological view of history' (534f.).

22. The quotations from letters in this section come from the so far unpublished letters of Troeltsch to Wilhelm Bousset. These are in the manuscript section of Göttingen university library and are restricted (until 2000). For viewing them and making use of them I am grateful to Herr H.Bousset and Frau Dr E.Dinkler-von Schubert. There are some quotations from the letters of 30 July and 12 August 1885 in E.Dinkler-von Schubert, 'Ernst Troeltsch. Briefe aus der Heidelberger Zeit an Wilhelm Bousset. 1894-1914', *Heidelberger Jahrbücher* 1976, 21f.

23. Review of W.Günther, *Die Grundlagen der Religionsphilosophie Troeltsch's*, Leipzig 1914. Troeltsch here says of his basic position that it can easily be caught in the dilemma of the church's presupposition of faith on the one hand and relativistic scepticism on the other, *TLZ* 1916, 448-50: 450.

24. 'My Books', *GS* IV, 15, *RH*, 376.

25. Letter of 6 November 1885. Reprinted in Dinkler-von Schubert, 'Troeltsch. Briefe' (n.22), 22 n.4. Apart from the reproduction of indivividual passages by E.Dinkler-von Schubert, so far Troeltsch's letters from Berlin are unpublished.

26. In the CV which Köberle sent when called for his ordination examination by the Landeskirche he wrote: 'When I returned to Berlin in the winter semester of 1885/86, some things changed in my life there. I now knew the city adequately, so I retreated more into my room. Nor was there any lack of the stimulation I needed, since my friend Ernst Troeltsch had come with me to Berlin, and our living together in the same house allowed very close companionship' (Examensakten Aufnahmeprüfung, 1887, no.3779, Landeskirchliches Archiv Nürnberg; I owe this reference to H.Renz).

27. Köberle in a later letter to his fellow-associate Julius Braun, 25 March 1887, unpublished; information from H.Renz.

28. Ernst Curtius (1814-1896) was a classical scholar; he had a particular interest in the history of art. Emil du Bois-Reymond (1818-1896) was professor of physiology. He stood out for the unusual breadth of his interests and fields of work. The combination of scientific questions with philosophy and history, characteristic of his work, was very attractive to Troeltsch.

29. Julius Kaftan (1848-1926) had been teaching in Berlin since 1883. Although he was not uncritical of Ritschl – through general reflections on the concept of religion and a mystical element in theology – he was regarded as the real dogmatic theologian of Ritschlianism. Among his writings special mention should be made of *Dogmatik* (1897), [8]1920; *Das Wesen der christlichen Religion*, 1881, [2]1888. The basic features of Kaftan's theological position became clear in his argument with Troeltsch (see the section 'The dispute with Kaftan' below). The correspondence with his brother Theodor (1847-1932), General Superintendent of Schleswig, offers some insight into his personal life and his views of church politics. Cf. *Kirche, Recht und Theologie*

in vier Jahrzehnten. Der Briefwechsel der Brüder Theodor und Julius Kaftan (two parts), ed. W.Göbell, Munich 1967.

30. Adolf Stöcker (1835-1909) was a Protestant theologian, court preacher and politician, a member of the Prussian Landtag (1879-1898) and the German Reichstag (1881-83, 1898-1908). Because of his manifest antisemitism he faded into the twilight and was dismissed as a court preacher. He was one of the initiators of the Evangelical Social Congress, which he left in 1896; after that he founded the Free Church Social Conference. In 1878 he left the Conservative Party and founded the Christian Social Party.

31. The essayist Rudolf Kassner gives the following account of Treitschke (1834-1896) and his effect on the students: 'In fact there was nothing Prussian about Treitschke, whose lectures I did not miss once, certainly not in language and accent. The Slavonic trait in his features which of course came from a long way back seemed to me to be unmistakable. And his whole drunken style, heightened – it must be said – by his deafness, was not really Prussian. He was a deaf hero. So Mommsen and Treitschke were the great opponents at the university. However, Treitschke won; he was the idol of the students. When they felt that their beloved teacher had thought enough about the past for that day and it was time to return to the present state of politics, they needed only to stamp their feet impatiently in the middle of the lecture for their wish to be fulfilled' (*Umgang der Jahre*, Erlenbach-Zurich 1949, 225).

Friedrich Meinicke gives a quite different verdict on Treitschke's lectures. He wrote that Treitschke lectured 'powerfully and eruptively with his dull droning voice, which he could not hear because he himself was deaf. But at that time I found his power violent, and the shrill judgments on the sins of parliamentarianism almost provoked something like a hidden critical undercurrent in me, for all my conservative training and disposition. Only in later semesters did I learn to admire what was really great in Treitschke when I read his *German History*... Indeed, according to all that I heard later, in his lectures he was quite an agitator and more concerned for immediate effect than in his writigs, where the clouds of his wrath alternated to good effect with the sunshine of a real dedication to great things and the artist in him restrained his own passion' (*Werke*, Vol.VIII, Stuttgart 1969, 54).

32. Archives of Uttenruthia, in Landeskirchliches Archiv Nürnberg.

33. Ibid. Information from H.Renz. He was also the first to identify Ernst Troeltsch as the author of the anonymous piece.

34. Johannes Weiss drew Troeltsch's attention to Göttingen as a place for study and in particular to Albrecht Ritschl. In a letter to his fellow associate Julius Braun, Troeltsch wrote: 'In addition, I have had my attention drawn to this remarkable man from the other side, by Weiss... who moved in Ritschl's family circles daily like a child of the house, and also knew this much-calumniated heretic in nightdress and nightcap. The same person, now at the end of his theological studies, is enthusiastic about Ritschlian theology with a remarkable certainty and hopes later to disseminate it as a lecturer. I cannot deny that this man, who is also personally very attractive and witty, has made a great impression on me and has confirmed and strengthened me in my thoughts about the relationship between theology and philosophy and metaphysics' (letter to Julius Braun, 24 December 1885; letter communicated through H.Renz).

35. R.Schäfer, *Ritschl. Grundlinien eines fast verschollenen dogmatischen Systems*, Tübingen 1968.

36. Cf. Troeltsch's CV on the occasion of his call to Bonn (Akten der preussischen Ministeriums für geistliche, Unterrichts- und Medizinalangelegenheiten, Central State Archive, Merseburg). For H.Reuter cf. T.Brieger, *ZKG* XI, 1889; T.Kolde, *RE*³ XVI, 696-703; C.Mirbt, *ADB* 53, 310-19.

37. 'Die "kleine Göttinger Fakultät" von 1890', *CW* 34, 1920, 282.

38. Cf. my 'Ernst Troeltsch und Paul de Lagarde', Mitteilungen der Ernst-Troeltsch-Gesellschaft III, 1984, 95-115.

39. Schultz began in Old Testament theology; however, the nature of his publications – the fourth edition of a *Theology of the Old Testament* appeared in 1889 – already showed that he was not least attracted by systematic topics. Apart from his works on systematic theology, an *Outline of Evangelical Dogmatics* and an *Outline of Evangelical Ethics* (1891 and 1892), he was also involved with practical theology; his sermons were published, as were statements on contemporary church questions.

40. Cf. H.Renz, 'Eine unbekannte Preisarbeit über Lotze', *TRST* 1, 33-47.

41. Cf. Akten des Universitätsarchivs, Göttingen; for the awarding of prizes see Pütter-Saalfeld-Oesterley, *Geschichte der Universität Göttingen*, 1838, Part 4, para 45, on 'The Royal Foundation of Annual Prize Essays for All Four Faculties'.

42. The prize essay is quoted by the page numbers of the original manuscript, which is in the university archive in Göttingen.

43. Cf. *Protestantisches Christentum und Kirche in der Neuzeit* (1906), 722: 'But on the whole theology follows... the development of general science and philosophy at a considerable distance. Its history is often only a history of the adoption and adaptation or contestation, and yet at the same time the plundering, of philosophical religion.'

44. In the second edition, the reference to the saying of Paul is omitted (cf. *AC*, 118). The passage above on p.118 is a modification of the text of the first edition, which has a more markedly confessional orientation.

45. This is shown particularly impressively by a letter from Troeltsch to Julius Braun (26 December 1887) which touches on central theological questions. Troeltsch writes: 'This much is clear, that the most varied images and comparisons, above all with the institutions of the Old Testament, are used for the enigma of the death of the messiah, nowhere as a doctrinal statement but always as a living image which is understandable in itself, always with a clear feeling of the discrepancy between the image and what is portrayed, and always as a basis for what is really decisive, Christ's call to obedience. You can imagine how important these observations are to me with my principle of forming no ideas which push aside those of the first interpreters of Christ. Here one problem above all has leapt out at me with almost disquieting earnestness, and that is the problem of the second coming. The usual silence on this point, or the reinterpretation of it, though it stood at the centre for the first Christians and Christ, goes very much against the grain. And it does not seem possible, even in a dream, to remove by criticism Jesus' prophecies of his second coming. Now there is no doubt that the Lord promised his return even in his disciples' lifetime and that the apostles held this hope high as their palladium. So was our Lord and Saviour, the only-begotten Son of our heavenly Father, wrong? I have to confess that I bow before the complete irrationality of this problem and infer from it that conceptions and theoretical fixations are purely subjective, purely human. I have ranged through a variety of books on the subject without finding any

essentially clearer insight. When we think of our theological squabbles on the real problems, this will be one of the most important. I do not know what to say about it, but I do not allow myself to be led astray by it in my faith' (this hitherto unpublished letter has been made available by H.Renz).

46. With this observation, on 12 March 1887 the dean sent Troeltsch's prize essay to the members of the faculty for examination. For this and for all the reports on the prize essay which follow see the proceedings of the Theological Faculty of the University of Göttingen, in the university archives.

47. For the event cf. also the description by H.Renz, 'Unbekannte Preisarbeit' (n.40), 33ff.

48. Julius Baumann (1837-1916), a pupil of Lotze's, had been professor of philosophy in Göttingen since 1869. He himself was very interested in the philosophy of religion. An anonymous work by him, *Das Evangelium der armen Seele*, appeared in 1871, with a foreword by Lotze.

49. *Chronik der Georg-August-Universität zu Göttingen für das Etatjahr 1887/88*, Göttingen 1888, 12. The 'Pro-Rector' was what would now be the Rector of the university. This designation came about because the local ruler was the 'Rector'. At the ceremony Ritschl spoke on 'Reformation in the Latin Church of the Middle Ages' (in *Drei Akademische Reden*, Bonn 1887, 30-46).

50. However, Troeltsch engaged in association life again. At the Uttenruthia meeting of 30 May 1888 he took on the task of composing a prologue for a beer festival with dancing (cf. *Versammlungsprotokolle der Uttenruthia*, Landeskirchliches Archiv, Nuremberg).

51. From 1868 August Köhler (1835-1897) was professor of Old Testament in Erlangen, and Leonhard Rabus (1835-1916) was teaching philosophy (as a Privatdozent).

52. For this, as for all the following passages quoted from Troeltsch's examination papers, see the records in the Landeskirchliches Archiv, Nuremberg, OKM, 1888, 4480.

53. All in all, the literature cited is: 'Kähler, *Das Gewissen*, very thorough with much historical material, used by everyone; Lotze, *Praktische Philosophie*, and various articles which seem to me to offer the best of the moderns; Kant, *Metaphysics of Morality* and *Critique of Practical Reason*, indispensable for the study of ethics; Wundt, *Ethik*, idealistic and optimistic but utterly empirical and not easy to make use of for the Christian approach; Schleiermacher's *Ethical Treatise on the Supreme Good*, etc., with Kant's writings the most important; lectures by Kaftan and Ritschl.'

54. A passage from a letter to Bousset of 12 September 1888 gives some indication of the position addressed in the last lines of the poem: ' "What is science?" is of course a basic question for me. It may be dimly evident to you from what I have written how it is to be answered. Here I am striving above all for hard facts and definite factual truth, renouncing the desire for cohesion. The everyday which imperceptibly underlies our lives is everywhere the most important, and everywhere there are only attempts, only approximations. All facts have to be recognized, however inconvenient they may seem to us.'

55. For Troeltsch's time at the Preachers' Seminary see W.Drechsel, 'Die Beziehungen Ernst Troeltschs zur bayerischen Landeskirche', *TRST* 1, 60-77.

56. With his ordination to the ministry Troeltsch had to have his name removed from the list of those aspiring to be officers in the reserve. He was assigned to the nursing

corps and from 1 to 18 August 1889 underwent training as a nursing auxiliary (cf. E.Troeltsch, personal records, Landeskirchliches Archiv, Nuremberg).

57. CV on his call to Bonn (Akten des preussischen Ministeriums der geistlichen, Unterrichts- und Medizinalangelegenheiten, Central State Archives, Merseburg).

58. Cf. W.Scherer, *Geschichte der deutschen Literatur (von der althochdeutschen Zeit bis zu Goethes Tod)*, Berlin 1883; H.Grimm, *Goethe* (2 vols.), Berlin 1887; W.Wundt, *Ethik. Eine Untersuchung der Tatsachen der Gesetze des sittlichen Lebens* (3 vols.), Stuttgart 1886; L.von Ranke, *Weltgeschichte* (9 vols.), Leipzig 1881-8.

59. Letter of 28 June 1899 (Akten des Königlichen Oberkonsistoriums, Landeskirchliches Archiv, Nuremberg).

60. Ibid.

61. In certain circumstances the licentiate examination and the Habilitation might coincide or overlap. That happened when there was a relevant qualification, for example an 'excellent' in the First Theological Examination, and an academic teaching post was being sought on this basis. In that case a disputation and a trial lecture were prescribed as additional tests. Special permission was necessary for the licentiate thesis to be written in German. For this see the letter to the University Curator of 1 March 1891 (Göttingen university archives, personal records of Ernst Troeltsch Az II b, no.90 UAG fol.19). For the procedure see also 348 below. Further references and supplementary information in F.W.Graf, '*Licentiatus theologiae* und Habilitation', *TRST* 1, 78ff.

62. Troeltsch had already expressed similar views in his prize essay, when he spoke somewhat vividly of the plundering of philosophy by theology. Cf. p.53 of the essay.

63. Cf. 'Die "Kleine Göttinger Fakultät" von 1890', *CW* 34, 1920, 282.

64. Later (in his *Social Teachings*), Troeltsch understood the identification of natural law, Christian law and Decalogue as a change from the early church and the Middle Ages; here Calvinism differed from Lutheranism by attaching greater importance to community organization on ethical principles. Troeltsch wrote that in his work on *Reason and Revelation in Johann Gerhard and Melanchthon* he had attempted to describe these connections but had not been 'sufficiently aware of the significance of the whole group of ideas relating to the Decalogue and natural law throughout the theological tradition, nor did I recognize it in Luther, and I attributed this doctrine too much to Melanchton. Here Luther's great innovation is a distinction between *justitia spiritualis* and *justitia civilis*, *motus spirituales* and the general natural moral obligations; the latter become good in a Christian sense if, as the First Tablet requires, they are "exercised in faith" ' (*GS* I, 494 n.225, *ST* II, 844 n.225).

65. For the passages quoted below from the reports by Hermann Schultz and Paul Tschackert see Troeltsch's personal records (Az II b, no.90 UAG fol.19).

66. In this connection Tschackert writes: 'At some points to which Herr Troeltsch's attention is drawn, the *genus dicendi* is not scholarly': p.34, 'a bad thing'; p.77, 'making elegantly plausible'; p.184, the dualism 'sits'; p.247 Melanchthon's 'Philistine' tendency.

67. For the reason why Troeltsch did his Habilitation in church history and the history of dogma and not, say, in systematic theology, cf. 348 n. 71.

68. For the topics of the oral examination see the proceedings of the theological faculty for 31 January 1891 (Dekanatsakten, University Archives, Göttingen).

69. The most important theses for Troeltsch's position and his further work are as follows (the numbering follows the order of the original).

1. Theology is a discipline of the history of religion; not, however, as an element in the construction of a universal history, but as a definition of the content of Christian religion by comparison with the few great religions which we know more precisely.

3. The religion of exilic and post-exilic Judaism is the soil of Christianity, to the degree that only from the former do the great historical foundations of the latter derive: belief in the resurrection, the concept of the messiah, apocalyptic, universal monotheism, religious individualism, the morality of proverbial wisdom.

12. The scientific element of dogmatics lies in the doctrine of principles; an account of the content of faith itself can no longer be said to be science in the strict sense.

13. To the degree to which it is advisable to systematize the Christian concepts of faith, eschatology must form the centre of relations.

14. Dogmatics and ethics can really be separated only if by ethics one understands an analysis and description of the process of ethicizing in terms of the history of philosophy.

15. Any positive doctrine of faith has a metaphysic of the philosophy of religion attached to it, even if the difference between religion and metaphysics has been understood very clearly.

16. Theology is as hard for the church to bear as it is for the church to do without.

17. The most important practical task for the theology of the present is to produce a method which is not artificial and an honest textbook for religious teaching in secondary schools (these theses are published in *TRST* 1, 299f., along with others by J.Weiss, W.Bousset, W.Wrede, A.Rahlfs and H.Hackmann, *TRST* 1, 296ff.).

70. For the context cf. F.W.Graf, 'Der "Systematiker" der "kleinen Göttinger Fakultät". Ernst Troeltschs Promotionsthesen und ihr Göttinger Kontext', *TRST* 1, 235-90, and my article 'Ernst Troeltsch und Paul de Lagarde', *Mitteilungen der Ernst Troeltsch Gesellschaft* III, 1984, 95-115.

71. Cf. the letter from the theological faculty to the University Curator of 1 March 1891, University Archives, Göttingen. The procedure of the faculty at the doctoral examination and the giving of the *venia legendi* is based on the 'regulations for the admission of Privatdozenten to the Theological Faculty in Göttingen', of 28 March 1831 (University Archives, Göttingen).

The regulation also explains why Troeltsch did his Habilitation in church history and the history of dogma. Paragraph 5 of the regulations reads: 'No Privatdozent may read systematic and practical theology, apart from ordinarius and extraordinarius professors of theology, without special permission from the theological faculty' (this regulation was changed in 1912). Permission to teach for two years was granted, with the mark 'excellent', and could be withdrawn before the end of this period. 'During this period the faculty will observe the application, the style of teaching, the scientific principles and the moral behaviour of the Dozent as closely as possible, to judge whether or not a definitie adoption can take place' (Regulations, para.4)

72. Letter to the Royal Bavarian Oberkonsistorium, 2 April 1891 (Landeskirchliches Archiv, Nuremberg).

73. The topic was set to bring out the special features of Protestant and Catholic understanding. For this and what follows see the examination papers for the 1891 examination (Landeskirchliches Archiv, Nuremberg).

74. The report is very critical: anyone who has looked round a school thoroughly cannot agree with Troeltsch. 'It would be very sad if the author's judgment were right that "according to experience, nine-tenths of all teaching given is boring".'

75. The structure of the sermon is as follows: 'Our text preaches the grace of God in Christ. We put two questions to it: I What is grace? Grace is 1. mercy, 2. great love, 3. life, 4. being transported into a heavenly state, 5. glorification in life in the world to come. II How do we come to grace? We come to grace 1. through resurrection and being given life, i.e. by a divine miracle, 2. not by works, 3. by faith.'
76. For the second examination a skeleton sermon also had to be prepared, on Mark 10.42-45. Troeltsch approached this dialectically: for him, on the one hand the petition of the apostles for greatness derives from a natural wish that is also recognized by Jesus; on the other the difference between the world and the kingdom of God and thus the estimation of greatness msut be perceived religiously on the basis of this difference.
77. Decision of the Oberkonsistorialrat, 18 June 1891 (Landeskirches Archiv, Nuremberg).
78. The travel grant came from a foundation instituted by Dean von Biarowsky, who in 1870 had donated 3000 guilders; from the interest on this, the best candidate of each theological examination was to receive 120 guilders for a trip to a place of his choosing. Troeltsch's travel account and his covering letter of 18 May 1895 have been preserved (Landeskirches Archiv, Nuremberg, Bestand Landeskirchenrat München XI, 1470a).

In his account Troeltsch combines personal impressions with general reflections on the situation in the church, church politics and culture. It is particularly worth mentioning that his first visit was to Strasbourg, where 'to my great delight I got to know Holtzmann and Spitta very well'. Possibly closer academic links were also established here, as feelers were also put out to Troeltsch over a professorship in Strasbourg. Moreover it is striking that Holtzmann was a former Heidelberg professor and was to go there soon after his call (I am grateful to H.Renz for drawing my attention to this travel account).
79. Report of the faculty, 21 July 1891 (University Archives, Göttingen). Making arrangements to supervise the Privatdozenten was one of the tasks of the faculty.
80. Ritschl's *Instruction in the Christian Religion* was conceived as a textbook for religious instruction in the upper classes of secondary schools. One has to point out how remarkable this is, since the account is a compressed version of his *Dogmatics* and hardly suitable for school use.
81. After the call to Bonn, which came so quickly, Troeltsch wrote in 1893 to Bousset, who had remained in Göttingen: 'Although I have made a number of very happy associations here, I do miss the great stimulation of our old group. Moreover since then my knowledge has perceptibly lagged behind' (card of 16 June 1893, UB Göttingen, unpublished).
82. Troeltsch mentions in a letter to Bousset how this introduction was made for him within the 'Little Faculty' especially through Alfred Rahlfs (1865-1935, from 1901 professor in Göttingen). 'Now of the little faculty only Rahlfs is left. I don't like to think about that. Theology is probably at a dead end. When his learning so impressed me and I seemed very uncouth and incompetent compared with him, I never thought that he would be the last. I shall never forget how much I owe to him and to the influence of Lagarde in terms of strictness and neatness, method and disposition which came to me through him' (letter of 27 May 1896, UB Göttingen 1896, unpublished).
83. *GS* II, viii.

84. Lagarde's critical reserve towards Ritschl derived from this renunciation of a dogmatically coloured view of the religious; however, feelings were mutual. G.von Selle has described this very vividly: 'Lagarde was of the opinion that Ritschl was not the right man... He complained that Ritschl had made the doctrine of justification and reconciliation the centre of a theology. That is not Protestant, but Pauline. And Lagarde had the the most passionate hatred of Paulinism. Paul falsified Christianity and Luther followed him. So Lagarde also rejected Luther. When the university celebrated the four hundredth anniversary of Luther's birth in 1883, Lagarde attempted to prevent this and make it the business of the theological faculty. From then on Ritschl cold-shouldered Lagarde and even ceased to return his greeting. Lagarde was a deeply pious person. But certainly he was not really justified in seeing Ritschl, of all people, as a man to whom religion meant nothing and theology everything, though Ritschl's concerns were probably more predominantly academic than with the realm of faith...' (*Die Georg-August-Universität zu Göttingen 1737-1937*, Göttingen 1937, 320f.).

85. In his memorial address on Wilhelm Bousset, Hermann Gunkel described the connections as follows: 'Our fathers were above all Harnack and Wellhausen. Wellhausen had introduced an authentic historical spirit into the Old Testament and rediscovered the history of Israelite religion. Following Baur, Harnack had recognized the origin of Christian dogma as a combination of primitive Christian thought with Greek philosophy. What was more obvious than that the historical spirit which had flowed from them to the young generation should now also take over the New Testament and there cast down all barriers...? At the same time, behind the new movement, but without knowing of it, were the many-sided and enigmatic Lagarde and the profound Duhm' (memorial address for Wilhelm Bousset, given in the University of Giessen on 9 May 1920, in *Evangelische Freiheit*, 1920, 146).

86. William Wrede (1859-1906), from 1891 Privatdozent in Göttingen, from 1893 Professor of New Testament in Breslau. Wrede achieved particular prominence as a result of his investigations into the messiahship of Jesus. According to Wrede, the idea of the messiahship of Jesus was incorporated into the Gospel as a result of the experience of the resurrection ('messianic secret'). In his view Paul was the founder of a new religion which was Christian in the narrower sense, in so far as in Pauline Christianity Christ became the centre, worshipped in the cult. Alfred Rahlfs (1865-1935) became the recognized specialist in Septuagint research, and in this continued the life-work of Paul de Lagarde. Hermann Gunkel (1862-1932) was Privatdozent in Göttingen from 1888 and professor from 1894 in Berlin, from 1907 in Giessen and from 1920 in Halle. Gunkel applied history-of-religions thought to the exegesis of Old Testament texts, wrote significant commentaries (Genesis, Psalms) and achieved particular prominence with his studies of tradition history and genre history.

87. Gressmann's summary verdict was: 'The axiom of the history-of-religions school was: there is no material in the world which does not have its prehistory, no concept which does not have its point of contact. This principle applies not only to small incidental things... but also to the great and central phenomena like Israelite prophecy or the rise of Christianity' (*Albert Eichhorn und die religionsgeschichtliche Schule*, Göttingen 1914, 35).

88. In this connection see Rade's critical definition of the history of religions as the 'science of the multiplicity of religions', *RGG*[1] IV, 2184.

89. Troeltsch's comments in the article 'The Dogmatics of the History-of-Religions School' (1913) are on the one hand a reflection of a prior judgment and on the other hand contributed to his label 'systematician of the history-of-religions school'. Troeltsch remarks: 'The writer of this article is regarded as the systematic and dogmatic theologian of this approach. Thus it is appropriate for him... to state the meaning of a dogmatics working with the presuppositions and in the spirit of this school' (*RH*, 87-108: 87).

90. Thus in 1896 Troeltsch wrote on the position of the theologians with a history-of-religions orientation: 'The Ritschlians are furious with us, which I had already expected in advance as a result of the Eisenach meetings [conferences of the 'Friends of *Christliche Welt*]. Wrede and Eichhorn, and also, say, Gunkel are regarded as quite dangerous and out-and-out opponents' (letter to Wilhelm Bousset, 27 May 1896, UB Göttingen, unpublished).

91. The deed of appointment dated 14 March 1892 reads: 'Since I have nominated Licentiate in Theology Ernst Troeltsch, hitherto Privatdozent at Göttingen, as Extraordinarius Professor in the Evangelical Faculty of Theology in the University of Bonn, I bestow on him the present chair in the trust that he will remain loyal to His Majesty the King and the royal house in steadfast truth and will perform the duties of the office bestowed on him to the full with unflagging zeal. In particular he will give without remuneration one lecture every six months on a branch of the disciplines to be taught by him, and also each semester will announce at least one private series of lectures in his discipline' (Akten des preussischen Ministeriums für geistliche, Unterrichts- und Medizinalangelegenheiten, Az UI.54/3: Central State Archives, Merseburg). As salary Troeltsch was granted 1800 marks from 1 April of that year in addition to the lodging allowance of 660 marks which was laid down by law. For this period cf. F.W.Graf, 'Profile: Spuren in Bonn', *TRST*1, 103-131.

92. *TLZ* 17, 1892, 208-12.

93. Ibid., 210.

94. From 1880-1899 Bernhard Weiss (1827-1918) was adviser to the Prussian Ministry of Culture and as such was joint head of the Department for Clergy Affairs. Since the head, Göppert, was a Catholic, he left it entirely to Weiss to deal with personnel questions in the Protestant faculties of theology. Cf. Bernhard Weiss, *Aus neunzig Lebensjahren. 1827-1918*, ed. H.G.Weiss, Leipzig 1927, 177.
Weiss's influential position changed little even after Göppert's death, when Althoff took over responsibility for personnel matters in the theological faculty, since, as Weiss wrote, Althoff was 'unfamiliar with these matters and usually followed my judgment' (ibid., 182).

95. Ibid., 177. Weiss's description of his meeting with Kaftan in Basel makes it clear how such a report was made: 'The very first morning there I heard Kaftan in a lecture and then went with him to my hotel, to examine his theological position from all sides. On the following days I heard him... again in dogmatics and in an exegetical study, in which again he pleased me very much' (ibid., 182).

96. 'Bericht über eine Reise nach Göttingen vom 2.November 1891', Ministerium für geistliche, Unterrichts- und Medizinalangelegenheiten, AZ U I 22003, Central State Archives, Merseburg.

97. The following remarks indicate how carefully Weiss used to make his reports, and with Prussian detachment: 'I also used my stay in Göttingen to listen to the two ordinarius professors [he means Bonwetsch and Haering] who have been there some time but were still unknown to me. I convinced myself that both were admirable acquisitions... I also listened again to my son *Johannes Weiss*, now that he has fully settled into his academic activity' (ibid).

98. Report of the Protestant theological faculty of the University of Bonn to the Ministerium für geistliche, Unterrichts- und Medizinalangelegenheiten, 30 June 1891, Az U 1 Z 102; Central State Archives, Merseburg.

99. Letter of 8 December 1891, records of the Prussian Ministerium für geistliche, Unterrichts- und Medizinalangelegenheiten, Az U 1 2203; Central State Archives, Merseburg).

100. Letter from the Bonn faculty to the Prussian Ministerium für geistliche, Unterrichts- und Medizinalangelegenheiten, 30 June 1891, Az U I 5020; Central State Archives, Merseburg.

101. Cf. the letter from the Ministry, 9 February 1892 (Az U I 519, 520 G I; Central State Archives, Merseburg).

102. Letter from the Evangelischer Oberkirchenrat to the Ministerium für geistliche, Unterrichts- und Medizinalangelegenheiten, Az U I 5413; Central State Archives, Merseburg (the date cannot be ascertained).

103. In his first semester in Bonn Troeltsch lectured for four hours a week on symbolics. In the winter semester of 1892/93 he lectured on the 'Life and Teaching of Schleiermacher' and 'Christian Ethics'; and in the next two semesters on 'Doctrine I' and 'Exercises on the History of Dogma'. In the summer semester of 1894 he left Bonn.

104. Troeltsch's colleague in the Bonn faculty, Arnold Meyer, later recalled this time. 'There was Grafe, whose hospitable home brought us together; his background was in Elberfeld pietism, but as Weizsäcker's pupil he was now a biblical scholar with a strictly critical bent; Sell, once church head at Darmstadt and now a simple professor, the man of witty parallels and points; Simons, with his acute knowledge of the history of the Rhineland Reformed community; in addition there was Ernst Troeltsch, only twenty-seven years old, full of the freshness of youth and of Swabian, Bavarian immediacy... The influence of the one who was then the youngest soon made itself felt; his clear thinking, his wealth of knowledge and his striking way of expressing himself easily overturned other views and always compelled one to reflect and dig deeper. In addition to theology he read quickly an amazing number of books, old and new, on related subjects, above all history and philosophy; here he had a special way of picking out specialists from all disciplines – theology, philosophy, the history of art and national economy – thus bringing himself up to date with the latest state of information. One occasion for this was the so-called "athletic club" which on Saturday afternoons took a whole cohort over hill and dale' ('Ernst Troeltsch nach persönlicher Erinnerung', *Neue Zürcher Zeitung*, 15 February 1923).

105. 'Positive' camp refers to 'positive' theology and its echo or parallels in church circles. Positive theology is to be seen less as a single theological trend than as a basic attitude concerned to preserve the theological tradition of the church which at the same time sought to keep free of the influence of modern science and the modern world-view in both theology and in church life.

106. Thus Troeltsch writes to his publisher Siebeck about the 'significantly increased

professional work' and describes this as the 'burden of lecture business' (letters to P.Siebeck of 5 May and 20 December 1892, Mohr/Siebeck archives, Tübingen, unpublished).

107. In 1895, Troeltsch wrote to Siebeck that 'in the last few months' he had been 'engaged by Holtzmann for the *Theologische Jahresbericht*' (letter of 15 October 1895, Mohr/Siebeck archives, Tübingen, unpublished).

108. To his friend Bousset Troeltsch speaks of the 'bone-breaking work of review' (card of 4 July 1896, UB Tübingen). And to Siebeck he writes: 'Unfortunately my capacity for work this summer has been very much diminished by marked nervousness, so that I was not able to do any work at all outside the penal colony for the *Jahresbericht*' (letter to P.Siebeck of 29 June 1899, Mohr/Siebeck archives, Tübingen).

109. Telegram of 6 November 1893 (records of the Prussian Ministerium für geistliche, Unterrichts- und Medizinalangelegenheiten, Az U I 7489; Central State Archives, Merseburg). Cf. also R.Schieder, 'Die Berufung Ernst Troeltschs nach Heidelberg', *TRST* I, 132-44.

110. Telegram of 6 November 1893, 5.20 p.m. (records of the Prussian Ministerium für geistliche, Unterrichts- und Medizinalangelegenheiten, Az U I 748793, Central State Archives, Merseburg).

111. Letter of 30 November 1893 to the Ministerium für geistliche, Unterrichts- und Medizinalangelegenheiten, Az U I 7552; Central State Archives, Merseburg.

112. Letter of 30 November 1893 to Minister Bosse (records of the Prussian Ministerium für geistliche, Unterrichts- und Medizinalangelegenheiten, Central State Archives, Merseburg).

113. The faculty in Bonn had suggested Clemen (Halle) and Titius (Berlin); if the post were changed into an ordinarius chair they suggested Herrmann (Marburg) and Reischle (Giessen). That the decision was made over the heads of the faculty is probably the result of Weiss's influence; to a letter to the Oberkirchenrat relating to the 'Nihil obstat' for O.Ritschl, Minister Bosse attached 'a note of my theological referees' (cf. letter of 19 March 1894, Az U I 7954; Central State Archives, Merseburg).

114. In a separate opinion Dean Ludwig Lemme – sure of the support of many clergy and laity within the Baden Landeskirche – proposed three theologians with a 'positive' orientation.
There was no agreement within the faculty as to whether the second chair of systematic theology should be occupied again at this point. The majority of the members were against, arguing that 'to have two chairs of systematic theology occupied would result in a flood of lectures, and given the state of theology at present and in the foreseeable future. five ordinarius professors are sufficient to meet all the demands of those studying theology'. However, two members of the faculty felt it necessary for the chair to be occupied (cf. the letter from the faculty dated 7 July 1893 to the Minsterium für Justiz, Kultur und Unterricht, Generallandesarchiv Karlsruhe, Dienstakte der theologischen Fakultät 235/3144).

115. Majority opinion of the faculty, 7 July 1893 (records of the Ministerium für Justiz, Kultus und Unterricht; Generallandesarchiv Karlsruhe, ibid.).

Part Two: Professor of Theology in Heidelberg

1. Heidelberg was referred to as a 'world village'. Cf. Camilla Jellinek, 'Georg Jellinek. Ein Lebensbild', in *Georg Jellinek, Ausgewählte Reden und Schriften* 1, Aalen 1970, 85. Hermann Glockner remarked on the Heidelberg climate: 'I had never come across such a mild, gentle climate anywhere; the breezes were light and sweet; it was like getting into a lukewarm bath...' (H.Glockner, *Heidelberger Bilderbuch*, Bonn 1969, 5).

2. Cf. P.Hensel, *Sein Leben in seinen Briefen*, Wolfenbüttel and Hanover 1947, 134: letter of Hensel to H.Rickert, 4 May 1899.

3. *CW* 1903, 355–6. These were two modern pictures which Troeltsch felt fitted the flowing character of the church well. The article shows a marked aesthetic sensitivity to both church and liturgy. For Hans Thoma, cf. also Carl Neumann, 'Über den Zusammenhang von Wissenschaft und Leben', in *Die Kunstwissenschaft der Gegenwart in Selbstdarstellungen*, Leipzig 1924, 9.

4. Cf. Jellinek, 'Georg Jellinek. Ein Lebensbild' (n.1), 85.

5. In the year 1900 Heidelberg had 1,500 students; in 1910 the number was already 2,370, 190 of them women. Women had the right to matriculate from summer 1900 onwards.

6. Letter to W.Bousset of 27 May 1986, UB Göttingen, unpublished.

7. Adolf Hausrath, Troeltsch's colleague in church history, said of Richard Rothe's *Ethics*: 'For the nineteenth century it is the last great evolution of that speculative movement which is marked by the names of Fichte, Schelling and Hegel' (*Geschichte der theologischen Facultät zu Heidelberg im neunzehnten Jahrhundert*, Heidelberg 1901, 13).

8. Richard Rothe, *Theologische Ethik* III, Wittenberg 1870, 173.

9. Thus we read: 'So in the development of the Christian life, whether of Christian humanity or the Christian individual, the nearer a point along the line of development lies to the beginning, the more the moral and the religious, morality and piety, diverge, and the nearer it comes to the end, the less this is the case' (ibid., 174).

10. 'He was one of those rare people who in the religious crisis of our time have never doubted in a supernatural revelation of redemption by God to human beings'(*RR*, 9f.).

11. 'That was the great basic notion of his inner life and of all his academic work: a recognition of the difference between church religion, which is isolated in itself and therefore seeks support and coherence in the church, and church-free religion, which takes upon itself tasks within the world and therefore emerges in life as a whole, stating that the supernatural saving form of the church with its dogmas, rites and clerics has only provisional significance and that what is of eternal significance is the religious and moral content of Christianity, which is even more recognizable in its fusion with modern humanity. On this principle rests its historical conception of the past, present and future of Christianity, its theological-philosophical doctrine of the nature of the world and the goals of life, and its practical work on the church problems of the present' (*RR*, 25f.)

Troeltsch's lecture shows where he feels in tune with Rothe's intentions and where he critically distances himself from them. It is an example of his capacity to adopt other positions sympathetically and at the same time to criticize them from within. In the end Rothe is counted one of the 'outsiders' in theology and put in a line with

Kierkegaard and Lagarde. Troeltsch concludes that 'all that is left for a later generation is to gather the kernels that he has ripened in his magic garden and plant them in ordinary soil' (*RR*, 42).

12. A.Hausrath remarks here: 'Strauss mocked that the critical results of the Tübingen school had swum up the Neckar to Heidelberg, there to be drawn into the region in a somewhat weakened state' (*Geschichte der theologischen Facultät zu Heidelberg im neunzehnten Jahrhundert*, Heidelberg 1901, 17).

13. Lemme's academic career took him to Heidelberg through Breslau (1876, Privatdozent; 1881, extraordinarius professor) and Bonn (1884, ordinarius professor).

14. Troeltsch received a salary of 4500 marks for his main post, a subsistence allowance of 500 marks and 760 marks accommodation allowance, and therefore was financially very much better off (cf. Personalakte Troeltsch 235/2599, Generallandesarchiv Karlsruhe).

15. His travelling companions were the archaeologist Löschke and the national economist Dietzel. On this trip – as in Bonn generally – Troeltsch found 'the company of non-theologians' very refreshing' (letter to W. Bousset of 12 October 1894, UB Göttingen). The stimuli which Troeltsch received with his travelling companions (and in part also through them) led him to renewed 'reflections on Greek culture, art and religion' (ibid.).

16. The faculty reported to the Ministry on 14 March 1894 that Troeltsch had asked for his appointment to be dated from 1 April and for this date to be put in the documents, although he only returned from his trip in the last week of April. That was done (cf. Generallandesarchiv Karlsruhe, Dienstakte der theologischen Fakultät 235/3144).

17. It was usual, and characteristic of conditions in the state, for the crown prince to give an audience to the newly appointed professors. Paul Hense, appointed professor of philosophy at Heidelberg in 1898, wrote an account in a letter to his mother. 'It was really a good effort by the old boy; he received me standing and did not just make small talk; he was admirably briefed and spoke with great thoroughness for about twenty minutes' (Paul Hensel, *Sein Leben in seinen Briefen*, Wolfenbüttel and Hanover 1947, 133). For Jellinek cf. Camilla Jellinek, 'Georg Jellinek. Ein Lebensbild' (n.1), 83.

18. Otto Frommel, 'Erinnerungen an Ernst Troeltsch', *Heidelberger Tageblatt*, 3 February 1923.

19. 'Lipsius, R.A., *Lehrbuch der evangelisch-protestantischen Dogmatik*, [3]1903', *GGA* 1894, 841-54.

20. To begin with, Troeltsch lived at 101a Gaisbergstrasse.

21. Letter to W.Bousset, 12 October 1894, UB Göttingen, printed in E.Dinkler-von Schubert, *Ernst Troeltsch. Briefe aus der Heidelberger Zeit an Wilhelm Bousset 1894-1914*, Heidelberger Jahrbücher XX, 1976, 24.

22. Letter to W.Bousset, 12 October 1894, UB Göttingen.

23. Letter to W.Bousset, 12 October 1894, UB Göttingen, printed in Dinkler-von Schubert, *Ernst Troeltsch* (n.21), 25f.

24. Letter to W.Bousset, 23 July 1895, UB Göttingen, printed in Dinkler-von Schubert, *Ernst Troeltsch* (n.21), 29.

25. In winter 1895/6 there followed History of Dogma (audience of 6) and in the summer semester of 1896 Doctrine I (audience of 15), which was continued with

part II in winter 1896-7; then Troeltsch gave four lectures a week on Symbolics (an audience of 14). Apart from his lectures on 'Theological Encyclopaedia', which were given for the first time in the winter semester of 1897-98, and 'Philosophy of Religion' (summer semester of 1902), by this point Troeltsch had given all his major theological lectures once; they were repeated in turn.

26. Letter to W.Bousset, 23 July 1895, UB Göttingen, printed in Dinkler-von Schubert, *Ernst Troeltsch* (n.21), 27.

27. Letter to W.Bousset, 1 October 1892, UB Göttingen, unpublished.

28. Letter to W.Bousset, 1 August 1897, UB Göttingen, unpublished.

29. Letter to W.Bousset, 3 September 1897, UB Göttingen, unpublished.

30. Ibid., unpublished.

31. 'Life in the faculty is extremely unpleasant. Bassermann cannot make up his mind to establish a *modus vivendi*, and persists in being very abrupt, although I have gone a long way to meet him. I won't even mention Lemme, who has scandalized us with his Rothe Jubilee. The only good thing is that Deissmann is a very pleasant colleague, indeed is already more to me than that. At last I have someone who gives me academic stimulation and discussion' (letter to W.Bousset, 5 August 1898, UB Göttingen, printed in Dinkler-von Schubert, *Ernst Troeltsch*, n.21, 32ff.).

32. Cf. the theses on the absoluteness of Christianity presented by Deissman as a basis for discussion on the occasion of Troeltsch's lecture on this theme. Cf. the section below on 'The absoluteness of Christianity and the history of religion'.

33. A resolution by the Prussian General Synod from 1903 makes clear the attitude prevailing here in church bodies: 'The synod expresses its thanks to all theologians who through their work help to endorse and defend the gospel faith. But it declares that the church cannot allow the contrast between the naturalistic and the Christian world views to be toned down. In lamenting the scandals which have occurred and which confuse the believing community, it expresses its certainty that even the present battles within theology will finally lead to a new foundation for and deepening of the unchanging truth of the gospel. It requests the state government not to appoint theologians who do not recognize that the saving acts of God and the character of the Holy Scriptures as revelation are the foundation of the church and of the certainty of salvation' (report of the *Allgemeine Zeitung*, Munich, 29 October 1903). A resolution from the 'Church-Positive Association of Adelsheim-Mosbach-Neckarbischofsheim' in 1908 shows the attitude of the 'positive' church circles in Baden. The association 'expresses its deep regret that in the most recent appointment to a theological chair in Heidelberg [the appointment of Johannes Weiss] no attention has been paid to either the confessional stance of our evangelical Landeskirche or the wishes of its positive members. We feel this a harsh injustice, and can only call on our members to work with all their might so that the pure gospel of the crucified and risen Son of God can win the victory in public preaching from pulpit and cathedra' (report in the *Deutsche Reichspost*, 7 March 1908).

34. Letter to W.Bousset, 27 January 1897, UB Göttingen, unpublished.

35. Letter to A.Jülicher, 27 January 1897, UB Marburg, unpublished.

36. Letter to W.Bousset, 12 Feburary 1897, UB Göttingen, unpublished.

37. Troeltsch makes a strict distinction between the purely theological task and theology as a profession from the perspective of interests in theological education and political activity. The latter must fade into the background when questions of appointment

become acute. If any alternatives emerge here, Troeltsch is clear which he himself must choose.

38. Letter to W.Bousset, 23 April 1897, UB Göttingen, unpublished.

39. Ibid.

40. E.Gustav Steude (1852-1907), seminary professor in Dresden, had produced some apologetic works. Paul Schmiedel (1851-1935), who is coupled with Bousset, was professor in Zurich at the time. His principal works were commentaries on the Gospels.

41. Proposal for the restoration of the New Testament chair, 14 September 1897, records of the theological faculty, Heidelberg University archives, H-1-201/53.

42. Report by Dean Troeltsch to the faculty members, 7 May 1899 (records of the theological faculty, Heidelberg University archives, H-1-201/54, p.236). Georg Jellinek, a lawyer who was close to both Troeltsch and Weber in Heidelberg, voted for the admission of women in his faculty – but with the minor qualification or request that they should take off their hats in the lecture theatre (cf. Camilla Jellinek, 'Georg Jellinek', n.1, 129).

43. This is best reflected in the following recollection of his Heidelberg student days by Max Weber, who was related to Hausrath (his mother and Hausrath's wife were sisters): 'Uncle suddenly came round on Sunday afternoon, called us down and took us off with him by the Philosophenweg to Neuenheim; I think that later he was as amazed at having done this as we were. On the way he gave free rein to his wit and let fly about humanity in general and the Heidelberg people in particular. Bassermann, Schenkel, Merx, Winkelmann and Kuno Fischer were taken up and their deeds of shame enumerated; if the person concerned was not a plagiarizer and a windbag, he was stupid. Anyway, the best comment was when he remarked in passing that he thought that he had last seen Otto [Otto Baumgarten, a cousin of the Webers], who had recently come to his lectures when he had time, at his church history lecture (of course he very carefully said that he could not prove this, since his lecture clashed with others). Uncle's reason for this was that sometimes he slept badly and was then distracted and did not want the relative concerned to write to his father later about the special expressions that he (i.e. the uncle) sometimes used. He also said in a very self-satisfied way that he had already offended almost all his colleagues when they had brought students to his lectures and finally declared that he would have each of his colleagues thrown out from within "his four walls" by the porters' (letter from Weber to his mother, 16 May 1882, in *Max Weber Jugendbriefe*, Tübingen nd [1934], 47f.).

44. 20 October 1898, Heidelberg University archives, H-I-201/50, p.144.

45. Letter to A.von Harnack, 13 November 1897, Deutsche Staatsbibliothek, Berlin, unpublished.

46. Letter to A.von Harnack, 27 April 1898, ibid.

47. Marianne Weber, *Max Weber*, Tübingen 1926, 240f.

48. Carl Neumann, *Rembrandt*, Munich 1902, ⁴1924.

49. Carl Neumann, 'Über den Zusammenhang von Wissenschaft und Leben', in *Die Kunstwissenschaft der Gegenwart in Selbstdarstellungen*, Leipzig 1924, 55.

50. Card to Bousset, 26 April 1903, UB Göttingen, unpublished. Neumann, who went from Göttingen to Kiel, returned to Heidelberg in 1911.

51. Letter to W.Bousset, 5 August 1898, UB Göttingen, printed in Dinkler-von Schubert, *Ernst Troeltsch* (n.21), 38f. Agnes von Zahn-Harnack writes of her father's

trip to Siebenbürgen: 'At the end of the old century (1899) he had been in Siebenbürgen together with his colleagues Troeltsch and von Schubert; the threads that he took up there lasted till the end of his life. The beautiful melody of the Saxon national anthem, "Siebenbürgen, land of blessing", often reminded him of the colourful, lively and moving images of those days' (A.von Zahn-Harnack, *Adolf von Harnack*, Berlin 1951, 297).

52. 'Erinnerung an Siebenbürgen', *CW* 13, 1899, 1233-8.

53. Ibid., 1236.

54. Letter to W.Bousset, 1 January 1900, UB Göttingen, printed in Dinkler-von Schubert, *Ernst Troeltsch* (n.21), 39.

55. Troeltsch shared this passion for travelling with Adolf von Harnack, of whom his daughter said: 'Travel – that was a magic word for Harnack!' (A.von Zahn-Harnack, *A.von Harnack*, n.51, 214).

56. These are the lectures given in 1893 at the Bonn vacation course which appeared later under the title 'Die christliche Weltanschauung und die wissenschaftlichen Gegenströmungen', cf. *ZTK* 3, 1893, 493-528; *ZTK* 4, 1894, 167-231, later reprinted in *GS* II, 227-327.

57. *GS* II, 247.

58. Cf. *GS* II, 268 and 301.

59. *GS* II, 319. Cf. also 318, where it is stated that no positive proof can be given for the character of the Christian religion as absolute revelation.

60. *GS* II, 318.

61. Albrecht Ritschl describes the connection as follows: 'For in doing good we are blessed, and the performance of our vocation assures us of our standing in the Kingdom of God, and that, too, so far as it is the fellowship of blessedness. But this is related to reconciliation as a consequence; with the appropriation of reconciliation, too, the will receives a direction towards the final end of the Kingdom of God. There is, therefore, no contradiction between the assertion that in reconciliation eternal life is bestowed by God through Christ, and completed consistently with the grace of God thus manifested, and the assertion that we reach the consummation of salvation through the development of the religious-moral character and through the life-performance – perfect in its own order – of our vocation' (*The Christian Doctrine of Justification and Reconciliation*, Vol. III, Edinburgh 1900, 669).

62. *GS* II, 285. 'It is here [the question whether or not the transcendent character of Christian ethics is recognized] that there also belongs above all the peculiar ascetic form of Christianity which on Protestant soil took the form of pietism and which Ritschl attempted to explain by such laborious detours only because he involuntarily toned down the marked historical peculiarity of both human ethics and Christian ethics' (*GS* II, 287). These criticisms of Ritschl expressed in 1893/94 became radical repudiation when the work was included in the *Gesammelte Schriften* in 1913. There we read, '... and which Ritschl attempted to explain by such laborious detours only because here he involuntarily failed to recognize the marked historical peculiarity of both humane and Christian ethics and obliterated the difference in a sober middle way, bourgeois professional morality with its trust in God. That is at best old Prussian morality, but it is neither Christian nor humanist' (ibid.).

63. Troeltsch noted various attempts in this direction in the theology of his time. 'Behind all theological systems today, in a more or less aphoristic presentation there is a philosophy of history or at least a philosophy of the history of religion in which

modern ideas of development are at work, either deliberately or in a concealed way. Even Ritschl's theology, which in other ways is so dry, has not been able to avoid this conflict' (*GS* II, 301).

64. *GS* II, 312.

65. *ZTK* 5, 1895, 361-436; 6, 1896, 71-110, 167-218; henceforth cited as *ZTK* 5 or 6. Troeltsch did not include either of the early articles from *ZTK*, 'The Independence of Religion', or 'Metaphysics and History', in the *Gesammelte Schriften*. In choosing the articles to be included he was guided by both principles and pragmatism. In this connection he wrote to his publisher Siebeck: 'Then [immediately after the publication of the first volume of the *Gesammelte Schriften*] we shall have to go straight on to the second volume. This will include works on the philosophy of religion and systematic theology. I do not want to publish the older works from *ZTK* again now. The main question is whether the works on the scientific situation and absoluteness can be published here... They give the perspective for the whole thing' (letter to P.Siebeck, 23 December 1908, Mohr/Siebeck archives, Tübingen, unpublished).

66. *ZTK* 5, 370. In 1918, in a review of Rudolf Otto's book *Das Heilige* (ET *The Idea of the Holy*, London 1923): 'Zur Religionsphilosophie', *Kantstudien* 23, 1918, 65ff., Troeltsch remarked that Otto – in contrast to Windelband, who raised the question of the validity of religion epistemologically on neo-Kantian presuppositions – was essentially making a psychological analysis of religion. This analysis led him to the idea of the independence of religion. Otto then resolved the epistemological and philosophical questions from this basic insight. Troeltsch thought that Otto's book – in contrast to the works of Windelband - 'offers a complete parallel to my investigations of the "independence of religion" published around twenty years ago... Still essentially following Dilthey, and equally purely on a historical and psychological basis, it asserted through analysis the peculiarity and underivability of religious phenomena. I still energetically maintain its main conclusions even now, though I think it necessary to set them in a broader, not merely psychological framework' (ibid., 65f.).

When Troeltsch says that Otto's philosophy of religion is close to his own he does not mean this in the sense that Otto's work develops the substance of his – the irrationality of the Holy stressed by Otto as compared with the rationality of the human view of reality is not in keeping with Troeltsch's basic view in the philosophy of religion – rather, he has in mind the approaches and the main result.

In coming to this conclusion I differ from the assessment by K.-E.Apfelbacher, who in his account of Troeltsch (*Frömmigkeit und Wissenschaft*, Paderborn 1978) appeals to the review of Otto's book to establish a 'persistent basic conception of the philosophy of religion' in Troeltsch (ibid., 90).

67. 'By itself and for itself, this value judgment of the community is not protected from the suspicion of exaggeration either by the inwardness of its conviction, or by its power to form community or by the number of those who confess it, and must at least prove itself in the struggle with the value judgments of other communities. The isolated individual element cannot in itself ever prove scientifically that it is the unconditional truth, least of all if it dispenses with the argument from miracle; reference to something more universal is then always necessary' (*ZTK* 5, 373f.).

68. In his philosophical foundation, which then at the same time provides the basis for specific ideas on the philosophy of religion, Troeltsch orientates himself more

markedly on the philosophy of Lotze than is the case with Ritschl. Ritschl used Lotze's philosophy essentially for his theory of the value judgment. Lotze's influence is more fundamental in Troeltsch.

69. As systematic thinking Wundt's philosophy arises from a basis in the individual sciences and clarifies their differing claims. For him an essential task of philosophy is the systematic and conceptual foundation of a philosophy of the spirit which arises from a basis in natural life. For Wundt, elemental subjective functions which underlie all thought are feelings, ideas and will. Thought rests on the content of ideas, is accompanied by feelings, and goes beyond the feelings to particular impulses of the will. Thought does not produce any objects, but rather is necessarily bound up with objects. Here the relationship to Troeltsch's own notions is clear.

70. The adoption of the idea of reciprocal relationship in the process of knowing and its extension to the philosophy of religion shows Troeltsch's borrowing from Lotze. Cf. H.Lotze, *Grundzüge der Metaphysik*, Leipzig 1901, 38ff.

71. The idea of elasticity and capacity to adapt to changing situations within the course of history which emerges in Troeltsch to some degree recalls Darwinian ideas, which here are transferred to the course of intellectual history. For the capacity of religion to adapt cf. especially *ZTK* 6, 78.

72. 'Its development [i.e. that of religion] must therefore be understood as a self-communiucation of the divine spirit, and there must be trust that in this self-communication the truth of religion reveals itself progressively' (*ZTK* 6, 80).

73. 'Religion approaches human beings, not with the necessity of a logical conclusion which establishes itself, but with the ideal demand of a creative content which is inwardly present to the disposition' (*ZTK* 6, 96).

74. In the ontological part of his *Grundzüge der Metaphysik*, Lotze speaks of a judgment which must be regarded as a presupposition of science and metaphysics, 'namely this: that if an ordered course of the world is to be conceivable at all, individual things cannot be completely as they want. Their natures cannot be created completely without respect for another or even otherwise, but that all things which are to belong to one and the same world must in respect of their qualities be members of a series or a system of series, so that one can move from the nature of each being to that of any other by more or less middle members in such a way that all the time two members following closely after each other allow a universal in common, from which the possibility derives that a particular consequence arises from their encounter' (ibid., 48f.).

75. In understanding this task as transcending theology in the narrower sense and being prior to it, Troeltsch dissociates himself increasingly more markedly from the Ritschlians, and not just from them. In theology and the philosophy of religion he adopts a position the breadth and development of which can be found paralleled only in Pfleiderer, who was strongly influenced by Hegel and 'liberal' elements, and within the philosophy of religion in Eucken.

76. Such a procedure, namely finding a place in the history of ideas or of theology and thus drawing out lines of development and going back to basic questions, is also evident in Troeltsch's review of the third edition of R.A.Lipsius' *Lehrbuch der evangelisch-protestantischen Dogmatik* in *GGA* 1894, 841-54. Troeltsch himself rated this review very highly. He wrote to Bousset: 'Now I'm working on my note on Lipsius, which will become more like an essay and will quite clearly spell out where I differ from the Ritschlians...' (card of 10 May 1894, UB Göttingen, unpublished).

Troeltsch ranged very wide: he set Lipsius' *Dogmatics* in the history of theology since Kant and Schleiermacher and then investigated its contribution to the contemporary theological situation. This review sheds light on Troeltsch's own position at this time, not least because it shows how Troeltsch's dissociation of himself from the theology of Ritschl and his school took place slowly and represents a process. So here the theology of Ritschl and his school is said to be characterized 'by brilliant historical conceptions and by the originality and energy of its positive construction' (ibid., 842). However, criticism also becomes clear when in connection with the Ritschlian orientation on practical church ends Troeltsch says that it is 'remote from all philosophical ingredients' (ibid.).

77. Cf. the section 'Collaboration with the Evangelical Social Congress'.
78. For the significance of Rade cf. Christoph Schwöbel, *Martin Rade. Das Verhältnis von Geschichte, Religion und Moral als Grundproblem seiner Theologie*, Gütersloh 1980. The personality and work of Rade are particularly interesting because he combined particular capacities and interests which led him beyond theology in the narrower, purely academic sense and also allowed him to take up practical questions of the church life of his time. He was a 'go-between' in the good sense – both personally in his relationship with others, and in the hermeneutical sense by perceiving the task of mediation imposed on theology and church in relation to his time.
79. Johannes Rathje, *Die Welt des freien Protestantismus*, Stuttgart 1952, 57, refers to this criticism. The journal originally did not set out 'to serve those in office and theologians, but the community and primarily its educated members. It seeks to edify them and help them to make a firm, clear Christian judgment. It hopes to achieve that through introduction to scripture, reports from the history of the church (especially the German Reformation) and a discussion of all the phenomena of our present as they call for or can bear a religious and moral assessment...' (Martin Rade, 'Christliche Welt und Freunde der christlichen Welt', *RGG*[1], 1703-8: 1704).
80. There is a good if not uncritical description of *Christliche Welt* in M.Reischle, *Theologie und Religionsgeschichte*, Tübingen and Leipzig 1904, 17: '*Christliche Welt* has so to speak put all these movements of the modern religious world on the stage for us; for that reason it is not so much a church paper which guides and educates us surely, as a reflection of the many efforts in the circles of those who, as members of this modern world, still remain Christians and want to find an appropriate form of Christianity for that world.'
81. The dismissal of the Württemberg pastor Christoph Schrempf because of his refusal to use the Apostles' Creed at baptisms and the dispute with the Württemberg church authorities which followed led to a statement by Harnack which was printed in the *Christliche Welt* ('In Sachen des Apostolikums', *CW*, 1892, 768-70). Harnack argued that it was quite possible for the German Evangelical Church to replace the Apostles' Creed with a short confession which would be more in accord with the Reformed confession of faith and which would do away with the problems associated with the wording of the Apostles' Creed. Although Harnack was concerned here with the positive adoption of the essential content of the Apostles' Creed, in right-wing church and theological circles more emphasis was put on the negative side of his standpoint. Harnack increasingly came into the firing line and the Schrempf case faded into the background. This dispute and its effects on church politics led on the one hand to a closer alliance between the theologians close to the journal and on the other to reflections on the principles and direction of the journal.

Notes to page 86

82. After the assembly convened in 1892, 'each year such a main meeting of the Friends took place; from autumn 1896 it was open to all, but the press were excluded. It usually took place in Eisenach' (cf. Martin Rade, '*Christliche Welt*', *RGG*[1], I, 1706). In 1903 a more markedly institutional link between the Friends was resolved on at the Eisenach conference. So in September of that year the 'Association of the Friends of *Christliche Welt*' was formed.

83. In a letter to Paul Drews (1858-1912) he observed that he himself was somewhat unhappy about the ideas of the left-wing group. 'Jülicher, Grafe, Krüger, Troeltsch, Johannes Weiss, Wrede, have a quite different stance from ours, and are stamped by a radicalism towards the Christ of faith which sooner or later will separate them from us or us from them' (Rathje, *Welt des freien Protestantismus*, n.79, 71). Rathje thought that in the long term Rade had increasingly dissociated himself from the old friends who had founded the journal with him and had increasingly come under the spell of the 'left'. W.Schneemelcher gives the same verdict in his article '*Christliche Welt* und Freunde der *Christlichen Welt*', *RGG*[3], Vol.1, 1737-9.

84. Cf. the account by Rathje, *Welt* (n.79), 84-95.

85. Letter of 17 January 1898, ibid., 94.

86. A note from Julius Kaftan is illuminating here: 'Then Gunkel lectured on the prophetical style... I have a formal horror of this history-of-religions method which ends up by treasuring and stressing most what is alien to us, as children do. Moreover everyone was agreed that it is stupid dogmatics which does all the damage' (letter to Martin Rade, 29 March 1901, from Rathje, *Welt*, n.79, 95).

87. A letter from Troeltsch to Martin Rade in which he comments on an article by Kattenbusch in *CW* ('In Sachen der Ritschlschen Theologie', *CW* 12, 1898, 59ff.) illustrates the sharpness of the confrontation: 'Such a small excommunication indeed had come to pass, and I am well aware what the tone of the gentlemen will prove to be... The consequence of all this will be that I shall ultimately be forced out of the "Friends of *Christliche Welt*". Fortunately I have no ambition to found a school or sect, but have purely academic interests, so such isolation will not bother me very much' (according to Rathje, *Welt*, n.79, 106. Rathje dates the letter New Year's Day 1898).

88. In 1893 Martin Rade had asked Troeltsch to give a lecture on the dogmatic significance of the historical Christ. In view of the differences in the Ritschlian school and especially the difference between the 'young' and the 'old' with its background in positions I have already mentioned, Rade probably hoped that a discussion would clear the air. Evidently he had a sure sense of issues which were controversial within the group of friends. Troeltsch wrote to Bousset that he had turned down Rade's request because of his 'personal scepticism about this question with its lack of results and the suspect nature of the undertaking generally' (letter to W.Bousset, 4 September 1893, UB Göttingen, unpublished).

89. Rathje, *Welt* (n.79), 90 n.31, gives a survey of the lecture topics at the Eisenach meetings up to the year 1903. In a letter to H.Delbrück, the editor of the *Preussische Jahrbücher*, Troeltsch himself gave another description of the topic, namely 'The Objective Element in Religion' (cf. the letter to H.Delbrück of 4 October 1985, Deutsche Staatsbibliothek Berlin, Delbrück archives). Troeltsch offered the lecture to Delbrück for publication as an expansion of the response to the article by J.Friedhelm on 'Atheism and Idealism', *PrJ* 82, 71-97, which Delbrück had asked for. Troeltsch only published the lecture in 1897, in the *Preussische Jahrbücher*, after

considerable rewriting. He changed the topic to 'Christianity and the History of Religion' (cf. the letter to H.Delbrück of 4 November 1896, ibid.).

90. W.Köhler, *Ernst Troeltsch*, Tübingen 1941, 1. Already a year earlier Troeltsch had evidently expected a dispute at the meeting of the Friends. He wrote telling Bousset that he should take part in the meeting, 'since I need some cover. I have the feeling that there will be a fight, and only hope that all turns out well' (card to W.Bousset, 25 September 1895, UB Göttingen).

91. Cf. Rathje, *Welt* (n.79), 91. Here of course it must be remembered that Rade's interest was to tone down the significance of any confrontation within the circle of friends in order to keep it together. But Julius Kaftan does not mention such a clash in the letters to his brother Theodore either. He merely criticizes Arthur Titius, who reported on the lecture in the *Vossische Zeitung* without having made notes during it. Kaftan was anxious that the lecture and discussion might have a negative effect on church politics. Troeltsch is not mentioned (in *Kirche, Recht und Theologie in vier Jahrzehnten. Der Briefwechsel der Brüder Theodor und Julius Kaftan*, ed. W.Göbell, Munich 1967, Part I, 143).

92. *CW* 7, 1893, 568-78. Troeltsch assesses the artistic qualities of the play very positively, in a way which is somewhat surprising for present-day readers. He says that in comparison with Sudermann's 'tendentious revolutionary play' *Ehre* (Honour), here the characters and structure of the play are better motivated and the dialogue is witty, apt and not bombastic. This positive assesment of Sudermann's play is in clear contrast to the review written by the critic Alfred Kerr in 1896. Kerr observes: 'His (Sudermann's) figures first of all commit the technical error of explaining themselves; in life we are never so foolish as to allow such characteristics. Secondly, however, the language in which they do this bears no relation to their nature. In all circumstances they speak international pamphlets in a tempered form' (A.Kerr, *Gesammelte Schriften*, first series, 1, *Das neue Drama*, Cologne and Berlin ²1964, 225f.).

93. Ibid., 570. Troeltsch stresses this notion because with the concept of type he associates the necessary expression of a view of life associated with a particular state.

94. Ibid., 571. Only the figure of the pastor is criticized and described as being remote from reality. According to Troeltsch, true Christianity is not affected here.

95. Ibid., 576.

96. 'He [Sudermann] means it honestly and really does not know the answer to the question that he poses in the title of his play. Pedantic criticism has accused him of caricaturing the petty-bourgeois world too much in a burlesque way. As if Sudermann could do anything else!... At one point his heroine says in her Nietzschean intoxication that one must become greater than one's guilt. Now Sudermann would have to be greater than his class if he really wanted to solve the riddle that nags at him. But he is not, and so he wanders helplessly in the petty-bourgeois "on the one hand – on the other hand"' (F.Mehring, *Gesammelte Schriften und Aufsätze* II, *Zur Literaturgeschichte von Hebbel bis Gorki*, Berlin 1929, 114).

97. Cf. *CW* 12, 1898, 627-31, 650-7.

98. *ZTK* 6, 1896, 373-94.

99. Here Kaftan allows an openness in principle in so far as he holds it to be possible that the claim to be the truth of all religion can also be found in other religions. Nevertheless it is the case that the claim to truth is raised by Christianity in a quite unique way. Cf. ibid., 378.

100. Ibid., 382.

101. Ibid.

102. 'On the contrary, I can only explain them [Troeltsch's accounts] to myself on the supposition that he has not progressed far enough to provide the presupposition for a further advance of knowledge. He has not made clear to himself the difference which exists between a simple scholarly development of the given material and a proclamation of the ideal. At least not all the way through. Or does he perhaps not recognize this distinction? As far as I am concerned – but in that case he would have to direct his criticism against himself. But that does not happen. Instead he presents his views with prophetic confidence' (ibid., 386).

103. Kaftan remarks somewhat condescendingly: 'Evidently Troeltsch's discussions represent a stage in their author's development which has not yet come to a conclusion. He started from a philosophical approach orientated on metaphysics. Then for a while in all kinds of theological distress he took refuge in the theology of Ritschl and his pupils. That is what he himself reports. But now the old tendencies have revived again, apparently under the influence of very wide reading and the impressions that he has gained from it. Nevertheless, he cannot really return to metaphysics. It emerges that he has not only found a temporary lodging among the theologians whom he criticizes but has appropriated their basic ideas and cannot get away from them. So he is caught between the devil and the deep blue sea' (ibid., 386f.).

104. Cf. ibid., 388.

105. Ibid., 387.

106. SR, *ZTK* 6,71.

107. Ibid., 389.

108. A comment in a letter to his publisher Siebeck shows how little Troeltsch liked the tone of Kaftan's criticism. 'I am writing a retort to Kaftan which I hope that Gottschick will print. It keeps off everything personal. But I find Kaftan's article, which I finally read a few weeks ago, infuriating. I would not have thought him capable of such mockery and pedantry' (letter to P.Siebeck of 9 December 1896, Mohr/Siebeck archives, Tübingen). For Gottschick cf. n.110.

109. Ibid., 391.

110. *ZTK* 8, 1898, 1-69. Troeltsch indicates the personal offence given by the publication of this article in a letter to Bousset: 'I have got into a very comic correspondence with Kaftan, which revolves around modifications to an article which I sent to Gottschick (a Ritschlian, editor of *ZTK*) refuting his attack. That has led to correspondence with all the members of the editorial committee [of *ZTK*] and Kaftan has written me a colossally coarse letter. He seems to be very worked up. I still hope to prevent a great explosion. I don't know what will come of it in the end. At any rate, I'm personally finished with Kaftan and don't want any more to do with him. But I would also find a public scene very unpleasant' (letter to Bousset, 27 January 1897, UB Göttingen, unpublished).

111. How Troeltsch sees the ideas of his article focussed on the question of method and the problems associated with the concept of development is shown once again in the review of his own work in *TJB* 18, 1898, 509-12. There he writes: 'Troeltsch [here Troeltsch speaks of himself in the third person] shows how alongside the modern method applied to the natural world an equally new and fruitful method has grown up applied to the historical world, the proven presupposition of which in

any application is the unity and equality of all human events. It possesses the only means of coping with this relativistic plurality in the concept of development... In this consistent application of the idea of development and the anti-supernaturalistic view of history and the foundation for religious norms which follows from it, Troeltsch sees the real difference between his position and that of Kaftan. He regards as a fundamental misunderstanding Kaftan's view of the essentials of his position in the derivation of Christianity from a philosophical ideal religion, on philosophical premises made the norm for judging history, with which Christianity is arbitrarily identified' (ibid., 509). He says that the consequence of the methodological approach which he has chosen in terms of historical comparison is that the 'form of Christianity given by naive self-isolation and self-absolutization undergoes considerable changes. But that is the effect of science on religion, which here as elsewhere does not do away with the view that is directly present, but alters it' (ibid., 511).

112. Ibid., 69.

113. *ZTK* 8, 1898, 70-96.

114. Cf. ibid., 74.

115. *Kirche, Recht und Theologie in vier Jahrzehnten. Der Briefwechsel der Brüder Theodor und Julius Kaftan*, edited with a commentary by W.Göbell, Munich 1967, Parts 1 and 2; cf. esp. Part 2, 463ff.

116. Ibid., 463.

117. Ibid., 465.

118. Ibid.

119. Ibid., 466. Theodor Kaftan published his Troeltsch lectures under the title *Ernst Tröltsch. Eine kritische Zeitstudie*, Schleswig 1912. Julius Kaftan later commented on this work by his brother on Troeltsch. 'You have caught Troeltsch admirably. In my view he should tell you how delighted he is that you have contributed to the dissemination of his true ideas. But his obscurity draws unsurmountable boundaries around him. He is neither wise nor inwardly free enough. Instead of that he threatens you with the verdict of science' (ibid., 507).

120. *Theologische Arbeiten aus dem rheinischen wissenschaftlichen Prediger-Verein*, Neue Folge 4, Tübingen and Leipzig 1900, 46-86.

121. Ibid., 50.

122. Ibid., 54f.

123. Ibid., 55.

124. Ibid., 56.

125. Troeltsch's article appeared first in the *Theologische Arbeiten aus dem rheinischen wissenschaftlichen Prediger-Verein* (NF 4, Tübingen and Leipzig 1900, 87-108) and was then included in *GS* II. Here it is quoted from *RH*.

126. In a letter to Adolf Jülicher, Troeltsch comments on his article; 'I did not think that from this hidden place it would provoke so much contradiction, and gave reasons for my own views elsewhere' (letter to A.Jülicher, 4 November 1901, UB Marburg H S 695/1136, quoted in Apfelbacher, *Frömmigkeit*, 211). In my view this remark should not be taken to indicate that in this article Troeltsch was not giving his real view of historical method – thus Apfelbacher, who therefore advises great caution in using it 'to define what Troeltsch means by "historical method"...' (ibid., 211). If this warning of Apfelbacher's were correct, it would be difficult to explain why elsewhere Troeltsch describes his view of the historical method in the same

terms and indeed the same phrases (cf. e.g. *TJB* 1897, 589, or II, 394). In my view, the purport of this comment in Troeltsch's letter is that the work is first to be seen in the context of the conversation or confrontation with Niebergall, and here his own position is expressed in a pointed way for clarification. Secondly, it is to be assumed that the emphasis in his remark lies on the 'gave reasons for', i.e. the wider framework. In other words, the wider setting for what he says here about methodology, against Niebergall, is described in other publications. In the light of this situation we can also understand why Troeltsch included the article in the *Gesammelte Schriften*, and indeed rated it highly. He wrote to his publisher Siebeck: 'I thought that "Historical and Dogmatic Method" should be included in the *Gesammelte Schriften*, but without the Niebergall work which goes with it. I personally do not think much of Niebergall's work, but the possibility cannot be excluded that the great public is more interested in it than in my work. You will be more in the picture than I am, and you will also know whether or not from your standpoint a new edition of the double publication is desirable. At any rate, I would be reluctant to omit from my *Gesammelte Schriften* an article which is important to me' (letter to P.Siebeck, 23 December 1908, Mohr/Siebeck archives, Tübingen).

127. E.Lessing rightly stresses that the individual characteristics of the historical method must be brought into a living connection (*Die Geschichtsphilosophie Ernst Troeltschs*, Hamburg 1965, 21f.).

128. In this connection Troeltsch speaks of the correlation of 'the importance of analogy, levelling all historical phenomena' (*GS* II, 733, *RH*, 14), whereas earlier he had said that the omnipotence of analogy includes the similarity of historical events in principle but not their equality. It transpires that the concept of 'levelling down' here also means the idea of the similarity of the events of tradition in principle. However, at the same time Troeltsch seems to be discussing a tendency which lies in the actual application of the method.

129. Thus Troeltsch speaks of the 'old dogmatic method' (*GS* II, 737, *RH*, 20) as it has built up a naive, old and assured relationship to tradition (*GS* II, 738, *RH*, 21). It is worth noting how near to Troeltsch is the view of the contemporary philosopher Friedrich Paulsen, also in aim and theoretical basis. Paulsen writes: 'There are two ways of considering and assessing historical things, the dogmatic and the historical.' The 'dogmatic' is the absolute method which determines truth and falsehood; for Paulsen it is a significant product of theological thought. By contrast, the 'historical method' allows one to do justice to history and moreover has a self-critical orientation ('Das jüngste Ketzergericht über die moderne Philosophie', *Deutsche Rundschau* 1898, reprinted in *Philosophia militans*, Berlin 1901, 3-28: 3).

130. Cf. 'The Debate on the Historical-Critical Method: Correspondence between Karl Barth and Adolf von Harnack', in *The Beginnings of Dialectic Theology* 1, ed. James M.Robinson, Richmond, Va 1968, 165-90.

131. Troeltsch gave a number of major public lectures, for example one to the Saxon Church Conference in Chemnitz in 1900 on 'The Scientific Situation and its Demands on Theology'. A good year later he then gave one to the friends of *Christliche Welt* in Mühlacker on 'The Absoluteness of Christianity and the History of Religion'. In 1904 Troeltsch first addressed the Evangelical Social Congress on 'Christian Ethics and Society', and then the World Congress in St Louis on 'Psychology and Epistemology in the Study of Religion'. Finally, mention should be made of the lecture given at the German Historians' Conference in Stuttgart on

'The Significance of Protestantism for the Rise of the Modern World'. All these works were later published later.

132. Letter to W.Bousset, 5 August 1898, UB Göttingen.

133. Letter to W.Bousset, 14 December 1909, UB Göttingen, published in E.Dinkler-von Schubert, *Ernst Troeltsch. Briefe*, 45f.

134. Letter card to W.Bousset, 22 August 1900, UB Göttingen, unpublished. Evidently the text was written very quickly and there is a slip of the pen in the last part of the first sentence quoted.

135. Baron Friedrich von Hügel, a Roman Catholic lay theologian living in England, played a great part in the rise and dissemination of the so-called Modernist movement. This could be described as a reform movement within Catholicism at the end of the nineteenth century. Von Hügel has been called the lay bishop of Modernism. This is Troeltsch's first letter to von Hügel (13 April 1910). The correspondence between Troeltsch and von Hügel came about on von Hügel's initiative. Troeltsch wrote openly to von Hügel on religious and theological matters in a way which is hardly to be found elsewhere in his writings, with the exception of those to Bousset. Evidently Troeltsch felt himself free from considerations of church and academic politics when writing to von Hügel.

136. Letter to F.von Hügel, 4 September 1913, Apfelbacher/Neuner, 100. Marta Fick was born on 24 April 1874; we do not know for what reason she was living in Heidelberg in 1900.

137. Troeltsch writes: 'With these lines I would like... to support the invitation to my wedding which is coming to you from my parents-in-law. You are relatively near, especially if you should be in Lübeck; in that case perhaps you could come. At all events, with these lines I want to tell you that I would very much like to have you with me on that day, both in rememberance of old times and also for the feeling of an ongoing bond in the present' (letter to Bousset, 31 March 1901, UB Göttingen, unpublished). Bousset could not accept the invitation. Cf Troeltsch's letter to Bousset of 22 July 1901.

138. Letter to W.Bousset, 22 July 1901, UB Göttingen, unpublished.

139. Letter to P.Siebeck, 16 July 1903, Mohr/Siebeck archives, Tübingen, unpublished. Fritz Schöll (1850–1919) was professor of classical philology in Heidelberg.

140. Troeltsch wrote to von Hügel about his wife's health problems: 'My wife's health received a setback through the death of her mother and even now, after a summer spent well, she is visited by a worrying heart condition. But the greatest pain is that our marriage, which is very happy in itself, is still childless, and grief about that is the reason for my wife's constant nervous illnesses. With the pressure of my academic work I do not suffer so much from this lack, though I too feel it oppressive to envisage going through life in this way without leaving any trace behind' (letter to F.von Hügel, 22 October 1905, Apfelbacher/Neuner, 70).

141. Neumann writes in a letter to Gertrud von le Fort: 'The first reunion [after Troeltsch's death] was deeply moving; her wild, unrestrained nature kept breaking through. She has read all her husband's writings and work and is herself looking after his papers' (letter of 26 April 1924, Deutsches Literaturarchiv Marbach, G.von le Fort papers, unpublished).

142. It is typical that the poet describes her relationship with the professor as that with a guardian and fatherly friend under whose protection she finds herself. This description of the relationship corresponds fully with another that she gives

elsewhere. In the preface to the *Glaubenslehre* which she edited she speaks of Troeltsch as the 'master'. Erika Dinkler-von Schubert's verdict is: 'Gertrud von le Fort always denied that Troeltsch lies behind a main character of the book, the Heidelberg scholar and guardian of Veronica. But his role as an *imago* is unmistakable' ('Heidelberg im Leben und Werk von Gertrud von le Fort', *Heidelberger Jahrbücher* XVI, 1972, 19).

143. The impressions of colleagues which are included in the book coincide with what can also be read in the memoirs of Gertrud von le Fort, giving the impression of a captivating style of lecturing, powerful eloquence which held the audience in its spell. The intense relationship with the students, the evenings with them, are probably very stylized; here Gertrud le Fort seems to have incorporated recollections of Niebergall. Cf. also the Marburg dissertation by F.Schmalenbach, *Das erzählende Werk Gertrud von le Forts*, 1956, 7ff.

144. From the sermon on Eph.2.4-9; qualifying examination papers, Landeskirchliches Archiv, Nuremberg.

145. Cf. Marianne Weber, *Max Weber*, Tübingen 1926, 240.

146. For a long time Troeltsch seems to have been neither a member of the Congress nor a speaker at it. That distinguishes him from Max Weber, and also from other theologians close to *Christliche Welt*, like Adolf von Harnack, Martin Rade and Julius Kaftan.

147. Cf. my article 'Demokratie, Konservatismus und Christentum. Ernst Troeltsch's Konzept zum Umgang mit politischer Ethik auf dem Evangelisch-sozialen Kongress 1904', *ZEE* 30, 1986, 84-98, which lists further literature.

148. Cf. *GS* I, 425 n.197.

149. Cf. Rathje, *Welt* (n.79), 79.

150. The text is included in *RH*, 173-209. Originally other titles had been discussed. Troeltsch's own suggestion had been to call his article 'Christian Ethics and Democracy'. Evidently a politically more innocent title was chosen. In connection with this Troeltsch wrote to the publishers, Vandenhoeck und Ruprecht in Göttingen, who published both the Congress papers and the separate volume: 'I would give the whole work a different title, since the title forced on me in Breslau does not fit at all' (letter of 13 June 1904, publishers' archive).

151. *RH*, 179f.

152. Troeltsch distinguishes between an older conservatism of Stahl's stamp and a more recent conservatism which represents a class-struggle variant of the old. The older conservatism feels responsible for those who are subjects because of a patriarchal view and disposition. The idea of the social and political inequality of human beings is compensated for by a personal responsibility which becomes effective in the sphere of private life. It is surprising how positive Troeltsch is about Stahl's conservatism. He does not comment critically on Stahl's reference to the significance of the 'inner' man as a relativizing of the social position.

153. Moreover Troeltsch did more work on the text and made some additions and modifications for publication; these indicate certain shifts in accent. He remarked that the additions that he made were 'very important for clarity' (letter to W.Ruprecht, June 1904, Vandenhoeck und Ruprecht archives, Göttingen). Troeltsch will have been led to the changes, among other things, by his lecture to the Congress.

154. Ibid., 192.

155. In Troeltsch's view there can be possible links between liberalism on the one hand and Catholicism and Puritanism on the other. Catholicism understands the state as an organized body of people which may not put religious values in question. In this respect liberalism and its understanding of the state is satisfactory for Catholicism. Puritanism stresses freedom of conviction over against the state and calls on the state to protect this. Here too there is a possible link. Troeltsch finds nationalism the only stance incompatible with Christian thought. For him, in principle a nationalistic orientation goes against the Christian ethos, because it requires something that this cannot give, namely a limitation to the nation.

156. Ibid., 202.

157. Ibid., 205f.

158. The subsequent highly illuminating discussion shows the degree to which Troeltsch's lecture gave the hearers the possibility of discovering themselves within the broad spectrum of the ideas which he presented and of relating what was said to their own interests. This is true of the contributions of both Julius Kaftan and Friedrich Neumann. Kaftan could agree with what Troeltsch said because he recognized his own view in it, namely that the natural ordinances represent only the material for the development of basic moral ideas.

   Naumann found in Troeltsch a clear sympathy for democratic trends. However, Martin Rade energetically contradicted this version. 'What I find utterly obvious in Naumann is not so obvious in Troeltsch, namely that in all circumstances his heart beats on the side of democracy. However, I am convinced that while Troeltsch's feelings are often infinitely democratic, and that in this respect he accepts anyone, he also has aristocratic sensibilities. And we may not restrict this tendency in the lecture' (*Protokoll der Verhandlungen des 15. Evangelisch-sozialen Kongresses*, Göttingen 1904, 52). In his closing statement, Troeltsch explained that for him the two principles of democracy and aristocracy had to remain, along with their possible links with Christian ideas. Each served as a corrective of the other. The compromise which became necessary in a historical situation made specific demands on each occasion.

159. *Die Verhandlungen des 18. Evangelisch-sozialen Kongresses, abgehalten in Strassburg (Elsass) 21. bis 23. Mai 1907*, Göttingen 1907, 38.

160. Cf. the letter to A. von Harnack of 25 June 1911, Deutsche Staatsbibliothek, Berlin, unpublished.

161. Letter to A.von Harnack, 23 June 1904, Deutsche Staatsbibliothek, Berlin, unpublished.

162. Ibid. For Münsterberg see n.164.

163. Paul Hensel, *Sein Leben in seinen Briefen*, Wolfenbüttel and Hanover 1947, 182ff.

164. From 1892 Hugo Münsterberg (1863-1916) had been professor of psychology at Harvard. Philosophically he belonged to south-west German neo-Kantianism (cf. *Philosophie der Werte*, 1908). For the organization of the Congress cf. *Congress of Arts and Science*, ed. H.J. Rogers, Boston and New York 1915, I, 17f.

165. Marianne Weber, *Max Weber*, Tübingen 1926, 292.

166. Letter from Troeltsch to his wife, 14 September 1904, unpublished. H.Renz kindly made this letter available to me.

167. Ibid.

168. Ibid.

169. Ibid.

170. Letter to H.Münsterberg, 15 October 1904, Boston Public Library, unpublished.

171. Weber continued the journey and attempted to gain a deeper insight into religious and social conditions in America. Cf. Marianne Weber, *Max Weber* (n.145), 303ff.

172. Letter to H.Münsterberg, 15 October 1904, Boston Public Library, unpublished.

173. 128 section meetings took place within 4 days; the Festival Hall seated 3000. The first Congress Volume (there were eight in all) gives the total cost as $138,761.22: H.J.Rogers (ed.), *Congress of Arts And Science*, I, Boston and New York 1905, 19ff.

174. The original title is a better indication of Troeltsch's intention or of the topic he was given than the one chosen for publication. The lecture was considerably expanded by Troeltsch for publication, but not changed much. Cf. further the section 'The approach and structure of Troeltsch's philosophy of religion'.

175. Letter to H.Münsterberg, 15 October 1904, Boston Public Library, unpublished.

176. Ibid.

177. Ibid.

178. The philosophy faculty arranged the appointment with the Ministry of the Grand Duchy (letter of 7 July 1909), referring to the proposed call to the philosophical faculty of the University of Berlin, which mentioned Troeltsch in first place. There is also mention of the nomination of Troeltsch in first place in the list of possibilities for the Berlin theological faculty. Neither nomination was successful (see below). The faculty's application was accepted in recognition of Troeltsch's 'teaching and research, which go beyond the sphere of the theological faculty', and he was appointed to teach four hours a week (letter of 21 July 1909, Ministerium des Justiz, des Kultur und der Unterrichts, Generallandesarchiv Karlsruhe, records of the philosophical faculty 235/3134). The appointment was made after the call of Georg Simmel to a philosophical chair in Heidelberg proved impracticable. Ernst Troeltsch, Max Weber and Eberhard Gothein were among those who support Simmel's call (cf. M.L.Gothein, *Eberhard Gothein*, Stuttgart 1931, 212).

179. On 20 April 1903, Troeltsch wrote to the Minister of Justice, Culture and Education: 'I have been strenuously involved in work on a major book and must make an effort to concentrate on it as far as possible. So I ask to be allowed to hand over to our new Privatdozent Licentiate Niebergall the classes in systematics in the practical theology seminar; on top of those in the scientific theological seminar these are always a great burden...' (Generallandesarchiv Karlsruhe, records of the theological faculty, 235/3144).

The problem cropped up again in 1908, when Ludwig Lemme no longer wanted to take on the duties of the seminar on practical theology. On 2 December Lemme wrote to Karlsruhe: 'Since Herr Geheimer Kirchenrat Dr Troeltsch, with whom I have alternated in supervising the classes in systematics in the seminar on practical theology since 1903, has given them up, I feel compelled to take the same action, since it is obvious that either both systematic theologians should supervise the classes, or neither' (ibid.).

180. Records of the theological faculty, Heidelberg University archives, H-I-201/59, p.22.

181. On 15 February 1902 Troeltsch commented on two grant applications: 'As Astor has kept playing truant since being given his report, I must withdraw the mark of excellent for Astor and recommend that he be put in the second class. Goldschmidt has come to my class for the second time in order to save lecture fees and has played

truant most of the time, so I cannot really recommend anything for him' (University archives, Heidelberg H-I-201/ 56, p.38).

All in all it is striking how different the levels were in the examinations for diligence. Notably thin work stands alongside very thoughtful and theologically impressive studies.

182. Notice of 10 or 12 July 1905, Heidelberg University archives, H-I-201/58, pp.173, 184.

183. Heidelberg University archives, H-I-201/58, p.39.

184. Heidelberg University archives, H-I-201/56, p.177.

185. Heidelberg University archives, H-I-201/58, pp.17f.

186. Letter to R.Otto, 17 November 1904, UB Marburg, HS 797/800; part of it is printed in K.E.Apfelbacher, *Frömmigkeit und Wissenschaft*, Münster 1978, 599.

187. Troeltsch wrote a note on J.Bestmann's *Protestantismus und die theologischen Fakultäten* which is interesting from an academic and a political point of view. Bestmann proposes that pastors should be appointed to the theological faculties as teachers, and 'believing students' as assistants. Troeltsch retorts: 'The proposal is made in the arrogant and affected tone of a head of theological conferences who is much admired in a small circle and completely forgets that the "critical theologians" are not dominant, but under pressure everywhere, and are appointed only because of a lack of academic talent among believers' (*TJB* 15, 1895, 423).

188. Lemme hardly minced matters in presenting his theological views. These are his comments on the Ritschlian school and Albert Ritschl as its head. 'For this school Ritschl is the canon, and to its principle that God is manifest in Christ one would have to add, to express its view, that Christ is manifest in Ritschl' (*Die Prinzipien der Ritschl'schen Theologie und ihr Werth*, Bonn 1891, iv). One can see particularly from Lemme's ethics how much he regarded himself so to speak as the theological counterpart to Troeltsch. For Lemme, the reference to sin and grace is ethically a clear expression of the 'contrast between the pre-Christian or the sub-Christian and the Christian' (*Die christliche Ethik* 1, 275). How markedly conservative Lemme's thought on politics and church politics was is clear from his criticism of Social Democracy and of democratic thought generally. Lemme energetically rejects any upheaval in society; he was particularly concerned for the family and for property. At the same time nationalistic and antisemitic features emerge quite openly in his work (cf. ibid., 497). That Lemme was also competent enough is evident from his remarks on the history of theology, for example in an account of the history of the theological faculty at Heidelberg. Cf. L.Lemme, 'Die Vertreter der systematischer Theologie', in *Heidelberger Professoren aus dem 19.Jahrhundert. Festschrift der Universität zur Zentenarfeier ihrer Erneuerung durch Karl Friedrich*, Heidelberg 1903, 77ff. Many apt comments are made here, and the account is vivid and instructive. I used to think that the critical comment about Friedrich Gogarten made in Marburg by Theodor Siegfried was original, but Lemme's article taught me better. There it is said of Carl Daub's changes of theological standpoint that he had been a kind of 'theological chameleon', the verdict Siegfried passed on Gogarten.

189. Quoted from M.Rade, 'Dr theol. von Bodelschwingh über die heutige Universitätstheologie', *CW* 18, 1904, 788.

190. Lemme was firmly against Bousset and had said that his call would be a 'personal insult to my person' (thus Troeltsch in a letter to Bousset, 1 March 1908, UB Göttingen, unpublished). Accordingly he announced that were Bousset nominated

he would put in a separate proposal. However, here the church-political situation, the mood at court and the actions of the 'believing circle' were also significant. Lemme abstained on the nomination of Weiss. Troeltsch spoke with deep resignation about this clash, which was both open and hidden: 'In the face of such pious boorishness as that of Lemme, who knows no objective reasons but only partisanship, one sometimes doubts the moral effects of faith' (ibid.). It should also be mentioned at this point that Bousset's call could not be secured even after the death of Johannes Weiss in 1914; the post went to Martin Dibelius. Bousset's academic career, his call to Giessen which came only in 1915, and the quarrels over questions relating to his call, are certainly no credit either to Protestant theology or to the theological faculties.

191. Letter to W.Bousset, 1 March 1908, UB Göttingen, published in Dinkler-von Schubert, *Briefe* (n.21), 44f.

192. See Troeltsch's letters to Hans von Schubert (private property of E.Dinkler-von Schubert).

193. Cf. A.Dietrich, 'Ernst Troeltsch', *Archiv für Politik und Geschichte* 1, Berlin 1923, 97-111: 103ff.

194. Ibid., 103. There is also a tradition that Troeltsch often improvised in his lectures. Thus Kuno Fischer's daughter said of both Troeltsch's and Gothein's lectures that both were 'comprehensible, but sloppy and often completely unprepared' (H.Glockner, *Heidelberger Bilderbogen*, Bonn 1969, 145).

195. So Dietrich thinks that Troeltsch's classes were very much a 'workshop'. In Dietrich's account, the problems arising from this approach are clear. 'Rightly, doubts were constantly raised about this highly personal form of direction; however, the pedagogics of the facts always kept breaking through again victoriously' ('Ernst Troeltsch', n.193, 104).

196. Nome gives the following picture: 'He was more concerned to stimulate them to work independently on the problems, and was content to refer to sources in which they could find the necessary material for forming their own judgment on the matter' (John Nome, *Det moderne Livsproblem hos Troeltsch og vat Tid*, Oslo 1950, 142).

197. References to the 'untheological' character of Troeltsch's appearance and his conduct run through almost all the biographical accounts. Thus Otto Frommel said that the first impression that the young Heidelberg professor of theology made on his students was that of being 'untheological' (*Heidelberger Tageblatt*, 3 February 1923). And Erich Marcks made the same comment in connection with the prospect of Troeltsch being called to a chair of philosophy in Berlin (meaning it positively). Cf. Ulrich Pretzel, 'Ernst Troeltschs Berufung an die Berliner Universität', in H.Leussink et al. (ed.), *Studium Berolinense*, Berlin 1960, 514. The reference to his capacity to be devastating comes from the description by Dietrich, 'Ernst Troeltsch' (n.193), 103ff.

198. G.Wünsch, 'Ernst Troeltsch', in W.Zorn (ed.), *Lebensbilder aus dem Bayerischen Schwaben*, Vol.9, 39. Wünsch then continues: 'Anyone who could not follow Troeltsch's intuition did not have a clue, and unfortunately this was true of many people.'

199. Nome, *Moderne Livsproblem* (n.196), 150. Nome's view is that there is a connection between the problems of Troeltsch's life, his personality and his understanding of faith. For Nome this last was the centre, and binds together the contrasts in his 'natural characteristics into a characterful physiognomy, thus giving a distinctive

personal centre to all the divergent tendencies which determined his interests, because it prompted the will to ethical action and was rooted in the awareness of something abiding and eternal which offered a goal to work for, in the midst of a world of transitory and changing relativities' (ibid., 242).

200. Cf. Troeltsch's remarks in the Baden First Chamber in which he countered the charge made in the chamber that the theology and church politics of the theological faculty was fixed and allowed no room for traditional church doctrine: 'From my personal experience I may say that I have constantly advised young people who by nature, disposition and temperament seemed particularly destined for a traditional attitude: "Gentlemen, keep to the right; your whole nature points you to the right" ' (Session of 26 February 1910, *Verhandlungen der Ersten Kammer der Stände-Versammlung des Grossherzogtums Baden*, Karlsruhe 1910, 179). Troeltsch's last (extant) letter to Wilhelm Herrmann is also of interest here. Troeltsch comments that in view of the polemic on both sides, students must 'work out the differences for themselves'. Moreover, he referred his students to Wilhelm Herrmann and advised them 'to study your letters as a supplement to my teaching' (letter to W.Herrmann, 10 March 1918, UB Marburg HS 691.499, printed in Apfelbacher, *Frömmigkeit*, n.66, 35).

201. However, distinctions need to be made here. Georg Wünsch felt other ties to Troeltsch than did, say, Friedrich Gogarten. Wünsch was influenced by Troeltsch's person and work, and this is evident even in the subject-matter of his books (e.g. *Luther and the Sermon on the Mount*, and *The Collapse of Lutheranism as a Social Form*). For Gogarten the impact of Troeltsch's person proved influential, and his work only partly so. Gogarten saw his proximity to and links with Troeltsch essentially in his historical work and diagnosis of the contemporary situation; Troeltsch's proposals for a theological solution for the most part seemed unacceptable to him. In connection with the problems of this assessment it should be observed here that Troeltsch's theological position is always also expressed in his historical work and contemporary studies, since it is bound up with these.

202. Troeltsch's later Berlin colleague Carl Stumpf describes in his recollections of Hermann Lotze what other presuppositions would be needed here: 'Nothing is more unattractive to the great mass of learners than the casting aside of caution; nothing is more desirable than a powerful dose of dogmatism' (in 'Zum Gedächtnis Lotzes', *Kantstudien* 22, 1918, 10).

203. Thus Harnack wrote in connection with Troeltsch: 'Indeed our best – and especially our best – are odd characters. No one wants to put his special characteristics on a chain; each carries his diamond wrapped in a slip of paper and presents it as a loose precious stone' (Harnack's card to Rade, 18 June 1904, UB Marburg, Rade collection).

204. 'Von der Münchener Kunstausstellung', *Korrespondenzblatt für die evangelische-lutherische Geistlichen in Bayern* 13, 393ff.

205. Cf. E.Rothacker, *Heitere Erinnerungen*, Bonn 1965, 57.

206. Cf. the school reports of the St Anna Gymnasium, Bundesarchiv Koblenz.

207. G.Wünsch has given me a detailed verbal account of this. So far, only two cards from Troeltsch have been found in Gogarten's papers. They refer to Gogarten's planned Promotion, which did not come about, above all because the Fichte work had already been published (in the possession of M.Bultmann).

208. Cf.the letter to F.von Hügel, 31 January 1920, Apfelbacher/Neuner, 105f.

209. In the 'personalia of the ordinand Ernst Troeltsch', under the rubric 'Knowledge of Music' appears the word 'without' (Akt des Königlich Bayerischen Oberkonsistoriums, Aufnahmsjahr 1888, Landeskirchliches Archiv, Nuremberg).

210. If music had no great practical and theoretical significance for Troeltsch, it did for Max Weber. The same can also be said of the Bassermann daughter, who was said to be a very musical woman, which indicates another difference between her and Troeltsch. She later married a Herr von Campenhausen, a lawyer in Heidelberg and uncle of the theologian Hans von Campenhausen. The marriage remained childless. Frau von Campenhausen gave piano lessons (verbal communication by E.Dinkler-von Schubert).

211. The 'Pro-Rector' would now be the Rector of the university; at that time the Rector was the local ruler. How great the interest of Grand Duke Friedrich of Baden was in the university, and particularly in the theological faculty, is evident from his letters to Wilhelm Herrmann, in which he supported Herrmann's proposed call to the University of Heidelberg (cf. 'Briefe Grossherzogs Friedrich von Baden an Wilhelm Herrmann', *CW* 54, 1940, 157ff.).

212. In the election of 1901, Lemme was passed over and Adolf Hausrath elected in his place (cf. *Chronik der christlichen Welt* 11, 1901, 293).

213. On the Grand Duke's eightieth birthday Troeltsch was nominated a Privy Councillor – one might say as a matter of routine (*Heidelberger Zeitung*, 8 September 1908). More important for him was the academic recognition he received from honorary doctorates (Doctor of Theology, Göttingen 1896; Doctor of Philosophy, Greifswald 1906; Doctor of Law, Breslau 1911) and his election as corresponding member of the Prussian Academy of Sciences in Berlin in 1912, on the proposal of Adolf von Harnack.

214. *Heidelberger Zeitung* 1906, 53, 3 March 1906: I owe this reference to H.Renz.

215. Ibid. Troeltsch made use of this aim as a transition to the praise of the local ruler which traditionally concluded the speech.

216. Cf. the account in the *Heidelberger Zeitung* of 26 September 1906, in which the text of Troeltsch's speech is printed.

217. *Die Trennung von Staat und Kirche, der staatliche Religionsunterricht und die theologischen Fakultäten*, Tübingen 1907; ET 'The Separation of Church and State and the Teaching of Religion', in *RH*, 109-17, quotation 109.

218. Thus in his 1901 rectoral address (*Die Aufgabe der theologischen Fakultäten und die allgemeine Religionsgeschichte*, Giessen 1901), Adolf von Harnack expressed the opinion that purely in theory there was something to be said for the expansion of the theological faculties in this direction. It would widen peoples' horizons beyond their own religions, and at the same time the consistent application of historical thought or method would be safeguarded. However, his own inclination was to keep to the previous solution. 'We want the theological faculties to remain faculties for research into the Christian religion, because in its pure form Christianity is not one religion alongside others, but is *the* religion' (ibid., 16).

219. In the first form the concept of truth is absolute; in the second it is relative, and in the third it is defined in both absolute and relative terms. The understanding of revelation is objective in the established church, subjective in the disestablished, free church, and a 'mixed form' in the state churches enjoying parity. Troeltsch's ideas on the understanding of revelation in this last form are quite difficult. He thinks that here too there could be said to be historical developments of revelation,

but not in a final sense detrimental to tolerance. The *Social Teachings* then enlarges on and supplements these ideas, as Troeltsch himself notes (cf. *GS* I, 872 n.478, *ST* II, 965f. n.478).

220. In view of Harnack's comments, Troeltsch's attitude to the question of changing theological faculties, say by making a history-of-religions section, is an interesting one. Troeltsch does not give such a possibility much of a chance. He thinks either that the result would be a disastrous dilettantism or that such a section would in practice take over the function of a theological faculty.

221. In a letter to Hans von Schubert, who had given a speech on the church-state relationship, Troeltsch remarks: 'Formulating the problem in a modern context is one of my most serious concerns. In "The Culture of the Present" I have explained why the situation seems to me to be completely different for Catholicism and old Protestantism, and I hope to return to the theme. I quite understand your hesitations about the separation and share them, though not unconditionally' (letter to H.von Schubert, 12 February 1906, in the possession of E.Dinkler-von Schubert, unpublished).

222. Accordingly Troeltsch says that the last part of his speech was 'a defence of the theological faculty' (letter to F.M.Schiele, 28 November 1906, Mohr/Siebeck archives, unpublished).

223. Cf. Troeltsch's remark in a letter to W.Köhler: 'Max Weber asked me to become actively involved in politics. I declined, explaining that despite many sympathies with liberalism I am not a liberal. The reason why I am not a liberal lies in my being a Christian and its effect on political thought' (Köhler, *Ernst Troeltsch*, n.90, 292). Troeltsch's article 'Political Ethics and Christianity', *RH*, 173-209: 180-4, indicates his objections to liberalism on religious grounds. Here we must take the criticisms of liberalism and nationalism together. Weber wanted Troeltsch to become active in the National Liberal Party. Troeltsch's attitude to membership of in the Baden First Chamber is evident from a later letter to the historian Hermann Oncken, after Oncken's election: 'I congratulate you warmly on the First Chamber. You will already see that though the state is small, it is quite a useful experience. One learns a great deal and develops iluminating relationships in a number of directions. Nor is the consolidation of one's position in Heidelberg which stems from it to be underestimated' (card to H.Oncken, 22 June 1915, Niedersaxony State Archives, Oldenburg, unpublished).

224. Thus he criticizes two calls which would not have given the faculty the 'significant professional colleagues' whom they had nominated but professors whose reputation was based more on their teaching than on their research. The Ministry, in agreement with the church authorities, had decided differently from the faculty and the senate. Troeltsch thought wrong the practice of the church authorities and the Ministry as far as possible to call people whose publications had given no cause for criticism. 'It has happened that fame and particularly brilliant contributions have been an obstacle' (*Verhandlungen der Ersten Kammer der Ständeversammlung des Grossherzogtums Baden in den Jahren 1909-1910, Protokollheft*, Karlsruhe 1910, 150). In this connection Troeltsch quotes the sarcastic comment by the head of a major educational institution: 'Gentlemen, for God's sake do not write any books; they only cause me and yourselves difficulties' (ibid.).

225. 'A faculty divided in itself and with its members at odds with one another not only

offends the other faculties but makes life unpleasant for scholars within such a faculty' (session of 26 February 1910, ibid., 179).

226. Ibid.

227. Ibid.

228. Proceedings, session of 9 April 1910, ibid., 260.

229. Proceedings, session of 18 July 1910, ibid., 640.

230. 'I believe that I can sympathize with and understand the church powers, approve of them and believe them to be in the right, treasure them and regard them as indispensable. But because here it is so difficult to distinguish between what is rich in blessing and what is dangerous, between spiritual inwardness and the organizational drive for power, between the furtherance of education and an unacceptable drive towards omnipotence, I believe that the protective means [of the state over against the church's claims to power] cannot be dispensed with' (ibid., 643).

231. Proceedings, session of 23 February 1912, ibid., 96.

232. Ibid., 97.

233. Ibid., 98.

234. Session of 12 June 1914, ibid., 515f. Finally it should be mentioned that Troeltsch was put forward within the Chamber as a spokesman on questions of public morality (a theologian was felt to be especially competent on this). He reported on a petition from the Popular Alliance for the Combatting of Obscenity in Word and Image. He was also spokesman of a commission which had to give advice on petitions from various associations in the state and on the 'brothel question'. Here Troeltsch leaves as little to be desired in oratorical vigour and liveliness as in his comments on questions of university and school politics.

235. That does not exclude a political link with the National Liberal Party. Troeltsch already seems to have been guided in this direction by home and school.

236. In 1909, in correspondence, the Heidelberg historian E.Marcks commented on Troeltsch's political attitude and tried to classify it. 'He has lively political interests which may be National Social...' (Ulrich Pretzel, 'Ernst Troeltschs Berufung an die Berliner Universität', in *Studium Berolinense. Aufsätze und Beiträge zur Probleme der Wissenschaft und zur Geschichte der Friedrich-Wilhelms-Universität zur Berlin*, ed. H.Leussink et al., Berlin 1960, 514).

237. At any rate Troeltsch seems to have had reservations here. At least, that is to be concluded from his remarks in 'Political Ethics and Christianity', here above all relating to the criticism of ideas of nationality. This criticism was also applied to Friedrich Naumannn, 'whose politics are not so much democratic or socialist as nationalistic, with a strong sense of solidarity with the rising classes' (179). Troeltsch seems to have been personally close to Naumann, but was not a member of his National Social Organization. At this point there are clear differences from Max Weber.

238. Letter to W.Bousset, 2 February 1912, UB Göttingen, unpublished.

239. Of 20 June 1920, published in *DG*, 247ff., 249.

240. The house in Ziegelhäuser Landstrasse 17 was an old family possession of the Fallensteins (Max Weber's mother was born a Fallenstein) and was lived in by Weber's uncle Adolf Hausrath until his death in 1909. Troeltsch moved into the upper storey of the house with his wife in spring 1910, and Weber and his wife into the dwelling below (cf. M.Weber, *Max Weber*, Tübingen 1926, 457ff.).

241. In *Die Religionswissenschaft der Gegenwart in Selbstdarstellungen*, Leipzig 1925, 65f. In addition to Max Weber and Ernst Troeltsch this circle included such prominent scholars as Wilhelm Windelband, Georg Jellinek, Eberhard Gothein and Karl Rathgen. Camilla Jellinek commented on the significance of the group and remarked in connection with the arguments presented in it: 'Firstfruits of the spirit were offered to this select circle which often became the nucleus of later works that also benefited the public' (*Georg Jellinek. Ein Lebensbild*, n.1, 31).
242. The description given by Max Weber of a visit to the philologist Ulrich von Wilamowitz-Moellendorf is also significant. In a letter to his father on 2 November 1885 he wrote: 'Today's visit to Wilamowitz... was not without its sensations. I went at the usual hour for visiting, and the maid showed me straight to his room without announcing me. I knocked, and when I went in I was met from a mass of folios, books, papers and scraps of paper which covered the desk and the floor by a tall figure clad in an approximately yellow smock, at any rate in highly primitive costume, who stared at me with the unconcealed indication of such enormous perplexity that I almost laguhed out loud, despite the somewhat difficult situation' (Max Weber, *Jugendbriefe*, Tübingen nd [1936], 183).
243. Karl Neumann commented critically on Troeltsch's and Weber's distancing of themselves from academic life and their bourgeois philistinism. In his memoirs of Heidelberg, Hermann Glockner puts Neumann's view like this: 'He felt to be a weakness the way in which Max Weber liked playing the powerful man and in every respect tended to excess. He thought that "in this respect Weber was like Troeltsch". "But you have to know that that came about over a period. Albrecht Dietrich and Windelband and Troeltsch and Weber, indeed the whole Eranos Society, were all a bit over the top, and in confidence, they acted more wild than they were. One says of children that their eyes are bigger than their bellies. But God alone knows how far the masculine, all-too-masculine goes and the vanity of the poor soul"' (Herrmann Glockner, *Heidelberger Bilderbuch*, Bonn 1969, 102).
244. Cf. on the one hand *DG*, 252, and on the other *GS* III, 161.
245. *DG*, 251.
246. Cf. E.Baumgarten, *Max Weber. Werk und Person*, Tübingen 1964, 624.
247. For details cf. the section on the *Social Teachings*.
248. C.Neumann, 'Zum Tode von Ernst Troeltsch', *Deutsche Vierteljahresschrift für Literaturwissenschaft und Geistesgeschichte* 1, 1923, 162.
249. Cf. F.K.Schumann, *Der Gottesgedanke und der Zerfall der Moderne*, Tübingen 1929, 276; there are similar comments in R.J.Rubanowice, *Crisis in Consciousness. The Thought of Ernst Troeltsch*, Tallahassee 1982, 45. F.W.Graf stresses that 'in scholarly exchanges with Max Weber Troeltsch was also the giver' ('Max Weber und die protestantische Theologie seiner Zeit', *ZRGG* 39, 1987, 134). In this connection see also the letter of condolence (previously unknown) written by Troeltsch to Marianne Weber, from which Graf quotes (ibid., 339).
250. Whereas Weber already had some interest in theology at the time they became acquainted, he laid the decisive foundations for the social and sociological orientation of Troeltsch's thought and encouraged him here. In an article, Graf has investigated this question, among others. He points out that Weber's understanding of religion came not least through his cousin, the theologian Otto Baumgartner, and was characterized by a proximity to the history-of-religions school. Religion was understood as a deep-seated human experience which has a specific effect on the

378 *Notes to pages 126-127*

way people live – that is the common background both for history-of-religions thought and for Weber's concept of religion as it emerged in his studies on the sociology of religion. Later, according to Graf, Ernst Troeltsch was Max Weber's 'professional adviser on literature', which for Graf also includes 'the relevance of its content' (F.W.Graf, 'Fachmenschenfreundschaft. Bemerkungen zu Max Weber und Ernst Troeltsch', in *Max Weber und seine Zeitgenossen*, ed. W.J.Mommsen and W.Schwendtker, Göttingen and Zurich 1988, 326).

251. Marianne Weber, *Max Weber* (n.240), 532. In a letter to his publisher Troeltsch writes: 'I also note that for the moment Weber is so offended that our relationship has suffered a heavy blow. Something connected with the military hospital led to a difference of opinion to which he gave such energetic expression that I could not but take offence to it. That has troubled my final days in Heidelberg' (letter to P.Siebeck, April 1915, Mohr/Siebeck archives, Tübingen, unpublished).

252. After Weber's sudden death in 1920, Troeltsch in his obituaries described him with deep understanding both as a man and as a scholar; at the same time he did not disguise what he had found dark and alien in Weber's nature. The remark which is occasionally made, that Troeltsch claimed to be ahead of Weber as a scholar and that this had burdened their relationship in the eyes of the Heidelberg public (cf. Baumgarten, *Max Weber*, n.246, 624), seems to me to be true only to a very limited degree and to have come more from outside. The remarks by Troeltsch which acknowledge Weber and stress his influence, not just in the obituaries, are difficult to harmonize with this.

253. In 1908 the question arose of a successor to O.Pfleiderer (1839-1900, Professor of Systematic Theology and New Testament). Although Harnack backed Troeltsch very vigorously, he could not get a majority for him in the faculty. J.Kaftan writes that there was therefore a 'regular dance'. In the end there was a compromise (cf. W.Göbell, ed., *Kirche, Recht und Theologie*, I, 47f.). The call to a chair in philosophy which came soon afterwards failed on the minority opinions put in by individual members of the faculty indicating reservations about Troeltsch's background in theology and his theological interest, which was still increasing. However, Dilthey voted for Troeltsch's appointment. Cf. U.Pretzel, 'Ernst Troeltschs Berufung an die Berliner Universität', in H.Leussink et al. (eds.), *Studium Berolinense* (n.236), 509ff.

254. Letter of 4 July 1914, Heidelberg University archives, Troeltsch personal records A-219. Troeltsch added that he felt strengthened by the marks of respect shown to him by his colleagues and the confidence which they indicated 'to go into the future, in which I want nothing but the best that the Heidelberg spirit has taught me, to win distinction in important places' (ibid.).

255. Letter to W.Bousset, 27 July 1914, UB Göttingen, partially published in E.Dinkler-von Schubert, *Ernst Troeltsch* (n.21), 47f. R.Seeberg (1859-1933) belonged to the 'modern-positivist' trend within theology. He saw himself as a Lutheran; politically he was conservative. Troeltsch seems to have been particularly disappointed by Deissmann's conduct. At least according to Troeltsch's information, Deissmann had vigorously supported Seeberg's campaign against him in Berlin (cf. Troeltsch's letter to his publisher P.Siebeck, 17 July 1914, Mohr/Siebeck archives, Tübingen).

256. Letter to W.Bousset, 27 July 1914, UB Göttingen, published in E.Dinkler-von Schubert, *Ernst Troeltsch* (n.21), 47f. With this step in view, Troeltsch is making

allies or companions in suffering, whatever one likes to call them. 'We must all, Naumann, Harnack, Traub, etc., get out of theology and are being more or less gently pushed.' The letter to C.H.Becker, Troeltsch's former Heidelberg colleague and later Minister of Culture, is also illuminating: Troeltsch writes: 'It [the decision to go to Berlin] was truly not an easy one, but I would have thought it cowardly to avoid the new demands at this central place of education. Moreover my outward farewell to theology brings not just pain but also some liberation from calculation and satiation. I have loved theology, at least as far as I have understood it, but with few exceptions not the theologians, i.e. the academics' (letter of 28 July 1914, Geheimes Staatsarchiv Berlin, unpublished).

257. Records of the theological faculty, 235/3145, Generallandesarchiv, Karlsruhe. Arthur Titius was nominated in next place, above all because, according to the report, he was one of the few theologians who understood something about modern science. Then in third place came Rudolf Otto; his systematic knowledge was stressed and reference was made to his acquisition of knowledge in the history of religions. Finally, mention was made of Hermann Süskind, who was counted one of the hopes of theology. It was said that of all those mentioned he was closest to the previous occupant of the chair, without having been his pupil or having started with him at all. One feels that one can hear Troeltsch, even down to the wording, above all in the opinion on Süskind. The proposal by the faculty does not seem to have followed Troeltsch's line. Leaving aside Hermann Süskind, his favourite was really Rudolf Otto, who was still too unknown. Troeltsch had struck up a close personal friendship with Rudolf Otto, and in particular had sympathized with his problems as a Privatdozent. Troeltsch's letters to Rudolf Otto are the most sympathetic and understanding that he wrote (or that have been preserved). He opened himself up personally to Otto in a way which we find elsewhere only with Friedrich von Hügel (cf. especially the letter of 17 November 1904, UB Marburg, HS 797/800, partly published in Apfelbacher, *Frömmigkeit*, 59). What seems to have attracted him theologically in Otto, so that he could see Otto as his genuine successor, was first Otto's history-of-religions orientation, and secondly the intellectual training that he had had through the study of Kant and Schleiermacher (also writing books on them). Troeltsch openly conceded to Bousset how little the faculty decision pleased him. 'Of course I wanted Otto above all to replace me. It was quite impossible. I do not know why. He is thought to be sick, and that is a vicious circle: he is sick because he cannot get a job and he cannot get a job because he is sick. It really is a wretched business. However, since his sprawling lecture at Eisenach I too have had some hesitations as to whether he can really form, shape and limit material. Now Wobbermin has accepted. He is not to my taste: honest, bold, but somewhat philistine' (letter to W.Bousset, 21 December 1914, UB Göttingen, published in E.Dinkler-von Schubert, *Ernst Troeltsch*, n.21, 49f.).

258. Records of the theological faculty, 235/3145, Generallandesarchiv, Karlsruhe.

259. The newspaper announcement mentions Troeltsch's mobilization speech (to be discussed below) and the effect that it had. 'Then for the first time Ernst Troeltsch became the preacher of the Fatherland, all our own' (from a newspaper cutting in the Troeltsch personal records, Heidelberg University archives).

Part Three: Main Works from the Heidelberg Period (1900-1914)

1. See xvii above.
2. In 'Ernst Troeltsch. Ein Gedenkwort', Becker Sachakten no.1559, Geheimes Staatsarchiv, Berlin. Similarly Max Scheler, who at the same time stresses Troeltsch's 'rare skill at sympathy' ('Ernst Troeltsch als Soziologe', *Kölner Vierteljahreshefte für Soziologie* 1923, 9).
3. *GS* II, vii.
4. Letter to F.von Hügel, 10 March 1903, Apfelbacher/Neuner, 61.
5. *GS* IV.3. As we saw, school and study abundantly fed this drive for knowledge. In one of his CVs Troeltsch mentions that having been a pupil of Ritschl and Reuter was particularly helpful for him. Of the latter he says: 'Reuter was a key model for method, and I follow him in my work on the history of dogma' (CV on the occasion of his call to Bonn, Central State Archives, Merseburg). This reference is above all to Reuter's basic idea that there can be only one historical method. According to Reuter, this applies to any subject and any discipline. Cf. Reuter's programmatic sketch for *ZKG* 1875, in T.Brieger, 'Nachruf auf Hermann Reuter', *ZKG* 11, 1889, no page number.
6. Letter to P.Siebeck, 1 August 1901, Mohr/Siebeck archives, Tübingen, unpublished. The project was originally part of a new textbook series 'Outlines of Theology', in which Troeltsch was to undertake the account of the history of theology. Troeltsch postponed the implementation of the plan well into the future. The real reason for this was that he did not want to put an account in outline form at the beginning but to begin with a major fundamental work. The outline then never materialized.
7. *Die Kultur der Gegenwart, ihre Entwicklung und ihre Ziele*, ed. P.Hinneberg, I.IV.1, Berlin and Leipzig 1906, 'Die Geschichte der Christlichen Religion', 253-458, [2]1909, 431-755; the quotations are from the latter.
8. Letter to W.Bousset, 12 October 1894, UB Göttingen, unpublished.
9. *PN*, 432.
10. Dilthey's concern with topical political and cultural questions is to be found less in his publications than in his diaries and letters, especially the letters to Count Yorck von Wartenburg.
11. For example when we read, 'However, the call to the gospel was its (i.e. the Reformation's) legal title. But this legal title was nothing new; it was simply the isolation and extraction of a basic element from the previous system' (*PN*, 436). The hermeneutic of G.Ebeling in his article 'Luther und der Anbruch der Neuzeit', *ZTK* 69, 1972, 185ff., is characterized by the idea of the 'soteriological situation of an age' which is the basis of the resolution of the controversial questions inherent in it. On this assumption Luther can be assigned neither to the Middle Ages nor to modern times. Rather, he occupies a 'highly complicated intermediate position'. Cf. ibid., 207: 'A view of history which is open to the breadth and depth of the controversies of an age will therefore have to note the controversial correlation between situation and word. With this slogan I am referring to the distinction used by Troeltsch for the sphere of problems with which we are concerned, between mediaeval questions and the unmediaeval answers which Luther gave to them... However, the critical comment must be made that the new answer also changes the question or already presupposes a change in the question. For an understanding of

the situation already betrays an intimation of what is needed to survive it' (ibid., 209f.). Ebeling is right in pointing out that a new answer also alters a question or presupposes a changed question. It is not enough simply to recognize a model of co-ordination. The change in both question and answer must be taken into account.

12. In the second edition of 1909 Troeltsch often made modifications to the text and incorporated additions. He also made a sharper conceptual distinction between old and new Protestantism, indicated the problem of 'defining the nature' of Protestantism, worked out the connection between religious idea and universal history of culture more strongly, and gave a more differentiated account of the social teachings.

13. *PN*, 431.

14. *PN*, 441.

15. *PN*, 444.

16. *PN*, 447. The supernatural concept of truth is characterized by the fact that the communication to human beings which takes place in it is regarded as a supernatural event.

17. *PN*, 449.

18. In this connection Hanns Rückert has underlined or even sharpened Troeltsch's verdict. 'There is much to be said for the view of Troeltsch, who generally gives the Reformation the role of once again delaying a late-mediaeval process of disintegration which was just about to break through in the Renaissance and humanism and in which the Western spirit already wanted to emancipate itself from its ties with the authority of the Christian church, once again bowing Europe under the Christian norm for no less than another 200 years' (Hanns Rückert, 'Geistesgeschichtliche Einordnung der Reformation', in *Vorträge und Aufsätze zur historischen Theologie*, Tübingen 1972, 59).

19. *PN*, 449. In the second edition Troeltsch added, by way of supplement and differentiation, that the practical implementation of the unity of state and church in Calvinism must be distinguished from that in Lutheranism. Luther attaches more importance to trust in the Word, while Calvin and Calvinism make more marked use of organizational means.

20. *PN*, 450.

21. Constant development of the material leads to breaks in Troeltsch's account which have different causes. On the one hand they are prompted by criticism; on the other hand new insights arise as a result of his reflections on social history. Many additions are made in the interest of a more marked historical differentiation, but at the same time their general tenor is to seek to reject possible or actual criticism of the wide generalization or to counter it effectively. To understand the account it is also important to note Troeltsch's distinction between the theological thought of Protestantism in the narrower sense and the general impact of Protestantism on cultural history.

22. Here is one example of the further work in the second edition: whereas originally Troeltsch spoke of the disintegration of the concept of the sacrament as the central religious idea of Protestantism, now, because he has probably sensed the inadequacy of the general term 'Protestantism' at this point, he has resorted to Luther both for differentiation and also as a basis (cf. *PN*, 456f.).

23. *PN*, 457.

24. H.Boehmer, *Luther im Lichte der neueren Forschung*, Leipzig and Berlin 1918, 230.

For Boehmer the so-called central idea consists 'in the new view of religion which found doctrinal expression in the statement about "justification by faith alone", i.e. in the view of "subjective religion" as a human disposition, and "objective religion" as a revelation of God's disposition' (ibid.).

25. *TR* 10, 1907, 51.

26. Ibid., 51ff. Hermann Fischer makes the criticism, already expressed in earlier literature, that Troeltsch's understanding of Luther is not derived directly from a thorough study of the sources ('Luther und sein Reformation in der Sicht Ernst Troeltschs', *NZST* 5, 1963, 132-72). Perhaps one can add that even where Troeltsch had a more precise knowledge of the sources, for example in the case of Melanchthon, Protestant orthodoxy and German Idealism, he tends towards sweeping verdicts and cites a good deal of secondary literature. Karl Holl also commented critically on the relationship between historical insights and systematic judgments in Troeltsch (cf. *Gesammelte Aufsätze zur Kirchengeschichte* I, 262 n.1). K.-E.Apfelbacher has put forward the theory that Troeltsch did not arrive at his historical verdict on the basis of a systematic viewpoint but, on the contrary, historical perceptions led him to systematic conclusions (*Frömmigkeit und Wissenschaft. Ernst Troeltsch und sein theologisches Programm*, Munich 1978, 121). In my view a sweeping statement about the dependence of systematic verdicts on historical insights does not help much here, because it does not make clear how closely historical and systematic statements are dovetailed in Troeltsch and how they stand in a living relationship of mutual influence in which the accents are placed differently.

27. *PN*, 460.

28. The following sentence makes clear what for Troeltsch was really new and thus to be accepted theologically: 'Here the new remains below the threshold of theology and often also below that of consciousness, because the doctrine of original sin makes impossible both the personalistic doctrine of immanence and the transcending and abolition of the order of law in the order of grace' (*PN*, 469). The result is a dualism, where a unitary view would have been appropriate.

29. *PN*, 481f.

30. According to this approach, the great figures of the history of religion are of crucial significance for the development of religious life. For example Bousset, *Das Wesen der Religion*, Halle 1904, 98, speaks of the 'prophetic Reformers' who ushered in a new era in the history of religion.

31. In Luther research both H.Rückert and G.Ebeling, along with F.Gogarten, pointed out that in Luther the new element lies in the use of traditional theological formulae. What is new is the principle of *pro me*, of personalism. So in the mediaeval notions an element is taken into Luther's theology which as it were explodes it from within. For Gogarten, here Luther in principle overcame metaphysical thought in theology (cf. *Verhängnis und Hoffnung der Neuzeit*, Stuttgart 1958, 168). Ebeling thinks that in a remarkable way Luther's thought leaves behind or is remote from both the spirit of the Middle Ages and that of modernity (cf. 'Luther und der Anbruch der Neuzeit', n.11, 207ff.). And Rückert emphasizes that with his idea of faith Luther breaks through the ontological scheme of thought which was dominant in the Middle Ages (cf. 'Geistesgschichtliche Einordnung der Reformation', n.18, 68).

In connection with Troeltsch's understanding of Luther there is unanimity that Luther's ideas have a close connection with the Middle Ages, while at the same time different elements are recognized which are grounded above all in his view of faith. The difference from Troeltsch lies where the elements which cannot be attributed to the Middle Ages are evaluated.

Troeltsch's cultural historical perspective which uses the Enlightenment as a criterion allows Luther to be associated with the modern world only conditionally and through historical intermediaries. By contrast, Gogarten, Ebeling and Rückert adopt an essentially theological approach to Luther which, while not leaving aside history and the question of historical connections, gives Luther – over and above his view of faith and the principle of the Word – a direct significance and authority for the present and for contemporary theology.

32. Cf. *PN*, 484ff.

33. Troeltsch commented on Luther's work 'On the Freedom of a Christian Man' (1520), above all in *PN*, 485f.

34. *PN*, 486.

35. Ibid.

36. Karl Holl in particular criticized Troeltsch's adoption of natural-law thinking in connection with both the historical derivation and definition of the concept and also the interpretation of Luther (cf. especially *Aufsätze zur Kirchengeschichte* I, 243f. n.2).

37. However, Troeltsch's accounts have emphases which sound contradictory in this connection. It is said that 'He (Luther) had also left them [his churches] a theology which, though completely occasional and unsystematic as a whole in general had a markedly uniform overall character and in the final shaping and consolidation of his works very naturally came to have a stronger force' (*PN*, 492). Or, 'Luther himself did not have a real theology, but only elements of one.' And then again later: 'Thus there came into being a very colourful mixture of sometimes very contradictory statements which nevertheless bore a unified stamp' (ibid.).

38. Troeltsch remarked that basically, all he had to say on the subject was already contained in the article 'Protestantisches Christentum und Kirche in der Neuzeit', but, given the 'enforced brevity' (though this was a work of over 300 large pages), the positive side, the new element in Protestantism, had not emerged so clearly. And at this point he says that his Stuttgart lecture on 'The Significance of Protestantism for the Rise of the Modern World' (1906) was 'not sufficiently transparent'. Troeltsch believed that he had now found 'essentially clearer formulations' ('Luther und die moderne Welt', in *Das Christentum*, 161). By way of amplification he referred to his article on 'The Essence of the Modern Spirit' (*PrJ* 1907), and added that after more recent reading he had noted how close his ideas were to those of Adolf von Harnack. But Troeltsch would not be Troeltsch if he did not make a further addition. So he judges above all 'the continuity between the Lutheran church and orthodoxy on the one hand and Luther's doctrine on the other to be considerably more marked than Harnack believes' (ibid., 161).

39. Thus Ebeling is almost certainly right in thinking that Troeltsch derives Luther's understanding of sin in a one-sided and sweeping way from the Augustinian-mediaeval tradition. Given that, it is impossible either to show where Luther's understanding differs from that of this tradition, or how it compares with modern thought (cf. Ebeling, 'Luther', n.11, 212f.). However, one can make two points on the attempt to understand Troeltsch. Troeltsch is not concerned to describe or take up the theological tradition in any great detail because he thinks that he can get by with a sweeping definition as compared to the idea of freedom on Enlightenment presuppositions. Furthermore he is basically driven by the fear of dogmatism and

of ecclesiastical or church-political narrowness and firmness, so that he makes a somewhat sweeping classification.

40. Cf. M.Welker, *Der Vorgang Autonomie*, Neukirchen 1975. Welker rightly emphasizes that the mere mention of the controversial word 'autonomy' does not exempt one from a detailed assessment of the formation of the theory from the perspective of the history of theology and philosophy.
In his article 'Autonomie und Rationalismus in der modernen Welt', *Internationale Wochenschrift für Wissenschaft, Kunst und Technik* 1, 1907, 199-210, Troeltsch differentiates between individualism and autonomy. Individualism is a general indication of direction and a global formula for modern feelings about the world. Troeltsch sees autonomy as a closer definition of this individualism on the basis of the charge that there must not be unlimited arbitratriness, but a bond to a law. So the idea of autonomy developed as a closer definition of individualism, because it can appropriately describe the relationship between the liberation of the individual and the individual's bond to a law.

41. Cf. 'Autonomie und Rationalismus in der modernen Welt' (n.40), 205. The task for the present is on the one hand to presuppose the idea of autonomy and on the other to transcend it. That means that the necessary 'transition' comes about through a theonomous foundation for culture which provides an ultimate root for the principle of autonomy through the idea of God.

42. *BP*, 77ff., *PP*, 80ff. Here Troeltsch is also concerned with the question of the unity of Luther's theology. He speaks of a concept underlying the whole, which runs through it but is not really formulated. H.Fischer, in his article 'Luther und seine Reformation in der Sicht Ernst Troeltschs', *NZST* 5, 1963, 132ff., assumes a development in Troeltsch which ends up in an increasingly strong emphasis on the connection between Reformation theology and modern thought. Here it does not seem to me to be possible to subsume Troeltsch's ideas under the heading of development. Troeltsch was influenced by particular thematic connections and the challenge of a particular contemporary situation, and in the light of that modified his basic view of the Reformation and its influence on the rise of the modern world.

43. Friedrich Loofs objected that Troeltsch's idea of a difference, indeed a contrast, between the authority of church culture and the modern notion of autonomy cannot really explain the wealth of actual conditions and circumstances, so that his one-sided view that a root of modernity lies in the idea of autonomy would take him beyond actual conditions. Loofs grants that there are elements of truth in Troeltsch's view that the decisive break in the history of culture should not be put with Luther. However, he still finds it questionable whether one can assume that a new epoch in the history of culture begins in the seventeenth century. He finds Troeltsch's idea of the modern world an artificial construction (cf. F.Loofs, *Luthers Stellung zum Mittelalter und zur Neuzeit*, Halle 1907, 14f., 26ff.).

44. Cf. from Vol. II of Dilthey's *Gesammelte Schriften* above all the article on 'The Natural System of the Humanities in the Seventeenth Century', 90-245.

45. *BP*, 16, *PP*, 26.

46. Cf. H.Blumenberg, *Die Legitimität der Neuzeit*, Frankfurt 1966.

47. F.Gogarten, *Verhängnis und Hoffnung der Neuzeit*, Stuttgart 1958, 123.

48. The changes which Troeltsch made here in the second edition of his article on 'The Significance of Protestantism for the Rise of the Modern World' (1911, translated into English as *Protestantism and Progress*, 1912) show his further work at

this point, which includes assimilation of the criticisms which had been made in the meantime. The Protestant 'special groups' which were of special significance for Troeltsch in the rise of modern Protestantism and the modern world generally are described in detail, a clear distinction being made between the Baptism movement and Spiritualism. Friedrich Loofs had criticized Troeltsch's original account vigorously (cf. F.Loofs, *Luthers Stellung*, n.43, 14f.).

49. *BP*, 85, *PP*, 87.

50. *Hälfte des Lebens*, Munich 1965, 88.

51. Apfelbacher, *Frömmigkeit* (n.26), 248.

52. The letter of 22 October 1905 is particularly important here. Troeltsch writes: 'I personally am a Protestant and have my roots in the religious individualism which grew out of Protestantism, though I do not fail to recognize the significance of the notions of solidarity and continuity. However, for me, the freedom of dogmatic thought from the determinations of the past and the ethical goal of the independence of the mature personality calls for a version of that notion of solidarity which makes institutional breaks and the formation of new institutions possible and makes individuals independent of the institution' (letter to F.von Hügel, 22 October 1905, Apfelbacher/Neuner, 7).

53. For Troeltsch, analysis of the time is bound up with the conditions for and possibilities of historical thinking. To turn one's gaze appropriately to the present means to see it with historical eyes and thus as a result and an expression of historical forces and movements.

54. Already in his work *Reason and Revelation in Johann Gerhard and Melanchthon* there are the first beginnings of a diagnosis of the time which rest on the perception of the changed form of Protestanism in modernity. The recognition of the lack of the 'old pillars' (cf. *VO*, 213) in theology and the history of theology implies an analysis of the period, and as such is bound to an interpretation of more recent intellectual history.

55. The extension and modification of the historical analysis is not to be understood as constructing stages which lead from an immanent theological view to a socio-historical one. Rather, at a very early stage there is implicit, or at least embryonic, a view which goes beyond that of theology and the history of ideas and incorporates an element of universal culture and social history. The work 'The Scientific Situation and Its Demands on Theology' (1900) has a programmatic character. The insights gained here were extended and modified on both the historical and the analytical side. This is shown by the lexicon articles on 'Deism' and 'English Moralists', the article on 'Basic Problems of Ethics' and *The Social Teachings of the Christian Churches and Groups*. According to Troeltsch's own estimation, his review of R.Seeberg's *Lehrbuch der Dogmengeschichte* II, in *GGA* 1901 (*GS* IV, 739–52), was particularly significant (see his comment in *GS* I, 950 n.510, *ST* II, 985f. n.510).

56. Troeltsch makes the following comment: 'It can merely be a matter of examining the situation as openly as possible without fixed presuppositions and prejudices and discovering the inner truth of the claims at war in it. On such a basis the individual can then form a verdict...'(*LT*, 11). However, here it should be noted critically that there is neither sufficient consideration of the possibility of conflict in the judgment assigned to the individual, nor is the requirement of consensus in one's own circle (of which Troeltsch goes on to speak) discussed further as a problem. Here Troeltsch

is evidently concerned with the fundamental considerations and the goals which are connected with them.

57. Cf. *GM*, *ZTK* 1898, 26. W.Köhler has referred to the distinction between internal and exclusive supernaturalism made by Troeltsch (*Ernst Troeltsch*, Tübingen 1941, 135). Apfelbacher has put this distinction at the centre of his account (*Frömmigkeit*, n.26, 191ff.). It is striking how, outside his usual generosity in conceptuality, Troeltsch is neither capable nor willing really to maintain this distinction. His reflections culminate in a polemic against 'exclusive' supernaturalism. The decision whether to accept a special character for Christian revelation does not stand at the beginning but at the end, and relates to the qualitative level, not to exclusiveness. 'Inner' supernaturalism is a personal religious experience, without the necessity and the dogmatic pressure to devalue other forms of religion. This distinction flourishes primarily from its opposite. It faces the theological task of defining the content of 'internal supernaturalism' and clarifying its relationship to 'external' formation in the form of teaching and cult.

58. Troeltsch says of the theology of the Enlightenment: 'Here only dogmatic reason or dogmatic revelation or a combination of the two as identical entities could be right. The latter was the solution to which theology finally saw itself forced and which more than any other furthered the Enlightenment' (*GS* IV, 372).

59. 'Culture Protestantism', understood as a polemical term used by dialectical theology, which criticized the close relationship between culture and Protestant theology or religion, while at the same time surrendering the radical other-wordliness of the Word of God.

60. Cf. the differentiated account in *LT*, 5ff. Troeltsch speaks of the effect of the monetary economy, of the new forms of production and distribution of commodities, points to the altered trading relations, and finally notes a change of mood which begins with the end of the Enlightenment and represents a 'conversion to the this-worldly'. In his 1893-4 article on 'The Christian World View and its Scietific Counter-Tendencies', Troeltsch had already protested that attempts were being made to derive the present crisis primarily from intrinsic theological factors. In *LT* he goes one step further, and extends his approach beyond theology and the history of ideas to social and political life.

61. *GS* IV, 311. As the objective powers and forces, they channel life, and give it an external framework and structure.

62. *GS* IV, 300f. Troeltsch's remarks on the whole correspond to what he says at the end of *The Social Teachings* about the 'brutal facts' of conditions which make all attempts to realize Christian social ideals shatter against them, as against a rock (cf. *GS* I, 984, *ST* II, 1013).

63. W.Dilthey, *Einleitung in die Geisteswissenschaften* (1883), *Gesammelte Schriften* I. Criticism in the form of the south-west German Kant school goes back to Wilhelm Windelband (1848-1915).

64. *GS* II, 227. Thus the comment made by Troeltsch on his early article on 'The Christian World View and its Scientific Counter Tendencies'.

65. Cf. *GS* IV, 9.

66. Cf. on the one hand the statement from the 1885 'Selbständigkeit der Religion' article, in which Troeltsch says of the psychology of religion that it seeks 'the place, the origin and the significance of religion in the human consciousness, and precisely in so doing can alone contribute what can be ascertained about the question of truth

in religion' (*ZTK* 5, 370) and on the other the formulation from the year 1904 according to which psychological work is the presupposition for posing the question of the 'value status or truth-content of religion' in an epistemology which is to be distinguished from it (RP, 475).

67. Max Weber, who came from Freiburg to Heidelberg in 1897, had close personal and scholarly ties with Heinrich Rickert. For their time together in Freiburg cf. Marianne Weber, *Max Weber*, Tübingen 1926, 213ff. Rickert, who later dedicated his work *Die Grenzen der Naturwissenschaftliche Begriffsbildung*, Freiburg 1896-1902, to the memory of Max Weber, comments on his 'close relationships with Max Weber', ibid., XIXff.

Paul Hensel (1860-1933) came to Heidelberg in 1898 as Extraordinarius Professor of Philosophy. Like Rickert, Hensel was a pupil of Wilhelm Windelband and had close contact with both philosophers, especially with Rickert. In his ethics Hensel was a neo-Kantian, and came to the philosophy of religion through ethical questions. Troeltsch describes the course of events somewhat generally in his autobiographical sketch like this: 'At the same time, through such investigations [into the "theory of validity"] I made the close acquaintance of Windelband and Paul Hensel, and independently of that I was strongly attracted and encouraged by Rickert's sharp logic' (*GS* IV, 9).

68. *GS* IV, 9.

69. The work is based on a lecture of Rickert's which he had given to the Freiburg 'Society of Cultural Science'. This society was a learned association whose members had in common that they were not natural scientists. The characteristic of and basis for the combination show something of the spirit of the time, and of the pressure from the natural sciences felt on the side of the humanities. Troeltsch reviewed the article (along with a work by Georg von Below on 'Die neue historische Methode') in *TLZ* 1899; here both assent and criticism are evident.

70. Instead of the term 'humanities', Rickert uses 'cultural science', because in his view this reflects the evaluative aspect better. The concept of culture is understood in this context to embrace the totality of universal objects, recognized as values.

71. Cf. H.Rickert, *Grenzen der naturwissenschaftlichen Begriffsbildung* (n.67), 305ff.

72. Cf. *TLZ*, 1899, 377. Here Troeltsch feels that the old division has to be kept, despite all the problems of the term 'Geisteswissenschaften'. A remark by Paul Hensel in a letter to Rickert points in the same direction: 'It seems to me that you have not got rid of a compulsive anxiety about "metaphysics" which now prevents you from drawing the last conclusions from your own standpoint' (letter of 15 November 1892, in *Paul Hensel, Sein Leben in seinen Briefen*, Wolfenbüttel and Hanover 1957, 76).

73. *TR* 6, 1903, 3-28; 37-72; 103-17; later in *GS* II, 673-728, with modifications and additions which indicate Troeltsch's later state of knowledge. The article can be said to have two functions. On the one hand it seeks to demonstrate the significance of Rickert's philosophy for theological work by the opportunities it offers in the face of scientific thinking and naturalism, and is a demand for a consistently historical methodology and conceptuality. On the other hand, it functions as self-assurance. It serves to adopt and assimilate Rickert's philosophy, with the aim of helping Troeltsch to find his own position by endorsing it and developing it.

74. In thus defining the concept of causality, Rickert dissociates himself from Karl Lamprecht's view (1856-1915). Lamprecht's aim was to elevate history to the

scientific status given to the natural sciences and to change its work from being a mere description of phenomena to being an 'explanation'. The great significance of Rickert's philosophy for most contemporary historians is due to Friedrich Meineke's *Erinnerungen*, and emerges from his reflections on the complex of themes. For the autobiographical element cf. *Werke* VIII, 166, 194; for the theme of causality and history cf. the important contribution on 'Kausalitäten und Werte in der Geschichte', *Werke* IV, 61-89.

75. On this cf. H.Rickert, *Grenzen der naturwissenschaftlichen Begriffsbildung* (n.67), first edition, 436ff.

76. Troeltsch made comments to this effect in his review of Seeberg, *GGA* 163, 1901, 15-30; *GS* IV, 739ff.

77. Rickert distinguishes seven different developmental concepts in all (cf. ibid., 472ff.). 1. Development as becoming generally; then 2. development understood as change. Further, 3. he can define development conceptually from a teleological aspect as the realization of a whole. Then there is 4. development as the summary of an individual historical process towards a teleological unity on the basis of a special value relationship, resulting in the special character and unity of a process of development. Next comes 5., as the assessment of a historical process on the basis of individual stages. Then, 6. development in the sense of the formation of different levels at which individual stages are judged on the basis of their orientation on a progress that is to be assumed. And finally, 7. as the constitution of a developmental series by a value. In being regarded as the cause of the whole series, this as it were realizes itself. In my view it is questionable whether all these concepts are independent. Above all, the first three hang closely together; indeed they follow from one another. For Rickert the fourth is the most important.

78. *GS* II, 722.

79. Ibid.

80. Cf. above all *GS* I, 362-77, 427ff., 794ff.; *ST*, 331ff., 461ff., 993ff.

81. *GS* II, 716.

82. *GS* II, 719.

83. Ibid.

84. *GS* II, 725. What significance Rickert has and retains for Troeltsch despite all critical modifications and ongoing intents is clear from the following page in a letter to Stefano Jacini Jr of 16 October 1909: 'I keep learning a great deal for my person, perhaps most from Rickert, and here I would mention "The Object of Knowledge", his great work *The Limits of Scientific Knowledge* (sic), and a small work "Two Kinds of Epistemology"' (in 'Ernst Troeltsch e il Modernismo', *Archivio di Filosofia* 1982, 75). This is Troeltsch's answer to the question of the best philosophical works in Germany at the time. There are similar comments by Troeltsch in letters to his publisher, e.g. in the letter of 5 April 1908. He then provided a large-scale critical discussion, both explicit and implicit, in the studies on historicism.

85. Troeltsch's work *Die Absolutheit des Christentums und die Religionsgeschichte* (1902) arose out of a lecture given on 3 October 1901 in Mühlacker to the 'Friends of *Christliche Welt*'. This lecture was expanded for publication; additions and alterations were made in 1912 for the second edition; the third edition of 1929, from which the English translation was made, is a reprint of the second. For the lecture Troeltsch developed theses which are as illuminating in their concentration and focus on the problems and suggestions for a solution as those of Adolf Deissmann. In principle

Deissmann takes a different course from Troeltsch by discussing research into the history of religion and historical method only after first having considered the character of the Christian religion as revelation, and examines the dimension of the confession in faith. Deissmann's theses, which were intended for a personal conversation with Troeltsch, are an interesting example of a position which, like Troeltsch's, recognizes the significance of history-of-religions research but nevertheless arrives at another foundation and puts the emphasis elsewhere. The theses of the two authors appeared in *CW*16, 1902, 923ff. and 1181f.

86. Troeltsch thinks that one could in fact say that Christianity is a relative phenomenon. 'For historical and relative are identical' (*AC*, 42).

87. According to Sarah Coakley, Troeltsch failed to keep apart different types of relativism which are to be distinguished logically. For this complex cf. the chapter 'The Nature of Troeltsch's Relativism', in *Christ without Absolutes*, Oxford 1988, 5–44. R.J.Rubanowice, *Crisis in Consciousness. The Thought of Ernst Troeltsch*, Talahassee 1982, 29, draws attention to parallel developments in contemporary physics (Planck, Einstein, Heisenberg). For the problem of absoluteness cf. also the work by G.von Schlippe, *Die Absolutheit des Christentums bei Ernst Troeltsch auf dem Hintergrund der Denkfelder des 19.Jahrhunderts*, Neustadt 1966.

88. W.Bodenstein, *Neige des Historismus*, Gütersloh 1958, 48, has drawn attention to this: 'Troeltsch's train of thought remains incomprehensible without the presupposition of a quite specific metaphysics.'

89. Cf. *AC*, 52.

90. *AC*, 77. In an expansion of the original text in the second edition Troeltsch remarks that here he has moved over from scientific to religious language. He thinks this justified by the subject matter and consistent (cf. *AC*, 77f.). In its apologetic and explanatory tendency the actual passage (from 77 bottom to 78 end of paragraph) sounds like a reaction to W.Herrmann's review, especially to the question raised in it about the relationship between personal conviction and scientific proof (cf. *TLZ* 27, 1902, 330-4, esp. 333).

91. There are similar notions in Harnack and Bousset (cf. A.von Zahn-Harnack, *Adolf von Harnack*, Berlin 1951, 184f.; W.Bousset, *Das Wesen der Religion*, Halle 1904, 196). 'Simple' naivety certainly has the magic of the beginning, and unbrokenness, but it is also uneducated, childishly ignorant. Education, including theological education, is naivety 'regained'.

92. *AC*, 92.

93. R.Bultmann, *Jesus and the Word*, New York and London 1934, reissued 1958, 66.

94. *AC*, 113.

95. *AC*, 112.

96. Cf. *AC*, 9.

97. The 'last' seems to me to address two things: first, validity on the basis of the individual decision, and second, finality in view of the goal of history.

98. In the second edition of 1911 Troeltsch made important changes to the text. Anything pointing in the direction of a special position for Christianity and its claim to revelation, or anything that could be understood in this sense was modified, so that in this way a merely gradual difference from the other religions emerged (cf. e.g. *AC*, 18, 103f.). Moreover a further differentiation was made in the category of claim. Now Troeltsch distinguished more clearly between Jesus' direct, naive idea of absoluteness and a claim on the basis of derived theological absoluteness. Jesus'

proclamation and the Hellenistic community, hitherto seen as supplementing each other, are now sharply distinguished (cf. *AC*, 70ff.; 107). Troeltsch's intention is now to stress the special nature of the substance of Christianity, its religious and ethical interpretation of life and the world. In its nature and strength the 'claim' is always a reflection of the situation; this can be detached from a particular historical form.

In Sarah Coakley's view, Troeltsch's first edition of the *Absoluteness* has 'strongly Herrmann-like passages'. For her, in this respect it represents a return to or a drawing closer to the Ritschlian school, for personal or political motives. She thinks that in the second edition Troeltsch attempted to bring the book in line with his christology which had developed in the meantime (*Christ without Absolutes*, n.87, 78).

99. In telling his friend Bousset that the book was on the way, Troeltsch remarked: 'As a *quid pro quo* [for a review which Bousset had sent him] you will soon be receiving a short new book, *The Absoluteness of Christianity and the History of Religion*, in which I take leave of this topic, but also think that I have really said something' (card to W.Bousset, 5 December 1901, UB Göttingen). All in all Troeltsch seems to have been content with its effect, in terms of both assent and criticism. He wrote to his publishers: 'So far I am very content with the reception of my *Absoluteness*. People seem to recognize the importance of the issue in principle and to occupy themselves with it accordingly' (letter to P.Siebeck, 27 December 1901, Mohr/Siebeck archives, Tübingen). For this section cf. also the chapter 'Kritische Stellungnahme', in von Schlippe, *Absolutheit* (n.87), 99-111.

100. W.Herrmann, *TLZ* 27, 330-4; reprinted in W.Herrmann, *Schriften zur Grundlegung der Theologie* I, Munich 1966, 193-9.

101. Herrmann himself developed this notion further in 'Der Glaube an Gott und die Wissenschaft unserer Zeit', *Schriften zur Grundlegung der Theologie* I, 242ff., and in the article 'Gottes Offenbarung an uns', ibid., II., 150ff.

102. Ibid., 197.

103. Ibid.

104. L.Ihmels, *Die Selbständigkeit der Dogmatik gegenüber der Religionsphilosophie*, Erlangen 1901.

105. R.Bultmann, 'On the Problem of Demythologizing', in *New Testament and Mythology and Other Basic Writings*, ed. Schubert M.Ogden, Philadelphia and London 1985, 119f.

106. Cf. U.Mann, *Das Christentum als absolute Religion*, Darmstadt 1970, esp. 78ff. Mann thinks that when he speaks of the 'absoluteness of Christianity' he is at the same time speaking about the content of Christian faith, and he thus arrives at his combination of the idea of absoluteness and tolerance.

107. A.von Harnack, *What is Christianity?*, New York 1957 [in view of the importance of the phrase 'essence of Christianity' in the discussion of this book, I have kept to a literal translation of the German title of the work, but references are to this edition, Tr.].

108. A.von Zahn-Harnack remarks: 'There was no pastors' conference and no synod, hardly a journal or newspaper, which did not comment on it' (*Adolf von Harnack*, n.91, 185). For the discussion generally cf. ibid., 181-8. J.Rathje, *Die Welt des freien Protestantismus*, Stuttgart 1952, 114ff., gives a vivid description of the debate and its effect on *Christliche Welt* or the Friends of *Christliche Welt*. H.W.Seidel's 'letters of

an assistant minister' (*Drei Stunden hinter Berlin*, Göttingen 1967) give a first-hand picture of the controversy more within the church. Seidel takes Harnack's side and regards the official responses as documentation of human offence and theological disputatiousness. However, he does not think that Harnack brought out clearly enough the practical and religious element that is present in his work (cf. ibid., 43f., 87).

109. *What is Christianity?* (n.107), 19.

110. Ibid., 63.

111. In a further memorandum which I shall not discuss further, Harnack described the 'main connections' of the gospel with the world, law and work.

112. *Das Wesen des Christentums und die Zukunftsreligion*, Gross-Lichterfelde and Berlin 1900.

113. Ibid., iv.

114. Ibid., 92-101.

115. Ibid., 98.

116. Ibid., 92.

117. Ibid., 16. For the discussion of Harnack's book cf. *Chronik der Christlichen Welt* 1, 1901, 307-11, 321-31, 339-43, 351f.

118. *GS* II, 387., *ETWTR*, 124. There is no reference to the controversy over 'The Essence of Christianity' in the correspondence between Troeltsch and Harnack. The letters we have were as a rule written for a specific reason, but *this* occasion probably did not prompt any correspondence. Troeltsch's letter to Harnack on the latter's sixtieth birthday sheds light on the professional and personal relationship between the two men. He writes: 'Along with Ritschl you are the next most important and crucial figure, and in relation to you, too, my work is often a deviation and a development which no longer follows your intentions. But that is inevitable in the pursuit of living knowledge' (letter to Adolf von Harnack, 8 May 1911, Deutsche Staatsbibliothek, Berlin, unpublished).

119. *GS* II, 393f., *ETWTR*, 130f. Unlike Troeltsch, Walther Köhler thinks that the concept or the formula 'essence of Christianity' did not first emerge with Romanticism (Chateaubriand's 'genius of Christianity', cf. *GS* II, 391f., *ETWTR*, 129), but can already be found in Bucer and his 'faith in Christ' as a shared formula in the disputes over the eucharist (cf. W.Köhler, *Ernst Troeltsch*, Tübingen 1941, 72). This argument seems problematical to me because the question here is a different one. It is *a priori* directed within Christianity, indeed within Protestantism, and is part of an attempt at union in the dispute over dogma.

120. *GS* II, 396, *ETWTR*, 132f.

121. Introduction by Rudolf Bultmann to *What is Christianity?* (n.107), cf. esp. 9.

122. *GS* II, 397, *ETWTR*, 133.

123. In his 1908 retrospect on a half-century of theological scholarship, Troeltsch argued against the Ritschl school that it accepted historical thought into theology only to the degree that it felt this necessary for religious purposes (*GS* II, 205, *ETWTR*, 63). Troeltsch includes Harnack among the historians of the school (as opposed to the dogmatic theologians). This makes a gradual distinction, but in terms of content the criticism remains. For Troeltsch, even the historians of the school 'treat those points of history given prominence by religious value judgments very differently from the rest of history. They thus make those high points into objective religious authorities...' (*GS* II, 205 n.7, *ETWTR*, 63 n.4).

124. *GS* II, 404, *ETWTR*, 139.
125. Troeltsch worked over passages concerned with this for the reprint in the *Gesammelte Schriften* and put some things more carefully and with more qualifications; others he attempted to explain or develop further by additions. For example, he had originally said: 'The portrait of Jesus is not directly presented in the sources, but is mediated and influenced by the faith of the community and above all by the faith of the great apostle whom he himself did not call and equip, but who worked his way through to the Exalted Christ in a struggle with his own heart' (*CW* 17, 1903, 580). To this he added in the *Gesammelte Schriften*: 'And... who, like the earliest original community, provided the picture of the risen Messiah with the most sublime divine predicates, as a result of which the latter came to replace the coming Kingdom of God as the object of faith and redeemer of the community who honoured him in the cult. This leads to a new picture of the Christ' (cf. *GS* II, 415, *ETWTR*, 148). S.W.Sykes has discussed the changes to the original text when it was included in the *Gesammelte Schriften* in 'Ernst Troeltsch and Christianity's Essence', in J.Clayton, *Ernst Troeltsch and the Future of Theology*, Cambridge 1976, 139-71. Sykes counts seventy alterations, though these are not all of equal importance (ibid., 143). When putting Troeltsch's alterations to the original text in a chronological context (for Sykes this is 1913, the year in which Volume II appeared), we must remember that Troeltsch had been occupied with the idea of bringing his work together since 1907. When we remember his habit of continually making alterations or changes in his manuscript copy, the question of the date to which to assign them becomes difficult.
126. *GS* II, 415, *ETWTR*, 149.
127. 'Modern Philosophy of History', *GS* II, 673ff., *RH*, 273ff.
128. *GS* II, 712, *RH*, 305.
129. Cf. *GS* II, 430. Troeltsch gives a relatively affirmative yet critical account of Bergson in his book on historicism (*GS* III, 632-49). However, Troeltsch's assent here is more marked than usual. For the significance of instinct and intuition in Bergson cf. especially *GS* III, 643ff.
130. *GS* II, 431, *ETWTR*, 162.
131. *GS* II, 430, *ETWTR*, 161.
132. *GS* II, 436, *ETWTR*, 166.
133. *GS* II, 449, *ETWTR*, 178.
134. Cf. *GS* II, 451, *ETWTR*, 179, and in addition 'Modern Philosophy of History', especially *GS* II, 691f. and *GS* II, 701-3, *RH* 292f., 301-3.
135. The idea of criticism of a historicizing approach on the one hand and a biblicistic approach on the other also appears in later articles by Troeltsch, as in 'The Dogmatics of the History of Religions School' (*RH*, 87-108). Here there is also clearer polemic against Harnack (cf. *RH*, 96f.). After a criticism of Schleiermacher, Hegel, Baur and Harnack we read: 'Thus the essence of Christianity can be understood only as the new interpretation and new adaptations, corresponding to each situation, produced by Christianity's historical power. The essence differs for every epoch, resulting from the totality of the influence in each age. The "essence", rather than simply the Bible or an ecclesiastical church's confession, must be the basis for a contemporary dogmatics. But this essence is actually the subjective, personal interpretation and synthesis which present thinking derives from the entire situation. with reference to the actual living issues and for the purpose of directing future activity' (*GS* II, 511, *RH*, 97).

136. Cf. especially R.Schäfer, 'Welchen Sinn hat es, nach einem Wesen des Christentums zu suchen?', *ZTK* 65, 1968, 329-47. Schäfer points out that the question of the essence of Christianity grows 'out of the history of Christianity, for where Christianity is defined, there one defines its essence. However, whereas people have spoken of the essence of Christanity only since Pietism and the Enlightenment, the concept of Christianity is almost as old as the phenomenon denoted by it' (ibid., 330). But this generalized statement does not help in any way towards the problems which have arisen for theology and the church on the presupposition of historical thought and historical methodology. There is further literature on the theme in Schäfer's article, 'Christentum, Wesen des', *HWP* 1, 1008-1016.

137. F.Gogarten, *Was ist Christentum?*, Göttingen 1956. Cf. especially 5ff., 10.

138. Cf. also Gogarten, *Verhängnis und Hoffnung der Neuzeit*, and especially the section on 'The Historicization of Human Existence', 103ff. H.Fischer, *Christlicher Glaube und Geschichte. Voraussetzungen und Folgen der Theologie Friedrich Gogartens*, Gütersloh 1967, has discussed the question of the relationship between Gogarten and Troeltsch in detail. For the problem of continuity, special mention should be made of W.Groll, *Ernst Troeltsch und Karl Barth – Kontinuität im Widerspruch*, Munich 1976.

139. For the question of the relationship between Tillich and Troeltsch cf. generally J.P.Clayton, 'Paul Tillich – ein "verjüngter Troeltsch" oder noch "ein Apfel vom Baume Kierkegaards"?', *TRST* 3, 259ff. Tillich's article, 'Biblische Religion und die Frage nach dem Sein', is in his *Gesammelte Werke* V, 138-84. Reference should also be made to G.Ebeling, *The Nature of Faith* (1959), London and New York 1966. Although Ebeling regards the concept of essence as 'heavily burdened as a result of its history' (ibid., 13) and is not concerned to discuss it, he stands in continuity with the questioning and in fact adopts a position by his move towards the personal, towards an orientation on faith.

140. Wilhelm Herrmann, who was born in 1846, was called as ordinarius to Marburg in 1879 and remained there until his death in 1922. In the long period of his activity Herrmann left a decisive stamp on the character and reputation of the Marburg faculty. A distinguished and theologically significant series of pupils bears witness to his great success as a teacher. Works of Herrmann which are relevant here are *Die Religion im Verhältnis zum Welterkennen und zur Sittlichkeit* (1897) and *The Communion of the Christian with God* (1886, ET London and Philadelphia 1971).

141. This later letter from Troeltsch to Herrmann is dated 23 September 1917. It is about the statement by German university teachers opposing the Reichstag majority in the interest of achieving an acceptable peace; here Troeltsch is seeking Herrmann's endorsement of this counter-statement. Cf. *Aufrufe und Reden deutscher Professoren im I.Weltkrieg*, Stuttgart 1975, 184.

142. *ZTK* 12, 1902, 44-94, 125-78, printed in altered form in *GS* II, 552-672.

143. Herrmann's *Ethik* appeared in the series Grundriss der theologischen Wissenschaften, which explains the form and purpose of the account. It was meant mainly for students and is based on the manuscript of earlier lectures.

144. One example is: 'So the moral commandment is the narrow door which leads into the beyond of the supernatural' (ibid., 57). This language, with its biblical colouring, takes up a basic notion in German idealism: moral action as the creative expression of human freedom is the point at which transcendence breaks into an immanent view of life and reality. Developing this idealistic approach further then leads

Herrmann beyond an idea of experience with existential colouring to a theological approach and interpretation.

145. Ibid., 83.

146. In his redemptive power, Jesus must be a fact which can define us for ourselves; we must experience the power of Jesus. The power concerned is his morality and the recognition of the loving concern of God for Jesus. The resort to principles of the inner life of Jesus through the concept of the 'fact' is formulated by Herrmann to counter historical criticism. In this way, for Herrmann Jesus becomes a clearly defined figure.

147. Ibid., 112. The passages in which Herrmann stresses the independence of religion from ethics and the remarks in which he links the two together are not very easy to understand. Herrmann thinks of the obedience of Christians as subjection to the will of God and human moral independence as the ingredient of Christian-moral life which results from that. It is by the subjection of human beings to the power of God that the supreme development of moral independence is achieved.

148. *GS* II, 570. The stimulus to tackle Herrmann's *Ethik* came from Johannes Gottschick, the editor of *ZTK*. Troeltsch wrote to his publisher: 'At the moment I am working on a lengthy article for Gottschick, at his request' (letter to P.Siebeck, 7 November 1901, Mohr/Siebeck archives, Tübingen). Gottschick evidently thought that this would be an interesting combination. Hitherto Troeltsch had written on ethical questions only in an article 'Atheistische Ethik' (originally in *PrJ* 82, 1895, 193-217). In it he commented critically on an article on 'Atheism and Idealism' published in the *Jahrbuch*, written by an older officer who described himself as a conservative and somewhat surprisingly advocated the thesis that atheism had greater ideal power and stronger ethics. One can see Troeltsch's article as cautious apologetic. He demonstrates the presuppositions and consequences of atheist ethics on the basis of their content and position in the history of ideas, and sees 'no impossibilities' in religious and metaphysical statements, even from the standpoint of an idealistic teleology (*GS* II, 549). It is enough for him to have struggled to establish a systematic and theoretical context for the decision of faith; the rest is a matter of personal conviction.

149. It is striking that Troeltsch does not include some important ideas from Herrmann in his reflections. One might think, for example, of Herrmann's interpretation of human existence by the demonstration of a restlessness in life for which the perspective of the 'end' has exemplary significance and in which Herrmann sees a stimulus towards human self-determination. On the basis of similar statements – albeit for the most part through the interpretation of the 'experience of faith' – Bultmann was able to give positive form to his relationship with his teacher Herrmann even after his shift to dialectical theology. At all events, if we look at Troeltsch, we see that sequence of some statements and the accentuation of others also sheds light on the critic himself. Since Troeltsch does not criticize Herrmann's remarks on the nation state, we may assume that the two essentially agree on the question of a nationalistic consciousness.

150. Cf. the account of the relationship betwen ethics and dogmatics in Troeltsch and the criticism of it by Karl Barth in Wilfried Groll, *Ernst Troeltsch und Karl Barth – Kontinuität im Widerspruch*, Munich 1976, 55ff., and in W.Pannenberg, 'Die Begründung der Ethik bei Ernst Troeltsch', in *Ethik und Ekklesiologie*, Göttingen 1977, 70ff.

151. Kant, *Critique of Judgment* (1790), ET by J.H.Bernard, London 1892, 359.

152. Thus at a significant point we read: 'But reason with its question of the final goal of willing must ultimately grasp each individual as an immortal conscience and make his helplessness a pain. It is by no means a matter of course that there must be a redemption from this moral misery. But it is a fact that the power of the personal life of Jesus gives new courage to people who cannot forget him, making it possible for them to be morally earnest and yet be happy' (ibid., 107f.). And at another point we read: 'So if our belief in the reality in which we stand recognizes the way to the eternal goal shown us by God, we are given our moral calling' (ibid., 116).

153. Accordingly we read: 'The basic concepts of Schleiermacher's general ethics are crossed by the theological scheme of the grounding of Christian ethics on the miracle of redemption. For that reason, the subordination and relationship of the science of religion and religious ethics to the general concepts of ethics required by its general ethic is not carried through' (*GS* II, 568).

154. *GS* II, 611.

155. *GS* II, 593.

156. *GS* II, 618.

157. Pannenberg comments critically, on Troeltsch's assumption that Troeltsch's own theological view of ethics is to be seen in connection with the adoption of objective goods as an expansion of subjectively formal ethics, that here he overlooks or wants to overlook the fact that he is thus addressing another ethical concept and cannot do justice to the burden of proof which falls on him as a result (cf. Pannenberg, 'Die Begründung der Ethik bei Ernst Troeltsch', n.150, 73f.).

158. Herrmann commented critically on Troeltsch's goal. He thought that while in ethics one could speak of 'goods', one could not speak of an 'ethic of goods'. For Herrmann, a moral good is something that is striven for by the will, with a moral aim. By contrast, an ethic of goods is excluded, because here the human will is governed by eudaemonism. From Troeltsch's draft criticism that in defining the ethical one must take note of the ideas of objective goods which come to us from history Herrmann simply inferred that the changes within Christian ethics must be seen in relation to culture. It is clear that this does not get to Troeltsch's basic notion. For the way in which later editions of Herrmann's *Ethik* take note of Troeltsch's criticism cf. W.Wiesenberg, *Das Verhältnis von Formal- und Materialethik, erörtert an dem Streit zwischen Wilhelm Herrmann und Ernst Troeltsch*, Königsberg 1934, 27ff.

159. *GS* II, 649.

160. *GS* II, 643.

161. *GS* II, 645.

162. *GS* II, 648.

163. Ibid.

164. *GS* II, 652.

165. *GS* II, 653.

166. H.Benckert was the first to make a scholarly study of drafts of Troeltsch's lectures on ethics and comment on them (cf. H.Benckert, *Ernst Troeltsch und das ethische Problem*, Göttingen 1923, especially 9f., 110f.).

167. Lecture draft on practical Christian ethics, WS 1911/12, UB Heidelberg Heid. HS.3653, no.3,4.

168. Ibid.

169. Thus he wrote in 1914: 'By these [he meant two outlines, one on ethics and one on dogmatics], I am clearing the way for my philosophy of religion, which is my dearest wish and plan. However, it needs time to mature' (letter to P.Siebeck, 8 January 1914, Mohr/Siebeck archives, Tübingen). Shortly before his death he affirmed once again: 'If life and strength are left me, I would love finally to return to the religious sphere and bring my philosophy of religion to a conclusion' (*GS* IV, 14f.) Special mention must be made of the following contributions to the more recent discussion of Troeltsch: K.E.Apfelbacher, *Frömmigkeit und Wissenschaft. Ernst Troeltsch und sein theologisches Programm*, Munich 1978; G.Becker, *Neuzeitliche Subjektivität und Religiosität. Die religionsphilosophische Bedeutung von Heraufkunft und Wesen der Neuzeit im Denken von Ernst Troeltsch*, Regensburg 1982; F W.Graf, 'Religion und Individualität. Bemerkungen zu einem Grundproblem der Religions-theorie Ernst Troeltschs', *TRST* 3, 207-30; F.W.Veauthier, 'Das Religiöse Apriori: Zur Ambivalenz von E.Troeltschs Analyse des Vernunftelementes in der Religion', *Kantstudien* 78, 1987, 42-63.

170. It originally appeared as a double issue in *Kantstudien* to commemorate the centenary of Kant's death. The subtitle is 'Also a Contribution to the Investigation of Kant's Philosophy of History'. Troeltsch later brought out the work as a separate publication. It played an important part in Troeltsch's academic life in that both a teaching appointment in the philosophical faculty in Heidelberg and above all his call to a chair of philosophy in Berlin could be attributed to this philosophical work.

171. It is important for him to note here that there are different views of the philosophy of religion, depending on whether the perspective is that of world-view, religion or science. The conclusion is the only point at which the outline of his position can be recognized. The conceptuality used by Troeltsch is coloured at many points by Baden Neo-Kantianism.

172. The subtitle runs: 'An Investigation of the Significance of Kantian Religious Theory for Contemporary Study of Religion'. Troeltsch considerably expanded the text of the lecture for German publication. It is particularly interesting that the criticism of James and the metaphysical passages were inserted later.

173. Thus we read: 'Today's philosophy of religion is philosophy of religion only to the degree that, and in the sense that, this word means "religious science" or "philosophy about religion" ' (*PE*, 5). Or: 'Both problems [which arise from the definition of a common scientific presupposition for the tasks of history and dogma] combine in producing a general science of religion or philosophy of religion which does not construct a knowledge of God by means of philosophy, but by critical analysis investigates the universal laws or historical gradations of value in the religious consciousness' (*GS* II, 224).

174. *PE*, 5: 'Both kinds of religious science are finished as far as modern science is concerned. The first was in truth mythological supernaturalist dogma, and the second in fact replaces religion with philosophy.'

175. *PE*, 11.

176. All in all, Troeltsch's criticism of Wilhelm Wundt's psychology can be derived from three basic notions. First, the special quality of the religious does not seem to him to be covered sufficiently by the designation of religion as a complex phenomenon. Secondly, the association of work in the psychology of religion with the psychology of peoples largely fails to take note of contemporary religious experience. And finally, Wundt's idea of a 'creative synthesis' presupposes a dogmatic notion of causality.

In Wundt the assumption of a 'creative synthesis' serves to explain psychological phenomena in which the fundamental notion is that, qualitatively speaking, the whole is more than the sum of its parts. Wundt defended himself against Troeltsch's interpretation (cf. W.Wundt, *Probleme der Völkerpsychologie*, 1911, 88-125).

177. Mention should be made here of W.James, *The Principles of Psychology* (2 vols), Boston 1890.

178. James made a name for himself with *The Varieties of Religious Experience*, which Troeltsch reviewed (*DLZ* 1904, 3021-7). The book was translated into German by Georg Wobbermin, on the remarkable principle of giving a free rendering of the original. A new translation of the book was eventually made by E.Herms, under the title *Die Vielfalt religiöser Erfahrung*, Hildesheim 1979.

179. *DLZ*, 1904, 3022.

180. A comparison with Wilhelm Herrmann is interesting here. Herrmann similarly understands the psychology of religion as an empirical science. The religious experience of the individual is to be distinguished fundamentally from this and its forms of scientific description. It is strictly tied to revelation. Its reality and its possibilities of expression are clearly distinct from what is possible scientifically or philosophically. However, in Herrmann the cost of this procedure is that a mystical experience is not thought to be accessible to a scientific approach. Eduard Spranger (1882-1963) advocated a completely different view of the possibilities of psychology. He criticized Troeltsch's notion of a development of the psychology of religion into an epistemology of religion in which universal validity can then be taken into account and a solution to the question of the norm can be arried at. For Spranger, a regulation of the multiplicity of values to be found in the psyche must follow from these values themselves and not through the adoption of other presuppositions (cf. E.Spranger, 'Ernst Troeltsch als Religionsphilosoph', *Philosophische Wochenschrift und Literaturzeitung* 1906, 56).

181. For Troeltsch, the account of the basic view of religion to be found in James comes about through the notion of a solemn sense of distance and enthusiastic elevation (*PE*, 16). Here Rudolf Otto's characterization of religion as *mysterium tremendum et fascinans* seems to be anticipated.

182. Troeltsch understands the term 'epistemology of religion' along the lines of Baden Neo-Kantianism. A theory of worth or validity in respect of the experience of reality claimed in religion has to be developed. Accordingly, 'it is impossible to keep to a merely empirical psychology; it is not just a matter of given facts, but of the epistemological content of these facts. But this question can no longer be answered by pure empiricism; the question of truth-content is always a question of validity. And the question of validity can only be decided through logical and general conceptual investigations' (*PE*, 18).

183. *PE*, 24.

184. *PE*, 26. Troeltsch tailors reception of Kant's philosophy above all to the philosophy of religion. In so doing he shifts the accents: while he takes over from Kant the transcendental philosophical approach and the aprioristic function of reason, he does not go on to develop this problem primarily in terms of epistemology, but in terms of the independence of the religious dimension. His use of Kantian philosophy and conceptuality is meant to serve to do justice to the wealth of religious experience from a rational perspective or in terms of the philosophy of consciousness.

185. *PE*, 28. For Troeltsch, value-judgment theology cannot appeal to the true intention

of Kantian philosophy: 'Kant himself... always stressed the necessity of aprioristic religious reason and the object posited in it, and therefore struggled to combine this necessary rational element with the empirical psychological element of concrete religious conceptions and feelings' (ibid.). We may doubt whether this really sees the significance of Ritschl's distinction, because the distinction between independent value judgments that direct religious knowledge and theoretical judgments, which goes back to the second edition of Ritschl's *Justification and Reconciliation*, attempts a differentiation from what is scientifically possible and at least partially touches on what Troeltsch intends here. Cf. Stephan-Schmidt, *Geschichte der evangelischen Theologie in Deutschland seit dem Idealismus*, Berlin and New York 1973, 267, and F.Mildenberger, *Geschichte der deutschen evangelischen Theologie im 19. und 20. Jahrhundert*, Stuttgart 1981, 128.

186. Cf. here H.Benckert, 'Der Begriff der Entscheidung bei Ernst Troeltsch', *ZTK* 12, 1931, 422-42. For Benckert, the last motives of Troeltsch's thought are connected with a contrast between 'science' on the one hand and 'life' on the other. Neither may be played off against the other or replaced by the other. According to Benckert, it is necessary to assume a polarity between the two basic motives which represents the 'mystery of Troeltsch's life and creative activity' (ibid., 425). In Benckert's view, however, for Troeltsch the sphere of life always had priority, 'for God encounters us in the sphere of life, but as thinkers we are obliged to make a connection between our insights' (ibid., 429). Here the concept of decision has an important function. Its necessity and possibility belong in the sphere of thought. By contrast, for Troeltsch practical decision is connected with the living quality of life.

187. Cf. *Critique of Pure Reason* B, 56off., ET by N.Kemp Smith, London ²1933, 464ff.

188. Cf. Troeltsch's comment: 'The psychology of religion shows us the basic feeling of all religion, not the product of a mechanical course, but an effect of that felt in it which transcends the senses; it seeks to derive from the intelligible "I" by virtue of some sort of a connection with the world beyod the senses.' But that becomes completely impossible in the Kantian theory of the empirical "I", and no distinction in the form of a twofold approach can alter the fact that these approaches are mutually quite exclusive. Here is the psychological evidence which can only confirm the expression of religious feeling... against the consequence of such an epistemology' (*PE*, 38).

189. Letter to R.Otto, UB Marburg HS 797/801, unpublished. Cf. also the folowing remark from another letter to Otto (no date, probably 1904, since it presupposes the appearance of Otto's book *Naturalistische und religiöse Weltansicht*, Tübingen 1904: Otto papers, UB Marburg HS 792/803), partly printed in Apfelbacher, *Frömmigkeit* (n.169), 48: 'Since I have radically broken with psychological mechanism and determinism, which I never shared but also never dared to reject firmly, I feel much freer. However, I now believe that mechanism and monism generally do not apply in principle over the whole of thought but that the concept of causality must be shaped in very different ascending forms.' Further reflection on the concept of causality follows in the framework of the studies on historicism. There it is stated that 'historical causality' should take up the element of the creative and thus make room for novelty (cf. *GS* III, 48ff.).

190. *PE*, 39.

191. *PE*, 26.

192. For this version of the *a priori* character of the religious in the context of an

interpretation of Kant see the critical questions by Rudolf Köhler: 'We had arrived at the conviction that Kant uses the concept *a priori* in the sense that under it the formal conditions of all experience are to be understood. These, even independent of all experience, are elements of reason and provide the possibility of making wider judgments with universal validity and necessity. Then I tried to make clear that the Kantian *a priori* is not a system of different *a prioris*; rather, the demonstration of aprioristic elements should serve to show the rational content of individual disciplines... In Kant the concept *a priori* is not the foundation for anything specific; on the contrary, it is the bracket which holds logic, ethics and aesthetics together in a system' (cf. Rudolf Köhler, *Der Begriff a priori in der modernen Religionsphilosophie*, Leipzig 1920, 63). Moreover, it should be pointed out that within his philosophical discussion of religious truth Kant himself is pursuing different goals and sees another possible basis for his goals, by understanding the existence of God as the expression of free rational activity with a link to human morality.

193. Cf. *GS* II, 757. Here the *a priori* acts as a 'synthetic unitary function of scientific understanding' (ibid.).

194. *PE*, 51.

195. Cf. *GS* II, 495.

196. Ibid.

197. Troeltsch was very reluctant to go into details, for example over the formation of concepts, in discussion with his theological and philosophical critics (e.g. in his answer to P.Spiess and also in his numerous reviews). Here he referred, rather, to his basic approach and the scope of his ideas. His response to an article by P.Spiess, 'Zur Frage des religiösen *a priori*', *Religion und Geisteskultur* 3, 1909, 207-15, is an example of this. In his reviews of books on the philosophy of religion Troeltsch attacked above all any one-sided criticism of his position. Three forms are characteristic for him: a theological emphasis on the notion of revelation (E.Schaeder); thought in terms of a philosophical understanding of truth (T.Oesterreich); and the construction of a 'dilemma' between belief in revelation and scepticism (W.Günther). Cf. his reviews in *TLZ* 1918, 11-12 (Schaeder); *TLZ* 1916, 231-3 (Österreich); and *TLZ* 1916, 448-50 (Günther). Troeltsch answered Spiess's criticism in the article 'Zur Frage des religiösen Apriori: Eine Erwiderung auf die Bemerkungen von Paul Spiess', *Religion und Geisteskultur*, 3, 1909, 263-73, later *GS* II, 754-68; ET 'On the Question of the Religious *A priori*', *RH* 33-45.

198. 'According to it [the epistemology of religion], having religion would be one and the same as having consciousness, and in fact that may be right here, as is the case with thought, morality and art. Religion resembles these latter only as they move from a state of rest into an actual state' (*RP*, 478).

199. Troeltsch's studies of historicism show how he continued to be occupied with the question of taking up and transforming the idea of development (cf. *GS* III, 464-72, 694-703).

200. On the basis of such considerations Troeltsch thought it possible and meaningful to engage in mission abroad. However, this was to be mission without any derogatory tendencies towards other religions, without fanaticism and without a zeal for conversion. Rather, an effort had to be made towards a more differentiated understanding of any existing religion with a view towards developing it and furthering it; in other words, this was to be mission more as an offer aimed at dialogue than as religious and cultural tutelage, combined with economic interests.

Troeltsch also understood his involvement in the Heidelberg missionary association in these terms. The association was called the Allgemeiner Evangelisch-Protestant-ischer Missionsverein, and Troeltsch became its president in 1903 (cf. *Jahreschronik der Evangelischer Gemeinde Heidelberg 1903*, 20. I am grateful for this reference to H.Renz; cf. also P.Tillich, *Vorlesungen über die Geschichte des Christlichen Denkens*, II, Stuttgart 1972, 193 and *GS* II, 795).

201. The statement 'the harmony of the *a priori*-rational-universal with the factual-irrational-unique is the mystery of reality and the fundamental problem of all knowledge' (*PE*, 49) points in this direction.

202. *PE*, 51.

203. *PE*, 52.

204. *PE*, 53.

205. Ibid.

206. RP, 484.

207. *PE*, 55.

208. Above all R.Otto (1869-1937) and A.Nygren (1890-1978) take up and develop ideas from the philosophy of religion in terms of a religious *a priori*. Otto and Troeltsch agree in taking the psychology and history of religion into account; they differ as a result of Otto's orientation on the philosophy of J.Fries and later his adoption of a specific religious category, that of the 'holy' (cf. R.Otto, *Kantisch-Fries'sche Religionsphilosophie und ihre Anwendung auf die Theologie*, 1909, and *The Idea of the Holy*, 1917, ET London 1923). Troeltsch reviewed Otto's book *The Idea of the Holy* in *Kantstudien* 1918, 65-76. For Otto cf. A.Paus, *Herkunft und Wesen der a priori-Theorie R.Ottos*, Leiden 1966, and H.Bräunlich, *Das Verhältnis von Religion und Theologie bei Ernst Troeltsch und Rudolf Otto*, Bonn Dissertation 1978. Nygren's interest was primarily in the scientific foundation of theology. For Nygren, religion has *a priori* validity because 'the religious experience is a transcendentally necessary and generally valid experience...' (in *Die Gültigkeit religiöser Erfahrung*, Studien des apologetischen Seminars in Wernigerode 8, Gütersloh 1922, here 51). For Nygren see especially G.Wingren, *Die Methodenfrage der Theologie*, 1957; for the theme generally see E.Lessing, 'Die Bedeutung des religiösen Apriori für wissenschafts-theoretische Überlegungen innerhalb der Theologie', *EvTh* 30, 1970, 355-67.

209. Letter to P.Siebeck, 23 March 1900, Mohr/Siebeck archives, Tübingen.

210. As time went on he expressed himself in different ways. Cf. the letter to F.M.Schiele of 4 November 1907 and to P.Siebeck of 18 January 1914 (Mohr/Siebeck archives, Tübingen). Here Troeltsch's purpose was also to retreat somewhat from the image of him which had developed in public. He did not want to be judged simply as a philosopher of religion and a historian, as a critic of theology and the church, but as a theologian who was able to develop a coherent picture of Christian faith and its significance for the present. One step in this direction was the fact that he had presented his view of Christian faith in the form of articles and lexicon articles (*RGG¹*). In addition there is the *Glaubenslehre* which appeared posthumously in 1925, edited by Gertrud von le Fort on the basis of lectures given in Heidelberg in 1911/12, and the lecture on 'The Significance of the Historical Existence of Jesus for Faith' (1911). Troeltsch's articles on dogma or dogmatics which appeared in *RGG* are particularly important for his understanding of dogmatic theology in the contemporary situation.

211. *RGG¹*, II, 109.

212. There was virtually no discussion of the *Glaubenslehre* at the time of its appearance: it did not fit well enough into the theological landscape of the time. From a more recent period the following articles should be mentioned: B.A.Gerrish, 'Ernst Troeltsch and the Possibility of a Historical Theology', in *Ernst Troeltsch and the Future of Theology*, ed. J.P.Clayton, 1976, 199-35; W.E.Wyman Jr, *The Concept of Glaubenslehre. Ernst Troeltsch and the Theological Heritage of Schleiermacher*, 1983; id., 'Troeltschs Begriff der Glaubenslehre', *TRST* 4, 352-73; H.J.Birkner, 'Glaubenslehre und Modernitätserfahrung... Ernst Troeltsch als Dogmatiker', *TRST* 4, 1987, 325-37; S.Coakley, 'Christologie "auf Triebsand"? Zur Aktualität von Troeltschs Christusdeutung', *TRST* 4, 338-51. Mention should also be made of the extended introduction by J.Klapwijk to the reprint, Aalen 1981, v-xxviii.

213. *GL*, 72.

214. *GL*, 167.

215. Cf. e.g. *GL*, 159ff.

216. *GL*, 4.

217. Cf. *GL*, 56, which reads: 'It [Christian doctrine] is a religious grasping, interpretation and assessment of reality, not a rational explanation... of reality.'

218. For Schleiermacher, religious feeling is a specific sphere of human mental activity and experience distinct from that of knowing and doing. Only if this special character is maintained can connecting links be drawn with other spheres of intellectual work and human experience. Cf. Friedrich Schleiermacher, *The Christian Faith*, Edinburgh 1928, 13ff.

219. *GS* II, 200.

220. Cf. *GS* II, 225.

221. Cf. 'Schleiermacher und die Kirche', in *Schleiermacher der Philosoph des Glaubens*, Berlin-Schöneberg 1910, 19ff.

222. Both assent to and criticism of Schleiermacher can also be found in a letter of Troeltsch's to Friedrich von Hügel. Troeltsch's concluding remark is particularly worth noting here. He writes: 'I have probably put myself too close to him; the reasons for that were partly tactical' (letter to F. von Hügel of 13 April 1901, Apfelbacher/Neuner, 55).

223. *GL*, 72.

224. Ibid.

225. The lexicon *Die Religion in Geschichte und Gegenwart* (1909ff.) was the direct expression in the form of an encyclopaedia of modern historical-critical theology with a history-of-religions approach. Many articles in the first edition, in which Troeltsch was involved, are still programmatical today.

226. Letter to F.M.Schiele, 2 September 1909, Mohr/Siebeck archives, Tübingen.

227. Thus he writes to Schiele: 'Of the articles, I have given Rade one ("Theodicy"); I would very much like to add "Grace", "Predestination" and "Eschatology" to it, because for once I would also like to hoist my really dogmatic banner in *Christliche Welt*' (letter to F.M.Schiele, 14 April 1906, Mohr/Siebeck archives, Tübingen).

228. *RGG*[1] II, 1448.

229. *RGG*[1] II, 1456.

230. Cf. *RGG*[1] II, 1450.

231. So we read: 'It [the autonomy achieved by the communication of religious power] is not the starting point but the culmination of religious upbringing, and as a result

often needs to refer back to the historical powers which stimulate faith, make it vivid and guarantee it' (*RGG*[1], II, 1452).

232. Given to the Christian Students' Conference in Aarau. Nine years later, in 1920, Karl Barth would similarly address a student conference in Aarau, on the topic of 'Biblical Questions, Inights, and Vistas'. The difference in approach becomes vividly clear when Barth says that the subject-matter makes the question of what he has to offer in the lecture unnecessary. For: 'It [the Bible] has already commanded, our whole knowledge lives from the knowledge of God. We are not outside but inside' (*The Word of God and the Word of Man*, New York 1957, 51f.). In connection with Troeltsch's approach from the history of religions which stresses religious experience, the following comment by Barth is of interest: 'In the Biblical experience there is a final element to which nothing in psychology corresponds, which cannot be reproduced in feeling. Biblical piety is not really pious... Biblical religious history has the distinction of being in its essence, in its inmost character, neither religion nor history – not religion but reality, not history but truth, one might say' (ibid., 66).

233. For details see A.Schweitzer, *Geschichte der Lebens-Jesu-Forschung*, Tübingen 1951, 444ff. (this account is not in the English translation).

234. So Troeltsch does not argue from an apologetic perspective with those who radically dispute the historicity of Jesus, like Drews and Jensen. He regards the present discussion as a consequence of the development. However, he can note a step beyond a critical standpoint, so that he can talk of 'a great exaggeration' and say that it is 'ludicrous' (cf. *GJ*, 4, *ETWTR*, 184).

235. Theologically this means: 'Granted this transformation [from the dogmatic-objective understanding of redemption to the personal understanding based on faith] there is no inner necessity for the appeal to a historical fact. The historical personality of Jesus and his saving work are not absolutely necessary' (*GJ*, 7, *ETWTR*, 185).

236. Troeltsch takes over the results of the critical quest of the historical Jesus. For him, historical criticism makes it impossible to know Jesus as a religious personality; the assumption of his ongoing influence as a person already comes to grief on that. Another phenomenon belongs in this context, which Troeltsch regards as the consequence of the theological line from Schleiermacher to Herrmann, and which he disputes vigorously, namely the assumption that outside the sphere of influence of Jesus and the Christian community there is only remoteness from God and inability to believe in God.

237. *GJ*, 15, *ETWTR*, 189.

238. *GJ*, 18f., *ETWTR*, 191.

239. *GJ*, 26, *ETWTR*, 194f.

240. *GJ*, 26, *ETWTR*, 195.

241. The historical reconstruction is hardly tenable in the form adopted by Troeltsch. Like Troeltsch, Hans Conzelmann is inclined to put in question the adoption of a cult in the earliest community. However, this assessment rests on the presupposition that cult is essentially to be understood as a means of influencing God, whereas the worship of the earliest community – without sacrifice, without fixed sacred times, without separate holy spaces and without mediation through priests – was essentially related to verbal elements, namely the exegesis of scripture, preaching and prayer (cf. H.Conzelmann, *An Outline of the Theology of the New Testament*, London and New York 1969, 53f.). In terms of the history of religion it is hardly possible to

sustain Troeltsch's general statement about a law of social psychology, since in the mystery religions there was community life and worship without any link to a historical person. Thus in his investigations into the Hellenistic mystery religions Richard Reitzenstein showed that the cultic actions to be found there (apart from penitence, repentance and prayer) represent a symbolic expression of the cosmic force of life (cf. R.Reitzenstein, *Die hellenistischen Mysterienreligionen*, Darmstadt 1973, 166).

242. *GJ*, 30, *ETWTR*, 196.

243. Letter to W.Bousset of 2 February 1912, UB Göttingen, unpublished. Troeltsch gives a qualified answer to this question: 'Not of course as a law of cultic worship of the founder but of the glorification and absolutizing of the period of foundation in which the cult always relates to itself, even if there is no worship of the founder' (ibid.).

244. Letter to W.Bousset of 2 September 1912. In his interpretation, K.E.Apfelbacher begins from the notion that the lecture is 'exclusively a study in the psychology of religion' (*Frömmigkeit*, n.169, 229). This view is problematical, because the lecture either contains or is influenced both implicitly and explicitly by theological interpretations. Moreover, theology can also consist in responding to a theological question in terms of the psychology of religion. For this see Troeltsch's letter to Bousset, where he says that his lecture is 'above all meant practically, as a guideline for students and clergy, who cannot work without a definite reference to Christ' (letter to W.Bousset, 2 February 1912, UB Göttingen, unpublished).

245. Cf. here above all Troeltsch's instructive and detailed letter to Bousset of 2 February 1912. It gains its special significance from the fact that it takes up some of Bousset's critical questions and goes into them in giving a precise answer. So at this point we gain an insight into the correspondence, and also see something of Bousset's manner of thinking and arguing.

246. Letter to W.Bousset of 2 February 1912, UB Göttingen.

247. Ibid.

248. Review of Troeltsch's lecture in *TLZ* 1912, 245-9, reprinted in *Schriften zur Grundlegung der Theologie*, ed. Fischer-Appelt, II, 282ff.

249. Ibid., 287. In the lecture itself Troeltsch showed how Herrmann's talk of the 'fact' of Jesus is to be accepted to the degree that here the cultic symbol is related to a real person (*GJ*, 321, *ETWTR*, 197f.). But in that case the 'fact' of the person understood in this way is not to be bracketted off from historical-critical research, but left free for it. According to Troeltsch, faith does not have to establish 'facts'; it can only interpret them, explain them. Thus Troeltsch sees the question of the effect of historical thought on theology as a point at issue between him and Herrmann.

250. The line of these ideas is developed by Herrmann's pupil Rudolf Bultmann; here the adoption and development of the historical progress from liberal to dialectical theology is significant. The attitude of the believer (or the person to be led to faith) in the present to the person of Jesus Christ is discussed under the heading 'Obedience to the truth which cannot be demonstrated' (cf. Bultmann's programmatic article from his early days, 'Liberal Theology and the Latest Theological Movement', 1920, *Faith and Understanding*, London and New York 1969, 28-53: 50). Bultmann connects the obedience in question with the kerygma as the living address of the Word of God, and 'experience' can be understood only as the existential grasping

Notes to pages 214–215

of the truth of faith. The kerymatic address and the idea of obedience gives the relationship between faith and history a radical existential solution which marks both the links with Herrmann's theology and the differences from it.

251. Reflections on the term 'Modernism' are fraught with difficulties. The definition of the term varies. In the papal condemnation in the form of the decree *Lamentabili* (3 July 1907) and the encyclical *Pascendi* (8 September 1907) Modernism is, to put it briefly, a disputing of absolute truths. This relates in particular to the saving function of Christ, his significance in founding the church, and the idea of tradition. The basis for disputing the absolute truth of faith is the acceptance of a critically analytical thought in theology, which leads to relativism through an inapproprate stress on the subjective element in faith and religion (cf. *The History of the Church*, ed. H.Jedin, Vol. IX, London and New York 1981, 420ff., which contains a further bibliography). Among more recent articles, mention should be made of those by E.Herms, 'Theologischer "Modernismus" und lehramtliche "Antimodernismus" in der römischen Kirche am Anfang des zwanzigsten Jahrhunderts', *TRST* 4, 13-55, and P.Neuner, 'Was ist Modernismus?', *TRST* 4, 56-66.

252. Troeltsch commmented on the problem in two publications, first in the article 'Katholizismus und Reformismus', *Internationale Wochenschrift für Wissenschaft, Kunst und Technik* 2, 1908, 15-26, and then in the article 'Modernismus', *Die neue Rundschau* 2, 1909, 456-81, reprinted in *GS* II, 45-67. It is worth noting that neither publication appeared in church or theological journals (e.g. *Christliche Welt*) but in cultural or scientific journals for a general readership. A personal letter to F.von Hügel of 4 April 1908 sheds substantial light on Troeltsch's overall assessment of the situation (Apfelbacher/Neuner 87-9).

253. Cf. 'Katholizismus und Reformismus', 17.

254. Ibid., 22.

255. So we read: 'Religious thought is the primal form of all human thought; it flows and springs from all the crannies of the human heart, even where it does not specifically end up in religion, as nowadays any real poet still shows. It is the glow of all great creative eras which realize an ideal because they believe it, and it is the salvation of all who are weary and overworked, who again want to gather and renew their strength. So it forms the basis of all popular feelings even now, keeps breaking out in all kinds of corners in the most colourful forms, and today in particular as a collective clearly elevates itself above the desolation and externality of a technical and material culture which is over-strained and dispersive' (*GS* II, 46f.).

256. So Troeltsch says on the one hand that Catholicism has a form of cult like 'all primitive and all pagan religion' (*GS* II, 50), or that compared with the original ideas of Christianity it represents a 'scandalous externalization' (*GS* II, 51). On the other hand, he points positively to the unbroken historical continuity in Catholicism. On the basis of this continuity there is a connection with the forces of the past and with the 'living-productive papal authority of the present' (ibid.).

257. *GS* II, 52. Both of Troeltsch's publications are very similar in the structure of their argument. The superiority of the article 'Modernism' is that its account of the political situation is more sophisticated; moreover it has an interesting critical attitude.

258. Karl Holl wrote an important contribution, restrained throughout, which saw events in a wider historical framework (*Der Modernismus*, Tübingen 1908, reprinted in *Gesammelte Aufsätze zur Kirchengeschichte* III, *Der Westen*, Tübingen, 1928, 437-

59). Holl depicted Modernism as a trend concerned for a 'balance between Catholic faith and modern thought' (*Gesammelte Aufsätze* III, 437) which in fact would inevitably end in a complete transformation of theology and the hierarchical system. Holl agreed with Troeltsch that any Protestant feeling of superiority forbids and similarly calls for Protestant self-criticism. At an essential point Holl went beyond Troeltsch's argument. In connection with the Modernist Roman Catholic theologians he observed that 'even among the most significant of them, the ultimate deepening of a personal religious sense as represented by Luther's doctrine of justification is missing' (ibid., 459). This could implicitly be the expression of a feeling of Protestant superiority, which was not Troeltsch's intention.

259. 'Catholizismus und Reformismus', 19f.

260. Friedrich Heiler, who was close to von Hügel and was also influenced by him, described his theology as a 'model of Catholic universality, synthesis and balance. With a strong emphasis on the transcendence and simultaneity of God and the inadequacy of all religious and dogmatic statements, it combines an energetic stress on the incarnation: the immersion of the infinite in the finite space and time of the historical, institutional and sacramental' (*RGG*² II, 2034f.).

261. Letter to F.von Hügel, 4 April 1908 (Apfelbacher/Neuner, 89).

262. However, here theologically one can note an unresolved juxtaposition. The retreat into an inner nucleus of piety remains possible at any time and is the last bastion. Especially at this time (1908) Troeltsch could probably have found some understanding for such a view in von Hügel, since von Hügel had quite clearly withdrawn into a religious individualism. Von Hügel however, then referred quite firmly to the forces of community and their significance for the Christian life of faith (cf. Peter Neuner, *Religiöse Erfahrung und geschichtliche Offenbarung. Friedrich von Hügels Grundlegung der Theologie*, Munich 1977). Cf. also H.Rollmann, 'Troeltsch, von Hügel and Modernism', *The Downside Review* 95, 1978, 35-60. For Troeltsch's relations with England and Scotland see *TRST* 3, 319-31; see also G.Moretto, 'Ernst Troeltsch in Italien', *TRST* 3, 283-307.

263. Apart from the letters to von Hügel, mention should also be made of those to Stefano Jacini (cf. the reprint of the letters in G.Moretto, 'Ernst Troeltsch e Il Modernismo', *Archivio di filosofia* 1982, 169ff.).

264. 'Katholizismus und Reformismus', 26.

265. Thus in the light of the situation in church politics he can say: 'So we must let things take their course' (*GS* II, 66). Or in the letter to F.von Hügel of 4 April 1908 (Apfelbacher/Neuner, 89) he says: 'What the world will make of these things is becoming increasingly obscure to me and also a matter of indifference. Everyone should see where he stands and not allow himself to be talked out of his religious possessions or to be led astray by political religion. I cannot say more, and I am content if at the same time I can help some other people to see where they stand.'

266. *GS* II, 66.

267. Jatho's characterization of the 'religion of Jesus' can serve as an example of his stress on personal experience. For him it cannot be 'shut up in a church, nor can it be made clear to anyone through a system, through proofs of faith or statements of faith. Jesus' religion is the free, bubbling life of a heart filled by God. Now it is in the nature of things for God to come to a special form of life in any human heart in which he is alive' (from the collection of sermons *Persönliche Religion*, NF, *Predigten*

von Carl Jatho, Cologne nd, 25; the collection contains sermons from the church year 1904/5).

268. Jatho saw himself exposed to vigorous criticism in the years before his trial and removal from office, from both conservative circles in the church and its official organs. In particular, a lecture of his on the eucharist provoked vigorous reactions from the 'positive' side and also brought him a warning from the Rhine Consistory (cf. F.Wiegand, *Kirchliche Bewegungen der Gegenwart* I, 1907, 7ff.; G.von Rohden, *Der Kölner Kirchenstreit. Pfarrer Jathos Amtsenthebung im Lichte der öffentlichen Meinung*, Berlin 1911). The sections on 'Agitation' and 'Jathos Lehre' in the last book are particularly relevant. H.Mulert, 'Lehrverpflichtung und Lehrfreiheit', *RGG*[1] III, 2033-44, is representative of liberal theological thought. In his article Mulert puts forward the view that not only such cases in which pastors advocated a 'critical theology' but – conversely and justly – also those invoving a 'retrogressive' theology came under the law of heresy (cf. ibid., 2043).

269. The chapter 'Der Fall Jatho' in Johannes Rathjes, *Die Welt des freien Protestantismus* (179-94), offers an insight into these connections. Rathje ends his account of the reactions in the circle of the 'Friends of *Christliche Welt*' or in the journal with the illuminating comment: 'It can be seen that there is no question of bridging over the oppositions' (ibid., 194).

270. *CW* 25, 1911, 677-82. When included in the *Gesammelte Schriften* the article was entitled 'On the Occasion of the Jatho Case from *Christliche Welt*', 1911 (*GS* II, 134-45). The title chosen is significant because Troeltsch sees behind the whole case and debate the question of the freedom of the conscience of the pastor and members of the community. Other works from this time belong within the themes touched on. Mention should be made above all of 'Religiöser Individualismus und Kirche' (1910) and 'Die Kirche im Leben der Gegenwart' (1911). The latter in particular is closely connected with the questions raised by the Jatho case. Here Troeltsch is speaking on the one hand of the autonomy of the person of the preacher and of religious individualism generally. Nevertheless, he sees limits to religious individualism, through the right of the religious community. He derives the foundation of the Christian community as church from the 'radiant spirit of Christ' (*GS* II, 126).

271. Jatho attempted to answer the theological queries about his teaching from the Oberkirchenrat very thoroughly. The enquiries were particularly directed at his concept of God, his understanding of the revelation of God in Christ, his view of human sin and guilt, and life after death (cf. *Chronik der Christlichen Welt* 1911, nos. 11, 12, 13). The protest from Protestant lay circles, including such significant people as the church lawyer Rudolf Sohm from Leipzig, the philosopher Paul Natorp from Marburg and the historian Max Lenz from Berlin, were also directed against the idea of a law on heresy within Protestantism. Harnack sought to defend the establishment of such a law in principle, because he thought an unprotected and disintegrating church worthless. Alongside Wilhelm Herrmann, whose argument was essentially based on a theological position, Julius Kaftan was also a resolute critic of Jatho's position and person – more on grounds of church law. But we shall hear more of this later. Just one word on the verdict of the tribunal: of its thirteen members only two, the lawyer W.Kahl and the theologian F.Loofs, voted that Jatho should remain in office.

272. Cf. *Jatho und Harnack. Ihr Briefwechsel. Mit einem Geleitwort*, ed. Martin Rade,

Tübingen 1911, 28. For the context cf. C.Schwöbel, *Martin Rade*, Gütersloh 1980, 140ff.

273. Here Troeltsch is influenced in his reflections by his *Social Teachings*. This affects above all his account of Congregationalism or the Independents. Here the demands for freedom of conscience or tolerance are expressed in a historically impressive and effective form. In particular there is stress on the right of the individual community and its independence over against both the state and the established church. However, the criticism of the Volkskirche inherent in the link with the ideal of earliest Christianity implies a tendency to a sectarian radicalization (cf. *GS* I, 738ff., 750f., 758f., *ST* II, 666ff., 677f., 688f.).

274. Kaftan indicates that he instituted the Jatho case together with the Court Preacher Dryander. 'I hewed into this notch with utter conviction, once I had come to know Jatho's standpoint impeccably in the green leaves of Cologne. Here the limits of the tolerable have been exceeded. If we did not intervene, we would be making the new disciplinary law no more than outward form. Or to put it more simply, we would be neglecting the duty imposed on us by this law' (letter from Julius Kaftan to his brother Theodore, 17 March 1911, *Kirche, Recht und Theologie* II, 484f.).

275. Hardly an appropriate context, given that Jatho without doubt did not have a materialistic view of the world. However, Haeckel was the best known agnostic as a result of his *magnum opus Die Welträtsel* (1899). Kaftan may have seen a connecting link here in the denial of transcendence expressed in his works.

276. Letter of 12 February 1911, ibid., 480.

277. Ibid.

278. Cf. *Jatho und Harnack. Ihr Briefwechsel*, edited with an introduction by Martin Rade, Tübingen 1911. However, note should be taken of Harnack's reaction to the lay vote on this matter, which has already been mentioned.

279. Ibid., 18.

280. Ibid., 62.

281. Ibid., 74.

282. Cf. the contribution 'Religiöser Individualismus und Kirche'. This arose out of a lecture which Troeltsch gave to the Wissenschaftliches Predigerverein of Baden in 1910. The quotation is on *GS* II, 126. These remarks indicate what basic presuppositions Troeltsch thought meaningful for practical involvement in the church. We might assume that the issue here was not influence from outside but also the 'symbolic representation' of liberal, academic theology in church bodies. It is perhaps because of this that towards the end of his time in Heidelberg Troeltsch was a member of the Baden General Synod (he was elected as a lay member on 12 June 1914: information supplied to me by H.Renz).

283. The book appeared in 1912 as the first volume of the *Gesammelte Schriften*: there had already been a partial publication. [The ET by Olive Wyon has the title *The Social Teaching* (in the singular) *of the Christian Churches*, 2 vols., London 1931. Olive Wyon was one of the heroic pioneering translators of German theology from the 1920s on, and we owe her a great deal. However, for modern scholarly usage her translation of Troeltsch's book poses some problems, so while I have given page references to it, the translation is sometimes my own. Tr.]

284. He writes to his publisher: 'Only a second edition of my *Social Teachings* could cause an interruption to this plan [to write an ethics, a dogmatics and a philosophy of religion]; that is in fact something I hope for and would welcome, since I am still

quietly working on this favourite book and collecting material for it' (letter to P.Siebeck, 18 January 1914, Mohr/Siebeck archives, Tübingen). The indication given at the end is impressively confirmed by Troeltsch's personal copy. In this he wrote additional comments to make some points more precisely or to develop them further, together with references to more recent literature. I shall go into these sometimes extensive additions above all at important points of my account. The copy was made available to me by H.Renz; it is in private hands.

285. *GS* IV, 11.

286. Cf. Troeltsch's letters to his publisher P.Siebeck, 23 December 1908 and 6 November 1910 (Mohr/Siebeck archives, Tübingen).

287. Letter to P.Siebeck, 6 January 1811 (Mohr/Siebeck archives, Tübingen).

288. In this connection see also Troeltsch's important articles in the *Realenzyklopädie* on the Enlightenment (1897) and the English moralists of the seventeenth and eighteenth centuries (1903).

289. Cf. M.von Nathusius, *Die Mitarbeit der Kirche an der Lösung der sozialen Frage*, 1893-95; ²1897; ³1904.

290. Cf. *GS* IV, 11.

291. Cf. H.Bosse, *Marx-Weber-Troeltsch*, Munich 1970. Bosse sees this limitation in Troeltsch and criticizes it with reference to Marx. Troeltsch's 'methodological standpoint' is depicted at length, above all by comparison with Rickert and Weber, in W.Gerhard, *Ernst Troeltsch als Soziologe* (Cologne dissertation 1975). Also important for understanding Troeltsch's *Social Teachings* or his significance for social ethics are: W.F.Kasch, *Die Sozialphilosophie von Ernst Troeltsch*, Tübingen 1973; M.Wichelhaus, *Kirchengeschichtsschreibung und Soziologie im 19.Jahrhundert und bei Ernst Troeltsch*, Heidelberg 1965; H.E.Tödt, 'Ernst Troeltschs Bedeutung für die evangelische Sozialethik', *ZEE* 10, 1966, 227-36; H.J.Gabriel, *Christlichkeit der Gesellschaft. Eine kritische Darstellung der Kulturphilosophie von Ernst Troeltsch*, Berlin 1975.

292. That is already evident from the lexicon article 'Aufklärung'. The review of Seeberg's *Dogmengeschichte* (1901), in which Troeltsch in principle advocates a cultural-historical approach, offers important additions or changes. What happens is the formation of an entity, each time from the womb of a particular culture, like the Eastern church, mediaeval Catholicism or Protestantism. In this article the approach in terms of cultural history is no longer seen as an extension of the history of ideas; it is directed towards the character and value of cultural epochs and phenomena.

293. Thus for example it is said in the account of the Middle Ages, in respect of the 'serfdom' to be found there, that religious conceptions had an indirect influence on conditions: not through 'legal consequences', but as an effect of the view of the family (cf. *GS* I, 299ff., *ST* I, 252ff.).

294. Lorenz von Stein (1815-90) was originally a national economist and professional administrator. He was one of the forerunners of sociology and laid foundations on which others could build (cf. *Geschichte der sozialen Bewegungen in Frankreich*, 1842, and especially the introduction to the third edition, on 'The Concept of Society and the Laws of the Social Movement'). Mention should also be made of *Das System der Staatswissenschaften* (1856), Vol.II, entitled *Die Gesellschaftslehre*. Lorenz von Stein recognized the way in which social situation and formation of consciousness were

interwoven and noted a separation of state and society on the basis of the special structure of the modern acquisitive society based on work and property.

295. Apart from von Stein, the works of M.Weber, G.Simmel and E.Gothein certainly lie in the background. It becomes clear how Troeltsch is taking a stand against a concept of society with a scientific orientation or determination, and instead of this favours a historical approach which takes up the notion of development, with echoes of the methodological discussion of the significance of the cultural sciences and the humanities.

296. *GS* I, 12, *ST* I, 32.

297. The dogmatic manner of assessment is expressed in the following verdict of Uhlhorn on the 'old' world: 'The world before Christ is a world without love' (ibid., 7).

298. Uhlhorn begins from the basic notion that the love of Christ has established itself in many shapes and forms, that the cross is at the same time a sign of victory over the world, and that there is rightly a Christian optimism about history.

299. He writes of his *Social Teachings*: 'It would be a history of the culture of the Christian church, a complete parallel to Harnack's *History of Dogma*' (*GS* IV, 11).

300. In Troeltsch's personal copy there is the draft for a 'new introduction' in which Troeltsch speaks of the 'limit of the history of dogma'. This emerges in the way in which such a history has assumed a dogmatic subject identical with itself for the historical changes in the framework and sphere of the church. It is therefore important to perceive the different churches and groups as phenomena existing independently alongside one another.

301. Paul Wernle, 'Vorläufige Anmerkungen zu den *Soziallehren der christlichen Kirchen und Gruppen* von Ernst Troeltsch', *ZTK* 22, 1912, 329-68; 23, 1913, 18-80. Of the large number of reviews of the *Social Teachings*, that by Reinhold Seeberg (*Theologisches Literaturblatt* 34, 1913, 169f.) should also be mentioned. The most interesting thing here is the assessment from two perspectives, on the one hand from the historical perspective and on the other in the spirit of that tradition of which Troeltsch was particularly critical: conservative Lutheranism. Cf. also W.Köhler's review in *HZ* 114, 1915, 598-605.

302. The research colloquium of the Ernst-Troeltsch-Gesellschaft, 26-29 September 1988, on the *Social Teachings* clarified some points of detail here. The results of this colloquium will be published.

303. Criticism that Troeltsch lacked knowledge of the sources was raised in particular from the side of historians or church historians. Cf. for example Karl Holl's comment that in connection with Luther, Troeltsch 'did not judge on the basis of the sources, but under the compulsion of concepts which were there *a priori*' (*Gesammelte Aufsätze* 1, 248 n.4). Max Scheler's judgment is to my mind more positive and more apt: 'The mighty work is not significant for its disclosure or evaluation of new sources but for its masterly synopses, and also for its seriousness about reality and its sociological and historical spirit' ('Ernst Troeltsch als Soziologe', *Kölner Vierteljahres-hefte für Soziologie*, 1923, 12). In a manuscript note to the planned second edition Troeltsch took up the question of the purpose and method of his account, not only by way of supplement but also with a recognizably apologetic tendency. He wrote (p.14 middle after 'ambiguous and misleading', *ST* 34, before 'Guiding Principles of this Survey'): 'That [i.e. the task of describing the actual historical signifance of the gospel and the history of its influence], however, seems to mean working through

the whole material of Christian history from new perspectives. That is also indeed the case, and precisely for that reason only the main points of the following accounts and investigations can rest on some personal research into the sources by the author. It would take more than a lifetime for situations and the ethical and dogmatic concept of doctrine which went with them to be subjected to original investigation in all their depth and breath. This can only be a first attempt, in which the fruitfulness of the new perspectives must be shown essentially with the help of material which is already available.'

304. Cf. *GS* I,27, *ST* I, 44f.

305. For Troeltsch, Jesus' preaching is significant here primarily from a sociological perspective, namely that it comes before the foundation of any community or communion (at any rate in the lasting sense). Moreover the preaching of Jesus is open in various directions through the religious ideal which constitutes it. We can conclude here that it can serve as a possible link in the direction of the church, the sect and also mysticism. In assessing the preaching of Jesus Troeltsch observes (in a manuscript note for the new edition): 'In particular, the preaching of Jesus still lies before any sociological formation of a Christian community and moves in so general and ideal a sphere that it must be taken quite independently as the starting point for the formation of various possible communities which could all in some way refer to it' (addition to the 'Introduction', 15, *ST* I, 34). This addition shows even more clearly that Troeltsch combines his theological verdict with a sociological one and draws consequences from this for his account.

306. For this question see also the section above on 'Troeltsch's "positive" views'.

307. To characterize this type he says: 'All action is the service of God and is a responsible office, authority as well as obedience. As stewards of God the great must care for the small, and as servants of God the little ones must submit to those who bear authority' (*GS* I, 68, *ST* I, 78).

308. The difference from what the gospel intended is to be described like this: 'The childlikeness, breadth and height of the gospel are already being expressed in the concrete and practical realm, and austere radicalism has already given way to compromise with, and the necessity of being terms of understanding with, the general life of the world' (*GS* I, 69, *ST* I, 80).

309. Such passages indicate in exemplary fashion how Troeltsch had a remarkably restricted understanding of Marx's ideas which was focussed on his purposes. A more penetrating understanding becomes evident only in the studies of historicism (cf. above all *GS* III, 315ff.).

310. *GS* I, 173, *ST* I, 160.

311. The idea of a unitary Christian or church culture in the Middle Ages already emerges, in substance or (in part) in so many words, in Troeltsch's earlier works. The Middle Ages is the era of church culture, while modern culture begins with the Enlightenment (cf. *PN*, 431, 600ff.).

312. *GS* I, 185f., *ST* I, 206.

313. Troeltsch energetically argues against Harnack that while Harnack has enriched the approach purely from the history of ideas by attempts at a psychologizing explanation, he has not gone far enough in his account because he has not taken note of the significance of sociological conditions for the development of dogma. That means 'that the special character of political and social development in the Middle Ages in the West is also the decisive factor for its basic ethical and spiritual

character. Here some "Marxism" is probably justified, over against the purely dialectical and ideological view of the history of the churches and dogmas' (*GS* I, 193 n.87a, *ST* I, 384 n.87a). This latter comment is directed against Seeberg in particular, but in principle it also applies to Harnack (cf. *GS* I, 209 n.98, *ST* 387f. n.98).

314. Here Troeltsch thinks that one cannot follow Seeberg in seeing the Middle Ages against the background of the Augustinian tradition. Rather, note should be taken of events in Western history generally in any definition of the relationship between state and church in the notion of a unitary culture. This also applies to the break in continuity with the idea of the Reich church through the rise of the Germano-Roman Landeskirchen. 'That too was a form of the state church, but it was quite unlike that of the East, since it was based, not on the strength of the state but on the inward permeation of the spiritual and the worldly...' (*GS* I, 195, *ST* I, 215).

315. Cf. *GS* I, 211, *ST* I, 229.

316. Cf. *GS* I, 217ff., *ST* I, 231ff.

317. According to Troeltsch, the idea of a unitary Christian culture may not claim to be influenced historically by a tradition going back to Augustine. Essentially, he subordinates Augustine to the ancient tradition, because Augustine is better understood from this context. His book *Augustin, die christliche Antike und das Mittelalter. Im Anschluss an die Schrift* De Civitate Dei, which appeared in 1915, represents an expansion of the *Social Teachings*. Here Troeltsch corrects his earlier interpretation that Augustine did not have an independent view of the life of the state and society. However, he maintains his view that in principle Augustine belongs to the ancient world, though for him this does not exclude the possibility that Augustine's ideas had an ongoing influence in the Middle Ages.

318. Troeltsch observes critically that the Protestant theologians are almost blind at this point. For them the idea of natural law had was virtually irrelevant to the rise of a Christian world-view (cf. *GS* I, 373 n.77, *ST* I, 197f. n.77). The criticism of Protestant theologians from Holl to Brunner then took the form that they could not detect to the same degree as Troeltsch the confusion in natural-law thinking which Troeltsch thought that he could perceive in historical reality. For Holl, the identification of Decalogue and natural law, like the distinction between relative and absolute natural law, is an invention of Troeltsch's which is historically untenable (cf. *Gesammelter Aufsätze* I, 243 n.2, 248 n.4).

Holl's criticism is that Troeltsch's use of the idea of natural law rests on an inconsistency to the degree that it contains natural conditions on the one hand and ethical questioning (in the sense of a 'should be') on the other (ibid., 243 n.2). However, Holl seems to misunderstand here, because by virtue of its disposition, in bringing together or combining the natural and the legal, the concept of natural law simultaneously presents a perspective of 'be' and 'should'. Brunner argues for dropping the concept of relative natural law introduced by Troeltsch, because it has only led to obscurity and confusion. 'The element of truth in the concept of "relative natural law" is none other than the necessary application of the "righteous in itself" to sinful historical reality' (Emil Brunner, *Gerechtigkeit*, Zurich 1943, 324 n.44).

319. In Thomistic ethics, according to Troeltsch, a gradual realization of the purposes of reason in reality is presupposed by the adoption of Aristotelian ideas, and in accord with this it is assumed that ethical demands are built up in stages. In these ethics the 'Aristotelian doctrine of virtue and of the end and the Stoic doctrine of

natural law and rational law are combined and fused' (*GS* I, 256, *ST* I, 260). Troeltsch assumes a bilinear tradition in the form of Aristotelianism on the one hand and Stoic tradition on the other, the two being combined in Thomism.

320. Despite Harnack's polemic (cf. 'Das Urchristentum und die sozialen Fragen', *PrZ* 131, 1908, 443f.), Troeltsch holds to his own view that Protestantism falls short of Augustinian ethics, because unlike the latter it could not combine the moral law and the Decalogue. Here he fails to find a clarity which can be provided by the acceptance of the idea of natural law. However, this also entails a critical view of the Catholic position. In Catholic ethics it becomes a real problem how the moral motivation resulting from religious aims can be combined with ethics. Troeltsch states pointedly: 'The scholastic-Augustinian statement of the problem itelf is in any case relevant, and corresponds to the fundamental tendency of Christian belief' (*GS* I, 267 n.120; here 268, *ST* I, 405f. n.120). In his interpretation of Augustine, Harnack is governed by the critical notion of measuring Augustinian conceptions by the position of Paul on the one hand and Lutheran theology on the other. For that very reason he provokes Troeltsch to contradict him.

321. *GS* I, 304, *ST* I, 298f.

322. The compromise character of mediaeval social philosophy is criticized by Troeltsch at the point where a given historical condition is rooted in natural law through a combination of providence and rationalism.

323. Troeltsch thinks that Karl Müller is the only church historian to have recognized the significance of the sects for mediaeval church history. However, he accuses him of having in the usual theological manner regarded 'the church type as the norm and the sects as a secondary phenomenon like monasticism and asceticism, from a popularization of which they are supposed to have emerged' (*GS* I, 360 n.163, *ST* I, 415 n.163).

324. The concept of the ideal type appears in Max Weber after 1903 (in the article 'Roscher und Knies und die logischen Probleme der historichen Nationalökonomie', 1903-6, included in *Gesammelte Aufsätze zur Wissenschaftslehre*, Tübingen 1903-6, 1ff.). Then in 1905 *Protestant Ethics and the Spirit of Capitalism* appeared (ET of [2]1920, London 1930). Finally, the article ' "Kirchen" und "Sekten" in Nordamerika', *Frankfurter Zeitung*, Easter 1906, revised version in *CW* 20, 1906, 558ff., under the title 'Kirchen und Sekten in Nordamerika. Eine kirchen- und sozialpolitische Skizze', is also important; the article was then considerably expanded for its inclusion in the *Gesammelte Aufsätze zur Religionssoziologie*. On the changes for the last version Max Weber commented: 'The revision was motivated by the fact that to my delight the concept of sect which I developed (in opposition to that of "church") has meanwhile been taken over and discussed thoroughly by Troeltsch in his *The Social Teachings of the Christian Churches*' (*Gesammelte Aufsätze zur Religionssoziologie* I, Tübingen 1973, 207 n.1).

325. For Max Weber, the 'ideal type' is arrived at through a 'one-sided accentuation of one or several perspectives and by the combination of a wealth of diffuse and discrete individual phenomena, here more present, there less, and in places not at all, which bring together perspectives with a one-sided emphasis into a unitary notion. In its conceptual purity this notion cannot be found anywhere in reality; it is a utopia, and for historical work the task is to establish in each individual case how near to or far from reality the ideal picture is' (*Gesammelte Aufsätze zur Wissenschaftslehre*, 191).

326. Cf. *GS* I, 364 n.164, *ST* I, 433f. n.164.

327. Troeltsch only recognized the significance of the formation of types – for the beginnings in the early church only church and sect are relevant – in the course of his work on the *Social Teachings*, and reacted accordingly. That he made insertions and additions here is clear from a comparison of the final version with the first printing in the *Archiv für Sozialwissenschaften und Sozialpolitik*.

328. Cf. *GS* I, 362, *ST* I, 331.

329. There is no account of the Eastern church. In the *Social Teachings* Troeltsch made only one brief reference to the different development and shaping of the Middle Ages in the East. In the East there is only a parallelism between the state and the Christian world of ideas, no intrinsic combination and association. 'This is why the Byzantine East lacks the deep inner conflict of the Middle Ages in the West and the development of phenomena like the Renaissance and the Reformation' (*GS* I, 194, *ST* I, 214). Troeltsch does not seem to have envisaged any fundamental change on this point even for the second edition. He suggests: 'It is not possible to follow the development in the East. Westerners do not have the linguistic knowledge, since such a study is impossible without a knowledge of the Russian literature. But at any rate it is necessary to point out that the programme of a Slavonic culture which is so important today, and a messianic role for Russia in the redemption of Europe, is only understandable in terms of these developments. Basically, the old Byzantine Christianity had only a monastic ethic' (addition in his own copy to *GS* I, 194, *ST* I, 214, after 'Renaissance and Reformation'; the quotation comes at the beginning of a lengthy insertion).

330. Paul Wernle criticized the emphasis on the concept of grace in Troeltsch's interpretation of Luther. 'To my mind that is too subtle and too theological. The *prius* seems to me to be only the radical thinking through of the law to the end, and as a result the collapse of the piety based on the law and sacramental grace and the new sense of the forgiving grace of the gospel' (*ZTK* 23, 1913, 18f.).

331. For Elert, Troeltsch's understanding of the Reformation, and especially of Luther's theology, comes to grief, first, on his inadequate knowledge of the sources and, second, on his understanding of justification. For Elert, the specific understanding of the doctrine of justification is connected with the difference betwen Luther and scholasticism. The important distinguishing mark for him here is the view of justification as *iustitia dei passiva*. However, according to Elert, in order to understand this connection properly, it is necessary to take note of Luther's distinctive concept of faith (cf. *Morphologie des Luthertums* I, Munich 1952, 357).

332. According to P.Wernle, Troeltsch's account of Luther's ethics is one of the sections in which he involuntarily asks himself 'whether Troeltsch has not made the issue even more complicated' (*ZTK* 23, 1931, 24). For Wernle, in assuming a twofold morality Troeltsch concentrated too strongly on Luther's work 'On Temporal Authority'. In his manuscript notes (for the second edition) Troeltsch attempts to explain and tone down the contradictions in Luther's ethics which he brought out so strongly. Thus we read (after 'difficulties of Protestant social philosophy', *GS* I, 475, *ST* I, 471f.): 'of course all this relates only to the old orthodox Lutheranism and the explicit formulations of Luther himself. If one considers Luther in the light of modern intellectual developments and goes back psychologically even beyond his formula to an unconscious unity in the human being, then one can probably attempt to construct a single basic direction behind this twofold ethics, which is directed

towards a inwardness of the I that takes up all tensions and oppositions in the assurance of God, which in its certainty also takes upon itself the alien, the mere "office", the necessities of the sinful life, and in the radical new freedom boldly directs itself only to the goal of the God-inwardness which is to be asserted in everything. For this one can appeal to all the statements in which Luther requires of the one who is free in God even the doing of what is sinful, i.e. what is required in practice by the concrete situation in an all-sinful (?) life. The paradoxical formulation alone shows that here we have reflections on an occasion and not a principle...'

333. Cf. *GS* I, 491, *ST* I, 489. Troeltsch saw the contrast between personal morality and the morality of office being increasingly weakened in the course of Luther's development. Luther himself, like his followers, increasingly accepted existing circumstances and attempted to breathe a Christian spirit into them and realize Christian charity in them. The result is obedience to the existing orders, and an acceptance of the existing authorities.

334. Cf. *GS* I, 447ff., *ST* I, 461ff.

335. The problems of this interpretation are connected with Troeltsch's structurally generalizing approach. Even if we recognize that many of the insights in this approach are correct, we have to indicate critically what Troeltsch is either blind to or puts in the background. In his work the doctrine of justification seems remarkably vague (as W.Elert saw rightly). The understanding of God introduced by the doctrine of the two kingdoms should fit more closely into the relationship between the *deus absconditus* and the *deus revelatus* and not just emphasize God's volitional nature and the anthropomorphism inherent in it. The christology appears reduced to the degree that it is regarded primarily as a solution to the difficulties of a combination of the order of retribution and the order of grace.

336. *GS* I, 513, *ST* II, 57f. In the face of this historical analysis, which takes note of reality, in Troeltsch's view, the paradox in Rudolf Sohm's theory comes out particularly clearly: the purely inward attitude of faith, without any support in definitions of church law and a corresponding understanding of state and society. Here Sohm assumes a purely intellectual or theological relationship between the Lutheran notion of the church and its foundation in earliest Christianity (cf. R.Sohm, *Kirchenrecht* I, 1892). Sohm's theory culminates in the much-discussed thesis that church law conflicts with the essence of the church. Troeltsch responds to this (cf. *GS* I, 520 n.236, *ST* II, 852 n.236).

337. Cf. in this connection for example Troeltsch's reference to F.J.Stahl, as the standard-bearer of the conservative party (*GS* I, 567 n.262, *ST* II, 867 n.262), or the remark that the further spread of serfdom among the peasants east of the Elbe after the sixteenth century was in no way opposed by Lutheranism. At this point there is also a clear criticism of Uhlhorn's account (cf. *GS* I, 589 n.289, *ST* II, 873 n.289).

338. For Troeltsch, new historical conditions arise for church and culture with the eighteenth century, so that there can no longer be any question of a single object of investigation. The close connection between church and state comes to an end; at the same time cultural life clearly becomes independent of church and confession. The last two chapters of the book are new additions as compared to the first publication in the 'Archiv'. Troeltsch explains that they had been planned from the beginning. What he would like to have had in a later new edition was a chapter on

Anglicanism. He also indicates (in the notes to his own copy) that he wanted to define the mysticism-type more closely, and began to move towards both a conceptual and a historical distinction. This remark is in keeping with his intent, also expressed in a letter, to describe mediaeval mysticism in more detail than through brief notes (letter to P.Siebeck, 2 January 1920, Mohr/Siebeck archives, Tübingen).

339. *GS* I, 605, *ST* II, 577.

340. The pattern is quite crude and does not correspond to historical reality. Of course Troeltsch saw this: he was concerned with basic characteristics. That in principle he shared the concern for historical differentiation and thus for closer definition called for in many reviews is evident, for example, from his distinction between original Calvinism with a Genevan stamp as a kind of modified Lutheranism and its further development in the form of neo-Calvinism. Only the latter then brings out more clearly the features which he indicates. In connection with the need to pay attention to economic conditions and questions of church law from a theological aspect while at the same time taking note of the sociological dimension, from the literature Troeltsch makes particular mention of Hundeshagen, who already adopts such a standpoint in his studies of church history (cf. *GS* I, 605 n.308, *ST* II, 879 n.308; cf. also M.Wichelhaus, *Kirchengeschichtsschreibung und Soziologie im neunzehnten Jahrhundert und bei Ernst Troeltsch*, Heidelberg 1965, 24ff.).

341. *GS* I, 702f., *ST* II, 640.

342. Cf. here F.Rachfahl, 'Nochmals Kalvinismus und Kapitalismus', in *Die protestant-ische Ethik* II, ed. J.Winckelmann, Hamburg 1972, 216ff.

343. In 'Die Kulturbedeutung des Calvinismus', 189; *GS* IV, 785.

344. M.Weber, 'Antikritisches zum "Geist" des Kapitalismus', ibid., 150f. We must not interpret Weber's comment as a noble gesture but as a statement of fact. It was only as a result of the irritation caused by Rachfahl's attack that what Baumgarten in his book on Weber presented as intellectual rivalry between the two (but then in a somewhat exaggerated way) came into being (cf. Baumgarten, *Max Weber*, Tübingen 1964, 624). In the argument with Rachfahl, Troeltsch went on to concede that he had made errors of judgment because of his tendency to generalize, especially in his account of Calvinism, its establishment and extension.

345. Troeltsch finds mixed forms e.g. among the Labadists, a monastic-like house community in Holland, or in the views of Sebastian Franck and Caspar Schwenkfeld. There was always a link between sect and mysticism (cf. *GS* I, 903ff., *ST* II, 799ff.).

346. *GS* I, 798 n.438, *ST* II, 694 n.438.

347. Suffering sects are mainly dominated by religious subjectivity and an orientation on close relations within a community. The aggressive sects proclaim ideas of renewing the world, with a critical impulse towards both church and state. The idea of the holy community and the militant approach is characteristic of this form.

348. In my view, at a meta-level Troeltsch could have accepted that there was a connection or a mediation between the suffering and the aggressive types: religious 'subjectivity' in life-style and roots in a familiar circle as one element; power to shape the world and the cultural criticism which results from adopting a detached position as the other.

349. Thus (in essence) in *GS* I, 938, *ST* II, 994, and literally in *GJ*, 8, *ETWTR*, 186. Rade's comments on the Jatho affair show that the designation is not an original formulation of Troeltsch's (cf. *CW* 1911, no.9, 212; *Jatho und Harnack*, Tübingen 1911, 72). Here Rade speaks of the 'mystery religion of our moderns'; for him it is

characterized by a tendency towards interiorization coupled with a deviation from the historical foundations of Christianity.

350. This basic trait beomes even clearer in Troeltsch's hand-written notes (on *GS* I, 849, *ST* II, 735). 'Mysticism is interiorization, presupposes objectification in cult, rites, dogmas. It is a secondary matter. Paradox of purpose and immediacy.' And further on: 'Mysticism as a concept in the philosophy of religion is to be distinguished from this elemental mysticism. Rise of the "I" to the Godhead and descent of the Godhead to the "I". Emanation and remanation, identity of the process of the soul with that within the Godhead and vice versa.'

351. L.Richter attempts to distinguish between an 'Eastern' kind of mysticism, in which the individual principle is dissolved, and a 'Western type' which brings with it a heightening of the principle of individuality (cf. *RGG*³ IV, 1259ff.). Moreover she distinguishes between a philosophical and a religious mysticism. This is an idea which can also be found in Troeltsch. The difficulties of giving a satisfactory general definition of mysticism are obvious. In connection with the distinction indicated, Troetsch points to the fundamental significance of the mystical union (cf. *GS* I, 851, *ST* II, 737f.).

352. It is another matter that here way and goal or form and content retrospectively coincide. F.Heiler also speaks of a fundamental paradox of mysticism. However, for him, in contrast to Troeltsch, it lies in the fact that the mystical communion with God is expressed only inadequately by the forms of the life of the senses (cf. *Erscheinungsformen und Wesen der Religion*, Stuttgart 1961, 22f.).

353. In this connection Troeltsch vigorously criticizes more recent writing in church history which has not seen the difference between the sect-type and mysticism clearly enough. As far as he is concerned, historical overlaps do not alter the urgent need for differentiation. Here, too, there is stress on the independence of his view from that of Max Weber (*GS* I, 957 n.512, here 958, *ST* II, 988f. n.512, here 989). Troeltsch's reference to a line of continuity in his own work seems to me to be justified here; it needs to be qualified only in the second instance, the Seeberg review (cf. *GS* I, 950 n.510, *ST* II, 987 n.510). The review in question does not yet explicitly contain the element of social history. He extends the approach in terms of the history of ideas in the direction of cultural history and the religious independence of individual epochs of history. Cf. his review of Seeberg's *Dogmengeschichte* in *GGA* 1901, 15-30 (*GS* IV, 739-52).

354. Cf. *GS* I, 864, *ST* II, 742. Troeltsch says critically of both Albrecht Ritschl and Max Weber that they have not paid enough attention to the changed attitude of the mystics to ethics. They have only referred to the absence of asceticism and the basic attitude to the world. But for Troeltsch the real grounds lie in the 'different kind of dogmatic idea and the social character of mysticism' (*GS* I, 921 n.499, here 923, *ST* II,979f. n.499, here 980).

355. Thus Wernle rightly noted in his review that Troeltsch devoted 100 pages of his large book to the Spiritualists, 'although virtually nothing emerges here for social teachings' (*ZTK* 23, 1913, 68). However, Wernle thinks that the description of the individual mystics and their positions is very successful, because it takes up the characteristic elements.

356. *GS* I, 871. The fundamental question is how an internalizing process which always brings God into thought or feeling and which is concerned to intensify

nearness to God or union with God can have any relationship with rational thought in its formal abstract form. Wernle criticizes Troeltsch at this point (cf. ibid., 78).

357. Cf. *GS* I, 926, *ST* II, 769.

358. *GS* I, 935 n.504a, here 936, *ST* II, 985 n.504a.

359. *GS* I, 978, *ST* II, 1004.

360. *GS* I, 981, *ST* II, 1008.

361. Cf. *GS* I, 983, *ST* II 1010. In this connection Troeltsch can make a positive reference to R.Rothe.

362. Cf. Max Weber, *The Protestant Ethic and the Spirit of Capitalism*, London 1930, 181. In Troeltsch we find: 'The Christian-Social ideals which developed alongside these two main types were unable in their day to make any impression on the hard mass of social reality: against this rock they fling themselves in vain today' (*GS* I, 984, *ST* II, 1012). In the handwritten notes to the second edition Troeltsch develops this thought: 'One could speak of a third type, at least to the degree that the romanticizing of the Christian social teachings in the Age of Restoration in fact made often made something new of them. Here it is significant that we also find this romanticizing at all confessional levels.'

363. 'They [the forces of the religious ethical idea] will no more create the kingdom of God on earth as a completed social-ethical organism than any other power in this world. One of the most serious and important insights to have emerged from our investigation is this: that all ideas come up against the brutal facts and all upward movement comes up against internal and external contrasts. There is no absolute Christian ethic which is simply waiting to be discovered: all we can do is control changing situations in the world...' (*GS* I, 985f., *ST* II, 1013).

364. Thus we find: 'The truth is – and this is the conclusion of the whole matter – that the kingdom of God is within us. But we must let our light shine before men in confident and untiring labour that they may see our good works and praise our Father in heaven. The final ends of all humanity are hidden in his hands' (*GS* I, 986, *ST* II, 1013).

Part Four: Philosopher of Culture in Berlin (1915-1923)

1. Letter to W.Bousset, 27 July 1914 (UB Göttingen, unpublished).

2. *Nach Erklärung der Mobilmachung*, Heidelberg 1914, 3. For Troeltsch's political attitude in the war cf. A.Rapp, *Il Problema della Germania negli Scritti Politici di Ernst Troeltsch (1914-1922)*, Rome 1978; R.J.Rubanowice, *Crisis In Consciousness: The Thought of Ernst Troeltsch*, Tallahassee 1982, 99-130; B.Sösemann, ' "Das erneuerte Deutschland". Ernst Troeltschs politisches Engagement in Ersten Weltkrieg', *TRST* 3, 120-44.

3. Ibid., 6. Later, after the war, there were to be criticisms of Troeltsch's formulation and he was asked how his statements then could be reconciled with his support of new conditions, the democratic and humanitarian element. Cf. Troeltsch's lecture 'Der Geist im neuen Deutschland' and the account of the ensuing discussion in *Verhandlungen der Freunde der christlichen Welt*, Marburg 1920, 74.

4. W.Köhler, *Ernst Troeltsch*, Tübingen 1941, 293.

5. Ibid., 13. The historical comparison which Troeltsch makes is significant for the political dimension of the speech. He sees a parallel between the present situation and that of Prussia at the time of the Third Silesian War. As this was a war to defend

possessions, we may conclude that Troeltsch regarded the First World War, too, as a defensive war. Whether it follows from this that all annexionist notions are to be rejected and the issue is merely one of defending territorial possesions is another question. Rather, it can be seen that Troeltsch has 'moderate' annexionist ideas, at least in the first period of the war.

6. *'Unser Volksheer', Rede gehalten am 3.November 1914 in der Vaterländischen Versammlung im Nibelungensaale zu Mannheim*, Heidelberg 1914.

7. Thus, for example we read: 'Only here [in the turning of the soul to the eternal] do we arrive at the point where we are completely at one with our army in the faith that God will sustain to the uttermost the life of our nation and in the obligation to suffer and to endure, to persist and to conquer for his sake' (ibid., 21).

8. *Das Wesen der Deutschen, Rede gehalten am 6.Dezember 1914 in der vaterländischen Versammlung in der Karlsruher Stadthalle*, Heidelberg 1915, 22ff.

9. Ibid., 26.

10. So we read: 'We are the most objective and broad-minded people in the world' (ibid., 27). In the course of these comments Troeltsch was not sparing in his criticism. He saw that there were many defects as well as vices among the Germans and he could connect this with the criticism which he had already directed against the 'neo-Germans'. Cf. here his major speech at the debate in the Evangelical Social Congress in 1907 (in *Verhandlungen des achtzehnten Evangelisch-sozialen Kongresses*, Göttingen 1907, 33-9, especially 34).

11. For Troeltsch, the narrow limits within which any people or nation thinks and lives are evident. The idea of Europeanness is clearly limited by this. According to Troeltsch, it calls for very careful political handling.

12. Troeltsch strikes a clearer note in his work *Deutscher Glaube und deutsche Sitte in unserem grossen Kriege*, which appeared among the Kriegsschriften des Kaiser-Wilhelm-Danks, Vol.9, 1914. Here he has more direct polemic and his concern is more clearly to provide political propaganda. There is a pointed mention of German loyalty and love of order, of German faith and German morality. 'It will be recognized that the secret of German power is not just our military drill, our systematic calculation and order, our cannons and field-grey uniforms, but primarily the holy faith of the German people in itself and the iron loyalty of our moral disposition' (ibid., 9f.). The Germans, he says, need an idea, a faith, from which to derive a moral justification and also a criterion for their action. So it is important to see that the law is morally right (cf. ibid., 18ff.). The discussion of the religious dimension of the war is particularly significant. For Troeltsch, the Christian view of faith in the narrower sense transcends all nationalistic thought and the ethic connected with it. But there is also a general religious dimension, which is arrived at by tracing a feeling of solidarity and a heroic disposition back to the depths of their origin, namely love of the Fatherland as the 'embodiment of the divine idea in the German being' (ibid., 28). Here Troeltsch is speaking of a form of the general revelation of history. Of such a manifestation of the divine he says: 'Here God turns his face to us in storm and fire. We will follow him as he speaks to us here. We know it is not his last nor his only word' (ibid.).

Granted, the universal religious dimension and the revelation that goes with it are transcended in the direction of the Christian understanding. This represents the highest stage. What lies below that, the general religious understanding, nevertheless has its own, albeit limited, function of providing a foundation. Troeltsch sees general religious feeling as a deeper form of patriotic disposition. It is obvious how problematical this notion is, and how open to misunderstanding or misuse. Moreover the difference, at any rate for the audience, between the general religious understanding and the specifically Christian understanding is very small, if it is seen at all. The general religious feeling and such a general religious interpretation of history bestow on the historical *kairos* a religious quality which ultimately remains without a criterion and can be claimed by anyone, even by opponents.

13. *CW* 29, 1915, 294-303. In the context of this question R.Rubanwice draws attention to Troeltsch's Christmas meditation, 'Friede auf Erden', *Die Hilfe*, 1914. His summary verdict is: 'Never able to reconcile satisfactorily the values of Christianity and nationalism, Troeltsch did admit that flag-waving patriotism might have its proper place, but he insisted that men owed their ultimate allegiance to something greater than the national Fatherland' (R.J.Rubanowice, *Crisis in Consciousness*, n.2, 101f.).

14. Letter to Elise Troeltsch, no date, presumably April 1915, Bundesarchiv Koblenz, unpublished.

15. Ibid.

16. Morning edition of the *Berliner Tageblatt*, 2 May 1915.

17. Ibid.

18. Thus in the view of L.Marcuse, *Mein zwangzigstes Jahrhundert*, Zurich 1975, 49.

19. Troeltsch writes: 'Above all, of course, the war and worry about how it will end is a burden. Nothing is clear' (letter to Elise Troeltsch, April 1915, Bundesarchiv Koblenz, unpublished). Troeltsch thinks that he can see a glimmer of hope in Hindenburg's promise that they can be finished with the Russians by May. 'But I am still very anxious for myself and fear the war. That would mean a terrible prolongation [if Italy entered the war]. Gradually the longing for peace is getting very great' (ibid.).

20. Letter to Elise Troeltsch, 14 June 1917; Bundesarchiv Koblenz, unpublished.

21. Ibid.

22. Ibid.

23. Ibid.

24. Letter to Elise Troeltsch, 10 July 1917; Bundesarchiv Koblenz, unpublished.

25. Karl Kaiser (1861-1933) was professor of medicine (physiology) in Heidelberg before moving to Berlin in 1902. His wife Mary (born 1865) was a friend of Getrud von le Fort.

26. Gertrud von le Fort, *Hälfte des Lebens. Erinnerungen*, Munich 1965, 130.

27. Card to G.von le Fort, 30 March 1917, UB Heidelberg, unpublished.

28. Letter to G.von le Fort, 5 November 1917, UB Heidelberg, unpublished.

29. Gertrud von le Fort, *Hälfte des Lebens* (n.26), 134.

30. Letter to G.von le Fort, 14 April 1916, Deutsches Literaturarchiv Marbach; unpublished.

31. Letter to F.Meinecke, 22 September 1915, Geheimes Staatsarchiv Berlin, unpublished.

32. Meinecke, who joined 'Gräca' after Troeltsch's letter of invitation, explains in a true historian's style: 'But there were two Gräcas which traced their origin to Schleiermacher, and each could claim to be the true heir, like the different Johann Maria Farinas in Cologne. In one the real pillars of German Greek scholarship of the time, Wilamowitz and Diels, were the dominant figures; the other, which now

welcomed Troeltsch and me with open arms, was composed of less illustrious figures. Its moving spirit was Otto Schroeder from the Joachimsthal Gymnasium, a humanist of the best kind, a person in whom love of Greece and Germanhood once again seemed to meet at a great depth' (*Werke*, VIII, 240). For relations between Troeltsch and Meinecke cf. H.Bögeholz, 'Berliner Zeitgenossenschaft. Erläuterungen zu Briefen von Ernst Troeltsch an Friedrich Meinecke', *TRST* I, 145-72.

33. *Werke*, VIII, 233.

34. *Werke*, VIII, 234. In Meinecke's Berlin memoirs there is also a reference to Walter Rathenau, who would join Troeltsch, Meinecke and Hintze on their walks, having lain in wait for them in Grunewald. Meinecke observed in a detached way. 'He was rather too witty and artificial for me, as the cultivated Jew sometimes is. Troeltsch yielded more readily to his blinding wisdom, just as Troeltsch in his openness generally was very happy as it were to walk on the Tauentzienstrasse of modern life and be greeted on it...' (*Werke*, VIII, 237).

35. Harnack's daughter wrote what a great gain her father had thought Troeltsch's call to Berlin to be. She quoted a letter from Harnack to Troeltsch: 'It goes without saying that I would have preferred to see you in the theological faculty, but I have always felt that you belonged to Berlin, and that the question of the "regiment" you serve in, while not a matter of indifference, is certainly secondary' (A.von Zahn-Harnack, *Adolf von Harnack*, Berlin ²1951, 340, letter of 29 April 1914. The date is certainly wrong, as Troeltsch's call did not come until July 1914). When the two figures are described in more detail, however, it emerges how different their temperaments were and how Harnack, who was certainly tolerant, judged Troeltsch with a mixture of benevolence and detachment. The following comment is also pertinent here: 'The contrast between the temperaments of Harnack and Troeltsch made their conversations particularly lively and exciting for the audience. Where they agreed on a work, as for example at the Dante celebrations in 1921, there was the most attractive harmony' (ibid., 341). Troeltsch's letters to Harnack also give the impression of detached respect for Harnack: in them the address 'Most respected colleague' or Troeltsch's reference to himself as a pupil are not just mere decoration.

36. Benno Erdmann (1851-1921) specialized in the field of logic and psychology. He made an appearance in the philosophy of history with a work on Kant (1904).

37. Alois Riehl (1844-1924) was a classical neo-Kantian of the 'realist' trend (T.Oesterreich). He was thought to be particularly sober and matter-of-fact in his philosophy. He saw epistemology as the main task of a scientific philosophy; behind this was the notion that experience had to be the foundation of any philosophizing which claimed to be scientific. In the last years of his activity Riehl turned to questions of world-view, in order to fulfil the duty of philosophy to show ways of living. Here his views went, among other things, in the direction of a free religious humanism. Riehl was a systematic philosopher of some status: Rickert praised his great breadth and tolerance (H.Rickert, *Kant als Philosoph der modernen Kultur*, 1924), 127f.
Carl Stumpf (1848-1936) taught in Berlin from 1894. Stumpf was interested in inter-disciplinary work, standing between psychology, music and philosophy, and influenced Husserl's phenomenology by his description of phenomena in the psyche. Mention should also be made of Ernst Cassirer (1874-1945), Privatdozent in philosophy from 1906-1919. Cassirer, who came from a background of Marburg Neo-Kantianism, had already made his mark in the pre-war period with two notable

works: the first was his *Substanzbegriff und Funktionsbegriff* (1910), which was concerned with the development of the scientific world-view and discussed questions of scientific epistemology in connection with this; the second was his great work on the philosophy of history: *Das Erkenntnisproblem in der Philosophie und Wissenschaft der neueren Zeit*, I, 1906; II, 1907. For Cassirer's Berlin period cf. Toni Cassirer, *Mein Leben mit Ernst Cassirer*, Hildesheim 1981, 100f.

38. Max Dessoir (1867-1947) made his mark with works on psychology and aesthetics. In the sphere of psychology he was especially interested in parapsychology, and in aesthetics in the question of a scientific basis for art. Cf. *Von Jenseits der Seele*, 1917, ⁶1931, and *Ästhetik und allgemeine Kunstwissenschaft*, 1906, ²1923.

39. Max Dessoir, *Buch der Erinnerung*, Stuttgart 1946, 177.

40. The topic from the summer semester of 1915, 'General Ethics and the Philosophy of Culture', was repeated three times, in SS 1917, 1919 and 1921. Troeltsch gave three main lecture courses on the philosophy of religion, in WS 1917/18, WS 1919/20 and SS 1922. He gave the course on the philosophy of history in WS 1921/22; he lectured twice on introduction to philosophy in SS 1916 and SS 1918. The seminars were either announced under the title 'Classes in Philosophy' or were concerned with topics wich he had discussed in his studies of historicism, e.g. the concept of a historical dialectic, the Marxist philosophy of history, Wilhelm Wundt's theory of history, Dilthey's theory of history, Simmel's theory of history. The contemporary background is recognizable in the production of the lecture list: the list keeps getting thinner and the paper worse.

41. Cf. also Meinecke, *Werke*. VIII, 245.

42. Dessoir, *Buch der Erinnerung* (n.39), 177.

43. Marcuse, *Mein Zwanzigste Jahrhundert* (n.18), 59. As here with Marcuse, despite the criticism which can be perceived throughout, sympathy for Troeltsch and fascination with his person are the decisive factors; this is evident not least in the incidental comments and the nuances. Thus we find in the continuation of the quotation, 'I had chosen this stormy academic as my mentor' (ibid.).

44. Letter to me from Gerhard Lehmann, 16 August 1985. Ludwig Marcuse reports the same thing (in his autobiography): 'Troeltsch, who examined me in his home on the Reichskanzlerplatz... put a great box of cigars between us, and only one question: on subjectivism in philosophy since Descartes. We conversed for two hours, talked a lot of shop, laughed a lot...' (ibid., 50). How Troeltsch nevertheless showed the flag in basics, in matters of conviction, and would not be manipulated or joked with, is shown by another small matter. He turned down an article by Ludwig Marcuse on Gerhard Hauptmann's *Der Narr in Christo Emmanuel Quint* 'because he found this religious poeticizing awful' (Marcuse, *Mein Zwanzigste Jahrhundert*, n.18, 49). According to Marcuse, the reason Troeltsch gave for this judgment was that 'he did not yet want to allow his religious substance to be destroyed' (ibid.).

45. Werner Sombart, a national economist and sociologist, had already published a variety of major works when he was called to a chair in the University of Berlin. Special mention should be made of *Der moderne Kapitalismus*, I and II (1902): *Sozialismus und soziale Bewegung im 19.Jahrhundert* (1896); *Der Bourgois* (1913). It is clear how close he came to Troeltsch's work and interests, especially his *Social Teachings*. This is further emphasized by the fact that Sombart's methodological standpoint was the Marxist theory of basis and superstructure.

46. Max Scheler gained his Promotion under Rudolf Eucken in Jena (with a thesis on relations between logical and ethical principles) and his Habilitation in Jena in 1899 ('The Transcendental and the Psychologische Method'), and started lecturing in Jena. He then moved to Munich. where in 1906 he lost his lectureship because of objections to his private life.

47. Letter to H.Delbrück, 17 June 1916, Deutsche Staatsbibliothek Berlin, unpublished. The letter also says: 'He called my account of themes and nuances "dogmatic", by which he probably meant "relating to the history of ideas", and essentially kept only to the outward effects. That was all right, as the idea of tolerance as such is economically indifferent...' (cf. W.Sombart, *Der moderne Kapitalismus* I, 1921, 448ff.).

48. Ibid.

49. Letter to C.H.Becker, 30 August 1918, Geheimes Staatsarchiv Berlin, unpublished. At this time (from 1916) Becker held office as the personnel adviser on appointments in the Ministry of Culture.

50. He comments: 'For my part I would very much like to see him appointed extraordinarius somewhere, but I do not think Berlin suitable, since there he would immediately become an agitator instead of getting down peacefully to work' (ibid.). Here Troeltsch is thinking particularly of Bonn, which he thought quite sterile philosophically and where Scheler's work could have been a real breath of fresh air in the desolation and fossilization prevalent there.

51. Friedrich Meinecke, *Werke*, VIII, 248. Things became more peaceful when appointments were discussed, but here too the main emphasis lay on the work of the committee.

52. Ibid., 249.

53. Thus Meinecke ends his vivid picture of relations in the faculty with the comment: 'Our quartet – Hitze, Troeltsch, Herkner and I – drew closer together in the face of the people from Göttingen and the sheepfarm (the reference is to Meinecke's fellow historian Dietrich Schäfer, with whom he fell out in 1915 on the question of war aims) as we called them, but remained quite quiet in the faculty and here at least caused no umbrage' (*Werke*, VIII, 250).

54. The speech on the Kaiser's birthday became a section in the studies of historicism (*GS* III, 111-220); it also appeared as a separate publication. The lecture 'Humanismus und Nationalismus in unserem Bildungswesen' was given at the assembly of the Vereinigung der Freunde des humanistischen Gymnasiums in Berlin and the province of Brandenburg on 28 November 1916 and published later (Berlin 1917, included in *DG*, 211-43). For Troeltsch, 'the gymnasium... is the real school in the scientific sense, and scientific education...' (*DG*, 212). He attacked excessive emphasis on the German self-understanding, but thought it necessary to indicate the distinctiveness of the German nature and the German spirit in the face of a one-sidedly humanistic view.

55. Pädagogische Konferenz im Ministerium der geistliche und Unterrichts-Angelegenheiten am 24. und 25.Mai 1917. Thesen und Verhandlungsbericht, Bundesarchiv Koblenz, NL 182 Spranger 135, Paket 1. For a printed version of the main statements (by Troeltsch and other members of the conference) cf. *ETB*, 235-7.

56. From no.2 of the 'Principles for the discussion on tasks of the professorial chairs for pedagogics at the university', developed by Troeltsch (ibid.).

57. Letter to G. von le Fort, 25 April 1917, UB Heidelberg, unpublished.

58. For this journey see the vivid account by Friedrich Meinecke in the letters to his wife (of 10 December 1917 and 3 December 1917), in Friedrich Meinecke, *Werke*, VI, 92-4. Troeltsch seems to have found little pleasure in the appearance of such colleagues as Eduard Meyer and Gustav Roethe, who hogged the conversation at lunch (cf. ibid., 94).

59. Troeltsch said of his journalistic work in the war that he had brought certain presuppositions to the observation of political phenomena as a result of his time in the Baden First Chamber and his *Social Teachings*. He then continued: 'On the other hand there was the circumstance that I could observe at least some of the great historical events very near to their source and thus gain a deep and vivid impression of the nature of historical destinies, developments and catastrophes in a way which is impossible from books and studies of sources.'

60. Cf. F.Meinecke, *Werke*, VIII, 235ff.

61. Ibid., 234.

62. Cf. Paul Rühlmann, 'Delbrücks Mittwochabend', in *Am Webstuhl der Zeit. Eine Erinnerungsgabe, Hans Delbrück, dem 80jährigen, von Freunden und Schülern dargebracht*, ed. E.Daniels and P.Rühlmann, Berlin 1928.

63. Hobohm was a Privatdozent in Berlin. The pressure group named after him was an attempt to influence public opinion in Germany by journalism. It embraced the 'moderate' trend and should be seen as close to, yet distinct from, the German National Committee for an Honourable Peace, which was founded at around the same time. Its influence was limited by lack of support given by the authorities, in particular the Reich government. Finally, mention should be made of a larger official organization, the Volksbund für Freiheit und Vaterland, but this was only founded in December 1917; it will be mentioned later.

64. 'Der Kulturkrieg. Rede vom 1.Juli 1915', *Deutsche Reden in schwerer Zeit*, Berlin 1915.

65. A letter to the Heidelberg historian Hermann Oncken shows how Troeltsch understood his task in political apologetic. Of the 'spirit of German culture' he wrote aptly that it was 'the sole object of attack in all more serious literature'. So these attacks had to be countered. He enjoyed this task very much. It emerges from the letter that Troeltsch took on commissions (letter to H.Oncken, 14 February 1915, Niedersächsisches Staatsarchiv in Oldenburg).

66. This Petition of the Intellectuals, which was delivered to the Reich Chancellor in 1915 and mainly corresponded with the associations addressed, contained 1,347 signatures, 352 from college teachers. The counter-declaration found far fewer supporters – only 141. The Petition of the Intellectuals was initiated by Reinhold Seeberg (1859-1935), professor of theology in Berlin. In political ideology and pragmatically this petition largely coincided with the views of the Pan-Germans. Maximum demands, like a protectorate for Belgium and the incorporation of Russian territory, were made. The text can be found in *Aufrufe und Reden deutscher Professoren im Ersten Weltkrieg*, ed. Klaus Böhme, Reclams Universal-Bibliothek 9787, 1975, 125-35. For details see above all B.Sösemann, who used the illuminating diaries of Theodor Wolff for his account, in 'Das "erneuerte Deutschland", Ernst Troeltschs politischen Engagement im Ersten Weltkrieg', *TRST* 3, 130ff.; cf. also A.von Zahn-Harnack, *Adolf von Harnack* (n.35), 361ff.

67. Cf. Sösemann, 'Das "Erneuerte Deutschland" ', 131.

68. Letter to G. Traub, 24 February 1915, Bundesarchiv Koblenz. I am grateful to

H.Renz for drawing my attention to this letter. Traub's political career, after supporting Naumann's ideas (cf. *Ethik und Kapitalismus*, 1904), led increasingly in a nationalist direction (Fatherland Party: Deutschnationale Volkspartei). There are further references in G.Mehnert, *Evangelische Kirche und Politik 1917-1919*, Düsseldorf 1959, 57ff., 145ff.

69. Ibid. These are the maximum demands which Troeltsch contemplated. At the same time it can be recognized that, given the general political spectrum, this is a moderate line. He significantly remarked that the German spirit should not be imposed on other peoples: 'it is for the Germans and not for the world'. According to Troeltsch, the Germans have enough to do keeping their own house in order. As the moral idea of German politics he gives 'that of the freedom of a state system in which there is mutual recognition'. In foreign policy, for him Austria is 'the black spot in our politics, above all Hungary'. It was Austria-Hungary which first produced the difficult situation in foreign politics. 'They [Austria and those who support its policy] brought the whole thing down on us with their crazy policy for southern Slavonia.'

70. F.Naumann, *Mitteleuropa*, Berlin 1915; *Werke*, IV, 491. Naumann wrote many articles on the question of Central Europe which appeared in *Die Hilfe* from February 1915 on before he brought out his book in October 1915. Hermann Oncken, in his work *Das alte und das neue Mitteleuropa. Historisch-politische Betrachtungen über Deutsche Bündnispolitik im Zeitalter Bismarcks und dem Zeitalter des Weltkrieges*, Gotha 1917, sought to expand Naumann's ideas both historically and politically. For Oncken, Naumann's 'sensitive deepening of such arguments' (ibid., 96) and his characteristic intellectual verve did not always bring the necessary clarity, and above all was not sufficiently close to reality. Troeltsch welcomed the appearance of Oncken's book on Central Europe. He thought it had appeared at just the right time (letter to H.Oncken, 20 November 1917, Niedersächsiches Staatsarchiv in Oldenburg). Compared with Troeltsch's approach, Oncken's lacks critical overtones, there is generally no reflection on a nationalistic attitude, which is evident throughout, and a 'victory-peace' is still (1917) thought attainable.

71. 'Imperialismus', *Die neue Rundschau* XXVI, January 1915, 8.

72. For this complex of questions see G.Schmidt, *Deutscher Historismus und der Übergang zur parlamentarischen Demokratie*, Lübeck and Hamburg 1964. Schmidt assumes that from 1917 on Troeltsch arrived at a different atittude, but qualifies this assumption in two ways. First he refers to the normativeness of facts which is perceived by Troeltsch, and secondly reflects whether 'his thought did not contain elements of different programmes which conversely allowed him a quite personal, conspicuous and relatively independent atttitude in situations' (ibid., 186). B.Sösemann indicates the perspectives to be noted in answering this question. First, attention must be paid to the various publications or organs of publication with their differing attitude and their specific publics; secondly, it must be noted that after moving to Berlin Troeltsch had far better sources of information. Accordingly, Sösemann assumes a change between the time in Heidelberg and that in Berlin. 'The statements from the last months of the Heidelberg period differ both in theme and in the accents of their rhetoric from those of the Berlin years, i.e. from spring 1915' (ibid., 127). The arguments advanced by both Schmidt and Sösemann deserve consideration. In my view this was a gradual – but not continuous – process which took place during 1916. The possibilities for this process were given by Troeltsch's

basic position, but he was encouraged above all by his insight into the military situation.

73. The reason given here by Troeltsch is one from history and the necessity imposed by it. At the same time he recalls the geographical location of Germany and the military situation connected with it. Troeltsch's argument is less political than apologetic and situational. But we might ask whether the monarchy as a state form must necesarily be seen in connection with a protective function and what political and military consequences can legitimately be drawn for Germany's geographical situation.

74. *DG*, 87f.

75. In 'Ideen von 1914', *Die neue Rundschau* 1916, 618. The phrase 'ideas of 1914' comes from a book by the Swedish constitutional lawyer Kjellén (*Die Ideen von 1915*, Leipzig 1915), who took the phrase from a book by the German sociologist J.Plenge, *Der Krieg und die Volkswirtschaft*, Münster ²1915. In his diagnosis of the time Plenge spoke of a 'spiritual revolution' and coined the expression in this connection.

76. Pacifism had very few supporters at that time among the professors, even among the theologians. But it was a tendency to be found among some significant liberal theologians, e.g. Martin Rade. For this intention in Rade and the problems associated with it cf. Christoph Schwöbel, *Martin Rade*, Gütersloh 1980, 176.

77. Thus we find in the article 'Der Völkerkrieg und das Christentum': 'We live in a double world, and through transition and detachment grow from the kingdom of ethicized nature into the kingdom of God, each in his own way...' (*CW* 1915, 15, 301).

78. That is shown, for example, by the remark, '...just as no one can break us in pieces, so we cannot break the others in pieces. People must somehow become aware of that and draw the necessary conclusions', in 'Politik des Mutes und Politik der Nüchternheit', *Das neue Deutschland. Wochenschrift für konservativen Fortschritt* 4, 1915/16, nos.41-5 (22 July 1916), 375.

79. Ibid., 376f.

80. The electoral reform was a reform of the Prussian three-class electoral system, which was to be modified in accordance with the Kaiser's Easter Message of 7 April 1917. This ran: 'After the tremendous contributions of the whole people in this fearful war it is my conviction that there is no longer any room for a class electoral system in Prussia. Furthermore, the draft law will have to provide for the direct and secret election of deputies' (from J.Hohlfeld, ed., *Dokumente der Deutschen Politik und Geschichte von 1848 bis zur Gegenwart*, II, Berlin nd, 345f.). In the view of the conservative party the reform was not in keeping with either the nature or the specific past of the Prussian state. Of contemporary authors, attention should be paid to F.Meinecke, 'Die Reform des preussischen Wahlrechts', *Werke*, II, 146ff.; his 'Osterbotschaft, Wahlreform und parlamentarisches Regime', ibid., 174ff., also deserves mention. The declaration on electoral reform (printed in ibid., 194) was signed among others by Hans Delbrück, Adolf von Harnack, Friedrich Meinecke and Ernst Troeltsch. There is a discussion of the question in connection with Meinecke and Troeltsch in G.Schmidt, *Deutscher Historismus und der Übergang zur Parlamentarischen Demokratie*, 103ff. (for Troeltsch in particular cf. 189). Cf. also Max Weber, 'Die Wahlrechtsnotgesetze des Reichs. Das Recht der heimkehrenden Krieger. Das preussische Wahlrecht', *Gesamtausgabe* I/15, 215-35.

81. Troeltsch will also have taken the audience into account above all in formulating

his third notion, and will also have had the readership of the journal ('conservative progressives') in view.

82. Ibid., 377. Furthermore, according to Troeltsch one can expect a reduction of the influence of individualistic democratic thought through the 'tradition of common sense and discipline' rooted in the German people. However, the critical undertones in this article are also evident.

83. Cf. Max Weber, 'Der Verschärfte U-Boot Krieg', in *Gesamtausgabe* I/15, 115ff. In March 1916 Weber had sent to party leaders, deputies he knew and the Foreign Office the text of a memorandum in which he discussed with convincing rational arguments the advantages and disadvantages of the military measures envisaged. His personal commitment and judgment emerge when he states: 'From the beginning of the war, the undersigned has had the unconditional confidence that we would come out of it with honour. For the first time, in view of such happenings and the chance that because of such an uncertain mission a war with America might come within the realms of possibility, he has serious anxiety both for the land and possibly for the future of the dynasty' (ibid., 152).

84. Cf. 'Der Ansturm der westlichen Demokratie', in *Deutsche Freiheit*, Gotha 1917, 80. However, it is equally clear that Troeltsch had strong political reservations about Tirpitz and his followers. Thus in a letter to Herrmann Oncken he says that a toing and froing between the exuberance of victory and political depression is characteristic of the Germans and then continues: 'In both the wire-pullers have their underlying purposes and the faction of Herr von Tirpitz thrives' (letter to H.Oncken, 20 November 1917, Niedersächsisches Staatsarchiv in Oldenburg, unpublished).

85. 'Der Ansturm der westlichen Demokratie' (n.84), 89.

86. Accordingly: 'There is no completely pure democracy in any major state in the world. It would be possible only in small, self-sufficient agricultural cantons, of the kind that only that enthusiastic chief theoretician of democracy, J.J.Rousseau, conjectured' ('Der Ansturm der westlichen Demokratie', n.84, 96).

87. It follows from this that future peace is not guaranteed 'intrinsically by any of the state forms' (ibid., 112).

88. Letter to Elise Troeltsch, 10 July 1917, Bundesarchiv Koblenz, unpublished. His obituary of Bethmann-Hollweg (10 January 1921) was more positive, but that is the case with obituaries. Critical comments are usually expressed in a veiled form. Thus Troeltsch thought that in Bethmann-Hollweg 'we have someone who was a great personality in his way. He mistrusted the famous Reichstag resolution because it did not have a favourable psychological effect on the army or abroad and disrupted the negotiations which he had in mind but could not yet hint at, though he agreed with its content' (*DG*, 256). After an interval of time and in view of the new circumstances Troeltsch could become more positive about Bethmann-Hollweg's personality, seeing how this man who was originally and by nature conservative put the emphasis on a moral renewal of the people, combining with it a degree of readiness for political reform.

89. *Werke*, VIII, 235.

90. Letter to H.von Schubert, 26 December 1917, in the possession of E.Dinkler-von Schubert, unpublished. Or he writes at the beginning of 1918 that the all-important thing is for the U-boat war still to have an effect in time, although a real assessment of the situation is hardly possible. He ends his remarks: 'Firm resolution without

illusions, that is now the only thing' (letter to H.von Schubert of 7 February 1918), in the possession of E.Dinkler-von Schubert, unpublished.

91. Cf. J.Rathje, *Die Welt des freien Protestantismus*, Stuttgart 1952, 256f.

92. Opening address to the Berlin assembly of the 'Volksbund für Freiheit und Vaterland', 7 January 1918, in *Deutsche Politik, Wochenschrift für Welt-und Kulturpolitik*, Berlin 1918, 73.

93. Ibid. It becomes clear how strongly these reflections sought to anticipate attacks from the conservative side and at the same time provide protection against exploitation from outside for propaganda purposes, when he says: 'That has nothing to do with the theories of English and French parliamentarianism, and the development is wholly dependent on the specific circumstances which come about on the basis of a changed Prussian electoral law' (ibid., 74).

94. Ibid., 76. The expression 'demobilization of spirits' was a phrase current at this time, and is to be regarded as a counter to the slogan 'mobilization of souls', used at the beginning of the war.

95. The degree to which Troeltsch is concerned not to terrify the nationalist thinkers in his audience but rather to win them over to the idea of the Volksbund becomes clear when he declares: 'We truly want to give nothing to the foe who sought and still seeks to annihilate us, and to give up nothing which is indispensable to us from the standpoint of the world situation' (ibid., 77).

96. Ibid., 78.

97. Cf. *The Times*, 10 May 1918.

98. The article states: 'It would be impossible to resume intercourse with German scholars until they had renounced the crimes against civilization which Germany had committed. But if such a change of mind should take place when Germans discovered the truth, British scholars might assist the process of conversion by which alone Germany could win readmission to the fellowship of civilized nations' (ibid.).

99. 'Through German Eyes', *The Times*, 11 May 1918, 5f.

100. *The Times*, 17 May, 5; cf. Hans Rollmann, 'Die Beziehungen Ernst Troeltschs zu England und Schottland', *TRST* 3, 319-31. Rollmann explains what significance this controversy had for the invitation of Troeltsch to a lecture tour in England in 1923.

101. *Frankfurter Zeitung und Handelsblatt*, 2 June 1918.

102. Hans Volkelt, *Demobilisierung der Geister? Eine Auseinandersetzung vornehmlich mit Geheimrat Prof. Dr. Ernst Troeltsch*, Munich 1918. Volkelt states that anyone who speaks of a compromise peace, as Troeltsch does, must be taught that he basically means a peace of renunciation. Anyone who talks of a demobilization of spirits in opposition to the slogan 'the mobilization of souls' at the beginning of the war, and thinks that 'this gentle disposition is... the right instrument for ending the war', is fundamentally mistaken (ibid., 10).

103. The charge is one of having an impracticable world-view which is incapable of action and in particular of lacking a healthy patriotic instinct. According to Volkelt, what the Fatherland needs are men with a hard will, men who are not moved by a gentle natural-law idealism but by a consistent nationalistic attitude. In practice this amounts to the propagation of an unbending will to endure. The way in which this work of Volkelt's and Troeltsch's view were judged around twenty-five years later in an official document sheds significant light on later political developments: Volkelt was being called to a chair of psychology in Leipzig. The report on Volkelt reads:

'From the platform of his psychological science, as early as 1918 for the first time he intervened in the political struggle by attacking in his brief work *Demobilization of Spirits?* the ideas of the Volksbund für Freiheit und Vaterland which had newly been founded at that time from the democratic and Marxist side and which were advocated by Troeltsch. In subtle yet sharp polemic he pointed out the dangers of the pacifism expressed there for our waging of the war' (letter of 23 December 1942 to the 'Hauptamt Wissenschaft', American Committee For The Study Of War Documents – T81 Roll nos.60, 61: I owe the reference to this and other sources to D.Piecha of Hagen).

104. 'Anklagen auf Defaitismus', *Deutsche Politik* 3, 661-9: 663.

105. Ibid., 667. 'Real political' means 'given the war situation', and 'moral' means that nothing is gained by a hardening of standpoints on either side. Rather, it is highly probable 'that the peoples will passionately rebel against this policy of hardening, if one has nothing else to say to them' (ibid., 669).

106. Letter to G.von le Fort of 11 November 1918, UB Heidelberg, unpublished.

107. Ibid. The example of Friedrich Meinecke shows that Troeltsch was not alone in expressing such deep concern and criticism and (initially) looking towards the future. On 21 October 1918 Meinecke wrote to the Marburg pathologist L.Aschoff: 'Each individual among us must now prefer to die honourably rather than to continue in a downtrodden national existence' (*Werke*, VI, 95). Meinecke then goes on: 'In any circumstances,a fearful, gloomy existence awaits us! And much as my hatred burns against the predatory nature of our enemies, my wrath and indignation is also hot against the German politicians of violence who have dragged us into this abyss through their arrogance and their stupidity' (ibid., 97).

108. *Spektator-Briefe* (= *SB*), 69.

109. The 'Spektator-Briefe', which appeared in *Kunstwart* between 1918 and 1922, give some impression of Troeltsch's political ideas and the attempt to influence the situation and people's thoughts by political journalism, above all in the sphere of citizenship and intelligence. The letters first appeared under the pseudonym 'Spectator'; later (from 1920) they were signed. From July 1920 they appeared at longer intervals. In addition to these 'Spectator Letters' we must consider other publications, some of which also appeared in *Kunstwart*, like the article on 'Aristocracy' or that on 'Madness or Development? The Decision of World History', 'Socialism', and 'The Intellectual Revolution'. The quotations are from Hans Baron's 1924 edition of the *Spektator-Briefe* because it is more easily accessible. Where other passages are cited, indications are given. One defect of the book edition (which Hans Baron describes as 'compiled by') is that Baron offers the reader a subsequent systematization, departing from the chronological sequence and inserting passges which indicate the development in retrospect. For further information and explanation see *ETB*, 6f.

110. Letter to H.Delbrück, 25 August 1919, Deutsche Staatsbibliothek Berlin, unpublished.

111. Thus Troeltsch's critical comment to Delbrück, ibid.

112. 16 November 1918, *SB*, 4. There is a link with the positive assessment of militarism in the war period in the form of some incidental comments. Troeltsch's political attitude after the war has been studied above all by E.Kollmann, 'Eine Diagnose der Weimarer Republik. Ernst Troeltschs politische Anschauungen', *HZ* 189, 1956, 291-319; G.Schwarz, 'Deutschland und Westeuropa bei Ernst

Troeltsch', *HZ* 191, 1960, 50-47; H.Ruddies, 'Soziale Demokratie und freier Protestantismus. Ernst Troeltsch in den Anfängen der Weimarer Republik', *TRST* 3, 145-74.

113. 30 November 1918, *SB*, 25.

114. 30 November 1918, *SB*, 26.

115. 30 November 1918, *SB*, 24. There are similar comments in the diaries of Harry Graf Kessler. He reports (12 November 1918) that during the days of revolution the trams kept running despite the street fights in Berlin. 'Nor did the electric light, water or telephone go off for a moment. The revolution was never more than a small whirlpool in the public life of the city, which flowed peacefully round it along its accustomed courses' (*Tagebücher 1918 bis 1937*, Frankfurt am Main 1982, 23). And on 17 November Graf Kessler comments: 'First Sunday after the Revolution. In the late afternoon great masses of walkers moved down the Linden as far as Marstall, to see the traces of the fights on the buildings. All very peaceful, with the usual bourgeois curiosity' (ibid., 30).

116. Cf. *SB* 22f., 125ff.

117. Of Delbrück's speech he says: 'He remarked that the faith of the historian in all his previous criteria and presuppositions is tottering. But here Goethe's saying applies: "And no power and no time fragments a shaped form which develops in a living way." I went away without faith in this shaped form, since we could see that it was precisely its "shape", the military form and the spirit among the masses which went with it, that was incurably shattered' (*SB* 24f.).

118. Accordingly, he says: 'I believe today that we will succeed in overcoming the Bolshevism among us...' (30 December 1918, *SB*, 28). Or he speaks of the 'threatening clouds which constantly rise again from the councils or the system of soviets' (20 March 1919, *SB*, 44). And on the two other points he comments: 'It is now hard to say how far elections and a national assembly can clarify this chaos [brought about by the politics of entente, the demobilization of the army and the changed relationships of political power]. Only one thing is evident: the unity and order of the Reich rest on the machinery of the Social Democratic party' (14 January 1919, *SB*, 32; cf. also 15 February 1919, *SB*, 42).

119. In these reflections Troeltsch regards the 'German spirit' more critically than he did during the war (cf. 20 April 1919, *SB*, 50).

120. 5 June 1919; *SB*, 61.

121. 23 May 1919; *SB*, 52.

122. 19 June 1991; *SB*, 314, 318.

123. There is repeatedly sharp criticism of the Centre Party generally and Erzberger in particular, cf. *SB*, 35, 68, 72f., 79, 112.

124. In the form of plans for the socialization of the economy; in tendencies to level out education and establish aims hostile to religion.

125. 19 December 1919, *SB*, 93.

126. 6 April 1920, *SB*, 129.

127. *Kunstwart* 33, 1919, 55.

128. He regards upbringing as upbringing for responsibility; at the same time part of the principle of upbringing must be the acceptance of others in their exalted position.

129. From this perspective, in his criticism Troeltsch can pick up his earlier view. Thus in 1907 he criticized 'democratic' individualism for its abstract, ordinary conception of equality and distinguished it from a view of personality which is

shaped by a sense of history and an understanding of art, by a power of sensitivity and a formative will. This 'other' individualism respects the individual in his particular intellectual and cultural capacities and at the same time takes seriously the power which the individual derives from the tradition (cf. *GS* IV, 5, 318ff., 335ff.).

130. The concrete political diagnosis is supported by a general theory. At all events, for him more recent history points in the direction of democratic thought and the democratic state form. The origin of the modern giant states, the concentration of · the populace in the great cities, the increasing industrialization, leave no alternative. The argument, the beginnings of which were present in the war publicity, becomes more significant.

131. 'Social democracy' must be distinguished from 'socialistic democracy', in which for Troeltsch the old power relationships are reversed and utopianism determines the formation of political ideas and aims. We should probably also interpret Troeltsch as saying that the notion of 'social' democracy takes up the specific possibilities of the German spirit to the degree that this favours the notion of community and thus represents a corrective to an abstract individualism backed up by ideology. If democracy is realized in Germany as social democracy, then for Troeltsch it 'will be able *a priori* to heal or exclude part of the affliction that clings to it' (29 December 1918, *SB*, 307). For Troeltsch, the expression 'social democracy' also implies a critical dissociation from the 'Western form', which on the basis of capitalist economic structure and praxis sets itself above the justified interests of the lower class.

132. E.g. *SB*, 68f., 223ff.

133. Friedrich Meinecke, Introduction to *Spektator-Briefe*, Tübingen 1924, vif.

134. It is evident that in his criticism Troeltsch did not stand alone in the bourgeois camp, above all among the intellectuals. One example out of many is to be found in Harry Graf Kessler's diaries. He gives a brief account of Ebert, ostensibly about his outward appearance, but saying considerably more. In a diary entry on 16 November 1918 Kessler wrote: 'Ebert with his black Van Dyke beard and his broad, stocky frame looks like someone from the south of France, a ship's captain from Marseilles' (*Tagebücher*, 29; cf. also ibid., 139).

135. There is no question that these are ideas from Naumann's thought-world, which Troeltsch already expressed in embryonic form during the war. Thus he remarked in 1921: 'Only a nationalistic feeling coming from the modern German worker and largely taking in the lower classes can be the basis for a real union [in view of the cultural and confessional differences in Germany] and a real resistance [to the political and economic pressure of the powers of the Entente]' (8 February 1921, *SB*, 175).

136. 11 September 1922; *SB*, 291.

137. Thus on 23 September 1919 he writes in a letter to Rudolf Paulus: 'I've now joined the editors, to help more in name than with work. I'm not a real democrat. I'm merely a rational democrat. Present-day parliamentarianism is just a caricature. But it is a price that we had to pay so as not all to be shot dead like the people in Russia' (this letter is in private hands; it was made available to me by H.Renz).

138. Cf. the remark by Hagen Schulze: 'It was a vicious circle: the less the Republic opposed suspicion and taunts, the more contemptible it appeared in public. Moreover, it was unable to gain a following or sympathy. It had no exciting ideas;

in a time when exaltation set the tone, a democracy with a concern for moderation and compromise found it hard to gain followers' (in *Weimar Deutschland 1917-1933. Die Deutschen und ihre Nation*, 4, Berlin 1982, 208).

139. The murder of Walter Rathenau in particular left a mark on Troeltsch, both politically and personally. He rightly saw the wide political implications of the event. His article in memory of Walter Rathenau (*Die Neue Rundschau* 2, 1922, 787ff., later *DG*, 258-64) shows how he could empathize with a man and his work and how he could also draw relevant political conclusions from the event. Because Troeltsch was ready to respect a person's characteristics, he could give an apt description of Rathenau's somewhat complex character and image. His assessment of Rathenau is an indirect critical indication of what he found lacking in other ministers of the Reich government, namely intellectual aristocracy and the capacity to cope with political tasks with a combination of relevant knowledge and diplomatic skill. Cf. also Troeltsch's comment in his article 'The Most Dangerous Times', the Spektator Brief of 7 July 1922, *SB*, 285. In his 'Memoirs of a Moralist', Hans Sahl reports that on the day of Walter Rathenau's murder Troeltsch began his lecture with the words 'The enemy is on the right wing' (cf. H.Sahl, *Memoiren eines Moralisten*, Darmstadt and Neuwied 1985, 62).

140. In an obituary of Max Weber, Troeltsch wrote: 'In the depths of his soul he was a politician, a natural ruler and an ardent patriot who saw his country on a false course and passionately desired to take over the leadership...' (*DG*, 250).

141. So we read: 'One cannot decide [on the renunciation of German political power] without deep resignation. But resignation seems to me to be necessary for the foreseeable future, and in my view German politics must in principle arrive at a similar conclusion' (8 February 1921, *SB*, 172).

142. Nowhere does the connection between political views, a philosophy of history and ethics become as evident in any of Troeltsch's last works as in his lecture on 'Natural Law and Humanity in World Politics' (1922). This shows all the merits of Troeltsch's way of thinking, the broad historical orientation, both intellectual and cultural, on these basic concepts of European and American thought. Reference to the historical development helps the political diagnosis of the time, and cultural history becomes politically relevant. Here we have the thesis, developed in detail in the *Social Teachings* and the works on the history of culture, that the ideas of individuality or humanity differ, depending on whether they are derived through Western European and American natural-law thinking or Romanticism, as in the case of Germany. The reflections take a course familiar from Troeltsch's works on cultural history and the philosophy of history: there is research into what has been and a concern for the will that is to shape the future. A cultural synthesis in the present must be orientated on the political and ethical ideas of the tradition, and must seek to embrace the dualism of German Romantic thinking and the Western European world of ideas without simply levelling out what has grown up through history. This outline of a synthesis is on the one hand conceived of in abstract terms, as it were as a play of ideas, yet on the other becomes effective in real politics as a background to thought and a political motive for the formation of the will. Thomas Mann, whose political development was similar to that of Troeltsch, evaluated the lecture in a newspaper article, 'Naturrecht und Humanität', *Frankfurter Zeitung*, 25 December 1923, reprinted in *Aufsätze, Reden, Essays*, Vol.3, Berlin 1986, 428-31.

143. The supporters of the German Democratic Party came from the camp of the

Progressive People's Party and the National Liberal Party. They had a liberal tendency in common. Freedom of mind was asked for, in order to arrive at an insight into the reasons for, and background to, the defeat of Germany and the need for change. The party history reports the difficulties which arose here, especially over the last point. Cf. above all W.Stephan, *Aufstieg und Verfall des Linksliberalismus 1918-1933*, Göttingen 1972; from contemporary literature mention should be made of T.Heuss, *Die neue Demokratie*, 1920; F.Naumann, *Die Demokratie in der Nationalversammlung*, 1920. For the foundation of the party cf. T.Wolff, *Die Wilhelminische Epoche, Fürst Bülow am Fenster und andere Begegnungen*, edited with an introduction by B.Sösemann, Frankfurt am Main 1989, XXVIff.

144. The ideas about the private economy have an anti-socialist bent and were already used in the election propaganda for the elections to the constituent National Assembly at the beginning of 1919.

145. Cf. the programme of the German Democratic Party, Leipzig, 13-15 November 1919, in *Deutsche Parteiprogramme seit 1861*, ed. W.Treue, Göttingen 1968, 135-40. The proximity to Naumann's ideas in the general points of social policy is unmistakable.

146. Troeltsch's critical reflections on the last point move in the direction of arguing that the church should now feel the same obligation to society as a whole as it had to the state previously (cf. 'Der Religionsunterricht und die Trennung von Staat und Kirchen', ed. F.Thimme and E.Rolffs, in *Revolution und Kirche*, Berlin 1919, 301ff.).

147. Letter to A.von Harnack, 28 March 1919, Deutsche Staatsbibliothek, Berlin, unpublished. Troeltsch takes the same line in a letter to the dean of the philosophy faculty on 23 April 1919: 'In the difficult situation of forming a coalition government, refuge would then be taken in the quite new creation of parliamentary secretaries of state to hold an essentially socialist government to the basic laws of the coalition and to control it. Like the membership of the Centre Party, I have adopted such a position so as not to allow it to fall into the hands of a radical state school teacher. For me personally it was a sacrifice, as it is an unpaid honorary office with much work' (Archiv der Humboldt-Universität Berlin, Bestand 1468, Blatt 57; I am grateful to H.Renz for the reference. There is also a reference in K.-E.Apfelbacher, *Frömmigkeit und Wissenschaft*, Munich 1978, 265).

148. The former Prussian Ministry of Clerical, Educational and Medical Affairs was renamed the Ministry of Science, Art and National Education, following the vocabulary of the time (Volksbildung) and in fact (without Clerical Affairs) corresponding to the principle of a separation of state and church.

149. Letter to A.von Harnack, 28 March 1919, Deutsche Staatsbibliothek Berlin, unpublished.

150. Letter to the dean, 23 April 1919, archive of the Humboldt-Universität, Berlin. Moreover in this letter Troeltsch assures the dean that he has taken into account all reservations in this direction and in particular asks his colleagues on the faculty to have confident in his tact. According to Troeltsch, in a real conflict of interests he would resign as under-secretary of state. In a supplementary letter of 19 May 1919, Troeltsch once again comments on the question: 'If the doubts have not been sufficiently dispelled, I would add that I have asked the Minister to inform me as little as possible about university matters out of a concern for the doubts which have

arisen in my faculty' (Archives of the Humboldt-Universität, philosophical faculty, Bestand 1468, p.61).

151. So he writes to the dean: 'I am also essentially concerned with developments in church matters which are so time-consuming that there is little time for anything else' (ibid.).

152. Cf. Emil Herrmann, *Über die notwendigen Grundlagen einer die konsistoriale und synodale Ordnung vereinigenden Kirchenverfassung*, 1862.

153. Günther Holstein thinks that for Emil Herrmann the consistorial element meets 'a real need in the Protestant church constitution' (*Die Grundlagen des Evangelischen Kirchenrechts*, Tübingen 1928, 200). He then continues: 'Indeed, even if the connection with church government by the local ruler which now exists should be lost. For it is not its nature to be an auxiliary institution for church government: church government by the local ruler and consistory are certainly connected in historical reality, but they do not necessarily belong together' (ibid.).

154. The justification for and significance of the status of a corporation in public law was the subject of controversy in the subsequent period from both the legal and the theological side. But there was widespread agreement that it understood the principle of the separation of state and church to be limited rather than radical, and that the status of a corporation in public law was given to the church in a special way, so that this status was *sui generis*. Cf. E.Forsthoff, *Lehrbuch des Verwaltungsrechts*, Vol.1, Munich and Berlin 1951, 373ff.; H.Liermann, *Deutsches Evangelisches Kirchenrecht*, Stuttgart 1933, 186ff.

155. 'Political parties are political and economic machines and their value lies primarily in their having some of the properties of organizations and machines', in *Bericht über die Verhandlungen des 2.Ausserordentlichen Parteitags der Deutschen Demokratischen Partei (13-15 Dezember 1919 in Leipzig)*, ed. Reichsgeschäftstelle, 166.

156. Relativizing words on ideology were probably also found because of the party-political situation, in view of both the Social Democrats, whose significance for the work of government was undisputed, and the Centre Party, which for Troeltsch was always also the vehicle of religious culture. However, the coalition question will not have been the only reason for Troeltsch to speak in this way. Rather, it shows that his thought also went beyond party lines, and that an interest merely in tactical voting was not enough for him.

157. Ibid., 179.

158. Ibid., 179f.

159. Cf. ibid., 181.

160. Ibid., 186. In the subsequent discussion Martin Rade took a positive attitude to the main content of the report, stressing its depth and breadth, and its indication of new cultural ideals. His criticism was in two directions: first, he felt that the renunciation of an ideological basis and orientation for the party was a notable lack; and secondly, he commented critically that Troeltsch had attempted to give the party as a whole a Protestant tone.

161. 'Die Religionsunterricht und die Trennung von Staat und Kirchen', in *Revolution und Kirche*, 323.

162. Cf. Troeltsch's comments in the lecture 'Der Geist im neuen Deutschland', *Verhandlungen der Freunde der christlichen Welt in Eisenach*, Marburg 1920, 17.

163. Thus Troeltsch in 'Briefe über religiöses Leben und Denken im gegenwärtigen

Deutschland (V)', *Schweizerische Theologische Zeitschrift* 36, 1919, 144. The article and the redactional note are dated 7 February 1919.

164. 'Die Kundgebungen des Dresdener Kirchentages', *Die Hilfe* 25, 1919, 565ff. Cf. Mehnert, *Evangelische Kirche und Politik* (n.68), 213-34, and K.Nowak, *Evangelische Kirche und Weimarer Republik*, 1981, 68-71.

165. Ibid. 567.

166. Report by Troeltsch on behalf of the Ministry for the Constituent Prussian Assembly, 8 July 1920. Cf. also his subsequent personal comment. Troeltsch criticizes the bureaucratic procedure 'that the electoral lists are compiled by the church authorities themselves from the taxation lists and other materials. I regard that as a significant flaw in the law, the consequence of which will be that a whole mass of people will not want to go through these formalities' (*Sitzungsbericht der Verfassunggebenden Preussischen Landesversammlung*, Vol.20, 11769).

167. See Mehnert, *Evangelische Kirche und Politik* (n.68), 16, who reports a similar initiative – relating to the Hesse Consistory in Kassel – by Kirchenrat Bernhard Ritter of Marburg. At the same time it is clear that Troeltsch took a critical view of the provisional transference of church government by the local ruler to three 'ministers *in evangelicis*'. The nomination of these ministers was a compromise over the transference of church government by the local ruler (state government on the one hand – church government on the other). Troeltsch, probably following an official line, sees here a transitional regulation 'so that the continuity of law can be restored and sustained' (ibid., 11768). J.R.C. Wright has found material which sheds more light on this question of church law. Troeltsch is in favour of the church deciding on what the electoral procedure is to be for the constituent church assembly. So in terms of church law a strengthening of the synodical principle is envisaged: all in all a compromise between state and church. Cf. J.R.C.Wright, 'Ernst Troeltsch als parlamentarischer Unterstaatssekretär im preussischen Ministerium für Wissenschaft, Kunst und Volksbildung', *TRST* 3, 175ff.

168. Letter from Troeltsch to Oberlehrer Reintjes, 22 June 1920, Haenisch papers, no.401, p.2, Central State Archive, Potsdam. On this occasion Troeltsch wrote a letter to Reintjes, who had been tough with him. The end of the letter shows Troeltsch's straight speaking and directness: 'You threaten me with "special steps by leading Democrats". I don't know what they might be. Presumably the *Berliner Tageblatt*. Nowadays such threats are part of the way of working which is common everywhere. I am not afraid of that and forbear to say what I think of the whole business of threats' (ibid). Troeltsch's behaviour in this matter, above all this letter, which was not an official one, prompted vigorous reactions, not least in the Ministry, against which Troeltsch vehemently defended himself.

169. All in all Troeltsch is concerned for fair and reasonable behaviour, which allows doubts about the accused. Because a divisional head in the Ministry had commented positively on Reintjes and negatively on Troeltsch, his behaviour and procedure, Troeltsch had to justify himself both to Secretary of State Becker and to the Minister.

170. From the statement asked for from Troeltsch by Becker, Central State Archive, Potsdam, Haenisch papers, no.401, p.6.

171. From Troeltsch's statement, 25 June 1920, ibid., 7.

172. Letter to Minister Haenisch, 15 October 1921, Central State Archive, Potsdam, Haenisch papers, 401, p.13.

173. The specific catalyst for this judgment was his experience with the head teacher

mentioned above. In conclusion Troeltsch remarks: 'But I regret the remark, because of course I did not intend to fuel a party-political battle by private comments.' This incident is reminiscent of Troeltsch's unconsidered remark at the World Congress in St Louis, because of which he felt it necessary to write a letter of apology to Hugo Münsterberg.

174. Thus F.Meinecke in his introduction to the Spectator Letters, written in 1923. J.R.C.Wright differs; he assumes that Troeltsch's period in office ended in July 1920, but does not give any further evidence. Cf. J.R.C.Wright, 'Ernst Troeltsch als parlamentarischer Unterstaatssekretär im preussischen Ministerium für Wissenschaft, Kunst und Volksbildung', TRST 3, 178f. B.Sösemann speaks of Troeltsch's resignation (but dates it to the year 1921); however, he does not give any explanation. Cf. B.Sösemann, 'Das "erneuerte Deutschland". Ernst Troeltschs politisches Engagement im Ersten Weltkrieg', *TRST* 3, 122 n.13. W.Köhler, who is evidently quoting from a letter from Troeltsch to him, writes: 'He announced his resignation from the Ministry as early as the end of March: "I now want to get out of politics and concentrate on my studies again"' (W.Köhler, *Ernst Troeltsch*, Heidelberg 1941, 293). In my view, the version of Troeltsch's contemporary and fellow party member, Meinecke, deserves priority. It is also supported by the fact that various newspaper articles which appeared at the beginning of 1921 have the addition 'Secretary of State' (cf. *ETB*, 218f.).

175. There was a vigorous discussion after a lecture given by Eric Kollmann in Marburg on 15 June 1955 on 'A Diagnosis of the Weimar Republic – Ernst Troeltsch and the Problem of the Political Professor'. In addition to Kollmann (a German American, a professor of history from Iowa and at that time a visiting professor in Marburg) the other speakers were Georg Wünsch (1887-1964, a systematic theologian and pupil of Troeltsch) and Adolf Grabowsky (1880-1969, a political scientist who with Troeltsch founded the Volksbund für Freiheit und Vaterland). According to my notes, Kollmann's view was positive. For him, Troeltsch was above all very active in his work at the Ministry and was known for his zeal for work; he was also able to get some things moving. Grabowsky differed, arguing that Troeltsch did not really get any response with his work, including his journalism in the Weimar period. According to Grabowsky, Troeltsch was a Tory conservative. In domestic politics one had to say that he did not move from advice to action. And he was not clear-sighted enough in foreign policy. Wünsch stressed three things in his contribution: Troeltsch was a man of reality, a man of truth, a man of synthesis.

176. *GS* II, viii.

177. Original title 'Das Ethos der hebräischen Propheten', *Logos. Internationale Zeitschrift für Philosophie der Kultur* 6, 1916/17, 1-28; later under the title 'Glaube und Ethos der hebräischen Propheten', in *GS* IV, 34-65. The full title of the other article was 'Die alte Kirche. Eine kulturphilosophische Studie', *Logos* 6, 265-314, later, without the addition, in *GS* IV, 65-121.

178. According to Herrmann Lübbe, Troeltsch's concept of secularization has an ambivalent structure, as it implies both the enriching of modern culture by a religious heritage and the negative element of an impoverishment. Troeltsch avoided all attempts at evasion in radical forms of thought and action, and remained rooted to the position of theological historicism. To this degree 'the concept of secularization which he occasionally used also remained a historical category; it was no longer the slogan of a militant progress nor yet the name of a history of decay lamented in a

criticism of civilization, but a neutralized term of scientific description' (Herrmann Lübbe, *Säkularisierung*, Munich 1965, 83f.). This judgment can be supplemented and corrected. The historical understanding of the term in Troeltsch is not exclusively neutral nor only concerned with description. Alongside the element of description and assertion, for Troeltsch the concept of secularization also has the character of an invitation: to take up secularization as a historical phenomenon and give it a new cultural form by exploiting the historical heritage. Cf. Trutz Rendtorff, *Theorie des Christentums. Historisch-theologische Studien zu seiner neuzeitlichen Verfassung*, Gütersloh 1972, 73ff. and 116ff.

179. There is further discussion of this question in G.Becker, *Neuzeitliche Subjektivität und Religiosität. Die religionsphilosophische Bedeutung von Heraufkunft und Wesen der Neuzeit im Denken von Ernst Troeltsch*, Regensburg 1982, 268ff., 285ff.

180. Card to W.Bousset, 28 December 1917, UB Göttingen, unpublished.

181. *GS* IV, 76.

182. *GS* IV, 95. For syncretism cf. Gunkel's formulation: 'Christianity is a syncretistic religion' (H.Gunkel, *Zum religionsgeschichtlichen Verständnis des Neuen Testaments*, Göttingen 1903, 95). For Bultmann, Christianity is not really a syncretistic religion. His explanation why differs from Troeltsch's: in Christianity a new, irreplaceable, unitary view of human existence emerges (R.Bultmann, *Primitive Christianity in its Contemporary Setting*, London 1956, 180ff.).

183. Ibid. For this connection see also Troeltsch's article 'Adolf von Harnack und Ferdinand Christian Baur',in *Festgabe von Fachgenossen und Freunden A.von Harnack zum siebzigsten Geburtstag dargebracht*, Tübingen 1921, 282-91; ET, 'Adolf von Harnack and F.C.von Baur 1921', in W.Pauck, *Harnack and Troeltsch: Two Historical Theologians*, New York 1968, 97-115.

184. *GS* IV, 97.

185. What Hans Baron later edited as the fourth volume of the *Gesammelte Schriften* in part goes in the direction indicated, but is no real substitute for what Troeltsch intended.

186. Letter to P.Siebeck, 2 January 1919, Mohr-Siebeck archives, Tübingen.

187. According to H.-J.Gabriel, the structure of the volume on historicism corresponds to that of the article on the 'Essence of Christianity'. The 'higher concepts' to be found there – criticism, the concept of development and the concept of the ideal – correspond in the volume on historicism to the discussion of criteria, the concept of development and the structure of European cultural history (cf. H.-J.Gabriel, *Christlichkeit der Gesellschaft?*, 207 n.390). There is in fact some similarity in formal method and also partially in content, which is not surprising against the background of Troeltsch's controversy with Harnack and his 'historicism'. As to content, Gabriel points out, in my view rightly, that Troeltsch's investigations into historicism are to be seen 'as a development and summary of his own presuppositions, aimed at a new attempt at a solution' (ibid., 158).

188. Here reference should be made to Rickert's work on 'The Limits of Scientific Conceptuality'. According to Rickert, in the formation of scientific concepts there is a combination of elements by the recognition of the necessity of natural laws and with reference to the Universal, or the general conceptual context. By contrast, in the formation of historical concepts individuality and vividness have priority, because through them the uniqueness and peculiarity of historical reality can be perceived (cf. *Die Grenzen der naturwissenschaftlichen Begriffsbildung*, 128ff.; 145ff.; [3/4]1921).

189. *GS* III, 38.

190. Here Troeltsch talks deliberately in the singular of the concept of originality and uniqueness. Of course one can ask what the 'more' of originality is in comparison with uniqueness. Troeltsch probably thinks that a historical phenomenon can be perceived by a reference back to the uniqueness of its origins.

191. *GS* III, 40.

192. Troeltsch had prefaced this with reflections on the balance between vividness and concept, the reality of experience and the ordering of this in categories, for example in the article on 'The Significance of the Concept of Contingency' (*GS* III, 769-78, esp. 774ff.). In connection with the course of his development one can say that he now once again returned more markedly to his theological beginnings and their proximity to Dilthey and Schleiermacher, but at the same time went beyond them in developing his theme, differentiating his conceptuality more markedly and also including new elements in his position, for example by taking in ideas from Bergson.

193. *GS* III, 67.

194. *GS* III, 48ff. Here Troeltsch evidently stands in a tradition which attempts to connect logic and feeling or intuition, and which in the history of philosophy goes back to Pascal. One possible factor here is his proximity to Bergson, who (in his theory of the comic) distinguishes a logic of reason from a logic of the imagination (cf. H.Holzhey, 'Logik des Gefühls', in *HWP* V, 411-14). For criticism of Troeltsch's understanding of logic cf. J.Schaaf, *Geschichte und Begriff*, Tübingen 1946, 6ff.; 15f. Schaaf sees it as a fundamental error of Troeltsch's that he does not envisage movement exclusively for corporeal things, but also in the realm of thought and imagination; here the term 'movement' should be banned in favour of talk of a succession of changes in the human consciousness. But this criticism, which seeks to allow movement in respect of history only metaphorically, gets in the way of access to Troeltsch's intention of going beyond mere forms of consciousness in the direction of real processes which result from the 'inner differentiations' in the world movement and the levels of reality connected with them (*GS* III, 632; cf. H.Demandt, *Metaphern der Geschichte*, Munich 1978). Philosophically, the clear application of the concept of movement to spatial changes does not correspond either to Bergson's intention or (in more recent times) to that of Whitehead, for whom both space and time are not localizable entities. For the argument cf. also Troeltsch's controversy with Rickert and Hegel (296ff. above).

195. Here Otto Hintze comments critically that Troeltsch did not take appropriate note of the different versions of the idea of evolution. For him, Troeltsch's criticism is mainly directed against Spencer's concept of evolution, whereas he is less opposed to an organological concept. However, for Hintze both types belong together, because they understand historical life 'by analogy with a biological organism'. On this common basis of interpretation neither is suitable for the practical work of the historian (cf. O.Hintze, 'Troeltsch und die Probleme des Historismus', in *Zur Theorie der Geschichte*, Tübingen 1978, 42ff.). Troeltsch's notion of understanding the concept of time in such a way that it allows a real understanding of history belongs in this context. In the background lies Bergson's distinction between chronometric mathematical time and time in the sense of duration (*la durée réelle*). For Troeltsch, this indicates a logic of life which transcends the spatial and which can take account of the continuity of contexts of life.

196. Troeltsch uses the term 'formal logic of history' as a synonym for 'formal

philosophy of history'. Here Rickert's reflections on the historical formation of
concepts lie in the background, albeit modified in a characteristic way. To sum up,
one can say that Troeltsch adds to Rickert's logical formation of conceptuality,
which starts from the subject, a variant from the philosophy of life and thus related
to the object, so as to be able to pay equal attention to historical life and to the
requirements of logic.

197. *GS* III, 66.

198. Cf. *GS* III, 104ff. Troeltsch's assumption that naturalism and historicism have
common roots is problematical. It can be accepted in connection with historicism
only to a very limited degree or in a broader sense. Hegel and Dilthey were with
good reason critics of Descartes.

199. E.Rothacker has referred to the ambivalence and the elusiveness of the term
'historicism'. He thinks that 'historicism can mean both a quite childlike naturalism
for which world history runs its course in accordance with the most primitive
mechanical analogies, and the peculiar concern of a Romantic for spiritual being or
an unfolding of reason as in Hegel's view of world history' (cf. *Einleitung in die
Geisteswissenschaften*, Tübingen 1920, 7).

200. However, the positive effect of historicism can only be recognized in a dialectical
process. For the perception of the fortuitousness of the individual historical event
at the same time amounts to its relativization. Only in a next, as it were contrary,
step can the contingent in turn be relativized, by the possibility of giving it a place
in a wider historical context.

201. The process which emerges here corresponds to the dialectic of change and
persistence. If it is to be possïble to speak of change, a substance must be presupposed
in which this change can take place or be perceived. Troeltsch applies this
. epistemological stucture of formal logic to the philosophy of history. Both a flux of
being and a firm standpoint are to be allowed: they are to correct each other and at
the same time to be combined and transcended in a system.

202. 'Die Entstehung des Historismus' (1936), *Werke*, III.

203. There is an account of the context and a criticism of Meinecke in my article 'Das
Problem der Geschichte bei Ernst Troeltsch', *ZTK* 57, 1960, 195f.

204. In connection with his planned philosophy of religion, Troeltsch gave his publisher
his own view as to whether in principle he belonged to the 'Windelband-Rickert
group'. He wrote: 'I do not have a basic plan, but intend a really full development
of the problem which is the philosophical basis of my whole standpoint. Essentially
I am very close to Rickert and belong to the whole of that group' (letter to P.Siebeck,
12 December 1911, Mohr/Siebeck archives, Tübingen). Troeltsch could not or
would not make more than a beginning at an approach to the phenomenological
school, though in retrospect he thought that it would have been possible (cf. *GS* III,
91f.; 596ff.).

205. Cf. *GS* III, 228. Troeltsch means a 'steeping' of formal logic in 'the content of
life'.

206. When in 1922 Troeltsch told Rickert that his book on historicism was soon to
appear, he described his work and manner of thought as follows: 'I am someone
who is less inclined to logic and sophistry than you are, and am more attached to
vividness and substance. I see Leibniz as a more central German philosopher than
Kant, and can only understand the latter on the basis of the former... Of course that
produces a position which is often different from yours, and of course I cannot

conceal the contradiction. But I am not very bothered about contradictions, since I too often develop my ideas through criticism of others. That comes about because I am basically always a conversationalist and think with the help of the tradition. Monologues mean nothing to me. This also leads to expressions of opposition. But as I know the difficulties, I am not surprised at any difference and take everything quite calmly. The main point is usually how different people are, something which again is disturbing for a pure logician, but which I have confirmed a hundred times by experience' (letter to H.Rickert, 15 May 1922, unpublished; communicated by H.Renz).

207. *GS* III, 232.

208. 'Historical logic must be the formation and selection of the historical picture from the subjectivities and conditions of the lives of past people as they are reproduced and subsequently experienced' (ibid.).

209. Troeltsch's critical investigation here goes in the direction of an 'as-if philosophy'. 'Development is an arrangement of the portrayer, who describes and treats the facts *as if* they served as a realization of values, indeed primarily of individual concrete historical values, and then of the universal human values which underlie them. By contrast, for the historian development is an inner movement of the object itself, in which one can and must intuitively immerse oneself, and from which further developments, which are new and lively each time, and therefore in turn individual, have to be formed' (*GS* III, 234f.). Max Weber also falls within the scope of this criticism: according to Troeltsch he cannot (or will not) consider the concept of development, its own logic and metaphysical depth. He rules out any assumption of an interweaving of being and value because there is a suspicion of a deviation into metaphysics and Romanticism. What remains is the contrast between pure research and value related to causality and a decision on values. The first is an expression of rationalism, the second of a heroic resolution combined with scepticism (cf. *GS* III, 568ff.). Troeltsch has rightly seen that in the long run the forced acknowledgment of values will not be able to assert itself against thought which is purely in terms of causality (cf. *GS* III, 49 n.219).

210. Troeltsch's argument with Rickert is focussed on a rooting of the philosophy of life in the theory of values. He can assent to a 'merging of values' along the lines of the phenomenological school to the degree that the significance of this is to show the living being as one which in principle does not contemplate and reflect but acts practically, selects, fights and strives, in which all mere intellectualism and contemplation is ultimately at the service of life, whether animal or spiritual and personal (*GS* III, 203).

211. *GS* III, 247.

212. *GS* III, 251.

213. Thus he says of Hegel's view of the state: 'In fact everything is combined in this notion. There has never been a greater synthesis. State and society, power and culture, nation and law, religion and the life of the world, one-sided power and a wealth of harmony, naivety and reflection, tradition and originality, historical sequence and system – everything is combined. No wonder that the impression was a tremendous one and worked even when it was like the distant sound of bells in the air' (*GS* III, 263). In accord with the spirit of the time Troeltsch regarded it as a positive factor that Hegel had seen Europeanism as the nucleus of world history (cf. *GS* III, 267).

214. In the book on historicism Troeltsch does not interpret Hegel as he did in his theological beginnings. Certainly in both cases he criticizes the working out of real history in the interest of the idea, but the accents are different. In particular, Hegel is later acquitted of a simple *a priori* construction of history; Troeltsch recognizes that he arrives at an *a posteriori* conceptual understanding of what actually happened through the idea. Among his new themes and purposes Troeltsch also recognizes the significance of Hegel's view of the state as a form of the relationship of the individual to society, including the idea of humanity as a unitary formation on a higher level transcending the state, namely the individuality of the people. Troeltsch adopts the idea of unity to be found here in Hegel in his notion of a 'construction of the cultural history of Europe'.

215. *GS* III, 167. The context is: 'The ultimate mystery of these processes is belief in the *momentaneous* reason which is manifest and compelling here and the power of the will to affirm such faith' (*GS* III, 167f.).

216. The closer definition of the concept of relativism is particularly significant here. For Mannheim this can be understood as the possibility of referring all the elements of meaning to one another, as a form of expression which is adequate to the system, time-conditioned and at the same time valid (*Ideology and Utopia*, London 1936, 76). For Mannheim, ideologizing is the adoption of time-conditioned contents or values as if they were timeless. True historical thinking de-ideologizes to the degree that it shows the particularity and time-conditioned nature of statements and forms of expression. Like Troeltsch, Mannheim aims at an appropriate knowledge of reality against the background of historical experience. In this context, ideological criticism is the unveiling of false forms of value-judgment (cf. especially, ibid., 77ff., and Karl Mannheim's article 'Historizismus', *Archiv für Sozialwissenschaft und Sozialpolitik* 52, 1924, 1-60).

217. For Troeltsch, in view of the second form of judgment it is necessary to accept the pendant of the *res gestae*, which are then understood hermeneutically through intellectual spontaneity as *historia rerum gestarum*. Otherwise free hypotheses and inventions would be possible. In Koselleck's words, 'the sources have a right of veto', which in Troeltsch takes the substance of things into account but is not always expressed with sufficient clarity (cf. R.Koselleck, *Vergangene Zukunft*, Frankfurt 1989, 206).

218. The discussions from the last perspective appear under the heading 'the concept of historical development and universal history' (cf. *GS* III, 221-693).

219. According to Troeltsch, in his philosophy of history Rudolf Eucken saw the significance of the individual and the special character of the life of the spirit, but a metaphysic of the spirit understood in dualistic terms prevented the formation of a universal notion of development. Eucken maintained the assumption of different stages of progress, a gradual development of values by stages, and thus largely renounced a universal overall development understood as a process in world history (cf. *GS* III, 485ff., esp. 490f.).

220. W.Köhler, *Ernst Troeltsch*, Tübingen 1941, 332ff.

221. This is shown with exemplary clarity in the account of Hegel's position.

222. Cf. *GS* III, 677.

223. *GS* III, 675.

224. The much-quoted central statement of a metaphysical solution to the philosophy of history runs: 'The key to the solution of our problem is not the Spinozan identity

of thought and being or nature and spirit, but the essential and individual identity of finite spirits with the infinite spirit and along with that intuitive participation in its concrete content and moved unity of life' (*GS* III, 677).

225. *Gesammelte Abhandlungen* 6, Leipzig 1942, 64.

226. *Werke* IV, 377.

227. F.Gogarten, *Verhängnis und Hoffnung der Neuzeit*, Stuttgart 1958, 118ff.

228. *GS* III, 263ff.

229. According to Antoni, the only original thought that Troeltsch offers in this connection is a religious one. The orientation on Western culture is understood as loyalty to the revelation of the Absolute which has been made to us. 'In this sermon there is perhaps a very remote echo of the Lutheran ethic of vocation: the European must remain European because that is his position in the world, because history has made him so, and because any deviation would be unnatural' (C.Antoni, *Von Historismus zur Soziologie*, Stuttgart nd [1939], 117).

230. Cf. K.Löwith, 'Weltgeschichte und Heilsgeschehen', in *Anteile. Martin Heidegger zum 60.Geburtstag*, Frankfurt am Main 1950, 130f., *Sämtliche Schriften* 2, 260.

231. *GS* III, 101.

232. Ibid. Such comments are reminiscent of Theodor Fontane (1819-1898) and his reflections on the human longing for happiness and meaning which he presented particularly in the works of his old age. Generally speaking, Troeltsch and Fontane closely resemble each other and have much in common. That is true both of their natures and their views of life, and of the way in which they perceived their times. Both tended towards a gentle melancholy which was checked by a more reflective trust in God. Both felt that their time was a time of revolution; both had deep roots in the past and attempted to make productive use of the new elements which were emerging, though they detected the ambivalence of such elements.

233. However, it is evident that here Troeltsch assumes a tension which can be interpreted in a positive sense (I find a situation, accept it, and thus in my sense make it new; I take up what is objectively there and transform it subjectively).

234. In terms of historical influence and motivation, one can say that in Troeltsch the heritage of the Enlightenment is combined with a second Enlightenment in a significant and characteristic combination of spontaneity and empathetic power with rationality and criticism. For this cf. T.Rendtorff, 'Theologische Orientierung im Prozess der Aufklärung. Eine Erinnerung an Ernst Troeltsch', *Aufklärung* 2, 1987, 19-33.

235. On the human side, the cultural-philosophical concept of revelation embraces both artistic sensitivity and a capacity for historical empathy, and on the divine side is the formation of the moment which is an expression of grace on the basis of a remarkable constellation of forces and events. One can speak of an implicit religious sense in Troeltsch's philosophy of history and culture (cf. *GS* III, 101, 213).

236. According to Troeltsch, while the concept of humanity has had its historical significance in more recent history, no solution of contemporary political and social questions is to be expected from it as a notion which goes into the inward and the personal dimension. The notion of humanity is not of fundamental significance for the creation of a cultural synthesis either understood in terms of natural law or incorporating the moral element. Rather, in substance it has only a limited historical significance.

237. Possibly we have here the influence of Oswald Spengler, who speaks of the

Western European-American stage of culture and for whom landscape and climatic conditions play a major role in cultural history (cf. O.Spengler, *The Decline of the West*, London 1926. See the introduction to Volume 1, 3ff., and Volume 2, Chapter 1, 'Origin and Landscape', 3-19). Troeltsch also saw such connections earlier, as for example in his work on absoluteness, but now he put them forward in a more pointed way.

238. *GS* III, 200. This version of the concept of individuality, in the sense both of existing facticity and of the ideal required, finds support from the philosophy of history above all in Fichte, especially in his concept of resistance. In Goethe and the Romantics the idea is then regarded as the individual element. For Troeltsch the concept of individuality forms the gateway to the theory of values from the double aspect indicated.

239. R.Röhricht rightly indicates the last aspect in his work *Zwischen Historismus und Existenzdenken*, Tübingen 1954. On the one hand there is the question of the apriorism and objectivity of the formation of criteria, which has objective presuppositions in the form of the development of historical complexes; on the other there is an emphasis on the decision and action of the individual on the basis of self-assurance and faith. However, one has to add that the approximations to existentialist philosophy in Troeltsch are toned down and broken by his inclusion of the existential in a wider context, whether on the basis of the notion of the cultural circle or through a monadological metaphysics.

240. *GS* III, 728. Troeltsch says of America that it has a great but incalculable future and that it has derived the powers for its cultural and political ambitions from the European tradition. For this reason he extended his notions of the cultural circle to America both in terms of its influence and on the assumption of actual connections and proximity.

241. *GS* III, 772. In his speech on the Dante Jubilee (1921), which has the significant title 'Mountain of Purification', Troeltsch sees the significance of Dante above all in the power of his poetic imagination to bring about unity. Dante can unite separate and conflicting elements like Christian mystical sensitivity, barbaric originality, poetic sensitivity and moral aims. Dante is a model of that synthesis for which Troeltsch strove in his time and which with poetic vividness arrives more at a combination of opposing elements of tradition than at an intellectual or abstract philosophical procedure. Troeltsch read Dante virtually as a textbook. He saw as a message for his time Dante's interpretation of life as a process of purification which goes through different stages and which, with unity as a goal before it, lives from the power of purification. According to Troeltsch there is no 'greater and more unitary summary of the ethical values of our cultural world down to the present day. Even Goethe's *Faust* does not contain anything higher. Basically, he presents the same thoughts, but with less cohesion and resolution' (*Berg der Läuterung*, Berlin 1921, 17).

242. *GS* IV, 14f.

243. When they had been worked out, the lectures went to Friedrich von Hügel for translation. Troeltsch chose as a topic 'Ethics and the Philosophy of History'; the two others, on 'The Place of Christianity among the World Religions' and 'Politics, Patriotism, and Religion' were given to him.

244. *SchmJb* 45, 1921, later in *GS* IV, 653ff.

245. *Die neue Rundschau* 1, 1922, 572-90.

246. On the surface, Troeltsch's comments on this theme are a discussion of two works which challenge Max Weber's theses on 'science as a profession'; more precisely, there is a criticism of Weber (E.von Kahler) and an anti-criticism (A.Salz). Cf. E.von Kahler, *Der Beruf der Wissenschaft*, Berlin 1920, and A.Salz, *Für die Wissenschaft. Gegen die Gebildeten unter ihren Verächtern*, Berlin 1921. Troeltsch uses the review to make some general criticisms of culture.

247. In this connection Troeltsch can refer to the works of Bergson, which aim at liberation from the fetters of naturalistic and mechanistic thought. These comments make his critical proximity to Bergson clear. Bergson's philosophy of life does not think in formalisms, like Neo-Kantianism apriorism, but its content is governed by the spiritual movement of phenomena. However, here Bergson ideologizes spontaneity and freedom and cannot avoid a lack of direction in his thought.

248. The lecture on 'German Education' given by Troeltsch on 3 October 1918 at the opening of the Volkshochschule in Görlitz is particularly significant in this connection. Here he refers to the pluralism in education on the basis of tradition and the different aims of the groups or institutions interested in education, and calls for a 'selection' from the wealth of material and a concentration on essentials. The simplification aimed at here must not be artificial, must not be a merely emotional presupposition or demand, but must come about through a division and gradation of the values in the tradition. The religious element must be dominant; the Christian element must have no confessional limits or dogmatic claims. The value of the person or personal life and the estimation of creative powers found an appropriate basis here, one which was essentially in tune with Western developments. Two remarks are worth special attention in this context. First, 'Here too it is important to become what one is' (*DG*, 195); and secondly, a remark which leads to the centre of his view of life: 'The supreme wisdom is to love one's destiny and at the same time cope with it creatively' (*DG*, 203). For further comment cf. E.Spranger, 'Ernst Troeltsch über Pädagogik als Universitätsfach', in J.Derbolac and F.Nicolin (eds.), *Erkenntnis und Verantwortung, Festschrift für Theodor Litt*, Düsseldorf 1960, 445ff.

249. Here Troeltsch refers to Nohl's article 'Die neue deutsche Bildung. Vortrag auf Einladung des Zentralinstituts für Erziehung und Unterricht', given as a lecture in Essen in 1920. It first appeared in *Pädagogisches Zentralblatt* 1921, 193ff., and was reprinted in *Pädagogik aus dreissig Jahren*, Frankfurt am Main 1949, 9-20.

250. Evidently Nohl had sent Troeltsch his lecture, in which he commented on Troeltsch both constructively and critically. Troeltsch reacted with a card. He wrote: 'All very true and admirable. I see things just like that. Only you have not formulated the "law" towards which you strive. In my view it cannot be formulated. It is a combination of different contents which can only be demonstrated in a leading person, a representative poet, just as the old revolutions in education found their culmination in Goethe. He is the law. Even he could not do away with the aristocratism in education. In my view no one can...' Troeltsch cannot recognize such a 'leading' person or force in the contemporary cultural situation. Neither Stefan George nor Max Scheler is a candidate here, so it cannot be a new Catholicism. Socialism, too, is excluded for Troeltsch. He concludes sceptically, 'I fear that we face a complete splitting instead of union' (card of 2 October 1921, UB Göttingen, Nohl papers, unpublished).

251. For example in the article already mentioned Nohl speaks of the nobility of the law or of a discipline of form through which a new will to formation is expressed

from the perspective of binding and unification. Troeltsch only hints at the help which emerges or offers itself in this crisis situation in the form of the phenomenological school, and does not discuss it further. A 'view of essence' directed against mere *a priori* thought-forms and a reference to laws of essence of the individual ontological regions – all this is in line with the direction of his thought and the criticism bound up with it.

252. For the controversy between Troeltsch and Gogarten see F.W.Graf, 'Kierkegaards junge Herren. Troeltschs Kritik der "Geistigen Revolution" im frühen 20.Jahrhundert', *TRST* 4, 172-92, and my article 'Entwicklungsdenken und Glaubensentscheidung. Troeltschs Kierkegaardverständnis und die Kontroverse Troeltsch – Gogarten', *ZTK* 79, 1982, 80-106.

253. *GS* IV, 666. Troeltsch thus classes 'followers of Kierkegaard' with thinkers with a mystical orientation like Jatho, Bonus and Johannes Müller, which is of course problematical. In any case it is more than questionable to call Heim a follower of Kierkegaard, because of his theological origin and aims. What Troeltsch is evidently concerned to do in his references is to understand the views of the theologians mentioned as an expression of the 'intellectual revolution' which is taking place in the cultural sphere.

254. Troeltsch commented both in his book on the problems of historicism and in a detailed review of Spengler's *Decline of the West* (*HZ* 1919, reprinted in *GS* IV,677ff.). For him Spengler's book is characteristic of the cultural situation of the time. His review is both sympathetic and critical. He stresses the author's independent thought and abundant knowledge, but criticizes the lack of scholarly solidity and the philosophical construction based on the assumption of a parallelism of cultures. For Troeltsch, Hermann Graf Keyserling is equally illuminating for the spirit of the time, both with his *Travel Diary of a Philosopher* and with the 'Society for Free Philosophy' founded on his initiative, and the 'School of Wisdom' which emerged from it. For Troeltsch, the books of the two authors Spengler and Keyserling are 'fashion books', but nevertheless (or precisely for that reason) their concept and style, and indeed their influence, allow conclusions to be drawn about the spirit of the time. What he thinks particularly symptomatic is that in both 'a philosophical intuition seeking out the essentials' (*GS* IV, 692) takes the place of careful detailed investigations and a critical examination of the source material, 'a philosophical intuition which picks out essentials' (*GS* IV, 692). Even if Troeltsch discovers similarities with his own philosophy of history, that does not alter his overall critical and detached verdict; his 'bourgeois conscientiousness and critical training' (*GS* IV, 693) simply will not let him go along with this any more.

255. 'Die Krisis des Historismus', *Die neue Rundschau* 1, 1922, 587. Here his reflections are supported by the hope that the political and cultural necessities of the issue will finally establish themselves. 'World political needs for converse between the peoples and the return to our great humane and universal history, which is certainly to be expected, will not allow the trees to grow up to heaven. There must also be a balance within our own people' (ibid.).

256. The German title presumably comes from Marta Troeltsch (cf. *ETB*, 6). [The sequence of lectures in the German is different from that in the English version, with the ethics lecture coming first.] The article already mentioned, on 'The Crisis of Historicism', is of great significance for the problems of historicism. It represents

a sovereign, free development of basic problems with a focus on the current situation of dialogue in philosophy and the humanities.

257. The individuality of moral conscience is as it were a second-order individuality, in so far as it only emerges in application, namely as the activity of the individual conscience. 'The ethic of cultural values, on the other hand, leads us into the realm of the historical particular in the much more radical sense of a moulding of universal tendencies into historical creations of culture – a moulding which is peculiar, unique and *sui generis...*' (*HÜ*, 30, *CT* 83).

258. *HÜ*, 32, *CT*, 86.

259. Cf. *HÜ*, 56f., *CT*, 123f.

260. With his reference to personal alliances, to germ-cells in which fellowship and community can be expressed individually, Troeltsch is taking up the longing of young people for intensive experience and the bonds of community which found varied expression in the German youth movement. The necessary process of training can come about through 'central personalities'. 'From these germ-cells there must proceed great fighting forces of public life. Since in the personal and particular they seek to find the universal and love, they will meet, embrace, and amalgamate' (*HÜ*, 58, *CT*, 126). Here Troeltsch focusses his thought on current problems and their solution, and attempts to occupy a mediating position between pure subjectivity and the assumption of an objective obligation through the common spirit.

261. Thus in connection with his lectures Troeltsch writes to Friedrich von Hügel, 'Of course with due respect to all churches and denominations I can only speak from a standpoint above the confessions for those who within, alongside or above the churches feel the need for a so to speak personal religion which can then content with the communities as they are, depending on circumstances and possibilities' (letter to F.von Hügel, presumably August 1921, Apfelbacher/Neuner, 115).

262. To this effect we read: 'We cannot live without a religion, yet the only one that we can endure is Christianity, because for Christianity has grown up with us and is part of us' (*HÜ*, 77, *CT*, 25).

263. This impression is confirmed by the closing thought: 'In our earthly experience the divine life is not one, but many. But to apprehend the one in the many constitutes the special character of love' (*HÜ*, 83, *CT*, 35).

264. *HÜ*, 101, *CT*, 160.

265. Ibid.

266. When one thinks of future developments, above all in Germany, a passage like the following was a word for the future: 'All radicalisms break down and lead to corruption' (*HÜ*, 104, *CT*, 165).

267. A visit to England had been planned in connection with the American trip in 1904. However, Troeltsch had returned home early because of the death of his mother-in-law (cf. Apfelbacher/Neuner, 39).

268. Letter to F. von Hügel, 29 December 1922, Apfelbacher/Neuner, 147.

269. Letter to von hügel, 11 january 1923, apfelbacher/neuner, 150.

270. *Berliner Tageblatt*, morning edition, 2 February 1923. Troeltsch saw his election as dean for the year 1923 as a positive sign of developments or of a change of mood in the University of Berlin. External honours which came to him in the last years of his life were an honorary doctorate in theology from the University of Oslo and his election as a member of the Academy of Sciences in Berlin (1922). For his election to the academy see the account in Meinecke, *Werke* VIII, 255f.

271. Letter from Marta Troeltsch to von Hügel, 10 February 1923, Apfelbacher/ Neuner 153. She adds: 'Now the burden of work, the struggle, the ardour of involvement which he took upon himself since 1914, have prematurely broken this strong heart' (ibid.).

272. Cf. Max Scheler, *Gesammelte Werke* 2, 24. The Reich President had sent a telegram of sympathy to Marta Troeltsch in which he referred to Troeltsch's scholarly importance and his political activity.

273. Reprinted in *CW* 37, 1923, 101-5.

274. Ibid., 103.

275. Ibid., 104.

276. *Deutsche Vierteljahresschrift* 1, 1921, 171.

277. Paul Tillich, 'Zum Tode von Ernst Troeltsch, 1923', in *Begegnungen, Gesammelte Werke* XII, 175.

Index of Names

Because of the frequency of appearances of his name, Ernst Troeltsch is not included. Recipients of letters from him are included, but not editors of them. English index by Susan J. Allen.

Adams, J.L., xiii
Althoff, F., 51, 351 n.94
Antoni, C., 304, 441 n.229
Apfelbacher, K.E., x, xiv, 149, 150, 341 n.3, 359 n.66, 365 n.126, 367 n.136, 367 n.141, 371 n.186, 373 nn.200, 208, 379 n.257, 380 n.4, 382 n.26, 385 nn.51, 52, 386 n.57, 395 n.169, 398 n.189, 401 n.222, 403 n.244, 432 n.147, 445, 446 n.271
Arnold, G., 239
Aschoff, L., 428 n.107
Augustine, 136, 235, 411 n.317, 412 n.320
Avenarius, F., 272

Baden, M. von, 271
Baron, H., 428 n.109, 436 n.185
Barth, K., 19, 71, 97, 175, 176, 204, 366 n.130, 393 n.139, 394 n.150, 402 n.232
Bassermann, H., 59, 62, 63, 64, 65, 66, 111, 356 n.31, 357 n.43
Baumann, J., 27, 346 n.48
Baumgarten, E., 377 n.246, 415 n.344
Baumgarten, O., 106, 357 n.43, 377 n.250, 378 n.252
Baur, F.C., 134, 350 n.85, 392 n.135, 436 n.183
Becker, C.H., 132, 259, 379 n.256, 422 n.49, 434 nn.169, 170
Becker, G., 395 n.169, 436 n.179
Bechmann, H., 342 n.19
Below, G. von, 387 n.69
Benckert, H., 186, 395 n.166, 398 n.186
Bense, W.F., xiii
Bergson, H., 174, 437, 443 n.247
Bestmann, J., 371 n.18
Bethmann-Hollweg, T. von, 268, 426 n.88
Biarowsky, W.J. von, 349 n.78
Biedermann, A.E., 78
Birkner, H.-J., 401 n.212

Bismarck, O. von, 5, 17
Blumenberg, H., 147, 148, 289, 294, 384 n.46
Bodelschwingh, F. von, 112
Bodenstein, W., 389 n.88
Boeckh, F., 6
Bögeholz, H., 420 n.32
Böhme, J. 147
Böhme, K., 423 n. 66
Boehmer, H., 139, 381 n.24, 382 n.24
Bonus, A., 218, 310, 444 n.253
Bornemann, W., 86
Bosse, F., 50, 51, 353 nn.112, 113
Bosse, H., 408 n.291
Bousset, H., 343 n.22
Bousset, W., 5, 10, 11 12, 14, 15, 17, 18, 19, 20, 26, 27, 28, 29, 32, 34, 35, 39, 45, 46, 47, 48, 49, 50, 51, 57, 58, 59, 62, 63, 64, 65, 67, 98, 99, 112, 121, 122, 127, 188, 211, 212, 249, 289, 341 nn.4, 6, 343 n.22, 346 n.54, 348 n.69, 349 nn.81, 82, 350 n.85, 351 n.90, 353 n.108, 354 n.6, 355, 356, 357, 358 n.54, 360 n.76, 362 n.88, 363 n.90, 364 n.110, 367, 371 n.190, 372 nn.190, 191, 376 n.238, 378, 379 n.257, 380 n.8, 382 n.30, 389 n.91, 390 n.99, 403 n.417 n.1, 436 n.180
Bräunlich, H., 400 n.208
Braun, I., 106
Braun, J., 342 n.15, 343 n.27, 344 n.34, 345 n.45
Brieger, T., 345 n.36, 380 n.5
Brunner, E., 411 n.318
Buchrucker, K.C.W., 34
Bultmann, M., 373 n.207
Bultmann, R., 71, 164, 168, 172, 175, 176, 290, 389 n.93, 390 n.105, 391 n.121, 394 n.149, 403 n.250, 436 n.182
Burckhardt, J., 67

Sources of Illustrations